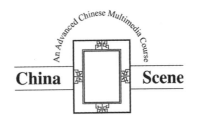

中国社会文化写实

China Scene: An Advanced Chinese Multimedia Course

Traditional & Simplified Characters

Hong Gang Jin, De Bao Xu, and James Hargett

CHENG & TSUI COMPANY
Boston

2007 printing with typographical corrections

20   19   18   17   16   15   9   10   11   12   13   14   15

Published by

Cheng & Tsui Company
25 West Street
Boston, MA 02111-1213 USA
Fax (617) 426-3669
www.cheng-tsui.com
"Bringing Asia to the World"™

ISBN-13: 978-0-88727-330-8

Printed in the United States of America

Acknowledgments

Many people have helped us prepare *China Scene: An Advanced Chinese Multimedia Course*. Most of them are ACC (Associated Colleges in China) teachers and our students at Hamilton College. Without their help, we never could have finished the textbook in a timely fashion. We are very grateful to ACC teachers Yin Zhang, Chunxue Yang and her husband Xie Li for their efforts in typing the latest revision and proofreading the Chinese portions of the book. We are also very grateful to our students Laurie A. Wittlinger for shooting wonderful photographs for the entire textbook, Megan Manchester for her great help in editing and proofreading the English translations of the footnotes, cultural notes, and sentence patterns; and Joshua R. Jenkins for skillfully proofreading the English translations of the earlier versions of sentence patterns. Many other ACC teachers and ACC students (too numerous to name here) also deserve thanks for their valuable feedback and comments on various aspects of the textbook during field testing.

Special thanks should go to Jill Cheng, President of Cheng & Tsui Company, who has been very enthusiastic and supportive during the textual preparation and editorial processes.

We also wish to extend our thanks to Ms. Chris Ingersoll, who designed the orginal logo (the window), which is used throughout the book, and to Ms. Ling Chen (University at Albany-SUNY), who helped with the preparation of the grammar and cultural notes.

Regarding the 2007 printing, we would like to thank ACC Intern Chuzhen Wang for her kind help in finding many of the mismatches in the traditional version of the texts (caused by the computer-programmed conversion from simplified characters to traditional characters), which were long overdue for correction since the first printing of the book in 2000.

Hong Gang Jin, De Bao Xu, and James M. Hargett

February 17, 2007

What's New in the 2007 Printing

I. AUDIO CDS
Recordings of each textbook lesson, complete with listening comprehension, are available as downloadable files at www.cheng-tsui.com.

II. CROSS-PLATFORM, MULTIMEDIA INTERACTIVE SOFTWARE *CHINA SCENE* (TEST VERSION)
is available and can be downloaded for free at: http://academics.hamilton.edu/eal/home//Software.html

III. CORRECTED TRADITIONAL TEXTS
Any mismatches in the traditional version of the texts (due to the computer-programmed conversion from simplified characters to traditional characters) have been corrected.

IV. CORRECTED FORMAT AND LAYOUT
The format and layout for both the traditional version and simplified version of the texts have been corrected.

目 錄

課文
(Texts)

目 录

课文
(Texts)

補充課文
(Supplementary Texts)

附錄
(Appendixes)

补充课文
(Supplementary Texts)

附录
(Appendixes)

前　言

　　《中國社會文化寫實》是為學過兩年以上中文的學生設計的一套多媒體語言文化教科書。這套教科書的目的是通過社會、文化多層面的教學內容，各種語體的多媒體真實語料，讓學生掌握高年級中文的語言結構、表達方法、以及交流方式。

　　自1996年開始這套教科書在美國一些大學及北京的幾個漢語中心進行試用，至今已修改了四版。全書由課本、配合課文的錄像帶、錄音光盤、以及多媒體互動光盤課文與練習（試用版）組成。

一、教學目的與教學設計

　　高年級的教學目的應從基本的、具體的功能性交際上升到有主題的、抽象的、與社會現實緊密結合的學術性交流上。因此高年級的教學重點應集中在以下四個方面：第一，利用不同的社會、文化內容幫助學生系統掌握正式場合以及學術交流時常用的詞彙、結構、慣用方法、文體及篇章結構；第二，有系統地讓學生了解掌握（正式的）書面語與口語在語言形式、功能、以及交際過程中的特點和區別；第三，通過各種交際練習逐步培養學生從句子、段落、一直到篇章的準確而又得體的表達能力；第四，通過精心選擇的各種課文幫助學生用中文原文學習一系列與中國文化觀念、社會變化、經濟發展、以及風土人情有關的課題，並幫助學生使用所學的語言進行學術性的交流。

　　為配合高年級中文的教學目的，本書在設計上力圖做到以下幾點：

　　（一）在選材上，力圖注意每篇文章的詞彙、結構、文體等具有一定的代表性。學完一課，學生即可以用所學詞彙與結構對與課文題目相關的各種社會、文化問題，進行口頭討論或者書面報告。

　　（二）課文採用對話、電視新聞原文兩種不同的語體，以幫助學生系統掌握中文口語與書面語在不同層次上（詞彙、結構、動賓搭配、語用等方面）的特點。在詞語解釋方面，採用以口語來解釋書面語的形式，並列出口語與書面語對照表讓學生清楚地了解二者的區別。在句型解釋方面，強調書面語的結構特點並同時指出其相應的口語結構。在語法解釋及練習方面，盡量使用各種形式以幫助學生充分掌握這兩種語體的使用。

　　（三）在課文編排上，盡量透過各種具有代表性的題材讓學生接觸中國的各種社會問題，同時也讓學生利用自己在美國大學所學的有關中國文化、歷史知識進行不同角度的討論。目的是避免單純語言學習的局面，讓學生通過對一系列有代表性的課題學會研究、討論、報告該課題所需的一套詞彙和結構。

　　（四）在練習設計上，採用以語言結構為中心和以語言使用為中心的兩類練習，以使學生通過不同目的語言活動來掌握高級中文。

　　（五）在教材設計上，注意選用當代中國大陸的各種電視新聞記實報導以便學生利用真實的語料學習中文。為強化此目的，這套教科書配備了相應的多媒體互動光盤課文與練習，其中包括全部簡繁體課文、逐句與全文聽力閱讀、與課文同步的全部生詞、語法逐項解釋、模擬對話練習、與課文逐句聯結的電視錄象、與上述各部分同步的錄音比較練習、以及全書生詞表和引得等（試用版），以便學生利用現代科技有效學習中文。

二、課文內容與設計：

　　這套教科書共有課文十四篇，補充課文兩篇，均由能反映當代中國社會及文化變遷的電視新聞報

前　言

　　《中国社会文化写实》是为学过两年以上中文的学生设计的一套多媒体语言文化教科书。这套教科书的目的是通过社会、文化多层面的教学内容，各种语体的多媒体真实语料，让学生掌握高年级中文的语言结构、表达方法、以及交流方式。

　　自1996年开始这套教科书在美国一些大学及北京的几个汉语中心进行试用，至今已修改了四版。全书由课本、配合课文的录像带、录音光盘、以及多媒体互动光盘课文与练习（试用版）组成。

一、教学目的与教学设计

　　高年级的教学目的应从基本的、具体的功能性交际上升到有主题的、抽象的、与社会现实紧密结合的学术性交流上。因此高年级的教学重点应集中在以下四个方面：第一，利用不同的社会、文化内容帮助学生系统掌握正式场合以及学术交流时常用的词汇、结构、惯用方法、文体及篇章结构；第二，有系统地让学生了解掌握（正式的）书面语与口语在语言形式、功能、以及交际过程中的特点和区别；第三，通过各种交际练习逐步培养学生从句子、段落、一直到篇章的准确而又得体的表达能力；第四，通过精心选择的各种课文帮助学生用中文原文学习一系列与中国文化观念、社会变化、经济发展、以及风土人情有关的课题，并帮助学生使用所学的语言进行学术性的交流。

　　为配合高年级中文的教学目的，本书在设计上力图做到以下几点：

　　（一）在选材上，力图注意每篇文章的词汇、结构、文体等具有一定的代表性。学完一课，学生即可以用所学词汇与结构对与课文题目相关的各种社会、文化问题，进行口头讨论或者书面报告。

　　（二）课文采用对话、电视新闻原文两种不同的语体，以帮助学生系统掌握中文口语与书面语在不同层次上（词汇、结构、动宾搭配、语用等方面）的特点。在词语解释方面，采用以口语来解释书面语的形式，并列出口语与书面语对照表让学生清楚地了解二者的区别。在句型解释方面，强调书面语的结构特点并同时指出其相应的口语结构。在语法解释及练习方面，尽量使用各种形式以帮助学生充分掌握这两种语体的使用。

　　（三）在课文编排上，尽量透过各种具有代表性的题材让学生接触中国的各种社会问题，同时也让学生利用自己在美国大学所学的有关中国文化、历史知识进行不同角度的讨论。目的是避免单纯语言学习的局面，让学生通过对一系列有代表性的课题学会研究、讨论、报告该课题所需的一套词汇和结构。

　　（四）在练习设计上，采用以语言结构为中心和以语言使用为中心的两类练习，以使学生通过不同目的语言活动来掌握高级中文。

　　（五）在教材设计上，注意选用当代中国大陆的各种电视新闻记实报道以便学生利用真实的语料学习中文。为强化此目的，这套教科书配备了相应的多媒体互动光盘课文与练习，其中包括全部简繁体课文、逐句与全文听力阅读、与课文同步的全部生词、语法逐项解释、模拟对话练习、与课文逐句联结的电视录象、与上述各部分同步的录音比较练习、以及全书生词表和引得等（试用版），以便学生利用现代科技有效学习中文。

二、课文内容与设计：

　　这套教科书共有课文十四篇，补充课文两篇，均由能反映当代中国社会及文化变迁的电视新闻报道導剪輯加工而成。題目涉及單親家庭、經濟改革、獨生子女政策、生活節奏變化、社會名人等等。每課包括三個主要部分：課文、語法重點、和練習。

（一）課文包括三個部分：對話、電視新聞原文、與生詞。對話包括一到兩個對話，目的是用口語對話的形式讓學生先接觸一些與課文主題、背景知識有關的主要詞彙和結構，為進一步系統學習本課涉及的敘述性正式語體打下基礎。在設計本部分內容時，注意做到下列四點：

第一，對話、電視新聞原文在內容上和背景知識上互相補充。例如：在"單親家庭"一課中，對話先介紹中國家庭結構的歷史變化，為學生在討論"單親家庭"時聯系背景進一步展開討論奠定了基礎。

第二，重點詞彙與結構在對話和電視新聞原文中循環使用。例如，每課的對話都在電視新聞原文的詞彙與結構基礎上編寫。除了有系統地增加一些與課文主題有關的詞彙以外，其它大多數詞彙、結構都是電視新聞原文的再循環。這種再循環在語言教學中十分必要：一方面可以最大限度地減少學生對大量生詞出現的畏懼心理；另一方面可以在不同的上下文中進一步加強對重點詞彙與結構的理解和使用。

第三，口語、書面語交錯使用，以使學生能在課文學習中學會區別兩種語體在詞彙和結構上的不同，並能正確使用兩種語體根據不同場合來表達自己的思想。

第四，生詞隨課文分批出現，分附於部分課文中，以便幫助學生分批掌握生詞同時避免課文后一次出現大批生詞的現象。

（二）語法要點分三大部分：詞語解釋、句型、與文化背景知識。

詞語解釋包括書面常用的文言詞、慣用詞的解釋和例句以及成語和專用語的英文解釋，並附有書面語、正式語與口語的對照表。部分課文中也列有方言詞與普通話對照表。

句型包括語法注釋、課文原文、與兩個例句。大多數句型之后還加有問答式的練習以幫助練習目標句型。在選擇句型上，重點從語體的角度突出強調結構的動賓搭配、語法限制、以及各種其他搭配。例如，解釋"受到十賓語"時就列出了可與"受到"搭配的所有名詞。只從語法規則上看，"受到十賓語"的結構很簡單，但從動賓搭配來看，"受到"可與很多名詞結合組成不同的句子以表達不同的思想。這種搭配組合練習是課堂句型練習的一個組成部分。

文化背景知識詳細解釋各種與文化、社會有關的觀念，為學生提供各種背景知識從而能正確理解課文。

（三）練習分為語言結構練習和語言實踐練習。

語言結構練習主要通過各種形式的練習幫助學生掌握每一課的詞彙及結構。練習方法大致有兩種：一是句子層次上的練習，包括短語翻譯、填空、完成句子、句子翻譯；另一個是段落、篇章層次上的練習，比如聽力練習（見錄音光盤）和閱讀練習等。

語言實踐練習主要建議各種實踐活動讓學生利用實際環境使用所學課文進行交流交際。練習形式包括根據課文回答問題、活動、討論題、報告、以及看圖討論。

《中國社會文化寫實》是對高年級中文教學的新嘗試。在很多方面，盡量突破一些舊的教學觀念，採用新的教學理論及方法。由於是新的探索，在很多方面還有待於進一步地完善和進一步地改進。

剪辑加工而成。题目涉及单亲家庭、经济改革、独生子女政策、生活节奏变化、社会名人等等。每课包括三个主要部分：课文、语法重点、和练习。

（一）课文包括三个部分：对话、电视新闻原文、与生词。对话包括一到两个对话，目的是用口语对话的形式让学生先接触一些与课文主题、背景知识有关的主要词汇和结构，为进一步系统学习本课涉及的叙述性正式语体打下基础。在设计本部分内容时，注意做到下列四点：

第一，对话、电视新闻原文在内容上和背景知识上互相补充。例如：在"单亲家庭"一课中，对话先介绍中国家庭结构的历史变化，为学生在讨论"单亲家庭"时联系背景进一步展开讨论奠定了基础。

第二，重点词汇与结构在对话和电视新闻原文中循环使用。例如，每课的对话都在电视新闻原文的词汇与结构基础上编写。除了有系统地增加一些与课文主题有关的词汇以外，其它大多数词汇、结构都是电视新闻原文的再循环。这种再循环在语言教学中十分必要：一方面可以最大限度地减少学生对大量生词出现的畏惧心理；另一方面可以在不同的上下文中进一步加强对重点词汇与结构的理解和使用。

第三，口语、书面语交错使用，以使学生能在课文学习中学会区别两种语体在词汇和结构上的不同，并能正确使用两种语体根据不同场合来表达自己的思想。

第四，生词随课文分批出现，分附于部分课文中，以便帮助学生分批掌握生词同时避免课文后一次出现大批生词的现象。

（二）语法要点分三大部分：词语解释、句型、与文化背景知识。

词语解释包括书面常用的文言词、惯用词的解释和例句以及成语和专用语的英文解释，并附有书面语、正式语与口语的对照表。部分课文中也列有方言词与普通话对照表。

句型包括语法注释、课文原文、与两个例句。大多数句型之后还加有问答式的练习以帮助练习目标句型。在选择句型上，重点从语体的角度突出强调结构的动宾搭配、语法限制、以及各种其他搭配。例如，解释"受到＋宾语"时就列出了可与"受到"搭配的所有名词。只从语法规则上看，"受到＋宾语"的结构很简单，但从动宾搭配来看，"受到"可与很多名词结合组成不同的句子以表达不同的思想。这种搭配组合练习是课堂句型练习的一个组成部分。

文化背景知识详细解释各种与文化、社会有关的观念，为学生提供各种背景知识从而能正确理解课文。

（三）练习分为语言结构练习和语言实践练习。

语言结构练习主要通过各种形式的练习帮助学生掌握每一课的词汇及结构。练习方法大致有两种：一是句子层次上的练习，包括短语翻译、填空、完成句子、句子翻译；另一个是段落、篇章层次上的练习，比如听力练习（见录音光盘）和阅读练习等。

语言实践练习主要建议各种实践活动让学生利用实际环境使用所学课文进行交流交际。练习形式包括根据课文回答问题、活动、讨论题、报告、以及看图讨论。

《中国社会文化写实》是对高年级中文教学的新尝试。在很多方面，尽量突破一些旧的教学观念，采用新的教学理论及方法。由于是新的探索，在很多方面还有待于进一步地完善和进一步地改进。

Preface

China Scene: An Advanced Chinese Multimedia Course is a set of language and cultural teaching materials designed for Chinese language students above the second-year level. The purpose of this textbook is to enable students to master advanced-level Chinese language structures, expressive styles, and conventions of communication through topics reflecting multiple aspects of society and culture, as well as various authentic multimedia materials in different linguistic registers. Beginning in 1996, this textbook was field tested in a number of American colleges and Chinese language centers in Beijing. It is now in its fourth version. Aside from the textbook itself, *China Scene* also offers a DVD, three audio CDs, and multimedia software with interactive video, audio, animation, texts, and exercises to accompany the textbook.

I. INSTRUCTIONAL PURPOSE AND DESIGN

We believe that the pedagogical goal in advanced language teaching should be to begin from basic, concrete, functional communication and progress through abstract, topic-oriented academic exchanges that are closely integrated with real society. Therefore, advanced-level language teaching should focus on the following four areas. First, teachers should utilize different socially and culturally relevant topics to help students systematically master the structures, vocabulary, use of idiomatic expressions, writing styles, and discourse structures commonly used in formal situations and academic exchanges. Second, students should be systematically exposed to the distinguishing features of written and spoken Chinese in terms of language form, function, and communication. Third, teachers should progressively foster students' ability to express themselves accurately and appropriately through communicative exercises at the sentence, paragraph, and discourse levels. Fourth, teachers should select original Chinese texts to help students learn about Chinese cultural concepts, social change, economic development, local customs, and human relationships, with the ultimate goal of enabling students to carry out academic exchanges using what they have learned.

For this purpose, in the design of this book we have tried to accomplish the following:

1. In selecting materials, we have tried to make sure that the vocabulary, structures, and writing style used in each text represent those frequently used in discussion of the topic. After completing a lesson, students should be able to use the structures they have learned to carry out in-depth discussions or write essays on social and cultural issues related to the lesson topics.

2. The content of each lesson is presented in two types of language settings--spoken dialogue and original television text--to help students systematically master the distinguishing features of spoken and written Chinese at the levels of vocabulary, structure, verb-object agreement, pragmatics, etc. For example, in explanations of words, not only have we used everyday speech to explain expressions used primarily in writing, we have also provided tables comparing the two registers to help students understand the differences between the two. Likewise, in explanations of sentence patterns, we have emphasized structural differences between written and spoken forms. Finally, in our grammar explanations and exercises, we have made every effort to include a variety of activities to help students master the usage of these two registers.

3. In choosing lessons, we have attempted to expose students to important issues in contemporary Chinese society and culture through various representative and authentic language materials. At the same time, students are involved in using what they have learned about Chinese culture and history in American universities to carry out discussions from different perspectives. In this way, advanced-level language study is not mere language learning, but rather teaches students, through representative topics and lessons, a cluster of structures and vocabulary necessary to discuss a given topic.

4. In designing exercises, we have given priority to dividing language activities into two types, which focus on language structure and language function respectively. In this way, students can master advanced-level Chinese through different form- and function-oriented activities.

5. In designing teaching materials, in order to make students use modern technology to study Chinese effectively, we have not only used broadcast media reports from contemporary Mainland China to provide students with authentic materials from the media in their study of Chinese; we have also created cross-platform, multimedia, interactive software to accompany the lessons. The software is a complete, multimedia, interactive version of the *China Scene* textbook. It includes simplified and traditional character texts, sentence-by-sentence listening exercises, pop-up vocabulary definitions, sentence explanations in the text, footnotes and cultural notes, conversational exercises, video presentation linked to individual sentences, voice-recording exercises, a vocabulary index, on-line instruction and help, and pop-up menus across lessons. It is a standalone program, and can be used in the classroom, language lab, or at home in lieu of the textbook, or to supplement it.

II. DESIGN OF THE LESSONS

China Scene includes fourteen lessons and two supplementary lessons. In creating these lessons, we have purposely drawn on television programs that reflect changes in contemporary Chinese society and culture as the basis for our editing and revision. The subject matter of the lessons touches upon single-parent families, economic reform, China's one-child policy, changes in the pace of everyday life, notable people in society, and other significant topics. Each lesson has three main sections: the lesson, key grammar points, and exercises.

1. The text of each lesson includes three parts: dialogue, original television text, and new vocabulary. The dialogue section normally includes one or two dialogues, the purpose of which is to use a conversational format to expose students to the main topic, background information, essential vocabulary, and structures in the lesson. From this initial stage, students proceed to the text to systematically study formal language in narrative formats such as news reports and interviews. In designing the content of this section, we have been mindful of accomplishing the following four points:

First, the content and background information in the dialogue and television news report complement each other. For example, in the dialogue of the lesson "Single-Parent Families" we have introduced information about structural changes in the Chinese family so that students can use this background to carry out in-depth discussions about single-parent families.

Second, key vocabulary and structures are purposely repeated throughout the dialogues and original television texts. For example, the dialogues in every lesson are written to incorporate vocabulary and structures from the original television texts. Aside from systematically adding vocabulary related to the main topic of the lesson, most of the remaining vocabulary and structures appear again in the television text. We believe that this type of repetition is absolutely essential in language teaching. On the one hand, this method can greatly reduce students' anxiety over having to learn large quantities of new vocabulary words; on the other hand, it can further strengthen students' mastery of key vocabulary and structures in different contexts.

Third, as for cross-usage between colloquial and written language, we believe this format can help students differentiate between the two language styles at the lexical and structural levels; moreover, students will be able to accurately utilize both language registers to express their own ideas in other settings.

Fourth, in order to avoid presenting one massive vocabulary list at the end of each lesson, new vocabulary words are listed after the section from which they are drawn, so that students master new vocabulary bit by bit.

2. Key grammar points are divided into three parts: "Words and Phrases", "Sentence Structures", and "Cultural Notes".

"Words and Phrases" includes explanations and examples of commonly used Classical Chinese expressions and fixed phrases, English explanations of idioms and specialized terms, and a table comparing formal and colloquial Chinese. In some lessons a table comparing dialectal and standard Chinese expressions is also provided.

"Sentence Structures" includes grammar notes, an example of the pattern as used in the lesson text, and two additional example sentences. Additionally, exercises in question-and-answer format have been added after sentence structures to help students practice target patterns. In selecting sentences structures, our focus is to stress verb-object agreement, grammatical constraints, and other appropriate word pairings in different linguistic contexts. For example, we have purposely selected 受到 (shòudào) + Object and listed all the nouns that may accompany 受到 (shòudào). If we only consider 受到 (shòudào) from the standpoint of grammatical rules, its structure is very simple. However, from the perspective of verb-object agreement, 受到 (shòudào) can be paired with many nouns to form different sentences and express different thoughts. We believe that this kind of classroom exercise enables students to draw connections between a variety of related structures. For this reason, they make up the sentence patterns in the lessons.

"Cultural Notes" specifically deals with cultural and social concepts relevant to the lesson topic. This section provides students with background information that can help them accurately understand each lesson.

3. The "Exercises" section is divided into two parts: "Language Structure" and "Language Practicum".

"Language Structure" helps students master the vocabulary and structures of each lesson, mainly though two different types of exercises: sentence-level and paragraph- or discourse-level. Sentence-level exercises include translation of short passages, fill-in-the-blank exercises, sentence completion, and translations. Paragraph- or discourse-level exercises include listening and reading comprehension.

"Language Practicum" mainly suggests different kinds of activities in which students may apply what they have learned in class to various real-life situations. Types of exercises include answering questions based on the lesson, task-based activities, topics for discussion, reports, and writing stories based on a series of pictures.

In short, *China Scene* represents a new attempt at advanced-level pedagogy. In many ways, we have made every effort to break away from old concepts of teaching, adopting new instructional theories and methods for advanced-level Chinese.

Throughout four years of field testing, we have come to realize that many areas of advanced-level Chinese language pedagogy still await further refinement and systematic research.

Hong Gang Jin, De Bao Xu, James M. Hargett

To Students

The suggestions below are intended to serve two related purposes: (1) to help you use this textbook effectively, and (2) to help you master as much of the material in the lessons as possible. Effective study time management is essential to success in these endeavors. "Study time management" means arranging your daily study schedule so as to maximize your command and retention of the material.

General Suggestions: The first thing you need to do is to familiarize yourself with the layout of the lessons in this textbook. Each lesson is organized in the same way: first come the dialogues and "television texts", each of which has its own separate vocabulary list. Next come explanations of words and phrases, a list of idioms, and key sentence structures. Finally, we provide a series of exercises (translations, dictation, fill-in-the-blank, answering questions based on the dialogue, etc.). Most of these exercises can be done either in class or at home. Also note that there is a vocabulary index at the end of the book. If you forget a word from a previous lesson, chances are good that you can quickly locate it in the index.

Arrange a daily study schedule. As you already know, it is impossible to "cram" Chinese. You must devise an organized and effective daily study schedule and you must stick to it. Try to apportion your study time so you devote equal attention to improving your speaking, reading, listening, and writing skills.

Specific Suggestions: Each lesson contains a wealth of material. How can you best deal with the lengthy vocabulary lists, grammar explanations, new sentence patterns, exercises, and assignments? Our suggestion is to approach the material in "blocks". In other words, do not attempt to master the entire lesson in one sitting. This is impossible. A more effective approach is to concentrate on one portion of the lesson at a time. For instance, start on the first dialogue (or a portion of the first dialogue). After mastering that text, move on to the second one, and so on. Whenever time permits, go back and review earlier material in the lesson.

Most of your daily assignments for class will probably be planned around the dialogues and television texts. Here are some suggestions on how to deal with this material: (1) Learn the vocabulary (or at least familiarize yourself with the new vocabulary). Keep in mind that it's easier to remember vocabulary if you know the root or generic meanings of the individual characters that comprise the new vocabulary items, most of which are made up of two characters. For instance, 補習／补习, meaning "to take lessons after school", appears in Lesson 1. 補／补 means "to mend" (see the "clothing" radical on the left side of the character), "replenish", "add to"; 習／习 means "study". You probably already know that 學習／学习 means "to study". So, in this instance you can use something you know (the 習／习 from 補習／学习) to help you learn something new. (Warning: Many single characters, such as 習／习, which can function as words in Classical Chinese, cannot be used alone as words in Modern Chinese, but must be combined with another character to form a word [補習／补习 is a good example].) If you are unsure whether a 字／字 [single character] can be used as a 詞／词 [word], check with your teacher! The idea here is to try and draw links between what you already know and the new words you encounter in the textbook. This approach will to help you to get a handle on the new vocabulary. (2) Read carefully through the key sentence structures (or sentence patterns). These are explained in each lesson. Again, the best way to do this is to make sure you know the meanings of the individual characters/words that form the structure. For instance, the pattern 發生…變化／发生…變化／变化 (Lesson 1) means "to undergo change". If you are aware that 發生／发生 is a verb meaning "to happen" or "take place" and that 變化／变化 ("change") functions as a noun-object for that verb, you'll easily remember the meaning of this structure. Take note of how the pattern works in the sample sentences; if you cannot understand the sample sentence, ask your teacher for help. (3) When preparing assignments, always read the material aloud! Do so with your best pronunciation and tones. With repetition, the sound and tonal qualities of the new vocabulary and sentence structures, along with the context in which they appear, can help you to remember the material. When focusing on the new vocabulary and patterns, try to devise your own sentences (say them aloud!).

Keep it simple at first. Remember, your ultimate goal is to master the patterns and vocabulary so you can use them to express your own thoughts and ideas.

Two final suggestions: First, you should strongly encourage your teacher(s) to correct you whenever you make a mistake. Believe it or not, many teachers are reluctant to correct students' errors because they fear the student will be offended. We contend that there is nothing "wrong" with making mistakes! The challenge, of course, is to learn from your mistakes (take notes, if necessary!) so you don't repeat them. So, tell your teacher(s) that you expect her or him to correct your mistakes! Second, you should make every possible effort to master all the material in the lessons. This is a daunting challenge. But even if you don't succeed, what is most essential is your total commitment to "learning everything". Don't let anything slip by you! Like any endeavor related to acquiring a new skill, attitude and commitment are key ingredients to success.

We hope the advice offered here will prove useful.

Good luck!

Hong Gang Jin, De Bao Xu, and James M. Hargett

课文
Texts

第一課

單親家庭

An Advanced Chinese Multimedia Course

China | Scene

第一课

单亲家庭

課文

一、對話  Dialogs

---

（一）

小麗：何茹，你為甚麼坐在這兒掉眼淚，一句話也不說？怎麼回事？

何茹：我爸爸昨天從美國來信了，他說他要留在美國，再也不回來了。我怎麼也沒想到[1]他會永遠也不回來了。

小麗：是嗎？他怎麼可以這樣呢？聽你說自從你爸走後，你媽媽就一個人挑起家庭的重擔，又要操持家務，又要教育孩子，把自己多少年的光陰都奉獻給了你們的家。

何茹：這還不算[2]，爸爸走後，我變得怪僻，不願念書，也不寫功課。媽為我急死了，花了很多錢，又請家教，又給我補習，才使我一天天好起來。我真想不通[3]，為甚麼我媽這麼無[4]私，可我爸卻這麼自私？為了留在美國，居然拋棄了自己的妻子和女兒。

小麗：你現在應該給你爸爸寫封信，告訴他你是怎麼想的，也許他會改變他的想法。

Notes [1]怎麼也沒想到 means "I never would have thought" or "I never would have expected". Here 怎麼 means "however", "no matter how" and must be used with either 也 or 都. Example: 怎麼說他都不聽. (No matter what I say, he never listens.)

[2]這還不算 means "what's more", "not only that", or "there's even more to what I just said". This colloquial expression is used to continue an explanation or to give additional examples or information. Example: 我要去城西，那個司機把我拉到了城東。這還不算，他還多要了二十塊！ (I wanted to go to the western part of the city, but the driver took me to the east. And what's more, he charged me an extra twenty *yuan*!)

[3]通, "to get through to" or "to understand", can be used as a complement in potential verb combinations. 想不通 translates as "unable （不） to figure something out （通） by thinking （想） about it". The corresponding positive form of this potential verb complement is 想得通 (able to figure something out by thinking about it). Examples: （電話）打得通 (able to dial through); 跟那個人說不通. (You can't get that person to understand anything.)

[4]無: The character 無 means "without" and is borrowed from Classical Chinese. It is often used in Modern Chinese to form disyllabic expressions such as 無限 (limitless, infinite) and 無私 (selfless) in this lesson. The second element in these disyllabic expressions is always a single-syllable noun, as in 無名 (nameless, anonymous) and 無法 (lacking a way to do something, incapable of).

课文

一、对话 Dialogs

（一）

小丽：何茹，你为什么坐在这儿掉眼泪，一句话也不说？怎么回事？

何茹：我爸爸昨天从美国来信了，他说他要留在美国，再也不回来了。我怎么也没想到[1]他会永远也不回来了。

小丽：是吗？他怎么可以这样呢？听你说自从你爸走后，你妈妈就一个人挑起家庭的重担，又要操持家务，又要教育孩子，把自己多少年的光阴都奉献给了你们的家。

何茹：这还不算[2]，爸爸走后，我变得怪僻，不愿念书，也不写功课。妈为我急死了，花了很多钱，又请家教，又给我补习，才使我一天天好起来。我真想不通[3]，为什么我妈这么无[4]私，可我爸却这么自私？为了留在美国，居然抛弃了自己的妻子和女儿。

小丽：你现在应该给你爸爸写封信，告诉他你是怎么想的，也许他会改变他的想法。

Notes: [1]怎么也没想到 means "I never would have thought" or "I never would have expected". Here 怎么 means "however", "no matter how" and must be used with either 也 or 都. Example: 怎么说他都不听. (No matter what I say, he never listens.)

[2]这还不算 means "what's more", "not only that", or "there's even more to what I just said". This colloquial expression is used to continue an explanation or to give additional examples or information. Example: 我要去城西，那个司机把我拉到了城东。这还不算，他还多要了二十块！ (I wanted to go to the western part of the city, but the driver took me to the east. And what's more, he charged me an extra twenty *yuan*!)

[3]通, "to get through to" or "to understand", can be used as a complement in potential verb combinations. 想不通 translates as "unable (不) to figure something out (通) by thinking (想) about it". The corresponding positive form of this potential verb complement is 想得通 (able to figure something out by thinking about it). Examples: （电话）打得通 (able to dial through); 跟那个人说不通. (You can't get that person to understand anything.)

[4]无: The character 无 means "without" and is borrowed from Classical Chinese. It is often used in Modern Chinese to form disyllabic expressions such as 无限 (limitless, infinite) and 无私 (selfless) in this lesson. The second element in these disyllabic expressions is always a single-syllable noun, as in 无名 (nameless, anonymous) and 无法 (lacking a way to do something, incapable of).

生詞

單親家庭	(dān qīn jiā tíng)	NP.	single-parent family
何茹	(hé rú)	N.	He Ru, name of a person 人名
掉眼淚	(diào yǎn lèi)	VO.	to shed tears
小麗	(xiǎo lì)	N.	Xiao Li, name of a person 人名
永遠	(yǒng yuǎn)	Adv.	forever, always
挑起	(tiāo qǐ)	V.	to carry, to shoulder
重擔	(zhòng dàn)	N.	burden
操持	(cāo chí)	V.	to take care of, to manage
家務	(jiā wù)	N.	household chores
教育	(jiào yù)	N/V.	education; to teach, to educate
光陰	(guāng yīn)	N.	lifetime, time
奉獻	(fèng xiàn)	V.	to devote to
怪僻	(guài pì)	Adj.	eccentric, weird, odd (of a person or his/her behaviors)
不願	(bù yuàn)	V.	to be unwilling
家教	(jiā jiào)	N.	family teacher, special tutor
補習	(bǔ xí)	V.	to take lessons after school
想不通	(xiǎng bù tōng)	VP.	cannot think through, cannot make sense out of
無私	(wú sī)	Adj.	selfless
自私	(zì sī)	Adj.	selfish
居然	(jū rán)	Adv.	unexpectedly, surprisingly, contrary to one's expectations
拋棄	(pāo qì)	V.	to abandon, to dump, to desert, to forsake
封	(fēng)	Classifier.	measure word for letters
改變	(gǎi biàn)	N/V.	change; to change, to alter, to correct

（二）

小麗：昨天我才知道我的朋友何茹的父親跟她母親離婚了，一個人留在美國不回來了。

我想問問你，這種現象在中國多嗎？

朱明：現在這種單親家庭的現象越來越多。

生词

单亲家庭	(dān qīn jiā tíng)	NP.	single-parent family
何茹	(hé rú)	N.	He Ru, name of a person 人名
掉眼泪	(diào yǎn lèi)	VO.	to shed tears
小丽	(xiǎo lì)	N.	Xiao Li, name of a person 人名
永远	(yǒng yuǎn)	Adv.	forever, always
挑起	(tiāo qǐ)	V.	to carry, to shoulder
重担	(zhòng dàn)	N.	burden
操持	(cāo chí)	V.	to take care of, to manage
家务	(jiā wù)	N.	household chores
教育	(jiào yù)	N/V.	education; to teach, to educate
光阴	(guāng yīn)	N.	lifetime, time
奉献	(fèng xiàn)	V.	to devote to
怪僻	(guài pì)	Adj.	eccentric, weird, odd (of a person or his/her behaviors)
不愿	(bù yuàn)	V.	to be unwilling
家教	(jiā jiào)	N.	family teacher, special tutor
补习	(bǔ xí)	V.	to take lessons after school
想不通	(xiǎng bù tōng)	VP.	cannot think through, cannot make sense out of
无私	(wú sī)	Adj.	selfless
自私	(zì sī)	Adj.	selfish
居然	(jū rán)	Adv.	unexpectedly, surprisingly, contrary to one's expectations
抛弃	(pāo qì)	V.	to abandon, to dump, to desert, to forsake
封	(fēng)	Classifier.	measure word for letters
改变	(gǎi biàn)	N/V.	change; to change, to alter, to correct

（二）

小丽：昨天我才知道我的朋友何茹的父亲跟她母亲离婚了，一个人留在美国不回来了。我想问问你，这种现象在中国多吗？

朱明：现在这种单亲家庭的现象越来越多。

小麗：是嗎？這是為甚麼？

朱明：你知道，這幾十年中國的家庭結構發生了很大的變化。以前是大家庭，三代同堂、四代同堂。那時候人們結婚、離婚都要受到家庭、社會和政治的限制。七十年代以後，出現了一家一個孩子的小家庭，但是離婚的人還是不多。

小麗：那現在呢？

朱明：從八十年代起，中國開放了，人們的生活條件也有了很大的改變，很多人開始對自己的婚姻不滿意，要求離婚。這樣由於離婚的增多，中國又出現了單親家庭的現象。

小麗：那這種現象對孩子的成長有影響嗎？

朱明：這種現象肯定對孩子的成長有影響。

生詞

朱明	(zhū míng)	N.	Zhu Ming, name of a person 人名
結構	(jié gòu)	N.	structure
三代同堂	(sān dài tóng táng)	Idiom.	three generations under one roof
政治	(zhèng zhì)	N.	politics
限制	(xiàn zhì)	V/N.	to limit; limit, limitation, restriction
開放	(kāi fàng)	V.	to open up, to open
條件	(tiáo jiàn)	N.	condition
滿意	(mǎn yì)	Adj/N.	to be satisfied; satisfaction
要求	(yāo qiú)	N/V.	demand, requirement
由於	(yóu yú)	Prep.	as a result of, due to, owing to
增多	(zēng duō)	V/N.	to increase; increase, growth in number or quantity
成長	(chéng zhǎng)	N/V.	growth, development; to grow

小丽：是吗？这是为什么？

朱明：你知道，这几十年中国的家庭结构发生了很大的变化。以前是大家庭，三代同堂、四代同堂。那时候人们结婚、离婚都要受到家庭、社会和政治的限制。七十年代以后，出现了一家一个孩子的小家庭，但是离婚的人还是不多。

小丽：那现在呢？

朱明：从八十年代起，中国开放了，人们的生活条件也有了很大的改变，很多人开始对自己的婚姻不满意，要求离婚。这样由于离婚的增多，中国又出现了单亲家庭的现象。

小丽：那这种现象对孩子的成长有影响吗？

朱明：这种现象肯定对孩子的成长有影响。

生词

朱明	(zhū míng)	N.	Zhu Ming, name of a person 人名
结构	(jié gòu)	N.	structure
三代同堂	(sān dài tóng táng)	Idiom.	three generations under one roof
政治	(zhèng zhì)	N.	politics
限制	(xiàn zhì)	V/N.	to limit; limit, limitation, restriction
开放	(kāi fàng)	V.	to open up, to open
条件	(tiáo jiàn)	N.	condition
满意	(mǎn yì)	Adj/N.	to be satisfied; satisfaction
要求	(yāo qiú)	N/V.	demand, requirement
由于	(yóu yú)	Prep.	as a result of, due to, owing to
增多	(zēng duō)	V/N.	to increase; increase, growth in number or quantity
成长	(chéng zhǎng)	N/V.	growth, development; to grow

二、電視原文 TV original

給爸爸的一封信

（根據原文改編）

爸爸：

您好嗎？我們遠隔千里，但是這封信寄去了女兒的思念與悲傷[5]，也許當您看完會想到很多很多……

90年，我才11歲，還是個天真頑皮的小姑娘。當媽媽將殘酷的現實告訴我時，雖然我不懂"離異"的含義，可我知道，我最愛、最崇拜的爸爸走了，他要"出差"，很長很長的時間，再也不回來了……

淚水淌過[6]我的面頰[7]，我撲在媽媽懷裡，無限傷心[8]地哭了一場[9]。

我變了，變得沉默，甚至有些怪僻，不愛學習，不寫作業。媽媽為這事急壞了。在媽媽和老師的關懷下，我又一天一天地好起來，可心靈上的創傷卻再也無法癒合……

上六年級時，媽媽花了五百多塊錢為我請來了兩個家教，幫我補習數學和語文。五百元錢也許對一個普通家庭不算甚麼，但對一個單身母親卻是一個不小的數字。然而媽媽卻不在乎為我花這些錢。只要孩子能受更好的教育，她心甘情願。這就是母愛，這就是母愛的無私和偉大。

Notes [5]悲傷 vs. 傷心: Both 悲傷 and 傷心 can function as adjectives meaning meaning "sad" 悲傷, however, can also function as a noun (sadness), while 傷心 cannot. Example: 女兒的思念與悲傷 (a daughter's longing and sadness).

[6]See Note (8).

[7]面頰 vs. 臉: 面頰 can mean either "face" or specifically "cheeks", depending on context. It is used exclusively in written Chinese. The colloquial word for face is 臉.

[8]淌過 vs. 流下: The verbs 淌過 and 流下 both mean "to drip", "to run down" and are used to mean "to cry". 淌过 is more common in written Chinese. The subject of a sentence using 淌過 is often "tears"; the object is often a place word. Example: 淚水淌過我的面頰. (Tears are running down my cheeks.) 流下, on the other hand, is more common in colloquial Chinese. Its subject is usually a person, and commonly used objects include 淚 (tears) and 熱淚 (hot tears). Example: 他高興得流下了眼淚. (He was so happy that he cried.)

[9]場: When describing events that take place for a period of time, such as sporting events and movies, the measure word 場 is often used. Examples: 她昨天看了三場電影. (She watched three movies yesterday.) 我今天下午看了一場球賽. (I went to a ball game this afternoon.) 場 is also used in reference to situations such as crying: 他哭了一場. (He cried a spell.)

二、电视原文 　 TV original

给爸爸的一封信

（根据原文改编）

爸爸：

　　您好吗？我们远隔千里，但是这封信寄去了女儿的思念与悲伤[5]，也许当您看完会想到很多很多……

　　90年，我才11岁，还是个天真顽皮的小姑娘。当妈妈将残酷的现实告诉我时，虽然我不懂"离异"的含义，可我知道，我最爱、最崇拜的爸爸走了，他要"出差"，很长很长的时间，再也不回来了……

　　泪水淌过[6]我的面颊[7]，我扑在妈妈怀里，无限伤心[8]地哭了一场[9]。

　　我变了，变得沉默，甚至有些怪僻，不爱学习，不写作业。妈妈为这事急坏了。在妈妈和老师的关怀下，我又一天一天地好起来，可心灵上的创伤却再也无法愈合……

　　上六年级时，妈妈花了五百多块钱为我请来了两个家教，帮我补习数学和语文。五百元钱也许对一个普通家庭不算什么，但对一个单身母亲却是一个不小的数字。然而妈妈却不在乎为我花这些钱。只要孩子能受更好的教育，她心甘情愿。这就是母爱，这就是母爱的无私和伟大。

Notes [5]悲伤 vs. 伤心: Both 悲伤 and 伤心 can function as adjectives meaning "sad". 悲伤, however, can also function as a noun (sadness), while 伤心 cannot. Example: 女儿的思念与悲伤 (a daughter's longing and sadness).

[6]See Note (8).

[7]面颊 vs. 脸: 面颊 can mean either "face" or specifically "cheeks", depending on context. It is used exclusively in written Chinese. The colloquial word for face is 脸.

[8]淌过 vs. 流下: The verbs 淌过 and 流下 both mean "to drip", "to run down" and are used to mean "to cry". 淌过 is more common in written Chinese. The subject of a sentence using 淌过 is often "tears"; the object is often a place word. Example: 泪水淌过我的面颊. (Tears are running down my cheeks.) 流下, on the other hand, is more common in colloquial Chinese. Its subject is usually a person, and commonly used objects include 泪 (tears) and 热泪 (hot tears). Example: 他高兴得流下了眼泪. (He was so happy that he cried.)

[9]场: When describing events that take place for a period of time, such as sporting events and movies, the measure word 场 is often used. Examples: 她昨天看了三场电影. (She watched three movies yesterday.) 我今天下午看了一场球赛. (I went to a ball game this afternoon.) 场 is also used in reference to situations such as crying: 他哭了一场. (He cried a spell.)

從這事以後，媽媽更加沉默了，她更老了，似乎又經歷了一次驚濤駭浪。為這事我一輩子也不能原諒自己。爸爸，任何人都有自私的時候，可也有應該奉獻的時候。媽媽無私地將十三年光陰奉獻給了這個家，她操持家務，教育孩子，唯一想得到的就是屬於自己的家，一個完整的家。然而，您沒有給她，您為了自己拋棄了妻子和女兒。

爸爸，這三年中，我給您寫過信，也寄過生日卡。可您不僅沒有看過我，甚至沒給我寫過一個字。別的孩子過生日都能得到父母雙雙的祝福，我卻只能得到母親的這一份。爸爸，我常想起我小的時候，想起和您在一起的情景。可惜那一切都成了過去。我希望您讀過這封信後，能記起您曾經有一個溫暖的家，一個可愛的女兒。

　　此致(10)

敬禮

　　　　　　　　　　您的女兒：何茹

生詞

原文	(yuán wén)	NP.	original text, the original
改編	(gǎi biān)	V.	to adapt, to revise
遠隔千里	(yuǎn gé qiān lǐ)	Idiom.	thousands of miles away
寄	(jì)	V.	to send, to mail
思念	(sī niàn)	V/N.	to miss, long for (somebody)
悲傷	(bēi shāng)	N.	sorrow, sadness
90年	(jiǔ líng nián)	Time N.	1990
天真	(tiān zhēn)	Adj.	naive
頑皮	(wán pí)	Adj.	mischievous
殘酷	(cán kù)	Adj.	cruel
現實	(xiàn shí)	N.	reality
離異	(lí yì)	N.	separation
含義	(hán yì)	N.	meaning, implication

Notes (10)此致, borrowed from Classical Chinese, is often used as a salutation at the close of a letter. Literally, it means "here （此） I convey （致）". 此致 is generally used in formal, written communications. It is indented at the bottom of a letter and followed by 敬禮 or 安康. People of lower social status often use this phrase in letters to a superior; for example, He Ru uses it when writing to her father.

　　从这事以后，妈妈更加沉默了，她更老了，似乎又经历了一次惊涛骇浪。为这事我一辈子也不能原谅自己。爸爸，任何人都有自私的时候，可也有应该奉献的时候。妈妈无私地将十三年光阴奉献给了这个家，她操持家务，教育孩子，唯一想得到的就是属于自己的家，一个完整的家。然而，您没有给她，您为了自己抛弃了妻子和女儿。

　　爸爸，这三年中，我给您写过信，也寄过生日卡。可您不仅没有看过我，甚至没给我写过一个字。别的孩子过生日都能得到父母双双的祝福，我却只能得到母亲的这一份。爸爸，我常想起我小的时候，想起和您在一起的情景。可惜那一切都成了过去。我希望您读过这封信后，能记起您曾经有一个温暖的家，一个可爱的女儿。

　　　　此致[10]

敬礼

　　　　　　　　　　　　　　　您的女儿：何茹

生词

原文	(yuán wén)	NP.	original text, the original
改编	(gǎi biān)	V.	to adapt, to revise
远隔千里	(yuǎn gé qiān lǐ)	Idiom.	thousands of miles away
寄	(jì)	V.	to send, to mail
思念	(sī niàn)	V/N.	to miss, long for (somebody)
悲伤	(bēi shāng)	N.	sorrow, sadness
90年	(jiǔ líng nián)	Time N.	1990
天真	(tiān zhēn)	Adj.	naive
顽皮	(wán pí)	Adj.	mischievous
残酷	(cán kù)	Adj.	cruel
现实	(xiàn shí)	N.	reality
离异	(lí yì)	N.	separation
含义	(hán yì)	N.	meaning, implication

Notes [10]此致, borrowed from Classical Chinese, is often used as a salutation at the close of a letter. Literally, it means "here （此） I convey （致）". 此致 is generally used in formal, written communications. It is indented at the bottom of a letter and followed by 敬礼 or 安康. People of lower social status often use this phrase in letters to a superior; for example, He Ru uses it when writing to her father.

崇拜	(chóng bài)	V.	to adore
出差	(chū chāi)	VO.	to be on a business trip, on business
淚水	(lèi shuǐ)	N.	tear, teardrop
淌	(tǎng)	V.	to fall
面頰	(miàn jiá)	N.	cheek, face
撲	(pū)	V.	to throw oneself into
懷裡	(huái lǐ)	PP.	in someone's arms or embrace
無限	(wú xiàn)	Adj.	infinite, without limit
傷心	(shāng xīn)	Adj.	sad
場	(chǎng)	Classifier.	measure word for a period of time
沉默	(chén mò)	N/Adj.	silence, silent
甚至	(shèn zhì)	Adv.	even, to the extent that
關懷	(guān huái)	VP.	show concern for, care
心靈	(xīn líng)	N.	heart and soul
創傷	(chuāng shāng)	N.	wound
無法	(wú fǎ)	VP.	unable, no way
瘉合	(yù hé)	V.	to heal, to recover
單身	(dān shēn)	Adj/N.	unmarried, single; an unmarried person
數字	(shù zì)	N.	number, amount
然而	(rán ér)	Adv.	but, however
不在乎	(bù zài hu)	VP.	not care
心甘情願	(xīn gān qíng yuàn)	Idiom.	be most willing to, willingness
偉大	(wěi dà)	Adj.	great, mighty
似乎	(sì hū)	V.	to seem as if
經歷	(jīng lì)	N./V.	experience; to experience
驚濤駭浪	(jīng tāo hài làng)	Idiom.	terrifying waves, hardship in one's life
原諒	(yuán liàng)	V.	to forgive, to excuse
唯一	(wéi yī)	Adj.	only, sole
屬於	(shǔ yú)	V.	to belong to, to be a part of
完整	(wán zhěng)	Adj.	whole, complete, entire
生日卡	(shēng rì kǎ)	N.	birthday card
雙雙	(shuāng shuāng)	Adv.	both, both of
祝福	(zhù fú)	N/V.	blessing, to bless

崇拜	(chóng bài)	*V.*	to adore
出差	(chū chāi)	*VO.*	to be on a business trip, on business
泪水	(lèi shuǐ)	*N.*	tear, teardrop
淌	(tǎng)	*V.*	to fall
面颊	(miàn jiá)	*N.*	cheek, face
扑	(pū)	*V.*	to throw oneself into
怀里	(huái lǐ)	*PP.*	in someone's arms or embrace
无限	(wú xiàn)	*Adj.*	infinite, without limit
伤心	(shāng xīn)	*Adj.*	sad
场	(chǎng)	*Classifier.*	measure word for a period of time
沉默	(chén mò)	*N/Adj.*	silence, silent
甚至	(shèn zhì)	*Adv.*	even, to the extent that
关怀	(guān huái)	*VP.*	show concern for, care
心灵	(xīn líng)	*N.*	heart and soul
创伤	(chuāng shāng)	*N.*	wound
无法	(wú fǎ)	*VP.*	unable, no way
愈合	(yù hé)	*V.*	to heal, to recover
单身	(dān shēn)	*Adj/N.*	unmarried, single; an unmarried person
数字	(shù zì)	*N.*	number, amount
然而	(rán ér)	*Adv.*	but, however
不在乎	(bù zài hu)	*VP.*	not care
心甘情愿	(xīn gān qíng yuàn)	*Idiom.*	be most willing to, willingness
伟大	(wěi dà)	*Adj.*	great, mighty
似乎	(sì hū)	*V.*	to seem as if
经历	(jīng lì)	*N./V.*	experience; to experience
惊涛骇浪	(jīng tāo hài làng)	*Idiom.*	terrifying waves, hardship in one's life
原谅	(yuán liàng)	*V.*	to forgive, to excuse
唯一	(wéi yī)	*Adj.*	only, sole
属于	(shǔ yú)	*V.*	to belong to, to be a part of
完整	(wán zhěng)	*Adj.*	whole, complete, entire
生日卡	(shēng rì kǎ)	*N.*	birthday card
双双	(shuāng shuāng)	*Adv.*	both, both of
祝福	(zhù fú)	*N/V.*	blessing, to bless

情景	(qíng jǐng)	N.	scene, situation
可惜	(kě xī)	Adv/Adj.	unfortunately; of pity, to be a pity
曾經	(céng jīng)	Adv.	once, in the past, formerly
溫暖	(wēn nuǎn)	Adj.	warm
此致	(cǐ zhì)	VP.	a salutation used at the end of a letter to indicate closure
敬禮	(jìng lǐ)	VO.	a salutation used at the end of a letter, meaning "respectfully, with best wishes"

情景	(qíng jǐng)	*N.*	scene, situation
可惜	(kě xī)	*Adv/Adj.*	unfortunately; of pity, to be a pity
曾经	(céng jīng)	*Adv.*	once, in the past, formerly
温暖	(wēn nuǎn)	*Adj.*	warm
此致	(cǐ zhì)	*VP.*	a salutation used at the end of a letter to indicate closure
敬礼	(jìng lǐ)	*VO.*	a salutation used at the end of a letter, meaning "respectfully, with best wishes"

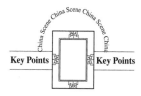

課文要點

一、詞語解釋  Words and Phrases

（一）文言詞、慣用詞 (Classical Chinese and idiomatic expressions)

1、同堂＝同在一個屋室裡
☞ 以前是大家庭，三代同堂、四代同堂。

2、与＝和、跟
☞ 这封信寄去了女儿的思念与悲伤。

3、將＝把
☞ 媽媽將殘酷的現實告訴了我。

4、無法（限）＝沒有（法子、限制）
☞ 我撲在媽媽懷裡，無限傷心地哭了一場。

5、時＝的時候
☞ 上六年級時，媽媽花了五百多塊錢為我請來了兩個家教。

6、然而＝但是
☞ 然而媽媽卻不在乎為我花這些錢。

7、此＝這、這兒
☞ 此致

（二）成語 (Idioms)

◆ 四代同堂 multi-generational family, four generations under one roof

◆ 遠隔千里 thousands of miles away, separated by great distance

◆ 天真頑皮 naive and mischievous

◆ 心甘情願 willing, agreeable, amenable

◆ 驚濤駭浪 trials and tribulations

课文要点

一、词语解释 Words and Phrases

（一）文言词、惯用词 (Classical Chinese and idiomatic expressions)

1、同堂 = 同在一个屋室里

☞ 以前是大家庭，三代同堂、四代同堂。

2、与 = 和、跟

☞ 这封信寄去了女儿的思念与悲伤。

3、将 = 把

☞ 妈妈将残酷的现实告诉了我。

4、无法（限）= 没有（法子、限制）

☞ 我扑在妈妈怀里，无限伤心地哭了一场。

5、时 = 的时候

☞ 上六年级时，妈妈花了五百多块钱为我请来了两个家教。

6、然而 = 但是

☞ 然而妈妈却不在乎为我花这些钱。

7、此 = 这、这儿

☞ 此致

（二）成语 (Idioms)

◆ 四代同堂 multi-generational family, four generations under one roof

◆ 远隔千里 thousands of miles away, separated by great distance

◆ 天真顽皮 naive and mischievous

◆ 心甘情愿 willing, agreeable, amenable

◆ 惊涛骇浪 trials and tribulations

二、書面語、正式語、口語對照表 ‖‖‖ Written/formal/colloquial Comparison

	書面／正式語	口語		書面／正式語	口語
1	淚水	眼淚	11	無限+adj.	非常／很
2	淌（眼淚）	掉（眼淚）	12	心靈	心裡
3	光陰	時間	13	無法	沒有法子
4	把…奉獻給…	把…都給…	14	癒合	好起來
5	思念	想	15	然而	可是
6	與	和／跟	16	似乎	好像
7	悲傷(adj)	難受	17	雙雙	兩個人
8	當…的時候	在…的時候	18	一切	所有的事情
9	面頰	臉	19	曾經	以前
10	卻 (adv.)	可是(conj.)			

三、句型 ✵ Sentence Structures

（一）發生（了）……的變化 (to undergo change, changes take place)

> ✎ 發生……的變化 is a structure used to describe changes （變化） taking place （發生） in something. The subject of 發生 can be a person, a place, or an institution. Examples: 何茹的母親這幾年發生了很大的變化. (He Ru's mother has undergone a major change in the last few years.) 中國這幾年的經濟制度發生了令人吃驚的變化. (In recent years, China's economic system has undergone some changes that have surprised people.) 學校裡發生了一些奇怪的變化. (The school experienced some unusual changes.)

☞ 這幾十年中國的家庭結構發生了很大的變化。

1、中國的社會結構由於西方的影響也發生了一些變化。

As a result of Western influence, changes have taken place within Chinese society.

2、單親家庭的出現說明中國的社會已經發生了變化。

The existence of single-parent families shows that changes have already taken place in Chinese society.

問：很多人一到國外就永遠不想回國了，這是為甚麼？
答：這是因為＿＿＿＿＿＿＿＿＿＿＿＿＿＿＿＿＿＿＿＿。

二、书面语、正式语、口语对照表 Written/formal/colloquial Comparison

	书面／正式语	口语		书面／正式语	口语
1	泪水	眼泪	11	无限+adj.	非常／很
2	淌（眼泪）	掉（眼泪）	12	心灵	心里
3	光阴	时间	13	无法	没有法子
4	把…奉献给…	把…都给…	14	愈合	好起来
5	思念	想	15	然而	可是
6	与	和／跟	16	似乎	好象
7	悲伤(adj.)	难受	17	双双	两个人
8	当…的时候	在…的时候	18	一切	所有的事情
9	面颊	脸	19	曾经	以前
10	却(adv.)	可是(conj.)			

三、句型 Sentence Structures

（一）发生（了）……的变化 (to undergo change, changes take place)

> ✍ 发生……的变化 is a structure used to describe changes（变化）taking place（发生）in something. The subject of 发生 can be a person, a place, or an institution. Examples: 何茹的母亲这几年发生了很大的变化. (He Ru's mother has undergone a major change in the last few years.) 中国这几年的经济制度发生了令人吃惊的变化. (In recent years, China's economic system has undergone some changes that have surprised people.) 学校里发生了一些奇怪的变化. (The school experienced some unusual changes.)

☞ 这几十年中国的家庭结构发生了很大的变化。

1、中国的社会结构由于西方的影响也发生了一些变化。
As a result of Western influence, changes have taken place within Chinese society.

2、单亲家庭的出现说明中国的社会已经发生了变化。
The existence of single-parent families shows that changes have already taken place in Chinese society.

问: 很多人一到国外就永远不想回国了，这是为什么？
答: 这是因为＿＿＿＿＿＿＿＿＿＿＿＿＿＿＿＿＿＿＿＿＿。

（二）受到……的限制 (to be limited by, to be restricted by)

> ✍ 受到……限制, "to be limited by" or "to be restricted by", is often used in a passive sense. Thus, English translations of this structure often include the passive voice indicator "by". 受到 here functions as a verb meaning "to suffer from" when followed by a noun with negative connotation, such as 限制 (restrictions) or 批評 (criticism). Examples: 離婚受到家庭的限制. (Divorce is restricted by families.) 這件事受到政府的批評. (This incident was criticized by the government.) 受到 can also mean "to receive" when followed by nouns with positive meanings such as 歡迎 (welcome) and 喜愛 (fondness). Examples: 這個生日卡受到很多人的歡迎. (This birthday card has been well received by many people.) 那件禮品受到人們的喜愛. (That gift was well liked by others.) When negating this pattern, the negative indicator 沒有 or 不 is normally placed before 受到.

☞ 那時候人們結婚、離婚都要受到家庭、社會和政治的限制。

1、以前中國的經濟受到很多的限制，所以發展得並不快。

In the past, China's economy was under many restrictions, so it has not developed quickly.

2、在結婚、離婚這樣的問題上，五十年代的中國人常常受到社會的限制嗎？

In terms of issues such as marriage and divorce, did Chinese people in the 1950s frequently suffer from social restrictions?

問：以前在中國找工作或者換工作受到一些甚麼限制？
答：＿＿＿＿＿＿＿＿＿＿＿＿＿＿＿＿＿＿＿＿＿＿。

（三）對……滿意／不滿意 (to be satisfied/dissatisfied with)

> ✍ 對……滿意／不滿意 is a structure used to express satisfaction （滿意） or dissatisfaction （不滿意） with a particular situation or person. Here, 對 literally means "toward" or "with respect to". Only the negative particle 不 can be used to negate this pattern, and it must be placed immediately before the verb.

☞ 很多人開始對自己的婚姻不滿意，要求離婚。

1、你對現在的學習條件和生活條件滿意不滿意？

Are you satisfied with the current studying and living conditions?

2、要是一個人對自己的生活不滿意，他就應該努力改變（它）。

If a person is dissatisfied with their life, they should try to change it.

問：你請家教給孩子補習數學已經三年了，你＿＿＿＿＿＿？
答：我覺得還不錯。孩子的學習成績還是有一定的提高。

11

（二）受到……的限制 (to be limited by, to be restricted by)

> ✍ 受到……限制, "to be limited by" or "to be restricted by", is often used in a passive sense. Thus, English translations of this structure often include the passive voice indicator "by". 受到 here functions as a verb meaning "to suffer from" when followed by a noun with negative connotation, such as 限制 (restrictions) or 批评 (criticism). Examples: 离婚受到家庭的限制. (Divorce is restricted by families.) 这件事受到政府的批评. (This incident was criticized by the government.) 受到 can also mean "to receive" when followed by nouns with positive meanings such as 欢迎 (welcome) and 喜爱 (fondness). Examples: 这个生日卡受到很多人的欢迎. (This birthday card has been well received by many people.) 那件礼品受到人们的喜爱. (That gift was well liked by others.) When negating this pattern, the negative indicator 没有 or 不 is normally placed before 受到.

☞ 那时候人们结婚、离婚都要受到家庭、社会和政治的限制。

1、以前中国的经济受到很多的限制，所以发展得并不快。

In the past, China's economy was under many restrictions, so it has not developed quickly.

2、在结婚、离婚这样的问题上，五十年代的中国人常常受到社会的限制吗？

In terms of issues such as marriage and divorce, did Chinese people in the 1950s frequently suffer from social restrictions?

问：以前在中国找工作或者换工作受到一些什么限制？
答：_____。

（三）对……满意／不满意 (to be satisfied/dissatisfied with)

> ✍ 对……满意／不满意 is a structure used to express satisfaction （满意） or dissatisfaction （不满意） with a particular situation or person. Here, 对 literally means "toward" or "with respect to". Only the negative particle 不 can be used to negate this pattern, and it must be placed immediately before the verb.

☞ 很多人开始对自己的婚姻不满意，要求离婚。

1、你对现在的学习条件和生活条件满意不满意？

Are you satisfied with the current studying and living conditions?

2、要是一个人对自己的生活不满意，他就应该努力改变（它）。

If a person is dissatisfied with their life, they should try to change it.

问：你请家教给孩子补习数学已经三年了，你_____？
答：我觉得还不错。孩子的学习成绩还是有一定的提高。

11

（四）　由於……的（增多／影響／變化／問題）　(because of, due to)

> ✍ 由於, "because of" or "due to", is often used in written or formal Chinese. It can be followed by a noun phrase, such as 由於人口的增多 (because of an increase in population), 由於政府的影響 (due to government influence), 由於社會的變化 (because of changes in society), and so on. 由於 can also be followed by a sentence, as in 由於他的經歷很特別 (because his experience is unique), 由於他想留在美國 (because he wants to remain in America). The 由於 clause can only be used as the first part of a sentence.

☞ 這樣由於離婚的增多，中國又出現了單親家庭的現象。

1、由於這件事的影響，我變得更沉默也更怪僻了。

Because of this incident, I have become more silent and eccentric.

2、由於功課的增多，很多學生都不看書就去做練習。

Because they have more homework, many students do exercises without even reading the book.

問：為甚麼現在中國三代同堂的大家庭越來越少？

答：＿＿＿＿＿＿＿＿＿＿＿＿＿＿＿＿＿＿＿＿＿＿＿。

（五）出現……（的）現象 (there occurs a phenomenon of)

> ✍ 出現……的現象 indicates that a certain phenomenon （現象） appeared or occurred （出現）. 出現 functions as an existential verb and can be followed by a noun phrase which describes a phenomenon or situation, often a noun indicating a place or time. Examples: 學校出現了一些奇怪的現象. (Some strange things have happened at school.) 這是八十年代出現的一個特殊的情況. (This is a special situation that occurred in the 1980s.) When negating this pattern, only 沒有 can be used before 出現.

☞ 這樣由於離婚的增多，中國又出現了單親家庭的現象。

1、八十年代中國出現了人人想出國留學的現象。

In the 1980s, the trend in China was for everyone to study abroad.

2、由於人們的想法改變了，社會上也出現了很多新現象，比方說，快餐、生日卡等等。

Because the way people think has changed, many new phenomena have appeared in society, such as fast food, birthday cards, etc.

問：最近校園裡有甚麼變化？我出國六個月甚麼都不知道。

答：＿＿＿＿＿＿＿＿＿＿＿＿＿＿＿＿＿＿＿＿＿＿。

（四）由于……的（增多／影响／变化／问题）(because of, due to)

> ✎ 由于, "because of" or "due to", is often used in written or formal Chinese. It can be followed by a noun phrase, such as 由于人口的增多 (because of an increase in population), 由于政府的影响 (due to government influence), 由于社会的变化 (because of changes in society), and so on. 由于 can also be followed by a sentence, as in 由于他的经历很特别 (because his experience is unique), 由于他想留在美国 (because he wants to remain in America). The 由于 clause can only be used as the first part of a sentence.

☞ 这样由于离婚的增多，中国又出现了单亲家庭的现象。

1、由于这件事的影响，我变得更沉默也更怪僻了。
　Because of this incident, I have become more silent and eccentric.
2、由于功课的增多，很多学生都不看书就去做练习。
　Because they have more homework, many students do exercises without even reading the book.

　问：为什么现在中国三代同堂的大家庭越来越少？
　答：＿＿＿＿＿＿＿＿＿＿＿＿＿＿＿＿＿＿＿＿＿。

（五）出现……（的）现象 (there occurs a phenomenon of)

> ✎ 出现……的现象 indicates that a certain phenomenon （现象） appeared or occurred （出现）. 出现 functions as an existential verb and can be followed by a noun phrase which describes a phenomenon or situation, often a noun indicating a place or time. Examples: 学校出现了一些奇怪的现象. (Some strange things have happened at school.) 这是八十年代出现的一个特殊的情况. (This is a special situation that occurred in the 1980s.) When negating this pattern, only 没有 can be used before 出现.

☞ 这样由于离婚的增多，中国又出现了单亲家庭的现象。

1、八十年代中国出现了人人想出国留学的现象。
　In the 1980s, the trend in China was for everyone to study abroad.
2、由于人们的想法改变了，社会上也出现了很多新现象，比方说，快餐、生日卡等等。
　Because the way people think has changed, many new phenomena have appeared in society, such as fast food, birthday cards, etc.
　问：最近校园里有什么变化？我出国六个月什么都不知道。
　答：＿＿＿＿＿＿＿＿＿＿＿＿＿＿＿＿＿＿＿＿＿。

（六）A 對 B 有（很大的）影響／A 對 B 影響很大 (A has an influence on B)

> ✍ A 對 B 有（很大）的影響 and A 對 B 影響很大 are interchangeable and mean the same thing: A has a strong influence on B, or A influences B in a profound way. When negating the first of these patterns, 沒 must be placed directly before the verb 有. Example: 我的家庭對我沒有影響。(My family has no influence on me.) In the second pattern, however, 不 must be used before 大. Example: 我的家庭對我影響不大。(My family has no significant influence on me.)

☞ 這種現象肯定對孩子的成長有影響。

1、父母離異無疑對孩子有很大的影響。

When parents separate, it has a strong influence on their children.

2、老師的好壞對學生的影響很大。

Whether the teacher is good or bad has a great influence on the students.

問：你認為_____？

答：我覺得政府的人口政策肯定對中國的家庭結構有影響。

（七）將（／把）……告訴…… (to tell someone about something)

> ✍ 將（／把）……告訴…… means "to tell someone about something". Either 將 or 把 can be used to introduce the object. 將 is normally used in formal or written Chinese, whereas 把 is used in colloquial Chinese. When negating this pattern, 不, 別, or 沒有 must be placed before 將 or 把. Example: 同學們沒有將此事告訴學校。(The classmates did not inform the school about this matter.)

☞ 當媽媽將殘酷的現實告訴我時，雖然我不懂"離異"的含義，可我知道，我最愛、最崇拜的爸爸走了。

1、當我將我的經歷告訴他時，他突然變得十分沉默。

When I told him about my experience, he immediately fell silent.

2、請你把一切都告訴我。

Please tell me everything.

問：小麗怎麼知道何茹父母離異的事？

答：_____。

（六）A 对 B 有（很大的）影响／A 对 B 影响很大 (A has an influence on B)

> ✍ A 对 B 有（很大）的影响 and A 对 B 影响很大 are interchangeable and mean the same thing: A has a strong influence on B, or A influences B in a profound way. When negating the first of these patterns, 没 must be placed directly before the verb 有. Example: 我的家庭对我没有影响. (My family has no influence on me.) In the second pattern, however, 不 must be used before 大. Example: 我的家庭对我影响不大. (My family has no significant influence on me.)

☞ 这种现象肯定对孩子的成长有影响。

1、父母离异无疑对孩子有很大的影响。

When parents separate, it has a strong influence on their children.

2、老师的好坏对学生的影响很大。

Whether the teacher is good or bad has a great influence on the students.

问：你认为＿＿＿＿＿＿＿＿＿＿＿＿＿＿＿＿＿＿＿？

答：我觉得政府的人口政策肯定对中国的家庭结构有影响。

（七）将（／把）……告诉…… (to tell someone about something)

> ✍ 将（／把）……告诉…… means "to tell someone about something". Either 将 or 把 can be used to introduce the object. 将 is normally used in formal or written Chinese, whereas 把 is used in colloquial Chinese. When negating this pattern, 不, 别, or 没有 must be placed before 将 or 把. Example: 同学们没有将此事告诉学校. (The classmates did not inform the school about this matter.)

☞ 当妈妈将残酷的现实告诉我时，虽然我不懂"离异"的含义，可我知道，我最爱、最崇拜的爸爸走了。

1、当我将我的经历告诉他时，他突然变得十分沉默。

When I told him about my experience, he immediately fell silent.

2、请你把一切都告诉我。

Please tell me everything.

问：小丽怎么知道何茹父母离异的事？

答：＿＿＿＿＿＿＿＿＿＿＿＿＿＿＿＿。

13

（八）……的含義 (the meaning of)

> ✍ 含義 here means "meaning" or "implication". Although 含義 and 意思 can both be translated as "meaning" in English, they are used in different senses in Chinese. 含義 is often modified by abstract nouns that refer to the deeper meaning of something. Examples: 離異的含義 (the real meaning of separation); 自由的含義 (the implications of freedom). On the other hand, 意思 may be modified by any kind of noun and refers to the literal meaning of a word or expression. Example: 崇拜的意思是甚麼? (What does *chongbai* mean?)

☞ 雖然我不懂"離異"的含義，可我知道，我最愛、最崇拜的爸爸走了。

1、我一點都不懂"痛苦"的含義。

I do not understand the meaning of suffering at all.

2、為甚麼你不能理解"奉獻"的含義？

Why can't you understand what it means to be devoted to something?

問：你真能理解他為甚麼說"我太對不起我的學校了"嗎？

答：雖然＿＿＿＿＿＿＿，可是＿＿＿＿＿＿＿＿＿＿。

（九）在……的關懷下 (under the care of)

> ✍ （九）在……的關懷下, "under the care of", is often used as a prepositional phrase at the beginning of a sentence. Unlike in English, this phrase can never be placed at the end of a Chinese sentence.

☞ 在媽媽和老師的關懷下，我又一天一天地好起來，可心靈上的創傷卻再也無法癒合……

1、在父母雙雙的關懷下，我一天天長大了。

Under both parents's care, I grew bigger each day.

2、在老師的關懷下，我的心靈創傷終於癒合了。

Under my teacher's care, my wounded heart finally healed.

問：你妹妹的學習成績是怎麼一天一天好起來的？

答：＿＿＿＿＿＿＿＿＿＿＿＿＿＿＿＿。

（十）在乎／不在乎 (to care/not care about)

> ✍ 在乎 (to care about) and 不在乎 (to not care about) are most often used in colloquial Chinese. The negative form is almost always 不在乎; 沒 is rarely used to negate 在乎.

（八）……的含义 (the meaning of)

> 含义 here means "meaning" or "implication". Although 含义 and 意思 can both be translated as "meaning" in English, they are used in different senses in Chinese. 含义 is often modified by abstract nouns that refer to the deeper meaning of something. Examples: 离异的含义 (the real meaning of separation); 自由的含义 (the implications of freedom). On the other hand, 意思 may be modified by any kind of noun and refers to the literal meaning of a word or expression. Example: 崇拜的意思是什么？ (What does *chongbai* mean?)

☞ 虽然我不懂"离异"的含义，可我知道，我最爱、最崇拜的爸爸走了。

1、我一点都不懂"痛苦"的含义。

I do not understand the meaning of suffering at all.

2、为什么你不能理解"奉献"的含义？

Why can't you understand what it means to be devoted to something?

问：你真能理解他为什么说"我太对不起我的学校了"吗？

答：虽然＿＿＿＿＿＿＿＿＿，可是＿＿＿＿＿＿＿＿＿＿。

（九）在……的关怀下 (under the care of)

> 在……的关怀下, "under the care of", is often used as a prepositional phrase at the beginning of a sentence. Unlike in English, this phrase can never be placed at the end of a Chinese sentence.

☞ 在妈妈和老师的关怀下，我又一天一天地好起来，可心灵上的创伤却再也无法愈合……

1、在父母双双的关怀下，我一天天长大了。

Under both parents' care, I grew bigger each day.

2、在老师的关怀下，我的心灵创伤终于愈合了。

Under my teacher's care, my wounded heart finally healed.

问：你妹妹的学习成绩是怎么一天一天好起来的？

答：＿＿＿＿＿＿＿＿＿＿＿＿＿＿＿＿＿。

（十）在乎／不在乎 (to care/not care about)

> 在乎 (to care about) and 不在乎 (to not care about) are most often used in colloquial Chinese. The negative form is almost always 不在乎；没 is rarely used to negate 在乎.

☞ 然而媽媽卻不在乎為我花這些錢。只要孩子能受更好的教育，她心甘情願。

1、他根本不在乎別人說甚麼，每天都在學他想學的東西。

He simply does not care what other people say. Every day he studies whatever he wants to study.

2、為了留在美國，他連拋棄妻子兒女都不在乎。

He did not even care that he deserted his wife and children to stay in the U.S.

問：＿＿＿＿＿＿＿＿＿＿＿＿＿＿＿＿＿＿＿＿＿＿＿？

答：因為他受爸爸的影響很大，他一點都不在乎自己的學習成績。

（十一）將（／把）……奉獻給…… (to be devoted or dedicated to)

> ✍ 將（／把）……奉獻給……, meaning "to be devoted or dedicated to", is most often used in formal or written Chinese. Grammatically, it follows the same rules as 將（把）……告訴…… (see Pattern 7 above). The two rules for using 把 and 將 still apply: 把 is more prevalent in spoken Chinese while 將 is more common in written Chinese; and the negative particle 不 or 沒 is normally placed before 將 or 把. Nouns which commonly follow 將 or 把 in this pattern are 時間, 心血, 光陰, 一生, 一切, etc. Example: 這位中學教師並沒有將自己的一切奉獻給學校. (This middle school teacher was really never completely devoted to the school.)

☞ 媽媽無私地將十三年光陰奉獻給了這個家。

1、我的爸爸將他的一顆心都奉獻給了這個家。

My father has devoted his heart to this family.

2、那個家教把她所有的時間都奉獻給了她的學生，使學生的成績一天天好起來。

That professor devotes all of her time to her students, which makes the students' grades improve daily.

問：你為甚麼會這麼崇拜你的老師？

答：＿＿＿＿＿＿＿＿＿＿＿＿＿我當然崇拜這樣的人。

☞ 然而妈妈却不在乎为我花这些钱。只要孩子能受更好的教育，她心甘情愿。

1、他根本不在乎别人说什么，每天都在学他想学的东西。

He simply does not care what other people say. Every day he studies whatever he wants to study.

2、为了留在美国，他连抛弃妻子儿女都不在乎。

He did not even care that he deserted his wife and children to stay in the U.S.

问: _____?

答: 因为他受爸爸的影响很大，他一点都不在乎自己的学习成绩。

（十一）将（／把）……奉献给…… (to be devoted or dedicated to)

✍ 将（／把）……奉献给……, meaning "to be devoted or dedicated to", is most often used in formal or written Chinese. Grammatically, it follows the same rules as 将（把）……告诉…… (see Pattern 7 above). The two rules for using 把 and 将 still apply: 把 is more prevalent in spoken Chinese while 将 is more common in written Chinese; and the negative particle 不 or 没 is normally placed before 将 or 把. Nouns which commonly follow 将 or 把 in this pattern are 时间, 心血, 光阴, 一生, 一切, etc. Example: 这位中学教师并没有将自己的一切奉献给学校. (This middle school teacher was really never completely devoted to the school.)

☞ 妈妈无私地将十三年光阴奉献给了这个家。

1、我的爸爸将他的一颗心都奉献给了这个家。

My father has devoted his heart to this family.

2、那个家教把她所有的时间都奉献给了她的学生，使学生的成绩一天天好起来。

That professor devotes all of her time to her students, which makes the students' grades improve daily.

问: 你为什么会这么崇拜你的老师？

答: _____我当然崇拜这样的人。

15

四、文化背景知識 Cultural Notes

1. 家教: this term literally means "family education" or "learning at home". It is also sometimes used in the broader sense of "family upbringing" (to say that a person "沒有家教" means that she has not received proper upbringing at home). Here, however, the term is used in the sense of "tutor": He Ru's mother has invited someone (家教) to come to their home to help He Ru with her studies. This is a common practice in China, especially when a student is having difficulty with his/her school work.

2. 三代同堂: Until quite recently, it was common for multiple generations of a family to live in the same household (同堂), usually with the senior male member serving as patriarch. Single-parent families (單親家庭) were uncommon, mainly because there were severe social and legal restraints against divorce (regardless of marriage problems, family unity was valued above all else). This situation changed with the sweeping economic reforms and social changes in the 1980s. Although there are more divorces now in China than at anytime in the past, the divorce rate in China is still low when compared with the United States.

3. Four-character idioms (成語 chéngyǔ) are common in Modern Chinese. Many of these expressions are drawn from Classical Chinese (古文 or 文言文). They provide a convenient means (only four characters) to describe a situation or a person. If possible, check the dictionary meanings of individual characters in the idioms you encounter. This will help you remember them and recognize them in other contexts. Important: Note that the language structure of many of these expressions is parallel or balanced. For instance, 驚濤駭浪 (translated in our text as "trials and tribulations") is comprised of two, balanced sets of adjectives + nouns (驚濤, literally, "torrential-billows"; and 駭浪, literally, "frightening-waves"). The structure of 心甘情願 (willing, agreeable, amenable) is also parallel. Try to figure it out.

四、文化背景知识 Cultural Notes

1. 家教: this term literally means "family education" or "learning at home". It is also sometimes used in the broader sense of "family upbringing" (to say that a person "没有家教" means that she has not received proper upbringing at home). Here, however, the term is used in the sense of "tutor": He Ru's mother has invited someone (家教) to come to their home to help He Ru with her studies. This is a common practice in China, especially when a student is having difficulty with his/her school work.

2. 三代同堂: Until quite recently, it was common for multiple generations of a family to live in the same household (同堂), usually with the senior male member serving as patriarch. Single-parent families (单亲家庭) were uncommon, mainly because there were severe social and legal restraints against divorce (regardless of marriage problems, family unity was valued above all else). This situation changed with the sweeping economic reforms and social changes in the 1980s. Although there are more divorces now in China than at anytime in the past, the divorce rate in China is still low when compared with the United States.

3. Four-character idioms (成语 chéngyǔ) are common in Modern Chinese. Many of these expressions are drawn from Classical Chinese (古文 or 文言文). They provide a convenient means (only four characters) to describe a situation or a person. If possible, check the dictionary meanings of individual characters in the idioms you encounter. This will help you remember them and recognize them in other contexts. Important: Note that the language structure of many of these expressions is parallel or balanced. For instance, 惊涛骇浪 (translated in our text as "trials and tribulations") is comprised of two, balanced sets of adjectives + nouns (惊涛, literally, "torrential-billows"; and 骇浪, literally, "frightening-waves"). The structure of 心甘情愿 (willing, agreeable, amenable) is also parallel. Try to figure it out.

練習

語言結構 Structures

一、短語翻譯 (Phrase translation)

1. to be thousands of miles away
2. love and sorrow
3. harsh reality
4. the meaning of "separation"
5. tears running down the face
6. to become quiet and eccentric
7. to hurt in one's heart
8. an ordinary family
9. a selfless mother
10. blessings from both parents
11. a warm and loving home
12. a scene of being with my mother
13. single parent
14. birthday card

二、聽力練習 (Listening comprehension)

1、聽寫 (Dictation)

2、聽錄音並回答問題 (Answering questions while listening to the audio CD)
   (1) 從信中你可以知道小麗跟何茹有甚麼樣的關係？
   (2) 寫出小麗給何茹的信的全文。

三、改寫下面劃線的詞 (Replace the underlined words)

　　當我把這個殘酷的現實告訴那個怪僻的人的時侯，他一下子變得十分沉默。從這事以後，誰都沒有法子跟他説話。

练习

语言结构 Structures

一、短语翻译 (Phrase translation)

1. to be thousands of miles away
2. love and sorrow
3. harsh reality
4. the meaning of "separation"
5. tears running down the face
6. to become quiet and eccentric
7. to hurt in one's heart
8. an ordinary family
9. a selfless mother
10. blessings from both parents
11. a warm and loving home
12. a scene of being with my mother
13. single parent
14. birthday card

二、听力练习 (Listening comprehension)

1、听写 (Dictation)

2、听录音并回答问题 (Answering questions while listening to the audio CD)
    (1) 从信中你可以知道小丽跟何茹有什么样的关系？
    (2) 写出小丽给何茹的信的全文。

三、改写下面划线的词 (Replace the underlined words)

当我把这个残酷的现实告诉那个怪僻的人<u>的时侯</u>，他一下子变得十分沉默。从<u>这事</u>以后，谁都<u>没有法子</u>跟他说话。

四、填空 (Fill in the blanks)

遠隔千里、天真頑皮、心甘情願、驚濤駭浪

1、我們這一代人經歷了一次又一次的＿＿＿＿＿＿＿，現在讓我們去再經歷這樣的生活，我想沒有一個人會＿＿＿＿＿＿＿。

2、雖然你與我分離十年，而且我們＿＿＿＿＿＿＿，可是我還記得你那＿＿＿＿＿＿＿的樣子。

五、完成句子 (Complete the sentences)

1、　　A：聽説你最近去中國了，情況怎麼樣？你給介紹介紹好嗎？
　　　　B：行啊。你知道在中國，＿＿＿＿＿＿＿＿＿＿＿＿＿＿＿＿＿＿＿

　　　　＿＿＿＿＿＿＿＿＿＿＿＿＿＿＿＿＿＿＿＿＿＿＿＿＿＿＿＿＿＿＿

　　　　（由於……的影響；發生……的變化）

2、　　A：你知道這張生日卡上寫的話有甚麼含義？
　　　　B：這張生日卡＿＿＿＿＿＿＿＿＿＿＿＿＿＿＿＿＿＿＿＿＿＿＿＿

　　　　＿＿＿＿＿＿＿＿＿＿＿＿＿＿＿＿＿＿＿＿＿＿＿＿＿＿＿＿＿＿＿

　　　　（似乎……；從此以後……）

3、　　A：聽説他爸爸和他媽媽離婚了。
　　　　B：是嗎？我真不明白，＿＿＿＿＿＿＿＿＿＿＿＿＿＿＿＿＿＿＿＿

　　　　＿＿＿＿＿＿＿＿＿＿＿＿＿＿＿＿＿＿＿＿＿＿＿＿＿＿＿＿＿＿＿

　　　　（將／把……奉獻給……；原諒……）

六、閱讀短文、回答問題 (Answering questions based on the reading passages)

自從改革開放以來，很多人有機會到國外去工作或者學習。由於人們的生活條件、環境和觀念都發生了很大的變化，而且也了解到了“自由”的含義，所以很多人願意留在國外再也不要回中國去了；還有些人為了留在美國甚至拋棄了自己的妻子和兒女。這樣，有很多中國家庭由於一個人出國另一個人不想出國而不得不分離，變成單親家庭。

問題
　　　　為甚麼有很多人希望留在美國？請從兩個方面説明。

四、填空 (Fill in the blanks)

远隔千里、天真顽皮、心甘情愿、惊涛骇浪

1、我们这一代人经历了一次又一次的＿＿＿＿＿＿，现在让我们去再经历这样的生活，我想没有一个人会＿＿＿＿＿＿。

2、虽然你与我分离十年，而且我们＿＿＿＿＿＿，可是我还记得你那＿＿＿＿＿＿的样子。

五、完成句子 (Complete the sentences)

1、　A：听说你最近去中国了，情况怎么样？你给介绍介绍好吗？
　　B：行啊。你知道在中国，＿＿＿＿＿＿＿＿＿＿＿＿＿＿＿＿
　　＿＿＿＿＿＿＿＿＿＿＿＿＿＿＿＿＿＿＿＿＿＿＿＿＿＿＿＿＿
　　（由于……的影响；发生……的变化）

2、　A：你知道这张生日卡上写的话有什么含义？
　　B：这张生日卡＿＿＿＿＿＿＿＿＿＿＿＿＿＿＿＿＿＿＿＿＿＿
　　＿＿＿＿＿＿＿＿＿＿＿＿＿＿＿＿＿＿＿＿＿＿＿＿＿＿＿＿＿
　　（似乎……；从此以后……）

3、　A：听说他爸爸和他妈妈离婚了。
　　B：是吗？我真不明白，＿＿＿＿＿＿＿＿＿＿＿＿＿＿＿＿＿＿
　　＿＿＿＿＿＿＿＿＿＿＿＿＿＿＿＿＿＿＿＿＿＿＿＿＿＿＿＿＿
　　（将／把……奉献给……；原谅……）

六、阅读短文、回答问题 (Answering questions based on the reading passages)

自从改革开放以来，很多人有机会到国外去工作或者学习。由于人们的生活条件、环境和观念都发生了很大的变化，而且也了解到了"自由"的含义，所以很多人愿意留在国外再也不要回中国去了；还有些人为了留在美国甚至抛弃了自己的妻子和儿女。这样，有很多中国家庭由于一个人出国另一个人不想出国而不得不分离，变成单亲家庭。

问题
　　为什么有很多人希望留在美国？请从两个方面说明。

中國的父母都認為孩子的教育是最重要的事情，除了幫孩子念書，做功課以外，很多家庭還要孩子下課以後念補習班，如果不上補習班，就給孩子每月花幾百元錢請個家教補習數學、語文、或者英文。幾百元錢對於一個中國家庭來説不是一個小數目，但是多數的中國父母並不在乎這些錢。只要孩子能受最好的教育，他們做甚麼事情都心甘情願。

問題
(1) 舉出三個例子説明中國的父母很注意孩子的教育。
(2) 用你的經歷談談美國人用甚麼方法讓孩子受到很好的教育。

七、翻譯 (Translate sentences)

1. Although my sister does not understand the meaning of "being thousands of miles away", she knows that our father will be away on business for a long time.

2. Under the care of my parents, the wound in my heart began to heal day by day.

3. I can never forgive my father because he is such a selfish person who never did housework and never paid attention to his children's education.

4. Unlike her father, her mother is a selfless person who devoted 30 years of her life to the family. All she wants is a warm and loving family.

中国的父母都认为孩子的教育是最重要的事情，除了帮孩子念书，做功课以外，很多家庭还要孩子下课以后念补习班，如果不上补习班，就给孩子每月花几百元钱请个家教补习数学、语文、或者英文。几百元钱对于一个中国家庭来说不是一个小数目，但是多数的中国父母并不在乎这些钱。只要孩子能受最好的教育，他们做什么事情都心甘情愿。

问题

(1) 举出三个例子说明中国的父母很注意孩子的教育。

(2) 用你的经历谈谈美国人用什么方法让孩子受到很好的教育。

七、翻译 (Translate sentences)

1. Although my sister does not understand the meaning of "being thousands of miles away", she knows that our father will be away on business for a long time.

2. Under the care of my parents, the wound in my heart began to heal day by day.

3. I can never forgive my father because he is such a selfish person who never did housework and never paid attention to his children's education.

4. Unlike her father, her mother is a selfless person who devoted 30 years of her life to the family. All she wants is a warm and loving family.

語言實踐 ⁝ Practice

一、根據課文回答問題 (Answering questions based on the dialogue)

1、何茹幾歲的時候就沒有爸爸了？那個時候她懂不懂甚麼叫"離異"？
2、爸爸走後，何茹有甚麼變化？她的母親為她做了些甚麼使她一天天好起來？
3、何茹對她的父親和母親的看法是甚麼？
4、何茹寫信給她父親，是要告訴他甚麼？
5、何茹給爸爸的信反映了中國一個甚麼社會問題？

二、活動 (Activities)

去北京的小學校，找小學的小朋友或者老師談談現在單親孩子多不多，他們的生活、學習怎麼樣？他們周圍的小朋友怎麼看單親家庭的孩子？

三、討論題 (Topics for discussion)

1、要是你是何茹，你會怎麼看你的父親？美國人對父母的觀念跟中國人有甚麼不同？
2、跟單親父母長大的孩子與別的孩子有甚麼不同？
3、學完這一課以後，你看到中國最近出現了一個甚麼社會問題？

四、報告 (Presentation)

你是何茹的爸爸，請你給何茹寫一封回信，跟她說明你為甚麼要跟何茹的母親分開。

语言实践：Practice

一、根据课文回答问题 (Answering questions based on the dialogue)

1、何茹几岁的时候就没有爸爸了？那个时候她懂不懂什么叫"离异"？
2、爸爸走后，何茹有什么变化？她的母亲为她做了些什么使她一天天好起来？
3、何茹对她的父亲和母亲的看法是什么？
4、何茹写信给她父亲，是要告诉他什么？
5、何茹给爸爸的信反映了中国一个什么社会问题？

二、活动 (Activities)

　　去北京的小学校，找小学的小朋友或者老师谈谈现在单亲孩子多不多，他们的生活、学习怎么样？他们周围的小朋友怎么看单亲家庭的孩子？

三、讨论题 (Topics for discussion)

1、要是你是何茹，你会怎么看你的父亲？美国人对父母的观念跟中国人有什么不同？
2、跟单亲父母长大的孩子与别的孩子有什么不同？
3、学完这一课以后，你看到中国最近出现了一个什么社会问题？

四、报告 (Presentation)

　　你是何茹的爸爸，请你给何茹写一封回信，跟她说明你为什么要跟何茹的母亲分开。

五、看圖討論 (Picto-discussion)

1

2

3

4

5

6

五、看图讨论 (Picto-discussion)

1

2

3

4

5

6

China Scene
An Advanced Chinese Multimedia Course

第二課

領養女嬰

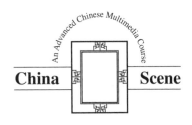

第二课

领养女婴

課文

一、對話  Dialogs

---

（一）

張東和：你知道現在美國有很多人去中國領養孩子，尤其是領養女嬰。

韓凱：　是嗎？中國不是有一家一個孩子的人口政策嗎？怎麼可能有那麼多被父母拋棄的孩子呢？

張東和：就是因為有一家一個孩子的政策，才有很多的女嬰被拋棄。我想在有些地方，人們的想法還很落後，所以，很多女孩子一生下來就被狠心的父母扔在醫院[1]或其它地方，尤其是一些有殘疾[2]的女孩子，她們的遭遇[3]就更不幸了。秋雲的故事就是一個很好的例子。

韓凱：　秋雲是誰？她怎麼了？

張東和：秋雲是一個孤兒，因為她右眼有殘疾，她的父母就把她扔在天津兒童醫院的大椅子上了。

韓凱：　真狠心哪！要是我沒有孩子我一定要領養一個，讓他（她）有一個溫暖的家庭。

張東和：我聽說天津有一個很好的兒童福利院，你可以去那裡領養。

Notes [1]院: In traditional China, an enclosed courtyard was called a 院. In Modern Chinese, this character is a suffix which denotes institutions, as in 醫院 (hospital), 老人院 (nursing home), 研究院 (research institute), and so on. In contrast, 園 means "garden" or "park", as 花園 (flower garden) and 公園 (public park). The only time 園 is used for an institution is in 幼兒園 (kindergarten).

[2]毛病, 殘疾, and 創傷: 毛病 refers to a defective physical condition or a psychological condition or insane behavior in a person. Examples: 我的車有毛病了. (There is something wrong with my car.) 她的腦筋有毛病. (She's messed up in the head.) 殘疾 refers to a physical handicap, as in 殘疾人 (a handicapped person) and 他身體有殘疾. (He is physically handicapped.) 創傷 refers to a physical injury or psychological trauma. Example: 他的創傷是打仗時候留下的. (His wounds are left over from his war days.)

[3]遭遇 vs. 經歷: 遭遇 and 經歷 can both be translated as the noun "experience", but differ in usage. 遭遇 refers to bitter or adverse experiences, as in 不幸的遭遇 (an unfortunate experience). 經歷, on the other hand, can refer to either positive or negative experiences, as in 幸福的經歷 (a happy experience); 可怕的經歷 (a frightening experience).

课文

一、对话 Dialogs

（一）

张东和：你知道现在美国有很多人去中国领养孩子，尤其是领养女婴。

韩凯：是吗？中国不是有一家一个孩子的人口政策吗？怎么可能有那么多被父母抛弃的孩子呢？

张东和：就是因为有一家一个孩子的政策，才有很多的女婴被抛弃。我想在有些地方，人们的想法还很落后，所以，很多女孩子一生下来就被狠心的父母扔在医院[1]或其它地方，尤其是一些有残疾[2]的女孩子，她们的遭遇[3]就更不幸了。秋云的故事就是一个很好的例子。

韩凯：秋云是谁？她怎么了？

张东和：秋云是一个孤儿，因为她右眼有残疾，她的父母就把她扔在天津儿童医院的大椅子上了。

韩凯：真狠心哪！要是我没有孩子我一定要领养一个，让他（她）有一个温暖的家庭。

张东和：我听说天津有一个很好的儿童福利院，你可以去那里领养。

Notes [1] 院: In traditional China, an enclosed courtyard was called a 院. In Modern Chinese, this character is a suffix which denotes institutions, as in 医院 (hospital), 老人院 (nursing home), 研究院 (research institute), and so on. In contrast, 园 means "garden" or "park", as 花园 (flower garden) and 公园 (public park). The only time 园 is used for an institution is in 幼儿园 (kindergarten).

[2] 毛病, 残疾, and 创伤: 毛病 refers to a defective physical condition or a psychological condition or insane behavior in a person. Examples: 我的车有毛病了. (There is something wrong with my car.) 她的脑筋有毛病. (She's messed up in the head.) 残疾 refers to a physical handicap, as in 残疾人 (a handicapped person) and 他身体有残疾. (He is physically handicapped.) 创伤 refers to a physical injury or psychological trauma. Example: 他的创伤是打仗时候留下的. (His wounds are left over from his war days.)

[3] 遭遇 vs. 经历: 遭遇 and 经历 can both be translated as the noun "experience", but differ in usage. 遭遇 refers to bitter or adverse experiences, as in 不幸的遭遇 (an unfortunate experience). 经历, on the other hand, can refer to either positive or negative experiences, as in 幸福的经历 (a happy experience); 可怕的经历 (a frightening experience).

生詞

領養	(lǐng yǎng)	*V.*	to adopt
女嬰	(nū yīng)	*N.*	baby girl
張東和	(zhāng dōng hé)	*N.*	Zhang Donghe, name of a person 人名
韓凱	(hán kǎi)	*N.*	Han Kai, name of a person 人名
政策	(zhèng cè)	*N.*	policy
落後	(luò hòu)	*Adj.*	backward
狠心	(hěn xīn)	*Adj.*	cruel, heartless
扔	(rēng)	*V.*	to throw away, to cast aside
殘疾	(cán jí)	*Adj/N.*	handicapped
遭遇	(zāo yù)	*N.*	(bitter) experience
不幸	(bù xìng)	*Adj.*	unfortunate
孤兒	(gū ér)	*N.*	orphan
天津	(tiān jīn)	*Place N.*	Tianjin, name of a city in China 地名
兒童醫院	(ér tóng yī yuàn)	*NP.*	children's hospital
福利院	(fú lì yuàn)	*NP.*	welfare institute

（二）

（幾年以後，在美國）

韓凱：你好！你叫甚麼名字？

秋雲：我叫秋雲。

韓凱：你是中國人，為甚麼你的父母都是美國人？

秋雲：因為我是被領養到美國來的。十五年前，我出生在天津。一生下來，我的父母就發現我的眼睛有毛病[4]，而且沒有治[5]，他們就把我扔在醫院的長椅上。醫院

✏️ **Notes** [4]See Note (2).

[5]沒（有）治 literally means "there is no cure", i.e., for a medical condition or disease. In colloquial Chinese, this expression is often used to mean that there is no way to deal with a certain person or situation. Example: 我們真拿他沒治. (We really can't do anything about him.) Yet another meaning of 沒治 is "terrific" or "outstanding". Example: 小李這個人好得簡直沒治了！(That Xiao Wang is simply terrific!) The opposite expression 有治 (there is a cure) can only be used when referring to diseases, not to people or situations.

生词

领养	(lǐng yǎng)	*V.*	to adopt
女婴	(nū yīng)	*N.*	baby girl
张东和	(zhāng dōng hé)	*N.*	Zhang Donghe, name of a person 人名
韩凯	(hán kǎi)	*N.*	Han Kai, name of a person 人名
政策	(zhèng cè)	*N.*	policy
落后	(luò hòu)	*Adj.*	backward
狠心	(hěn xīn)	*Adj.*	cruel, heartless
扔	(rēng)	*V.*	to throw away, to cast aside
残疾	(cán jí)	*Adj/N.*	handicapped
遭遇	(zāo yù)	*N.*	(bitter) experience
不幸	(bù xìng)	*Adj.*	unfortunate
孤儿	(gū ér)	*N.*	orphan
天津	(tiān jīn)	*Place N.*	Tianjin, name of a city in China 地名
儿童医院	(ér tóng yī yuàn)	*NP.*	children's hospital
福利院	(fú lì yuàn)	*NP.*	welfare institute

（二）

（几年以后，在美国）

韩凯：你好！你叫什么名字？

秋云：我叫秋云。

韩凯：你是中国人，为什么你的父母都是美国人？

秋云：因为我是被领养到美国来的。十五年前，我出生在天津。一生下来，我的父母就发现我的眼睛有毛病[4]，而且没有治[5]，他们就把我扔在医院的长椅上。医院

✎ **Notes** [4]See Note (2).

[5]没（有）治 literally means "there is no cure", i.e., for a medical condition or disease. In colloquial Chinese, this expression is often used to mean that there is no way to deal with a certain person or situation. Example: 我们真拿他没治. (We really can't do anything about him.) Yet another meaning of 没治 is "terrific" or "outstanding". Example: 小李这个人好得简直没治了！(That Xiao Wang is simply terrific!) The opposite expression 有治 (there is a cure) can only be used when referring to diseases, not to people or situations.

的人發現以後，就把我送到天津兒童福利院。

韓凱：原來你就是那個"秋雲"。我在我的中文課本裡讀到過你的故事。你不是讓《天津日報》社以集體的名義領養了嗎？你怎麼又來美國了？

秋雲：後來我的遭遇在電視上發表了，一個美國教授聽說了以後就決定申請義務領養我。兩年以後，也就是我七歲的時候來到了美國。

韓凱：你喜歡你的美國爸爸媽媽嗎？

秋雲：當然，我的爸爸媽媽對我非常好，我的父母用他們的愛心和溫暖讓我覺得我是天下最幸福的孩子。可是，我也想回中國去找找我真正的父母。

生詞

秋雲	(qiū yún)	N.	Qiu Yun, name of a person 人名
毛病	(máo bìng)	N.	defect
沒有治	(méi yǒu zhì)	Adj.	incurable
扔在	(rēng zài)	V.	to throw on
課本	(kè běn)	N.	textbook
日報社	(rì bào shè)	NP.	newspaper agency
集體	(jí tǐ)	Adj/Adv.	collective, collectively
名義	(míng yì)	N.	in the name of
發表	(fā biǎo)	V.	to publish
申請	(shēn qǐng)	V/N.	to apply for; application
義務	(yì wù)	Adj/Adv.	voluntary, voluntarily

二、電視原文 🖥 TV original

秋雲

（根據原文改編）

　　六年前的一個秋天，一個剛剛出生六個月的女嬰由於右眼的天生殘疾被狠心的父母拋棄在了天津兒童醫院。女嬰被送到了天津兒童福利院，生活了六年。

的人发现以后，就把我送到天津儿童福利院。

韩凯：　原来你就是那个"秋云"。我在我的中文课本里读到过你的故事。你不是让
　　　　《天津日报》社以集体的名义领养了吗？你怎么又来美国了？

秋云：　后来我的遭遇在电视上发表了，一个美国教授听说了以后就决定申请义务领养
　　　　我。两年以后，也就是我七岁的时候来到了美国。

韩凯：　你喜欢你的美国爸爸妈妈吗？

秋云：　当然，我的爸爸妈妈对我非常好，我的父母用他们的爱心和温暖让我觉得我是
　　　　天下最幸福的孩子。可是，我也想回中国去找找我真正的父母。

生词

秋云	(qiū yún)	N.	Qiu Yun, name of a person 人名
毛病	(máo bìng)	N.	defect
没有治	(méi yǒu zhì)	Adj.	incurable
扔在	(rēng zài)	V.	to throw on
课本	(kè běn)	N.	textbook
日报社	(rì bào shè)	NP.	newspaper agency
集体	(jí tǐ)	Adj/Adv.	collective, collectively
名义	(míng yì)	N.	in the name of
发表	(fā biǎo)	V.	to publish
申请	(shēn qǐng)	V/N.	to apply for; application
义务	(yì wù)	Adj/Adv.	voluntary, voluntarily

二、电视原文 💻 TV original

秋云

（根据原文改编）

六年前的一个秋天，一个刚刚出生六个月的女婴由于右眼的天生残疾被狠心的父
母抛弃在了天津儿童医院。女婴被送到了天津儿童福利院，生活了六年。

　　那裡的阿姨們給她起了一個很好聽的名字：秋雲。一個偶然的機會，秋雲被帶到了《天津日報》社。秋雲的不幸遭遇打動了日報社的記者們，於是一個以《天津日報》社的名義義務領養秋雲的計劃開始醞釀。

　　字幕：1994年5月20日，天津兒童福利院

　　這是一個普通的日子，然而對於生活在天津兒童福利院的六歲孤兒秋雲來說卻有著特殊的意義。正是在這一天她有了自己溫暖的家。從這一天開始，《天津日報》社的近千名工作人員將擁有⁽⁶⁾一個共同的女兒—秋雲。

　　天津兒童福利院副院長⁽⁷⁾嚴繼英：“秋雲是88年的2月12號在兒童醫院的大椅子上（被）發現的。她當時呢，就是因為眼部⁽⁸⁾有毛病，估計她家屬認為她的眼沒有治了，就把她扔到兒童醫院的長椅子上。醫院發現以後，就把她送到馬場派出所，又送到兒童福利院來了。她的智商也不低，其它方面都很正常，就是眼部有毛病，別的都挺好的。甚麼唱歌、跳舞都行，感情也挺豐富的。”

　　5月16號天津市第一份以集體名義領養孤兒協議書簽訂了。根據協議，《天津日報》社將對秋雲負有撫養、教育、醫療保健，以及監護責任，直至她成人為止。《天津日報》社的記者和工作人員，也就是秋雲的“爸爸媽媽”，早已為她的日後生活做好了安排。秋雲將被寄宿到天津市第十一幼兒園，每逢公休日、節假日，報社將安排假日父母活動。日報社已婚職工輪流接秋雲回家，帶她享受家庭生活。南開中學康校長當場⁽⁹⁾表示，直到秋雲長大，南開中學將免費為她提供中學教育。

Notes ⁽⁶⁾有 vs. 擁有: 有 and 擁有 both mean "to have" or "to possess", but differ in usage. Objects taken by the verb 有 are usually concrete and commonplace, such as 紙, 桌子, or 椅子. 擁有 takes more formal objects, such as 工作人員 (working staff), 財產 (property), 土地 (land).

⁽⁷⁾長 (zhǎng) can function as a suffix meaning "the person in charge". In the text, 校長 means "principal" or "headmaster"; it can also refer to a college or university president. Other examples using 長 include: 船長 (boat captain), 外交部長 (Minister of Foreign Affairs), 研究所所長 (director of a research institute).

⁽⁸⁾部 means "part" or "section of a whole". When used with words which refer to parts of the body, it can mean "section" or "area", as in 眼部 (the area around the eyes). 眼部 is different in meaning from 眼上 (the surface of the eyes). Such words are usually only used in the medical field, seldom in colloquial Chinese. When attached to words related to institutions or organizations, 部 refers to an individual department, as in 外交部 (Ministry of Foreign Affairs), 門診部 (outpatient services department). Finally, 部 can used to refer to geographical sections of a country, as in 中國北部 (Northern China).

⁽⁹⁾當場 means "right there", "on the spot" and is usually followed by a verb. Example: 校長當場表示同意. (The president consented immediately.) The related term 現場 is sometimes used to mean "live" or "spontaneous" in reference to performances, as in 現場直播 (live broadcast).

　　那里的阿姨们给她起了一个很好听的名字：秋云。一个偶然的机会，秋云被带到了《天津日报》社。秋云的不幸遭遇打动了日报社的记者们，于是一个以《天津日报》社的名义义务领养秋云的计划开始酝酿。

　　字幕：1994年5月20日，天津儿童福利院

　　这是一个普通的日子，然而对于生活在天津儿童福利院的六岁孤儿秋云来说却有着特殊的意义。正是在这一天她有了自己温暖的家。从这一天开始，《天津日报》社的近千名工作人员将拥有⁽⁶⁾一个共同的女儿—秋云。

　　天津儿童福利院副院长⁽⁷⁾严继英："秋云是88年的2月12号在儿童医院的大椅子上（被）发现的。她当时呢，就是因为眼部⁽⁸⁾有毛病，估计她家属认为她的眼没有治了，就把她扔到儿童医院的长椅子上。医院发现以后，就把她送到马场派出所，又送到儿童福利院来了。她的智商也不低，其它方面都很正常，就是眼部有毛病，别的都挺好的。什么唱歌、跳舞都行，感情也挺丰富的。"

　　5月16号天津市第一份以集体名义领养孤儿协议书签订了。根据协议，《天津日报》社将对秋云负有抚养、教育、医疗保健，以及监护责任，直至她成人为止。《天津日报》社的记者和工作人员，也就是秋云的"爸爸妈妈"，早已为她的日后生活做好了安排。秋云将被寄宿到天津市第十一幼儿园，每逢公休日、节假日，报社将安排假日父母活动。日报社已婚职工轮流接秋云回家，带她享受家庭生活。南开中学康校长当场⁽⁹⁾表示，直到秋云长大，南开中学将免费为她提供中学教育。

Notes (6)有 vs. 拥有: 有 and 拥有 both mean "to have" or "to possess", but differ in usage. Objects taken by the verb 有 are usually concrete and commonplace, such as 纸, 桌子, or 椅子. 拥有 takes more formal objects, such as 工作人员 (working staff), 财产 (property), 土地 (land).

(7)长 (zhǎng) can function as a suffix meaning "the person in charge". In the text, 校长 means "principal" or "headmaster"; it can also refer to a college or university president. Other examples using 长 include: 船长 (boat captain), 外交部长 (Minister of Foreign Affairs), 研究所所长 (director of a research institute).

(8)部 means "part" or "section of a whole". When used with words which refer to parts of the body, it can mean "section" or "area", as in 眼部 (the area around the eyes). 眼部 is different in meaning from 眼上 (the surface of the eyes). Such words are usually only used in the medical field, seldom in colloquial Chinese. When attached to words related to institutions or organizations, 部 refers to an individual department, as in 外交部 (Ministry of Foreign Affairs), 门诊部 (outpatient services department). Finally, 部 can used to refer to geographical sections of a country, as in 中国北部 (Northern China).

(9)当场 means "right there", "on the spot" and is usually followed by a verb. Example: 校长当场表示同意. (The president consented immediately.) The related term 现场 is sometimes used to mean "live" or "spontaneous" in reference to performances, as in 现场直播 (live broadcast).

在捐款儀式中，《天津日報》社職工當場捐資23,000多元作為秋雲的首批⁽¹⁰⁾撫養基金，領秋雲回家的首批"假日父母"名單已排至9月份。

生詞

天生	(tiān shēng)	*Adj.*	congenital, to be born with
阿姨們	(ā yí mén)	*N.*	nurse, aunt, nursemaid
起名字	(qǐ míng zì)	*V.*	to name (someone)
偶然	(ǒu rán)	*Adv.*	accidental, by chance
打動	(dǎ dòng)	*V.*	to move, to touch (emotionally)
記者	(jì zhě)	*V.*	reporter
於是	(yú shì)	*Conj.*	therefore, consequently, as a result
醞釀	(yùn niàng)	*V.*	under discussion, to discuss, to deliberate on
字幕	(zì mù)	*N.*	caption
普通	(pǔ tōng)	*Adj.*	ordinary, common
特殊	(tè shū)	*Adj.*	special
意義	(yì yì)	*N.*	meaning, significance
工作人員	(gōng zuò rén yuán)	*NP.*	working staff
擁有	(yōng yǒu)	*V.*	to possess, to have
共同	(gòng tóng)	*Adj.*	common, shared
副院長	(fù yuàn zhǎng)	*N.*	deputy director
嚴繼英	(yán jì yīng)	*N.*	Yan Jiying, name of a person 人名
家屬	(jiā shǔ)	*N.*	spouse, family members
馬場	(mǎ chǎng)	*Place N.*	Machang, name of a place 地名
派出所	(pài chū suǒ)	*NP.*	the security office
智商	(zhì shāng)	*N.*	IQ
感情	(gǎn qíng)	*N.*	emotion, feeling
豐富	(fēng fù)	*Adj.*	rich, abundant
協議	(xié yì)	*N.*	agreement

Notes [10]The prefix 首 literally means "primary", "head", or "first". It must be followed by a monosyllabic word, as in 首先 (first), 首次 (the first time), 首批 (the first group of people), 首都 (national capital).

在捐款仪式中，《天津日报》社职工当场捐资23,000多元作为秋云的首批⁽¹⁰⁾抚养基金，领秋云回家的首批"假日父母"名单已排至9月份。

生词

天生	(tiān shēng)	*Adj.*	congenital, to be born with
阿姨们	(ā yí mén)	*N.*	nurse, aunt, nursemaid
起名字	(qǐ míng zì)	*V.*	to name (someone)
偶然	(ǒu rán)	*Adv.*	accidental, by chance
打动	(dǎ dòng)	*V.*	to move, to touch (emotionally)
记者	(jì zhě)	*V.*	reporter
于是	(yú shì)	*Conj.*	therefore, consequently, as a result
酝酿	(yùn niàng)	*V.*	under discussion, to discuss, to deliberate on
字幕	(zì mù)	*N.*	caption
普通	(pǔ tōng)	*Adj.*	ordinary, common
特殊	(tè shū)	*Adj.*	special
意义	(yì yì)	*N.*	meaning, significance
工作人员	(gōng zuò rén yuán)	*NP.*	working staff
拥有	(yōng yǒu)	*V.*	to possess, to have
共同	(gòng tóng)	*Adj.*	common, shared
副院长	(fù yuàn zhǎng)	*N.*	deputy director
严继英	(yán jì yīng)	*N.*	Yan Jiying, name of a person 人名
家属	(jiā shǔ)	*N.*	spouse, family members
马场	(mǎ chǎng)	*Place N.*	Machang, name of a place 地名
派出所	(pài chū suǒ)	*NP.*	the security office
智商	(zhì shāng)	*N.*	IQ
感情	(gǎn qíng)	*N.*	emotion, feeling
丰富	(fēng fù)	*Adj.*	rich, abundant
协议	(xié yì)	*N.*	agreement

✎ **Notes** ⁽¹⁰⁾The prefix 首 literally means "primary", "head", or "first". It must be followed by a monosyllabic word, as in 首先 (first), 首次 (the first time), 首批 (the first group of people), 首都 (national capital).

簽訂	(qiān dìng)	*V.*	to sign
負有	(fù yǒu)	*V.*	to shoulder, to bear
撫養	(fǔ yǎng)	*V.*	to raise, to foster
醫療保健	(yī liáo bǎo jiàn)	*NP.*	medical treatment
以及	(yǐ jí)	*Conj.*	and, as well as
監護	(jiān hù)	*N.*	guardianship
為止	(wéi zhǐ)	*VP.*	until
成人	(chéng rén)	*N.*	adult
日後	(rì hòu)	*Adj.*	in the future
寄宿	(jì sù)	*V.*	to lodge, to put up
幼兒園	(yòu ér yuán)	*N.*	nursery school, kindergarten
每逢	(měi féng)	*Adv.*	every (+ time expression)
節假日	(jié jià rì)	*N.*	holidays
公休日	(gōng xiū rì)	*N.*	week-end, public holidays
已婚	(yǐ hūn)	*Adj.*	married
職工	(zhí gōng)	*N.*	staff, workers
輪流	(lún liú)	*Adv.*	to take turns
享受	(xiǎng shòu)	*V.*	to enjoy
校長	(xiào zhǎng)	*N.*	president of a school, school principal, headmaster
免費	(miǎn fèi)	*Adv.*	free of charge, free
提供	(tí gōng)	*V.*	to provide
儀式	(yí shì)	*N.*	ceremony
當場	(dāng chǎng)	*Adv.*	on the spot, right there
捐資	(juān zī)	*VO.*	to donate money
首批	(shǒu pī)	*NP.*	first group of
基金	(jī jīn)	*N.*	fund
名單	(míng dān)	*N.*	list of names, name list
排	(pái)	*V.*	to arrange, to put in order

签订	(qiān dìng)	*V.*	to sign
负有	(fù yǒu)	*V.*	to shoulder, to bear
抚养	(fǔ yǎng)	*V.*	to raise, to foster
医疗保健	(yī liáo bǎo jiàn)	*NP.*	medical treatment
以及	(yǐ jí)	*Conj.*	and, as well as
监护	(jiān hù)	*N.*	guardianship
为止	(wéi zhǐ)	*VP.*	until
成人	(chéng rén)	*N.*	adult
日后	(rì hòu)	*Adj.*	in the future
寄宿	(jì sù)	*V.*	to lodge, to put up
幼儿园	(yòu ér yuán)	*N.*	nursery school, kindergarten
每逢	(měi féng)	*Adv.*	every (+ time expression)
节假日	(jié jià rì)	*N.*	holidays
公休日	(gōng xiū rì)	*N.*	week-end, public holidays
已婚	(yǐ hūn)	*Adj.*	married
职工	(zhí gōng)	*N.*	staff, workers
轮流	(lún liú)	*Adv.*	to take turns
享受	(xiǎng shòu)	*V.*	to enjoy
校长	(xiào zhǎng)	*N.*	president of a school, school principal, headmaster
免费	(miǎn fèi)	*Adv.*	free of charge, free
提供	(tí gōng)	*V.*	to provide
仪式	(yí shì)	*N.*	ceremony
当场	(dāng chǎng)	*Adv.*	on the spot, right there
捐资	(juān zī)	*VO.*	to donate money
首批	(shǒu pī)	*NP.*	first group of
基金	(jī jīn)	*N.*	fund
名单	(míng dān)	*N.*	list of names, name list
排	(pái)	*V.*	to arrange, to put in order

課文要點

一、詞語解釋（文言詞、慣用詞）Words and Phrases

1、名＝個
　☞ 《天津日報》社的近千名工作人員將擁有一個共同的女兒秋雲。

2、以＝用
　☞ 5月16號天津市第一份以集體名義領養孤兒協議書簽訂了。

3、直至＝直到
　☞ 根據協議，《天津日報》社將對秋雲負有撫養教育、醫療保健，以及監護責任，直至她成人為止。

4、為＝是
　☞ 根據協議，《天津日報》社將對秋雲負有撫養教育、醫療保健，以及監護責任，直至她成人為止。

5、止＝停止，結束
　☞ 根據協議，《天津日報》社將對秋雲負有撫養教育、醫療保健，以及監護責任，直至她成人為止。

6、逢＝到
　☞ 每逢公休日、節假日，報社將安排"假日父母"活動。

7、已婚＝已經結婚
　☞ 已婚職工輪流接秋雲回家。

8、首批＝第一批
　☞ 首批"假日父母"名單已排至9月份。

9、排至＝排到
　☞ 領秋雲回家的首批"假日父母"名單已排至9月份。

10、逢＝到
　☞ 每逢公休日、節假日，報社將安排"假日父母"活動。

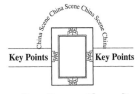

课文要点

一、词语解释（文言词、惯用词）Words and Phrases

1、名 = 个
- ☞ 《天津日报》社的近千名工作人员将拥有一个共同的女儿秋云。

2、以 = 用
- ☞ 5月16号天津市第一份以集体名义领养孤儿协议书签订了。

3、直至 = 直到
- ☞ 根据协议，《天津日报》社将对秋云负有抚养教育、医疗保健，以及监护责任，直至她成人为止。

4、为 = 是
- ☞ 根据协议，《天津日报》社将对秋云负有抚养教育、医疗保健，以及监护责任，直至她成人为止。

5、止 = 停止，结束
- ☞ 根据协议，《天津日报》社将对秋云负有抚养教育、医疗保健，以及监护责任，直至她成人为止。

6、逢 = 到
- ☞ 每逢公休日、节假日，报社将安排"假日父母"活动。

7、已婚 = 已经结婚
- ☞ 已婚职工轮流接秋云回家。

8、首批 = 第一批
- ☞ 首批"假日父母"名单已排至9月份。

9、排至 = 排到
- ☞ 领秋云回家的首批"假日父母"名单已排至9月份。

10、逢 = 到
- ☞ 每逢公休日、节假日，报社将安排"假日父母"活动。

二、書面語、正式語、口語對照表 ⊪⊪ Written/formal/colloquial Comparison

	書面/正式語	口語		書面/正式語	口語
1	由於	因為	6	直至	直到
2	於是	所以	7	早已	早就
3	醞釀	討論	8	日後	以後
4	擁有	有	9	首批	第一批
5	以及	和/跟	10	排至	排到

三、句型 ❀ Sentence Structures

（一）⋯⋯是一個（很好的）例子 (to be a [good] example of)

> ✍ ⋯⋯是一個（很好）的例子, "to be a (good) example of", is often used for illustration. The subject of such a sentence can be a noun, a VO structure, or a sentence. The modifying element of 例子 can be an adjective, adverb, or a VO phrase. Examples: 鄧小平就是一個改革者的例子. (Deng Xiaoping is an example of a reformer.) 請客是其中的一個例子. (Inviting someone to dinner is one example among them.) 他留在美國不回來就是一個出國熱的例子. (His remaining in America and not returning is an example of the study abroad craze.)

☞ 秋雲的故事就是一個很好的例子。

1、現在中國的單親家庭越來越多，何茹的家庭就是一個很好的例子。

Nowadays, single-parent families are more and more common in China. He Ru's family is a good example.

2、拋棄女嬰的現象在中國還是有的，秋雲就是一個很好的例子。

The phenomenon of abandoning baby girls still exists in China; Qiu Yun is a good example.

問：現在在中國為了出國而離婚的人越來越多嗎？
答：對。由於＿＿＿＿＿＿＿＿＿＿＿＿＿＿＿＿＿。

（二）A 被 B 拋棄（／領養） or B 拋棄 A or B 領養 A (to be deserted by)

> ✍ In the structure A 被 B 拋棄／領養, 被 is used to create a passive structure. The noun that immediately follows 被 serves as the agent of the verb. The 被 structure is not always associated with words indicating adversity, such as 拋棄 (to throw away, to abandon), 打了 (beaten), and 扔

二、书面语、正式语、口语对照表 ‖‖ Written/formal/colloquial Comparison

	书面／正式语	口语		书面／正式语	口语
1	由于	因为	6	直至	直到
2	于是	所以	7	早已	早就
3	酝酿	讨论	8	日后	以后
4	拥有	有	9	首批	第一批
5	以及	和／跟	10	排至	排到

三、句型 ✼ Sentence Structures

（一）……是一个（很好的）例子 (to be a [good] example of)

> ✍ ……是一个（很好）的例子, "to be a (good) example of", is often used for illustration. The subject of such a sentence can be a noun, a VO structure, or a sentence. The modifying element of 例子 can be an adjective, adverb, or a VO phrase. Examples: 邓小平就是一个改革者的例子. (Deng Xiaoping is an example of a reformer.) 请客是其中的一个例子. (Inviting someone to dinner is one example among them.) 他留在美国不回来就是一个出国热的例子. (His remaining in America and not returning is an example of the study abroad craze.)

☞ 秋云的故事就是一个很好的例子。

1、现在中国的单亲家庭越来越多，何茹的家庭就是一个很好的例子。
Nowadays, single-parent families are more and more common in China. He Ru's family is a good example.

2、抛弃女婴的现象在中国还是有的，秋云就是一个很好的例子。
The phenomenon of abandoning baby girls still exists in China; Qiu Yun is a good example.

问：现在在中国为了出国而离婚的人越来越多吗？
答：对。由于＿＿＿＿＿＿＿＿＿＿＿＿＿＿＿＿＿。

（二）A 被 B 抛弃（／领养）or B 抛弃 A or B 领养 A (to be deserted by)

> ✍ In the structure A 被 B 抛弃／领养, 被 is used to create a passive structure. The noun that immediately follows 被 serves as the agent of the verb. The 被 structure is not always associated with words indicating adversity, such as 抛弃 (to throw away, to abandon), 打了 (beaten), and 扔

31

> 了 (thrown). It can also carry a neutral or positive meaning. Examples: 他終於被一個好心人領養了. (Finally he was adopted by a good person.) 這個好消息被人們傳到了他的學校. (This good news was spread to his school by some people.) The active counterpart of this pattern is B 拋棄 A or B 領養 A.

☞ 六年前的一個秋天，一個剛剛出生六個月的女嬰由於右眼的天生殘疾被狠心的父母拋棄在了天津兒童醫院。

1、兩年前，我跟我的媽媽都被我爸爸拋棄了。

Two years ago, my mother and I were deserted by my father.

2、這個女嬰被她的狠心的父母拋棄了。

This little girl was abandoned by her heartless parents.

問：聽説十年前＿＿＿＿＿＿＿＿＿＿＿＿＿＿＿＿＿＿？
答：對啊。當時就因為我是女的，我狠心的父母就把我扔在了醫院裡。

（三）估計 (to estimate, to guess, to reckon)

> 估計, "to estimate", "to guess", or "to reckon", is often followed by a sentence, although it may also be followed by other elements, such as a noun or VO structure. The subject of 估計 is often omitted, especially when the subject is the first-person pronoun "I", referring to the speaker. Example: 估計他明天一早就會去日報社看看. (I suppose first thing tomorrow morning he will go to the newspaper agency and have a look.) When the subject of 估計 is the second-person (you) or third-person pronoun (he, she, or they), it is usually included. Example: 他估計這種離婚會越來越多. (He estimates that these types of divorces will become more and more common.)

☞ 她（秋雲）當時呢，就是因為眼部有毛病，估計她家屬認為她的眼沒有治了，就把她扔到兒童醫院的長椅子上。

1、估計現在去中國領養孩子的人超過了十萬。

It is estimated that more than 100,000 people have gone to China to adopt children.

2、你估計中國一家一個孩子的政策這幾年會改變嗎？

Do you suppose that China's one-child policy will change in the next few years?

問：＿＿＿＿＿＿＿＿＿＿＿＿＿＿＿＿＿＿＿＿？
答：據估計，現在中國的兒童福利院共有三十多個。

了 (thrown). It can also carry a neutral or positive meaning. Examples: 他终于被一个好心人领养了. (Finally he was adopted by a good person.) 这个好消息被人们传到了他的学校. (This good news was spread to his school by some people.) The active counterpart of this pattern is B 抛弃 A or B 领养 A.

☞ 六年前的一个秋天，一个刚刚出生六个月的女婴由于右眼的天生残疾被狠心的父母抛弃在了天津儿童医院。

1、两年前，我跟我的妈妈都被我爸爸抛弃了。

Two years ago, my mother and I were deserted by my father.

2、这个女婴被她的狠心的父母抛弃了。

This little girl was abandoned by her heartless parents.

问：听说十年前＿＿＿＿＿＿＿＿＿＿＿＿＿＿＿＿＿＿＿？

答：对啊。当时就因为我是女的，我狠心的父母就把我扔在了医院里。

（三）估计 (to estimate, to guess, to reckon)

估计, "to estimate", "to guess", or "to reckon", is often followed by a sentence, although it may also be followed by other elements, such as a noun or VO structure. The subject of 估计 is often omitted, especially when the subject is the first-person pronoun "I", referring to the speaker. Example: 估计他明天一早就会去日报社看看. (I suppose first thing tomorrow morning he will go to the newspaper agency and have a look.) When the subject of 估计 is the second-person (you) or third-person pronoun (he, she, or they), it is usually included. Example: 他估计这种离婚会越来越多. (He estimates that these types of divorces will become more and more common.)

☞ 她（秋云）当时呢，就是因为眼部有毛病，估计她家属认为她的眼没有治了，就把她扔到儿童医院的长椅子上。

1、估计现在去中国领养孩子的人超过了十万。

It is estimated that more than 100,000 people have gone to China to adopt children.

2、你估计中国一家一个孩子的政策这几年会改变吗？

Do you suppose that China's one-child policy will change in the next few years?

问：＿＿＿＿＿＿＿＿＿＿＿＿＿＿＿＿＿＿＿＿＿？

答：据估计，现在中国的儿童福利院共有三十多个。

（四）給……起（／取）……名字 (to give someone the name of)

> ✍ 給……起（／取）……名字, "to give someone the name of", is an idiomatic expression in which the verb 起 or 取 must be used to indicate the action of giving a name or naming someone. The verb 給 cannot be used directly with 名字. Adjectives, numbers, measure words, and other modifying elements can be inserted between 起 or 取 and 名字. Example: 誰給你起的這麼好聽的名字？ (Who gave you such a pretty name?)

☞ 那裡的阿姨們給她起了一個很好聽的名字，秋雲。

1、你給你的兒子起名字了嗎？叫甚麼？

Have you given your son a name yet? What have you named him?

2、我給我的小貓起了一個很好聽的名字叫"咪咪"。

I gave my cat a pretty name, "Mimi".

問：你的中文名字真有意思，不但好聽，而且容易記，_____？
答：是我的中文老師給我起的。

（五）一個偶然的機會…… (by chance, accidentally)

> ✍ 一個偶然的機會, "by chance", "accidentally" (literally, "a random opportunity"), can only be used at the beginning of a sentence. To place the phrase elsewhere would result in an odd or unacceptable sentence. Here 偶然 is an adjective modifying a noun, as in 偶然的現象 (accidental phenomenon). In addition, it can function as a predicate. Example: 這件事非常偶然. (This event is very fortuitous.)

☞ 一個偶然的機會，秋雲被帶到了《天津日報》社。

1、一個偶然的機會，兒童福利院的人把她帶到了日報社。

The people at the Children's Welfare Institute happened to take her to the daily newspaper agency.

2、一個偶然的機會，我在這兒碰到了一對美國夫婦，他們把我帶到了美國。所以這個地方對我有著特殊的意義。

I chanced upon an American couple here who brought me to the U.S.; therefore this place has special significance to me.

問：你是怎麼被天津兒童福利院領養的呢？
答：_____。

（四）给……起（／取）……名字 (to give someone the name of)

> ✎ 给……起（／取）……名字, "to give someone the name of", is an idiomatic expression in which the verb 起 or 取 must be used to indicate the action of giving a name or naming someone. The verb 给 cannot be used directly with 名字. Adjectives, numbers, measure words, and other modifying elements can be inserted between 起 or 取 and 名字. Example: 谁给你起的这么好听的名字？(Who gave you such a pretty name?)

☞ 那里的阿姨们给她起了一个很好听的名字，秋云。

1、你给你的儿子起名字了吗？叫什么？

Have you given your son a name yet? What have you named him?

2、我给我的小猫起了一个很好听的名字叫"咪咪"。

I gave my cat a pretty name, "Mimi".

问：你的中文名字真有意思，不但好听，而且容易记，_____?
答：是我的中文老师给我起的。

（五）一个偶然的机会……(by chance, accidentally)

> ✎ 一个偶然的机会, "by chance", "accidentally" (literally, "a random opportunity"), can only be used at the beginning of a sentence. To place the phrase elsewhere would result in an odd or unacceptable sentence. Here 偶然 is an adjective modifying a noun, as in 偶然的现象 (accidental phenomenon). In addition, it can function as a predicate. Example: 这件事非常偶然. (This event is very fortuitous.)

☞ 一个偶然的机会，秋云被带到了《天津日报》社。

1、一个偶然的机会，儿童福利院的人把她带到了日报社。

The people at the Children's Welfare Institute happened to take her to the daily newspaper agency.

2、一个偶然的机会，我在这儿碰到了一对美国夫妇，他们把我带到了美国。所以这个地方对我有着特殊的意义。

I chanced upon an American couple here who brought me to the U.S.; therefore this place has special significance to me.

问：你是怎么被天津儿童福利院领养的呢？
答：_____。

（六）對……來說，…… (to, for)

> ✎ 對……來說, "to" or "for", is often usedat the beginning of a sentence to introduce a topic or point of view. Normally, the preposition 對 is followed by a personal noun, pronoun, country, or institution, as in 對孩子們來說 (as for the children), 對我來說 (to me), 對美國來說 (for the United States), 對我們的大學來說 (as for our university). Example: 對美國來說，人口問題還不是一個很大的社會問題. (For America, the population question is not a major social problem.)

☞ 這是一個普通的日子，然而對於生活在天津兒童福利院的六歲孤兒秋雲來說卻有著特殊的意義。

1、對一個離婚的人來說，他仍然對他孩子的教育、撫養和監護負有責任。
As a divorcé, he still has the responsibility of educating, raising, and serving as guardian of his children.

2、對一個孤兒來說，有一個溫暖的家，享受家庭生活是她最大的希望。
As an orphan, having a warm and loving family and a prosperous life are her greatest hopes.

問：你以前在這個老人福利院工作過五年，為甚麼離開三年後還要回來？
答：＿＿＿＿＿＿＿＿＿＿＿＿＿＿＿＿＿＿＿＿＿＿＿。

（七）以……的名義 (in the name of)

> ✎ 以……的名義, "in the name of", is a prepositional phrase normally used either before the verb and after the subject, or before the subject of a sentence. Example: 以集體的名義日報社跟兒童醫院簽訂了一項協議 or 日報社以集體的名義跟兒童醫院簽訂了一項協議. (The newspaper, under its own name, signed an agreement with the Children's Hospital.)

☞ 秋雲的不幸遭遇打動了日報社的記者們，於是一個以《天津日報》社的名義義務領養秋雲的計劃開始醞釀。

1、這個醫院以集體的名義跟報社簽訂了一項協議。
The hospital, in its own collective name, reached an agreement with the newspaper agency.

2、我以個人的名義領養孤兒，可以嗎？
I want to adopt an orphan in my own name; is that possible?

問：這篇文章寫得很好，是以誰的名義發表的？
答：＿＿＿＿＿＿＿＿＿＿＿＿＿＿＿＿＿＿＿。

（六）对……来说，……(to, for)

> ✍ 对……来说，"to" or "for", is often used at the beginning of a sentence to introduce a topic or point of view. Normally, the preposition 对 is followed by a personal noun, pronoun, country, or institution, as in 对孩子们来说 (as for the children), 对我来说 (to me), 对美国来说 (for the United States), 对我们的大学来说 (as for our university). Example: 对美国来说，人口问题还不是一个很大的社会问题。(For America, the population question is not a major social problem.)

☞ 这是一个普通的日子，然而对于生活在天津儿童福利院的六岁孤儿秋云来说却有着特殊的意义。

1、对一个离婚的人来说，他仍然对他孩子的教育、抚养和监护负有责任。
　　As a divorcé, he still has the responsibility of educating, raising, and serving as guardian of his children.

2、对一个孤儿来说，有一个温暖的家，享受家庭生活是她最大的希望。
　　As an orphan, having a warm and loving family and a prosperous life are her greatest hopes.

问：你以前在这个老人福利院工作过五年，为什么离开三年后还要回来？
答：＿＿＿＿＿＿＿＿＿＿＿＿＿＿＿＿＿＿＿＿＿＿＿。

（七）以……的名义 (in the name of)

> ✍ 以……的名义，"in the name of", is a prepositional phrase normally used either before the verb and after the subject, or before the subject of a sentence. Example: 以集体的名义日报社跟儿童医院签订了一项协议 or 日报社以集体的名义跟儿童医院签订了一项协议. (The newspaper, under its own name, signed an agreement with the Children's Hospital.)

☞ 秋云的不幸遭遇打动了日报社的记者们，于是一个以《天津日报》社的名义义务领养秋云的计划开始酝酿。

1、这个医院以集体的名义跟报社签订了一项协议。
　　The hospital, in its own collective name, reached an agreement with the newspaper agency.

2、我以个人的名义领养孤儿，可以吗？
　　I want to adopt an orphan in my own name; is that possible?

问：这篇文章写得很好，是以谁的名义发表的？
答：＿＿＿＿＿＿＿＿＿＿＿＿＿＿＿＿＿＿＿＿＿＿＿。

（八）對……（負）有（……的）責任 (to have a certain responsibility for someone)

> ✍ 對……負有（……的）責任, "to have a certain responsibility for someone", is a set phrase that is used most often in written or formal Chinese. Its colloquial counterpart is 對……有（……的）責任. The preposition 對 must be used to introduce the person or target for which the subject is responsible. A modifying element between 負有 and 責任 is optional.

☞ 《天津日報》社將對秋雲負有撫養教育、醫療保健，以及監護責任，直至她成人為止。

1、只要你是父母，你就對你的孩子負有責任，直至他們成人為止。

As long as you are a parent, your children are your responsibility until they become adults.

2、這個單位的已婚職工都對這個孩子負有監護的責任。

The married workers of this work unit all have the responsibility of serving as this child's guardians.

問：你認為政府對老百姓的生活負有甚麼責任？

答：_____。

（九）直至（／到）……（為止） (up until)

> ✍ 直至（／到）……為止, "up until", is an adverbial phrase that is normally placed at the beginning of a sentence to introduce the ending phase of an event. Occasionally, this phrase can be placed at the end of a sentence. See the example below.

☞ 《天津日報》社將對秋雲負有撫養教育、醫療保健，以及監護責任，直至她成人為止。

1、直至今年為止，我父親每年都給我寄一張生日卡。

Up until this year, my father sent me a birthday card every year.

2、直到昨天為止，你一直跟我說他的智商很低，也很奇怪。

Up until yesterday, you were always telling me that his IQ was very low and he was very strange.

問：美國和中國已經建立了多長時間的外交關係？

答：_____。

（八）对……（负）有（……的）责任 (to have a certain responsibility for someone)

> ✍ 对……负有（……的）责任, "to have a certain responsibility for someone", is a set phrase that is used most often in written or formal Chinese. Its colloquial counterpart is 对……有（……的）责任. The preposition 对 must be used to introduce the person or target for which the subject is responsible. A modifying element between 负有 and 责任 is optional.

☞ 《天津日报》社将对秋云负有抚养教育、医疗保健，以及监护责任，直至她成人为止。

1、只要你是父母，你就对你的孩子负有责任，直至他们成人为止。
As long as you are a parent, your children are your responsibility until they become adults.

2、这个单位的已婚职工都对这个孩子负有监护的责任。
The married workers of this work unit all have the responsibility of serving as this child's guardians.

问：你认为政府对老百姓的生活负有什么责任？
答：＿＿＿＿＿＿＿＿＿＿＿＿＿＿＿＿＿＿＿＿。

（九）直至（／到）……（为止）(up until)

> ✍ 直至（／到）……为止, "up until", is an adverbial phrase that is normally placed at the beginning of a sentence to introduce the ending phase of an event. Occasionally, this phrase can be placed at the end of a sentence. See the example below.

☞ 《天津日报》社将对秋云负有抚养教育、医疗保健，以及监护责任，直至她成人为止。

1、直至今年为止，我父亲每年都给我寄一张生日卡。
Up until this year, my father sent me a birthday card every year.

2、直到昨天为止，你一直跟我说他的智商很低，也很奇怪。
Up until yesterday, you were always telling me that his IQ was very low and he was very strange.

问：美国和中国已经建立了多长时间的外交关系？
答：＿＿＿＿＿＿＿＿＿＿＿＿＿＿＿＿＿＿。

（十）每逢 + N/S (every time, whenever)

> ✍ 每逢, "every time" or "whenever", is used to indicate a cycle of repeated events. 每逢 can be followed by a time word or a sentence. Examples: 每逢星期五我們都有考試. (We have exams every Friday.) 每逢工作有困難，他總來幫忙. (Every time we have some trouble at work, he always comes over to help.) 每逢 is normally placed at the beginning of a sentence, either before the subject, as in the examples below, or after the subject and before the verb. Example: 他每逢周五都要去看電影. (He goes to see a movie every Friday.)

☞ 每逢公休日、節假日，報社將安排假日父母活動。

1、每逢周末，我們都會以個人的名義去附近的兒童福利院訪問。

Every weekend we visit the nearby orphanage.

2、每逢學校放假，他都會坐火車去城裡做義務工作。

Whenever vacation comes around, he takes the train to town to do volunteer work.

問：學校一般甚麼時候給學生安排校外活動？

答：＿＿＿＿＿＿＿＿＿＿＿＿＿＿＿＿＿＿。

（十一）輪流 + V (to take turns doing something)

> ✍ 輪流 is an adverb meaning "to take turns". It must be followed immediately by a verb, even if the verb is a generic one, such as 輪流來, 輪流做 (to take turns doing something). Sometimes 輪著 can be used in place of 輪流 in colloquial Chinese.

☞ 日報社已婚職工輪流接秋雲回家，帶她享受家庭生活。

1、為了讓孤兒有一個溫暖的家，日報社的職工輪流接他回家過周末。

In order to give the orphan a loving family, the workers at the newspaper agency took turns bringing him home on weekends.

2、學校的老師當場表示，他們會每個星期輪流給生病的同學補習。

The teachers announced right then and there that every week they would take turns giving supplemental lessons to the sick students.

問：你父母離婚了，那你現在住在哪兒呢？跟你爸還是你媽？

答：雖然我父母離婚了，但是他們仍然對我的生活、教育負有責任，所以

＿＿＿＿＿＿＿＿＿＿＿＿＿＿＿＿＿。

（十）每逢 + N/S (every time, whenever)

> ✍ 每逢, "every time" or "whenever", is used to indicate a cycle of repeated events. 每逢 can be followed by a time word or a sentence. Examples: 每逢星期五我们都有考试. (We have exams every Friday.) 每逢工作有困难，他总来帮忙. (Every time we have some trouble at work, he always comes over to help.) 每逢 is normally placed at the beginning of a sentence, either before the subject, as in the examples below, or after the subject and before the verb. Example: 他每逢周五都要去看电影. (He goes to see a movie every Friday.)

☞ 每逢公休日、节假日，报社将安排假日父母活动。

1、每逢周末，我们都会以个人的名义去附近的儿童福利院访问。

   Every weekend we visit the nearby orphanage.

2、每逢学校放假，他都会坐火车去城里做义务工作。

   Whenever vacation comes around, he takes the train to town to do volunteer work.

问：学校一般什么时候给学生安排校外活动？

答：_____。

（十一）轮流 + V (to take turns doing something)

> ✍ 轮流 is an adverb meaning "to take turns". It must be followed immediately by a verb, even if the verb is a generic one, such as 轮流来, 轮流做 (to take turns doing something). Sometimes 轮着 can be used in place of 轮流 in colloquial Chinese.

☞ 日报社已婚职工轮流接秋云回家，带她享受家庭生活。

1、为了让孤儿有一个温暖的家，日报社的职工轮流接他回家过周末。

   In order to give the orphan a loving family, the workers at the newspaper agency took turns bringing him home on weekends.

2、学校的老师当场表示，他们会每个星期轮流给生病的同学补习。

   The teachers announced right then and there that every week they would take turns giving supplemental lessons to the sick students.

问：你父母离婚了，那你现在住在哪儿呢？跟你爸还是你妈？

答：虽然我父母离婚了，但是他们仍然对我的生活、教育负有责任，所以

_____。

（十二）免費 + V (to do something free of charge)

> ✍ 免費, "for free" or "free of charge", is most often used in formal or written Chinese. 免 is a Classical Chinese word meaning 不要. While 免費 is normally placed immediately before a verb, it can also be used before a prepositional phrase introduced by 為 or 讓, as in 免費為學生安排旅行 (to arrange free travel for students). When negating the structure, 不 or 沒有 must be placed before 免費.

☞ 南開中學康校長當場表示，直到秋雲長大，南開中學將免費為她提供中學教育。

1、這個飯館不能為無家的人提供免費早飯和午飯。

This restaurant cannot provide free breakfast and lunch for the homeless.

2、這個福利院為孤兒安排免費寄宿學校。

This welfare institute provides free living arrangements at school for orphans.

問：醫院建造這座24層的大樓是誰提供的捐款？

答：＿＿＿＿＿＿＿＿＿＿＿＿＿＿＿＿＿＿＿＿。

四、文化背景知識 Cultural Notes

1. Americans adopting Chinese children: Many Americans now travel to China to adopt Chinese children. Most of the children are healthy infant girls, 3-6 months old. The overall cost is approximately $15,000-$20,000. Eligibility and requirements for prospective parents are the following: (1) must be over 35 years of age; (2) must be physically and mentally healthy; (3) must not have any infectious or contagious diseases. Typically, prospective parents first prepare a dossier of various medical records and official documents, then travel to China to meet the child and complete the adoption process.

2. China's One-Child Policy: Faced with severe over-population problems, in the 1970s China promulgated a new "one-child policy". Families could now only have one child. Although some exceptions are made (in the case of twins, for example, or when a child is born with severe defects), this policy has been enforced strictly, more successfully in the cities, less successfully in the countryside.

3. The expression "以集體的名義 + V" is often used to describe a collective or joint effort. For instance, in our text we learn that the orphanage (as an organization) has adopted Qiu Yun.

4. 阿姨 (or "aunt") has three uses as a form of address: (1) aunt (referring specifically to the sister of one's mother); (2) "aunt" (referring generally to any woman of one's mother's generation); and (3) nurse (in a family). In our text it is used by children in the orphanage to address the women who work there and look after them (the same practice is followed in nursery schools and child care centers).

5. 派出所 are smaller, local precincts of China's primary police organization, the Public Security Bureau (公安局 Gōngānjú). 派出所 serve both police and welfare functions, dealing mainly with neighborhood matters such as domestic (family) problems, petty theft, and so on. They also help older residents (especially those without children or relatives nearby) who might need assistance of some kind (buying food, seeing a doctor, and so on).

（十二）免费 + V (to do something free of charge)

> ✍ 免费, "for free" or "free of charge", is most often used in formal or written Chinese. 免 is a Classical Chinese word meaning 不要. While 免费 is normally placed immediately before a verb, it can also be used before a prepositional phrase introduced by 为 or 让, as in 免费为学生安排旅行 (to arrange free travel for students). When negating the structure, 不 or 没有 must be placed before 免费.

☞ 南开中学康校长当场表示，直到秋云长大，南开中学将免费为她提供中学教育。

1、这个饭馆不能为无家的人提供免费早饭和午饭。

This restaurant cannot provide free breakfast and lunch for the homeless.

2、这个福利院为孤儿安排免费寄宿学校。

This welfare institute provides free living arrangements at school for orphans.

问：医院建造这座24层的大楼是谁提供的捐款？

答：_____。

四、文化背景知识 Cultural Notes

1. Americans adopting Chinese children: Many Americans now travel to China to adopt Chinese children. Most of the children are healthy infant girls, 3-6 months old. The overall cost is approximately $15,000-$20,000. Eligibility and requirements for prospective parents are the following: (1) must be over 35 years of age; (2) must be physically and mentally healthy; (3) must not have any infectious or contagious diseases. Typically, prospective parents first prepare a dossier of various medical records and official documents, then travel to China to meet the child and complete the adoption process.

2. China's One-Child Policy: Faced with severe over-population problems, in the 1970s China promulgated a new "one-child policy". Families could now only have one child. Although some exceptions are made (in the case of twins, for example, or when a child is born with severe defects), this policy has been enforced strictly, more successfully in the cities, less successfully in the countryside.

3. The expression "以集体的名义 + V" is often used to describe a collective or joint effort. For instance, in our text we learn that the orphanage (as an organization) has adopted Qiu Yun.

4. 阿姨 (or "aunt") has three uses as a form of address: (1) aunt (referring specifically to the sister of one's mother); (2) "aunt" (referring generally to any woman of one's mother's generation); and (3) nurse (in a family). In our text it is used by children in the orphanage to address the women who work there and look after them (the same practice is followed in nursery schools and child care centers).

5. 派出所 are smaller, local precincts of China's primary police organization, the Public Security Bureau (公安局 Gōngānjú). 派出所 serve both police and welfare functions, dealing mainly with neighborhood matters such as domestic (family) problems, petty theft, and so on. They also help older residents (especially those without children or relatives nearby) who might need assistance of some kind (buying food, seeing a doctor, and so on).

練習

語言結構 Structures

一、短語翻譯 (Phrase translation)

1. an orphan in the Children's Hospital
2. to find a female baby on the chair
3. birth defect in one's left eye
4. unfortunate experience
5. an unexpected opportunity
6. to be under discussion within the company
7. a day with special meaning
8. a child with a normal IQ and rich feelings
9. in the name of the community (collectively)
10. to assume responsibility for the child's education
11. the married staff
12. during the donation ceremony

二、聽力練習 (Listening comprehension)

1、聽寫 (Dictation)

2、聽錄音並回答問題 (Answering questions while listening to the audio CD)
    (1)《人民日報》社對它的職工有甚麼要求和規定？
    (2) 你所知道的美國報社或者電台對他們的職工有甚麼規定？跟中國的有甚麼不同？

三、改寫下面劃線的詞 (Replace the underlined words)

1、去年<u>首批</u>教師已向學校<u>以</u>各種理由提出辭掉工作，其中<u>已婚</u>教師占百分之二十。

2、<u>每逢</u>周五，他都<u>以</u>有病的藉口不來上課。<u>然而</u>老師從不過問。

练习

语言结构 Structures

一、短语翻译 (Phrase translation)

1. an orphan in the Children's Hospital
2. to find a female baby on the chair
3. birth defect in one's left eye
4. unfortunate experience
5. an unexpected opportunity
6. to be under discussion within the company
7. a day with special meaning
8. a child with a normal IQ and rich feelings
9. in the name of the community (collectively)
10. to assume responsibility for the child's education
11. the married staff
12. during the donation ceremony

二、听力练习 (Listening comprehension)

1、听写 (Dictation)

2、听录音并回答问题 (Answering questions while listening to the audio CD)
(1)《人民日报》社对它的职工有什么要求和规定？
(2) 你所知道的美国报社或者电台对他们的职工有什么规定？跟中国的有什么不同？

三、改写下面划线的词 (Replace the underlined words)

1、去年<u>首批</u>教师已向学校<u>以</u>各种理由提出辞掉工作，其中<u>已婚</u>教师占百分之二十。

2、<u>每逢</u>周五，他都<u>以</u>有病的借口不来上课。<u>然而</u>老师从不过问。

四、完成句子 (Complete the sentences)

1、　　A：＿＿＿＿＿＿＿＿＿＿＿＿＿，我知道了你的不幸遭遇。

　　　　B：是啊，你知道，＿＿＿＿＿＿＿＿＿＿＿＿＿＿＿＿＿＿

　　　　（一個偶然的機會……；對……來説）

2、　　A：聽説你們買了一張生日卡，要送給老師。是真的嗎？

　　　　B：對。＿＿＿＿＿＿＿＿＿＿＿＿＿＿＿＿＿＿＿＿＿＿＿

　　　　（以……的名義；有著……的意義）

3、　　A：這家報社最近在醖釀一件甚麼事情？

　　　　B：報社覺得＿＿＿＿＿＿＿＿＿＿＿＿＿＿＿＿＿，我覺得這個做法非常好。

　　　　（對……負有責任；為……提供……）

五、閲讀短文、回答問題 (Answering questions based on the reading passage)

孤兒大多數是被父母拋棄的孩子，他們的生活遭遇可以説是最不幸的了。在中國，要是一個孤兒有殘疾，又是女的，那就更不幸了。在一些兒童福利院裡，女嬰占百分之七十，殘疾兒童占百分之三十。中國為甚麼會有這樣的現象呢？第一，因為中國很多地方人們的思想還很落後，還有重男輕女的想法，加上這幾年"一家一個孩子"的人口政策，要是生了女孩子就沒有機會要男孩子，所以，只好拋棄女嬰。第二，中國的殘疾人往往被人看不起，也受到不公平的待遇。由於這種情況，一些父母在孩子生下來以後，一發現他們有殘疾或者是女嬰就想法把孩子扔掉。有的被拋棄在醫院裡，有的被扔在火車站。這樣的孩子可以説是最不幸的孩子了。儘管這幾年政府在各個地方建立了很多兒童福利院來收養孤兒，但是中國無家的孩子仍然不少。

問題

　　(1) 被拋棄的孤兒多數是甚麼樣的孩子？

　　(2) 為甚麼人們會拋棄他們自己的孩子？

　　(3) 用你自己的話説説美國在 "foster home" 的孩子。

六、翻譯 (Translate sentences)

1. June 26 is a day that has special meaning to this female orphan. By chance, her experience was told to a couple in Beijing and they decided to adopt her on that very day.

四、完成句子 (Complete the sentences)

1、　　A：_____，我知道了你的不幸遭遇。
　　　　B：是啊，你知道，_____
　　　　（一个偶然的机会……；对……来说）

2、　　A：听说你们买了一张生日卡，要送给老师。是真的吗？
　　　　B：对。_____
　　　　（以……的名义；有着……的意义）

3、　　A：这家报社最近在酝酿一件什么事情？
　　　　B：报社觉得_____，我觉得这个做法非常好。
　　　　（对……负有责任；为……提供……）

五、阅读短文、回答问题 (Answering questions based on the reading passage)

　　　　孤儿大多数是被父母抛弃的孩子，他们的生活遭遇可以说是最不幸的了。在中国，要是一个孤儿有残疾，又是女的，那就更不幸了。在一些儿童福利院里，女婴占百分之七十，残疾儿童占百分之三十。中国为什么会有这样的现象呢？第一，因为中国很多地方人们的思想还很落后，还有重男轻女的想法，加上这几年"一家一个孩子"的人口政策，要是生了女孩子就没有机会要男孩子，所以，只好抛弃女婴。第二，中国的残疾人往往被人看不起，也受到不公平的待遇。由于这种情况，一些父母在孩子生下来以后，一发现他们有残疾或者是女婴就想法把孩子扔掉。有的被抛弃在医院里，有的被扔在火车站。这样的孩子可以说是最不幸的孩子了。尽管这几年政府在各个地方建立了很多儿童福利院来收养孤儿，但是中国无家的孩子仍然不少。

问题
　　(1) 被抛弃的孤儿多数是什么样的孩子？
　　(2) 为什么人们会抛弃他们自己的孩子？
　　(3) 用你自己的话说说美国在"foster home"的孩子。

六、翻译 (Translate sentences)

1. June 26 is a day that has special meaning to this female orphan. By chance, her experience was told to a couple in Beijing and they decided to adopt her on that very day.

2. According to the agreement, the Children's Welfare Institute will be responsible for this orphan's education and medical expenses until she becomes an adult.

3. During the adoption ceremony, the staff members contributed 20,000 dollars to the newspaper agency right on the spot.

4. A plan is under discussion with Nankai Middle School about providing tuition and fees for the orphan free of charge for three years.

2. According to the agreement, the Children's Welfare Institute will be responsible for this orphan's education and medical expenses until she becomes an adult.

3. During the adoption ceremony, the staff members contributed 20,000 dollars to the newspaper agency right on the spot.

4. A plan is under discussion with Nankai Middle School about providing tuition and fees for the orphan free of charge for three years.

語言實踐 ：Practice

一、根據課文回答問題 (Answering questions based on the dialogue)

1、秋雲是誰？她有甚麼不幸的遭遇？
2、秋雲六歲的時候，有一件甚麼事發生了？
3、秋雲除了右眼有毛病以外，別的方面怎麼樣？
4、領養孤兒協議是由哪兩家簽定的？
5、協議規定了甚麼？
6、誰是秋雲的爸爸媽媽？秋雲以後被寄養在哪兒？節日怎麼辦？
7、你覺得秋雲的命運好不好？她真的不是孤兒了嗎？

二、活動 (Activities)

出去跟殘疾人談談，看看社會為他們提供的幫助和設備。再了解一下中國的正常人對殘疾人的看法和態度。

三、討論題 (Topics for discussion)

1、你覺得秋雲讓《天津日報》社領養是不是一件好事？秋雲需要不需要這麼多父母？
2、一個孤兒到底需要一個甚麼樣的家？單位除了有義務之外，應該不應該有權力領養孩子？
3、像秋雲這樣的殘疾孤兒在美國會有甚麼遭遇？女嬰和男嬰有沒有區別？

四、報告 (Presentation)

《中國和美國殘疾人的生活》

语言实践 Practice

一、根据课文回答问题 (Answering questions based on the dialogue)

1、秋云是谁？她有什么不幸的遭遇？
2、秋云六岁的时候，有一件什么事发生了？
3、秋云除了右眼有毛病以外，别的方面怎么样？
4、领养孤儿协议是由哪两家签定的？
5、协议规定了什么？
6、谁是秋云的爸爸妈妈？秋云以后被寄养在哪儿？节日怎么办？
7、你觉得秋云的命运好不好？她真的不是孤儿了吗？

二、活动 (Activities)

出去跟残疾人谈谈，看看社会为他们提供的帮助和设备。再了解一下中国的正常人对残疾人的看法和态度。

三、讨论题 (Topics for discussion)

1、你觉得秋云让《天津日报》社领养是不是一件好事？秋云需要不需要这么多父母？
2、一个孤儿到底需要一个什么样的家？单位除了有义务之外，应该不应该有权力领养孩子？
3、象秋云这样的残疾孤儿在美国会有什么遭遇？女婴和男婴有没有区别？

四、报告 (Presentation)

《中国和美国残疾人的生活》

五、看圖討論 (Picto-discussion)

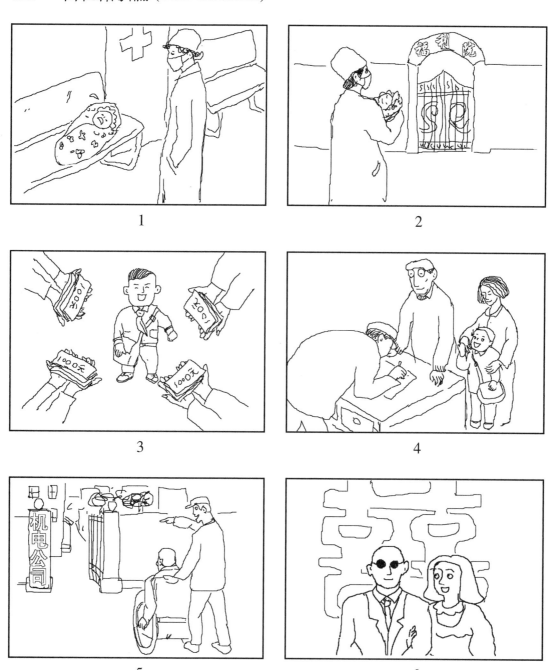

五、看图讨论 (Picto-discussion)

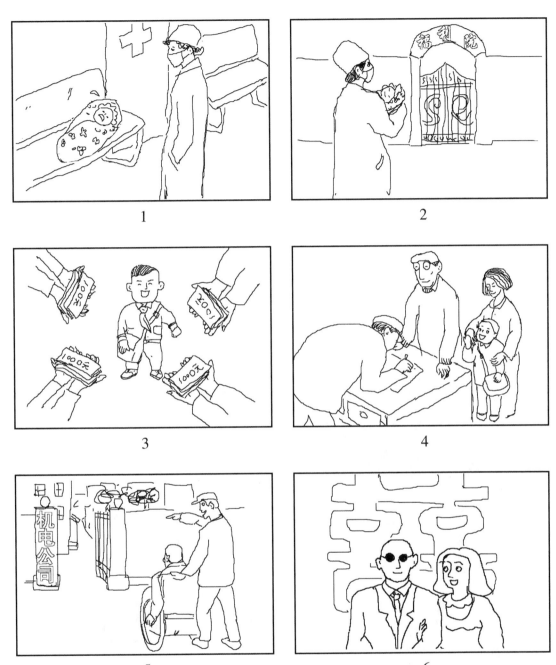

1

2

3

4

5

6

China Scene

An Advanced Chinese Multimedia Course

第三課

私營企業

China Scene
An Advanced Chinese Multimedia Course

第三课

私营企业

課文

一、對話  Dialogs

---

（一）

周班： 中國政府的改革開放政策對農民的觀念和生活有甚麼影響？

王老師：那影響可大了。比如從八十年代開始，政府允許農民承包土地，實行⁽¹⁾責任制。到後來農民還可以自己創辦⁽²⁾企業，很多農民靠自己的本事⁽³⁾，從種責任田逐步發展成私營企業⁽⁴⁾家或個體戶。

周班： 那農民的生活是不是越來越好呢？

王老師：是啊！就拿我們課文裡的王雙貴來說吧，他家原來是一個地地道道的農民家庭，從他爸爸開始就一直在農村種地過日子。八十年代，中國經濟開放了。王雙貴大學畢業以後，辭去公職，回家跟他爸爸辦起了花卉企業。

周班： 看來中國大陸的經濟改革給農民帶來了不少的自由和新的生活。

生詞

私營	(sī yíng)	*Adj.*	privately owned
企業	(qǐ yè)	*N.*	enterprise, business
周班	(zhōu bān)	*N.*	Zhou Ban, name of a person 人名

Notes ⁽¹⁾實行, "to implement" or "to carry out", typically takes disyllabic objects such as 政策 (policy) and 制度 (system). Its use is restricted to formal situations, such as in discussing new policies implemented by the government or an institution.

⁽²⁾創辦 vs. 開辦: 創辦 and 開辦, meaning "to start up", "to found", "to open", are often used to describe the formation of a new business （企業） or project （項目）. These verbs are commonly used in written Chinese. The verbs 辦 and 辦起 are similar in meaning and usage to 創辦 and 開辦, but sound more colloquial.

⁽³⁾The nouns 才能, 本事, and 能力 all share the same English translation, "ability". The most informal of the three terms is 本事, which refers to a native ability or inborn talent that not everyone has. Example: 她很有本事. (She is very capable.) A slightly more formal term is 能力, which refers to universal abilities which everyone has, as in 管理的能力 (managerial ability). The formal term 才能 may also be translated as "talent" or "skill". Example: 他的指揮才能得到了充分發揮. (His skill in conducting has been fully realized.)

⁽⁴⁾私營企業 is interchangeable with 私有企業, meaning "privately-owned business". 私營, however, focuses on the management of a business, while 私有 focuses on ownership.

课文

一、对话 Dialogs

（一）

周班：　中国政府的改革开放政策对农民的观念和生活有什么影响？

王老师：那影响可大了。比如从八十年代开始，政府允许农民承包土地，实行⁽¹⁾责任
制。到后来农民还可以自己创办⁽²⁾企业，很多农民靠自己的本事⁽³⁾，从种责任
田逐步发展成私营企业⁽⁴⁾家或个体户。

周班：　那农民的生活是不是越来越好呢？

王老师：是啊！就拿我们课文里的王双贵来说吧，他家原来是一个地地道道的农民家
庭，从他爸爸开始就一直在农村种地过日子。八十年代，中国经济开放了。
王双贵大学毕业以后，辞去公职，回家跟他爸爸办起了花卉企业。

周班：　看来中国大陆的经济改革给农民带来了不少的自由和新的生活。

生词

私营	(sī yíng)	*Adj.*	privately owned
企业	(qǐ yè)	*N.*	enterprise, business
周班	(zhōu bān)	*N.*	Zhou Ban, name of a person 人名

Notes ⁽¹⁾实行, "to implement" or "to carry out", typically takes disyllabic objects such as 政策 (policy) and 制度 (system). Its use is restricted to formal situations, such as in discussing new policies implemented by the government or an institution.

⁽²⁾创办 vs. 开办: 创办 and 开办, meaning "to start up", "to found", "to open", are often used to describe the formation of a new business（企业）or project（项目）. These verbs are commonly used in written Chinese. The verbs 办 and 办起 are similar in meaning and usage to 创办 and 开办, but sound more colloquial.

⁽³⁾The nouns 才能, 本事, and 能力 all share the same English translation, "ability". The most informal of the three terms is 本事, which refers to a native ability or inborn talent that not everyone has. Example: 她很有本事. (She is very capable.) A slightly more formal term is 能力, which refers to universal abilities which everyone has, as in 管理的能力 (managerial ability). The formal term 才能 may also be translated as "talent" or "skill". Example: 他的指挥才能得到了充分发挥. (His skill in conducting has been fully realized.)

⁽⁴⁾私营企业 is interchangeable with 私有企业, meaning "privately-owned business".　私营, however, focuses on the management of a business, while 私有 focuses on ownership.

政府	(zhèng fǔ)	*N.*	government
改革	(gǎi gé)	*V/N.*	to reform; reform
農民	(nóng mín)	*N.*	peasants
允許	(yǔn xǔ)	*V.*	to allow, to permit
承包	(chéng bāo)	*V.*	to contract
土地	(tǔ dì)	*N.*	land
實行	(shí xíng)	*V.*	to implement, to carry out
責任制	(zé rèn zhì)	*NP.*	responsibility system
創辦	(chuàng bàn)	*V.*	to start, to found, to open
靠	(kào)	*V.*	to rely on, to depend on
本事	(běn shì)	*N.*	ability, capability
種地	(zhòng dì)	*VO.*	to till, to cultivate land
責任田	(zé rèn tián)	*NP.*	land for which one is responsible
逐步	(zhú bù)	*Adv.*	gradually
企業家	(qǐ yè jiā)	*N.*	entrepreneur
個體戶	(gè tǐ hù)	*N.*	(small) businessman/entrepreneur
地地道道	(dì dì dào dào)	*Adj.*	typical
農村	(nóng cūn)	*N.*	countryside
辭去	(cí qù)	*V.*	to resign
公職	(gōng zhí)	*N.*	public post, job in a state-owned enterprise
花卉	(huā huì)	*N.*	flowers and plants, floral
大陸	(dà lù)	*N.*	Mainland China

(二)

周班： 國營企業和私營企業在中國有甚麼不同[5]？

王老師：國營企業是由國家或政府管理經營的企業，私營企業是個人投資個人負責管理的企業。現在這種私營企業在中國十分活躍，主要是因為私營企業在管理

✎ **Notes** [5]區別 vs. 不同: 區別 and 不同 can both function as either nouns or verbs. As nouns, they mean "difference" and are used in the same way. Example: 這個跟那個有區別 or 這個跟那個有不同. (This one is different from that one.) As a verb, however, 區別 means "to distinguish" or "to differentiate" and takes an object directly. Example: 你能不能區別私營企業和國營企業的不同？ (Can you distinguish the differences between private and state-owned businesses?) 不同, on the other hand, means "to be different from" and requires the preposition 和, 跟, or 與 to introduce an object. Example: 大學校和小學校很不同. (Large schools are very different from small schools.)

政府	(zhèng fǔ)	*N.*	government
改革	(gǎi gé)	*V/N.*	to reform; reform
农民	(nóng mín)	*N.*	peasants
允许	(yǔn xǔ)	*V.*	to allow, to permit
承包	(chéng bāo)	*V.*	to contract
土地	(tǔ dì)	*N.*	land
实行	(shí xíng)	*V.*	to implement, to carry out
责任制	(zé rèn zhì)	*NP.*	responsibility system
创办	(chuàng bàn)	*V.*	to start, to found, to open
靠	(kào)	*V.*	to rely on, to depend on
本事	(běn shì)	*N.*	ability, capability
种地	(zhòng dì)	*VO.*	to till, to cultivate land
责任田	(zé rèn tián)	*NP.*	land for which one is responsible
逐步	(zhú bù)	*Adv.*	gradually
企业家	(qǐ yè jiā)	*N.*	entrepreneur
个体户	(gè tǐ hù)	*N.*	(small) businessman/entrepreneur
地地道道	(dì dì dào dào)	*Adj.*	typical
农村	(nóng cūn)	*N.*	countryside
辞去	(cí qù)	*V.*	to resign
公职	(gōng zhí)	*N.*	public post, job in a state-owned enterprise
花卉	(huā huì)	*N.*	flowers and plants, floral
大陆	(dà lù)	*N.*	Mainland China

（二）

周班： 国营企业和私营企业在中国有什么不同[5]？

王老师： 国营企业是由国家或政府管理经营的企业，私营企业是个人投资个人负责管理的企业。现在这种私营企业在中国十分活跃，主要是因为私营企业在管理

✏️ **Notes** [5]区别 vs. 不同: 区别 and 不同 can both function as either nouns or verbs. As nouns, they mean "difference" and are used in the same way. Example: 这个跟那个有区别 or 这个跟那个有不同. (This one is different from that one.) As a verb, however, 区别 means "to distinguish" or "to differentiate" and takes an object directly. Example: 你能不能区别私营企业和国营企业的不同？ (Can you distinguish the differences between private and state-owned businesses?) 不同, on the other hand, means "to be different from" and requires the preposition 和, 跟, or 与 to introduce an object. Example: 大学校和小学校很不同. (Large schools are very different from small schools.)

> 上有自己的優勢，自己説了算⁽⁶⁾，職工能進也能出，而且幹部能上能下，完全
> 靠自己的本事吃飯。
>
> 周班：　看來只有這種管理方法才能⁽⁷⁾讓市場經濟很快地發展。

生詞

國營	(guó yíng)	*Adj.*	state owned
國家	(guó jiā)	*N.*	country, nation
管理	(guǎn lǐ)	*N/V.*	management; to manage
經營	(jīng yíng)	*V/N.*	to run, to engage in (pertaining to selling); management
投資	(tóu zī)	*V/N.*	to invest; investment
負責	(fù zé)	*Adj.*	to be responsible
活躍	(huó yuè)	*Adj.*	active, dynamic
優勢	(yōu shì)	*N.*	advantage, strong point
説了算	(shuō le suàn)	*VP.*	to keep one's word
市場經濟	(shì chǎng jīng jì)	*NP.*	market economy

二、電視原文 💻 TV original

農民創辦花卉企業

（根據原文改編）

　　十幾年前，在中國大陸，私人辦企業是不可⁽⁸⁾想像的事情。當時實行的是排斥私人經濟的社會主義計劃經濟。改革開放使私營經濟逐漸活躍起來，成為社會主義市場經濟的重要組成部分。如今私營企業已經走上了從無到有，逐漸成熟的道路。

✏️ **Notes** ⁽⁶⁾自己説了算 is a colloquial expression meaning "Whatever you say, goes" or "You have the final say". Example: 他在家裡甚麼事情都是他説了算！(In his family, whatever he says, goes!)

⁽⁷⁾See Note (3).

⁽⁸⁾The prefix 不可, "impossible to", can be attached to certain disyllabic verbs to form new fixed expressions such as 不可想像 (unimaginable), 不可名狀 (indescribable), 不可收拾 (unable to remedy, out of hand).

上有自己的优势，自己说了算⁽⁶⁾，职工能进也能出，而且干部能上能下，完全靠自己的本事吃饭。

周班：　看来只有这种管理方法才能⁽⁷⁾让市场经济很快地发展。

生词

国营	(guó yíng)	*Adj.*	state owned
国家	(guó jiā)	*N.*	country, nation
管理	(guǎn lǐ)	*N/V.*	management; to manage
经营	(jīng yíng)	*V/N.*	to run, to engage in (pertaining to selling); management
投资	(tóu zī)	*V/N.*	to invest; investment
负责	(fù zé)	*Adj.*	to be responsible
活跃	(huó yuè)	*Adj.*	active, dynamic
优势	(yōu shì)	*N.*	advantage, strong point
说了算	(shuō le suàn)	*VP.*	to keep one's word
市场经济	(shì chǎng jīng jì)	*NP.*	market economy

二、电视原文 TV original

农民创办花卉企业

（根据原文改编）

　　十几年前，在中国大陆，私人办企业是不可⁽⁸⁾想象的事情。当时实行的是排斥私人经济的社会主义计划经济。改革开放使私营经济逐渐活跃起来，成为社会主义市场经济的重要组成部分。如今私营企业已经走上了从无到有，逐渐成熟的道路。

Notes ⁽⁶⁾自己说了算 is a colloquial expression meaning "Whatever you say, goes" or "You have the final say". Example: 他在家里什么事情都是他说了算！(In his family, whatever he says, goes!)

⁽⁷⁾See Note (3).

⁽⁸⁾The prefix 不可, "impossible to", can be attached to certain disyllabic verbs to form new fixed expressions such as 不可想象 (unimaginable), 不可名状 (indescribable), 不可收拾 (unable to remedy, out of hand).

（採訪一）

記者： "當初您大學本科畢業以後就分到了東營，是不是？"

被採訪者： "東營地質研究院。"

記者： "在那邊工作情況怎麼樣？"

被採訪者： "在那邊工作是挺好，後來我家的花卉企業越搞越大，我覺得呢，丟了那個專業倒是也有點可惜。"

記者： "你學的甚麼專業？"

被採訪者： "學的古生物專業。我是南京大學畢業的。"

記者： "最初[9]這個公司是你父親創辦的吧？"

被採訪者： "我父親創辦的。1981年，當時咱們不是整個國家剛開始農村承包地嗎？我家（是）從三畝地自家責任田，逐步逐步發展起來的。"

記者： "他對你辭去公職，回到家鄉跟他幹抱甚麼態度呢？"

被採訪者： "我父親（跟我這個觀點）基本上是一樣的，就是覺得咱們私營企業在咱們國家雖然起步時間不很長，但是前景非常廣大。"

記者： "你已經在私營企業裡幹了一段時間了，你能談談你在這裡有甚麼好處嗎？"

被採訪者： "我經過[10]這一年多的工作，我覺得幹私營企業前景非常大；再一個呢，管理上，我覺得比管理國營企業要容易得多。因為私營企業說到底在管理上有自己的優勢，自己說了算，確實有權力，職工能進能出，這是一個；再一個呢，幹部能上能下，技術員也能上能下，完全靠自己的本事吃飯。"

　　作為一名私有企業的經營者，既要有創業精神又要有管理才能，因為私有企業的風險是壓在個人身上的。

Notes [9]最初: 初 means "first", "at the beginning", "at the outset". Thus, 最初 means "at the very beginning". The related term 當初 is similar to 當時 and can mean "at the outset", "in the first place", or "at that time", depending on context.

[10]The verb 經過 can mean "to pass through a place". Example: 他經過紐約兩次但都沒機會下來看看. (He has passed through New York twice, but has never had a chance to look around.) It can also mean "to go through an experience". Example: 經過多年的學習他有了管理企業的能力. (After many years of study, he acquired the ability to manage a business.) A related term is the verb 經歷 (to experience), as in 他經歷過很多政治運動. (He has experienced many political campaigns.)

（采访一）

记者： "当初您大学本科毕业以后就分到了东营，是不是？"

被采访者： "东营地质研究院。"

记者： "在那边工作情况怎么样？"

被采访者： "在那边工作是挺好，后来我家的花卉企业越搞越大，我觉得呢，丢了那个专业倒是也有点可惜。"

记者： "你学的什么专业？"

被采访者： "学的古生物专业。我是南京大学毕业的。"

记者： "最初⁽⁹⁾这个公司是你父亲创办的吧？"

被采访者： "我父亲创办的。1981年，当时咱们不是整个国家刚开始农村承包地吗？我家（是）从三亩地自家责任田，逐步逐步发展起来的。"

记者： "他对你辞去公职，回到家乡跟他干抱什么态度呢？"

被采访者： "我父亲（跟我这个观点）基本上是一样的，就是觉得咱们私营企业在咱们国家虽然起步时间不很长，但是前景非常广大。"

记者： "你已经在私营企业里干了一段时间了，你能谈谈你在这里有什么好处吗？"

被采访者： "我经过⁽¹⁰⁾这一年多的工作，我觉得干私营企业前景非常大；再一个呢，管理上，我觉得比管理国营企业要容易得多。因为私营企业说到底在管理上有自己的优势，自己说了算，确实有权力，职工能进能出，这是一个；再一个呢，干部能上能下，技术员也能上能下，完全靠自己的本事吃饭。"

作为一名私有企业的经营者，既要有创业精神又要有管理才能，因为私有企业的风险是压在个人身上的。

Notes ⁽⁹⁾最初: 初 means "first", "at the beginning", "at the outset". Thus, 最初 means "at the very beginning". The related term 当初 is similar to 当时 and can mean "at the outset", "in the first place", or "at that time", depending on context.

⁽¹⁰⁾The verb 经过 can mean "to pass through a place". Example: 他经过纽约两次但都没机会下来看看. (He has passed through New York twice, but has never had a chance to look around.) It can also mean "to go through an experience". Example: 经过多年的学习他有了管理企业的能力. (After many years of study, he acquired the ability to manage a business.) A related term is the verb 经历 (to experience), as in 他经历过很多政治运动. (He has experienced many political campaigns.)

（採訪二）

記者：　　　　“原來從事甚麼工作啊？”

被採訪者：“我原來上學，畢業以後就到這邊來工作。”

記者：　　　　“上甚麼學？”

被採訪者：“我是上高中。”

記者：　　　　“待遇怎麼樣？”

被採訪者：“待遇還可以。”

記者：　　　　“現在每個月工資多少錢？”

被採訪者：“每月現在工資300多塊錢。”

記者：　　　　“噢，300多，比一般的職工要高得多。”

被採訪者：“是的。”

記者：　　　　“其它福利待遇呢？”

被採訪者：“其它福利待遇，像一般的生活（方面），工裝服甚麼的，也都有。”

記者：　　　　“平時你們都在不同的崗位[11]上工作，回到家裡聊起天以後，你們比較一下你們的單位和別的單位有甚麼區別[12]沒有？”

被採訪者：“有時候也談起來他們單位機制方面可能存在一些問題，像個人有長處，有時候不能得到[13]及時[14]的發揮。我們這邊有甚麼意見和建議，可以馬上向公司提出來，如果比較合理，公司就馬上採納[15]，並且對我們有時候還有獎勵。”

Notes [11]崗位 originally referred to a military outpost. Since 1949, however, it has been used to mean one's workplace, as in 走上新的崗位 (to take up a new post, to get a new job).

[12]See Note (5).

[13]得 (dé) 到, "to acquire", "to attain", or "to get", is a formal verb which always precedes an abstract noun. Example: 病人得到了治療. (The patient received medical treatment.) 得到 usually takes objects with positive connotations, as in 得到支持 (to receive support) and 得到幫助 (to receive help), or with objects which, while not positive, the speaker may feel are deserved, as in 得到懲罰 (to receive punishment). However, 得到 is never used to indicate that someone has caught a disease. Sentences containing 得到 can either be translated literally, as shown above, or as passive sentences. (The patient was treated.)

[14]As an adverb, 及時 means "on time", "immediately". Example: 請你及時告訴我！ (Please tell me immediately!) As an adjective, it means "timely", "immediate". Example: 病人得到及時的治療. (The patient received immediate treatment.)

[15]採納 means "to adopt", but is only used with objects such as 意見 (opinions), 建議 (suggestions), 提議 (proposals), or 要求 (demands). The verb used to describe the adoption of a child is 領養.

（采访二）

记者：　　　"原来从事什么工作啊？"

被采访者："我原来上学，毕业以后就到这边来工作。"

记者：　　　"上什么学？"

被采访者："我是上高中。"

记者：　　　"待遇怎么样？"

被采访者："待遇还可以。"

记者：　　　"现在每个月工资多少钱？"

被采访者："每月现在工资300多块钱。"

记者：　　　"噢，300多，比一般的职工要高得多。"

被采访者："是的。"

记者：　　　"其它福利待遇呢？"

被采访者："其它福利待遇，象一般的生活（方面），工装服什么的，也都有。"

记者：　　　"平时你们都在不同的岗位⁽¹¹⁾上工作，回到家里聊起天以后，你们比较一下你们的单位和别的单位有什么区别⁽¹²⁾没有？"

被采访者："有时候也谈起来他们单位机制方面可能存在一些问题，象个人有长处，有时候不能得到⁽¹³⁾及时⁽¹⁴⁾的发挥。我们这边有什么意见和建议，可以马上向公司提出来，如果比较合理，公司就马上采纳⁽¹⁵⁾，并且对我们有时候还有奖励。"

Notes ⁽¹¹⁾岗位 originally referred to a military outpost. Since 1949, however, it has been used to mean one's workplace, as in 走上新的岗位 (to take up a new post, to get a new job).

⁽¹²⁾See Note (5).

⁽¹³⁾得 (dé) 到, "to acquire", "to attain", or "to get", is a formal verb which always precedes an abstract noun. Example: 病人得到了治疗. (The patient received medical treatment.) 得到 usually takes objects with positive connotations, as in 得到支持 (to receive support) and 得到帮助 (to receive help), or with objects which, while not positive, the speaker may feel are deserved, as in 得到惩罚 (to receive punishment). However, 得到 is never used to indicate that someone has caught a disease. Sentences containing 得到 can either be translated literally, as shown above, or as passive sentences. (The patient was treated.)

⁽¹⁴⁾As an adverb, 及时 means "on time", "immediately". Example: 请你及时告诉我！ (Please tell me immediately!) As an adjective, it means "timely", "immediate". Example: 病人得到及时的治疗. (The patient received immediate treatment.)

⁽¹⁵⁾采纳 means "to adopt", but is only used with objects such as 意见 (opinions), 建议 (suggestions), 提议 (proposals), or 要求 (demands). The verb used to describe the adoption of a child is 领养.

生詞

辦	(bàn)	*V.*	to run, to handle
不可想像	(bù kě xiǎng xiàng)	*Adj.*	unthinkable, unimaginable
排斥	(pái chì)	*V.*	to exclude, to repel
社會主義	(shè huì zhǔ yì)	*Adj/NP.*	socialist, socialism
計劃經濟	(jì huà jīng jì)	*NP.*	planned economy
組成部分	(zǔ chéng bù fèn)	*NP.*	component
逐漸	(zhú jiàn)	*Adv.*	gradually
從無到有	(cóng wú dào yǒu)	*Idom.*	to spring from nothing, from nonexistence to existence
如今	(rú jīn)	*Adv.*	now
成熟	(chéng shú)	*Adj.*	mature, maturity
道路	(dào lù)	*N.*	road, route, path
採訪	(cǎi fǎng)	*V/N.*	to interview, to gather material; interview
當初	(dāng chū)	*Adv.*	at that time, originally
本科	(běn kē)	*N.*	undergraduate
分	(fēn)	*V.*	to assign
東營	(dōng yíng)	*Place N.*	Dongying, name of a place 地名
地質	(dì zhì)	*N.*	geology
研究院	(yán jiū yuàn)	*NP.*	research institute
專業	(zhuān yè)	*N.*	specialty, major, field of study
古生物	(gǔ shēng wù)	*NP.*	paleontology
最初	(zuì chū)	*Adv.*	at the beginning, initially
承包地	(chéng bāo dì)	*NP.*	contracted land
畝	(mǔ)	*Classifier.*	measurement for land
自家	(zì jiā)	*NP.*	one's own family
基本上	(jī běn shàng)	*Adv.*	basically
起步	(qǐ bù)	*VO.*	starting step, initial step
前景	(qián jǐng)	*N.*	future, prospects
經過	(jīng guò)	*V.*	to pass, to go through, to undergo
說到底	(shuō dào dǐ)	*VP.*	bottom line
創業	(chuàng yè)	*VO.*	to do pioneering work, to start an undertaking, to start a business
精神	(jīng shén)	*N.*	spirit

生词

办	(bàn)	*V.*	to run, to handle
不可想象	(bù kě xiǎng xiàng)	*Adj.*	unthinkable, unimaginable
排斥	(pái chì)	*V.*	to exclude, to repel
社会主义	(shè huì zhǔ yì)	*Adj/NP.*	socialist, socialism
计划经济	(jì huà jīng jì)	*NP.*	planned economy
组成部分	(zǔ chéng bù fèn)	*NP.*	component
逐渐	(zhú jiàn)	*Adv.*	gradually
从无到有	(cóng wú dào yǒu)	*Idom.*	to spring from nothing, from nonexistence to existence
如今	(rú jīn)	*Adv.*	now
成熟	(chéng shú)	*Adj.*	mature, maturity
道路	(dào lù)	*N.*	road, route, path
采访	(cǎi fǎng)	*V/N.*	to interview, to gather material; interview
当初	(dāng chū)	*Adv.*	at that time, originally
本科	(běn kē)	*N.*	undergraduate
分	(fēn)	*V.*	to assign
东营	(dōng yíng)	*Place N.*	Dongying, name of a place 地名
地质	(dì zhì)	*N.*	geology
研究院	(yán jiū yuàn)	*NP.*	research institute
专业	(zhuān yè)	*N.*	specialty, major, field of study
古生物	(gǔ shēng wù)	*NP.*	paleontology
最初	(zuì chū)	*Adv.*	at the beginning, initially
承包地	(chéng bāo dì)	*NP.*	contracted land
亩	(mǔ)	*Classifier.*	measurement for land
自家	(zì jiā)	*NP.*	one's own family
基本上	(jī běn shàng)	*Adv.*	basically
起步	(qǐ bù)	*VO.*	starting step, initial step
前景	(qián jǐng)	*N.*	future, prospects
经过	(jīng guò)	*V.*	to pass, to go through, to undergo
说到底	(shuō dào dǐ)	*VP.*	bottom line
创业	(chuàng yè)	*VO.*	to do pioneering work, to start an undertaking, to start a business
精神	(jīng shén)	*N.*	spirit

才能	(cái néng)	*N.*	capability, ability, talent
風險	(fēng xiǎn)	*N.*	risk
壓	(yā)	*V.*	to weigh on (someone), to place, to press on
從事	(cóng shì)	*V.*	to be engaged in
福利待遇	(fú lì dài yù)	*NP.*	fringe benefits
工裝服	(gōng zhuāng fú)	*NP.*	work uniform
崗位	(gǎng wèi)	*N.*	post
單位	(dān wèi)	*N.*	work unit
區別	(qū bié)	*N/V.*	difference; to differentiate, to distinguish
機制	(jī zhì)	*N.*	system
長處	(cháng chù)	*NP.*	strong point, advantage
及時	(jí shí)	*Adv.*	on time, timely, immediately
存在	(cún zài)	*V/N.*	to exist, existence
發揮	(fā huī)	*V.*	to bring into play, to give play to
意見	(yì jiàn)	*N.*	opinion
建議	(jiàn yì)	*N/V.*	suggestion; to suggest
提	(tí)	*V.*	to put forward, to raise, to propose
合理	(hé lǐ)	*Adj.*	reasonable, rational
採納	(cǎi nà)	*V.*	to adopt, to take in
獎勵	(jiǎng lì)	*N/V*	award, reward; to reward

才能	(cái néng)	*N.*	capability, ability, talent
风险	(fēng xiǎn)	*N.*	risk
压	(yā)	*V.*	to weigh on (someone), to place, to press on
从事	(cóng shì)	*V.*	to be engaged in
福利待遇	(fú lì dài yù)	*NP.*	fringe benefits
工装服	(gōng zhuāng fú)	*NP.*	work uniform
岗位	(gǎng wèi)	*N.*	post
单位	(dān wèi)	*N.*	work unit
区别	(qū bié)	*N/V.*	difference; to differentiate, to distinguish
机制	(jī zhì)	*N.*	system
长处	(cháng chù)	*NP.*	strong point, advantage
及时	(jí shí)	*Adv.*	on time, timely, immediately
存在	(cún zài)	*V/N.*	to exist, existence
发挥	(fā huī)	*V.*	to bring into play, to give play to
意见	(yì jiàn)	*N.*	opinion
建议	(jiàn yì)	*N/V.*	suggestion; to suggest
提	(tí)	*V.*	to put forward, to raise, to propose
合理	(hé lǐ)	*Adj.*	reasonable, rational
采纳	(cǎi nà)	*V.*	to adopt, to take in
奖励	(jiǎng lì)	*N/V*	award, reward; to reward

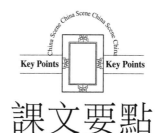

課文要點

一、詞語解釋 ✎ Words and Phrases

（一）文言詞、慣用詞 (Classical Chinese and idiomatic expressions)

1、辭去＝辭掉
- ☞ 他對你辭去公職，回到家鄉跟他幹抱甚麼態度呢？

2、當初＝在那個時候
- ☞ 當初您大學本科畢業以後就分到了東營。

3、向＝跟
- ☞ 我們這邊有甚麼意見和建議，可以馬上向公司提出來。

（二）成語、專用語 (idioms and specialized words)

- ◆ 地地道道 typical
- ◆ 不可想像 unimaginable
- ◆ 計劃經濟 planned economy
- ◆ 市場經濟 market economy
- ◆ 從無到有 spring from nothing
- ◆ 福利待遇 fringe benefits

二、書面語、正式語、口語對照表 ⅲⅲ Written/formal/colloquial Comparison

	書面／正式語	口語		書面／正式語	口語
1	辭去	辭／辭掉	6	前景／將來	以後的情況
2	當初	在那個時候	7	一名	一個
3	如今	現在	8	從事（工作）	做（工作）
4	十分	很	9	區別	不同
5	起步	開始			

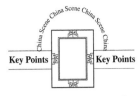

课文要点

一、词语解释 Words and Phrases

（一）文言词、惯用词 (Classical Chinese and idiomatic expressions)

1、辞去 = 辞掉

☞ 他对你辞去公职，回到家乡跟他干抱什么态度呢？

2、当初 = 在那个时候

☞ 当初您大学本科毕业以后就分到了东营。

3、向 = 跟

☞ 我们这边有什么意见和建议，可以马上向公司提出来。

（二）成语、专用语 (idioms and specialized words)

◆ 地地道道 typical

◆ 不可想象 unimaginable

◆ 计划经济 planned economy

◆ 市场经济 market economy

◆ 从无到有 spring from nothing

◆ 福利待遇 fringe benefits

二、书面语、正式语、口语对照表 Written/formal/colloquial Comparison

	书面／正式语	口语		书面／正式语	口语
1	辞去	辞／辞掉	6	前景／将来	以后的情况
2	当初	在那个时候	7	一名	一个
3	如今	现在	8	从事（工作）	做（工作）
4	十分	很	9	区别	不同
5	起步	开始			

三、句型 Sentence Structures

（一）就拿……來說 (to take someone or something for example)

> 就拿……來説, "to take someone or something for example", is used to further explain a statement made previously by giving a specific figure or example. Example: 來美國以後，他的英文有了很大的進步。就拿寫報告來説，現在差不多都不用改了. (Since coming to the United States, his English has improved a lot. Take writing reports for example; he hardly ever needs to make any revisions anymore.) 就拿……來説 is a set phrase that must be placed at the beginning of a sentence, before the subject of the main clause.

☞ 就拿我們課文裡的王雙貴來説吧，他家原來是一個地地道道的農民家庭。

1、中國改革開放以後，私營企業越來越多。就拿農村來説，很多農民創辦了自己的企業。

  Since China's economic reforms, more and more private businesses have appeared. For example, in the countryside, many peasants have started their own businesses.

2、國營企業也有一定的優勢。就拿福利待遇來説，國營企業就可以為職工提供醫療保險。

  State-owned enterprise also has certain advantages. For example, in terms of fringe benefits, they can provide health insurance for their workers.

  問：亞洲現在的經濟情況怎麼樣？
  答：＿＿＿＿＿＿＿＿＿＿＿＿＿＿＿＿＿＿＿＿＿＿。

（二）靠…… + VO (to rely on, to depend on something to do something)

> 靠…… + VO, "to rely on" or "to depend on someone or something", is the same as 憑……＋VO (see Lesson 7, Pattern 6). While the element following 靠 can be a noun or another VO structure, the phrase must be placed after the subject and immediately before the main verb. Examples: 靠自己的本事吃飯 (to rely on one's own skills to make a living); 他靠騙人過日子。(He makes a living merely by cheating others.)

☞ 很多農民靠自己的本事，從種責任田逐步發展成私營企業家或個體戶。

1、一個人應該靠自己的才能和本事生活。

  A person should rely on their own talents and abilities to survive.

2、私營企業是完全靠個人投資和個人管理的。

  Private enterprise depends completely on individual investment and management.

三、句型 Sentence Structures

（一）就拿……来说 (to take someone or something for example)

> 就拿……来说, "to take someone or something for example", is used to further explain a statement made previously by giving a specific figure or example. Example: 来美国以后，他的英文有了很大的进步。就拿写报告来说，现在差不多都不用改了。(Since coming to the United States, his English has improved a lot. Take writing reports for example; he hardly ever needs to make any revisions anymore.) 就拿……来说 is a set phrase that must be placed at the beginning of a sentence, before the subject of the main clause.

☞ 就拿我们课文里的王双贵来说吧，他家原来是一个地地道道的农民家庭。

1、中国改革开放以后，私营企业越来越多。就拿农村来说，很多农民创办了自己的企业。

Since China's economic reforms, more and more private businesses have appeared. For example, in the countryside, many peasants have started their own businesses.

2、国营企业也有一定的优势。就拿福利待遇来说，国营企业就可以为职工提供医疗保险。

State-owned enterprise also has certain advantages. For example, in terms of fringe benefits, they can provide health insurance for their workers.

问：亚洲现在的经济情况怎么样？

答：_____。

（二）靠…… + VO (to rely on, to depend on something to do something)

> 靠…… + VO, "to rely on" or "to depend on someone or something", is the same as 凭…… + VO (see Lesson 7, Pattern 6). While the element following 靠 can be a noun or another VO structure, the phrase must be placed after the subject and immediately before the main verb. Examples: 靠自己的本事吃饭 (to rely on one's own skills to make a living); 他靠骗人过日子。(He makes a living merely by cheating others.)

☞ 很多农民靠自己的本事，从种责任田逐步发展成私营企业家或个体户。

1、一个人应该靠自己的才能和本事生活。

A person should rely on their own talents and abilities to survive.

2、私营企业是完全靠个人投资和个人管理的。

Private enterprise depends completely on individual investment and management.

問：你的公司是用甚麼方法逐步發展起來的？

答：＿＿＿＿＿＿＿＿＿＿＿＿＿＿＿＿＿＿＿＿＿。

（三）給……帶來（了）…… (to bring something for someone)

> ✍ 給……帶來（了），"to bring something for someone", is a structure in which the preposition 給 must be used to indicate the recipient of the verb. The aspect marker 了 often follows 帶來 to indicate completion of the action. The object of 帶來 can be a concrete or abstract noun, as in 帶來一些書 (to bring a few books), 帶來變化 (to bring changes), 帶來幸福 (to bring good fortune). When negating the sentence, 不 or 沒 should be placed before 給, and 了 must be omitted. Example: 這種產品沒有給家庭帶來更多的方便. (This kind of product has not brought more convenience to families.)

☞ 看來中國大陸的經濟改革給農民帶來了不少的自由和新的生活。

1、社會主義計劃經濟給你帶來了甚麼好處？

What benefits has the socialist planned economy provided for you?

2、自己辦花卉公司給你帶來甚麼優勢？

What benefits does running your own flower shop provide?

問：何茹的爸爸出國給何茹帶來了甚麼？

答：＿＿＿＿＿＿＿＿＿＿＿＿＿＿＿＿＿＿＿＿＿。

（四）……是不可想像的…… (to be unimaginable)

> ✍ 不可想像 here means "unimaginable". 不可 is often used with another disyllabic word to indicate "impossible", as in 不可理解 (impossible to understand, incomprehensible), 不可思議 (unthinkable). ……是不可想像的…… is usually preceded by a sentence or a VO structure, as in the examples below. Sometimes the subject may be a noun, which is always followed by another modifying element. Example: 汽車在中國人的生活中不再是不可想像的事情了. (Cars are no longer unimaginable in the lives of most Chinese people.)

☞ 十幾年前，在中國大陸，私人辦企業是不可想像的事情。

1、幾年前大學本科畢業生幹私營企業是不可想像的。

A few years ago, it was unimaginable for an undergraduate to start a private business.

2、在幾年前，辭去國營企業的工作回農村去是不可想像的事。

A few years ago, leaving a job at a state-owned company to return to the countryside was unimaginable.

问：你的公司是用什么方法逐步发展起来的？

答：＿＿＿＿＿＿＿＿＿＿＿＿＿＿＿＿＿。

（三）给……带来（了）…… (to bring something for someone)

> ✍ 给……带来（了），"to bring something for someone", is a structure in which the preposition 给 must be used to indicate the recipient of the verb. The aspect marker 了 often follows 带来 to indicate completion of the action. The object of 带来 can be a concrete or abstract noun, as in 带来 一些书 (to bring a few books), 带来变化 (to bring changes), 带来幸福 (to bring good fortune). When negating the sentence, 不 or 没 should be placed before 给, and 了 must be omitted. Example: 这种产品没有给家庭带来更多的方便. (This kind of product has not brought more convenience to families.)

☞ 看来中国大陆的经济改革给农民带来了不少的自由和新的生活。

1、社会主义计划经济给你带来了什么好处？

What benefits has the socialist planned economy provided for you?

2、自己办花卉公司给你带来什么优势？

What benefits does running your own flower shop provide?

问：何茹的爸爸出国给何茹带来了什么？

答：＿＿＿＿＿＿＿＿＿＿＿＿＿＿＿＿＿。

（四）……是不可想象的…… (to be unimaginable)

> ✍ 不可想象 here means "unimaginable". 不可 is often used with another disyllabic word to indicate "impossible", as in 不可理解 (impossible to understand, incomprehensible), 不可思议 (unthinkable). ……是不可想象的…… is usually preceded by a sentence or a VO structure, as in the examples below. Sometimes the subject may be a noun, which is always followed by another modifying element. Example: 汽车在中国人的生活中不再是不可想象的事情了. (Cars are no longer unimaginable in the lives of most Chinese people.)

☞ 十几年前，在中国大陆，私人办企业是不可想象的事情。

1、几年前大学本科毕业生干私营企业是不可想象的。

A few years ago, it was unimaginable for an undergraduate to start a private business.

2、在几年前，辞去国营企业的工作回农村去是不可想象的事。

A few years ago, leaving a job at a state-owned company to return to the countryside was unimaginable.

問：在美國，如果政府不給老百姓說話的自由，美國人會覺得怎麼樣？

答：＿＿＿＿＿＿＿＿＿＿＿＿＿＿＿＿＿＿＿＿＿＿＿。

（五）A 使（／讓）B 活躍起來 (A makes B active)

> ✍ A 使（／讓）B 活躍起來 is a causative structure meaning "A makes B active". 起來 here indicates that becoming active is a gradual process. The verb 讓 can be substituted for the more formal 使. The negation for this structure is A 沒有使（／讓）B 活躍起來. The negative particle 不 is rarely used with this structure.

☞ 改革開放使私營經濟逐漸活躍起來。

1、他說的那句話使整個班的氣氛都活躍起來了。

His remark livened the atmosphere of the whole class.

2、經濟改革，國家開放使中國的經濟活躍起來了。

Economic reform and the opening up of the nation have made China's economy active.

問：你認為甚麼樣的經濟可以＿＿＿＿＿＿＿＿＿＿＿＿？

答：＿＿＿＿＿＿＿＿＿＿＿＿＿＿＿＿＿＿＿。

（六）成為／是……的組成部分 (to become/to be an integral part of)

> ✍ 成為／是……的組成部分, "to become or to be an integral part of", is a structure used commonly in written and formal Chinese. Either 成為 or 是 may be used as a verb, depending on whether the emphasis is on gradual change or the identity of the object.

☞ 改革開放使私營經濟逐漸活躍起來，成為社會主義市場經濟的重要組成部分。

1、私營企業和國營企業是中國經濟最重要的組成部分。

Private and state-owned enterprise are the most important components of China's economy.

2、幹部、職工、技術員是一個企業最重要的組成部分。

Cadres, workers, and technicians are the most important components of a business.

問：美國總統的新經濟政策是甚麼？它的重要組成部分是甚麼？

答：＿＿＿＿＿＿＿＿＿＿＿＿＿＿＿＿＿＿＿＿。

问：在美国，如果政府不给老百姓说话的自由，美国人会觉得怎么样？

答：＿＿＿＿＿＿＿＿＿＿＿＿＿＿＿＿＿＿＿＿。

（五）A 使（／让）B 活跃起来 (A makes B active)

> ✍ A 使（／让）B 活跃起来 is a causative structure meaning "A makes B active". 起来 here indicates that becoming active is a gradual process. The verb 让 can be substituted for the more formal 使. The negation for this structure is A 没有使（／让）B 活跃起来. The negative particle 不 is rarely used with this structure.

☞ 改革开放使私营经济逐渐活跃起来。

1、他说的那句话使整个班的气氛都活跃起来了。

His remark livened the atmosphere of the whole class.

2、经济改革，国家开放使中国的经济活跃起来了。

Economic reform and the opening up of the nation have made China's economy active.

问：你认为什么样的经济可以＿＿＿＿＿＿＿＿＿＿＿？

答：＿＿＿＿＿＿＿＿＿＿＿＿＿＿＿＿＿＿。

（六）成为／是……的组成部分 (to become/to be an integral part of)

> ✍ 成为／是……的组成部分, "to become or to be an integral part of", is a structure used commonly in written and formal Chinese. Either 成为 or 是 may be used as a verb, depending on whether the emphasis is on gradual change or the identity of the object.

☞ 改革开放使私营经济逐渐活跃起来，成为社会主义市场经济的重要组成部分。

1、私营企业和国营企业是中国经济最重要的组成部分。

Private and state-owned enterprise are the most important components of China's economy.

2、干部、职工、技术员是一个企业最重要的组成部分。

Cadres, workers, and technicians are the most important components of a business.

问：美国总统的新经济政策是什么？它的重要组成部分是什么？

答：＿＿＿＿＿＿＿＿＿＿＿＿＿＿＿＿＿＿＿。

（七）走上……的道路 (to take the road of, to get on the path of)

> ✍ 走上……的道路, "to take the road of" or "to get on the path of", is a set phrase that is often used in a figurative sense. In English it often translates as "to become", as in 走上致富的道路 (to become rich), 走上犯罪的道路 (to become a criminal). The modifying element before 道路 is often a disyllabic VO construction, such as 致富 (wealth) or 犯罪 (crime).

☞ 如今私營企業已經走上了從無到有，逐漸成熟的道路。

1、作為一個公司的經營者，沒有創造精神和管理才能就不能走上致富的道路。

Acting as a manager in a company without a pioneering spirit and good business sense cannot lead down a path to fortune.

2、他大學本科畢業以後找不到工作，最後走上了犯罪的道路。

After graduating from college, he could not find a job; finally, he became a criminal.

問：真沒想到去年他還是一個天真、活潑的孩子，今年就成了這個公司的經理了。
這是怎麼回事？

答：_____。

（八）（是／）由……創辦的 (to be established by; to be created by)

> ✍ （是／）由……創辦, meaning "to be established by" or "to be created by", is a passive structure often used with 是……的 to emphasize the agent of the verb 創辦. When the agent is not the focus of the sentence, either B 由 A 創辦 or the active form A 創辦 B can be used. 創辦 is interchangeable with 辦, but 創辦 is used in both spoken and written Chinese, whereas 辦 is used only in colloquial Chinese.

☞ 最初這個公司是你父親創辦的吧？

1、這個學校是由地方企業創辦的，雖然時間不長，可是前景很好。

This school was established by a local business. Although it has not been in existence for very long, its prospects are good.

2、這個公司是由那個農民自己創辦的，似乎風險很大。

That farmer established this company by himself. It appears that there were great risks involved.

問：請你談談美國的福特汽車公司的創辦歷史。

答：_____。

（七）走上……的道路 (to take the road of, to get on the path of)

> ✍ 走上……的道路, "to take the road of" or "to get on the path of", is a set phrase that is often used in a figurative sense. In English it often translates as "to become", as in 走上致富的道路 (to become rich), 走上犯罪的道路 (to become a criminal). The modifying element before 道路 is often a disyllabic VO construction, such as 致富 (wealth) or 犯罪 (crime).

☞ 如今私营企业已经走上了从无到有，逐渐成熟的道路。

1、作为一个公司的经营者，没有创造精神和管理才能就不能走上致富的道路。
Acting as a manager in a company without a pioneering spirit and good business sense cannot lead down a path to fortune.

2、他大学本科毕业以后找不到工作，最后走上了犯罪的道路。
After graduating from college, he could not find a job; finally, he became a criminal.

问： 真没想到去年他还是一个天真、活泼的孩子，今年就成了这个公司的经理了。这是怎么回事？

答： _____。

（八）（是／）由……创办的 (to be established by; to be created by)

> ✍ （是／）由……创办, meaning "to be established by" or "to be created by", is a passive structure often used with 是……的 to emphasize the agent of the verb 创办. When the agent is not the focus of the sentence, either B 由 A 创办 or the active form A 创办 B can be used. 创办 is interchangeable with 办, but 创办 is used in both spoken and written Chinese, whereas 办 is used only in colloquial Chinese.

☞ 最初这个公司是你父亲创办的吧？

1、这个学校是由地方企业创办的，虽然时间不长，可是前景很好。
This school was established by a local business. Although it has not been in existence for very long, its prospects are good.

2、这个公司是由那个农民自己创办的，似乎风险很大。
That farmer established this company by himself. It appears that there were great risks involved.

问： 请你谈谈美国的福特汽车公司的创办历史。

答： _____。

（九）對……抱……的態度 (to take an attitude toward something)

> ✍ 對……抱……的態度, "to take an attitude toward something", is often used to ask a question in a spoken or informal setting. The elements used to modify 態度 are normally disyllabic words such as 支持 or 反對. The verb 抱 can often be replaced by the more formal word 採取 (to select, to adopt). Example: 你對美國政府的經濟政策採取甚麼態度？ (What is your attitude toward American economic policy?) When used to ask a question, this pattern is usually not repeated in the answer. See the examples below.

☞ 他對你辭去公職，回到家鄉跟他幹抱甚麼態度呢？

1、你對中國的人口政策抱甚麼態度？

What do you think of China's population policy?

2、你父母對你學習中文和中國文化抱甚麼態度？

What is your parents' attitude toward your studying Chinese language and culture?

問：＿＿＿＿＿＿＿＿＿＿＿＿＿＿＿＿＿＿？

答：我認為中國的人口政策是必要的。

（十）説到底 (ultimately, the bottom line is)

> ✍ 説到底, "ultimately", "the bottom line is", often functions as an inserted element to point out the most basic truth or fact of a situation. It can occur at the beginning of a sentence or immediately precede a verb. It is more commonly used in colloquial Chinese than in written Chinese.

☞ 因為私營企業説到底在管理上有自己的優勢，自己説了算，確實有權力。

1、私營企業的風險説到底是壓在個人身上的。

In a private business, the risk ultimately falls on the individual.

2、説到底，幹私營企業是為了提高自己的工資和福利待遇。

Ultimately, we are starting a private business in order to improve our salaries and fringe benefits.

問：你總説國營企業有前景，有優勢。國營企業的優勢到底在哪兒？

答：＿＿＿＿＿＿＿＿＿＿＿＿＿＿＿＿＿＿＿。

（九）对……抱……的态度 (to take an attitude toward something)

> ✍ 对……抱……的态度, "to take an attitude toward something", is often used to ask a question in a spoken or informal setting. The elements used to modify 态度 are normally disyllabic words such as 支持 or 反对. The verb 抱 can often be replaced by the more formal word 采取 (to select, to adopt). Example: 你对美国政府的经济政策采取什么态度？ (What is your attitude toward American economic policy?) When used to ask a question, this pattern is usually not repeated in the answer. See the examples below.

☞ 他对你辞去公职，回到家乡跟他干抱什么态度呢？

1、你对中国的人口政策抱什么态度？
   What do you think of China's population policy?
2、你父母对你学习中文和中国文化抱什么态度？
   What is your parents' attitude toward your studying Chinese language and culture?

问：_____？
答：我认为中国的人口政策是必要的。

（十）说到底 (ultimately, the bottom line is)

> ✍ 说到底, "ultimately", "the bottom line is", often functions as an inserted element to point out the most basic truth or fact of a situation. It can occur at the beginning of a sentence or immediately precede a verb. It is more commonly used in colloquial Chinese than in written Chinese.

☞ 因为私营企业说到底在管理上有自己的优势，自己说了算，确实有权力。

1、私营企业的风险说到底是压在个人身上的。
   In a private business, the risk ultimately falls on the individual.
2、说到底，干私营企业是为了提高自己的工资和福利待遇。
   Ultimately, we are starting a private business in order to improve our salaries and fringe benefits.

问：你总说国营企业有前景，有优势。国营企业的优势到底在哪儿？
答：_____。

（十一）在……方面有……（的）優勢 (to have the advantage in an area)

> ✎ 在……方面有……的優勢, "to have an advantage in the area of", is a structure often used in formal or written Chinese. 在……方面 must be placed before the main verb to indicate the area or aspect in which the advantage lies. The element between 有 and 優勢 is optional and often disyllabic. Examples: 在資金方面有優勢 (to have an advantage in capital); 在教育孩子方面有顯著的優勢 (to have an obvious advantage in educating children); 在學習方面有很大的優勢 (to have a great advantage in one's studies). 很 cannot be omitted in the last sentence, because 很 helps form a disyllabic phrase.

☞ 因為私營企業説到底在管理上有自己的優勢，自己説了算，確實有權力。

1、這種小學校在一些方面也有它的優勢，學生很少，老師跟學生的關係很近。

This type of small school also has its advantages in certain aspects: There are not many students, and relationships between professors and students are very close.

2、這種機制在管理上有一個很大的優勢，就是技術員能上能下，完全靠自己的本事吃飯。

This type of system has a great advantage in management. Technicians can be promoted or demoted depending on their own capabilities.

問：你認為計劃經濟在甚麼方面有優勢？
答：我認為＿＿＿＿＿＿＿＿＿＿＿＿＿＿＿＿＿＿＿＿＿。

（十二）（在……方面）存在……問題 (problems exist in an area or aspect)

> ✎ 存在……問題 means that a problem （問題） exists （存在） in some area or aspect （方面） of something. The subject can be present or absent (see Example 2). The element between 存在 and 問題 is optional and often disyllabic. Example: 他們的考試制度還存在不少問題。(Problems still persist in their exam system.)

☞ 有時候也談起來他們單位機制方面可能存在一些問題。

1、在管理制度方面，這家公司還存在很多問題。

This company has many problems with its management system.

2、雖然在組織方面還存在不少的問題，但是這幾年政府已經發生了很大的變化。

Although many organizational problems still exist, great changes have taken place in the government during recent years.

問：＿＿＿＿＿＿＿＿＿＿＿＿＿＿＿＿＿＿＿＿＿＿＿＿＿？
答：我認為這種老人福利院雖然在機制上存在一些問題，但是在管理上有一定的優

（十一）在……方面有……（的）优势 (to have the advantage in an area)

> ✍ 在……方面有……的优势, "to have an advantage in the area of", is a structure often used in formal or written Chinese. 在……方面 must be placed before the main verb to indicate the area or aspect in which the advantage lies. The element between 有 and 优势 is optional and often disyllabic. Examples: 在资金方面有优势 (to have an advantage in capital); 在教育孩子方面有显著的优势 (to have an obvious advantage in educating children); 在学习方面有很大的优势 (to have a great advantage in one's studies). 很 cannot be omitted in the last sentence, because 很 helps form a disyllabic phrase.

☞ 因为私营企业说到底在管理上有自己的优势，自己说了算，确实有权力。

1、这种小学校在一些方面也有它的优势，学生很少，老师跟学生的关系很近。
   This type of small school also has its advantages in certain aspects: There are not many students, and relationships between professors and students are very close.

2、这种机制在管理上有一个很大的优势，就是技术员能上能下，完全靠自己的本事吃饭。
   This type of system has a great advantage in management. Technicians can be promoted or demoted depending on their own capabilities.

问：你认为计划经济在什么方面有优势？
答：我认为_____。

（十二）（在……方面）存在……问题 (problems exist in an area or aspect)

> ✍ 存在……问题 means that a problem （问题）exists （存在）in some area or aspect （方面）of something. The subject can be present or absent (see Example 2). The element between 存在 and 问题 is optional and often disyllabic. Example: 他们的考试制度还存在不少问题。(Problems still persist in their exam system.)

☞ 有时候也谈起来他们单位机制方面可能存在一些问题。

1、在管理制度方面，这家公司还存在很多问题。
   This company has many problems with its management system.

2、虽然在组织方面还存在不少的问题，但是这几年政府已经发生了很大的变化。
   Although many organizational problems still exist, great changes have taken place in the government during recent years.

问：_____？
答：我认为这种老人福利院虽然在机制上存在一些问题，但是在管理上有一定的优勢。

（十三）作為……(as, being, to serve as)

> ✍ 作為 means "as", "being", "to serve as". This adverbial phrase is often used to introduce a topic at the beginning of a sentence. It never appears after a verb or at the end of a sentence. Occasionally, the 作為 phrase may also be placed after the subject. Example: 你作為父親不應該這樣啊！(As a father, you really shouldn't act like this!)

☞ 作為一名私有企業的經營者，既要有創業精神又要有管理才能。

1、作為一名大學生，你應該靠自己的能力去學習。

　　As a college student, you should depend on your own ability to study.

2、作為一個九十年代的農民，他不應該有這種落後的觀念。

　　As a farmer in the nineties, he should not have such backward ideas.

　　問：＿＿＿＿＿＿＿＿＿＿＿＿＿＿＿＿＿＿＿＿＿＿？

　　答：我認為一個九十年代的企業家應該有創業精神，要不怕擔風險。

（十四）向……提出 (to bring up something, to suggest something to someone)

> ✍ 向……提出 means "to bring up something, to suggest something to someone". In this structure, 向 indicates that the recipient of the suggestion is superior or senior to the speaker. 跟 or 給 can alternately be used in this structure to indicate that the recipient of the suggestion or opinion is of the same age or status as the speaker. Examples: 他跟他的女朋友提出一些條件. (He brought up some conditions with his girlfriend.) 他給班上的同學提出一些問題. (He raised some questions with his classmates.) 他向老板提了一些建議. (He offered some suggestions to his boss.) When negating such sentences, 不 or 沒 should be placed before 向.

☞ 我們這邊有甚麼意見和建議，可以馬上向公司提出來。

1、我打算明天向單位提出辭職，回家跟我老爸幹個體了。

　　I plan to present my resignation to the work unit tomorrow and return home to start a business with my dad.

2、要是你對我們的課有甚麼建議，請你向教課的老師提出來。

　　If you have any suggestions for our class, please mention them to the professor.

　　問：要是你想辭去公職，創辦自己的公司，應該向誰提出來？

　　答：＿＿＿＿＿＿＿＿＿＿＿＿＿＿＿＿＿＿＿＿。

势。

（十三）作为…… (as, being, to serve as)

> ✍ 作为 means "as", "being", "to serve as". This adverbial phrase is often used to introduce a topic at the beginning of a sentence. It never appears after a verb or at the end of a sentence. Occasionally, the 作为 phrase may also be placed after the subject. Example: 你作为父亲不应该这样啊！ (As a father, you really shouldn't act like this!)

☞ 作为一名私有企业的经营者，既要有创业精神又要有管理才能。

1、作为一名大学生，你应该靠自己的能力去学习。
   As a college student, you should depend on your own ability to study.

2、作为一个九十年代的农民，他不应该有这种落后的观念。
   As a farmer in the nineties, he should not have such backward ideas.

问: ＿＿＿＿＿＿＿＿＿＿＿＿＿＿＿＿＿＿＿？
答: 我认为一个九十年代的企业家应该有创业精神，要不怕担风险。

（十四）向……提出 (to bring up something, to suggest something to someone)

> ✍ 向……提出 means "to bring up something, to suggest something to someone". In this structure, 向 indicates that the recipient of the suggestion is superior or senior to the speaker. 跟 or 给 can alternately be used in this structure to indicate that the recipient of the suggestion or opinion is of the same age or status as the speaker. Examples: 他跟他的女朋友提出一些条件. (He brought up some conditions with his girlfriend.) 他给班上的同学提出一些问题. (He raised some questions with his classmates.) 他向老板提了一些建议. (He offered some suggestions to his boss.) When negating such sentences, 不 or 没 should be placed before 向.

☞ 我们这边有什么意见和建议，可以马上向公司提出来。

1、我打算明天向单位提出辞职，回家跟我老爸干个体了。
   I plan to present my resignation to the work unit tomorrow and return home to start a business with my dad.

2、要是你对我们的课有什么建议，请你向教课的老师提出来。
   If you have any suggestions for our class, please mention them to the professor.

问: 要是你想辞去公职，创办自己的公司，应该向谁提出来？
答: ＿＿＿＿＿＿＿＿＿＿＿＿＿＿＿＿＿＿＿。

（十五）對⋯⋯有獎勵：A 獎勵 B (to reward someone, to award something to someone)

> ✍ 對⋯⋯有獎勵 or A 獎勵 B may be used interchangeably to mean "to reward someone" or "to award something to someone". In the first pattern, 獎勵 functions as a noun; in the second, it is a verb. When negating the structure 對⋯⋯有獎勵, the particle 沒 is normally placed before 有 instead of 對. Example: 他們的公司對工作努力的人也沒有獎勵. (Their company does not provide awards even for people who work hard.)

☞ 如果比較合理，公司就馬上採納，並且對我們有時候還有獎勵。

1、這種企業的優勢是老板有權力獎勵工作努力的人。

One of the advantages of this type of business is that the boss has the power to reward hard workers.

2、只要你有好的管理辦法，向公司提出來，公司就會獎勵你。

As long as your managerial ideas are good, if you suggest them to the company, the company will reward you.

問：如果一個家庭只生一個孩子，政府對他們有沒有獎勵？

答：_____。

（十五）对……有奖励；A 奖励 B (to reward someone, to award something to someone)

> ✍ 对……有奖励 or A 奖励 B may be used interchangeably to mean "to reward someone" or "to award something to someone". In the first pattern, 奖励 functions as a noun; in the second, it is a verb. When negating the structure 对……有奖励, the particle 没 is normally placed before 有 instead of 对. Example: 他们的公司对工作努力的人也没有奖励. (Their company does not provide awards even for people who work hard.)

☞ 如果比较合理，公司就马上采纳，并且对我们有时候还有奖励。

1、这种企业的优势是老板有权力奖励工作努力的人。

One of the advantages of this type of business is that the boss has the power to reward hard workers.

2、只要你有好的管理办法，向公司提出来，公司就会奖励你。

As long as your managerial ideas are good, if you suggest them to the company, the company will reward you.

问：如果一个家庭只生一个孩子，政府对他们有没有奖励？

答：_____。

四、文化背景知識 Cultural Notes

1. As mentioned in the opening lines of Lesson 3, the reforms initiated by China's government have had a major impact on China's farmers (or peasants). Strictly speaking, prior to the reforms virtually all farm land was government controlled. Beginning in the 1980s, however, this situation changed with reforms such as the "contracting land" (承包土地) policy, whereby farmers could contract (that is, rent from the government) a parcel of land for which they would be responsible (責任田, or or "being responsible for the fields [they contract for]"). This new system created incentives for farmers, who could now engage in private enterprise and, using their talents and hard work, could make much more money.

2. 單位 is usually translated as "unit", referring to organizations, departments, divisions, sections, and so on. When a Chinese person mentions his or her "單位", they are usually talking about the place where they work. Until recently, almost everyone in China was employed in a "unit" that was essentially financed and run and by state. Typically, one's *danwei* would provide virtually all the services one would need, including housing and health care. The strong growth of China's market economy in recent years, however, has inspired more and more people to leave their work unit and 下海, or or "take a plunge into the sea" (that is, try their hand at making money in the private sector). Although many have succeeded, the risks and costs (losing one's essentially free housing, medical care, and so on) of leaving one's 單位 are substantial.

3. The expressions "能進", "能出" and "能上", "能下" are related (note the parallel "能-verb1, 能-verb2"structure). They are often used to describe the choices (能進, 能出) and mobility (能上, 能下) one has when working for a organization of company that engages in private enterprise (this could be a company that is 100% privately owned, or a state-run organization that allows a certain amount of private investment in some of its enterprises). That is to say, one can "go in" (進) or "leave" (出), just as one can "advance" (上) or "fail" (下). The idea here is that success or failure depends mainly on one's talents and capabilities (本事) and not on one's family or work connections.

四、文化背景知识 Cultural Notes

1. As mentioned in the opening lines of Lesson 3, the reforms initiated by China's government have had a major impact on China's farmers (or peasants). Strictly speaking, prior to the reforms virtually all farm land was government controlled. Beginning in the 1980s, however, this situation changed with reforms such as the "contracting land" (承包土地) policy, whereby farmers could contract (that is, rent from the government) a parcel of land for which they would be responsible (责任田, or "being responsible for the fields [they contract for]"). This new system created incentives for farmers, who could now engage in private enterprise and, using their talents and hard work, could make much more money.

2. 单位 is usually translated as "unit", referring to organizations, departments, divisions, sections, and so on. When a Chinese person mentions his or her "单位", they are usually talking about the place where they work. Until recently, almost everyone in China was employed in a "unit" that was essentially financed and run and by state. Typically, one's *danwei* would provide virtually all the services one would need, including housing and health care. The strong growth of China's market economy in recent years, however, has inspired more and more people to leave their work unit and 下海, or "take a plunge into the sea" (that is, try their hand at making money in the private sector). Although many have succeeded, the risks and costs (losing one's essentially free housing, medical care, and so on) of leaving one's 单位 are substantial.

3. The expressions "能进", "能出" and "能上", "能下" are related (note the parallel "能-verb1, 能-verb2" structure). They are often used to describe the choices (能进, 能出) and mobility (能上, 能下) one has when working for a organization of company that engages in private enterprise (this could be a company that is 100% privately owned, or a state-run organization that allows a certain amount of private investment in some of its enterprises). That is to say, one can "go in" (进) or "leave" (出), just as one can "advance" (上) or "fail" (下). The idea here is that success or failure depends mainly on one's talents and capabilities (本事) and not on one's family or work connections.

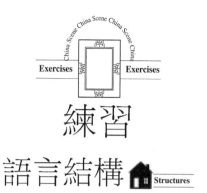

練習

語言結構 Structures

一、短語翻譯 (Phrase translation)

1. private enterprise in Mainland China
2. a socialist planned economy
3. to gradually mature and become active
4. an important component of the country's economy
5. undergraduate student from Nanjing University
6. to study biology
7. contracted land
8. to resign from a public position
9. a manager with a bright future
10. to have the advantage of using flexible technicians
11. management capability
12. the salary and fringe benefits of private enterprise

二、聽力練習 (Listening comprehension)

1、聽寫 (Dictation)

2、聽錄音並回答問題 (Answering questions while listening to the audio CD)
    (1) 私營企業的優勢是甚麼？
    (2) 要是你要在中國找工作，你會找國營還是私營企業的工作？為甚麼？

三、填空 (Fill in the blanks)

地地道道、不可想像、市場經濟、從無到有

十幾年前，一個_____的農民要想辦私營企業是_____的，現在中國搞了

练习

语言结构 Structures

一、短语翻译 (Phrase translation)

1. private enterprise in Mainland China
2. a socialist planned economy
3. to gradually mature and become active
4. an important component of the country's economy
5. undergraduate student from Nanjing University
6. to study biology
7. contracted land
8. to resign from a public position
9. a manager with a bright future
10. to have the advantage of using flexible technicians
11. management capability
12. the salary and fringe benefits of private enterprise

二、听力练习 (Listening comprehension)

1、听写 (Dictation)

2、听录音并回答问题 (Answering questions while listening to the audio CD)
   (1) 私营企业的优势是什么？
   (2) 要是你要在中国找工作，你会找国营还是私营企业的工作？为什么？

三、填空 (Fill in the blanks)

地地道道、不可想象、市场经济、从无到有

十几年前，一个_____的农民要想办私营企业是_____的，现在中国搞了

_____，各種個體戶、私營企業也走上了_____，逐漸成熟的道路。

四、完成句子 (Complete the sentences)

1、　　Ａ：我想採訪一下你。_____

　　　　Ｂ：我是1988年從北大畢業的，分配到了經濟研究所。當時中國的市場經濟十
分活躍，所以_____

_____

　　　（從……畢業；對……抱……態度；向……提出……；走上了……的道路）

2、　　Ａ：請你說說，義務領養孩子說到底能給你帶來甚麼好處？

　　　　Ｂ：你知道在十年前，_____，

現在，_____

　　　（是……不可想像的……；對……有獎勵）

五、閱讀短文、回答問題 (Answering questions based on the reading passages)

過去中國實行的是社會主義的計劃經濟，計劃經濟就是說政府說了算，企業必須根據國家和政府的要求進行生產或者管理，企業和個人的權力都很小。此外，要是有合理的意見或者建議，一般要以集體的名義提出，因為個人的意見和建議多數是不會被採納的。所以這種機制下的企業不需要管理者個人的創業精神和經營才能，管理者也完全不能發揮個人的能力。改革開放以後，中國的各種不同的企業機制逐漸活躍起來，尤其是私營企業，已經成為市場經濟的一個重要組成部分。

問題

中國的經濟制度有甚麼樣的變化？過去的制度有甚麼特點？現在呢？

"我在中國做生意快兩年了，和很多中國的企業家一塊兒工作過。我覺得這些人當中懂國際商業法和企業管理的人還不夠多，不少人連一份正式的銷售計劃書都做不出來。另外，中國商人的英語水平也還急需提高。我認為，中國商人應該建立一個觀念，即把自己當作一種產品。產品質量好，銷路就可能好。有很多產品推銷的方法和技巧可以用來推銷自我。"

問題

　　　　(1) 從這一段話你可以看出是誰說的話？
　　　　(2) 你認為他的話有沒有道理？為甚麼？

_____，各种个体户、私营企业也走上了_____，逐渐成熟的道路。

四、完成句子 (Complete the sentences)

1、　A：我想采访一下你。_____

　　B：我是1988年从北大毕业的，分配到了经济研究所。当时中国的市场经济十
分活跃，所以_____

_____

　　（从……毕业；对……抱……态度；向……提出……；走上了……的道路）

2、　A：请你说说，义务领养孩子说到底能给你带来什么好处？

　　B：你知道在十年前，_____，

现在，_____

　　（是……不可想象的……；对……有奖励）

五、阅读短文、回答问题 (Answering questions based on the reading passages)

> 　　过去中国实行的是社会主义的计划经济，计划经济就是说政府说了算，企业必须根据国家和政府的要求进行生产或者管理，企业和个人的权力都很小。此外，要是有合理的意见或者建议，一般要以集体的名义提出，因为个人的意见和建议多数是不会被采纳的。所以这种机制下的企业不需要管理者个人的创业精神和经营才能，管理者也完全不能发挥个人的能力。改革开放以后，中国的各种不同的企业机制逐渐活跃起来，尤其是私营企业，已经成为市场经济的一个重要组成部分。

问题

　　中国的经济制度有什么样的变化？过去的制度有什么特点？现在呢？

> 　　"我在中国做生意快两年了，和很多中国的企业家一块儿工作过。我觉得这些人当中懂国际商业法和企业管理的人还不够多，不少人连一份正式的销售计划书都做不出来。另外，中国商人的英语水平也还急需提高。我认为，中国商人应该建立一个观念，即把自己当作一种产品。产品质量好，销路就可能好。有很多产品推销的方法和技巧可以用来推销自我。"

问题

　　(1) 从这一段话你可以看出是谁说的话？
　　(2) 你认为他的话有没有道理？为什么？

六、翻譯 (Translate sentences)

1. When the country was implementing the socialist planned economy a decade ago, it was unimaginable for someone to start a private business in the countryside.

2. I believe that a private enterprise has its advantages in terms of its management. A manager in a private enterprise has the power to make decisions to hire and fire a person according to the needs of the company.

3. In 1989, you resigned from a public post and started your own business. What did your friends and relatives think of you?

4. Recently, private enterprises have grown from non-existence to an abundance, from small to big. They have gradually matured and now play an important role in China's economy.

六、翻译 (Translate sentences)

1. When the country was implementing the socialist planned economy a decade ago, it was unimaginable for someone to start a private business in the countryside.

2. I believe that a private enterprise has its advantages in terms of its management. A manager in a private enterprise has the power to make decisions to hire and fire a person according to the needs of the company.

3. In 1989, you resigned from a public post and started your own business. What did your friends and relatives think of you?

4. Recently, private enterprises have grown from non-existence to an abundance, from small to big. They have gradually matured and now play an important role in China's economy.

語言實踐 ：Practice

一、根據課文回答問題 (Answering questions based on the dialogue)

1、十幾年前為甚麼私人辦企業是不可想像的？
2、請你說說王雙貴的家庭和他上大學前後的經歷。
3、王雙貴家的花卉公司是從甚麼時候、怎麼發展起來的？
4、王雙貴的父親對他辭去公職、回到家鄉抱甚麼態度？
5、王雙貴覺得私營企業的好處是甚麼？
6、記者覺得要辦私營企業要有甚麼才能？為甚麼？
7、用你自己的話說說採訪（二）中被採訪者的經歷和他對公司的看法。
    (1) 學歷
    (2) 工資
    (3) 福利待遇
    (4) 公司對職工的態度

二、活動 (Activities)

到街上去採訪一個私營企業家、合資公司職工、或個體戶，再採訪一個在國營單位工作的工人。採訪問題：

1、原來從事甚麼工作？
2、原來是哪個學校畢業的？
3、你是甚麼專業？
4、每月工資怎麼樣？福利待遇好不好？
5、有些甚麼福利待遇？
6、你對於幹……抱甚麼態度？你的家人呢？
7、你這個公司是怎麼創辦的？
8、……的好處（優勢）有哪些？
9、你們對自己的工作和單位的看法。

三、討論題 (Topics for discussion)

1、你認為中國的私營企業是不是中國經濟發展的希望？這種私營企業有甚麼特點？
2、如果你是一個大學畢業生，你願意回家跟父母幹，還是願意去大公司工作？為甚麼？
3、中國農民從七十年代初到現在都經歷了哪些經濟改革和社會變化？

语言实践 ：Practice

一、根据课文回答问题 (Answering questions based on the dialogue)

1、十几年前为什么私人办企业是不可想象的？
2、请你说说王双贵的家庭和他上大学前后的经历。
3、王双贵家的花卉公司是从什么时候、怎么发展起来的？
4、王双贵的父亲对他辞去公职、回到家乡抱什么态度？
5、王双贵觉得私营企业的好处是什么？
6、记者觉得要办私营企业要有什么才能？为什么？
7、用你自己的话说说采访（二）中被采访者的经历和他对公司的看法。
    (1) 学历
    (2) 工资
    (3) 福利待遇
    (4) 公司对职工的态度

二、活动 (Activities)

      到街上去采访一个私营企业家、合资公司职工、或个体户，再采访一个在国营单位工作的工人。采访问题：

1、原来从事什么工作？
2、原来是哪个学校毕业的？
3、你是什么专业？
4、每月工资怎么样？福利待遇好不好？
5、有些什么福利待遇？
6、你对于干……抱什么态度？你的家人呢？
7、你这个公司是怎么创办的？
8、……的好处（优势）有哪些？
9、你们对自己的工作和单位的看法。

三、讨论题 (Topics for discussion)

1、你认为中国的私营企业是不是中国经济发展的希望？这种私营企业有什么特点？
2、如果你是一个大学毕业生，你愿意回家跟父母干，还是愿意去大公司工作？为什么？
3、中国农民从七十年代初到现在都经历了哪些经济改革和社会变化？

四、報告 (Presentation)

《兩個人物採訪：國營企業和私營企業的工人》

五、看圖討論 (Picto-discussion)

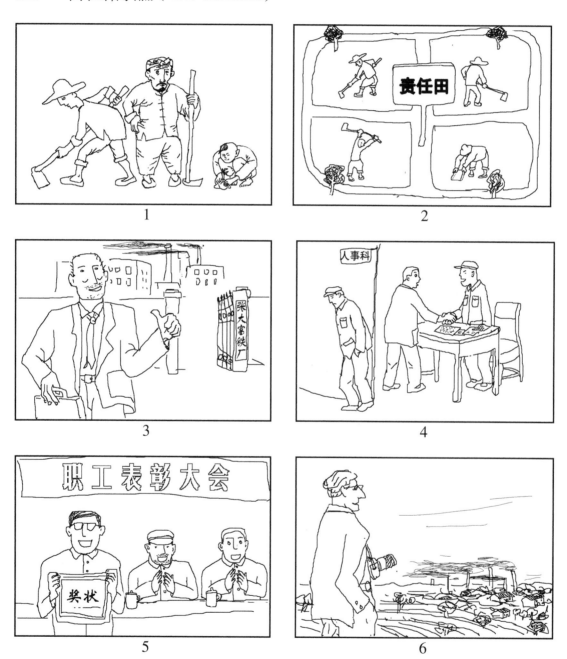

1

2

3

4

5

6

四、报告 (Presentation)

《两个人物采访：国营企业和私营企业的工人》

五、看图讨论 (Picto-discussion)

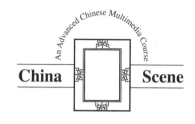

第四課

農民個體戶

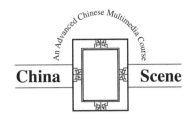

China Scene

An Advanced Chinese Multimedia Course

第四课

农民个体户

課文

一、對話  Dialogs

---

（一）

王志仁：對不起，打擾一下。你在這兒做小商品生意⁽¹⁾做了兩年了，我想跟您談談您從農民到當個體戶的生活⁽²⁾。

張田青：好啊！你要問些甚麼？我盡量回答。

王志仁：你為甚麼要當個體戶呢？

張田青：你知道，地少人多是中國農村的一個普遍現象，所以單靠土地我們農民很難致富。我自己也認為只有當個體戶才能擺脫土地的束縛。

王志仁：你主要經營⁽³⁾甚麼？

張田青：我主要經營副食品，也就是一些點心、水果啦，等。有時候我也做些茶葉生意。

王志仁：那你覺得當個體戶怎麼樣？

張田青：我們也有我們的難處⁽⁴⁾，像我們這種不起眼的小店，規模不大，比不上商業街上的繁華氣派的大店；可是也有我們的好處，職工人數不多也好管理。

Notes　⁽¹⁾生意, 買賣, and 業務 are all nouns meaning "business". The verbs 做, 幹 and 搞 may all be used to express the idea of doing business, as in 搞生意, 做買賣, etc. In some contexts, 業務 can modify another noun, in which case it means "professional" or "vocational", as in 業務能力 (professional ability), 業務學習 (vocational study). 業務 can also mean "business" or "industry" in titles such as 保險業務 (the insurance business) and 運輸業務 (the shipping industry).

　　⁽²⁾The adjective 活 can mean "alive" or "living", as in 他爺爺還活著 (his grandfather is still alive) or "flexible", as in 我們的想法變活了 (our thinking has become flexible).

　　⁽³⁾經營 vs. 專營: 經營 can function either as a noun (management) or as a verb (to run, to engage in sales). Examples: 這幾年他們的經營不錯. (Their management has been pretty good these past few years.) 我們公司經營運輸業務. (Our company is engaged in the shipping business.) 專營, on the other hand, is a verb which means "to specialize in selling something", as in 他的辦公室專營杭州絲綢. (His office specializes in selling Hangzhou silk.)

　　⁽⁴⁾The suffix 處 (chù) is often appended to monosyllabic adjectives to form nouns, as in 好處 (good points), 長處 (strong points), 短處 (weak points), 難處 (difficulties).

课文

一、对话 Dialogs

（一）

王志仁：对不起，打扰一下。你在这儿做小商品生意[1]做了两年了，我想跟您谈谈您从农民到当个体户的生活[2]。

张田青：好啊！你要问些什么？我尽量回答。

王志仁：你为什么要当个体户呢？

张田青：你知道，地少人多是中国农村的一个普遍现象，所以单靠土地我们农民很难致富。我自己也认为只有当个体户才能摆脱土地的束缚。

王志仁：你主要经营[3]什么？

张田青：我主要经营副食品，也就是一些点心、水果啦，等。有时候我也做些茶叶生意。

王志仁：那你觉得当个体户怎么样？

张田青：我们也有我们的难处[4]，象我们这种不起眼的小店，规模不大，比不上商业街上的繁华气派的大店；可是也有我们的好处，职工人数不多也好管理。

Notes [1]生意, 买卖, and 业务 are all nouns meaning "business". The verbs 做, 干 and 搞 may all be used to express the idea of doing business, as in 搞生意, 做买卖, etc. In some contexts, 业务 can modify another noun, in which case it means "professional" or "vocational", as in 业务能力 (professional ability), 业务学习 (vocational study). 业务 can also mean "business" or "industry" in titles such as 保险业务 (the insurance business) and 运输业务 (the shipping industry).

[2]The adjective 活 can mean "alive" or "living", as in 他爷爷还活着 (his grandfather is still alive) or "flexible", as in 我们的想法变活了 (our thinking has become flexible).

[3]经营 vs. 专营: 经营 can function either as a noun (management) or as a verb (to run, to engage in sales). Examples: 这几年他们的经营不错. (Their management has been pretty good these past few years.) 我们公司经营运输业务. (Our company is engaged in the shipping business.) 专营, on the other hand, is a verb which means "to specialize in selling something", as in 他的办公室专营杭州丝绸. (His office specializes in selling Hangzhou silk.)

[4]The suffix 处 (chù) is often appended to monosyllabic adjectives to form nouns, as in 好处 (good points), 长处 (strong points), 短处 (weak points), 难处 (difficulties).

王志仁：那你對今後有甚麼看法呢？

張田青：我們只希望國家的政策越來越開放，這樣，我們的小商品個體戶的日子也能
好一些。

生詞

王志仁	(wáng zhì rén)	N.	Wang Zhiren, name of a person 人名
打擾	(dǎ rǎo)	V.	to trouble, to disturb
小商品	(xiǎo shāng pǐn)	NP.	small commodities
生意	(shēng yì)	N.	business
張田青	(zhāng tián qīng)	N.	Zhang Tianqing, name of a person 人名
盡量	(jìn liàng)	V.	to try one's best
地少人多	(dì shǎo rén duō)	Idiom.	densely populated, overpopulation with a limited amount of arable land
普遍	(pǔ biàn)	Adj.	widespread, common
現象	(xiàn xiàng)	N.	phenomenon
單	(dān)	Adv.	solely
致富	(zhì fù)	V.	to become rich
擺脫	(bǎi tuō)	V.	to get rid of, to shake off, to cast off
束縛	(shù fù)	N/V.	control, restriction, fetter; to control, to restrict
副食品	(fù shí pǐn)	NP.	non-staple food
點心	(diǎn xīn)	N.	pastry, snack
不起眼	(bù qǐ yǎn)	Adj.	unnoticeable
規模	(guī mó)	N.	scale, scope
商業街	(shāng yè jiē)	NP.	commercial drive
繁華	(fán huá)	Adj.	flourishing, bustling
氣派	(qì pài)	Adj.	stylish, extravagant
人數	(rén shù)	N.	number of people

王志仁： 那你对今后有什么看法呢？

张田青： 我们只希望国家的政策越来越开放，这样，我们的小商品个体户的日子也能
好一些。

生词

王志仁	(wáng zhì rén)	N.	Wang Zhiren, name of a person 人名
打扰	(dǎ rǎo)	V.	to trouble, to disturb
小商品	(xiǎo shāng pǐn)	NP.	small commodities
生意	(shēng yì)	N.	business
张田青	(zhāng tián qīng)	N.	Zhang Tianqing, name of a person 人名
尽量	(jìn liàng)	V.	to try one's best
地少人多	(dì shǎo rén duō)	Idiom.	densely populated, overpopulation with a limited amount of arable land
普遍	(pǔ biàn)	Adj.	widespread, common
现象	(xiàn xiàng)	N.	phenomenon
单	(dān)	Adv.	solely
致富	(zhì fù)	V.	to become rich
摆脱	(bǎi tuō)	V.	to get rid of, to shake off, to cast off
束缚	(shù fù)	N/V.	control, restriction, fetter; to control, to restrict
副食品	(fù shí pǐn)	NP.	non-staple food
点心	(diǎn xīn)	N.	pastry, snack
不起眼	(bù qǐ yǎn)	Adj.	unnoticeable
规模	(guī mó)	N.	scale, scope
商业街	(shāng yè jiē)	NP.	commercial drive
繁华	(fán huá)	Adj.	flourishing, bustling
气派	(qì pài)	Adj.	stylish, extravagant
人数	(rén shù)	N.	number of people

（二）

王志仁：忙著呢，李伯父，我有幾個有關[5]個體戶的問題一直想問問您。您家祖祖輩
　　　　輩都是地地道道的農民，那麼現在突然幹起買賣[6]來了，您覺得觀念上是不
　　　　是發生了很大的變化？

李伯父：是啊，中國農村的情況你也知道，以前出門做買賣是想也不敢想的事[7]。現
　　　　在政策開放了，我們農民的想法也活[8]了。有的人利用當地的情況做些小生
　　　　意，有的人出門去闖世界，日子都過得不錯。

王志仁：那您家裡都主要經營甚麼？

李伯父：我們主要經營禮品、花卉。

王志仁：一般的年收入是多少？

李伯父：一般年收入都能達到兩萬多元，營業額每年差不多是六萬，流動資金[9]十萬
　　　　左右。

生詞

伯父	(bó fù)	N.	uncle, father's elder brother
有關	(yǒu guān)	V.	to relate to, to concern
祖祖輩輩	(zǔ zǔ bèi bèi)	Idiom.	for all generations
突然	(tū rán)	Adv.	suddenly, unexpectedly
敢	(gǎn)	V/Adj.	to dare; daring, bold,

Notes [5]有關 vs. 關於: 有關 functions as a predicate in the pattern A 跟 B 有關 (A is connected to B). Example: 秋雲被拋棄跟她的眼部有毛病有關. (Qiu Yun's abandonment was connected to her eyes being defective.) 關於, on the other hand, is a preposition meaning "concerning", "about". Example: 他昨天談了關於去昆明的計劃. (Yesterday he talked about his plans to go to Kunming.) When placed at the beginning of a sentence, however, 有關 and 關於 are interchangeable, as in 有關經濟政策的問題，我一會兒再談 (I will speak on the issue of economic policy momentarily); 關於他對人權的態度，我這裡就不多說了. (I have nothing more to say about his attitude toward human rights.)

[6]See Note (1).

[7]The pattern V + 也不 + V appears in the text in the sentence 以前出門做買賣是想也不敢想的事. (In the past, the idea of leaving home to start a business was something that I would never have dared to consider.) The phrase 想也不敢想 here means "in one's thinking one would never dare to think about" and emphasizes the verb 想. The V + 也不 + V pattern can also be used as a noun modifier, as in 聽也不要聽的事情 (something you would never want to hear about).

[8]See Note (2).

[9]資金 vs. 本錢: Both 資金 and 本錢 mean "capital". 資金, however, is a more formal term that refers to the capital held by a company. 本錢 refers to capital held by an individual or a small business.

（二）

王志仁：忙着呢，李伯父，我有几个有关[5]个体户的问题一直想问问您。您家祖祖辈辈都是地地道道的农民，那么现在突然干起买卖[6]来了，您觉得观念上是不是发生了很大的变化？

李伯父：是啊，中国农村的情况你也知道，以前出门做买卖是想也不敢想的事[7]。现在政策开放了，我们农民的想法也活[8]了。有的人利用当地的情况做些小生意，有的人出门去闯世界，日子都过得不错。

王志仁：那您家里都主要经营什么？

李伯父：我们主要经营礼品、花卉。

王志仁：一般的年收入是多少？

李伯父：一般年收入都能达到两万多元，营业额每年差不多是六万，流动资金[9]十万左右。

生词

伯父	(bó fù)	N.	uncle, father's elder brother
有关	(yǒu guān)	V.	to relate to, to concern
祖祖辈辈	(zǔ zǔ bèi bèi)	Idiom.	for all generations
突然	(tū rán)	Adv.	suddenly, unexpectedly
敢	(gǎn)	V/Adj.	to dare; daring, bold,

Notes [5] 有关 vs. 关于: 有关 functions as a predicate in the pattern A 跟 B 有关 (A is connected to B). Example: 秋云被抛弃跟她的眼部有毛病有关. (Qiu Yun's abandonment was connected to her eyes being defective.) 关于, on the other hand, is a preposition meaning "concerning", "about". Example: 他昨天谈了关于去昆明的计划. (Yesterday he talked about his plans to go to Kunming.) When placed at the beginning of a sentence, however, 有关 and 关于 are interchangeable, as in 有关经济政策的问题，我一会儿再谈 (I will speak on the issue of economic policy momentarily); 关于他对人权的态度，我这里就不多说了. (I have nothing more to say about his attitude toward human rights.)

[6] See Note (1).

[7] The pattern V + 也不 + V appears in the text in the sentence 以前出门做买卖是想也不敢想的事. (In the past, the idea of leaving home to start a business was something that I would never have dared to consider.) The phrase 想也不敢想 here means "in one's thinking one would never dare to think about" and emphasizes the verb 想. The V + 也不 + V pattern can also be used as a noun modifier, as in 听也不要听的事情 (something you would never want to hear about).

[8] See Note (2).

[9] 资金 vs. 本钱: Both 资金 and 本钱 mean "capital". 资金, however, is a more formal term that refers to the capital held by a company. 本钱 refers to capital held by an individual or a small business.

			courageous
出門	(chū mén)	VO.	to go out, to get out of one's house
活	(huó)	Adj.	flexible
利用	(lì yòng)	V.	to utilize
當地的情況	(dāng dì de qíng kuàng)	NP.	the local situation
闖世界	(chuǎng shì jiè)	VO.	to explore the world
禮品	(lǐ pǐn)	N.	gift, present
達	(dá)	V.	to reach, to attain
營業額	(yíng yè é)	NP.	sales quota
流動	(liú dòng)	Adj.	circulating (funds), floating
資金	(zī jīn)	N.	funds, capital

二、電視原文 💻 TV original

瓜市村變遷
（根據原文改編）

　　觀眾[10]朋友，我身後這條繁忙熱鬧的街道就是遠近聞名的瓜市商業批發街。也許它比不上大都市商業街的繁華與氣派，但它卻是瓜市村農民創辦的第一條專營[11]小商品批發業務[12]的商業街。就是這樣一條不起眼的商業街每年的營業額達到近四億元。

（採訪一）

記者：　師傅，打擾一下，我們是山東電視台的記者，想採訪一下您。我想問一下您現在主要經營甚麼呢？

男農民：我現在主要經營副食品。

🖊 **Notes** [10]The suffix 眾, meaning "a collective group of people", may be appended to a verb to form a noun, as in 觀眾 (viewing audience), 聽眾 (listening audience), 大眾 (the masses).

[11]See Note (3).

[12]See Note (1).

			courageous
出门	(chū mén)	VO.	to go out, to get out of one's house
活	(huó)	Adj.	flexible
利用	(lì yòng)	V.	to utilize
当地的情况	(dāng dì de qíng kuàng)	NP.	the local situation
闯世界	(chuǎng shì jiè)	VO.	to explore the world
礼品	(lǐ pǐn)	N.	gift, present
达	(dá)	V.	to reach, to attain
营业额	(yíng yè é)	NP.	sales quota
流动	(liú dòng)	Adj.	circulating (funds), floating
资金	(zī jīn)	N.	funds, capital

二、电视原文 TV original

瓜市村变迁

（根据原文改编）

观众⁽¹⁰⁾朋友，我身后这条繁忙热闹的街道就是远近闻名的瓜市商业批发街。也许它比不上大都市商业街的繁华与气派，但它却是瓜市村农民创办的第一条专营⁽¹¹⁾小商品批发业务⁽¹²⁾的商业街。就是这样一条不起眼的商业街每年的营业额达到近四亿元。

（采访一）

记者： 师傅，打扰一下，我们是山东电视台的记者，想采访一下您。我想问一下您现在主要经营什么呢？

男农民：我现在主要经营副食品。

Notes ⁽¹⁰⁾The suffix 众, meaning "a collective group of people", may be appended to a verb to form a noun, as in 观众 (viewing audience), 听众 (listening audience), 大众 (the masses).

⁽¹¹⁾See Note (3).

⁽¹²⁾See Note (1).

記者：　您是從甚麼時候開始做買賣的？

男農民：我從87年。

記者：　剛開始是不是也規模這麼大呢？

男農民：當時規模很小，慢慢越來越大。

記者：　您是本村的村民嗎？是不是咱們村裡家家都做買賣，而且都是咱們村的村民在擺攤呢？

男農民：大部分是我們本村的村民，也有外邊的，有福建的，有浙江的，外地的來做生意的。

記者：　您87年以前做甚麼呢？

男農民：原先我們是地地道道的農戶。

記者：　過去你們家祖祖輩輩都是種地的，也包括你愛人都是種地的。那麼你突然想做買賣，他們能同意你的做法嗎？

男農民：一開始，她不是十分同意，因為啥呢，因為以前的思想很陳舊。現在呢，政策好了，她也大部分同意。

記者：　每年收入達多少呢？

男農民：一年收入一萬多塊錢。

記者：　有多少流動資金？

男農民：總共有五、六萬。

（採訪二）

記者：　忙著呢，你從哪兒來？

女農民：我從浙江啊。

記者：　您怎麼想起到這兒來呢？

女農民：因為國家政策開放了嘛，所以出來幹點買賣。

記者：　你怎麼知道青州有個瓜市街，專營私人擺攤的呢？

记者：　您是从什么时候开始做买卖的？

男农民：我从87年。

记者：　刚开始是不是也规模这么大呢？

男农民：当时规模很小，慢慢越来越大。

记者：　您是本村的村民吗？是不是咱们村里家家都做买卖，而且都是咱们村的村民在摆摊呢？

男农民：大部分是我们本村的村民，也有外边的，有福建的，有浙江的，外地的来做生意的。

记者：　您87年以前做什么呢？

男农民：原先我们是地地道道的农户。

记者：　过去你们家祖祖辈辈都是种地的，也包括你爱人都是种地的。那么你突然想做买卖，他们能同意你的做法吗？

男农民：一开始，她不是十分同意，因为啥呢，因为以前的思想很陈旧。现在呢，政策好了，她也大部分同意。

记者：　每年收入达多少呢？

男农民：一年收入一万多块钱。

记者：　有多少流动资金？

男农民：总共有五、六万。

（采访二）

记者：　忙着呢，你从哪儿来？

女农民：我从浙江啊。

记者：　您怎么想起到这儿来呢？

女农民：因为国家政策开放了嘛，所以出来干点买卖。

记者：　你怎么知道青州有个瓜市街，专营私人摆摊的呢？

女農民：我們也是由親戚帶出來的。

記者：　噢，親戚給介紹過來的。

記者：　到了這裡以後，你覺得買賣好做嗎？

女農民：反正是買賣呢，像我們來，本錢[13]不大，買賣不太好做啊。

記者：　你原來在浙江幹甚麼？

女農民：農村裡的。

記者：　種地的，那麼你從種地到這兒來做買賣，觀念上發生了很大變化，你覺得比你原來的日子怎麼樣？

女農民：那比原來的日子肯定好的。原先我們是農村裡的，農村的嘛，一般比城裡肯定差好多。現在麼，反正穿啊、吃啊、都挺好（的）。就是一年餘下來的錢不是很多。

記者：　一個女同志自己出來闖世界是不是很不容易？

女農民：也行，這裡的人挺好。反正是我們外地的，他們很照顧，市場秩序也挺好，沒人搗亂。

記者：　你想不想繼續在這做下去。

女農民：也想啊，最好麼，就繼續在這裡做下去。

　　觀眾朋友們，地少人多是中國農村存在的一種普遍現象。瓜市村有人口一千四百多，耕地十三公頃，人均只有0.01 公頃。很顯然，要單靠這0.01公頃土地，農民致富是非常難的。而發展商業使村民們擺脫了土地的束縛，走上了致富之路。

生詞

瓜市村	(guā shì cūn)	*Place N.*	Guashicun, name of a village 地名
變遷	(biàn qiān)	*N.*	historical changes, vicissitudes
觀眾	(guān zhòng)	*N.*	audience, viewers
繁忙	(fán máng)	*Adj.*	busy, bustling

Notes　[13]See Note (9).

女农民：我们也是由亲戚带出来的。

记者：　噢，亲戚给介绍过来的。

记者：　到了这里以后，你觉得买卖好做吗？

女农民：反正是买卖呢，象我们来，本钱[13]不大，买卖不太好做啊。

记者：　你原来在浙江干什么？

女农民：农村里的。

记者：　种地的，那么你从种地到这儿来做买卖，观念上发生了很大变化，你觉得比你原来的日子怎么样？

女农民：那比原来的日子肯定好的。原先我们是农村里的，农村的嘛，一般比城里肯定差好多。现在么，反正穿啊、吃啊、都挺好（的）。就是一年余下来的钱不是很多。

记者：　一个女同志自己出来闯世界是不是很不容易？

女农民：也行，这里的人挺好。反正是我们外地的，他们很照顾，市场秩序也挺好，没人捣乱。

记者：　你想不想继续在这做下去。

女农民：也想啊，最好么，就继续在这里做下去。

　　观众朋友们，地少人多是中国农村存在的一种普遍现象。瓜市村有人口一千四百多，耕地十三公顷，人均只有0.01公顷。很显然，要单靠这0.01公顷土地，农民致富是非常难的。而发展商业使村民们摆脱了土地的束缚，走上了致富之路。

生词

瓜市村	(guā shì cūn)	*Place N.*	Guashicun, name of a village 地名
变迁	(biàn qiān)	*N.*	historical changes, vicissitudes
观众	(guān zhòng)	*N.*	audience, viewers
繁忙	(fán máng)	*Adj.*	busy, bustling

Notes [13]See Note (9).

熱鬧	(rè nào)	*Adj.*	busy, crowded
遠近聞名	(yuǎn jìn wén míng)	*Idiom.*	famous far and wide, to be known far and wide
批發	(pī fā)	*NP.*	wholesale
大都市	(dà dū shì)	*N/Adj.*	big city; metropolitan
業務	(yè wù)	*N.*	business
師傅	(shī fù)	*N.*	term of address, master worker
電視台	(diàn shì tái)	*NP.*	TV station
擺攤	(bǎi tān)	*VO.*	to set up a stand
本	(běn)	*Pron.*	this (including the speaker)
大部分	(dà bù fèn)	*Adj.*	for the most part, mostly
福建	(fú jiàn)	*Place N.*	Fujian (Province)
浙江	(zhè jiāng)	*Place N.*	Zhejiang (Province), name of a province in South China 地名
原先	(yuán xiān)	*Adv.*	originally, formerly
農戶	(nóng hù)	*N.*	peasant, farmer
包括	(bāo kuò)	*V.*	to include, to contain
愛人	(ài rén)	*N.*	wife or husband (used on the mainland)
陳舊	(chén jiù)	*Adj.*	outdated, obsolete
總共	(zǒng gòng)	*Adv.*	in all, altogether
專營	(zhuān yíng)	*VP.*	to specialize in selling (something)
親戚	(qīn qì)	*N.*	relative
本錢	(běn qián)	*N.*	capital
反正	(fǎn zhèng)	*Adv.*	anyway, anyhow, in any case
餘	(yú)	*N.*	surplus
照顧	(zhào gù)	*V.*	to take care of
秩序	(zhì xù)	*N.*	order
搗亂	(dǎo luàn)	*V.*	to make trouble
繼續	(jì xù)	*V.*	to continue, to go on
耕地	(gēng dì)	*N.*	arable land
公頃	(gōng qǐng)	*N.*	hectare (approx. 16.5 acres)
人均	(rén jūn)	*NP.*	average per person
顯然	(xiǎn rán)	*Adv/Adj.*	obviously, obvious

热闹	(rè nào)	*Adj.*	busy, crowded
远近闻名	(yuǎn jìn wén míng)	*Idiom.*	famous far and wide, to be known far and wide
批发	(pī fā)	*NP.*	wholesale
大都市	(dà dū shì)	*N/Adj.*	big city; metropolitan
业务	(yè wù)	*N.*	business
师傅	(shī fù)	*N.*	term of address, master worker
电视台	(diàn shì tái)	*NP.*	TV station
摆摊	(bǎi tān)	*VO.*	to set up a stand
本	(běn)	*Pron.*	this (including the speaker)
大部分	(dà bù fèn)	*Adj.*	for the most part, mostly
福建	(fú jiàn)	*Place N.*	Fujian (Province)
浙江	(zhè jiāng)	*Place N.*	Zhejiang (Province), name of a province in South China 地名
原先	(yuán xiān)	*Adv.*	originally, formerly
农户	(nóng hù)	*N.*	peasant, farmer
包括	(bāo kuò)	*V.*	to include, to contain
爱人	(ài rén)	*N.*	wife or husband (used on the mainland)
陈旧	(chén jiù)	*Adj.*	outdated, obsolete
总共	(zǒng gòng)	*Adv.*	in all, altogether
专营	(zhuān yíng)	*VP.*	to specialize in selling (something)
亲戚	(qīn qì)	*N.*	relative
本钱	(běn qián)	*N.*	capital
反正	(fǎn zhèng)	*Adv.*	anyway, anyhow, in any case
余	(yú)	*N.*	surplus
照顾	(zhào gù)	*V.*	to take care of
秩序	(zhì xù)	*N.*	order
捣乱	(dǎo luàn)	*V.*	to make trouble
继续	(jì xù)	*V.*	to continue, to go on
耕地	(gēng dì)	*N.*	arable land
公顷	(gōng qǐng)	*N.*	hectare (approx. 16.5 acres)
人均	(rén jūn)	*NP.*	average per person
显然	(xiǎn rán)	*Adv/Adj.*	obviously, obvious

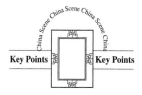

課文要點

一、詞語解釋 Words and Phrases

（一）文言詞、方言詞、慣用詞 (Classical Chinese, dialect and idiomatic expressions)

1、有關＝關於
  ☞ 我有幾個有關個體戶的問題一直想問問您。

2、啥＝甚麼
  ☞ 因為啥呢，因為以前的思想很陳舊。

3、之＝的
  ☞ 發展商業使村民們擺脫了土地的束縛，走上了致富之路。

（二）成語、慣用語 (idioms and fixed expressions)

◆ 人多地少: overpopulation with a limited amount of arable land
◆ 祖祖輩輩: for all generations, every generation
◆ 遠近聞名: famous far and wide, widely known
◆ 致富之路: road to riches, path to wealth

二、書面語、正式語、口語對照表 Written/formal/colloquial Comparison

	書面／正式語	口語		書面／正式語	口語
1	單靠、只靠	就靠	6	原先	原來／本來
2	專營	專門經營	7	…之路	…的道路
3	有關	關於	8	總共	一共
4	致富	發財	9	今後	以後
5	本+N.	這兒的+N.			

＊方言、普通話對照表 Putonghua/dialect Comparison

	方言	普通話		方言	普通話
1	啥	甚麼			

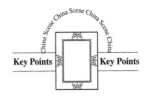

Key Points   Key Points

课文要点

一、词语解释 Words and Phrases

（一）文言词、方言词、惯用词 (Classical Chinese, dialect and idiomatic expressions)

> 1、有关 = 关于
>
> ☞ 我有几个有关个体户的问题一直想问问您。
>
> 2、啥 = 什么
>
> ☞ 因为啥呢，因为以前的思想很陈旧。
>
> 3、之 = 的
>
> ☞ 发展商业使村民们摆脱了土地的束缚，走上了致富之路。

（二）成语、惯用语 (idioms and fixed expressions)

> ◆ 人多地少: overpopulation with a limited amount of arable land
>
> ◆ 祖祖辈辈: for all generations, every generation
>
> ◆ 远近闻名: famous far and wide, widely known
>
> ◆ 致富之路: road to riches, path to wealth

二、书面语、正式语、口语对照表 Written/formal/colloquial Comparison

	书面／正式语	口语		书面／正式语	口语
1	单靠、只靠	就靠	6	原先	原来／本来
2	专营	专门经营	7	…之路	…的道路
3	有关	关于	8	总共	一共
4	致富	发财	9	今后	以后
5	本+N.	这儿的+N.			

＊方言、普通话对照表 Putonghua/dialect Comparison

	方言	普通话		方言	普通话
1	啥	什么			

三、句型 Sentence Structures

（一）擺脫……的束縛（／困難／限制）(to break away from the restrictions of)

> ✎ 擺脫……的束縛, "to break away from the restrictions of", is a VO structure in which 擺脫 indicates that the subject must use its will or determination to shake off, break away from, or free itself from something. 擺脫 is often followed by disyllabic words associated with undesirable situations, such as 束縛, 困難 or 限制. Modifying elements for 束縛 can be nouns or adjectives, such as 政府的束縛 (government restrictions), 父母的限制 (limitations from parents), 重重束縛 (layer upon layer of restrictions). This structure is often used in formal or written Chinese.

☞ 我自己也認為只有當個體戶才能擺脫土地的束縛。

1、為了擺脫國營企業在管理上的束縛，我辭去公職，開始創辦自己的企業。

In order to avoid management restrictions on state-owned enterprises, I am resigning from a public post to start my own business.

2、為了擺脫貧困的束縛，現在很多中國人都開始做買賣、"向錢看"。

In order to avoid poverty, many Chinese people have now begun to do business "looking toward money".

問：你為甚麼有了孩子還要離婚出國？你的出國是不是跟你的家庭、丈夫有關係？

答：＿＿＿＿＿＿＿＿＿＿＿＿＿＿＿＿＿＿＿＿＿＿＿。

（二）比得上／比不上……（條件／情況）(can/cannot be compared with)

> ✎ 比得上／比不上, "can/cannot be compared with", is a potential complement structure which indicates whether or not it is possible to compare two things in terms of a particular aspect. 比得上 indicates that it is possible to compare the two things mentioned; 比不上 implies that the first item is not comparable to or not as good as the second. This pattern is often used in conjunction with 在……方面 or 在……上. The object following the verb phrase 比得上 and 比不上 can be anything that has comparative value.

☞ 像我們這種不起眼的小店，規模不大，比不上商業街上的繁華氣派的大店。

1、在福利待遇方面，私營企業比得上國營企業嗎？

In terms of fringe benefits, are private enterprises comparable to state-owned enterprises?

2、農村的生活條件說到底比不上城裡的生活條件。

Living conditions in the countryside simply can't compare to those in the city.

問：＿＿＿＿＿＿＿＿＿＿＿＿＿＿＿＿＿＿＿？

答：我們這兒的宿舍條件比美國一些學校的條件還要好。

三、句型 Sentence Structures

（一）摆脱……的束缚（／困难／限制）(to break away from the restrictions of)

> 摆脱……的束缚, "to break away from the restrictions of", is a VO structure in which 摆脱 indicates that the subject must use its will or determination to shake off, break away from, or free itself from something. 摆脱 is often followed by disyllabic words associated with undesirable situations, such as 束缚, 困难 or 限制. Modifying elements for 束缚 can be nouns or adjectives, such as 政府的束缚 (government restrictions), 父母的限制 (limitations from parents), 重重束缚 (layer upon layer of restrictions). This structure is often used in formal or written Chinese.

☞ 我自己也认为只有当个体户才能摆脱土地的束缚。

1、为了摆脱国营企业在管理上的束缚，我辞去公职，开始创办自己的企业。
   In order to avoid management restrictions on state-owned enterprises, I am resigning from a public post to start my own business.

2、为了摆脱贫困的束缚，现在很多中国人都开始做买卖、"向钱看"。
   In order to avoid poverty, many Chinese people have now begun to do business "looking toward money".

问：你为什么有了孩子还要离婚出国？你的出国是不是跟你的家庭、丈夫有关系？
答：_____。

（二）比得上／比不上……（条件／情况）(can/cannot be compared with)

> 比得上／比不上, "can/cannot be compared with", is a potential complement structure which indicates whether or not it is possible to compare two things in terms of a particular aspect. 比得上 indicates that it is possible to compare the two things mentioned; 比不上 implies that the first item is not comparable to or not as good as the second. This pattern is often used in conjunction with 在……方面 or 在……上. The object following the verb phrase 比得上 and 比不上 can be anything that has comparative value.

☞ 象我们这种不起眼的小店，规模不大，比不上商业街上的繁华气派的大店。

1、在福利待遇方面，私营企业比得上国营企业吗？
   In terms of fringe benefits, are private enterprises comparable to state-owned enterprises?

2、农村的生活条件说到底比不上城里的生活条件。
   Living conditions in the countryside simply can't compare to those in the city.

问：_____？
答：我们这儿的宿舍条件比美国一些学校的条件还要好。

（三）利用……的情況 （／條件／機會） (to take advantage of a situation)

> ✍ 利用, "to take advantage of", often forms a VO structure in which the object of 利用 can be 機會, 情況, 條件 or 環境. 利用 and 用 share the same meaning, but 利用 is more formal than 用. In addition to its positive meaning, which implies that something is being or should be utilized to its fullest, 利用 can also have the negative connotation of "to use" when followed by objects such as 人 or 關係. Example: 他很會利用人. (He is good at using people.) The 利用 phrase can also be followed by a verb phrase to indicate the purpose of 利用. Example: 他常常利用去批發市場的機會買一些禮品. (He often takes advantage of a trip to the wholesale market to buy some gifts.)

☞ 有的人利用當地的情況做些小生意，有的人出門去闖世界，日子都過得不錯。

1、這個人很有管理才能，當廠長才一年，就利用當地的情況，又創辦了一家食品廠，年收入達80萬。

This person really has a knack for management. After one year as factory manager, he took advantage of the local situation to set up a food factory which brings in 800,000 *yuan* in profit a year.

2、既然你來了北京，你就要利用北京的條件，多交中國朋友，練習說話。

Now that you are in Beijing, you should take advantage of the environment to make many friends and practice speaking Chinese.

問：你為甚麼放棄美國的工作，來中國創辦外資公司？
答：＿＿＿＿＿＿＿＿＿＿＿＿＿＿＿＿＿＿＿＿＿。

（四）我想問一下…… (may I ask, I would like to ask)

> ✍ 我想問一下, "I would like to ask" or "may I ask", is an expression used at the beginning of a conversation to attract someone's attention before asking a question. It is interchangeable with 打擾一下 and 對不起，請問.

☞ 我想問一下，您現在主要經營甚麼呢？

1、我想問一下，你當個體戶以前做甚麼？
May I ask, what did you do before you became a private entrepreneur?

2、我想問一下，你家祖祖輩輩是農民，現在想當個體戶，有風險，家裡能同意你的做法嗎？

For generations your family were farmers; now you want to risk being an entrepreneur. May I ask, does your family agree with what you are doing?

問：＿＿＿＿＿＿＿＿＿＿＿＿＿＿＿＿＿＿＿＿？
答：我出生在天津，後來有一對美國夫婦領養了我。

（三）利用……的情况 （／条件／机会） (to take advantage of a situation)

> ✍ 利用, "to take advantage of", often forms a VO structure in which the object of 利用 can be 机会, 情况, 条件 or 环境. 利用 and 用 share the same meaning, but 利用 is more formal than 用. In addition to its positive meaning, which implies that something is being or should be utilized to its fullest, 利用 can also have the negative connotation of "to use" when followed by objects such as 人 or 关系. Example: 他很会利用人. (He is good at using people.) The 利用 phrase can also be followed by a verb phrase to indicate the purpose of 利用. Example: 他常常利用去批发市场的机会买一些礼品. (He often takes advantage of a trip to the wholesale market to buy some gifts.)

☞ 有的人利用当地的情况做些小生意，有的人出门去闯世界，日子都过得不错。

1、这个人很有管理才能，当厂长才一年，就利用当地的情况，又创办了一家食品厂，年收入达80万。

This person really has a knack for management. After one year as factory manager, he took advantage of the local situation to set up a food factory which brings in 800,000 *yuan* in profit a year.

2、既然你来了北京，你就要利用北京的条件，多交中国朋友，练习说话。

Now that you are in Beijing, you should take advantage of the environment to make many friends and practice speaking Chinese.

问：你为什么放弃美国的工作，来中国创办外资公司？

答：_____。

（四）我想问一下…… (may I ask, I would like to ask)

> ✍ 我想问一下, "I would like to ask" or "may I ask", is an expression used at the beginning of a conversation to attract someone's attention before asking a question. It is interchangeable with 打扰一下 and 对不起，请问.

☞ 我想问一下，您现在主要经营什么呢？

1、我想问一下，你当个体户以前做什么？

May I ask, what did you do before you became a private entrepreneur?

2、我想问一下，你家祖祖辈辈是农民，现在想当个体户，有风险，家里能同意你的做法吗？

For generations your family were farmers; now you want to risk being an entrepreneur. May I ask, does your family agree with what you are doing?

问：_____？

答：我出生在天津，后来有一对美国夫妇领养了我。

（五）包括 (to include)

> ✍ 包括, "to include", is often used as a verb. Examples: 我們說的大家庭包括三代同堂，四代同堂的家庭. (The large families we are referring to include families with three or four generations living under one roof.) 中國的企業形式有三種，這裡包括國營，私營和合資. (There are three types of Chinese businesses: state-owned, private, and joint-venture.)

☞ 過去你們家祖祖輩輩都是種地的，也包括你愛人都是種地的。

1、中國的經濟包括計劃經濟和市場經濟兩種。

The Chinese economy includes both planned and market economies.

2、作為一個小商品批發商，你的工作包括甚麼？

As a wholesale dealer of small commodities, what does your work entail?

問：你在中國留學的學費包括甚麼？
答：＿＿＿＿＿＿＿＿＿＿＿＿＿＿＿＿＿＿＿＿＿。

（六）同意……的意見（／意思／作法／說法／看法） (to agree with someone's opinion)

> ✍ 同意, "to agree with", is a verb that can be used alone, as in 我同意 (I agree), or can take objects such as 意見, 意思, 作法, or 說法. Unlike in English, the object of 同意 cannot be a person. Two common errors made by English speakers studying Chinese are to place a noun indicating a person after 同意, or to place the preposition 跟 before 同意. Many of the adverbs we have learned so far can be placed before 同意, including 大部分, 基本上, 十分, 完全, etc. Example: 我基本上同意你的意見. (I essentially agree with your opinion.)

☞ 那麼你突然想做買賣，她們能同意你的作法嗎？

1、你同意這種落後、陳舊的看法嗎？

Do you agree with this kind of backward, out-of date view?

2、政府現在還不同意國營企業由私人管理的作法。

The government has not yet approved independent management of state-owned businesses.

問：現在很多人因為國營企業前景不好而辭職，你同意他們的作法嗎？
答：＿＿＿＿＿＿＿＿＿＿＿＿＿＿＿＿＿＿＿＿＿。

（五）包括 (to include)

> ✍ 包括, "to include", is often used as a verb. Examples: 我们说的大家庭包括三代同堂，四代同堂的家庭. (The large families we are referring to include families with three or four generations living under one roof.) 中国的企业形式有三种，这里包括国营，私营和合资. (There are three types of Chinese businesses: state-owned, private, and joint-venture.)

☞ 过去你们家祖祖辈辈都是种地的，也包括你爱人都是种地的。

1、中国的经济包括计划经济和市场经济两种。
The Chinese economy includes both planned and market economies.

2、作为一个小商品批发商，你的工作包括什么？
As a wholesale dealer of small commodities, what does your work entail?

问：你在中国留学的学费包括什么？
答：＿＿＿＿＿＿＿＿＿＿＿＿＿＿＿＿＿＿＿＿＿。

（六）同意……的意见（／意思／作法／说法／看法）(to agree with someone's opinion)

> ✍ 同意, "to agree with", is a verb that can be used alone, as in 我同意 (I agree), or can take objects such as 意见, 意思, 作法, or 说法. Unlike in English, the object of 同意 cannot be a person. Two common errors made by English speakers studying Chinese are to place a noun indicating a person after 同意, or to place the preposition 跟 before 同意. Many of the adverbs we have learned so far can be placed before 同意, including 大部分, 基本上, 十分, 完全, etc. Example: 我基本上同意你的意见. (I essentially agree with your opinion.)

☞ 那么你突然想做买卖，她们能同意你的作法吗？

1、你同意这种落后、陈旧的看法吗？
Do you agree with this kind of backward, out-of date view?

2、政府现在还不同意国营企业由私人管理的作法。
The government has not yet approved independent management of state-owned businesses.

问：现在很多人因为国营企业前景不好而辞职，你同意他们的作法吗？
答：＿＿＿＿＿＿＿＿＿＿＿＿＿＿＿＿＿＿＿＿＿。

78

（七）很顯然……(obviously)

> ✍ 顯然, "obviously", is an adverb normally placed either at the beginning of a sentence as a topic starter or immediately before a verb. Example: 顯然報社不同意你的看法. (Obviously, the newspaper does not agree with your view.) Occasionally, 很顯然 can be placed after the subject. Example: 這家企業，很顯然，已經改變了他們的經營方式. (It is obvious that this enterprise has already changed its managerial style.)

☞ 很顯然，要單靠這0.01公頃土地，農民致富是非常難的。

1、很顯然，創辦自己的公司會有很大的風險，可是年收入也會很好。

Obviously, establishing your own company involves great risks, but the annual income will be good.

2、很顯然，只有擺脫陳舊的觀念，才能發揮個人的能力，走上致富的道路。

Obviously, only by getting rid of obsolete ideas can people bring their abilities into play and be able to walk the road to riches.

問：為甚麼現在有很多人離開自己的家到外地去找工作？

答：＿＿＿＿＿＿＿＿＿＿＿＿＿＿＿＿＿＿＿。

（八）繼續 (to continue, to go on, to keep doing)

> ✍ 繼續, meaning "to continue", is a verb which is often followed by a VO, an adverb, a place + VO, or a place + V, as in 繼續學中文 (to continue studying Chinese), 繼續努力 (to continue to be diligent), 繼續在這兒找工作 (to continue looking for work here), 繼續在這兒工作 (to continue working here).

☞ 你想不想繼續在這兒做下去。

1、很顯然，這家公司的經營體制改革還要繼續，不能到這兒為止。

It is very obvious that reforms of this company's managerial system must continue; they cannot just stop at this point.

2、我並不同意你的看法，我認為夫妻的關係不好，就應該離婚，不應該繼續這種不健康的婚姻。

I disagree with your view. I think that if a relationship is bad between a husband and wife, they should divorce. They should not continue this sort of unhealthy marriage.

問：你對美國這幾年的電腦發展有甚麼看法？

答：＿＿＿＿＿＿＿＿＿＿＿＿＿＿＿＿＿＿＿。

（七）很显然……(obviously)

> ✍ 显然, "obviously", is an adverb normally placed either at the beginning of a sentence as a topic starter or immediately before a verb. Example: 显然报社不同意你的看法. (Obviously, the newspaper does not agree with your view.) Occasionally, 很显然 can be placed after the subject. Example: 这家企业, 很显然, 已经改变了他们的经营方式. (It is obvious that this enterprise has already changed its managerial style.)

☞ 很显然, 要单靠这0.01公顷土地, 农民致富是非常难的。

1、很显然, 创办自己的公司会有很大的风险, 可是年收入也会很好。
   Obviously, establishing your own company involves great risks, but the annual income will be good.

2、很显然, 只有摆脱陈旧的观念, 才能发挥个人的能力, 走上致富的道路。
   Obviously, only by getting rid of obsolete ideas can people bring their abilities into play and be able to walk the road to riches.

问：为什么现在有很多人离开自己的家到外地去找工作？
答：_____。

（八）继续 (to continue, to go on, to keep doing)

> ✍ 继续, meaning "to continue", is a verb which is often followed by a VO, an adverb, a place + VO, or a place + V, as in 继续学中文 (to continue studying Chinese), 继续努力 (to continue to be diligent), 继续在这儿找工作 (to continue looking for work here), 继续在这儿工作 (to continue working here).

☞ 你想不想继续在这儿做下去。

1、很显然, 这家公司的经营体制改革还要继续, 不能到这儿为止。
   It is very obvious that reforms of this company's managerial system must continue; they cannot just stop at this point.

2、我并不同意你的看法, 我认为夫妻的关系不好, 就应该离婚, 不应该继续这种不健康的婚姻。
   I disagree with your view. I think that if a relationship is bad between a husband and wife, they should divorce. They should not continue this sort of unhealthy marriage.

问：你对美国这几年的电脑发展有什么看法？
答：_____。

四、文化背景知識 Cultural Notes

1. The expression 本地人 (literally, "people of this place") is used to describe persons who are native to the hometown of the speaker; conversely, 外地人 refers to persons who are not native to the speaker's hometown. Use of these terms requires a proper geographical reference. For instance, a native of Beijing would have to be physically in Beijing when using these expressions to refer to "natives" or "non-natives" of that city.

2. Strictly speaking, 伯父 refers to the elder brother of one's father (uncle). Here the term is used as a respectful form of address for an elderly man. The female counterpart is 伯母.

3. The term 愛人 is used generally to introduce either husband or wife. Unlike most forms of address in China, 愛人 can refer to a man or a woman. Note that 愛人 is not used in Taiwan, where 先生 is preferred for "husband" and 太太 for "wife". These terms of address are now being used more frequently on the Mainland.

4. In the past 師傅 meant "master". For instance, if a student enlisted a teacher to teach him a particular skill such as 功夫, handicrafts 手藝, or smithing (that is, a person who does the work of a blacksmith) 打鐵, he would address is teacher as "master" or 師傅. Students of such masters were known as 學徒, or "apprentices". Recently, however, the scope of reference for 師傅 has expanded considerably, so as to now include almost any middle-aged or older working people (both male and female).

5. The term 同志, or "comrade", was common in China during the 1950s, '60s, and '70s. Since the 1980s, however, its use has diminished greatly.

四、文化背景知识 Cultural Notes

1. The expression 本地人 (literally, "people of this place") is used to describe persons who are native to the hometown of the speaker; conversely, 外地人 refers to persons who are not native to the speaker's hometown. Use of these terms requires a proper geographical reference. For instance, a native of Beijing would have to be physically in Beijing when using these expressions to refer to "natives" or "non-natives" of that city.

2. Strictly speaking, 伯父 refers to the elder brother of one's father (uncle). Here the term is used as a respectful form of address for an elderly man. The female counterpart is 伯母.

3. The term 爱人 is used generally to introduce either husband or wife. Unlike most forms of address in China, 爱人 can refer to a man or a woman. Note that 爱人 is not used in Taiwan, where 先生 is preferred for "husband" and 太太 for "wife". These terms of address are now being used more frequently on the Mainland.

4. In the past, 师傅 meant "master". For instance, if a student enlisted a teacher to teach him a particular skill such as 功夫, handicrafts 手艺, or smithing (that is, a person who does the work of a blacksmith) 打铁, he would address his teacher as "master", or 师傅. Students of such masters were known as 学徒, or "apprentices". Recently, however, the scope of reference for 师傅 has expanded considerably, so as to now include almost any middle-aged or older working people (both male and female).

5. The term 同志, or "comrade", was common in China during the 1950s, '60s, and '70s. Since the 1980s, however, its use has diminished greatly.

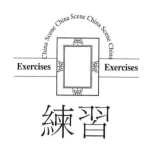

練習

語言結構 Structures

一、短語翻譯 (Phrase translation)

1. overpopulation with a limited amount of arable land
2. a widespread problem in the countryside
3. to make use of the local conditions
4. to sell goods on a busy and crowded street
5. an enterprise which is not noticeable
6. yearly sales quota
7. a reporter from the TV station
8. a typical farming family for generations
9. the income and capital of the shop
10. to set up a stand in the market
11. average per person
12. to get rid of poverty

二、聽力練習 (Listening comprehension)

1、聽寫 (Dictation)

2、聽錄音並回答問題 (Answering questions while listening to the audio CD)
  (1) 過去中國的農民有甚麼特點？現在呢？
  (2) 既然當個體戶很辛苦，為甚麼還是有很多農民願意當？

三、改寫下面劃線的詞 (Replace the underlined words)

　　這個報導是<u>有關</u>一個地地道道的農民怎麼<u>以</u>自己的能力，<u>將</u>一個很小的花店發展成一個大的花卉企業，走上了致富<u>之</u>路的。

练习

语言结构 Structures

一、短语翻译 (Phrase translation)

1. overpopulation with a limited amount of arable land
2. a widespread problem in the countryside
3. to make use of the local conditions
4. to sell goods on a busy and crowded street
5. an enterprise which is not noticeable
6. yearly sales quota
7. a reporter from the TV station
8. a typical farming family for generations
9. the income and capital of the shop
10. to set up a stand in the market
11. average per person
12. to get rid of poverty

二、听力练习 (Listening comprehension)

1、听写 (Dictation)

2、听录音并回答问题 (Answering questions while listening to the audio CD)
   (1) 过去中国的农民有什么特点？现在呢？
   (2) 既然当个体户很辛苦，为什么还是有很多农民愿意当？

三、改写下面划线的词 (Replace the underlined words)

这个报道是<u>有关</u>一个地地道道的农民怎么<u>以</u>自己的能力，<u>挬</u>一个很小的花店发展成一个大的花卉企业，走上了致<u>富之路</u>的。

四、填空 (Fill in the blanks)

遠近聞名、地地道道、祖祖輩輩

我認識他，我們這兒的人都認識他，因為他家＿＿＿＿都是＿＿＿＿賣副食的，他家賣的油＿＿＿＿。

五、完成句子 (Complete the sentences)

1、　A：你覺得單靠你一個人的資金能致富嗎？
　　B：＿＿＿＿＿＿＿＿＿＿＿＿＿＿＿＿＿＿＿＿＿＿＿，我們還必須把大家聯合起來，才能＿＿＿＿＿＿＿＿＿＿＿＿＿＿＿＿＿＿＿
　　（很顯然……；　單靠……；　擺脫……）

2、　A：＿＿＿＿＿＿＿＿＿＿＿＿＿＿＿＿＿＿＿＿＿＿＿
　　B：我一年的流動資金是三萬，收入是一萬。
　　（打擾一下……）

3、　A：我想問一下現在辭去公職，當個體戶的人很多嗎？
　　B：對。＿＿＿＿＿＿＿＿＿＿＿＿＿＿＿＿＿＿＿＿＿＿＿
　　（是……普遍的現象）

六、閱讀短文、回答問題 (Answering questions based on the reading passage)

北京的西城有一個紅橋市場。這個市場是一個國內外聞名的商業批發市場。

這個市場最初是由幾個農民創辦的。也許在很多方面，這個市場沒有北京其它大商店那麼繁華氣派，但它是一個既繁忙熱鬧又經濟實惠的市場。去那兒的人有外地人，也有北京人，有外國人，也有中國人，有農村的，也有城裡的。大家都知道在紅橋市場可以買到很多又便宜又實用的東西，比方說，禮品、箱子、和珍珠（pearl）等等。紅橋市場雖然從外面看好像不起眼，規模也不大，但是經營的商品有五萬多種，每年的營業額大概是六十億元。

就拿在紅橋市場三樓幹買賣的張新明來說，他從八十年代末就跟著親戚出來闖北京，幹了幾年小商品批發，有了些資本。三年前他在紅橋市場租了個櫃台，專營小禮品。買賣做了才三年的時間，張新明就"發"了。他現在每年的年收入達到二十萬，流動資金也在四十萬左右。

四、填空 (Fill in the blanks)

远近闻名、地地道道、祖祖辈辈

我认识他，我们这儿的人都认识他，因为他家_____都是_____卖副食的，他家卖的油_____。

五、完成句子 (Complete the sentences)

1、　　A：你觉得单靠你一个人的资金能致富吗？
　　　　B：_____，我们还必须把大家联合起来，才能_____
　　　　（很显然……；单靠……；摆脱……）

2、　　A：_____
　　　　B：我一年的流动资金是三万，收入是一万。
　　　　（打扰一下……）

3、　　A：我想问一下现在辞去公职，当个体户的人很多吗？
　　　　B：对。_____
　　　　（是……普遍的现象）

六、阅读短文、回答问题 (Answering questions based on the reading passage)

北京的西城有一个红桥市场。这个市场是一个国内外闻名的商业批发市场。

这个市场最初是由几个农民创办的。也许在很多方面，这个市场没有北京其它大商店那么繁华气派，但它是一个既繁忙热闹又经济实惠的市场。去那儿的人有外地人，也有北京人，有外国人，也有中国人，有农村的，也有城里的。大家都知道在红桥市场可以买到很多又便宜又实用的东西，比方说，礼品、箱子、和珍珠（pearl）等等。红桥市场虽然从外面看好象不起眼，规模也不大，但是经营的商品有五万多种，每年的营业额大概是六十亿元。

就拿在红桥市场三楼干买卖的张新明来说，他从八十年代末就跟着亲戚出来闯北京，干了几年小商品批发，有了些资本。三年前他在红桥市场租了个柜台，专营小礼品。买卖做了才三年的时间，张新明就"发"了。他现在每年的年收入达到二十万，流动资金也在四十万左右。

問題

 (1) 請你説説紅橋市場是一個甚麼樣的市場。（地點、誰創辦的、經營甚麼、有甚麼特點等等）

 (2) 張新明是怎麼"發"的？

 (3) 請你用書上的話説説美國的跳蚤市場（Flea Market）。

七、翻譯 (Translate sentences)

1. In order to free themselves from the restrictions of the socialist planned economy and get rich, many peasants began to leave their land to start their own businesses by making use of local conditions.

2. Obviously, this unnoticeable business street was created by several local peasants. People here mainly specialize in wholesale dealing of everyday goods.

3. This typical shop owner has a family which has been engaged in farming for many generations. Now he has a shop which generates $10,000 in annual income.

4. Limited arable land and overpopulation are widespread problems in China. Breaking away from these problems is the most important issue facing the government.

问题
>   (1) 请你说说红桥市场是一个什么样的市场。（地点、谁创办的、经营什么、有什么
>   特点等等）
>   (2) 张新明是怎么"发"的？
>   (3) 请你用书上的话说说美国的跳蚤市场（Flea Market）。

七、翻译 (Translate sentences)

1. In order to free themselves from the restrictions of the socialist planned economy and get rich, many peasants began to leave their land to start their own businesses by making use of local conditions.

2. Obviously, this unnoticeable business street was created by several local peasants. People here mainly specialize in wholesale dealing of everyday goods.

3. This typical shop owner has a family which has been engaged in farming for many generations. Now he has a shop which generates $10,000 in annual income.

4. Limited arable land and overpopulation are widespread problems in China. Breaking away from these problems is the most important issue facing the government.

語言實踐： Practice

一、根據課文回答問題 (Answering questions based on the dialogue)

1、說說瓜市村有甚麼？它的特點是甚麼？它每年營業額是多少？
2、說說被採訪的男農民以前做甚麼？現在經營甚麼？從甚麼時候開始？每年收入多少？流動資金多少？
3、女農民是從哪來的？她是怎麼來到瓜市村的？她對做買賣的看法是甚麼？她想以後做甚麼？
4、用瓜市村的例子說明為甚麼單靠土地農民很難致富？為甚麼做個體戶可以致富？

二、活動 (Activities)

去菜市場或者小商品市場找一個從農村來的個體戶聊聊，問他下面幾個問題：

1、從哪兒來？
2、以前做甚麼？
3、他的村子有多大，耕地多少，人口多少？
4、他為甚麼做個體戶？
5、每年收入多少，流動資金多少？
6、他覺得做個體戶的前景怎麼樣？

三、討論題 (Topics for discussion)

1、中國人多地少的問題從哪些方面可以知道？舉例說明。
2、以前農民很少走出自己的家門，離開自己的土地到外地去，更不要說做買賣。你覺得課文中的農民個體戶的現象對中國以後的發展有沒有好處？為甚麼？
3、你跟街上的農民談過嗎？能不能談談他們做生意的情況？

四、報告 (Presentation)

《賣菜農民的一天》
《小商品批發農民的生活》

语言实践 : Practice

一、根据课文回答问题 (Answering questions based on the dialogue)

1、说说瓜市村有什么？它的特点是什么？它每年营业额是多少？
2、说说被采访的男农民以前做什么？现在经营什么？从什么时候开始？每年收入多少？流动资金多少？
3、女农民是从哪来的？她是怎么来到瓜市村的？她对做买卖的看法是什么？她想以后做什么？
4、用瓜市村的例子说明为什么单靠土地农民很难致富？为什么做个体户可以致富？

二、活动 (Activities)

去菜市场或者小商品市场找一个从农村来的个体户聊聊，问他下面几个问题:

1、从哪儿来？
2、以前做什么？
3、他的村子有多大，耕地多少，人口多少？
4、他为什么做个体户？
5、每年收入多少，流动资金多少？
6、他觉得做个体户的前景怎么样？

三、讨论题 (Topics for discussion)

1、中国人多地少的问题从哪些方面可以知道？举例说明。
2、以前农民很少走出自己的家门，离开自己的土地到外地去，更不要说做买卖。你觉得课文中的农民个体户的现象对中国以后的发展有没有好处？为什么？
3、你跟街上的农民谈过吗？能不能谈谈他们做生意的情况？

四、报告 (Presentation)

《卖菜农民的一天》
《小商品批发农民的生活》

五、看圖討論 (Picto-discussion)

五、看图讨论 (Picto-discussion)

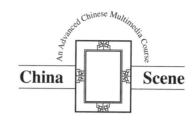

第五課

獨生子女文化

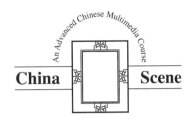

第五课

独生子女文化

課文

一、對話  Dialogs

---

（一）

莫根：　王老師，今天星期天，又出去啊？

王老師：是啊，孩子今天去參加鋼琴考試。

莫根：　是嗎？考幾級？考得怎麼樣？

王老師：想考個五級，可是現在成績還沒下來。

莫根：　考試都考些甚麼？

王老師：一般都考練習曲和樂曲兩部分。

莫根：　評委⁽¹⁾嚴格嗎？

王老師：你知道，評委都是國家一流的鋼琴演奏家和教育家，他們的責任感⁽²⁾都很強，
　　　　要求很嚴格。

生詞

莫根	(mò gēn)	N.	Mo Gen, name of a person 人名
鋼琴	(gāng qín)	N.	piano
練習曲	(liàn xí qǔ)	N.	etude
樂曲	(yuè qǔ)	N.	musical composition
部分	(bù fèn)	N.	part
評委	(píng wěi)	N.	the evaluation committee
一流	(yī liú)	N.	first rate

Notes ⁽¹⁾評委 is an abbreviation of the title 評比委員會 (Evaluation Committee). Abbreviations, such as 北大 for 北京大學 (Beijing University) and 北師大 for 北京師範大學 (Beijing Normal University), are common in Chinese.

⁽²⁾The suffix 感 often translates as "sense of", as in 責任感 (sense of responsibility), 方向感 (sense of direction), 競爭感 (sense of competition), and 義務感 (sense of obligation).

课文

一、对话 Dialogs

（一）

莫根：　王老师，今天星期天，又出去啊？

王老师：是啊，孩子今天去参加钢琴考试。

莫根：　是吗？考几级？考得怎么样？

王老师：想考个五级，可是现在成绩还没下来。

莫根：　考试都考些什么？

王老师：一般都考练习曲和乐曲两部分。

莫根：　评委[1]严格吗？

王老师：你知道，评委都是国家一流的钢琴演奏家和教育家，他们的责任感[2]都很强，
要求很严格。

生词

莫根	(mò gēn)	N.	Mo Gen, name of a person 人名
钢琴	(gāng qín)	N.	piano
练习曲	(liàn xí qǔ)	N.	etude
乐曲	(yuè qǔ)	N.	musical composition
部分	(bù fèn)	N.	part
评委	(píng wěi)	N.	the evaluation committee
一流	(yī liú)	N.	first rate

✎ **Notes** [1]评委 is an abbreviation of the title 评比委员会 (Evaluation Committee). Abbreviations, such as 北大 for 北京大学 (Beijing University) and 北师大 for 北京师范大学 (Beijing Normal University), are common in Chinese.

[2]The suffix 感 often translates as "sense of', as in 责任感 (sense of responsibility), 方向感 (sense of direction), 竞争感 (sense of competition), and 义务感 (sense of obligation).

演奏	(yǎn zòu)	N/V.	performance; to perform with a musical instrument
家	(jiā)	N.	specialist in a certain field
責任感	(zé rèn gǎn)	N.	sense of responsibility
嚴格	(yán gé)	Adj.	strict, rigorous, stringent

（二）

莫根： 王老師，常聽人說起"獨生子女文化"，甚麼是"獨生子女文化"？

王老師："獨生子女文化"是指中國在培養獨生子女時形成的一種特殊文化。這種文化的特點是父母對他們孩子的智力發展和非智力發展採取不同的態度。在智力發展方面是三個"捨得"。

莫根： 甚麼是三個"捨得"？

王老師： 三個"捨得"是說孩子的父母為了孩子的學習"捨得花錢"、"捨得花精力"、"捨得花時間"。比如送孩子上補習班、星期日學校學鋼琴、提琴等。可是在其它方面，像社會公德、勞動觀念和生活習慣卻一點精力和時間都不花，使孩子的發展很不平衡。

莫根： 現在中國是不是已經開始注意到這個問題了？

王老師： 是啊，這種現像使很多社會學[3]家都很擔心。這就是為甚麼這幾年中國到處都在組織一些活動，提高兒童在各方面的素質[4]，讓兒童得到平衡發展。

生詞

獨生子女	(dú shēng zǐ nǚ)	NP.	single child
指	(zhǐ)	V.	to refer to
培養	(péi yǎng)	V.	to cultivate, to nurture, to foster, cultivation

---

✏ **Notes** [3]學 here functions as a suffix referring to branches of learning or academic disciplines. It is similar to the suffix "-ology" in English. Examples: 社會學 (sociology), 比較文學 (comparative literature), 經濟學 (economics), 心理學 (psychology).

[4]素質 vs. 質量: Both 素質 and 質量 are nouns meaning "quality". 素質 refers to the quality of a person, taking into account their education, integrity, moral standards, etc. 質量 indicates the overall quality of a product, service, or profession, as in 藥品質量 (the quality of a brand of medicine), 服務質量 (quality of service), and 教學質量 (the quality of someone's teaching).

演奏	(yǎn zòu)	*N/V.*	performance; to perform with a musical instrument
家	(jiā)	*N.*	specialist in a certain field
责任感	(zé rèn gǎn)	*N.*	sense of responsibility
严格	(yán gé)	*Adj.*	strict, rigorous, stringent

（二）

莫根： 王老师，常听人说起"独生子女文化"，什么是"独生子女文化"？

王老师： "独生子女文化"是指中国在培养独生子女时形成的一种特殊文化。这种文化的特点是父母对他们孩子的智力发展和非智力发展采取不同的态度。在智力发展方面是三个"舍得"。

莫根： 什么是三个"舍得"？

王老师： 三个"舍得"是说孩子的父母为了孩子的学习"舍得花钱"、"舍得花精力"、"舍得花时间"。比如送孩子上补习班、星期日学校学钢琴、提琴等。可是在其它方面，象社会公德、劳动观念和生活习惯却一点精力和时间都不花，使孩子的发展很不平衡。

莫根： 现在中国是不是已经开始注意到这个问题了？

王老师： 是啊，这种现象使很多社会学[3]家都很担心。这就是为什么这几年中国到处都在组织一些活动，提高儿童在各方面的素质[4]，让儿童得到平衡发展。

生词

独生子女	(dú shēng zǐ nǚ)	*NP.*	single child
指	(zhǐ)	*V.*	to refer to
培养	(péi yǎng)	*V.*	to cultivate, to nurture, to foster, cultivation

---

✏️ **Notes** [3]学 here functions as a suffix referring to branches of learning or academic disciplines. It is similar to the suffix "-ology" in English. Examples: 社会学 (sociology), 比较文学 (comparative literature), 经济学 (economics), 心理学 (psychology).

[4]素质 vs. 质量: Both 素质 and 质量 are nouns meaning "quality". 素质 refers to the quality of a person, taking into account their education, integrity, moral standards, etc. 质量 indicates the overall quality of a product, service, or profession, as in 药品质量 (the quality of a brand of medicine), 服务质量 (quality of service), and 教学质量 (the quality of someone's teaching).

形成	(xíng chéng)	*V.*	to form
特點	(tè diǎn)	*N.*	characteristics, attributes
智力	(zhì lì)	*N.*	intelligence, intellect
非	(fēi)	*Adv.*	non, not
採取	(cǎi qǔ)	*V.*	to adopt, to take
態度	(tài dù)	*N.*	attitude
捨得	(shě dé)	*V.*	to be willing to part with, to not grudge
精力	(jīng lì)	*N.*	energy
比如	(bǐ rú)	*Adv.*	for example
星期日學校	(xīng qī rì xué xiào)	*NP.*	weekend school
提琴	(tí qín)	*N.*	violin
公德	(gōng dé)	*N.*	social morals
勞動	(láo dòng)	*N.*	labor, work
平衡	(píng héng)	*N/V.*	balance; to balance
社會學	(shè huì xué)	*N.*	sociology
組織	(zǔ zhī)	*V/N.*	to organize; organization
各方面	(gè fāng miàn)	*NP.*	various aspects
素質	(sù zhì)	*N.*	quality, diathesis

形成	(xíng chéng)	*V.*	to form
特点	(tè diǎn)	*N.*	characteristics, attributes
智力	(zhì lì)	*N.*	intelligence, intellect
非	(fēi)	*Adv.*	non, not
采取	(cǎi qǔ)	*V.*	to adopt, to take
态度	(tài dù)	*N.*	attitude
舍得	(shě dé)	*V.*	to be willing to part with, to not grudge
精力	(jīng lì)	*N.*	energy
比如	(bǐ rú)	*Adv.*	for example
星期日学校	(xīng qī rì xué xiào)	*NP.*	weekend school
提琴	(tí qín)	*N.*	violin
公德	(gōng dé)	*N.*	social morals
劳动	(láo dòng)	*N.*	labor, work
平衡	(píng héng)	*N/V.*	balance; to balance
社会学	(shè huì xué)	*N.*	sociology
组织	(zǔ zhī)	*V/N.*	to organize; organization
各方面	(gè fāng miàn)	*NP.*	various aspects
素质	(sù zhì)	*N.*	quality, diathesis

二、電視原文 💻 TV original

日記—未來[5]與希望

（根據原文改編）

1994年4月24日　　　　星期天　　　大風

這是一場特殊的音樂會，登[6]台亮相的演員全是孩子。

很多孩子都是頭一回登這麼大的台，彈[7]這麼大的琴。他們大的十幾歲，小的只有五歲，都是從全國業餘鋼琴考級中選拔出來的優秀生。

（採訪）

記者："你考級了嗎，這次？"

兒童："沒有。"

記者："為甚麼沒考？"

兒童："因為我想上來就考一個五級、八級的。"

（採訪）

記者："你周圍[8]小朋友裡邊彈鋼琴的人多嗎？"

兒童："不算多，差不多十來個吧。"

✏️ Notes [5]將來, 未來, 以後, 今後: 將來 and 未來 both mean "in the future". These expressions are used in formal settings and can be used to modify nouns, as in 未來的變遷 (future changes). Two less formal expressions meaning "future" are 以後 and 今後. When used as adverbs, these time expressions must appear either before or after the subject and always before the main verb.

[6]登 vs. 爬: The verb 登 or 登上 carries a formal tone and means "to climb up" or "to step up". Example: 我登上了萬里長城. (I climbed the Great Wall.) 爬 also means "to climb", but suggests clambering or scrambling, as in 爬樹 (to climb a tree) and 爬山 (to hike up a mountain).

[7]彈: Several Chinese verbs are used to mean "to play (an instrument)". Each verb is particular to a type of instrument, and they cannot be used interchangeably: 彈鋼琴 (to play the piano), 彈吉他 (to play the guitar), 拉小提琴 (to play the violin), 拉二胡 (to play the *erhu*), 打鼓 (to play the drums), 敲鼓 (to play the drums). The verb 玩 (to play, to have fun, to socialize) may be used to indicate playing an instrument in a fun or frivolous way, but never to refer to serious playing.

[8]周圍: 附近 and 周圍, both meaning "nearby" or "in the vicinity", are interchangeable. Both should be placed after a noun referent, as in 學校附近 or 學校周圍 (near the school).

二、电视原文 💻 **TV original**

日记—未来⁽⁵⁾与希望

（根据原文改编）

　　　1994年4月24日　　　　　星期天　　　大风

这是一场特殊的音乐会，登⁽⁶⁾台亮相的演员全是孩子。

很多孩子都是头一回登这么大的台，弹⁽⁷⁾这么大的琴。他们大的十几岁，小的只有五岁，都是从全国业余钢琴考级中选拔出来的优秀生。

（采访）

记者：　"你考级了吗，这次？"

儿童：　"没有。"

记者：　"为什么没考？"

儿童：　"因为我想上来就考一个五级、八级的。"

（采访）

记者：　"你周围⁽⁸⁾小朋友里边弹钢琴的人多吗？"

儿童：　"不算多，差不多十来个吧。"

✏️ **Notes** ⁽⁵⁾将来, 未来, 以后, 今后: 将来 and 未来 both mean "in the future". These expressions are used in formal settings and can be used to modify nouns, as in 未来的变迁 (future changes). Two less formal expressions meaning "future" are 以后 and 今后. When used as adverbs, these time expressions must appear either before or after the subject and always before the main verb.

　　⁽⁶⁾登 vs. 爬: The verb 登 or 登上 carries a formal tone and means "to climb up" or "to step up". Example: 我登上了万里长城. (I climbed the Great Wall.) 爬 also means "to climb", but suggests clambering or scrambling, as in 爬树 (to climb a tree) and 爬山 (to hike up a mountain).

　　⁽⁷⁾弹: Several Chinese verbs are used to mean "to play (an instrument)". Each verb is particular to a type of instrument, and they cannot be used interchangeably: 弹钢琴 (to play the piano), 弹吉他 (to play the guitar), 拉小提琴 (to play the violin), 拉二胡 (to play the *erhu*), 打鼓 (to play the drums), 敲鼓 (to play the drums). The verb 玩 (to play, to have fun, to socialize) may be used to indicate playing an instrument in a fun or frivolous way, but never to refer to serious playing.

　　⁽⁸⁾周围: 附近 and 周围, both meaning "nearby" or "in the vicinity", are interchangeable. Both should be placed after a noun referent, as in 学校附近 or 学校周围 (near the school).

記者：“他們中有幾個考級的嗎？”

兒童：“有，有一個。”

誰也說不清[9]，現在究竟有多少孩子在學琴，為了促進業餘音樂教育的科學化[10]、規範化，八十年代後期中國也開始建立了自己的考級制度。

1994年2月18日　　　　　　星期五　　　　大霧

這是今年鋼琴考級的最後一天，一進大廳頓時[11]讓人感到一種臨戰前的緊張氣氛。

（採訪）

記者：“哎，你好，你考幾級啊？”

兒童：“四級。”

記者：“你考得怎麼樣？”

兒童：“還行。”

考試的內容一般由基本練習和樂曲兩部分組成。評委們都是國家一流的鋼琴演奏家和鋼琴教育家，他們以強烈的責任感，把心血浸注在鋼琴教育事業上。

Notes [9]誰也說不清, "no one can say for sure", is one of many inserted elements in Chinese. This kind of phrase is used to introduce one's own commentary on a subject. Another example of an inserted element is 早就聽說 (I heard long ago), discussed in Key Sentence Structure 14 of this lesson.

[10]化 is a suffix meaning "to change" or "to transform". English translations of words with the suffix 化 often end with "-ize", "-ation", or "-ization". Thus, 科學 + 化 yields the word "scientification" or "to make something scientific". Other examples include 現代化 (modernization), 多樣化 (to diversify; diversification).

[11]頓時, meaning "immediately", "at once", can only be used to recount something that has already happened or become a fact. Example: 決定剛一做出，頓時就傳開了. (As soon as the decision was made, it spread around immediately.) A common synonym is 一下子.

记者：　"他们中有几个考级的吗？"

儿童：　"有，有一个。"

　　谁也说不清[9]，现在究竟有多少孩子在学琴，为了促进业余音乐教育的科学化[10]、规范化，八十年代后期中国也开始建立了自己的考级制度。

1994年2月18日　　　　　　星期五　　　　大雾

这是今年钢琴考级的最后一天，一进大厅顿时[11]让人感到一种临战前的紧张气氛。

（采访）

记者：　"哎，你好，你考几级啊？"

儿童：　"四级。"

记者：　"你考得怎么样？"

儿童：　"还行。"

　　考试的内容一般由基本练习和乐曲两部分组成。评委们都是国家一流的钢琴演奏家和钢琴教育家，他们以强烈的责任感，把心血浸注在钢琴教育事业上。

Notes [9]谁也说不清, "no one can say for sure", is one of many inserted elements in Chinese. This kind of phrase is used to introduce one's own commentary on a subject. Another example of an inserted element is 早就听说 (I heard long ago), discussed in Key Sentence Structure 14 of this lesson.

[10]化 is a suffix meaning "to change" or "to transform". English translations of words with the suffix 化 often end with "-ize", "-ation", or "-ization". Thus, 科学 + 化 yields the word "scientification" or "to make something scientific". Other examples include 现代化 (modernization), 多样化 (to diversify; diversification).

[11]顿时, meaning "immediately", "at once", can only be used to recount something that has already happened or become a fact. Example: 决定刚一做出，顿时就传开了. (As soon as the decision was made, it spread around immediately.) A common synonym is 一下子.

早就聽説京城有個小神童，學琴三年，這次報考了七級和八級。她叫王羽佳，報名時不到七歲。

（採訪）

記者： "你自己願意彈，還是你爸爸媽媽讓你彈的？"

王羽佳："我自己願意彈。"

記者： "為甚麼願意呢？"

王羽佳："很有趣。"

記者： "你長大想幹甚麼呢？彈琴？"

王羽佳："想（當）指揮、鋼琴家。"

記者： "上幾年級呀？"

王羽佳："一年級。"

記者： "學習怎麼樣？考試考得怎麼樣？"

王羽佳："雙百。"

看來家長們也正是意識到了彈鋼琴的這些好處，加上經濟條件的改善和對精神生活需求的上升，鋼琴正在悄悄地進入到中國的尋常百姓家。多了不説，就是這回報考的三千人，一家一台鋼琴，您閉上眼睛想一下，得占多大地方？

（採訪）

記者： "您和孩子有沒有認為練琴是件很苦的事呢？"

家長： "是件很苦的事。本身學琴[12]呢，也是對他意志品質的鍛煉。我認為應該從小培養孩子，從小就提高他的競爭的意識。另外呢，對提高孩子的素質也有好處。"

Notes [12]本身學琴: The term 本身 means "itself" or "in itself". In most cases, the referent of this term directly precedes it, as in 條約本身 (the treaty itself); 學琴本身很困難. (Studying the violin in and of itself is very difficult.) The form 本身學琴 found in the text of the lesson is an uncommon, casual form.

早就听说京城有个小神童，学琴三年，这次报考了七级和八级。她叫王羽佳，报名时不到七岁。

（采访）

记者：　　"你自己愿意弹，还是你爸爸妈妈让你弹的？"

王羽佳："我自己愿意弹。"

记者：　　"为什么愿意呢？"

王羽佳："很有趣。"

记者：　　"你长大想干什么呢？弹琴？"

王羽佳："想（当）指挥、钢琴家。"

记者：　　"上几年级呀？"

王羽佳："一年级。"

记者：　　"学习怎么样？考试考得怎么样？"

王羽佳："双百。"

看来家长们也正是意识到了弹钢琴的这些好处，加上经济条件的改善和对精神生活需求的上升，钢琴正在悄悄地进入到中国的寻常百姓家。多了不说，就是这回报考的三千人，一家一台钢琴，您闭上眼睛想一下，得占多大地方？

（采访）

记者：　"您和孩子有没有认为练琴是件很苦的事呢？"

家长：　"是件很苦的事。本身学琴(12)呢，也是对他意志品质的锻炼。我认为应该从小培养孩子，从小就提高他的竞争的意识。另外呢，对提高孩子的素质也有好处。"

Notes (12)本身学琴: The term 本身 means "itself" or "in itself". In most cases, the referent of this term directly precedes it, as in 条约本身 (the treaty itself); 学琴本身很困难. (Studying the violin in and of itself is very difficult.) The form 本身学琴 found in the text of the lesson is an uncommon, casual form.

記者："您認為花點錢，受點累是非常值得的。"

家長："要三個捨得，捨得花錢，捨得花精力，捨得花時間。"

看著這演出，看著台下觀眾，我想像著中國的未來，21世紀是屬於他們的。

生詞

日記	(rì jì)	N.	diary
未來	(wèi lái)	N.	future
音樂會	(yīn yuè huì)	N.	concert
登台亮相	(dēng tái liàng xiàng)	VP.	to appear on the stage
演員	(yǎn yuán)	N.	actor or actress, performer
頭一回	(tóu yī huí)	Adv.	for the first time
彈	(tán)	V.	to play (musical instrument)
琴	(qín)	N.	piano, musical instrument
業餘	(yè yú)	Adj.	amateur
考級	(kǎo jí)	VO.	to take a test to be placed at a certain level or group
選拔	(xuǎn bá)	V.	to select, to choose (usually of person)
優秀生	(yōu xiù shēng)	NP.	outstanding student
周圍	(zhōu wéi)	Adv.	nearby, in the vicinity of
究竟	(jiū jìng)	Adv.	after all
促進	(cù jìn)	V.	to promote
科學化	(kē xué huà)	NP.	"scientification", make more scientific
規範化	(guī fàn huà)	NP.	standardization
建立	(jiàn lì)	V.	to establish
制度	(zhì dù)	N.	system
大霧	(dà wù)	NP.	foggy
大廳	(dà tīng)	N.	hall
頓時	(dùn shí)	Adv.	at once
臨戰	(lín zhàn)	Adv.	prior to battle, before battle
氣氛	(qì fēn)	N.	atmosphere
內容	(nèi róng)	N.	content

记者：　"您认为花点钱，受点累是非常值得的。"

家长：　"要三个舍得，舍得花钱，舍得花精力，舍得花时间。"

　　看着这演出，看着台下观众，我想象着中国的未来，21世纪是属于他们的。

生词

日记	(rì jì)	N.	diary
未来	(wèi lái)	N.	future
音乐会	(yīn yuè huì)	N.	concert
登台亮相	(dēng tái liàng xiàng)	VP.	to appear on the stage
演员	(yǎn yuán)	N.	actor or actress, performer
头一回	(tóu yī huí)	Adv.	for the first time
弹	(tán)	V.	to play (musical instrument)
琴	(qín)	N.	piano, musical instrument
业余	(yè yú)	Adj.	amateur
考级	(kǎo jí)	VO.	to take a test to be placed at a certain level or group
选拔	(xuǎn bá)	V.	to select, to choose (usually of person)
优秀生	(yōu xiù shēng)	NP.	outstanding student
周围	(zhōu wéi)	Adv.	nearby, in the vicinity of
究竟	(jiū jìng)	Adv.	after all
促进	(cù jìn)	V.	to promote
科学化	(kē xué huà)	NP.	"scientification", make more scientific
规范化	(guī fàn huà)	NP.	standardization
建立	(jiàn lì)	V.	to establish
制度	(zhì dù)	N.	system
大雾	(dà wù)	NP.	foggy
大厅	(dà tīng)	N.	hall
顿时	(dùn shí)	Adv.	at once
临战	(lín zhàn)	Adv.	prior to battle, before battle
气氛	(qì fèn)	N.	atmosphere
内容	(nèi róng)	N.	content

基本	(jī běn)	Adj.	basic
強烈	(qiáng liè)	Adj.	strong, intense
浸注	(jìn zhù)	V.	to pour in, to devote to
事業	(shì yè)	N.	undertaking, cause
京城	(jīng chéng)	Place N.	the capital city
神童	(shén tóng)	N.	prodigy
王羽佳	(wáng yǔ jiā)	N.	Wang Yujia, name of a person 人名
報名	(bào míng)	V.	to register
指揮	(zhǐ huī)	V.	to conduct
意識	(yì shì)	N.	sense, realization
改善	(gǎi shàn)	N/V.	improvement; to improve
需求	(xū qiú)	N.	need
上升	(shàng shēng)	N.	increase
悄悄地	(qiāo qiāo de)	Adv.	quietly
尋常	(xún cháng)	Adj.	ordinary, common
百姓	(bǎi xìng)	N.	people
台	(tái)	Classifier.	a classifier for piano
占	(zhàn)	V.	to occupy, to take up
苦	(kǔ)	Adj.	bitter, causing hardship or suffering
意志	(yì zhì)	N.	will power, will
品質	(pǐn zhì)	N.	quality, character
鍛煉	(duàn liàn)	V.	to train, to forge, to temper
競爭	(jìng zhēng)	N.	competition
值得	(zhí dé)	Adj.	worth, worthwhile
演出	(yǎn chū)	V.	to perform
世紀	(shì jì)	N.	century

基本	(jī běn)	*Adj.*	basic
强烈	(qiáng liè)	*Adj.*	strong, intense
浸注	(jìn zhù)	*V.*	to pour in, to devote to
事业	(shì yè)	*N.*	undertaking, cause
京城	(jīng chéng)	*Place N.*	the capital city
神童	(shén tóng)	*N.*	prodigy
王羽佳	(wáng yǔ jiā)	*N.*	Wang Yujia, name of a person 人名
报名	(bào míng)	*V.*	to register
指挥	(zhǐ huī)	*V.*	to conduct
意识	(yì shì)	*N.*	sense, realization
改善	(gǎi shàn)	*N/V.*	improvement; to improve
需求	(xū qiú)	*N.*	need
上升	(shàng shēng)	*N.*	increase
悄悄地	(qiāo qiāo de)	*Adv.*	quietly
寻常	(xún cháng)	*Adj.*	ordinary, common
百姓	(bǎi xìng)	*N.*	people
台	(tái)	*Classifier.*	a classifier for piano
占	(zhàn)	*V.*	to occupy, to take up
苦	(kǔ)	*Adj.*	bitter, causing hardship or suffering
意志	(yì zhì)	*N.*	will power, will
品质	(pǐn zhì)	*N.*	quality, character
锻炼	(duàn liàn)	*V.*	to train, to forge, to temper
竞争	(jìng zhēng)	*N.*	competition
值得	(zhí dé)	*Adj.*	worth, worthwhile
演出	(yǎn chū)	*V.*	to perform
世纪	(shì jì)	*N.*	century

課文要點

一、詞語解釋 Words and Phrases

（一）文言詞、慣用詞 (Classical Chinese and idiomatic expressions)

1、頭一回＝第一次
☞ 很多孩子都是頭一回登這麼大的台。

2、頓時＝馬上、一下子
☞ 一進大廳頓時讓人感到一種臨戰前的緊張氣氛。

3、入＝到……裡
☞ 鋼琴正在悄悄地進入到中國的尋常百姓家。

4、尋常＝普通、一般（的）
☞ 尋常百姓的意思就是普通老百姓的意思。

（二）成語 (idioms)

◆ 登台亮相: to appear on stage

◆ 多了不說: no need to say more

二、書面語、正式語、口語對照表 Written/formal/colloquial Comparison

	書面／正式語	口語		書面／正式語	口語
1	未來／將來	以後	6	究竟	到底
2	登台亮相	在台上表演	7	頓時	一下子
3	第一次	頭一次	8	以	用
4	登	上	9	京城	北京城（裡）
5	選拔	選			

课文要点

一、词语解释 Words and Phrases

（一）文言词、惯用词 (Classical Chinese and idiomatic expressions)

1、头一回 = 第一次
　☞ 很多孩子都是头一回登这么大的台。
2、顿时 = 马上、一下子
　☞ 一进大厅顿时让人感到一种临战前的紧张气氛。
3、入 = 到……里
　☞ 钢琴正在悄悄地进入到中国的寻常百姓家。
4、寻常 = 普通、一般（的）
　☞ 寻常百姓的意思就是普通老百姓的意思。

（二）成语 (idioms)

◆ 登台亮相: to appear on stage

◆ 多了不说: no need to say more

二、书面语、正式语、口语对照表 Written/formal/colloquial Comparison

	书面／正式语	口语		书面／正式语	口语
1	未来／将来	以后	6	究竟	到底
2	登台亮相	在台上表演	7	顿时	一下子
3	第一次	头一次	8	以	用
4	登	上	9	京城	北京城（里）
5	选拔	选			

三、句型 Sentence Structures

（一）……是指…… (to refer to)

> ✍ ……是指……, "to refer to", is a verb phrase used for definition. The term to be defined is placed before 是指 and the definition of the term is placed after it. The negative structure is ……不是指 ……. Example: 獨生子女文化不是指一個人，而是指一種現象. ("Single-child culture" does not refer to a particular person, but rather refers to a phenomenon.)

☞ "獨生子女文化"是指中國在培養獨生子女時形成的一種特殊文化。

1、"孤兒"是指沒有父母的孩子。

"Orphan" refers to a child who does not have any parents.

2、"獨生子女文化"是指中國在培養獨生子女時形成的一種特殊文化。

"Single-child culture" refers to the special culture formed in the process of raising single children in China.

問：中國人常常用"單位"這個詞，它到底有甚麼意思？

答：＿＿＿＿＿＿＿＿＿＿＿＿＿＿＿＿＿＿＿＿＿。

（二）……的特點是…… (the characteristics of something are)

> ✍ ……的特點是……, "the characteristics of something are", is a set phrase used to list or to state characteristics of an object or event. It is usually followed by a list of adjectives or a clause. Examples: 這種公司的特點是小而精. (The characteristics of this company are that it is both small and self-selected.) 這種小店的特點是收入穩定，風險不大. (The characteristics of this small shop are that its income is steady and its risks are small.)

☞ 這種文化的特點是父母對他們孩子的智力發展和非智力發展採取不同的態度。

1、單親家庭的特點之一是孩子不能受到父母雙雙的關心。

One of the characteristics of the single-parent family is that children cannot receive both parents' care.

2、個體戶的特點是靠自己的本事做生意。

The distinguishing characteristic of entrepreneurs is that they use their own abilities to do business.

問：美國老年人的生活有甚麼特點？

答：＿＿＿＿＿＿＿＿＿＿＿＿＿＿＿＿＿＿＿＿＿。

97

三、句型 ⁂ Sentence Structures

（一）……是指…… (to refer to)

> ✍ ……是指……, "to refer to", is a verb phrase used for definition. The term to be defined is placed before 是指 and the definition of the term is placed after it. The negative structure is ……不是指……. Example: 独生子女文化不是指一个人，而是指一种现象. ("Single-child culture" does not refer to a particular person, but rather refers to a phenomenon.)

☞ "独生子女文化"是指中国在培养独生子女时形成的一种特殊文化。

1、 "孤儿"是指没有父母的孩子。

"Orphan" refers to a child who does not have any parents.

2、 "独生子女文化"是指中国在培养独生子女时形成的一种特殊文化。

"Single-child culture" refers to the special culture formed in the process of raising single children in China.

问：中国人常常用"单位"这个词，它到底有什么意思？

答：＿＿＿＿＿＿＿＿＿＿＿＿＿＿＿＿＿＿＿＿＿。

（二）……的特点是…… (the characteristics of something are)

> ✍ ……的特点是……, "the characteristics of something are", is a set phrase used to list or to state characteristics of an object or event. It is usually followed by a list of adjectives or a clause. Examples: 这种公司的特点是小而精. (The characteristics of this company are that it is both small and self-selected.) 这种小店的特点是收入稳定，风险不大. (The characteristics of this small shop are that its income is steady and its risks are small.)

☞ 这种文化的特点是父母对他们孩子的智力发展和非智力发展采取不同的态度。

1、单亲家庭的特点之一是孩子不能受到父母双双的关心。

One of the characteristics of the single-parent family is that children cannot receive both parents' care.

2、个体户的特点是靠自己的本事做生意。

The distinguishing characteristic of entrepreneurs is that they use their own abilities to do business.

问：美国老年人的生活有什么特点？

答：＿＿＿＿＿＿＿＿＿＿＿＿＿＿＿＿＿＿＿＿＿。

（三）對……採取……（的）態度 (to adopt an attitude toward something)

✐ 對……採取……的態度, "to adopt an attitude toward something", is similar to the pattern 對……抱……的態度 reviewed in Lesson 5, Pattern 9, but is more formal. Modifying elements between 採取 and 態度 are often disyllabic words such as 反對, 支持, or 相反. The noun phrase placed after 對 is usually a person, event, or object. The negative particle 不 or 沒 can be placed either before 對 or before the verb 採取. Examples: 他沒有對這件事採取任何態度. (He has not adopted any particular attitude toward this matter.) 他對這件事沒有採取任何態度. (As for this matter, he has not adopted any particular attitude.).

☞ 這種文化的特點是父母對他們孩子的智力發展和非智力發展採取不同的態度。

1、以前人們對離婚採取反對的態度。

In the past, people opposed divorce.

2、你為甚麼對孩子的非智力發展採取這樣的態度呢？我不同意。

Why do you have this kind of attitude toward children's intellectual development? I don't agree.

問：＿＿＿＿＿＿＿＿＿＿＿＿＿＿＿＿＿＿？

答：我當然反對這種人口政策，因為我認為生孩子是夫妻之間的事而不是政府的事。

（四）頭一回…… (the first time, the first instance) = 第一次（多用在口語中）

✐ 頭一回, "the first time" or "the first instance", is a time adverb normally placed either at the beginning of a sentence or immediately before a verb. It has the same meaning and usage as 第一次, but is often used in colloquial Chinese.

☞ 很多孩子都是頭一回登這麼大的台，彈這麼大的琴。

1、這是我頭一回來北京，買了不少生活和學習用品。

This is my first time in Beijing. I bought lots of articles for daily use and school supplies.

2、打擾一下，這是你頭一回在中國登台演出嗎？緊張不緊張？

Excuse me, is this your first time performing on stage in China? Are you nervous?

問：這是你頭一回登台講話嗎？感覺怎麼樣？

答：是的。＿＿＿＿＿＿＿＿＿＿＿＿＿。

（三）对……采取……（的）态度 (to adopt an attitude toward something)

> 对……采取……的态度, "to adopt an attitude toward something", is similar to the pattern 对……抱……的态度 reviewed in Lesson 5, Pattern 9, but is more formal. Modifying elements between 采取 and 态度 are often disyllabic words such as 反对, 支持, or 相反. The noun phrase placed after 对 is usually a person, event, or object. The negative particle 不 or 没 can be placed either before 对 or before the verb 采取. Examples: 他没有对这件事采取任何态度. (He has not adopted any particular attitude toward this matter.) 他对这件事没有采取任何态度. (As for this matter, he has not adopted any particular attitude.)

☞ 这种文化的特点是父母对他们孩子的智力发展和非智力发展采取不同的态度。

1、以前人们对离婚采取反对的态度。

In the past, people opposed divorce.

2、你为什么对孩子的非智力发展采取这样的态度呢？我不同意。

Why do you have this kind of attitude toward children's intellectual development? I don't agree.

问: _____?

答: 我当然反对这种人口政策，因为我认为生孩子是夫妻之间的事而不是政府的事。

（四）头一回…… (the first time, the first instance) = 第一次（多用在口语中）

> 头一回, "the first time" or "the first instance", is a time adverb normally placed either at the beginning of a sentence or immediately before a verb. It has the same meaning and usage as 第一次, but is often used in colloquial Chinese.

☞ 很多孩子都是头一回登这么大的台，弹这么大的琴。

1、这是我头一回来北京，买了不少生活和学习用品。

This is my first time in Beijing. I bought lots of articles for daily use and school supplies.

2、打扰一下，这是你头一回在中国登台演出吗？紧张不紧张？

Excuse me, is this your first time performing on stage in China? Are you nervous?

问: 这是你头一回登台讲话吗？感觉怎么样？

答: 是的。_____。

（五）捨得 + VO/N (to be willing to part with, to not grudge)

> ✍ 捨得, "to be willing to part with" or "to not grudge", is a verb that can be followed by either a VO structure or a noun, as in 捨得花精力 (to be willing to expend energy), 捨得這點兒錢 (to be willing to spend this much). The negative form is usually 捨不得. Example: 這個人捨不得吃，也捨不得穿，就知道攢錢. (This person is reluctant to spend money on food and clothing; all he cares about is saving money.)

☞ 這種文化的特點是父母對他們孩子的智力發展和非智力發展採取不同的態度。在智力發展方面是三個"捨得"。

1、你捨得花五百元請家教幫助你孩子學語文嗎？

Are you willing to spend 500 *yuan* to hire a tutor to help your child learn Chinese?

2、要想學會一種外語，你一定要捨得花精力和時間天天練習。

If you want to master a foreign language, you certainly must be willing to spend energy and time studying every day.

問：現在的家長們都願意送孩子出國嗎？
答：當然＿＿＿＿＿＿＿＿＿＿＿＿＿＿＿。

（六）使……得到……（／平衡／健康／快速）發展 (to cause something to develop)

> ✍ 使……得到……發展, "to cause something to develop", is typically used in written or formal settings. The English translation of 得到 varies depending on the noun that follows 得到, e.g., 得到支持 (to receive support), 得到照顧 (to be well taken care of). The modifying elements that can be placed before 發展 include 平衡, 健康, and 快速, among others.

☞ 這就是為甚麼這幾年中國到處都在組織一些活動，提高兒童在各方面的素質，讓兒童得到平衡發展。

1、政府新的匯率政策真能使經濟得到快速發展嗎？

Can the government's new exchange rate policy really accelerate economic development?

2、報社為秋雲做的安排真能讓她在報社的大家庭中得到健康發展嗎？

Can the arrangements the newspaper made for Qiu Yun really allow her to develop vigorously within the newspaper's "big family"?

問：你認為甚麼辦法能使孩子比較平衡、健康地發展？
答：＿＿＿＿＿＿＿＿＿＿＿＿＿＿＿。

（五）舍得 + VO/N (to be willing to part with, to not grudge)

> ✍ 舍得, "to be willing to part with" or "to not grudge", is a verb that can be followed by either a VO structure or a noun, as in 舍得花精力 (to be willing to expend energy), 舍得这点儿钱 (to be willing to spend this much). The negative form is usually 舍不得. Example: 这个人舍不得吃，也舍不得穿，就知道攒钱. (This person is reluctant to spend money on food and clothing; all he cares about is saving money.)

☞ 这种文化的特点是父母对他们孩子的智力发展和非智力发展采取不同的态度。在智力发展方面是三个"舍得"。

1、你舍得花五百元请家教帮助你孩子学语文吗？

Are you willing to spend 500 *yuan* to hire a tutor to help your child learn Chinese?

2、要想学会一种外语，你一定要舍得花精力和时间天天练习。

If you want to master a foreign language, you certainly must be willing to spend energy and time studying every day.

问：现在的家长们都愿意送孩子出国吗？
答：当然＿＿＿＿＿＿＿＿＿＿＿＿＿＿＿＿。

（六）使⋯⋯得到⋯⋯（/平衡/健康/快速）发展 (to cause something to develop)

> ✍ 使⋯⋯得到⋯⋯发展, "to cause something to develop", is typically used in written or formal settings. The English translation of 得到 varies depending on the noun that follows 得到, e.g., 得到支持 (to receive support), 得到照顾 (to be well taken care of). The modifying elements that can be placed before 发展 include 平衡, 健康, and 快速, among others.

☞ 这就是为什么这几年中国到处都在组织一些活动，提高儿童在各方面的素质，让儿童得到平衡发展。

1、政府新的汇率政策真能使经济得到快速发展吗？

Can the government's new exchange rate policy really accelerate economic development?

2、报社为秋云做的安排真能让她在报社的大家庭中得到健康发展吗？

Can the arrangements the newspaper made for Qiu Yun really allow her to develop vigorously within the newspaper's "big family"?

问：你认为什么办法能使孩子比较平衡、健康地发展？
答：＿＿＿＿＿＿＿＿＿＿＿＿＿＿＿＿。

（七）從……（中）選拔（出）…… (to select from, to choose from)

> ✍ 從……（中）選拔（出） means "to select from" or "to choose from". The adverbs 中 (among) and 出 (out) are optional in this structure. There are, however, special rules for the use of 中 in this pattern. When the name of a country, city, or large place follows 從, 中 must be omitted, as in 從中國選拔三個運動員 (to select three athletes from China). When other place words follow 從, 中 should always follow the place words. Example: 這三個鋼琴家都是從音樂學院的學生中選拔的. (These three pianists were selected from among the students at the conservatory of music.)

☞ 他們大的十幾歲，小的只有五歲，都是從全國業餘鋼琴考級中選拔出來的優秀生。

1、從學校的中文比賽活動中，我們選拔了四位優秀生去參加北京電視台的表演。

We selected the four most outstanding students from the school's Chinese language competition to take part in a performance at the Beijing Television Station.

2、在這條商品批發街上，我們選拔出五個個體戶代表我們向當地政府提出我們的要求。

On this wholesale market street, we selected five entrepreneurs to represent us in bringing up our suggestions to the local government.

問：你知道這些台上表演的學生都是誰嗎？
答：知道。＿＿＿＿＿＿＿＿＿＿＿＿＿＿＿。

（八）促進……（的發展／進步／交流） (to promote)

> ✍ The verb 促進 is often followed by certain nouns such as 發展, 進步, 交流, or 關係. Modifying elements are inserted between the verb 促進 and the object.

☞ 為了促進業餘音樂教育的科學化、規範化，八十年代後期中國也開始建立了自己的考級制度。

1、為了促進私營企業的發展，這個地方的政府特意批准建立瓜市批發街。

In order to promote the development of private enterprise, the local government approved the establishment of a wholesale street in Melon Town.

2、為了促進兒童的競爭意識，很多家長讓兒童放學以後再去學鋼琴，或補習其它功課。

In order to foster their children's competitive spirit, many parents make them learn to play the piano or go to tutorials after school.

問：創辦這樣的小商品批發店究竟是為了甚麼？
答：＿＿＿＿＿＿＿＿＿＿＿＿＿＿＿＿＿。

（七）从……（中）选拔（出）…… (to select from, to choose from)

> ✍ 从……（中）选拔（出） means "to select from" or "to choose from". The adverbs 中 (among) and 出 (out) are optional in this structure. There are, however, special rules for the use of 中 in this pattern. When the name of a country, city, or large place follows 从, 中 must be omitted, as in 从中国选拔三个运动员 (to select three athletes from China). When other place words follow 从, 中 should always follow the place words. Example: 这三个钢琴家都是从音乐学院的学生中选拔的. (These three pianists were selected from among the students at the conservatory of music.)

☞ 他们大的十几岁，小的只有五岁，都是从全国业余钢琴考级中选拔出来的优秀生。

1、从学校的中文比赛活动中，我们选拔了四位优秀生去参加北京电视台的表演。
We selected the four most outstanding students from the school's Chinese language competition to take part in a performance at the Beijing Television Station.

2、在这条商品批发街上，我们选拔出五个个体户代表我们向当地政府提出我们的要求。
On this wholesale market street, we selected five entrepreneurs to represent us in bringing up our suggestions to the local government.

问：你知道这些台上表演的学生都是谁吗？
答：知道。_____。

（八）促进……（的发展／进步／交流） (to promote)

> ✍ The verb 促进 is often followed by certain nouns such as 发展, 进步, 交流, or 关系. Modifying elements are inserted between the verb 促进 and the object.

☞ 为了促进业余音乐教育的科学化、规范化，八十年代后期中国也开始建立了自己的考级制度。

1、为了促进私营企业的发展，这个地方的政府特意批准建立瓜市批发街。
In order to promote the development of private enterprise, the local government approved the establishment of a wholesale street in Melon Town.

2、为了促进儿童的竞争意识，很多家长让儿童放学以后再去学钢琴，或补习其它功课。
In order to foster their children's competitive spirit, many parents make them learn to play the piano or go to tutorials after school.

问：创办这样的小商品批发店究竟是为了什么？
答：_____。

（九）初期、中期、後期 (the beginning, middle, and end periods)

> ✍ 初期, 中期, and 後期 are terms used specifically for divisions of decades, dynasties, or periods of illness. 九十年代初期 (the early 1990s), 唐朝中期 (the middle years of the Tang dynasty), and 癌症後期 (the late stage of cancer) are all acceptable expressions, but these terms cannot be used for divisions of months or weeks.

☞ 為了促進業餘音樂教育的科學化、規範化，八十年代後期中國也開始建立了自己的考級制度。

1、八十年代初期，中國開始實行經濟開放，到現在中國的經濟已經發生了很大的變化。
During the early '80s, China started to open up its economy. Now China's economy has already undergone major changes.

2、九十年代中期，世界各國都十分關注大陸和台灣的關係問題。
In the mid-'90s, every nation in the world took interest in the relationship between Mainland China and Taiwan.

問：中國的經濟改革大概是從甚麼時候開始的？
答：＿＿＿＿＿＿＿＿＿＿＿＿＿＿＿＿＿＿＿＿＿＿。

（十）建立……制度 （／關係／機制） (to establish)

> ✍ 建立, "to establish", is a verb that normally takes objects such as 制度, 關係, or 組織, referring to systems, relationships, organizations, or institutions, as in 建立科學的管理制度 (to establish a scientific management system), 建立合作關係 (to establish a cooperative relationship), 建立新中國 (to establish a new China). 建立, however, cannot take 規定 (regulations) or 條文 (rules) as its object, although such objects can be used with "to establish" in English. Other impossible expressions include "to establish credit" and "to establish oneself".

☞ 為了促進業餘音樂教育的科學化、規範化，八十年代後期中國也開始建立了自己的考級制度。

1、從五十年代中期開始，中國就建立了社會主義計劃經濟的制度。
China established a socialist planned economic system in the mid-'50s.

2、現在中國人都在討論怎麼建立一個合理的醫療保險制度。
These days, Chinese people are all discussing how to establish a reasonable system of health insurance.

（九）初期、中期、后期 (the beginning, middle, and end periods)

> ✍ 初期, 中期, and 后期 are terms used specifically for divisions of decades, dynasties, or periods of illness. 九十年代初期 (the early 1990s), 唐朝中期 (the middle years of the Tang dynasty), and 癌症后期 (the late stage of cancer) are all acceptable expressions, but these terms cannot be used for divisions of months or weeks.

☞ 为了促进业余音乐教育的科学化、规范化，八十年代后期中国也开始建立了自己的考级制度。

1、八十年代初期，中国开始实行经济开放，到现在中国的经济已经发生了很大的变化。

During the early '80s, China started to open up its economy. Now China's economy has already undergone major changes.

2、九十年代中期，世界各国都十分关注大陆和台湾的关系问题。

In the mid-'90s, every nation in the world took interest in the relationship between Mainland China and Taiwan.

问：中国的经济改革大概是从什么时候开始的？
答：＿＿＿＿＿＿＿＿＿＿＿＿＿＿＿＿＿＿＿＿。

（十）建立……制度（／关系／机制）(to establish)

> ✍ 建立, "to establish", is a verb that normally takes objects such as 制度, 关系, or 组织, referring to systems, relationships, organizations, or institutions, as in 建立科学的管理制度 (to establish a scientific management system), 建立合作关系 (to establish a cooperative relationship), 建立新中国 (to establish a new China). 建立, however, cannot take 规定 (regulations) or 条文 (rules) as its object, although such objects can be used with "to establish" in English. Other impossible expressions include "to establish credit" and "to establish oneself".

☞ 为了促进业余音乐教育的科学化、规范化，八十年代后期中国也开始建立了自己的考级制度。

1、从五十年代中期开始，中国就建立了社会主义计划经济的制度。
China established a socialist planned economic system in the mid-'50s.

2、现在中国人都在讨论怎么建立一个合理的医疗保险制度。
These days, Chinese people are all discussing how to establish a reasonable system of health insurance.

問：＿＿＿＿＿＿＿＿＿＿＿＿＿＿＿＿＿＿＿＿？

答：這種買房制度大概是在九十年代末開始建立的。

（十一）讓……感到……（的）氣氛 (to give someone a sense of something)

> ✍ 讓……感到……（的）氣氛, "to give someone a sense of something", is a set phrase in which the recipient of 感到 must precede the verb and follow 讓. The negative particle 不 or 沒 is normally placed before 讓. Modifying elements for 氣氛 can be adjectives, such as 緊張 and 輕鬆, or nouns, such as 家庭, 課堂, and 大學. Example: 這個小大學讓學生感到一種大家庭的氣氛. (This small college makes students feel like they are part of a big family.)

☞ 這是今年鋼琴考級的最後一天，一進大廳頓時讓人感到一種臨戰前的緊張氣氛。

1、考試前，我去了教室，在那兒，我感到一種緊張的氣氛。

Before the test, I went into the classroom, where I could sense a kind of intense atmosphere.

2、鋼琴考級比賽以前，人人都感到一種臨戰前的氣氛。

Before the piano competition, the room was as tense as a battlefield.

問：你為甚麼進去一會兒就出來了，這個會讓你不舒服嗎？

答：＿＿＿＿＿＿＿＿＿＿＿＿＿＿＿＿＿＿＿＿。

（十二）由……組成 (to be composed of)

> ✍ 由……組成, "to be composed of", is an example of a passive sentence introduced by 由. The people, categories, or things which the subject is composed of must be placed before 組成 and following the preposition 由. Example: 我們的評委由八個人組成. (Our evaluation committee is composed of eight people.) The preposition 由, although translated as "by" in English, cannot be replaced by 被.

☞ 考試的內容一般由基本練習和樂曲兩部分組成。

1、這次考試由三部分組成：聽寫、翻譯和寫作。

The test is divided into three parts: dictation, translation, and composition.

2、鋼琴考級的評委由八個有名的鋼琴演奏家和教育家組成。

The evaluation committee of the piano competition is composed of eight famous pianists and music educators.

問：美國高中生考 SAT 一般都分幾個部分？

答：＿＿＿＿＿＿＿＿＿＿＿＿＿＿＿＿＿＿。

问: _____?
答: 这种买房制度大概是在九十年代末开始建立的。

（十一）让……感到……（的）气氛 (to give someone a sense of something)

> ✍ 让……感到……（的）气氛, "to give someone a sense of something", is a set phrase in which the recipient of 感到 must precede the verb and follow 让. The negative particle 不 or 没 is normally placed before 让. Modifying elements for 气氛 can be adjectives, such as 紧张 and 轻松, or nouns, such as 家庭, 课堂, and 大学. Example: 这个小大学让学生感到一种大家庭的气氛. (This small college makes students feel like they are part of a big family.)

☞ 这是今年钢琴考级的最后一天，一进大厅顿时让人感到一种临战前的紧张气氛。

1、考试前，我去了教室，在那儿，我感到一种紧张的气氛。
Before the test, I went into the classroom, where I could sense a kind of intense atmosphere.

2、钢琴考级比赛以前，人人都感到一种临战前的气氛。
Before the piano competition, the room was as tense as a battlefield.

问: 你为什么进去一会儿就出来了，这个会让你不舒服吗？
答: _____。

（十二）由……组成 (to be composed of)

> ✍ 由……组成, "to be composed of", is an example of a passive sentence introduced by 由. The people, categories, or things which the subject is composed of must be placed before 组成 and following the preposition 由. Example: 我们的评委由八个人组成. (Our evaluation committee is composed of eight people.) The preposition 由, although translated as "by" in English, cannot be replaced by 被.

☞ 考试的内容一般由基本练习和乐曲两部分组成。

1、这次考试由三部分组成: 听写、翻译和写作。
The test is divided into three parts: dictation, translation, and composition.

2、钢琴考级的评委由八个有名的钢琴演奏家和教育家组成。
The evaluation committee of the piano competition is composed of eight famous pianists and music educators.

问: 美国高中生考SAT一般都分几个部分？
答: _____。

（十三）把……浸注在……上 (to devote something to, to dedicate something to)

> ✍ 把……浸注在……上, "to devote something to" or "to dedicate something to", is a structure used mostly in written or formal settings. The objects commonly used with 浸注 are similar to those used with 奉獻 (see Lesson 1, Pattern 11). The 把 construction is required before the verb to indicate the object of the verb "to devote". To negate this structure, 沒有 must be placed before the 把 construction. Example: 他並沒有把心血浸注在教育事業上. (He never really devoted his heart and soul to teaching.) The directional complement 上 can be replaced by 中 or 裡, depending on context.

☞ 他們以強烈的責任感，把心血浸注在鋼琴教育事業上。

1、從兒童彈琴這件事上可以看出現在家長把他們的精力和時間全部浸注在孩子身上了。

Watching a child playing the piano, one can see that today's parents devote all their time and energy to their children.

2、我的老師把他的全部心血都浸注在教學上了。

My professor devotes all of his energy to his teaching.

問：你能跟我談談你的父親嗎？為甚麼你這麼崇拜他？
答：＿＿＿＿＿＿＿＿＿＿＿＿＿＿＿＿＿＿＿＿＿＿。

（十四）早就聽説…… (I heard it said long ago, it was said long ago)

> ✍ 早就聽説, "I heard it said long ago" or "it was said long ago", is a set phrase normally used to introduce a topic at the beginning of a sentence. In addition to 聽説, 早就 can also be followed by expressions such as 傳説. Examples: 早就聽説(/傳説), 中國的住房政策要改革了. (It has been rumored for a long time that China has to reform its housing policies.)

☞ 早就聽説京城有個小神童，學琴三年，這次報考了七級和八級。

1、早就聽説鋼琴已經進入了中國的尋常百姓家，平均三家就有一台鋼琴。

A while ago, I heard that pianos had already entered the homes of China's common people, and that on average, one out of every three households has a piano.

2、早就聽説他從小就是一個"神童"，現在他已經是中國的最優秀的音樂家了。

I heard long ago that he was a child prodigy when he was a child, and that now he is China's most outstanding musician.

問：＿＿＿＿＿＿＿＿＿＿＿＿＿＿＿＿＿＿＿＿＿＿？
答：你說喬丹嗎？他是美國最優秀的籃球手。我怎麼會不知道？

（十三）把……浸注在……上 (to devote something to, to dedicate something to)

> ✐ 把……浸注在……上, "to devote something to" or "to dedicate something to", is a structure used mostly in written or formal settings. The objects commonly used with 浸注 are similar to those used with 奉献 (see Lesson 1, Pattern 11). The 把 construction is required before the verb to indicate the object of the verb "to devote". To negate this structure, 没有 must be placed before the 把 construction. Example: 他并没有把心血浸注在教育事业上. (He never really devoted his heart and soul to teaching.) The directional complement 上 can be replaced by 中 or 里, depending on context.

☞ 他们以强烈的责任感，把心血浸注在钢琴教育事业上。

1、从儿童弹琴这件事上可以看出现在家长把他们的精力和时间全部浸注在孩子身上了。

Watching a child playing the piano, one can see that today's parents devote all their time and energy to their children.

2、我的老师把他的全部心血都浸注在教学上了。

My professor devotes all of his energy to his teaching.

问：你能跟我谈谈你的父亲吗？为什么你这么崇拜他？

答：_____。

（十四）早就听说…… (I heard it said long ago, it was said long ago)

> ✐ 早就听说, "I heard it said long ago" or "it was said long ago", is a set phrase normally used to introduce a topic at the beginning of a sentence. In addition to 听说, 早就 can also be followed by expressions such as 传说. Examples: 早就听说(/传说)，中国的住房政策要改革了. (It has been rumored for a long time that China has to reform its housing policies.)

☞ 早就听说京城有个小神童，学琴三年，这次报考了七级和八级。

1、早就听说钢琴已经进入了中国的寻常百姓家，平均三家就有一台钢琴。

A while ago, I heard that pianos had already entered the homes of China's common people, and that on average, one out of every three households has a piano.

2、早就听说他从小就是一个"神童"，现在他已经是中国的最优秀的音乐家了。

I heard long ago that he was a child prodigy when he was a child, and that now he is China's most outstanding musician.

问：_____?

答：你说乔丹吗？他是美国最优秀的篮球手。我怎么会不知道？

103

（十五）……值得…… (to be worthwhile)

> ✍ 值得, "to be worthwhile", is a special verb that can be used in both active and passive sentences. In either case, it can be followed by a verb or verb phrase. Examples: 為了了解中國，值得花時間交中國朋友 (active). (In order to better understand China, it is worthwhile to spend time making Chinese friends.) 中國文化很值得研究 (passive). (Chinese culture is worth studying.) The difference between active and passive usages of 值得 is that in the latter, the subject is actually the object of 值得 or the object of the verb following 值得. The verb 值得 cannot be followed immediately by a noun, such as 錢 or 時間. The negative form of 值得 is always 不值得.

☞ 您認為花點錢，受點累是非常值得的。

1、現在的家長覺得在孩子身上花精力、花錢最值得。

Today's parents feel that spending time and money on children is the most worthwhile thing to do.

2、在北京住一個夏天學中文，我覺得非常值得。

I feel that living in Beijing for a summer to study Chinese is very worthwhile.

問：你認為去北京學習中文值得不值得？為甚麼？
答：＿＿＿＿＿＿＿＿＿＿＿＿＿＿＿＿＿＿＿＿＿。

四、文化背景知識 Cultural Notes

> 1. Diary format in China: The first line of an entry always carries the date (year, month, day–in that order), day of the week, and a brief description of the weather. A prose entry would then follow.
>
> 2. Most of the print media in the United States–newspapers, magazines, and so on–are owned either by individuals or by private corporations. The Bill of Rights guarantees Americans "Freedom of the Press", which means that national, state, and local governments have little or no control over what is published in American newspapers. As is well known, American publications frequently carry editorials that voice criticisms of government leaders and their policies. In China, the situation is much different. Virtually all legal publications in China are controlled by the government. Moreover, strict policies determine what is appropriate and inappropriate for publication. As a result, one rarely finds negative accounts of government policies in Chinese newspapers.

（十五）……值得…… (to be worthwhile)

> ✍ 值得, "to be worthwhile", is a special verb that can be used in both active and passive sentences. In either case, it can be followed by a verb or verb phrase. Examples: 为了了解中国，值得花时间交中国朋友 (active). (In order to better understand China, it is worthwhile to spend time making Chinese friends.) 中国文化很值得研究 (passive). (Chinese culture is worth studying.) The difference between active and passive usages of 值得 is that in the latter, the subject is actually the object of 值得 or the object of the verb following 值得. The verb 值得 cannot be followed immediately by a noun, such as 钱 or 时间. The negative form of 值得 is always 不值得.

☞ 您认为花点钱，受点累是非常值得的。

1、现在的家长觉得在孩子身上花精力、花钱最值得。

Today's parents feel that spending time and money on children is the most worthwhile thing to do.

2、在北京住一个夏天学中文，我觉得非常值得。

I feel that living in Beijing for a summer to study Chinese is very worthwhile.

问：你认为去北京学习中文值得不值得？为什么？

答：_____。

四、文化背景知识 Cultural Notes

1. Diary format in China: The first line of an entry always carries the date (year, month, day–in that order), day of the week, and a brief description of the weather. A prose entry would then follow.

2. Most of the print media in the United States–newspapers, magazines, and so on–are owned either by individuals or by private corporations. The Bill of Rights guarantees Americans "Freedom of the Press", which means that national, state, and local governments have little or no control over what is published in American newspapers. As is well known, American publications frequently carry editorials that voice criticisms of government leaders and their policies. In China, the situation is much different. Virtually all legal publications in China are controlled by the government. Moreover, strict policies determine what is appropriate and inappropriate for publication. As a result, one rarely finds negative accounts of government policies in Chinese newspapers.

練習

語言結構 Structures

一、短語翻譯 (Phrase translation)

1. a special concert in Beijing
2. to perform on stage
3. an amateur pianist
4. excellent students
5. to play the piano at age 5
6. friends around school
7. "scientification" and standardization
8. a tense atmosphere
9. etude
10. the top notch piano performer
11. a strong sense of responsibility and competition
12. one's good will and fine character

二、聽力練習 (Listening comprehension)

1、聽寫 (Dictation)

2、聽錄音並回答問題 (Answering questions while listening to the audio CD)
    (1) 寫出聽力的原文
    (2) 請你想出一個在美國的工作，也有考級制度。談談這個工作的考級要求和評委。

三、改寫下面劃線的詞 (Replace the underlined words)

這是他頭一回登台說話，一上台他頓時心跳得很快。不知為啥他甚麼也說不出來了。

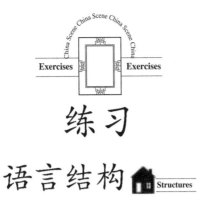

练习

语言结构 Structures

一、短语翻译 (Phrase translation)

1. a special concert in Beijing
2. to perform on stage
3. an amateur pianist
4. excellent students
5. to play the piano at age 5
6. friends around school
7. "scientification" and standardization
8. a tense atmosphere
9. etude
10. the top notch piano performer
11. a strong sense of responsibility and competition
12. one's good will and fine character

二、听力练习 (Listening comprehension)

1、听写 (Dictation)

2、听录音并回答问题 (Answering questions while listening to the audio CD)
(1) 写出听力的原文
(2) 请你想出一个在美国的工作，也有考级制度。谈谈这个工作的考级要求和评委。

三、改写下面划线的词 (Replace the underlined words)

这是他<u>头一回</u>登台说话，一上台他<u>顿时</u>心跳得很快。不知为啥他什么也说不出来了。

四、完成句子 (Complete the sentences)

1、　　A：你們為甚麼組織這個鋼琴考試？

　　　　B：_____

　　　　（為了……促進……的發展；……後期……）

2、　　A：中國的經濟由哪兩個部分組成？搞這兩種經濟能不能促進中國社會的發展？

　　　　B：_____

　　　　（由……組成；擺脫……的束縛）

3、　　A：_____

　　　　B：是啊，我的老師為了學生，他甚麼都願意奉獻。

　　　　（早就聽説；把……浸注在……）

五、閱讀短文、回答問題 (Answering questions based on the reading passages)

你要我跟你説説對彈琴的看法？好吧。你説得很對，這幾年，人們對孩子的素質培養很重視，加上人們的經濟條件有了改善，所以家家都買鋼琴讓孩子學彈琴。你大概覺得我很幸運，爸爸、媽媽花這麼多錢給我買琴，還給我交學費上鋼琴課。可是我認為學琴，尤其是在中國學彈琴，是一件很苦的事，也不一定是一件好事。一方面父母給我們很大的壓力，為了讓我們變成小神童，每天要花三～五個鐘頭練琴，別的甚麼事都不能做；另一方面我們也有同學之間的競爭。父母説得好聽，練琴有三大好處：一個是鍛煉意志，一個是提高素質，還有一個是提高競爭意識。為了讓我們練琴，所有的父母都捨得花時間、花錢、花精力。可我們覺得，練琴不一定真有那麼多好處，其實壞處倒很多。比方説，我們沒有機會學別的東西，我們的興趣都是父母的興趣，我們的發展很單一，還有我們都覺得現在的生活太沒有意思了。

問題

　　(1) 在孩子的父母看來，彈琴的好處是甚麼？

　　(2) 在孩子看來，彈琴的壞處是甚麼？

　　(3) 在你看來，對孩子的最好的教育方法是甚麼？談談你自己少年時的經驗。

甚麼是"獨生子女問題"呢？獨生子女問題是指很大一部分獨生子女存在著明顯的個性品質問題，如自私、任性、不獨立等。在現實生活中，一方面，獨生子女家庭都有"望子成龍"的心態；另一方面，對孩子是"含在嘴裡怕化了，抱在懷裡怕摔了"。這樣，在期待獨生子女個個成為小神童的同時，許多家庭陷入了過分溺愛和過分管制的教育誤區。

四、完成句子 (Complete the sentences)

1、　　A：你们为什么组织这个钢琴考试？

　　　　B：＿＿＿＿＿＿＿＿＿＿＿＿＿＿＿＿＿＿＿＿＿＿＿＿＿＿＿＿＿

　　　　（为了……促进……的发展；……后期……）

2、　　A：中国的经济由哪两个部分组成？搞这两种经济能不能促进中国社会的发展？

　　　　B：＿＿＿＿＿＿＿＿＿＿＿＿＿＿＿＿＿＿＿＿＿＿＿＿＿＿＿＿＿

　　　　（由……组成；摆脱……的束缚）

3、　　A：＿＿＿＿＿＿＿＿＿＿＿＿＿＿＿＿＿＿＿＿＿＿＿＿＿＿＿＿＿

　　　　B：是啊，我的老师为了学生，他什么都愿意奉献。

　　　　（早就听说；把……浸注在……）

五、阅读短文、回答问题 (Answering questions based on the reading passages)

你要我跟你说说对弹琴的看法？好吧。你说得很对，这几年，人们对孩子的素质培养很重视，加上人们的经济条件有了改善，所以家家都买钢琴让孩子学弹琴。你大概觉得我很幸运，爸爸、妈妈花这么多钱给我买琴，还给我交学费上钢琴课。可是我认为学琴，尤其是在中国学弹琴，是一件很苦的事，也不一定是一件好事。一方面父母给我们很大的压力，为了让我们变成小神童，每天要花三～五个钟头练琴，别的什么事都不能做；另一方面我们也有同学之间的竞争。父母说得好听，练琴有三大好处：一个是锻炼意志，一个是提高素质，还有一个是提高竞争意识。为了让我们练琴，所有的父母都舍得花时间、花钱、花精力。可我们觉得，练琴不一定真有那么多好处，其实坏处倒很多。比方说，我们没有机会学别的东西，我们的兴趣都是父母的兴趣，我们的发展很单一，还有我们都觉得现在的生活太没有意思了。

问题

　　(1) 在孩子的父母看来，弹琴的好处是什么？

　　(2) 在孩子看来，弹琴的坏处是什么？

　　(3) 在你看来，对孩子的最好的教育方法是什么？谈谈你自己少年时的经验。

什么是"独生子女问题"呢？独生子女问题是指很大一部分独生子女存在着明显的个性品质问题，如自私、任性、不独立等。在现实生活中，一方面，独生子女家庭都有"望子成龙"的心态；另一方面，对孩子是"含在嘴里怕化了，抱在怀里怕摔了"。这样，在期待独生子女个个成为小神童的同时，许多家庭陷入了过分溺爱和过分管制的教育误区。

問題

(1) 甚麼是"獨生子女問題"？

(2) 這個問題是由於甚麼導致的？

六、翻譯 (Translate sentences)

1. The campaign is composed of two parts: one is to choose excellent students from among the nation's amateur piano players, the other is to cultivate the children's fine character and sense of competition.

2. People here are beginning to realize the advantages of piano lessons for a child. Pianos quietly begin to appear in common people's houses.

3. Along with the improvement of the economic situation and the need for a spiritual life, more and more parents are willing to spend their money and energy on their children.

问题
   (1) 什么是"独生子女问题"？
   (2) 这个问题是由于什么导致的？

六、翻译 (Translate sentences)

1. The campaign is composed of two parts: one is to choose excellent students from among the nation's amateur piano players, the other is to cultivate the children's fine character and sense of competition.

2. People here are beginning to realize the advantages of piano lessons for a child. Pianos quietly begin to appear in common people's houses.

3. Along with the improvement of the economic situation and the need for a spiritual life, more and more parents are willing to spend their money and energy on their children.

語言實踐：Practice

一、根據課文回答問題 (Answering questions based on the dialogue)

1、甚麼是日記體？它的特點是甚麼？
2、從第一則日記中能知道現在中國家庭中流行讓孩子做甚麼嗎？現在孩子學鋼琴的人數
　　比率是多大？
3、根據報導，建立鋼琴考級制度的目的是甚麼？
4、鋼琴考級最後一天，走進考試大廳給人一種甚麼感覺？
5、考試的內容有甚麼？評委都是誰？
6、用你自己的話說說京城小神童的故事：她今年幾歲？為甚麼想彈琴？她長大想幹甚麼？
　　她學習怎麼樣？她報考幾級？
7、在家長看來，學鋼琴的好處是甚麼？
8、讓孩子學鋼琴，家長得捨得甚麼？

二、活動 (Activities)

　　　找一個中國家庭的孩子，了解一下他（她）的生活、學習、和其它活動。記下他
（她）的生活、學習、和其它活動。用日記的形式寫一下你所認識的中國小孩子的生活。

三、討論題 (Topics for discussion)

1、從這篇課文裡我們知道中國的父母為了孩子的智力發展甚麼都捨得。你覺得這種方法
　　真能鍛煉孩子的競爭意識嗎？為甚麼？
2、"獨生子女"政策會給中國社會帶來甚麼現象？你認為父母應該怎麼平衡孩子的智力
　　發展和非智力發展？
3、談談兒童的不平衡發展所帶來的問題？

四、報告 (Presentation)

　　　對兒童的培養，尤其是對獨生子女的培養，你覺得應該不應該只注意智力發展，而不
　　注意非智力發展？為甚麼？

语言实践 ⋮ Practice

一、根据课文回答问题 (Answering questions based on the dialogue)

1、什么是日记体？它的特点是什么？
2、从第一则日记中能知道现在中国家庭中流行让孩子做什么吗？现在孩子学钢琴的人数比率是多大？
3、根据报道，建立钢琴考级制度的目的是什么？
4、钢琴考级最后一天，走进考试大厅给人一种什么感觉？
5、考试的内容有什么？评委都是谁？
6、用你自己的话说说京城小神童的故事：她今年几岁？为什么想弹琴？她长大想干什么？她学习怎么样？她报考几级？
7、在家长看来，学钢琴的好处是什么？
8、让孩子学钢琴，家长得舍得什么？

二、活动 (Activities)

　　找一个中国家庭的孩子，了解一下他（她）的生活、学习、和其它活动。记下他（她）的生活、学习、和其它活动。用日记的形式写一下你所认识的中国小孩子的生活。

三、讨论题 (Topics for discussion)

1、从这篇课文里我们知道中国的父母为了孩子的智力发展什么都舍得。你觉得这种方法真能锻炼孩子的竞争意识吗？为什么？
2、"独生子女"政策会给中国社会带来什么现象？你认为父母应该怎么平衡孩子的智力发展和非智力发展？
3、谈谈儿童的不平衡发展所带来的问题？

四、报告 (Presentation)

　　对儿童的培养，尤其是对独生子女的培养，你觉得应该不应该只注意智力发展，而不注意非智力发展？为什么？

五、看圖討論 (Picto-discussion)

五、看图讨论 (Picto-discussion)

1

2

3

4

5

6

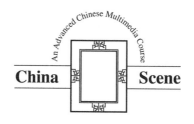

第六課

兒童教育

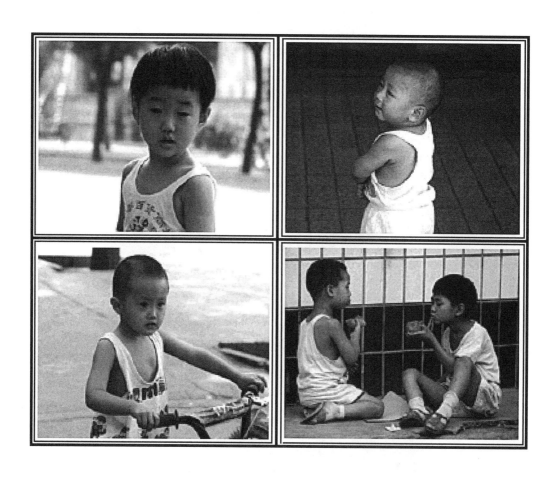

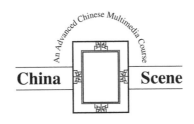

第六课

儿童教育

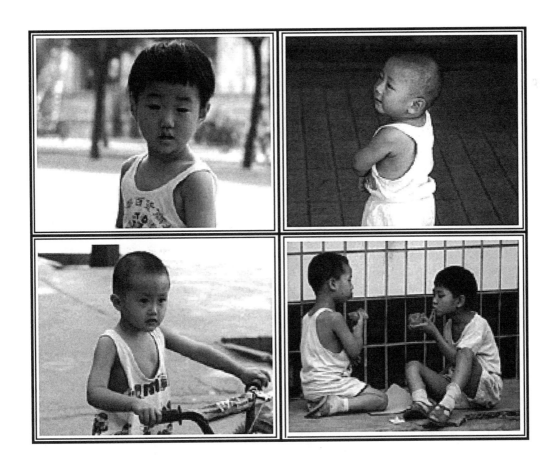

課文

一、對話  Dialogs

---

（一）

趙華：　　你對中國的人口政策有甚麼看法？

李子慶：我覺得中國的人口政策雖然在[1]一定的時間內可以控制人口，可是也許會引起很多社會問題。

趙華：　　比方說甚麼問題？

李子慶：獨生子女的問題。現在的家庭都是一個孩子。一方面，父母對孩子的期望太高，給孩子很大的壓力；另一方面，父母又對孩子過分[2]溺愛，甚麼事都替孩子幹，因此造成了中國兒童自主能力差[3]的問題。

趙華：　　看來，一家一個孩子的政策控制了人口，可是也造成了很多社會問題。

生詞

| 趙華 | (zhào huá) | N. | Zhao Hua, name of a person 人名 |
| 李子慶 | (lǐ zǐ qìng) | N. | Li Ziqing, name of a person 人名 |

Notes [1]一定 can be used either as an adverb or as an adjective. When used as an adverb, it means "definitely" or "certainly" and must precede a verb. Example: 人口政策一定可以控制人口. (Population policy can certainly control population size.) As an adjective, 一定 must precede a noun and may be followed by 的. In such cases, it means "given", "particular", "certain", as in 在一定時間內 (within a given time), 在一定程度上 (to a particular level), 有一定的好壞 (to have a certain advantage).

[2]過分, literally "to exceed（過）the usual allotment（分）", has two functions, both of which carry negative meanings. When used as an adverb before a verb or adjective, 過分 means "excessively", as in 過分討厭 (excessively disgusting), 過分溺愛 (spoiling a child too much), 過分長 (way too long). As an adjective, 過分 means "too much", "overboard". Examples: 他這個人真是太過分了! (He is really too much!) 提意見可以，但是你的話太過分了. (It's okay to raise your opinion, but you've gone overboard.)

[3]差 (chà) can be used in several ways. First, it can function as an adjective meaning "inferior" or "substandard". Example: 那家公司的產品很差. (That company's products are no good.) In constructions like this, 很 almost always precedes 差. Second, as a verb, 差 can mean "to be short of" or "to lack", as in 差一個人 (to be short one person). Third, 差 appears in the bound expression 差不多, which means "more or less the same". Example: 他現在的情況跟以前差不多. (His situation now is about the same as before.) In this construction, 差不多 never takes a negative or adverbial modifier.

课文

一、对话 Dialogs

（一）

赵华：　你对中国的人口政策有什么看法？

李子庆：我觉得中国的人口政策虽然在[(1)]一定的时间内可以控制人口，可是也许会引起很多社会问题。

赵华：　比方说什么问题？

李子庆：独生子女的问题。现在的家庭都是一个孩子。一方面，父母对孩子的期望太高，给孩子很大的压力；另一方面，父母又对孩子过分[(2)]溺爱，什么事都替孩子干，因此造成了中国儿童自主能力差[(3)]的问题。

赵华：　看来，一家一个孩子的政策控制了人口，可是也造成了很多社会问题。

生词

赵华	(zhào huá)	N.	Zhao Hua, name of a person 人名
李子庆	(lǐ zǐ qìng)	N.	Li Ziqing, name of a person 人名

Notes [(1)]一定 can be used either as an adverb or as an adjective. When used as an adverb, it means "definitely" or "certainly" and must precede a verb. Example: 人口政策一定可以控制人口. (Population policy can certainly control population size.) As an adjective, 一定 must precede a noun and may be followed by 的. In such cases, it means "given", "particular", "certain", as in 在一定时间内 (within a given time), 在一定程度上 (to a particular level), 有一定的好坏 (to have a certain advantage).

[(2)]过分, literally "to exceed （过） the usual allotment （分）", has two functions, both of which carry negative meanings. When used as an adverb before a verb or adjective, 过分 means "excessively", as in 过分讨厌 (excessively disgusting), 过分溺爱 (spoiling a child too much), 过分长 (way too long). As an adjective, 过分 means "too much", "overboard". Examples: 他这个人真是太过分了! (He is really too much!) 提意见可以，但是你的话太过分了. (It's okay to raise your opinion, but you've gone overboard.)

[(3)]差 (chà) can be used in several ways. First, it can function as an adjective meaning "inferior" or "substandard". Example: 那家公司的产品很差. (That company's products are no good.) In constructions like this, 很 almost always precedes 差. Second, as a verb, 差 can mean "to be short of" or "to lack", as in 差一个人 (to be short one person). Third, 差 appears in the bound expression 差不多, which means "more or less the same". Example: 他现在的情况跟以前差不多. (His situation now is about the same as before.) In this construction, 差不多 never takes a negative or adverbial modifier.

控制	(kòng zhì)	*N/V.*	control; to control
期望	(qī wàng)	*N/V.*	expectation; to expect
壓力	(yā lì)	*N.*	pressure
過分	(guò fèn)	*Adj.*	excessive, over, too much
溺愛	(nì ài)	*V.*	to spoil (a child), to be excessively fond of
替	(tì)	*V.*	to take the place of, to substitute for
造成	(zào chéng)	*V.*	to cause, to result in
自主能力	(zì zhǔ néng lì)	*N.*	independence
差	(chà)	*Adj.*	lacking, poor

（二）

趙華：　中國常常説現在的兒童是"小皇帝"、"小太陽"，這到底是甚麼意思？

李子慶：這主要是説中國從七十年代末以後出生的孩子，大多都是獨生子女，雖然他們也許在學習成績上不錯，但是多數自主性[4]很差，不會做家務，不會做飯，甚至連學習、生活用品[5]都不會整理，農村的孩子也不會幹農活。

趙華：　是嗎？這些問題會不會導致兒童心理不健全？

李子慶：對。這個問題已經引起了社會各界的重視。針對這些問題，很多學校都在開展各種活動，"小能手"活動就是其中的一種。

生詞

皇帝	(huáng dì)	*N.*	emperor
太陽	(tài yáng)	*N.*	the sun
末	(mò)	*N.*	end
用品	(yòng pǐn)	*N.*	articles for use
農活	(nóng huó)	*N.*	farm work
導致	(dǎo zhì)	*V.*	to cause, to result in, to lead to

Notes [4]When attached to a verb or adjective, 性 functions as a suffix meaning "basic nature", "essential characteristic", or "-ability", as in 獨立性 (independent spirit), 依賴性 (dependability), 可能性 (possibility).

[5]The suffix 品 may be attached to nouns or verbs to form nouns referring to products or commodities, as in 生活用品 (products used in everyday life), 商品 (commercial products), 工業產品 (industrial goods), 農產品 (produce). In the common expression 人品, however, 品 refers specifically to the moral character or qualities of a person. Example: 她人品很好 (She is a person of good moral character).

控制	(kòng zhì)	*N/V.*	control; to control
期望	(qī wàng)	*N/V.*	expectation; to expect
压力	(yā lì)	*N.*	pressure
过分	(guò fèn)	*Adj.*	excessive, over, too much
溺爱	(nì ài)	*V.*	to spoil (a child), to be excessively fond of
替	(tì)	*V.*	to take the place of, to substitute for
造成	(zào chéng)	*V.*	to cause, to result in
自主能力	(zì zhǔ néng lì)	*N.*	independence
差	(chà)	*Adj.*	lacking, poor

（二）

赵华： 中国常常说现在的儿童是"小皇帝"、"小太阳"，这到底是什么意思？

李子庆： 这主要是说中国从七十年代末以后出生的孩子，大多都是独生子女，虽然他们也许在学习成绩上不错，但是多数自主性[4]很差，不会做家务，不会做饭，甚至连学习、生活用品[5]都不会整理，农村的孩子也不会干农活。

赵华： 是吗？这些问题会不会导致儿童心理不健全？

李子庆： 对。这个问题已经引起了社会各界的重视。针对这些问题，很多学校都在开展各种活动，"小能手"活动就是其中的一种。

生词

皇帝	(huáng dì)	*N.*	emperor
太阳	(tài yáng)	*N.*	the sun
末	(mò)	*N.*	end
用品	(yòng pǐn)	*N.*	articles for use
农活	(nóng huó)	*N.*	farm work
导致	(dǎo zhì)	*V.*	to cause, to result in, to lead to

Notes [4]When attached to a verb or adjective, 性 functions as a suffix meaning "basic nature", "essential characteristic", or "-ability", as in 独立性 (independent spirit), 依赖性 (dependability), 可能性 (possibility).

[5]The suffix 品 may be attached to nouns or verbs to form nouns referring to products or commodities, as in 生活用品 (products used in everyday life), 商品 (commercial products), 工业产品 (industrial goods), 农产品 (produce). In the common expression 人品, however, 品 refers specifically to the moral character or qualities of a person. Example: 她人品很好 (She is a person of good moral character).

心理	(xīn lǐ)	*N/Adj.*	psychology; psychological
健全	(jiàn quán)	*Adj.*	normal and healthy, of sound mind and body
引起	(yǐn qǐ)	*V.*	to lead to, to arouse
社會各界	(shè huì gè jiè)	*NP.*	people from all walks of life
重視	(zhòng shì)	*V.*	to emphasize, to attach importance to
針對	(zhēn duì)	*V.*	to be aimed at, to be directed against
開展	(kāi zhǎn)	*V.*	to launch, to start
能手	(néng shǒu)	*N.*	a dab, a goodhand, a crackerjack, an expert

二、電視原文 ▯ TV original

讓兒童變成小能手
（根據原文改編）

　　在中國流行著這樣一句話：兒童是國家的未來。可見在這個世界上人口最多的國家對兒童教育的重視。但是由於近幾年生活水準(6)的提高和獨生子女家庭的增多，父母對孩子過分的溺愛和由此(7)產生孩子自主性差的現象也逐漸明顯起來。

　　前不久，天津舉辦了一次小能手活動，就是為了讓近幾年中國出現的這種孩子自主性差的趨勢得到某些程度的好轉。

　　由天津市婦女聯合會和教育局舉辦的家庭勞動小能手活動至今已進行了三屆。近些年，中國兒童自主能力差的現象已引起社會各界的重視。中國政府1992年在九十年代中國兒童發展規劃綱要中提出了提高全民族素質從兒童抓起的方針。

🖉 **Notes** (6)水準 vs. 水平: Both 水準 and 水平 mean "level" or "standard" and are generally interchangeable, as in 生活水平 or 生活水準 (standard of living), 文化水平 or 文化水準 (cultural level, level of refinement). The one exception is level of language proficiency, as in 中文水平 (proficiency level in Chinese), for which 水平 must be used.

　　(7)The expression 由此, derived from Classical Chinese, means 從這兒 and is used only in written settings. Examples: 由此向前 (to go forward from here); 由此往北 (to proceed north from here).

心理	(xīn lǐ)	N/Adj.	psychology; psychological
健全	(jiàn quán)	Adj.	normal and healthy, of sound mind and body
引起	(yǐn qǐ)	V.	to lead to, to arouse
社会各界	(shè huì gè jiè)	NP.	people from all walks of life
重视	(zhòng shì)	V.	to emphasize, to attach importance to
针对	(zhēn duì)	V.	to be aimed at, to be directed against
开展	(kāi zhǎn)	V.	to launch, to start
能手	(néng shǒu)	N.	a dab, a goodhand, a crackerjack, an expert

二、电视原文 🖥 TV original

让儿童变成小能手
（根据原文改编）

　　在中国流行着这样一句话：儿童是国家的未来。可见在这个世界上人口最多的国家对儿童教育的重视。但是由于近几年生活水准⑹的提高和独生子女家庭的增多，父母对孩子过分的溺爱和由此⑺产生孩子自主性差的现象也逐渐明显起来。

　　前不久，天津举办了一次小能手活动，就是为了让近几年中国出现的这种孩子自主性差的趋势得到某些程度的好转。

　　由天津市妇女联合会和教育局举办的家庭劳动小能手活动至今已进行了三届。近些年，中国儿童自主能力差的现象已引起社会各界的重视。中国政府1992年在九十年代中国儿童发展规划纲要中提出了提高全民族素质从儿童抓起的方针。

✎ **Notes** ⑹水准 vs. 水平: Both 水准 and 水平 mean "level" or "standard" and are generally interchangeable, as in 生活水平 or 生活水准 (standard of living), 文化水平 or 文化水准 (cultural level, level of refinement). The one exception is level of language proficiency, as in 中文水平 (proficiency level in Chinese), for which 水平 must be used.

　　⑺The expression 由此, derived from Classical Chinese, means 从这儿 and is used only in written settings. Examples: 由此向前 (to go forward from here); 由此往北 (to proceed north from here).

生活的富裕使不少的孩子產生了依賴的行為，而大部分的家長在教育觀念和方法上也顯露出許多問題。據天津市有關資料顯示，40%的家長怕影響孩子學習而不願意讓孩子參加勞動，50%多的家長每天替孩子整理學習生活用品。而在1,500名被調查的學生當中，47%不會做飯，農村70%多的不會幹農活。這些導致了少兒心理素質的不健全，對孩子甚至對一個國家的未來無疑是一種很大的隱患[8]，與今後社會對他們的要求也形成了很大的反差。

針對這一現象，天津市從1992年起開始了家庭勞動小能手的活動。規模由最初的十五萬人發展到今年的四十萬人，涉及到全市各個區縣，內容上也從過去的家務勞動、自我服務、工藝[9]製作發展到社會公益[10]勞動和素質培養等方面。

在小能手活動中，發現了許多自食其力的典型孩子。這個保定道小學的學生小時候因事故失去了雙臂，而他卻學會了用雙腳疊被子、洗臉、寫字。可惜由於本次節目時間有限，我們只有留在以後再向您作介紹了。

在動手能力差的問題上，城鎮孩子和農村（孩子）相比，可能體現得更明顯。但隨著農村生活結構的變化，鄉村孩子也出現了依賴性強的趨勢。這座農村小學校為了增強學生的自主能力，特意在校內開闢了一塊學農基地，承包給各班，並聘請[11]農民當輔導教師，這無疑給他們的今後奠定了一點基礎。

今年的"天津小能手活動"要到10月份才告結束，所以我們還有機會再向大家介紹這方面的情況。

Notes [8]隱患: 隱 means "hidden"; 患 means "calamity", "trouble", "peril". Originally a medical term, 隱患 is now used to refer to a hidden disease, or to undetected troubles or dangers in a person or organization, as in 社會的隱患 (hidden dangers in society). Unlike 問題, which can refer to problems in any area, 隱患 cannot be used for minor or everyday situations.

[9]公益 vs. 工藝: 公益 means "public interests" or "public welfare", as in 社會公益 (social welfare), 熱心公益 (enthusiastic about public welfare). Its homophone 工藝 means "craft" or "technology" in expressions such as 手工藝 (handicrafts), 工藝品 (industrial products, manufactured goods), 工藝水平 (level of craftsmanship).

[10]See Note (9).

[11]聘請, 邀請, and 請: 聘請, meaning "to appoint", "to hire", refers to taking up an official post or position, as in 聘請一位老師任校長 (to appoint a teacher to serve as university president). 邀請 is used to invite someone to a special event, as in 邀請她參加我們學校的大會 (to invite her to participate in our school conference), or to invite someone to do something that does not require a formal invitation, as in 邀請他來家中吃晚飯 (to invite him home for dinner). 請 also meeans "to request", "to invite", "to ask", but is less formal than 聘請 or 邀請. In colloquial Chinese it can mean either 聘請 or 邀請, depending on context. Examples: 我們請他當顧問。(We hired him as a consultant.) 我請他來家里吃飯。(I invited him to come over to the house to eat.)

生活的富裕使不少的孩子产生了依赖的行为，而大部分的家长在教育观念和方法上也显露出许多问题。据天津市有关资料显示，40%的家长怕影响孩子学习而不愿意让孩子参加劳动，50%多的家长每天替孩子整理学习生活用品。而在1,500名被调查的学生当中，47%不会做饭，农村70%多的不会干农活。这些导致了少儿心理素质的不健全，对孩子甚至对一个国家的未来无疑是一种很大的隐患[8]，与今后社会对他们的要求也形成了很大的反差。

针对这一现象，天津市从1992年起开始了家庭劳动小能手的活动。规模由最初的十五万人发展到今年的四十万人，涉及到全市各个区县，内容上也从过去的家务劳动、自我服务、工艺[9]制作发展到社会公益[10]劳动和素质培养等方面。

在小能手活动中，发现了许多自食其力的典型孩子。这个保定道小学的学生小时候因事故失去了双臂，而他却学会了用双脚叠被子、洗脸、写字。可惜由于本次节目时间有限，我们只有留在以后再向您作介绍了。

在动手能力差的问题上，城镇孩子和农村（孩子）相比，可能体现得更明显。但随着农村生活结构的变化，乡村孩子也出现了依赖性强的趋势。这座农村小学校为了增强学生的自主能力，特意在校内开辟了一块学农基地，承包给各班，并聘请[11]农民当辅导教师，这无疑给他们的今后奠定了一点基础。

今年的"天津小能手活动"要到10月份才告结束，所以我们还有机会再向大家介绍这方面的情况。

Notes [8]隐患: 隐 means "hidden"; 患 means "calamity", "trouble", "peril". Originally a medical term, 隐患 is now used to refer to a hidden disease, or to undetected troubles or dangers in a person or organization, as in 社会的隐患 (hidden dangers in society). Unlike 问题, which can refer to problems in any area, 隐患 cannot be used for minor or everyday situations.

[9]公益 vs. 工艺: 公益 means "public interests" or "public welfare", as in 社会公益 (social welfare), 热心公益 (enthusiastic about public welfare). Its homophone 工艺 means "craft" or "technology" in expressions such as 手工艺 (handicrafts), 工艺品 (industrial products, manufactured goods), 工艺水平 (level of craftsmanship).

[10]See Note (9).

[11]聘请, 邀请, and 请: 聘请, meaning "to appoint", "to hire", refers to taking up an official post or position, as in 聘请一位老师任校长 (to appoint a teacher to serve as university president). 邀请 is used to invite someone to a special event, as in 邀请她参加我们学校的大会 (to invite her to participate in our school conference), or to invite someone to do something that does not require a formal invitation, as in 邀请他来家中吃晚饭 (to invite him home for dinner). 请 also means "to request", "to invite", "to ask", but is less formal than 聘请 or 邀请. In colloquial Chinese it can mean either 聘请 or 邀请, depending on context. Examples: 我们请他当顾问. (We hired him as a consultant.) 我请他来家里吃饭. (I invited him to come over to the house to eat.)

生詞

流行	(liú xíng)	*Adj.*	popular, trendy, fashionable, in vogue
水準	(shuǐ zhǔn)	*N.*	standard, level
由此	(yóu cǐ)	*PrepP.*	from this, because of
產生	(chǎn shēng)	*V.*	to occur, to appear
明顯	(míng xiǎn)	*Adj.*	obvious, obviously, clearly
舉辦	(jǔ bàn)	*V.*	to hold, to sponsor
趨勢	(qū shì)	*N.*	tendency
某些	(mǒu xiē)	*Pron.*	some
程度	(chéng dù)	*N.*	degree
好轉	(hǎo zhuǎn)	*NP.*	positive changes, better, improvement
聯合會	(lián hé huì)	*NP.*	association, federation, union
教育局	(jiào yù jú)	*NP.*	education bureau
至今	(zhì jīn)	*Adv.*	up to today, up to now
屆	(jiè)	*Classifier.*	session
規劃	(guī huà)	*N.*	program, plan
綱要	(gāng yào)	*N.*	outline
民族	(mín zú)	*N.*	nation, nationality, race
方針	(fāng zhēn)	*N.*	guiding principle, policy
富裕	(fù yù)	*Adj.*	well-to-do, prosperous, well-off
依賴	(yī lài)	*V.*	to rely on, to depend on
行為	(xíng wéi)	*N.*	action, behavior
顯露	(xiǎn lù)	*V.*	to reveal, to demonstrate
資料	(zī liào)	*N.*	statistics, data, information
顯示	(xiǎn shì)	*V.*	to indicate, to show
調查	(diào chá)	*N/V.*	investigation; to investigate
無疑	(wú yí)	*Adv.*	undoubtedly, doubtless
隱患	(yǐn huàn)	*N.*	hidden disease, undetected disease
反差	(fǎn chā)	*N.*	contrast
涉及	(shè jí)	*V.*	to involve, to relate to
區縣	(qū xiàn)	*N.*	districts and counties
工藝	(gōng yì)	*N.*	handicraft, technology

生词

流行	(liú xíng)	Adj.	popular, trendy, fashionable, in vogue
水准	(shuǐ zhǔn)	N.	standard, level
由此	(yóu cǐ)	PrepP.	from this, because of
产生	(chǎn shēng)	V.	to occur, to appear
明显	(míng xiǎn)	Adj.	obvious, obviously, clearly
举办	(jǔ bàn)	V.	to hold, to sponsor
趋势	(qū shì)	N.	tendency
某些	(mǒu xiē)	Pron.	some
程度	(chéng dù)	N.	degree
好转	(hǎo zhuǎn)	NP.	positive changes, better, improvement
联合会	(lián hé huì)	NP.	association, federation, union
教育局	(jiào yù jú)	NP.	education bureau
至今	(zhì jīn)	Adv.	up to today, up to now
届	(jiè)	Classifier.	session
规划	(guī huà)	N.	program, plan
纲要	(gāng yào)	N.	outline
民族	(mín zú)	N.	nation, nationality, race
方针	(fāng zhēn)	N.	guiding principle, policy
富裕	(fù yù)	Adj.	well-to-do, prosperous, well-off
依赖	(yī lài)	V.	to rely on, to depend on
行为	(xíng wéi)	N.	action, behavior
显露	(xiǎn lù)	V.	to reveal, to demonstrate
资料	(zī liào)	N.	statistics, data, information
显示	(xiǎn shì)	V.	to indicate, to show
调查	(diào chá)	N/V.	investigation; to investigate
无疑	(wú yí)	Adv.	undoubtedly, doubtless
隐患	(yǐn huàn)	N.	hidden disease, undetected disease
反差	(fǎn chā)	N.	contrast
涉及	(shè jí)	V.	to involve, to relate to
区县	(qū xiàn)	N.	districts and counties
工艺	(gōng yì)	N.	handicraft, technology

製作	(zhì zuò)	N.	make, manufacture
公益	(gōng yì)	NP.	public welfare
自食其力	(zì shí qí lì)	Idiom.	self-supporting, self-reliant
典型	(diǎn xíng)	Adj.	typical
保定道	(bǎo dìng dào)	Place N.	name of a street
事故	(shì gù)	N.	accident
雙臂	(shuāng bì)	NP.	both arms
疊	(dié)	V.	to fold, to make
被子	(bèi zi)	N.	quilt
本次	(běn cì)	Pron.	this time
節目	(jié mù)	N.	program
城鎮	(chéng zhèn)	NP.	cities and towns
體現	(tǐ xiàn)	V.	to represent, to embody
座	(zuò)	Classifier.	measure word for buildings
特意	(tè yì)	Adv.	for a special purpose, specially
開闢	(kāi pì)	V.	to open up, to start
基地	(jī dì)	N.	base
聘請	(pìn qǐng)	V.	to invite, to hire
輔導	(fǔ dǎo)	V.	to instruct, to tutor
奠定	(diàn dìng)	V.	to lay, to pave, to establish
基礎	(jī chǔ)	N.	basis, foundation

制作	(zhì zuò)	*N.*	make, manufacture
公益	(gōng yì)	*NP.*	public welfare
自食其力	(zì shí qí lì)	*Idiom.*	self-supporting, self-reliant
典型	(diǎn xíng)	*Adj.*	typical
保定道	(bǎo dìng dào)	*Place N.*	name of a street
事故	(shì gù)	*N.*	accident
双臂	(shuāng bì)	*NP.*	both arms
叠	(dié)	*V.*	to fold, to make
被子	(bèi zi)	*N.*	quilt
本次	(běn cì)	*Pron.*	this time
节目	(jié mù)	*N.*	program
城镇	(chéng zhèn)	*NP.*	cities and towns
体现	(tǐ xiàn)	*V.*	to represent, to embody
座	(zuò)	*Classifier.*	measure word for buildings
特意	(tè yì)	*Adv.*	for a special purpose, specially
开辟	(kāi pì)	*V.*	to open up, to start
基地	(jī dì)	*N.*	base
聘请	(pìn qǐng)	*V.*	to invite, to hire
辅导	(fǔ dǎo)	*V.*	to instruct, to tutor
奠定	(diàn dìng)	*V.*	to lay, to pave, to establish
基础	(jī chǔ)	*N.*	basis, foundation

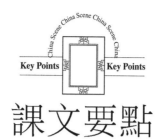

課文要點

一、詞語解釋 Words and Phrases

（一）文言詞、慣用詞 (Classical Chinese and idiomatic expressions)

> 1、各界＝各行各業、各個領域
>
> ☞ 中國兒童自主能力差的現象已引起社會各界的重視。
>
> 2、可見＝可以看見、想見
>
> ☞ 可見在這個世界上人口最多的國家對兒童教育的重視。
>
> 3、由此＝從這一點（方面）
>
> ☞ 由此產生的孩子自主性差的現象也逐漸明顯起來。
>
> 4、至今＝到現在
>
> ☞ 由天津市婦女聯合會和教育局舉辦的家庭勞動小能手活動至今已進行了三屆。
>
> 5、據＝根據
>
> ☞ 據天津市有關資料顯示，50%多的家長每天替孩子整理學習生活用品。
>
> 6、而＝但是
>
> ☞ 而在1500名被調查的學生當中，47%不會做飯。
>
> 7、與＝跟
>
> ☞ 與今後社會對他們的要求也形成了很大的反差。
>
> 8、由＝從
>
> ☞ 規模由最初的十五萬人發展到今年的四十萬人。

（二）成語 (idioms)

> ◆ 自食其力: earn one's living, self-supporting

课文要点

一、词语解释 Words and Phrases

（一）文言词、惯用词 (Classical Chinese and idiomatic expressions)

1、各界 = 各行各业、各个领域

☞ 中国儿童自主能力差的现象已引起社会各界的重视。

2、可见 = 可以看见、想见

☞ 可见在这个世界上人口最多的国家对儿童教育的重视。

3、由此 = 从这一点（方面）

☞ 由此产生的孩子自主性差的现象也逐渐明显起来。

4、至今 = 到现在

☞ 由天津市妇女联合会和教育局举办的家庭劳动小能手活动至今已进行了三届。

5、据 = 根据

☞ 据天津市有关资料显示，50%多的家长每天替孩子整理学习生活用品。

6、而 = 但是

☞ 而在1500名被调查的学生当中，47%不会做饭。

7、与 = 跟

☞ 与今后社会对他们的要求也形成了很大的反差。

8、由 = 从

☞ 规模由最初的十五万人发展到今年的四十万人。

（二）成语 (idioms)

◆ 自食其力: earn one's living, self-supporting

二、書面語、正式語、口語對照表 ⅢⅢⅢWritten/formal/colloquial Comparison

	書面／正式語	口語		書面／正式語	口語
1	針對…問題	對…問題	11	隱患	將來的大問題／不容易覺察的大問題
2	可見	可以看到／知道	12	由	從
3	由此	從這兒	13	最初	一開始
4	逐漸／漸漸	一點兒一點兒地	14	涉及／遍及到	影響到
5	前不久	不久以前	15	因	因為
6	舉／開辦	辦	16	失去／失掉	沒有了
7	某些程度	一定程度	17	本次	這一次
8	至今	到今天	18	由於…有限	因為…不夠
9	已	已經	19	今後	以後
10	無疑／肯定	一定			

三、句型 ❖Sentence Structures

（一）造成／導致（……的問題／情況／困難）(to lead to the consequences of, to result in)

> ✍ 造成／導致（的問題／情況／困難）means "to lead to the consequences of", "to result in". The two verbs 造成 and 導致 are interchangeable in most cases. They can take object phrases such as 的問題, 的情況, 的困難, and 的現象. Unlike their English counterpart, 造成 and 導致 can only take nouns that indicate undesirable situations, problems, or difficulties. Positive and even neutral nouns are not normally used as objects of 造成 or 導致.

☞ 看來，一家一個孩子的政策控制了人口，可是也造成了很多社會問題。

1、父母對孩子過分溺愛，甚麼事都替孩子幹，因此造成了中國兒童自主能力差的問題。
Parents spoil their children and do everything for them. As a result, Chinese children lack independence.

2、中國政府的開放政策雖然促進了經濟發展，可是也造成了很多社會問題，流動人口問題就是一個很好的例子。
Although Chinese government policy has promoted economic development, it has also caused many social problems. The floating population is a good example.

119

二、书面语、正式语、口语对照表 ▦ Written/formal/colloquial Comparison

	书面／正式语	口语		书面／正式语	口语
1	针对…问题	对…问题	11	隐患	将来的大问题／不容易觉察的大问题
2	可见	可以看到／知道	12	由	从
3	由此	从这儿	13	最初	一开始
4	逐渐／渐渐	一点儿一点儿地	14	涉及／遍及到	影响到
5	前不久	不久以前	15	因	因为
6	举／开办	办	16	失去／丢掉	没有了
7	某些程度	一定程度	17	本次	这一次
8	至今	到今天	18	由于…有限	因为…不够
9	已	已经	19	今后	以后
10	无疑／肯定	一定			

三、句型 ▦ Sentence Structures

（一）造成／导致（……的问题／情况／困难）(to lead to the consequences of, to result in)

> ✍ 造成／导致（的问题／情况／困难）means "to lead to the consequences of", "to result in". The two verbs 造成 and 导致 are interchangeable in most cases. They can take object phrases such as 的问题, 的情况, 的困难, and 的现象. Unlike their English counterpart, 造成 and 导致 can only take nouns that indicate undesirable situations, problems, or difficulties. Positive and even neutral nouns are not normally used as objects of 造成 or 导致.

☞ 看来，一家一个孩子的政策控制了人口，可是也造成了很多社会问题。

1、父母对孩子过分溺爱，什么事都替孩子干，因此造成了中国儿童自主能力差的问题。

Parents spoil their children and do everything for them. As a result, Chinese children lack independence.

2、中国政府的开放政策虽然促进了经济发展，可是也造成了很多社会问题，流动人口问题就是一个很好的例子。

Although Chinese government policy has promoted economic development, it has also caused many social problems. The floating population is a good example.

119

問：為甚麼現在單親家庭越來越多？是甚麼原因造成的？

答：＿＿＿＿＿＿＿＿＿＿＿＿＿＿＿＿＿＿＿＿＿＿＿　。

（二）重視 (to emphasize, to place emphasis on)

> ✍ 重視, "to emphasize", "to place emphasis on", can take an object either preverbally or postverbally. Examples: 家長對孩子的教育都很重視. (All parents place emphasis on their children's education.) 家長都很重視孩子的教育. (All parents emphasize their children's education.) When 重視 is preceded by its object, the object must be introduced by 對. When negating this structure, the negative particle is placed before the verb. Example: 有些家長對孩子的教育不重視. (Some parents do not place emphasis on their children's education.)

☞ 在中國流行著這樣一句話：兒童是國家的未來。可見在這個世界上人口最多的國家對兒童教育的重視。

1、你覺得中國政府對人口控制非常重視嗎？

Do you think that the Chinese government places enough emphasis on population control?

2、現在的家長對孩子的自主性培養很不重視。很多孩子只會念書，其它甚麼都不會做。

Parents these days do not emphasize teaching their children to be independent. Therefore, many children know nothing but study.

問：＿＿＿＿＿＿＿＿＿＿＿＿＿＿＿＿＿＿＿＿＿＿＿？

答：我們單位對職工提出的建議既不重視也不採納。真讓人幹得沒意思。

（三）舉辦……活動（／比賽／會議）(to sponsor, to organize)

> ✍ 舉辦, "to sponsor", "to organize", is a verb that normally takes objects such as 活動, 比賽 or 會議. In most situations, 舉辦 is interchangeable with 舉行. With the passive use of 舉辦, 由 must be used to introduce the agent. Example: 這個活動由教育局舉辦. (This activity was organized by the Education Bureau.)

☞ 前不久，天津舉辦了一次小能手活動，就是為了讓近幾年中國出現的這種孩子自主性差的趨勢得到某些程度的好轉。

1、明天我們學校舉辦中文比賽活動，你要參加嗎？

Our school will be holding a Chinese language contest tomorrow. Would you like to attend?

120

问：为什么现在单亲家庭越来越多？是什么原因造成的？

答：_____。

（二）重视 (to emphasize, to place emphasis on)

✍ 重视, "to emphasize", "to place emphasis on", can take an object either preverbally or postverbally. Examples: 家长对孩子的教育都很重视. (All parents place emphasis on their children's education.) 家长都很重视孩子的教育. (All parents emphasize their children's education.) When 重视 is preceded by its object, the object must be introduced by 对. When negating this structure, the negative particle is placed before the verb. Example: 有些家长对孩子的教育不重视. (Some parents do not place emphasis on their children's education.)

☞ 在中国流行着这样一句话：儿童是国家的未来。可见在这个世界上人口最多的国家对儿童教育的重视。

1、你觉得中国政府对人口控制非常重视吗？

Do you think that the Chinese government places enough emphasis on population control?

2、现在的家长对孩子的自主性培养很不重视。很多孩子只会念书，其它什么都不会做。

Parents these days do not emphasize teaching their children to be independent. Therefore, many children know nothing but study.

问：_____?

答：我们单位对职工提出的建议既不重视也不采纳。真让人干得没意思。

（三）举办……活动（／比赛／会议）(to sponsor, to organize)

✍ 举办, "to sponsor", "to organize", is a verb that normally takes objects such as 活动, 比赛 or 会议. In most situations, 举办 is interchangeable with 举行. With the passive use of 举办, 由 must be used to introduce the agent. Example: 这个活动由教育局举办. (This activity was organized by the Education Bureau.)

☞ 前不久，天津举办了一次小能手活动，就是为了让近几年中国出现的这种孩子自主性差的趋势得到某些程度的好转。

1、明天我们学校举办中文比赛活动，你要参加吗？

Our school will be holding a Chinese language contest tomorrow. Would you like to attend?

2、天津舉辦的小能手活動就是要解決兒童自主性差的問題。

Tianjin is sponsoring a campaign to solve the problems caused by lack of independence in children.

問：最近幾年你們學生會都做了些甚麼事情？

答：＿＿＿＿＿＿＿＿＿＿＿＿＿＿＿＿＿＿＿＿＿。

（四）使（／讓）⋯⋯得到⋯⋯好轉 (to improve something, to make something take a turn for the better)

> ✍ 使（／讓）⋯⋯得到⋯⋯好轉, "to improve something", "to make something take a turn for the better", is often used in formal and written settings. While 使 and 讓 are interchangeable, 使 is more formal than 讓. The verb 得到, "to receive" or "to get", usually takes a verb phrase as its object, indicating the passive voice, as in 得到好轉 (to be improved), 得到解決 (to be resolved), 得到支持 (to receive support). The modifying elements often inserted between 得到 and 好轉 include 一定程度的 (a definite level), 一些 (some), and 某些程度的 (a certain level). Examples: 中國的人口過多的趨勢最近得到一些好轉. (China's population problem has recently improved somewhat.) 這家公司的資金問題最近得到某些程度的好轉. (This company's financial difficulty has recently experienced some degree of improvement.)

☞ 前不久，天津舉辦了一次小能手活動，就是為了讓近幾年中國出現的這種孩子自主性差的趨勢得到某些程度的好轉。

1、為了讓這個問題得到好轉，學校組織了很多反對喝酒的活動。

In order to bring about improvement, the school has organized a campaign against drinking.

2、農民下海當個體戶讓這個地方的土地緊張問題得到了一定程度的好轉。

Farmers who have become entrepreneurs have helped improve the land shortage situation.

問：現在亞洲的經濟情況不太好，你知道中國政府做了些甚麼事情讓這種情況得到好轉嗎？

答：＿＿＿＿＿＿＿＿＿＿＿＿＿＿＿＿＿＿＿＿＿。

（五）據有關資料顯示 (according to relevant statistics or data)

> ✍ 據有關資料顯示, "according to relevant statistics or data", is an adverbial phrase often placed at the beginning of a sentence. Unlike English, such phrases have a fixed position before the subject. A comma is always inserted between the phrase and the subject that follows.

2、天津举办的小能手活动就是要解决儿童自主性差的问题。

Tianjin is sponsoring a campaign to solve the problems caused by lack of independence in children.

问：最近几年你们学生会都做了些什么事情？

答：_____。

（四）使（／让）……得到……好转 (to improve something, to make something take a turn for the better)

> ✍ 使（／让）……得到……好转, "to improve something", "to make something take a turn for the better", is often used in formal and written settings. While 使 and 让 are interchangeable, 使 is more formal than 让. The verb 得到, "to receive" or "to get", usually takes a verb phrase as its object, indicating the passive voice, as in 得到好转 (to be improved), 得到解决 (to be resolved), 得到支持 (to receive support). The modifying elements often inserted between 得到 and 好转 include 一定程度的 (a definite level), 一些 (some), and 某些程度的 (a certain level). Examples: 中国的人口过多的趋势最近得到一些好转. (China's population problem has recently improved somewhat.) 这家公司的资金问题最近得到某些程度的好转. (This company's financial difficulty has recently experienced some degree of improvement.)

☞ 前不久，天津举办了一次小能手活动，就是为了让近几年中国出现的这种孩子自主性差的趋势得到某些程度的好转。

1、为了让这个问题得到好转，学校组织了很多反对喝酒的活动。

In order to bring about improvement, the school has organized a campaign against drinking.

2、农民下海当个体户让这个地方的土地紧张问题得到了一定程度的好转。

Farmers who have become entrepreneurs have helped improve the land shortage situation.

问：现在亚洲的经济情况不太好，你知道中国政府做了些什么事情让这种情况得到好转吗？

答：_____。

（五）据有关资料显示 (according to relevant statistics or data)

> ✍ 据有关资料显示, "according to relevant statistics or data", is an adverbial phrase often placed at the beginning of a sentence. Unlike English, such phrases have a fixed position before the subject. A comma is always inserted between the phrase and the subject that follows.

☞ 據天津市有關資料顯示，40%的家長怕影響孩子學習而不願意讓孩子參加勞動，50%多的家長每天替孩子整理學習生活用品。

1、據有關資料顯示，美國50%的中學生都吸過毒，80%的中學生吸過煙。

According to relevant statistics, 50% of middle school students in the U.S. have used drugs, and 80% have smoked cigarettes.

2、據有關資料顯示，中國的獨生子女生活能力差、依賴性很強。這個問題已引起了社會的重視。

According to relevant data, China's single children lack the ability to take care of themselves and are very dependent. This problem has attracted society's attention.

問：你知道一般的美國人平均每個禮拜吃幾次快餐？

答：＿＿＿＿＿＿＿＿＿＿＿＿＿＿＿＿＿＿＿＿＿。

（六）與⋯⋯形成反差（／對比）(to form a contrast between)

✍ A 與 B 形成反差（／對比），"to form a contrast between A and B", is used to express drastic differences or extremes between two things. The preposition 與 can be used interchangeably with 和 and 跟, but 與 is more formal. The modifying elements inserted between 形成 and 反差 can be 很大的 (big, major), 強烈的 (strong), 令人吃驚的 (surprising), etc. Example: 這幾年中國的計劃經濟和市場經濟發展形成了強烈的反差。(Over the last few years, the development of China's market economy has contrasted sharply with that of the planned economy.)

☞ 這些導致了少兒心理素質的不健全，對孩子甚至對一個國家的未來無疑是一種很大的隱患，與今後社會對他們的要求也形成了很大的反差。

1、在管理方法上，私營企業與國營企業形成了很大的反差。

Private enterprise contrasts sharply with state-owned enterprise with respect to management style.

2、獨生子女的問題與今後社會對他們的要求形成了很大的反差。

The problems of single children are incompatible with the future demands of society.

問：你認為政府的住房政策和老百姓的實際買房能力反差很大嗎？

答：當然。＿＿＿＿＿＿＿＿＿＿＿＿＿＿＿＿＿＿＿。

☞ 据天津市有关资料显示，40%的家长怕影响孩子学习而不愿意让孩子参加劳动，50%多的家长每天替孩子整理学习生活用品。

1、据有关资料显示，美国50％的中学生都吸过毒，80%的中学生吸过烟。
According to relevant statistics, 50% of middle school students in the U.S. have used drugs, and 80% have smoked cigarettes.

2、据有关资料显示，中国的独生子女生活能力差、依赖性很强。这个问题已引起了社会的重视。
According to relevant data, China's single children lack the ability to take care of themselves and are very dependent. This problem has attracted society's attention.

问：你知道一般的美国人平均每个礼拜吃几次快餐？
答：＿＿＿＿＿＿＿＿＿＿＿＿＿＿＿＿＿。

（六）与……形成反差（／对比）(to form a contrast between)

✍ A 与 B 形成反差（／对比），"to form a contrast between A and B", is used to express drastic differences or extremes between two things. The preposition 与 can be used interchangeably with 和 and 跟, but 与 is more formal. The modifying elements inserted between 形成 and 反差 can be 很大的 (big, major), 强烈的 (strong), 令人吃惊的 (surprising), etc. Example: 这几年中国的计划经济和市场经济发展形成了强烈的反差。(Over the last few years, the development of China's market economy has contrasted sharply with that of the planned economy.)

☞ 这些导致了少儿心理素质的不健全，对孩子甚至对一个国家的未来无疑是一种很大的隐患，与今后社会对他们的要求也形成了很大的反差。

1、在管理方法上，私营企业与国营企业形成了很大的反差。
Private enterprise contrasts sharply with state-owned enterprise with respect to management style.

2、独生子女的问题与今后社会对他们的要求形成了很大的反差。
The problems of single children are incompatible with the future demands of society.

问：你认为政府的住房政策和老百姓的实际买房能力反差很大吗？
答：当然。＿＿＿＿＿＿＿＿＿＿＿＿＿＿＿＿＿。

（七）由（／從）……發展到…… (to develop from A to B)

> ✍ 由（／從）A 發展到 B, "to develop from A to B" is a structure indicating a gradual change or expansion. The two referents of 發展到, A and B, must be split by the verb. The object indicating the original state A is placed before the verb and introduced with the preposition 由 or 從. The object indicating the changed state B must appear after the verb. Examples: 在這十年中，他的家從三口人發展成十五口人. (Over the last decade, the size of his family has expanded from three people to fifteen people.) 沒想到何茹已經從不做功課發展到不去上學，也不要考試. (I never would have thought that He Ru already has gone from not doing her homework to not wanting to go to school or take exams.) While the prepositions 由 and 從 are interchangeable in this structure, 由 is more formal than 從.

☞ 規模由最初的十五萬人發展到今年的四十萬人，涉及到全市各個區縣，內容上也從過去的家務勞動、自我服務、工藝製作發展到社會公益勞動和素質培養等方面。

1、在短短的三十年中，中國的人口從九百六十萬發展到十三億。

Within thirty years, China's population has grown from 9.6 million to 1.3 billion.

2、這種小能手活動由一個學校發展到今天的15萬人的大規模。

This type of activity began with one school and now involves 150,000 people.

問：你們學校從建立到現在已經多少年了？發展得怎麼樣？
答：＿＿＿＿＿＿＿＿＿＿＿＿＿＿＿＿＿＿＿＿＿＿＿＿。

（八）涉及到…… (to involve, to touch upon, to be tied to)

> ✍ 涉及（到）, "to involve", "to be tied to", "to touch upon", is a verb phrase in which 到 can be omitted. This phrase can be used as a main verb, as in 這種規模的改革會涉及很多問題 (reform of this scope touches upon many problems); or a secondary verb supplementing the main verb, as in 這樣的計劃太復雜，涉及到很多問題. (These kinds of plans are too complicated; they are tied to too many other issues.) When negating 涉及, either 不 or 沒有 can be used. Examples: 這次人口討論不夠成功，沒有涉及到有關人口政策的問題. (The discussions on population have not been successful enough this time around; they did not touch on questions related to population policy.) 這個政策並不涉及國營企業的工作人員. (This policy does not really involve the workers at state-owned businesses.)

☞ 規模由最初的十五萬人發展到今年的四十萬人，涉及到全市各個區縣，內容上也從過去的家務勞動，自我服務，工藝製作發展到社會公益勞動和素質培養等方面。

1、中國的經濟問題總是涉及到中國的管理機制問題。

China's economic problems are always tied to problems in its management system.

（七）由（／从）……发展到…… (to develop from A to B)

> ✍ 由（／从）A 发展到 B, "to develop from A to B" is a structure indicating a gradual change or expansion. The two referents of 发展到, A and B, must be split by the verb. The object indicating the original state A is placed before the verb and introduced with the preposition 由 or 从. The object indicating the changed state B must appear after the verb. Examples: 在这十年中，他的家从三口人发展成十五口人。 (Over the last decade, the size of his family has expanded from three people to fifteen people.) 没想到何茹已经从不做功课发展到不去上学，也不要考试。 (I never would have thought that He Ru already has gone from not doing her homework to not wanting to go to school or take exams.) While the prepositions 由 and 从 are interchangeable in this structure, 由 is more formal than 从.

☞ 规模由最初的十五万人发展到今年的四十万人，涉及到全市各个区县，内容上也从过去的家务劳动、自我服务、工艺制作发展到社会公益劳动和素质培养等方面。

1、在短短的三十年中，中国的人口从九百六十万发展到十三亿。

Within thirty years, China's population has grown from 9.6 million to 1.3 billion.

2、这种小能手活动由一个学校发展到今天的15万人的大规模。

This type of activity began with one school and now involves 150,000 people.

问：你们学校从建立到现在已经多少年了？发展得怎么样？

答：_____。

（八）涉及到…… (to involve, to touch upon, to be tied to)

> ✍ 涉及（到），"to involve", "to be tied to", "to touch upon", is a verb phrase in which 到 can be omitted. This phrase can be used as a main verb, as in 这种规模的改革会涉及很多问题 (reform of this scope touches upon many problems); or a secondary verb supplementing the main verb, as in 这样的计划太复杂，涉及到很多问题. (These kinds of plans are too complicated; they are tied to too many other issues.) When negating 涉及, either 不 or 没有 can be used. Examples: 这次人口讨论不够成功，没有涉及到有关人口政策的问题. (The discussions on population have not been successful enough this time around; they did not touch on questions related to population policy.) 这个政策并不涉及国营企业的工作人员. (This policy does not really involve the workers at state-owned businesses.)

☞ 规模由最初的十五万人发展到今年的四十万人，涉及到全市各个区县，内容上也从过去的家务劳动，自我服务，工艺制作发展到社会公益劳动和素质培养等方面。

1、中国的经济问题总是涉及到中国的管理机制问题。

China's economic problems are always tied to problems in its management system.

2、管理問題也涉及到幹部、職工、和技術員的工資和福利問題。

Problems of management involve issues such as wages and fringe benefits of cadres, workers, and technicians.

問：這次學生會開會討論涉及到一些甚麼問題？
答：＿＿＿＿＿＿＿＿＿＿＿＿＿＿＿＿＿＿＿＿。

（九）隨著⋯⋯的（變化／發展／改善／進步）(accompanying, along with, related to)

> ✍ 隨著, "accompanying", "along with", "related to", is normally used to form an adverbial structure before the subject of a main clause. 隨著 is often followed by nouns such as 發展, 變化, 改善, 提高, 進步, indicating that one situation changes along with another. It is usually used in formal contexts. Example: 隨著市場經濟的發展，中國人的想法越來越活。(Following the development of China's market economy, Chinese people have begun to think more and more flexibly.) The 隨著 phrase can never be placed after the subject or at the end of a sentence.

☞ 但隨著農村生活結構的變化，鄉村孩子也出現了依賴性強的趨勢。

1、隨著中國人口問題的出現，中國的經濟問題、住房問題、工作問題也同時出現了。

China's economic, housing, and employment problems have emerged simultaneously as a result of the population problem.

2、隨著中國經濟改革的快速發展，中國的家庭結構也發生了變化。

A change in China's family structure has occurred as a result of rapid economic reform.

問：這幾年人們的錢好像越來越多，多貴的東西都有人買。
答：是啊。＿＿＿＿＿＿＿＿＿＿＿＿＿＿＿＿＿＿＿。

（十）無疑 (undoubtedly, without a doubt)

> ✍ 無疑, "undoubtedly", "without a doubt", is an adverb which can be placed before or after a subject and immediately before a verb. Examples: 無疑，這種自主能力要靠家長來培養。(Without a doubt, this sort of independence depends on nurturing from one's parents.) 這種自主能力無疑要靠家長來培養。(This sort of independence undoubtedly depends on nurturing from one's parents.) 無疑 is more commonly used in formal and written Chinese.

☞ 這座農村小學校為了增強學生的自主能力，特意在校內開闢了一塊學農基地，承包給各班，並聘請農民當輔導教師。這無疑給他們的今後奠定了一點基礎。

2、管理问题也涉及到干部、职工、和技术员的工资和福利问题。
Problems of management involve issues such as wages and fringe benefits of cadres, workers, and technicians.

问：这次学生会开会讨论涉及到一些什么问题？
答：_____。

（九）随着……的（变化／发展／改善／进步）(accompanying, along with, related to)

> ✐ 随着, "accompanying", "along with", "related to", is normally used to form an adverbial structure before the subject of a main clause. 随着 is often followed by nouns such as 发展, 变化, 改善, 提高, 进步, indicating that one situation changes along with another. It is usually used in formal contexts. Example: 随着市场经济的发展，中国人的想法越来越活. (Following the development of China's market economy, Chinese people have begun to think more and more flexibly.) The 随着 phrase can never be placed after the subject or at the end of a sentence.

☞ 但随着农村生活结构的变化，乡村孩子也出现了依赖性强的趋势。

1、随着中国人口问题的出现，中国的经济问题、住房问题、工作问题也同时出现了。
China's economic, housing, and employment problems have emerged simultaneously as a result of the population problem.
2、随着中国经济改革的快速发展，中国的家庭结构也发生了变化。
A change in China's family structure has occurred as a result of rapid economic reform.

问：这几年人们的钱好象越来越多，多贵的东西都有人买。
答：是啊。_____。

（十）无疑 (undoubtedly, without a doubt)

> ✐ 无疑, "undoubtedly", "without a doubt", is an adverb which can be placed before or after a subject and immediately before a verb. Examples: 无疑，这种自主能力要靠家长来培养. (Without a doubt, this sort of independence depends on nurturing from one's parents.) 这种自主能力无疑要靠家长来培养. (This sort of independence undoubtedly depends on nurturing from one's parents.) 无疑 is more commonly used in formal and written Chinese.

☞ 这座农村小学校为了增强学生的自主能力，特意在校内开辟了一块学农基地，承包给各班，并聘请农民当辅导教师。这无疑给他们的今后奠定了一点基础。

1、他無疑是我最崇拜、最喜歡的人。

He is undoubtedly the person I most love and adore.

2、從表情看，他無疑又經歷了一次驚濤駭浪。

It is apparent from his facial expression that he has undoubtedly experienced great hardship.

問：你認為中國的經濟在亞洲經濟危機中又經歷了一次驚濤駭浪嗎？

答：＿＿＿＿＿＿＿＿＿＿＿＿＿＿＿＿＿＿＿＿＿＿。

（十一）給（／為）……奠定……基礎 (to establish a foundation for, to lay a foundation for)

> ✍ 給（／為）……奠定……基礎, "to establish a foundation for" or "to lay a foundation for", is a structure often used in formal and written Chinese. The prepositions 給 and為 are interchangeable. 為, however, is more formal than 給. When negating this pattern, the negative particle must be placed before 給 or 為 instead of before 奠定. The spoken version of this structure is 打基礎.

☞ 這座農村小學校為了增強學生的自主能力，特意在校內開闢了一塊學農基地，承包給各班，並聘請農民當輔導教師。這無疑給他們的今後奠定了一點基礎。

1、這種小能手活動真能給兒童以後的獨立生活奠定基礎嗎？

Can this type of skills campaign really provide a foundation for children's independent lives later on?

2、我們上的一對一的單班課為我們的中文奠定了很好的基礎。

Our one-on-one session provides a very good foundation for our Chinese.

問：中學的送報工作對你日後的生活有甚麼幫助？

答：＿＿＿＿＿＿＿＿＿＿＿＿＿＿＿＿＿＿＿＿＿＿。

1、他无疑是我最崇拜、最喜欢的人。

He is undoubtedly the person I most love and adore.

2、从表情看，他无疑又经历了一次惊涛骇浪。

It is apparent from his facial expression that he has undoubtedly experienced great hardship.

问：你认为中国的经济在亚洲经济危机中又经历了一次惊涛骇浪吗？

答：_____。

（十一）给（／为）……奠定……基础 (to establish a foundation for, to lay a foundation for)

✍ 给（／为）……奠定……基础, "to establish a foundation for" or "to lay a foundation for", is a structure often used in formal and written Chinese. The prepositions 给 and 为 are interchangeable. 为, however, is more formal than 给. When negating this pattern, the negative particle must be placed before 给 or 为 instead of before 奠定. The spoken version of this structure is 打基础.

☞ 这座农村小学校为了增强学生的自主能力，特意在校内开辟了一块学农基地，承包给各班，并聘请农民当辅导教师。这无疑给他们的今后奠定了一点基础。

1、这种小能手活动真能给儿童以后的独立生活奠定基础吗？

Can this type of skills campaign really provide a foundation for children's independent lives later on?

2、我们上的一对一的单班课为我们的中文奠定了很好的基础。

Our one-on-one session provides a very good foundation for our Chinese.

问：中学的送报工作对你日后的生活有什么帮助？

答：_____。

四、文化背景知識 Cultural Notes

1. The Women's Federation (婦女聯合會), or 婦聯 for short, is a government-sponsored organization found in most cities in China. It seeks to promote and advance issues that will improve the working and social conditions of women.

2. The government organization in China that oversees all matters regarding education is called 教育部, or State Education Council. 教育局 (Education Bureaus), mentioned in our text, are local-level organs of the 教育部. They enforce government policies regarding education and manage all local matters regarding education.

3. The highest level of local administration in China is the province (省). Just three examples would be 廣東, 山西, and 台灣 (altogether, China has 22 provinces if not including 台灣, 5 autonomous regions, 4 municipalities 北京, 上海, 天津, and 重慶 (chóng qìng) directly under the central government, and 2 special autonomous regions Hong Kong and Macau). Provinces are in turn divided into a number of different smaller administrative units, such as counties (縣 xiàn), cities (城市 chéngshì), towns (鎮 zhèn), and villages (村 cūn).

四、文化背景知识 Cultural Notes

1. The Women's Federation (妇女联合会), or 妇联 for short, is a government-sponsored organization found in most cities in China. It seeks to promote and advance issues that will improve the working and social conditions of women.

2. The government organization in China that oversees all matters regarding education is called 教育部, or State Education Council. 教育局 (Education Bureaus), mentioned in our text, are local-level organs of the 教育部. They enforce government policies regarding education and manage all local matters regarding education.

3. The highest level of local administration in China is the province (省). Just three examples would be 广东, 山西, and 台湾 (altogether, China has 22 provinces if not including 台湾, 5 autonomous regions, 4 municipalities 北京, 上海, 天津, and 重庆 (chóng qìng) directly under the central government, and 2 special autonomous regions Hong Kong and Macau). Provinces are in turn divided into a number of different smaller administrative units, such as counties (县 xiàn), cities (城市 chéngshì), towns (镇 zhèn), and villages (村 cūn).

練習

語言結構 Structures

一、短語翻譯 (Phrase translation)

1. handicraft-making activities
2. standard of living
3. to be excessively fond of, to spoil
4. to result in being dependent on
5. the phenomenon of lacking independence
6. a tendency among Chinese children
7. to a certain degree
8. people from all walks of life
9. psychological state and behavior
10. doubtless
11. societal demand
12. self-supporting students
13. the structure of one's life

二、聽力練習 (Listening comprehension)

1、聽寫 (Dictation)

2、聽錄音並回答問題 (Answering questions while listening to the audio CD)
   (1) B 的甚麼經歷為他的今後生活奠定了很好的基礎？
   (2) 你在上大學前有過一些甚麼工作或者社會的經歷，這些經歷對你今後的生活有甚麼好處？

三、改寫下面劃線的詞 (Replace the underlined words)

　　從中國開放<u>至今</u>十多年了，中國<u>各界</u>都有很大的變化。人們<u>由</u>窮變富，想法也開放多了。<u>由此可見</u>，中國的改革開放是有必要的。

练习

语言结构 Structures

一、短语翻译 (Phrase translation)

1. handicraft-making activities
2. standard of living
3. to be excessively fond of, to spoil
4. to result in being dependent on
5. the phenomenon of lacking independence
6. a tendency among Chinese children
7. to a certain degree
8. people from all walks of life
9. psychological state and behavior
10. doubtless
11. societal demand
12. self-supporting students
13. the structure of one's life

二、听力练习 (Listening comprehension)

1、听写 (Dictation)

2、听录音并回答问题 (Answering questions while listening to the audio CD)
   (1) B 的什么经历为他的今后生活奠定了很好的基础？
   (2) 你在上大学前有过一些什么工作或者社会的经历，这些经历对你今后的生活有什么好处？

三、改写下面划线的词 (Replace the underlined words)

从中国开放<u>至今</u>十多年了，中国<u>各界</u>都有很大的变化。人们<u>由</u>穷变富，想法也开放多了。<u>由此可见</u>，中国的改革开放是有必要的。

四、完成句子 (Complete the sentences)

1、　　A：_____

　　　　B：是嗎？那中國人是怎麼對待這種出國熱的呢？

　　　　（隨著……，出現了……的趨勢）

2、　　A：你知道現在中國獨生子女有哪兩方面的問題？

　　　　B：_____

　　　　（據……資料顯示；由於……；導致了……）

3、　　A：舉辦這種家務勞動活動有甚麼好處？

　　　　B：舉辦這種活動一是＿＿＿＿＿＿＿＿＿＿，二是＿＿＿＿＿＿＿＿＿＿＿＿＿

　　　　（讓……得到好轉；奠定……基礎）

五、閱讀短文、回答問題 (Answering questions based on the reading passages)

據有關資料顯示，中國的人口有十三億，是世界上人口最多的一個國家。從六十年代起，中國就開始實行控制人口的政策。最早實行的是"一個不少，兩個正好"和晚婚的政策。這種政策在一定程度上控制了一些人口的增長，但是中國的人口在七十代仍然增長得很快。政府不得不實行"一家一個孩子"的政策。盡管這個政策已經實行了二十幾年了，人口的控制仍然很難。而"一家一個孩子"的政策給社會帶來的隱患也越來越明顯。比方說，很多孩子從小被父母過分溺愛，自主性很差，依賴性也很強。我們後街的王朋朋就是一個典型。朋朋今年十一歲了，雖然書念得不錯，常常考雙百，可是吃飯還要媽媽餵，衣服還要奶奶給穿；長這麼大，從來沒自己洗過臉，疊過被子。像他這樣的孩子怎麼可能知道"自食其力"的含義？無疑，中國現在不但面臨人口過多的問題，而且也面臨如何解決人口政策帶來的其他社會問題。

問題

(1) 請你談談中國的人口政策的發展和結果。

(2) 請你用學過的話談談美國的社會福利（Social Security）給社會帶來的問題。

有人調查了北京2294名小學生參加家務勞動的情況，結果發現這些學生平均每天幹家務的時間只有0.2小時，遠遠低於美國同齡孩子的人均1.2小時。某小學一低年級班共有32名學生，其中有20名不會穿衣，有10名需要父母幫助洗臉洗腳。

問題

(1) 這個調查說明了一個甚麼問題？

(2) 你認為中國應該怎麼解決這個問題？

四、完成句子 (Complete the sentences)

1、　A：_____

　　B：是吗？那中国人是怎么对待这种出国热的呢？

　　（随着……，出现了……的趋势）

2、　A：你知道现在中国独生子女有哪两方面的问题？

　　B：_____

　　（据……资料显示；由于……；导致了……）

3、　A：举办这种家务劳动活动有什么好处？

　　B：举办这种活动一是_____，二是_____

　　（让……得到好转；奠定……基础）

五、阅读短文、回答问题 (Answering questions based on the reading passages)

据有关资料显示，中国的人口有十三亿，是世界上人口最多的一个国家。从六十年代起，中国就开始实行控制人口的政策。最早实行的是"一个不少，两个正好"和晚婚的政策。这种政策在一定程度上控制了一些人口的增长，但是中国的人口在七十代仍然增长得很快。政府不得不实行"一家一个孩子"的政策。尽管这个政策已经实行了二十几年了，人口的控制仍然很难。而"一家一个孩子"的政策给社会带来的隐患也越来越明显。比方说，很多孩子从小被父母过分溺爱，自主性很差，依赖性也很强。我们后街的王朋朋就是一个典型。朋朋今年十一岁了，虽然书念得不错，常常考双百，可是吃饭还要妈妈喂，衣服还要奶奶给穿；长这么大，从来没自己洗过脸，叠过被子。象他这样的孩子怎么可能知道"自食其力"的含义？无疑，中国现在不但面临人口过多的问题，而且也面临如何解决人口政策带来的其他社会问题。

问题

　(1) 请你谈谈中国的人口政策的发展和结果。

　(2) 请你用学过的话谈谈美国的社会福利（Social Security）给社会带来的问题。

有人调查了北京2294名小学生参加家务劳动的情况，结果发现这些学生平均每天干家务的时间只有0.2小时，远远低于美国同龄孩子的人均1.2小时。某小学一低年级班共有32名学生，其中有20名不会穿衣，有10名需要父母帮助洗脸洗脚。

问题

　(1) 这个调查说明了一个什么问题？

　(2) 你认为中国应该怎么解决这个问题？

六、翻譯 (Translate sentences)

1. Recently, because of the enhanced standard of living and the increased number of single-child families, there is a tendency for children to be overly dependent on their parents.

2. The phenomenon of children's lack of independence caught the attention of people from all walks of life. The local government began to sponsor campaigns to help children learn to do housework.

3. As a result of economic reform and the opening of the country, the problems of state-owned businesses have become more and more obvious.

4. The scale of this enterprise has grown from an annual income of $60,000 to $100,000. Their business ranges from everyday goods to handicrafts.

六、翻译 (Translate sentences)

1. Recently, because of the enhanced standard of living and the increased number of single-child families, there is a tendency for children to be overly dependent on their parents.

2. The phenomenon of children's lack of independence caught the attention of people from all walks of life. The local government began to sponsor campaigns to help children learn to do housework.

3. As a result of economic reform and the opening of the country, the problems of state-owned businesses have become more and more obvious.

4. The scale of this enterprise has grown from an annual income of $60,000 to $100,000. Their business ranges from everyday goods to handicrafts.

語言實踐：Practice

一、根據課文回答問題 (Answering questions based on the dialogue)

1、中國近幾年的兒童普遍有一些甚麼問題？
2、針對這個問題，中國天津市婦女聯合會和教育局組織了一些甚麼活動？這些活動是根據甚麼方針組織的？
3、據有關資料顯示，家長在教育孩子的觀念上和方法上有甚麼問題？
4、這些問題對孩子、對國家、對社會有甚麼影響？
5、請你說說天津家庭勞動小能手活動的規模和內容。
6、保定道小學有一個典型學生，請你說說他的故事。
7、農村孩子現在有甚麼問題？學校用甚麼方法解決這個問題？

二、活動 (Activities)

　　去街道或者學校調查一下現在的獨生子女有甚麼優點，有甚麼問題。他們常做哪些家務？自主能力怎麼樣？他們的父母都希望他們怎麼樣？跟蹤一個五歲的小孩子一天，看他（她）一天都做些甚麼？

三、討論題 (Topics for discussion)

1、中國孩子，尤其是獨生子女生活能力差，自主性差，依賴性強的問題是怎麼產生的？
2、美國有沒有這個問題？美國父母的教育觀念和方法跟中國父母有甚麼不同？
3、你覺得小能手活動對小孩子的自主性有幫助嗎？你覺得除了小能手活動以外，社會還應該做些甚麼？

四、報告 (Presentation)

　　《獨生子女政策的好處和壞處》

语言实践 Practice

一、根据课文回答问题 (Answering questions based on the dialogue)

1、中国近几年的儿童普遍有一些什么问题？
2、针对这个问题，中国天津市妇女联合会和教育局组织了一些什么活动？这些活动是根据什么方针组织的？
3、据有关资料显示，家长在教育孩子的观念上和方法上有什么问题？
4、这些问题对孩子、对国家、对社会有什么影响？
5、请你说说天津家庭劳动小能手活动的规模和内容。
6、保定道小学有一个典型学生，请你说说他的故事。
7、农村孩子现在有什么问题？学校用什么方法解决这个问题？

二、活动 (Activities)

　　去街道或者学校调查一下现在的独生子女有什么优点，有什么问题。他们常做哪些家务？自主能力怎么样？他们的父母都希望他们怎么样？跟踪一个五岁的小孩子一天，看他（她）一天都做些什么？

三、讨论题 (Topics for discussion)

1、中国孩子，尤其是独生子女生活能力差，自主性差，依赖性强的问题是怎么产生的？
2、美国有没有这个问题？美国父母的教育观念和方法跟中国父母有什么不同？
3、你觉得小能手活动对小孩子的自主性有帮助吗？你觉得除了小能手活动以外，社会还应该做些什么？

四、报告 (Presentation)

　　《独生子女政策的好处和坏处》

五、看圖討論 (Picto-discussion)

1

2

3

4

5

6

五、看图讨论 (Picto-discussion)

1

2

3

4

5

6

第七課

午餐與社會變化

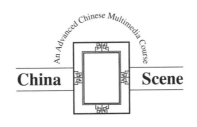

第七课

午餐与社会变化

課文

一、對話  Dialogs

---

（一）

安喜：　張老師，請教⁽¹⁾您一個問題：中國的流動人口多嗎？

張老師：多。自從改革開放以來，很多人的想法不知不覺有了很大的變化。他們不想待在家裡，所以就跑到外地去闖世界、作個體戶、開私營企業。這種情況在中國的大城市很普遍。就拿北京這個大都市來說吧，流動人口就有幾百萬。

安喜：　那大部分的流動人口都是從哪兒來的呢？

張老師：大多都是從農村來的。中國農村地少人多，要想致富，不那麼容易。很多人得跑到別的地方去工作，流動人口也就越來越多。

安喜：　中國的經濟發展給中國帶來了很多新鮮事。

生詞

請教	(qǐng jiào)	V.	to ask advice, to consult
安喜	(ān xǐ)	N.	An Xi, name of a person 人名
不知不覺	(bù zhī bù jué)	Adv.	unconsciously, without noticing
外地	(wài dì)	Adj.	part of the country other than where one is
新鮮事	(xīn xiān shì)	NP.	new things, fresh things

Notes ⁽¹⁾請教 is a verb meaning "to seek advice" or "to consult". Example: 關於這個問題我請教了很多農民專家. (I have sought advice on this issue from many agriculture experts.) When placed at the beginning of a sentence, 請教 forms a polite request meaning "may I ask", as in 請教一下，您知道這個字怎麼讀嗎？ (Excuse me, do you know how to pronounce this word?)

课文

一、对话  Dialogs

---

（一）

安喜：　张老师，请教⁽¹⁾您一个问题：中国的流动人口多吗？

张老师：多。自从改革开放以来，很多人的想法不知不觉有了很大的变化。他们不想
　　　　待在家里，所以就跑到外地去闯世界、作个体户、开私营企业。这种情况在
　　　　中国的大城市很普遍。就拿北京这个大都市来说吧，流动人口就有几百万。

安喜：　那大部分的流动人口都是从哪儿来的呢？

张老师：大多都是从农村来的。中国农村地少人多，要想致富，不那么容易。很多人
　　　　得跑到别的地方去工作，流动人口也就越来越多。

安喜：　中国的经济发展给中国带来了很多新鲜事。

生词

请教	(qǐng jiào)	*V.*	to ask advice, to consult
安喜	(ān xǐ)	*N.*	An Xi, name of a person 人名
不知不觉	(bù zhī bù jué)	*Adv.*	unconsciously, without noticing
外地	(wài dì)	*Adj.*	part of the country other than where one is
新鲜事	(xīn xiān shì)	*NP.*	new things, fresh things

Notes ⁽¹⁾请教 is a verb meaning "to seek advice" or "to consult". Example: 关于这个问题我请教了很多农民专家. (I have sought advice on this issue from many agriculture experts.) When placed at the beginning of a sentence, 请教 forms a polite request meaning "may I ask", as in 请教一下，您知道这个字怎么读吗？(Excuse me, do you know how to pronounce this word?)

（二）

安喜：　李師傅，你在吃飯[2]哪？對不起，打擾了。

李師傅：安喜，是你啊！沒關係，請坐，請坐。

安喜：　李師傅，你每天中午都在這兒吃盒飯嗎？

李師傅：對。這種盒飯有葷有素，花樣也很多，我很喜歡。

安喜：　李師傅，我有個問題想問問您，現在北京人都怎麼吃午飯？

李師傅：現在北京人吃午飯有這麼幾種：一是自己帶飯，二是在單位食堂[3]吃，三是買街頭盒飯，四是去酒樓吃，五是公司提供工作午餐，憑卡吃飯。

安喜：　那現在單位食堂還多嗎？

李師傅：不多了。很多人在個體戶、私營企業上班，沒有食堂，所以午餐都得在外邊吃。

安喜：　這樣看來，北京人的午餐已經走向社會化了。

李師傅：對。另外呢，改革開放了，老百姓的生活節奏也加快了，這種變化也要求人們吃又快又方便的午餐。

安喜：　那快速化也是北京人午餐的一個特點吧？

李師傅：對。還有一個特點，就是人們的收入增多了，要求也就高了，不但要吃飽，而且要有檔次[4]和品種，這樣午餐也就越來越多樣化了。

安喜：　真有意思，現在北京人的午餐有三化：社會化、快速化、多樣化。

生詞

| 盒飯 | (hé fàn) | *NP.* | boxed meal |

Notes [2]See Note (7).

[3]食堂 vs. 飯館: In most circumstances, 食堂 refers to a cafeteria associated with a work unit or school, as in 單位食堂 (work unit cafeteria). 飯館 usually refers to an independent restaurant. Two similar terms are 飯店 (large restaurant and hotel) and 酒樓 (fancy restaurant).

[4]檔次 vs. 質量: 檔次 means "quality", "ranking", or "grade". It refers specifically to a level of quality and carries implications about the social ranking of a product and the status of the people who use it. Example: 那家酒樓檔次很高。(That hotel is very high-class.) 質量, on the other hand, focuses on the intrinsic quality of something, not on its ranking or status. Example: 產品質量很高。(This product is high in quality.)

（二）

安喜： 李师傅，你在吃饭[2]哪？对不起，打扰了。

李师傅：安喜，是你啊！没关系，请坐，请坐。

安喜： 李师傅，你每天中午都在这儿吃盒饭吗？

李师傅：对。这种盒饭有荤有素，花样也很多，我很喜欢。

安喜： 李师傅，我有个问题想问问您，现在北京人都怎么吃午饭？

李师傅：现在北京人吃午饭有这么几种：一是自己带饭，二是在单位食堂[3]吃，三是买街头盒饭，四是去酒楼吃，五是公司提供工作午餐，凭卡吃饭。

安喜： 那现在单位食堂还多吗？

李师傅：不多了。很多人在个体户、私营企业上班，没有食堂，所以午餐都得在外边吃。

安喜： 这样看来，北京人的午餐已经走向社会化了。

李师傅：对。另外呢，改革开放了，老百姓的生活节奏也加快了，这种变化也要求人们吃又快又方便的午餐。

安喜： 那快速化也是北京人午餐的一个特点吧？

李师傅：对。还有一个特点，就是人们的收入增多了，要求也就高了，不但要吃饱，而且要有档次[4]和品种，这样午餐也就越来越多样化了。

安喜： 真有意思，现在北京人的午餐有三化：社会化、快速化、多样化。

生词

盒饭	(hé fàn)	NP.	boxed meal

Notes [2]See Note (7).

[3]食堂 vs. 饭馆: In most circumstances, 食堂 refers to a cafeteria associated with a work unit or school, as in 单位食堂 (work unit cafeteria). 饭馆 usually refers to an independent restaurant. Two similar terms are 饭店 (large restaurant and hotel) and 酒楼 (fancy restaurant).

[4]档次 vs. 质量: 档次 means "quality", "ranking", or "grade". It refers specifically to a level of quality and carries implications about the social ranking of a product and the status of the people who use it. Example: 那家酒楼档次很高. (That hotel is very high-class.) 质量, on the other hand, focuses on the intrinsic quality of something, not on its ranking or status. Example: 产品质量很高. (This product is high in quality.)

有葷有素	(yǒu hūn yǒu sù)	VP.	to have both meat and vegetable
花樣	(huā yàng)	N.	variety
食堂	(shí táng)	N.	cafeteria
街頭	(jiē tóu)	N.	on the street
酒樓	(jiǔ lóu)	N.	restaurant
憑卡	(píng kǎ)	V.	to use a card
社會化	(shè huì huà)	N.	to be socialized; socialization
節奏	(jié zòu)	N.	pace, rhythm
快速化	(kuài sù huà)	N.	to become fast-paced
檔次	(dàng cì)	N.	quality, high quality level
品種	(pǐn zhǒng)	N.	variety, assortment
多樣化	(duō yàng huà)	N.	to have variety

二、電視原文　TV original

北京人的午餐
（根據原文改編）

隨著中國改革開放的深入，北京已經步入了世界大都市的行列。這個大都市有著一千多萬的固定人口和幾百萬的流動人口。這麼大的城市吃午飯是個大問題，那麼北京人是怎麼樣解決午餐問題的呢？

（採訪）
甲："自己帶飯。"
乙："我中飯在家吃，因為我在機關[5]上班。"
丙："有時上食堂。要是高興，就和朋友在外頭個體炒點菜吃。"
丁："我們吃快餐。"

這裡的一些單位已經開始向午餐社會化邁進。沒有了食堂，於是便有了這種街頭盒飯。

Notes [5]機關 refers to a public or government body that serves an administrative function, as in 政府機關 (government organs) and 領導機關 (leadership groups). 機關 is never used for private enterprises.

136

有荤有素	(yǒu hūn yǒu sù)	*VP.*	to have both meat and vegetable
花样	(huā yàng)	*N.*	variety
食堂	(shí táng)	*N.*	cafeteria
街头	(jiē tóu)	*N.*	on the street
酒楼	(jiǔ lóu)	*N.*	restaurant
凭卡	(píng kǎ)	*V.*	to use a card
社会化	(shè huì huà)	*N.*	to be socialized; socialization
节奏	(jié zòu)	*N.*	pace, rhythm
快速化	(kuài sù huà)	*N.*	to become fast-paced
档次	(dàng cì)	*N.*	quality, high quality level
品种	(pǐn zhǒng)	*N.*	variety, assortment
多样化	(duō yàng huà)	*N.*	to have variety

二、电视原文 🖥 **TV original**

北京人的午餐

（根据原文改编）

随着中国改革开放的深入，北京已经步入了世界大都市的行列。这个大都市有着一千多万的固定人口和几百万的流动人口。这么大的城市吃午饭是个大问题，那么北京人是怎么样解决午餐问题的呢？

（采访）

甲："自己带饭。"

乙："我中饭在家吃，因为我在机关[5]上班。"

丙："有时上食堂。要是高兴，就和朋友在外头个体炒点菜吃。"

丁："我们吃快餐。"

这里的一些单位已经开始向午餐社会化迈进。没有了食堂，于是便有了这种街头盒饭。

✏ **Notes** [5]机关 refers to a public or government body that serves an administrative function, as in 政府机关 (government organs) and 领导机关 (leadership groups). 机关 is never used for private enterprises.

被採訪者："一般都是上班的，帶飯不方便，涼啊，有的單位沒法熱飯，結果出來買一點，挺便宜的，三塊錢。"

　　這家位於地安門繁華大街的不足十幾坪米的小店就專供盒飯午餐，品種比街頭的多，檔次也提高了。於是乎(6)周圍遠近大小的公司職員們紛紛來此就餐(7)或訂餐。

（採訪）

記者：　　　"您是光賣盒飯？"

被採訪者："對，我們專營盒飯。"

記者：　　　"一天做幾頓啊？"

被採訪者："一天供應一頓。"

記者：　　　"為甚麼就供應一頓？"

被採訪者："因為我們下午的工作量(8)很大，老得準備明天的菜，所以必須盯著一整下午到晚上，準備的全是明天的。你這是要甚麼？丸子和甚麼？"

買飯者：　　"丸子油菜。"

記者：　　　"你好，打擾一下你吃飯。你是常來這兒吃飯嗎？"

被採訪者："對，我常來這兒吃飯。"

記者：　　　"那你平常中飯都怎麼吃？"

被採訪者："平常在公司的時候旁邊有酒樓甚麼的，就在酒樓吃。自從這兒盒飯開了以後就方便了我們周圍這些公司的人。"

Notes (6)於是乎 means the same as 於是 (consequently, as a result), but is more formal. The character 乎, a particle from Classical Chinese, carries no meaning here.

(7)就餐 vs. 吃飯: 就 here is a verb meaning "to undertake" or "engage in", as in the formal expression 就餐 (to eat, to dine). 吃飯 is much more colloquial and informal.

(8)量 is a suffix used to form nouns. It refers to an amount of or capacity to do something, as in 飯量 (appetite), 酒量 (alcohol tolerance), 工作量 (work capacity).

被采访者：　"一般都是上班的，带饭不方便，凉啊，有的单位没法热饭，结果出来买
　　　　　　　一点，挺便宜的，三块钱。"

　　这家位于地安门繁华大街的不足十几平米的小店就专供盒饭午餐，品种比街头的
多，档次也提高了。于是乎[6]周围远近大小的公司职员们纷纷来此就餐[7]或订餐。

（采访）

记者：　　　"您是光卖盒饭？"

被采访者：　"对，我们专营盒饭。"

记者：　　　"一天做几顿啊？"

被采访者：　"一天供应一顿。"

记者：　　　"为什么就供应一顿？"

被采访者：　"因为我们下午的工作量[8]很大，老得准备明天的菜，所以必须盯着一整下
　　　　　　　午到晚上，准备的全是明天的。你这是要什么？丸子和什么？"

买饭者：　　"丸子油菜。"

记者：　　　"你好，打扰一下你吃饭。你是常来这儿吃饭吗？"

被采访者：　"对，我常来这儿吃饭。"

记者：　　　"那你平常中饭都怎么吃？"

被采访者：　"平常在公司的时候旁边有酒楼什么的，就在酒楼吃。自从这儿盒饭开了
　　　　　　　以后就方便了我们周围这些公司的人。"

✎ **Notes** [6]于是乎 means the same as 于是 (consequently, as a result), but is more formal. The character 乎, a particle from Classical Chinese, carries no meaning here.

[7]就餐 vs. 吃饭：就 here is a verb meaning "to undertake" or "engage in", as in the formal expression 就餐 (to eat, to dine). 吃饭 is much more colloquial and informal.

[8]量 is a suffix used to form nouns. It refers to an amount of or capacity to do something, as in 饭量 (appetite), 酒量 (alcohol tolerance), 工作量 (work capacity).

　　洋快餐吃長了總覺得不那麼對勁，有了這家盒飯大王[9]，這家通訊公司的職員們便放棄了吃洋快餐。中國人的肚子嘛，還是吃米飯炒菜習慣。

（採訪）

記者：　　　　"哎，你們好。每天你都吃這兒的飯嗎？"

被採訪者：　"是啊，幾乎每天都是吃這些盒飯。因為原先我們吃過其它的快餐，其它快餐有牛肉麵、包子，但是對這些呢，感到時間吃長了有點膩了。這些盒飯呢，有些炒菜，葷素搭配得比較好，可選的餘地也比較大；再一個呢，就是說，這種盒飯比較簡潔。"

　　憑卡吃飯是國外引進的，北京燕莎友誼商城便引進了這種午餐制度。餐廳內我們看到員工們有秩序地排隊打卡領飯，這種葷素合理搭配的配餐制度，使得三千名員工一小時內就能就餐完畢，適應了當今商品社會的快節奏。

　　白領人的午餐卻又有所不同，他們出沒於賓館、飯店之間，高效的工作使得他們只有很短的午餐時間，一般，飯店通常為他們提供工作午餐。

　　北京人的午餐，在不知不覺中變化著，人們不再為吃午餐而發愁，而且越吃越講究，吃的去處也越來越多，種類越來越全。市場經濟使得北京人的午餐豐富多彩，日新月異，午餐作為一天中必要的食物和營養補充，越來越多地受到人們的重視。

　　午餐社會化會隨著改革開放的進程一起加快。

生詞

隨著	(suí zhe)	*Adv.*	along with, accompanying
深入	(shēn rù)	*V.*	to deepen
步入	(bù rù)	*V.*	to step into

Notes [9]大王, "the king of" or "the best of", is a suffix often used in the names of restaurants or businesses, such as 盒飯大王 (The Boxed Lunch King), 餃子大王 (The Dumpling King), 快餐大王 (The King of Fast Food), 茶葉大王 (The Tea King).

洋快餐吃长了总觉得不那么对劲，有了这家盒饭大王⁽⁹⁾，这家通讯公司的职员们便放弃了吃洋快餐。中国人的肚子嘛，还是吃米饭炒菜习惯。

（采访）

记者：　　　　"哎，你们好。每天你都吃这儿的饭吗？"

被采访者：　　"是啊，几乎每天都是吃这些盒饭。因为原先我们吃过其它的快餐，其它快餐有牛肉面、包子，但是对这些呢，感到时间吃长了有点腻了。这些盒饭呢，有些炒菜，荤素搭配得比较好，可选的余地也比较大；再一个呢，就是说，这种盒饭比较简洁。"

凭卡吃饭是国外引进的，北京燕莎友谊商城便引进了这种午餐制度。餐厅内我们看到员工们有秩序地排队打卡领饭，这种荤素合理搭配的配餐制度，使得三千名员工一小时内就能就餐完毕，适应了当今商品社会的快节奏。

白领人的午餐却又有所不同，他们出没于宾馆、饭店之间，高效的工作使得他们只有很短的午餐时间，一般，饭店通常为他们提供工作午餐。

北京人的午餐，在不知不觉中变化着，人们不再为吃午餐而发愁，而且越吃越讲究，吃的去处也越来越多，种类越来越全。市场经济使得北京人的午餐丰富多采，日新月异，午餐作为一天中必要的食物和营养补充，越来越多地受到人们的重视。

午餐社会化会随着改革开放的进程一起加快。

生词

随着	(suí zhe)	*Adv.*	along with, accompanying
深入	(shēn rù)	*V.*	to deepen
步入	(bù rù)	*V.*	to step into

Notes ⁽⁹⁾大王, "the king of" or "the best of", is a suffix often used in the names of restaurants or businesses, such as 盒饭大王 (The Boxed Lunch King), 饺子大王 (The Dumpling King), 快餐大王 (The King of Fast Food), 茶叶大王(The Tea King).

行列	(háng liè)	N.	ranks
固定	(gù dìng)	Adj.	fixed
機關	(jī guān)	N.	office
炒	(chǎo)	V.	to stir fry
邁進	(mài jìn)	V.	to stride forward
便	(biàn)	Adv.	then
上班	(shàng bān)	VO.	to go to work
位於	(wèi yú)	V.	to be located, to be situated
地安門	(dì ān mén)	Place N.	Di'anmen, name of a street in Beijing 地名
不足	(bù zú)	Adv.	less than
坪米	(píng mǐ)	N.	square meter
專供	(zhuān gòng)	V.	to specialize in supplying
於是乎	(yú shì hū)	Adv.	then
紛紛	(fēn fēn)	Adv.	one after another
此	(cǐ)	Pron.	this
就餐	(jiù cān)	V.	to eat, to dine
訂餐	(dìng cān)	VO.	to order food
光	(guāng)	Adv.	only
供應	(gòng yìng)	V.	to supply
工作量	(gōng zuò liàng)	NP.	work load, amount of work
盯著	(dīng zhe)	VP.	to keep the focus on
丸子	(wán zi)	N.	meatball
油菜	(yóu cài)	N.	rape (a kind of vegetable)
洋	(yáng)	Adj.	western, foreign
對勁（兒）	(dùi jìng (er))	V.	to suit, to be fitting
盒飯大王	(hé fàn dà wáng)	NP.	King of Boxed Lunches, name of a restaurant
通訊公司	(tōng xùn gōng sī)	NP.	communication company
放棄	(fàng qì)	V.	to give up, to renounce
米飯	(mǐ fàn)	N.	rice
牛肉麵	(niú ròu miàn)	NP.	beef noodle
包子	(bāo zi)	N.	steamed buns with meat, vegetable, or sweet filling
膩	(nì)	Adj.	to be bored of, to be tired of

行列	(háng liè)	N.	ranks
固定	(gù dìng)	Adj.	fixed
机关	(jī guān)	N.	office
炒	(chǎo)	V.	to stir fry
迈进	(mài jìn)	V.	to stride forward
便	(biàn)	Adv.	then
上班	(shàng bān)	VO.	to go to work
位于	(wèi yú)	V.	to be located, to be situated
地安门	(dì ān mén)	Place N.	Di'anmen, name of a street in Beijing 地名
不足	(bù zú)	Adv.	less than
平米	(píng mǐ)	N.	square meter
专供	(zhuān gòng)	V.	to specialize in supplying
于是乎	(yú shì hū)	Adv.	then
纷纷	(fēn fēn)	Adv.	one after another
此	(cǐ)	Pron.	this
就餐	(jiù cān)	V.	to eat, to dine
订餐	(dìng cān)	VO.	to order food
光	(guāng)	Adv.	only
供应	(gòng yìng)	V.	to supply
工作量	(gōng zuò liàng)	NP.	work load, amount of work
盯着	(dīng zhe)	VP.	to keep the focus on
丸子	(wán zi)	N.	meatball
油菜	(yóu cài)	N.	rape (a kind of vegetable)
洋	(yáng)	Adj.	western, foreign
对劲（儿）	(dùi jìng (er))	V.	to suit, to be fitting
盒饭大王	(hé fàn dà wáng)	NP.	King of Boxed Lunches, name of a restaurant
通讯公司	(tōng xùn gōng sī)	NP.	communication company
放弃	(fàng qì)	V.	to give up, to renounce
米饭	(mǐ fàn)	N.	rice
牛肉面	(niú ròu miàn)	NP.	beef noodle
包子	(bāo zi)	N.	steamed buns with meat, vegetable, or sweet filling
腻	(nì)	Adj.	to be bored of, to be tired of

搭配	(dā pèi)	V.	to match, to balance
可選	(kě xuǎn)	Adj.	selectable
餘地	(yú dì)	N.	leeway, room, latitude
引進	(yǐn jìn)	V.	to introduce from, to import
燕莎友誼商城	(yàn shā yǒu yì shāng chéng)	NP.	Lufthansa Friendship Shopping Center, name of a shopping center
員工	(yuán gōng)	N.	staff member
排隊	(pái duì)	VO.	to line up, to form a waiting line
配餐	(pèi cān)	V.	to provide meals
完畢	(wán bì)	V.	to finish, to complete
適應	(shì yìng)	V.	to fit in, to be suitable for
節奏	(jié zòu)	NP.	fast pace
白領人	(bái lǐng rén)	NP.	white collar worker
出沒於	(chū mò yú)	VP.	to be in and out of
賓館	(bīn guǎn)	N.	guest house, hotel
高效	(gāo xiào)	NP.	high efficiency
發愁	(fā chóu)	V.	to worry, to be concerned about
去處	(qù chù)	N.	place to go
種類	(zhǒng lèi)	N.	type, variety
豐富多彩	(fēng fù duō cǎi)	Adj.	rich and colorful
日新月異	(rì xīn yuè yì)	V.	to change by days and months, to change continuously
營養	(yíng yǎng)	N.	nutrition
補充	(bǔ chōng)	N.	supplement, addition, complement
進程	(jìn chéng)	N.	process

搭配	(dā pèi)	*V.*	to match, to balance
可选	(kě xuǎn)	*Adj.*	selectable
余地	(yú dì)	*N.*	leeway, room, latitude
引进	(yǐn jìn)	*V.*	to introduce from, to import
燕莎友谊商城	(yàn shā yǒu yì shāng chéng)	*NP.*	Lufthansa Friendship Shopping Center, name of a shopping center
员工	(yuán gōng)	*N.*	staff member
排队	(pái duì)	*VO.*	to line up, to form a waiting line
配餐	(pèi cān)	*V.*	to provide meals
完毕	(wán bì)	*V.*	to finish, to complete
适应	(shì yìng)	*V.*	to fit in, to be suitable for
节奏	(jié zòu)	*NP.*	fast pace
白领人	(bái lǐng rén)	*NP.*	white collar worker
出没于	(chū mò yú)	*VP.*	to be in and out of
宾馆	(bīn guǎn)	*N.*	guest house, hotel
高效	(gāo xiào)	*NP.*	high efficiency
发愁	(fā chóu)	*V.*	to worry, to be concerned about
去处	(qù chù)	*N.*	place to go
种类	(zhǒng lèi)	*N.*	type, variety
丰富多采	(fēng fù duō cǎi)	*Adj.*	rich and colorful
日新月异	(rì xīn yuè yì)	*V.*	to change by days and months, to change continuously
营养	(yíng yǎng)	*N.*	nutrition
补充	(bǔ chōng)	*N.*	supplement, addition, complement
进程	(jìn chéng)	*N.*	process

課文要點

一、詞語解釋 <small>Words and Phrases</small>

（一）文言詞、慣用詞 (Classical Chinese and idiomatic expressions)

1、便＝就
☞ 於是便有了這種街頭盒飯。

2、於＝在
☞ 這家位於地安門繁華大街的不足十幾坪米的小店就專供盒飯午餐。

3、不足＝不夠、不到
☞ 這家小店不足十幾坪米。

4、於是乎＝於是、因此，"乎"在這裡是助詞，沒有意思
☞ 於是乎周圍遠近大小的公司職員們紛紛來此就餐或訂餐。

5、此＝這（個地方、件事等）
☞ 人們紛紛來此就餐或訂餐。

6、光＝只
☞ 您是光賣盒飯？

7、可選＝可以選擇的
☞ 可選的餘地比較大。

8、憑＝靠
☞ 憑卡吃飯是國外引進的。

9、畢＝完
☞ 使得三千名員工一小時內就能就餐完畢。

10、所＋動詞＝……的地方、東西等
☞ 白領人的午餐卻又有所不同。

11、出沒於＝在……地方出現
☞ 他們出沒於賓館、飯店之間。

（二）成語、慣用語 (idioms and fixed expressions)

◆ 流動人口: floating population
◆ 固定人口: permanent population
◆ 葷素搭配: to balance between meat and vegetables
◆ 不知不覺: without noticing
◆ 日新月異: constant changes
◆ 豐富多彩: rich and colorful

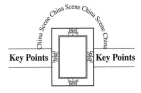

课文要点

一、词语解释 Words and Phrases

（一）文言词、惯用词 (Classical Chinese and idiomatic expressions)

1、便 = 就
  ☞ 于是便有了这种街头盒饭。

2、于 = 在
  ☞ 这家位于地安门繁华大街的不足十几平米的小店就专供盒饭午餐。

3、不足 = 不够、不到
  ☞ 这家小店不足十几平米。

4、于是乎 = 于是、因此，"乎"在这里是助词，没有意思
  ☞ 于是乎周围远近大小的公司职员们纷纷来此就餐或订餐。

5、此 = 这（个地方、件事等）
  ☞ 人们纷纷来此就餐或订餐。

6、光 = 只
  ☞ 您是光卖盒饭？

7、可选 = 可以选择的
  ☞ 可选的余地比较大。

8、凭 = 靠
  ☞ 凭卡吃饭是国外引进的。

9、毕 = 完
  ☞ 使得三千名员工一小时内就能就餐完毕。

10、所 + 动词 = ……的地方、东西等
  ☞ 白领人的午餐却又有所不同。

11、出没于 = 在……地方出现
  ☞ 他们出没于宾馆、饭店之间。

（二）成语、惯用语 (idioms and fixed expressions)

◆ 流动人口: floating population
◆ 固定人口: permanent population
◆ 荤素搭配: to balance between meat and vegetables
◆ 不知不觉: without noticing
◆ 日新月异: constant changes
◆ 丰富多采: rich and colorful

二、書面語、正式語、口語對照表 Written/formal/colloquial Comparison

	書面／正式語	口語		書面／正式語	口語
1	請教	問	10	光	只
2	便(adv.)	就	11	或	或者
3	位於	在	12	幾乎	差不多
4	於	在	13	可選	可以選擇的
5	不足	不到	14	使得	使／讓
6	專供	專賣／專門供應	15	三千名	三千個
7	於是乎	於是／所以	16	完畢	完
8	來此	來這兒	17	當今	現在
9	就餐	吃飯			

三、句型 Sentence Structures

（一）步入（／進入）……的行列 (to step into the ranks of, to be among)（多用在書面／正式語體）

> 步入（／進入）……的行列, meaning "to step into the ranks of" or "to be among", is a structure most often used in formal or written settings. A similar but less formal structure studied earlier is 成為……之一. The subject of 步入 is often the name of a country, city, institution, or enterprise. Examples: 上海已經步入經濟發展最快的行列. (Shanghai has already stepped into the ranks of cities with the fastest economic growth.) 這個大學步入美國前二十五名大學的行列. (This college has already entered the ranks of America's top twenty five universities.) 步入 can also be replaced with 進入. The character 行 in the combination 行列 reads háng (not xíng).

☞ 隨著中國改革開放的深入，北京已經步入了世界大都市的行列。

1、中國現在已經步入世界經濟大國的行列。

China has already stepped into the ranks of world economic powers.

2、廣東已經步入中國重要經濟省份的行列。

Guangdong is among China's most important provinces.

二、书面语、正式语、口语对照表 ▂▃▅▆ Written/formal/colloquial Comparison

	书面／正式语	口语		书面／正式语	口语
1	请教	问	10	光	只
2	便（adv.）	就	11	或	或者
3	位于	在	12	几乎	差不多
4	于	在	13	可选	可以选择的
5	不足	不到	14	使得	使／让
6	专供	专卖／专门供应	15	三千名	三千个
7	于是乎	于是／所以	16	完毕	完
8	来此	来这儿	17	当今	现在
9	就餐	吃饭			

三、句型 ❋ Sentence Structures

（一）步入（／进入）……的行列 (to step into the ranks of, to be among)（多用在书面／正式语体）

> ✍ 步入（／进入）……的行列, meaning "to step into the ranks of" or "to be among", is a structure most often used in formal or written settings. A similar but less formal structure studied earlier is 成为……之一. The subject of 步入 is often the name of a country, city, institution, or enterprise. Examples: 上海已经步入经济发展最快的行列. (Shanghai has already stepped into the ranks of cities with the fastest economic growth.) 这个大学步入美国前二十五名大学的行列. (This college has already entered the ranks of America's top twenty five universities.) 步入 can also be replaced with 进入. The character 行 in the combination 行列 reads háng (not xíng).

☞ 随着中国改革开放的深入，北京已经步入了世界大都市的行列。

1、中国现在已经步入世界经济大国的行列。

China has already stepped into the ranks of world economic powers.

2、广东已经步入中国重要经济省份的行列。

Guangdong is among China's most important provinces.

（二）解決……問題（／困難／難點）(to resolve a problem, to solve a problem)

> 解決 "to resolve" or "to solve", is a verb that most often takes 問題, 困難, or 難點 as its object. A modifying phrase can be placed before the object to specify the kind of problem or difficulties being described. Occasionally, speakers may use a jocular tone to say: 你打算在哪兒解決午餐? (So where do you plan to eat lunch?) 解決 here is used as an equivalent of 吃. In order to emphasize the result of 解決, resultative complements such as 好 and 掉 can be added to the verb. Examples: 中國必須解決好國營企業的問題. (China must resolve the issue of state-owned enterprise.) 你能不能把 職工住房問題解決掉? (Can you solve the employees' housing problem?)

☞ 這麼大的城市吃午飯是個大問題，那麼北京人是怎麼樣解決午餐問題的呢？

1、中國要解決十億人吃飯穿衣的問題，就必須向現代化邁進。

If China wants to resolve the problem of feeding and clothing one billion people, it must work toward modernization.

2、如果企業能解決好午餐的問題，工作也會向前邁進。

If a company can make sure that its workers get a good lunch, productivity will increase.

問：中國已經邁入世界經濟大國的行列，這樣的大國能不能在經濟發展的基礎上解決人口問題呢？

答：_____。

（三）向……邁進 (to march toward, to forge ahead)

> 向……邁進, "to march toward" or "to forge ahead", is a structure used mostly in formal settings. It has the same meaning as 向/往……方向/爭取/發展. 向……邁進 expresses a kind of determination to strive for better results. The negative particle 不 or 沒 must be placed before 向. Example: 考上指揮以後，他不再向前邁進了. (After passing the exam for commander, he no longer strived to get ahead.)

☞ 這裡的一些單位已經開始向午餐社會化邁進。

1、步入經濟大國行列以後，中國還要向世界先進國家的行列邁進。

Having stepped into rank with other economic powers, China still wants to become one of the world's most advanced countries.

2、十歲的小南考了鋼琴八級以後，還不滿足，還要向九級、十級邁進。

Ten-year-old Xiao Nan is still not satisfied after passing the piano exam at level eight. He wants to take the exams for levels nine and ten.

問：現在你這個公司已經辦得很不錯了，還要向哪兒再發展呢？

答：_____。

143

（二）解决……问题（／困难／难点）(to resolve a problem, to solve a problem)

> ✍ 解决, "to resolve" or "to solve", is a verb that most often takes 问题, 困难, or 难点 as its object. A modifying phrase can be placed before the object to specify the kind of problem or difficulties being described. Occasionally, speakers may use a jocular tone to say: 你打算在哪儿解决午餐？(So where do you plan to eat lunch?) 解决 here is used as an equivalent of 吃. In order to emphasize the result of 解决, resultative complements such as 好 and 掉 can be added to the verb. Examples: 中国必须解决好国营企业的问题. (China must resolve the issue of state-owned enterprise.) 你能不能把 职工住房问题解决掉? (Can you solve the employees' housing problem?)

☞ 这么大的城市吃午饭是个大问题，那么北京人是怎么样解决午餐问题的呢？

1、中国要解决十亿人吃饭穿衣的问题，就必须向现代化迈进。
If China wants to resolve the problem of feeding and clothing one billion people, it must work toward modernization.

2、如果企业能解决好午餐的问题，工作也会向前迈进。
If a company can make sure that its workers get a good lunch, productivity will increase.

问：中国已经迈入世界经济大国的行列，这样的大国能不能在经济发展的基础上解决人口问题呢？

答：＿＿＿＿＿＿＿＿＿＿＿＿＿＿＿＿＿＿＿＿＿＿＿＿。

（三）向……迈进 (to march toward, to forge ahead)

> ✍ 向……迈进, "to march toward" or "to forge ahead", is a structure used mostly in formal settings. It has the same meaning as 向／往……方向／争取／发展. 向……迈进 expresses a kind of determination to strive for better results. The negative particle 不 or 没 must be placed before 向. Example: 考上指挥以后，他不再向前迈进了. (After passing the exam for commander, he no longer strived to get ahead.)

☞ 这里的一些单位已经开始向午餐社会化迈进。

1、步入经济大国行列以后，中国还要向世界先进国家的行列迈进。
Having stepped into rank with other economic powers, China still wants to become one of the world's most advanced countries.

2、十岁的小南考了钢琴八级以后，还不满足，还要向九级、十级迈进。
Ten-year-old Xiao Nan is still not satisfied after passing the piano exam at level eight. He wants to take the exams for levels nine and ten.

问：现在你这个公司已经办得很不错了，还要向哪儿再发展呢？
答：＿＿＿＿＿＿＿＿＿＿＿＿＿＿＿＿＿＿＿＿＿＿＿＿。

（四）位於…… (to be located at or in)

> ✍ 位於, "to be located at or in", is a verb used mostly in written Chinese to indicate the location of something. Example: 這家小店位於市中心. (This small shop is located in the heart of the city.) Since 位於 is a formal term used only in written settings, it should not be used in conversation. Its spoken equivalent is 在. Example: 這家小店在市中心. (This small shop is in the heart of the city.)

☞ 這家位於地安門繁華大街的不足十幾坪米的小店就專供盒飯午餐。

1、車站位於市區，那個地方總是很熱鬧。

The train station is located in the city. It is always crowded and bustling.

2、這個商城位於大都市的繁重街道上，所以人們紛紛來此購買東西。

This mall is located on a busy street. People come in steady streams to shop here.

問：請你向觀眾簡單地介紹一下北京的秀水市場。

答：_____ 。

（五）……的餘地 (room for, margin of, leeway to)

> ✍ ……的餘地, "room for", "margin of", "leeway to", is an expression that often follows phrases such as 可選, 發展, 商量, 發揮, or 改變. It can function as either a subject or an object. Examples: 你認為計劃經濟的發展餘地大不大? (Do you think there is much room for development in the planned economy?) 考級的通知已經發出了，可以說現在沒有甚麼商量的餘地了. (The examination scores have already been announced; you could say that there's no more room for discussion.)

☞ 這些盒飯呢，有些炒菜，葷素搭配的比較好，可選的餘地也比較大。

1、這樣的東西都要過海關，沒有商量的餘地。

These kinds of things must go through Customs; there is no room for discussion.

2、那個批發市場很大，挑選的餘地自然也很大。

That wholesale market is huge, so naturally there is plenty of selection.

問：你對台灣的問題有甚麼看法？你認為政府會考慮他們的獨立要求嗎？

答：_____ 。

（四）位于…… (to be located at or in)

> ✍ 位于, "to be located at or in", is a verb used mostly in written Chinese to indicate the location of something. Example: 这家小店位于市中心. (This small shop is located in the heart of the city.) Since 位于 is a formal term used only in written settings, it should not be used in conversation. Its spoken equivalent is 在. Example: 这家小店在市中心. (This small shop is in the heart of the city.)

☞ 这家位于地安门繁华大街的不足十几平米的小店就专供盒饭午餐。

1、车站位于市区，那个地方总是很热闹。

The train station is located in the city. It is always crowded and bustling.

2、这个商城位于大都市的繁重街道上，所以人们纷纷来此购买东西。

This mall is located on a busy street. People come in steady streams to shop here.

问：请你向观众简单地介绍一下北京的秀水市场。

答：＿＿＿＿＿＿＿＿＿＿＿＿＿＿＿＿＿＿＿＿＿。

（五）……的余地 (room for, margin of, leeway to)

> ✍ ……的余地, "room for", "margin of", "leeway to", is an expression that often follows phrases such as 可选, 发展, 商量, 发挥, or 改变. It can function as either a subject or an object. Examples: 你认为计划经济的发展余地大不大? (Do you think there is much room for development in the planned economy?) 考级的通知已经发出了，可以说现在没有什么商量的余地了. (The examination scores have already been announced; you could say that there's no more room for discussion.)

☞ 这些盒饭呢，有些炒菜，荤素搭配的比较好，可选 的余地也比较大。

1、这样的东西都要过海关，没有商量的余地。

These kinds of things must go through Customs; there is no room for discussion.

2、那个批发市场很大，挑选的余地自然也很大。

That wholesale market is huge, so naturally there is plenty of selection.

问：你对台湾的问题有什么看法？你认为政府会考虑他们的独立要求吗？

答：＿＿＿＿＿＿＿＿＿＿＿＿＿＿＿＿＿＿＿＿＿。

（六）憑…… VO (to rely on something to do something, to use something as proof)

> 憑 is a verb meaning "to rely on", "to use something as proof". It is similar to 靠 in Lesson 3 in that both are secondary verbs that indicate the means by which something is achieved. 憑 is different, however, because in addition to meaning "to rely on" in phrases such as 憑本事吃飯 (to rely on one's talents to make a living) and 憑能力工作 (rely on one's abilities to work), 憑 also indicates a means of proof or eligibility to do something, as in 憑卡吃飯 (to need a card to eat somewhere), 憑票上車 (to need a ticket to board a bus). 憑 cannot be replaced with 靠 in such sentences.

☞ 憑卡吃飯是國外引進的，北京燕莎友誼商城便引進了這種午餐制度。

1、在私營企業工作要憑自己的本事，所以管理才能很重要。

In a private company, one must rely on one's own abilities. Managerial skills are thus very important.

2、食堂可以憑卡吃飯，圖書館可以憑卡借書，所以很方便。

You can use your card to eat in the cafeteria and take out books at the library; so having a card is very convenient.

問：你為甚麼說在美國買東西很方便，連現金都不用帶？
答：＿＿＿＿＿＿＿＿＿＿＿＿＿＿＿＿＿＿＿＿＿＿＿。

（七）（從）……引進…… (to introduce, to import from)

> （從）……引進, "in the middle of", "in the process of", is a verb structure that often takes a place word to indicate where something is imported from. （從）……引進 can be used with the emphatic 是……的 structure. Example: 這種產品是從美國引進的. (These kinds of products are imported from America.) Negation occurs before 從 rather than before the main verb. Example: 中國不能從西方國家引進民主. (China cannot import democracy from Western countries.)

☞ 憑卡吃飯是國外引進的，北京燕莎友誼商城便引進了這種午餐制度。

1、這些技術都是從美國引進的，對中國人來說還很新鮮。

These technologies were introduced from the United States. They are new to the Chinese.

2、中國開放了，技術、管理都可以從外國引進，連快餐都可以從外國引進。

Because China has opened up, technology, management, and even fast food can all be imported from abroad.

問：這種電腦的技術是從哪兒來的？
答：＿＿＿＿＿＿＿＿＿＿＿＿＿＿＿＿＿。

（六）凭⋯⋯ VO (to rely on something to do something, to use something as proof)

> ✍ 凭 is a verb meaning "to rely on", "to use something as proof". It is similar to 靠 in Lesson 3 in that both are secondary verbs that indicate the means by which something is achieved. 凭 is different, however, because in addition to meaning "to rely on" in phrases such as 凭本事吃饭 (to rely on one's talents to make a living) and 凭能力工作 (rely on one's abilities to work), 凭 also indicates a means of proof or eligibility to do something, as in 凭卡吃饭 (to need a card to eat somewhere), 凭票上车 (to need a ticket to board a bus). 凭 cannot be replaced with 靠 in such sentences.

☞ 凭卡吃饭是国外引进的，北京燕莎友谊商城便引进了这种午餐制度。

1、在私营企业工作要凭自己的本事，所以管理才能很重要。
In a private company, one must rely on one's own abilities. Managerial skills are thus very important.

2、食堂可以凭卡吃饭，图书馆可以凭卡借书，所以很方便。
You can use your card to eat in the cafeteria and take out books at the library; so having a card is very convenient.

问：你为什么说在美国买东西很方便，连现金都不用带？
答：＿＿＿＿＿＿＿＿＿＿＿＿＿＿＿＿＿＿＿＿＿。

（七）（从）⋯⋯引进⋯⋯ (to introduce, to import from)

> ✍ （从）⋯⋯引进, "to introduce", "to import from", is a verb structure that often takes a place word to indicate where something is imported from. （从）⋯⋯引进 can be used with the emphatic 是⋯⋯的 structure. Example: 这种产品是从美国引进的. (These kinds of products are imported from America.) Negation occurs before 从 rather than before the main verb. Example: 中国不能从西方国家引进民主. (China cannot import democracy from Western countries.)

☞ 凭卡吃饭是国外引进的，北京燕莎友谊商城便引进了这种午餐制度。

1、这些技术都是从美国引进的，对中国人来说还很新鲜。
These technologies were introduced from the United States. They are new to the Chinese.

2、中国开放了，技术、管理都可以从外国引进，连快餐都可以从外国引进。
Because China has opened up, technology, management, and even fast food can all be imported from abroad.

问：这种电脑的技术是从哪儿来的？
答：＿＿＿＿＿＿＿＿＿＿＿＿＿＿＿＿＿。

（八）在……中 (in the middle of, in the process of)

> ✍ 在……中, "in the middle of", "in the process of", is a prepositional phrase which indicates that one action or event takes place while another is going on. The phrases which can be inserted after 在 include verbs such as 工作, 學習, 變化, etc. The 在……中 phrase often functions as an adverbial phrase and must be placed before the main clause. Example: 美國人的生活在緊張的節奏中發生著變化. (Americans' lives are changing in the midst of their fast-paced life-styles.) The colloquial versions of this structure are ……當中 and 正在……的時候.

☞ 北京人的午餐，在不知不覺中變化著。

1、中國人對孩子獨立的觀念在改革中變化了很多。

Chinese people's ideas about children's independence changed greatly during the reforms.

2、中國人的午餐在改革開放中變化了很多，多數人願意在街上吃快餐。

What Chinese people eat for lunch changed greatly during economic reforms. Many people are willing to eat fast food on the street.

問：在你們的討論中，你發現了一些甚麼問題？

答：在＿＿＿＿＿＿＿＿＿＿＿＿＿＿＿＿＿＿＿＿。

（九）為……而…… (to do something because of something, to be in a particular state because of something)

> ✍ 為……而…… means "to do something because of something" or "to be in a particular state because of something". 為 indicates the reason or cause of the action or state, and 而 introduces the result or effect. This structure can take verbs such as 發愁 and 擔心, and adjectives such as 緊張 and 害怕. The prepositional phrase 為…… must be placed before the verb, and the negative particle 不 or 沒有 must be placed before the 為 phrase. Example: 我並不為以後的出路而發愁. (I am really not worried about a way out in the future.) On less formal occasions, 而 can be omitted. Example: 他現在還為家庭擔心嗎？ (Is he still worried about his family?)

☞ 人們不再為吃午餐而發愁，而且越吃越講究，吃的去處也越來越多，種類越來越全。

1、為學中文而來中國的美國學生越來越多。

More and more American students are coming to China to study Chinese.

2、為買東西而來白溝的人每天達4萬人次。

Up to 40,000 people a day come to White Gully to shop.

問：這些流動人口多數是為甚麼而來北京的？

答：＿＿＿＿＿＿＿＿＿＿＿＿＿＿＿＿＿＿＿＿。

（八）在……中 (in the middle of, in the process of)

> ✍ 在……中, "in the middle of", "in the process of", is a prepositional phrase which indicates that one action or event takes place while another is going on. The phrases which can be inserted after 在 include verbs such as 工作, 学习, 变化, etc. The 在……中 phrase often functions as an adverbial phrase and must be placed before the main clause. Example: 美国人的生活在紧张的节奏中发生着变化. (Americans' lives are changing in the midst of their fast-paced life-styles.) The colloquial versions of this structure are ……当中 and 正在……的时候.

☞ 北京人的午餐，在不知不觉中变化着。

1、中国人对孩子独立的观念在改革中变化了很多。
   Chinese people's ideas about children's independence changed greatly during the reforms.

2、中国人的午餐在改革开放中变化了很多，多数人愿意在街上吃快餐。
   What Chinese people eat for lunch changed greatly during economic reforms. Many people are willing to eat fast food on the street.

   问：在你们的讨论中，你发现了一些什么问题？
   答：在＿＿＿＿＿＿＿＿＿＿＿＿＿＿＿＿＿＿。

（九）为……而…… (to do something because of something, to be in a particular state because of something)

> ✍ 为……而…… means "to do something because of something" or "to be in a particular state because of something". 为 indicates the reason or cause of the action or state, and 而 introduces the result or effect. This structure can take verbs such as 发愁 and 担心, and adjectives such as 紧张 and 害怕. The prepositional phrase 为…… must be placed before the verb, and the negative particle 不 or 没有 must be placed before the 为 phrase. Example: 我并不为以后的出路而发愁. (I am really not worried about a way out in the future.) On less formal occasions, 而 can be omitted. Example: 他现在还为家庭担心吗？ (Is he still worried about his family?)

☞ 人们不再为吃午餐而发愁，而且越吃越讲究，吃的去处也越来越多，种类越来越全。

1、为学中文而来中国的美国学生越来越多。
   More and more American students are coming to China to study Chinese.

2、为买东西而来白沟的人每天达4万人次。
   Up to 40,000 people a day come to White Gully to shop.

   问：这些流动人口多数是为什么而来北京的？
   答：＿＿＿＿＿＿＿＿＿＿＿＿＿＿＿＿＿＿。

（十）適應 (to fit, to adjust to, to be adaptable to)

> ✍ 適應, meaning "to fit", "to adjust to", "to be adaptable to", is a verb which normally takes objects such as 生活, 環境, 生活節奏, 需要, and 變化. Unlike "to fit" in English, 適應 cannot be used with nouns that do not allow adjustment or change of some sort. 適合 must be used for sentences such as 適合我的性格 (to fit my personality), 適合我的樣子 (to go with my appearance or style).

☞ 餐廳內我們看到員工們有秩序地排隊打卡領飯，這種葷素合理搭配的配餐制度，使得三千名員工一小時內就能就餐完畢，適應了當今商品社會的快節奏。

1、很多人初來北京的時候，很不適應這裡的交通情況。

When people first arrive in Beijing, many are not well adjusted to the traffic situation here.

2、這種快節奏的學習方法對低年紀的學生來說很難適應。

It is difficult for lower-level students to adapt to this kind of fast-paced study method.

問：你覺得這種快餐，老百姓會歡迎嗎？

答：是的＿＿＿＿＿＿＿＿＿＿＿＿＿＿＿＿＿＿＿＿＿＿。

（十一）講究 (to be picky about, to be meticulous about)

> ✍ 講究, "to be picky about" or "to be meticulous about", is a verb which can take verbs, concrete nouns, and abstract nouns as its object, as in 講究吃穿 (to be particular about what one eats and wears); 講究品種 (to be picky about varieties); 講究營養 (to be meticulous about nutrition). 講究 can also be used as an adjective. Example: 她對吃穿很講究. (She is meticulous about what she eats and wears.)

☞ 北京人的午餐，在不知不覺中變化著，人們不再為吃午餐而發愁，而且越吃越講究，吃的去處也越來越多，種類越來越全。

1、在中國的社會，人們很講究人與人之間的關係。

In Chinese society, people pay a lot of attention to relationships between people.

2、他這個人對於吃飯穿衣都講究得很。

He is extremely picky about the food he eats and the clothes he wears.

問：＿＿＿＿＿＿＿＿＿＿＿＿＿＿＿＿＿＿＿＿＿＿。

答：這些小問題我一點兒都不在乎。

（十）适应 (to fit, to adjust to, to be adaptable to)

> ✎ 适应, meaning "to fit", "to adjust to", "to be adaptable to", is a verb which normally takes objects such as 生活, 环境, 生活节奏, 需要, and 变化. Unlike "to fit" in English, 适应 cannot be used with nouns that do not allow adjustment or change of some sort. 适合 must be used for sentences such as 适合我的性格 (to fit my personality), 适合我的样子 (to go with my appearance or style).

☞ 餐厅内我们看到员工们有秩序地排队打卡领饭，这种荤素合理搭配的配餐制度，使得三千名员工一小时内就能就餐完毕，适应了当今商品社会的快节奏。

1、很多人初来北京的时候，很不适应这里的交通情况。

When people first arrive in Beijing, many are not well adjusted to the traffic situation here.

2、这种快节奏的学习方法对低年纪的学生来说很难适应。

It is difficult for lower-level students to adapt to this kind of fast-paced study method.

问：你觉得这种快餐，老百姓会欢迎吗？

答：是的 _____。

（十一）讲究 (to be picky about, to be meticulous about)

> ✎ 讲究, "to be picky about" or "to be meticulous about", is a verb which can take verbs, concrete nouns, and abstract nouns as its object, as in 讲究吃穿 (to be particular about what one eats and wears); 讲究品种 (to be picky about varieties); 讲究营养 (to be meticulous about nutrition). 讲究 can also be used as an adjective. Example: 她对吃穿很讲究. (She is meticulous about what she eats and wears.)

☞ 北京人的午餐，在不知不觉中变化着，人们不再为吃午餐而发愁，而且越吃越讲究，吃的去处也越来越多，种类越来越全。

1、在中国的社会，人们很讲究人与人之间的关系。

In Chinese society, people pay a lot of attention to relationships between people.

2、他这个人对于吃饭穿衣都讲究得很。

He is extremely picky about the food he eats and the clothes he wears.

问：_____。

答：这些小问题我一点儿都不在乎。

四、文化背景知識 Cultural Notes

1. The term 戶口 literally means the number of households (戶) and the total population (口). Every citizen in China must register his/her place of residence with the government. Afterwards they are issued a permeanent resident (戶口 hùkǒu) within certain area. A family is issued a booklet (戶口簿 hùkǒubù) in which each member of the family has a page recording his/her birth date, sex, and relationship with the other members of the family. Among China's 戶口 are two varieties of population: the first is those persons who are part of China's fixed population (固定人口); the second is those who are part of China's floating population (流動人口). The former refers to persons who live and work in a fixed place (and have a 戶口 in that place); the latter refers to persons who move from place to place seeking work (and who do not have a 戶口 there or anywhere else).

2. Chinese eating habits: Most Chinese people do not like to eat cold food (unless it can be heated up). In fact, many Chinese have an aversion to any food or drink that is cold. This is because many Chinese believe that cold food and drink are bad for one's health.

四、文化背景知识 Cultural Notes

1. The term 户口 literally means the number of households (户) and total population (口). Every citizen in China must register his/her place of residence with the government. Afterwards they are issued a permeanent resident (户口 hùkǒu) within certain area. A family is issued a booklet (户口簿 hùkǒubù) in which each member of the family has a page recording his/her birth date, sex, and relationship with the other members of the family. Among China's 户口 are two varieties of population: the first is those persons who are part of China's fixed population (固定人口); the second is those who are part of China's floating population (流动人口). The former refers to persons who live and work in a fixed place (and have a 户口 in that place); the latter refers to persons who move from place to place seeking work (and who do not have a 户口 there or anywhere else).

2. Chinese eating habits: Most Chinese people do not like to eat cold food (unless it can be heated up). In fact, many Chinese have an aversion to any food or drink that is cold. This is because many Chinese believe that cold food and drink are bad for one's health.

練習

語言結構 Structures

一、短語翻譯 (Phrase translation)

1. fixed population and floating population
2. to work in an office or in a company
3. one of the largest metropolitan areas in the world
4. to be located on a crowded street
5. to specialize in selling fast food
6. to increase the quality and variety of food
7. working capacity in this fast food store
8. Western fast food and Chinese boxed lunches
9. beef noodles and steamed buns
10. a balanced meal with meat and vegetables
11. to eat using one's card
12. to fit into a fast-paced life
13. to line up in an orderly fashion
14. white collar and blue collar workers

二、聽力練習 (Listening comprehension)

1、聽寫 (Dictation)

2、聽錄音並回答問題 (Answering questions while listening to the audio CD)
  (1) 對話
      寫出對話的全文
  (2) 短文
      a. 北京的流動人口都有哪幾類人？
      b. 談談紐約或者你所熟悉的大城市的流動人口和固定人口的情況。

练习

语言结构 Structures

一、短语翻译 (Phrase translation)

1. fixed population and floating population
2. to work in an office or in a company
3. one of the largest metropolitan areas in the world
4. to be located on a crowded street
5. to specialize in selling fast food
6. to increase the quality and variety of food
7. working capacity in this fast food store
8. Western fast food and Chinese boxed lunches
9. beef noodles and steamed buns
10. a balanced meal with meat and vegetables
11. to eat using one's card
12. to fit into a fast-paced life
13. to line up in an orderly fashion
14. white collar and blue collar workers

二、听力练习 (Listening comprehension)

1、听写 (Dictation)

2、听录音并回答问题 (Answering questions while listening to the audio CD)
   (1) 对话
     写出对话的全文
   (2) 短文
     a. 北京的流动人口都有哪几类人？
     b. 谈谈纽约或者你所熟悉的大城市的流动人口和固定人口的情况。

三、改寫下面划線的詞 (Replace the underlined words)

　　　　隨著中國生活節奏的加快，人們的生活也不知不覺起了變化。以前人們很少出去到飯館吃飯，因為一個月掙的錢<u>不足</u>五十元。現在人們錢多了，<u>便</u>想花錢出去吃點兒好的。<u>於是乎</u>飯店的生意也好起來了。拿<u>此</u>飯店來說，以前，位<u>於</u>一條小街上，不足十坪米，一年流動資金才兩千。現在不但在熱鬧的大街上有店，而且每年收入有五十萬。

四、完成句子 (Complete the sentences)

1、　　　A：這家私營企業是怎麼進入大企業的行列的？
　　　　　B：他們＿＿＿＿＿＿＿＿＿＿＿＿＿＿＿＿＿＿＿＿＿＿＿＿＿＿
　　　　（從……引進……；憑……）

2、　　　A：你聽說過燕沙商城嗎？在哪兒？他們的商品怎麼樣？
　　　　　B：＿＿＿＿＿＿＿＿＿＿＿＿＿＿＿＿＿＿＿＿＿＿＿＿＿＿＿＿＿
　　　　（位於……；受到……的歡迎）

五、閱讀短文、回答問題 (Answering questions based on the reading passages)

　　　　說起吃午餐，我覺得在首都經貿大學最方便。因為吃的種類很全，吃的去處也很多。要是不想出校門，你不但可以在外國留學生餐廳吃午餐，而且也可以去中國學生食堂買飯票吃飯。這兩個地方的飯菜雖然檔次不太高，但是品種和花樣都還不錯。要是這兩個地方的飯你都吃膩了，想吃一點講究的菜，還可以走出校門，到學校對面的飯館吃米飯炒菜，或者去東邊的餃子館點菜就餐。除了上面四種午餐外，你還可以在路邊買包子，盒飯，花個兩三塊錢，就可以吃得很飽，營養也很豐富。要是你想吃洋快餐，也很容易，麥當勞就在前邊不遠的地方。在北京六個月，我從來沒為我的午餐發過愁，而且越吃越會吃，越吃越講究。

問題
　　(1) 在首都經貿大學校內校外，有幾個吃午飯的地方？
　　(2) 在你看來，甚麼樣的飯菜經濟實惠？甚麼樣的飯菜營養豐富，檔次很高？
　　(3) 談談你在美國大學上學時有幾種解決午餐的辦法。（最少寫三種）

　　　　隨著生活、工作節奏的加快，人們吃的飯也開始簡化。一種叫"快餐"的食品應運而生。這種食品的最大特點是方便、衛生、便宜和快捷。此外，由於快餐質量穩定，供應快速，服務周到，也很受老百姓的歡迎。因此在世界上很多國家，尤其是經濟發達的國家，發展得很快。在美國，無論你走到哪兒，都可以找到吃快餐的地方。據有關資料顯示，美國人每月吃的快餐占食物總量的三分之一；從東海岸到西海岸，飯店百分之八十是快餐店。從八十年代末以來，很多美國快餐企業打入了中國，比如，麥當勞、肯德基家鄉雞、意大利比薩餅等。這些洋快餐使中國人的吃飯習慣有了很大的改變。

三、改写下面划线的词 (Replace the underlined words)

随着中国生活节奏的加快，人们的生活也不知不觉起了变化。以前人们很少出去到饭馆吃饭，因为一个月挣的钱<u>不足</u>五十元。现在人们钱多了，<u>便</u>想花钱出去吃点儿好的。<u>于是乎</u>饭店的生意也好起来了。拿<u>此</u>饭店来说，以前，位<u>于</u>一条小街上，不足十平米，一年流动资金才两千。现在不但在热闹的大街上有店，而且每年收入有五十万。

四、完成句子 (Complete the sentences)

1、　A：这家私营企业是怎么进入大企业的行列的？
　　B：他们＿＿＿＿＿＿＿＿＿＿＿＿＿＿＿＿＿＿＿＿
　　（从……引进……；凭……）

2、　A：你听说过燕沙商城吗？在哪儿？他们的商品怎么样？
　　B：＿＿＿＿＿＿＿＿＿＿＿＿＿＿＿＿＿＿＿＿＿＿＿
　　（位于……；受到……的欢迎）

五、阅读短文、回答问题 (Answering questions based on the reading passages)

说起吃午餐，我觉得在首都经贸大学最方便。因为吃的种类很全，吃的去处也很多。要是不想出校门，你不但可以在外国留学生餐厅吃午餐，而且也可以去中国学生食堂买饭票吃饭。这两个地方的饭菜虽然档次不太高，但是品种和花样都还不错。要是这两个地方的饭你都吃腻了，想吃一点讲究的菜，还可以走出校门，到学校对面的饭馆吃米饭炒菜，或者去东边的饺子馆点菜就餐。除了上面四种午餐外，你还可以在路边买包子，盒饭，花个两三块钱，就可以吃得很饱，营养也很丰富。要是你想吃洋快餐，也很容易，麦当劳就在前边不远的地方。在北京六个月，我从来没为我的午餐发过愁，而且越吃越会吃，越吃越讲究。

问题
(1) 在首都经贸大学校内校外，有几个吃午饭的地方？
(2) 在你看来，什么样的饭菜经济实惠？什么样的饭菜营养丰富，档次很高？
(3) 谈谈你在美国大学上学时有几种解决午餐的办法。（最少写三种）

随着生活、工作节奏的加快，人们吃的饭也开始简化。一种叫"快餐"的食品应运而生。这种食品的最大特点是方便、卫生、便宜和快捷。此外，由于快餐质量稳定，供应快速，服务周到，也很受老百姓的欢迎。因此在世界上很多国家，尤其是经济发达的国家，发展得很快。在美国，无论你走到哪儿，都可以找到吃快餐的地方。据有关资料显示，美国人每月吃的快餐占食物总量的三分之一；从东海岸到西海岸，饭店百分之八十是快餐店。从八十年代末以来，很多美国快餐企业打入了中国，比如，麦当劳、肯德基家乡鸡、意大利比萨饼等。这些洋快餐使中国人的吃饭习惯有了很大的改变。

問題

(1) 快餐是在甚麼情況下產生的？

(2) 快餐有些甚麼特點？

(3) 你認為作者對美國人吃快餐的討論對不對。你覺得這幾年人們對快餐的看法有沒有改變？

六、翻譯 (Translate sentences)

1. With its development of a market economy and private enterprise, China has been ranked as one of the largest economic powers in the world.

2. This fast food store is located on a busy and crowded street. The variety and quality of the food is known to everyone near and far.

3. Because there is a large floating population of workers living nearby, they frequently come to this boxed lunch place to eat or to order food.

4. In order for people to adapt to the society's fast-paced life, the Lufthansa Friendship Shopping Center imported a new system for getting money: withdrawing it with a card.

问题

    (1) 快餐是在什么情况下产生的？

    (2) 快餐有些什么特点？

    (3) 你认为作者对美国人吃快餐的讨论对不对。你觉得这几年人们对快餐的看法有没有改变？

六、翻译 (Translate sentences)

1. With its development of a market economy and private enterprise, China has been ranked as one of the largest economic powers in the world.

2. This fast food store is located on a busy and crowded street. The variety and quality of the food is known to everyone near and far.

3. Because there is a large floating population of workers living nearby, they frequently come to this boxed lunch place to eat or to order food.

4. In order for people to adapt to the society's fast-paced life, the Lufthansa Friendship Shopping Center imported a new system for getting money: withdrawing it with a card.

語言實踐 Practice

一、根據課文回答問題 (Answering questions based on the dialogue)

1、北京作為一個世界大都市，有多少固定人口？多少流動人口？
2、根據採訪，你知道一般北京人怎麼解決午餐？
　　(1)
　　(2)
　　(3)
　　(4)
3、根據採訪，你知道為甚麼人們都出來買午餐？
　　(1)
　　(2)
4、用你自己的話來說說地安門繁華大街上的那家小店。
5、根據這篇報導，快餐有幾種？為甚麼人們不常去吃洋快餐和其它快餐，而要吃盒飯呢？
6、北京燕沙商城引進了一種甚麼午餐制度？這個制度的特點和好處各是甚麼？
7、白領人的午餐是甚麼？
8、北京人的午餐現在發生了甚麼變化？有甚麼特點？

二、活動 (Activities)

　　去麥當勞、盒飯大王、街上的快餐點吃飯，順便問問中國人他們一般午餐都吃甚麼？他們在哪兒吃？他們喜歡洋快餐，中快餐，還是快餐盒飯？對現在午餐的品種、檔次和可選餘地有甚麼看法？

三、討論題 (Topics for discussion)

1、你吃過北京的幾種快餐？吃快餐的好處是甚麼？壞處是甚麼？你覺得單位食堂和街頭快餐各有甚麼好處？
2、現在美國的快餐都被引進到了中國，例如麥當勞、肯德基，你覺得這些快餐會不會對中國人的吃飯習慣有影響？你跟中國人討論過這個問題嗎？他們對這種現象抱甚麼態度？

四、報告 (Presentation)

　　《比較一下洋快餐、中國普通快餐和盒飯的不同。談談人們生活節奏的變化和快餐的發展》

语言实践 ⋮ Practice

一、根据课文回答问题 (Answering questions based on the dialogue)

1、北京作为一个世界大都市，有多少固定人口？多少流动人口？
2、根据采访，你知道一般北京人怎么解决午餐？
   (1)
   (2)
   (3)
   (4)
3、根据采访，你知道为什么人们都出来买午餐？
   (1)
   (2)
4、用你自己的话来说说地安门繁华大街上的那家小店。
5、根据这篇报道，快餐有几种？为什么人们不常去吃洋快餐和其它快餐，而要吃盒饭呢？
6、北京燕莎商城引进了一种什么午餐制度？这个制度的特点和好处各是什么？
7、白领人的午餐是什么？
8、北京人的午餐现在发生了什么变化？有什么特点？

二、活动 (Activities)

去麦当劳、盒饭大王、街上的快餐点吃饭，顺便问问中国人他们一般午餐都吃什么？他们在哪儿吃？他们喜欢洋快餐，中快餐，还是快餐盒饭？对现在午餐的品种、档次和可选余地有什么看法？

三、讨论题 (Topics for discussion)

1、你吃过北京的几种快餐？吃快餐的好处是什么？坏处是什么？你觉得单位食堂和街头快餐各有什么好处？
2、现在美国的快餐都被引进到了中国，例如麦当劳、肯德基，你觉得这些快餐会不会对中国人的吃饭习惯有影响？你跟中国人讨论过这个问题吗？他们对这种现象抱什么态度？

四、报告 (Presentation)

《比较一下洋快餐、中国普通快餐和盒饭的不同。谈谈人们生活节奏的变化和快餐的发展》

五、看圖討論 (Picto-discussion)

1

2

3

4

5

6

五、看图讨论 (Picto-discussion)

1

2

3

4

5

6

中国社会文化写实　第七课

China Scene

An Advanced Chinese Multimedia Course

第八課

結婚 "保險"

第八课

结婚 "保险"

課文

一、對話  Dialogs

高邁：小李，剛才有你一個電話。好像是你的老同學梁為民來的。

小李：是的，你猜對了。我已經給他回過電話了。我們一個同學春節要結婚，我們得商量一下買甚麼禮品送給他。

高邁：是嗎？這幾年買結婚[1]禮品可是個傷腦筋的事情。我的一個親戚夏天結婚，我們跑了十幾家禮品店，也沒找到一種拿得出手的禮品。

小李：是啊，為這事，我一直在發愁。可是今天梁為民說我們就買一份結婚保險送給他們。

高邁：甚麼結婚保險？我聽說過汽車保險、房子保險，從來沒聽說過結婚保險。真新鮮，現在連結婚都有了保險了。

小李：是啊，這是近幾年中國出現的新鮮事。

高邁：為甚麼中國會出現這種保險呢？老百姓真有這種需求嗎？

小李：據說這跟中國現在離婚率[2]高、家庭不穩定有一定的關係，結婚保險滿足了人們在這方面的心理需求。你看，這是北京人民保險公司新開設的保險項目。保險費分別是66塊和88塊，6和8都是吉利數字。

高邁：這種保險真能保得住婚姻[3]嗎？

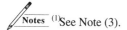 [1]See Note (3).

[2]When used as a suffix, 率 means "rate of" or "proportion of", as in 離婚率 (divorce rate), 畢業率 (graduation rate), 出國率 (emigration rate), 匯率 (exchange rate).

[3]結婚, 婚姻 and 婚禮: 結婚 is a VO structure meaning "to get married". The structure A 跟 B 結婚 is usually used to say that Person A married Person B. 婚姻 is a noun meaning "marriage", as in 婚姻制度(marriage system), 婚姻法 (marriage law), 婚姻有問題 (to have marital problems). 婚禮 means "wedding ceremony" or "wedding". Example: 他們結婚的時候婚禮很排場. (When they got married, the ceremony was very extravagant.)

156

课文

一、对话  Dialogs

高迈：小李，刚才有你一个电话。好象是你的老同学梁为民来的。

小李：是的，你猜对了。我已经给他回过电话了。我们一个同学春节要结婚，我们得商量一下买什么礼品送给他。

高迈：是吗？这几年买结婚[1]礼品可是个伤脑筋的事情。我的一个亲戚夏天结婚，我们跑了十几家礼品店，也没找到一种拿得出手的礼品。

小李：是啊，为这事，我一直在发愁。可是今天梁为民说我们就买一份结婚保险送给他们。

高迈：什么结婚保险？我听说过汽车保险、房子保险，从来没听说过结婚保险。真新鲜，现在连结婚都有了保险了。

小李：是啊，这是近几年中国出现的新鲜事。

高迈：为什么中国会出现这种保险呢？老百姓真有这种需求吗？

小李：据说这跟中国现在离婚率[2]高、家庭不稳定有一定的关系，结婚保险满足了人们在这方面的心理需求。你看，这是北京人民保险公司新开设的保险项目。保险费分别是66块和88块，6和8都是吉利数字。

高迈：这种保险真能保得住婚姻[3]吗？

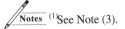 **Notes** [1]See Note (3).

[2]When used as a suffix, 率 means "rate of" or "proportion of", as in 离婚率 (divorce rate), 毕业率 (graduation rate), 出国率 (emigration rate), 汇率 (exchange rate).

[3]结婚, 婚姻 and 婚礼: 结婚 is a VO structure meaning "to get married". The structure A 跟 B 结婚 is usually used to say that Person A married Person B. 婚姻 is a noun meaning "marriage", as in 婚姻制度(marriage system), 婚姻法 (marriage law), 婚姻有问题 (to have marital problems). 婚礼 means "wedding ceremony" or "wedding". Example: 他们结婚的时候婚礼很排场. (When they got married, the ceremony was very extravagant.)

小李：哪裡，這種保險不起法律作用，就是賺老百姓的錢唄。

高邁：誰讓我們老百姓有這種心理需求呢[4]？

生詞

保險	(bǎo xiǎn)	N.	insurance
高邁	(gāo mài)	N.	Gao Mai, name of a person 人名
梁為民	(liáng wéi mín)	N.	Liang Weimin, name of a person 人名
春節	(chūn jié)	N.	Spring Festival (New Year's)
商量	(shāng liáng)	V.	to discuss, to talk over
傷腦筋	(shāng nǎo jīn)	VO.	to search one's brain, to use one's brain, to think hard, bothersome
拿得出手	(ná de chū shǒu)	Adj.	presentable
率	(lǜ)	N.	rate
穩定	(wěn dìng)	Adj.	stable, steady
滿足	(mǎn zú)	V.	to satisfy
開設	(kāi shè)	V.	to open
分別	(fēn bié)	Adj.	separately, respectively
項目	(xiàng mù)	N.	item, a list of items
吉利	(jí lì)	Adj.	fortunate, lucky, auspicious
起	(qǐ)	V.	to become, to take (the effect of)
法律	(fǎ lǜ)	N.	law
作用	(zuò yòng)	N.	function, role
賺	(zhuàn)	V.	to make (money)

Notes [4]誰讓……呢？, "Who made you do something?" is a rhetorical question used to express the speaker's belief that a mistake or unfortunate event is a person's own fault. By asking "Who made you do this?" the speaker is implying that no one did. Examples: 誰讓你沒有早一點兒來呢？ (Who kept you from coming earlier? You should have come earlier!) 誰讓你相信他呢？ (Who made you believe him? You shouldn't have believed him!)

小李: 哪里，这种保险不起法律作用，就是赚老百姓的钱呗。

高迈: 谁让我们老百姓有这种心理需求呢⁽⁴⁾?

生词

保险	(bǎo xiǎn)	*N.*	insurance
高迈	(gāo mài)	*N.*	Gao Mai, name of a person 人名
梁为民	(liáng wéi mín)	*N.*	Liang Weimin, name of a person 人名
春节	(chūn jié)	*N.*	Spring Festival (New Year's)
商量	(shāng liáng)	*V.*	to discuss, to talk over
伤脑筋	(shāng nǎo jīn)	*VO.*	to search one's brain, to use one's brain, to think hard, bothersome
拿得出手	(ná de chū shǒu)	*Adj.*	presentable
率	(lǜ)	*N.*	rate
稳定	(wěn dìng)	*Adj.*	stable, steady
满足	(mǎn zú)	*V.*	to satisfy
开设	(kāi shè)	*V.*	to open
分别	(fēn bié)	*Adj.*	separately, respectively
项目	(xiàng mù)	*N.*	item, a list of items
吉利	(jí lì)	*Adj.*	fortunate, lucky, auspicious
起	(qǐ)	*V.*	to become, to take (the effect of)
法律	(fǎ lǜ)	*N.*	law
作用	(zuò yòng)	*N.*	function, role
赚	(zhuàn)	*V.*	to make (money)

Notes ⁽⁴⁾谁让……呢？, "Who made you do something?" is a rhetorical question used to express the speaker's belief that a mistake or unfortunate event is a person's own fault. By asking "Who made you do this?" the speaker is implying that no one did. Examples: 谁让你没有早一点儿来呢？(Who kept you from coming earlier? You should have come earlier!) 谁让你相信他呢？(Who made you believe him? You shouldn't have believed him!)

二、電視原文 TV original

給結婚保個險
（根據原文改編）

　　結婚歷來被視為中國人一生中的頭等[5]大事。對於大多數新婚夫婦來說，一個熱熱鬧鬧，有模有樣的婚禮是少不了的。近些年來，盡管政府大力[6]提倡節儉辦[7]婚事，但隨著人們物質生活條件的改善，婚禮的排場還是一年比一年氣派。而作為新人的親朋好友，有幸被邀請參加婚禮竟很難說是好事還是壞事。

　　雖然在結婚禮品商店裡，各種各樣的禮品擺滿了櫃台。可是要挑上一件既不加重經濟負擔，又拿得出手的禮品還真挺傷腦筋。眼下在北京，就有這樣一種禮品受到了越來越多人的歡迎。

（採訪）

梁為民：　"我結婚的時候呢，我們一個同學買了一份婚姻保險送給我。這個婚姻保險我是頭一回收到，這個禮物給我感覺挺新穎的。它的價值是66塊錢，數字很吉利，很吉祥，而且也比較經濟。同時它也有比較好的意義在裡頭，它給人一種挺好的祝福，當時我心裡感覺特別好。等今年春節時候，我們的一個同學結婚，我去了。我當時買禮物的時候，首先就想到要給他買一份婚姻保險。在我給他禮物的時候，他很高興，他也覺得很新奇，就像當時我收到這種禮物的時候那種感覺一樣，我從他的表情[8]裡能看出來。"

Notes [5]頭等 means "top level", 頭 meaning "head" or "first" and 等 meaning "category" or "level", as in 頭等大事 (a matter of prime importance) and 頭等重要(of utmost significance). 頭等 is used mostly in formal and written contexts. It means the same as the colloquial terms 第一 and 最.

[6]大力 means "strongly", "with great force". It is used exclusively as an adverb preceding verbs, as in 大力提倡 (to vigorously advocate), 大力支持 (to vigorously support), 大力鼓勵 (to strongly encourage). 大力 is used in formal and written Chinese and often is followed by disyllabic verbs.

[7]The verb 辦 means "to handle", "to arrange", "to deal with". It is used in situations where there is paperwork or a bureaucratic process to deal with, as in 辦保險 (to get insurance). 買保險 can be used for "to purchase insurance".

[8]表情 vs 感情: 表情 means "facial expression". It may be used alone or in the phrase 臉上的表情 (the expression on someone's face). 感情 carries the more general meaning "affection" or "emotion", as in 何茹對她母親的感情 (He Ru's love for her mother).

二、电视原文 TV original

给结婚保个险

（根据原文改编）

结婚历来被视为中国人一生中的头等[5]大事。对于大多数新婚夫妇来说，一个热热闹闹，有模有样的婚礼是少不了的。近些年来，尽管政府大力[6]提倡节俭办[7]婚事，但随着人们物质生活条件的改善，婚礼的排场还是一年比一年气派。而作为新人的亲朋好友，有幸被邀请参加婚礼竟很难说是好事还是坏事。

虽然在结婚礼品商店里，各种各样的礼品摆满了柜台。可是要挑上一件既不加重经济负担，又拿得出手的礼品还真挺伤脑筋。眼下在北京，就有这样一种礼品受到了越来越多人的欢迎。

（采访）

梁为民：　"我结婚的时候呢，我们一个同学买了一份婚姻保险送给我。这个婚姻保险我是头一回收到，这个礼物给我感觉挺新颖的。它的价值是66块钱，数字很吉利，很吉祥，而且也比较经济。同时它也有比较好的意义在里头，它给人一种挺好的祝福，当时我心里感觉特别好。等今年春节时候，我们的一个同学结婚，我去了。我当时买礼物的时候，首先就想到要给他买一份婚姻保险。在我给他礼物的时候，他很高兴，他也觉得很新奇，就象当时我收到这种礼物的时候那种感觉一样，我从他的表情[8]里能看出来。"

Notes [5]头等 means "top level", 头 meaning "head" or "first" and 等 meaning "category" or "level", as in 头等大事 (a matter of prime importance) and 头等重要(of utmost significance). 头等 is used mostly in formal and written contexts. It means the same as the colloquial terms 第一 and 最.

[6]大力 means "strongly", "with great force". It is used exclusively as an adverb preceding verbs, as in 大力提倡 (to vigorously advocate), 大力支持 (to vigorously support), 大力鼓励 (to strongly encourage). 大力 is used in formal and written Chinese and often is followed by disyllabic verbs.

[7]The verb 办 means "to handle", "to arrange", "to deal with". It is used in situations where there is paperwork or a bureaucratic process to deal with, as in 办保险 (to get insurance). 买保险 can be used for "to purchase insurance".

[8]表情 vs 感情: 表情 means "facial expression". It may be used alone or in the phrase 脸上的表情 (the expression on someone's face). 感情 carries the more general meaning "affection" or "emotion", as in 何茹对她母亲的感情 (He Ru's love for her mother).

　　梁為民送給朋友的結婚禮品是北京市人民保險公司新近開設的結婚紀念保險。保險費分為66元、88元和100元三種。8和6都是吉祥的數字，如果夫婦雙方不離婚而迎來了二十五年銀婚紀念日，那麼交付66元保險的，可以領到460元的返還金；四十年紅寶石婚和五十年金婚紀念時可以分別領到2,000元和7,000元。如果考慮到物價上漲的因素，幾百幾千元保險金或許算不了甚麼[9]。然而作為結婚禮品，結婚紀念保險所蘊含的文化氛圍卻渲染了一種新婚的喜悅和神聖感。

（採訪）

記者：　　　　“你辦這個結婚保險是送朋友的還是為個人保險呢？”

被採訪者：“是為我們自己。”

記者：　　　　“那你們出於甚麼目的來辦這個結婚保險？”

被採訪者：“因為我覺得現在社會上離婚的也挺多的。我們辦這個保險主要是為我們自己，主要是說我們以後能白頭偕老，能共同度過我們的一生。就是這麼想的。”

　　北京東城區結婚登記處趙秀梅：“我們北京婚姻登記處自從92年的9月份，受人民保險公司的委託，開辦這種結婚紀念保險業務以來，受到新婚夫婦熱烈歡迎。雖然這個東西不起法律的約束作用，但是來登記結婚的人都有一個心理需求，就是願意白頭偕老，地久天長，圖一種吉利。購買這麼一份東西，能夠滿足他們這樣的心理需求。”

生詞

歷來	(lì lái)	*Adv.*	all along, always
被視為	(bèi shì wéi)	*VP.*	to be considered as
頭等大事	(tóu děng dà shì)	*NP.*	the most important thing

Notes [9] 算不了甚麼 is a fixed colloquial expression meaning "this is nothing" or "no big deal". 甚麼 here is an indefinite referent meaning "anything". Example: 在這種飯館吃飯，花幾百塊算不了甚麼。(It's nothing to spend a few hundred *yuan* eating in a restaurant like this.) The positive form 算得了甚麼 usually functions as a rhetorical question and means the same as the negative form. Example: 你算得了甚麼？還要來管我？(Who are you to tell me what to do?)

梁为民送给朋友的结婚礼品是北京市人民保险公司新近开设的结婚纪念保险。保险费分为66元、88元和100元三种。8和6都是吉祥的数字，如果夫妇双方不离婚而迎来了二十五年银婚纪念日，那么交付66元保险的，可以领到460元的返还金；四十年红宝石婚和五十年金婚纪念时可以分别领到2,000元和7,000元。如果考虑到物价上涨的因素，几百几千元保险金或许算不了什么[9]。然而作为结婚礼品，结婚纪念保险所蕴含的文化氛围却渲染了一种新婚的喜悦和神圣感。

（采访）

记者： "你办这个结婚保险是送朋友的还是为个人保险呢？"

被采访者： "是为我们自己。"

记者： "那你们出于什么目的来办这个结婚保险？"

被采访者： "因为我觉得现在社会上离婚的也挺多的。我们办这个保险主要是为我们自己，主要是说我们以后能白头偕老，能共同度过我们的一生。就是这么想的。"

北京东城区结婚登记处赵秀梅： "我们北京婚姻登记处自从92年的9月份，受人民保险公司的委托，开办这种结婚纪念保险业务以来，受到新婚夫妇热烈欢迎。虽然这个东西不起法律的约束作用，但是来登记结婚的人都有一个心理需求，就是愿意白头偕老，地久天长，图一种吉利。购买这么一份东西，能够满足他们这样的心理需求。"

生词

历来	(lì lái)	Adv.	all along, always
被视为	(bèi shì wéi)	VP.	to be considered as
头等大事	(tóu děng dà shì)	NP.	the most important thing

Notes [9]算不了什么 is a fixed colloquial expression meaning "this is nothing" or "no big deal". 什么 here is an indefinite referent meaning "anything". Example: 在这种饭馆吃饭，花几百块算不了什么. (It's nothing to spend a few hundred *yuan* eating in a restaurant like this.) The positive form 算得了什么 usually functions as a rhetorical question and means the same as the negative form. Example: 你算得了什么？还要来管我？ (Who are you to tell me what to do?)

新婚夫婦	(xīn hūn fū fù)	NP.	newly-married couple, newlyweds
熱熱鬧鬧	(rè rè nào nào)	Adj.	lively and thrilling
有模有樣	(yǒu mó yǒu yàng)	Adj/N.	stylish, stylishness
婚禮	(hūn lǐ)	N.	wedding, wedding ceremony
大力	(dà lì)	Adv.	strongly, vigorously
提倡	(tí chàng)	V.	to advocate, to promote
節儉	(jié jiǎn)	Adj.	thrifty, frugal
物質	(wù zhì)	N.	material, materialistic
排場	(pái chǎng)	N.	ostentation and extravagance
親朋好友	(qīn péng hǎo yǒu)	NP.	friends and relatives
新人	(xīn rén)	N.	newlyweds
有幸	(yǒu xìng)	Adj/Adv.	fortunate, lucky; fortunately
邀請	(yāo qǐng)	V.	to invite
竟	(jìng)	Adv.	even
各種各樣	(gè zhǒng gè yàng)	AdjP.	a variety of, various kinds of
擺滿	(bǎi mǎn)	V.	to place all over
櫃台	(guì tái)	N.	sales counter
挑	(tiāo)	V.	to select
加重	(jiā zhòng)	V.	to add, to increase
經濟	(jīng jì)	N/Adj.	economy; economical
負擔	(fù dān)	N.	burden, load
新穎	(xīn yǐng)	Adj.	new, novel
價值	(jià zhí)	N.	value
首先	(shǒu xiān)	Adv.	first
表情	(biǎo qíng)	N.	facial expression
新近	(xīn jìn)	Adj/Adv.	recent; recently
迎來	(yíng lái)	V.	to welcome (a time, festival, event, etc.)
銀婚	(yín hūn)	NP.	silver wedding anniversary
紀念日	(jì niàn rì)	NP.	day of commemoration, anniversary
交付	(jiāo fù)	V.	to pay for
領	(lǐng)	V.	to receive (salary, fund)
返還金	(fǎn huán jīn)	NP.	refund, returning fee
紅寶石婚	(hóng bǎo shí hūn)	NP.	red diamond wedding anniversary
金婚	(jīn hūn)	NP.	golden wedding anniversary
物價	(wù jià)	N.	price

新婚夫妇	(xīn hūn fū fù)	NP.	newly-married couple, newlyweds
热热闹闹	(rè rè nào nào)	Adj.	lively and thrilling
有模有样	(yǒu mó yǒu yàng)	Adj/N.	stylish, stylishness
婚礼	(hūn lǐ)	N.	wedding, wedding ceremony
大力	(dà lì)	Adv.	strongly, vigorously
提倡	(tí chàng)	V.	to advocate, to promote
节俭	(jié jiǎn)	Adj.	thrifty, frugal
物质	(wù zhì)	N.	material, materialistic
排场	(pái chǎng)	N.	ostentation and extravagance
亲朋好友	(qīn péng hǎo yǒu)	NP.	friends and relatives
新人	(xīn rén)	N.	newlyweds
有幸	(yǒu xìng)	Adj/Adv.	fortunate, lucky; fortunately
邀请	(yāo qǐng)	V.	to invite
竟	(jìng)	Adv.	even
各种各样	(gè zhǒng gè yàng)	AdjP.	a variety of, various kinds of
摆满	(bǎi mǎn)	V.	to place all over
柜台	(guì tái)	N.	sales counter
挑	(tiāo)	V.	to select
加重	(jiā zhòng)	V.	to add, to increase
经济	(jīng jì)	N/Adj.	economy; economical
负担	(fù dān)	N.	burden, load
新颖	(xīn yǐng)	Adj.	new, novel
价值	(jià zhí)	N.	value
首先	(shǒu xiān)	Adv.	first
表情	(biǎo qíng)	N.	facial expression
新近	(xīn jìn)	Adj/Adv.	recent; recently
迎来	(yíng lái)	V.	to welcome (a time, festival, event, etc.)
银婚	(yín hūn)	NP.	silver wedding anniversary
纪念日	(jì niàn rì)	NP.	day of commemoration, anniversary
交付	(jiāo fù)	V.	to pay for
领	(lǐng)	V.	to receive (salary, fund)
返还金	(fǎn huán jīn)	NP.	refund, returning fee
红宝石婚	(hóng bǎo shí hūn)	NP.	red diamond wedding anniversary
金婚	(jīn hūn)	NP.	golden wedding anniversary
物价	(wù jià)	N.	price

上漲	(shàng zhǎng)	*N/V.*	inflation, increase; to increase
因素	(yīn sù)	*N.*	factor
或許	(huò xǔ)	*Adv.*	maybe
蘊含	(yùn hán)	*V.*	to contain
氛圍	(fèn wéi)	*N.*	atmosphere
渲染	(xuàn rǎn)	*V.*	to play up, to heighten
喜悦	(xǐ yuè)	*N.*	happiness
神聖感	(shén shèng gǎn)	*NP.*	sacred sense, holy sense
出於⋯的目的	(chū yú...de mù dì)	*Prep.*	out of
白頭偕老	(bái tóu xié lǎo)	*Idiom.*	to live together until death
度過	(dù guò)	*V.*	to spend, to pass
東城區	(dōng chéng qū)	*Place N.*	east district
趙秀梅	(zhào xiù méi)	*N.*	Zhao Xiumei, name of a person 人名
登記處	(dēng jì chù)	*NP.*	registration office
委託	(wěi tuō)	*V.*	to entrust
約束	(yuē shù)	*N/V.*	control, restriction; to restrain
地久天長	(dì jiǔ tiān cháng)	*Idiom.*	to last as long as heaven and earth
圖	(tú)	*V.*	to seek for
購買	(gòu mǎi)	*V.*	to purchase

上涨	(shàng zhǎng)	N/V.	inflation, increase; to increase
因素	(yīn sù)	N.	factor
或许	(huò xǔ)	Adv.	maybe
蕴含	(yùn hán)	V.	to contain
氛围	(fèn wéi)	N.	atmosphere
渲染	(xuàn rǎn)	V.	to play up, to heighten
喜悦	(xǐ yuè)	N.	happiness
神圣感	(shén shèng gǎn)	NP.	sacred sense, holy sense
出于…的目的	(chū yú...de mù dì)	Prep.	out of
白头偕老	(bái tóu xié lǎo)	Idiom.	to live together until death
度过	(dù guò)	V.	to spend, to pass
东城区	(dōng chéng qū)	Place N.	east district
赵秀梅	(zhào xiù méi)	N.	Zhao Xiumei, name of a person 人名
登记处	(dēng jì chù)	NP.	registration office
委托	(wěi tuō)	V.	to entrust
约束	(yuē shù)	N/V.	control, restriction; to restrain
地久天长	(dì jiǔ tiān cháng)	Idiom.	to last as long as heaven and earth
图	(tú)	V.	to seek for
购买	(gòu mǎi)	V.	to purchase

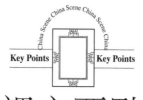

課文要點

一、詞語解釋 Words and Phrases

（一）文言詞、慣用詞 (Classical Chinese and idiomatic expressions)

> 1、被視為＝被看成是
> ☞ 結婚歷來被視為中國人一生中的頭等大事。
> 2、竟＝居然
> ☞ 有幸被邀請參加婚禮竟很難說是好事還是壞事。
> 3、眼下＝現在
> ☞ 眼下在北京，就有這樣一種禮品受到了越來越多人的歡迎。

（二）成語 (idioms)

> ◆ 親朋好友: relatives and friends
> ◆ 經濟負擔: economic burden
> ◆ 白頭偕老: to live together until death
> ◆ 地久天長: to last as long as heaven and earth

二、書面語、正式語、口語對照表 Written/formal/colloquial Comparison

	書面／正式語	口語		書面／正式語	口語
1	歷來	一直	7	新近	最近
2	被視為…	被看成是…／被認為是…	8	交付	給／付
3	頭等大事	最要緊的事	9	或許	也許／可能
4	有幸+V.	很榮幸地+V.	10	出於…目的	為了…
5	竟	竟然／居然	11	購買	買
6	目前	眼下／現在			

课文要点

一、词语解释 Words and Phrases

（一）文言词、惯用词 (Classical Chinese and idiomatic expressions)

1、被视为 = 被看成是

☞ 结婚历来被视为中国人一生中的头等大事。

2、竟 = 居然

☞ 有幸被邀请参加婚礼竟很难说是好事还是坏事。

3、眼下 = 现在

☞ 眼下在北京，就有这样一种礼品受到了越来越多人的欢迎。

（二）成语 (idioms)

◆ 亲朋好友: relatives and friends

◆ 经济负担: economic burden

◆ 白头偕老: to live together until death

◆ 地久天长: to last as long as heaven and earth

二、书面语、正式语、口语对照表 Written/formal/colloquial Comparison

	书面／正式语	口语		书面／正式语	口语
1	历来	一直	7	新近	最近
2	被视为…	被看成是…／被认为是…	8	交付	给／付
3	头等大事	最要紧的事	9	或许	也许／可能
4	有幸+V.	很荣幸地+V.	10	出于…目的	为了…
5	竟	竟然／居然	11	购买	买
6	目前	眼下／现在			

三、句型 ❀❀ Sentence Structures

（一）為……傷腦筋 (to be troubled, bothered, or annoyed by something; to have a headache over)

> ✍ 為……傷腦筋, "to be troubled, bothered, or annoyed by something", "to have a headache over", is most often used in colloquial Chinese. The noun following 為 can be a person or a thing. The negative particle 不 or 沒 must be placed before the preposition 為. Example: 他並沒有為獨立報告傷腦筋，他覺得這種報告是一種很好的經驗. (He is not really stressed out about writing an independent report. He thinks that writing this kind of report is a good experience.) This structure is similar to the pattern 為……而發愁 (see Lesson 7, Pattern 9). A more formal version of 為……傷腦筋 is 因……而煩惱. Example: 政府常常因流動人口過多而煩惱. (The government is often troubled by the size of the migrant population.)

☞ 這幾年買結婚禮品可是個傷腦筋的事情。

1、很多父母都為自己孩子的將來傷腦筋。

Many parents get headaches over their children's future.

2、自從有了出租車北京人一點都不用為出門坐車傷腦筋了。

Since the advent of taxis, people in Beijing don's have to worry about getting a ride when they go out.

問：每逢聖誕節，你總是為甚麼事傷腦筋？

答：＿＿＿＿＿＿＿＿＿＿＿＿＿＿＿＿＿＿＿＿。

（二）（對）……起……（的）作用 (to play a role in, to function as, to have an effect on)

> ✍ （對）……起……(的)作用, "to play a role in", "to function as", "to have an effect on", is used in both spoken and written Chinese. 作用 can be used either as a simple object, as in 起作用, or with certain modifying elements. Typical examples of elements that can precede 作用 include 法律, 促進, 保護, and 約束. Negative particles 不 or 沒 must be placed before the verb 起, as in 不起甚麼作用 (to serve no function whatsoever, to have no effect at all). The target of 作用 is placed before the verb 起 and is introduced by the preposition 對. Example: 這種政策對經濟不起促進作用. (This kind of policy has no role in advancing the economy.)

☞ 雖然這個東西不起法律的約束作用，但是來登記結婚的人都有一個心理需求，就是願意白頭偕老，地久天長，圖一種吉利。

1、這種保險是不起法律約束作用的。

This type of insurance is not protected by law.

三、句型 ∅ Sentence Structures

（一）为……伤脑筋 (to be troubled, bothered, or annoyed by something; to have a headache over)

> ✍ 为……伤脑筋,"to be troubled, bothered, or annoyed by something", "to have a headache over", is most often used in colloquial Chinese. The noun following 为 can be a person or a thing. The negative particle 不 or 没 must be placed before the preposition 为. Example: 他并没有为独立报告伤脑筋，他觉得这种报告是一种很好的经验. (He is not really stressed out about writing an independent report. He thinks that writing this kind of report is a good experience.) This structure is similar to the pattern 为……而发愁 (see Lesson 7, Pattern 9). A more formal version of 为……伤脑筋 is 因……而烦恼. Example: 政府常常因流动人口过多而烦恼. (The government is often troubled by the size of the migrant population.)

☞ 这几年买结婚礼品可是个伤脑筋的事情。

1、很多父母都为自己孩子的将来伤脑筋。
Many parents get headaches over their children's future.

2、自从有了出租车北京人一点都不用为出门坐车伤脑筋了。
Since the advent of taxis, people in Beijing don't have to worry about getting a ride when they go out.

问：每逢圣诞节，你总是为什么事伤脑筋？
答：＿＿＿＿＿＿＿＿＿＿＿＿＿＿＿＿＿＿＿。

（二）（对）……起……（的）作用 (to play a role in, to function as, to have an effect on)

> ✍ （对）……起……(的)作用, "to play a role in", "to function as", "to have an effect on", is used in both spoken and written Chinese. 作用 can be used either as a simple object, as in 起作用, or with certain modifying elements. Typical examples of elements that can precede 作用 include 法律, 促进, 保护, and 约束. Negative particles 不 or 没 must be placed before the verb 起, as in 不起什么作用 (to serve no function whatsoever, to have no effect at all). The target of 作用 is placed before the verb 起 and is introduced by the preposition 对. Example: 这种政策对经济不起促进作用. (This kind of policy has no role in advancing the economy.)

☞ 虽然这个东西不起法律的约束作用，但是来登记结婚的人都有一个心理需求，就是愿意白头偕老，地久天长，图一种吉利。

1、这种保险是不起法律约束作用的。
This type of insurance is not protected by law.

163

2、讓孩子學鋼琴到底對孩子的智力發展起不起作用？

Does making a child play the piano ultimately have an effect on the child's intellectual development?

問：你吃的這種藥到底對你的病起不起作用？要是不起作用，你怎麼辦？

答：＿＿＿＿＿＿＿＿＿＿＿＿＿＿＿＿＿＿＿＿＿＿。

（三）滿足……的需求（／要求）(to satisfy or meet the need of, to fulfill the demand for)

> ✍ 滿足……需求, "to satisfy or meet the need of", "to fulfill the demand for", is a verb phrase that may alternately take 要求, 需要, or 條件 as an object. The auxiliary verb 能 can be used with 滿足 to indicate possibility. Negation must occur directly before the verb 滿足. In this pattern, 滿足 cannot be replaced by 滿意, although both often share the same English translation.

☞ 購買這麼一份東西，能夠滿足他們這樣的心理需求。

1、結婚保險能夠滿足新婚夫婦的心理需求。

Marriage insurance can satisfy the psychological needs of a newly-married couple.

2、為了滿足女兒的學琴要求，老王決定送女兒去上鋼琴課。

In order to satisfy his daughter's demand to study piano, Lao Wang decided to send her to piano classes.

問：很多人去看心理醫生是為了滿足一種心理要求，還是真的讓醫生看病？

答：＿＿＿＿＿＿＿＿＿＿＿＿＿＿＿＿＿＿＿＿＿。

（四）……被視為……／A 被 B 視為……(to be considered)

> ✍ 被視為, "to be considered", forms a passive sentence which lacks the adverse or negative tone associated with most 被 structures. It can be used with or without an agent. If the agent is used, it must be placed after 被 and before the verb 視為. Example: 現在找工作被年青人視為一生中的頭等大事. (For young people, finding a job is now considered the first priority in life.) This pattern is often used in both spoken and written Chinese. A more colloquial version is 把……看成是……. Example: 他把找工作看成是頭等重要的事. (He thinks finding a job is an extremely important thing.)

☞ 結婚歷來被視為中國人一生中的頭等大事。

1、以前下海幹個體戶被視為讓人吃驚的舉動。

In the past, to become an entrepreneur was considered shocking.

2、让孩子学钢琴到底对孩子的智力发展起不起作用？

Does making a child play the piano ultimately have an effect on the child's intellectual development?

问：你吃的这种药到底对你的病起不起作用？要是不起作用，你怎么办？

答：＿＿＿＿＿＿＿＿＿＿＿＿＿＿＿＿＿＿＿＿＿＿。

（三）满足……的需求（／要求）(to satisfy or meet the need of, to fulfill the demand for)

> ✍ 满足……需求, "to satisfy or meet the need of", "to fulfill the demand for", is a verb phrase that may alternately take 要求, 需要, or 条件 as an object. The auxiliary verb 能 can be used with 满足 to indicate possibility. Negation must occur directly before the verb 满足. In this pattern, 满足 cannot be replaced by 满意, although both often share the same English translation.

☞ 购买这么一份东西，能够满足他们这样的心理需求。

1、结婚保险能够满足新婚夫妇的心理需求。

Marriage insurance can satisfy the psychological needs of a newly-married couple.

2、为了满足女儿的学琴要求，老王决定送女儿去上钢琴课。

In order to satisfy his daughter's demand to study piano, Lao Wang decided to send her to piano classes.

问：很多人去看心理医生是为了满足一种心理要求，还是真的让医生看病？

答：＿＿＿＿＿＿＿＿＿＿＿＿＿＿＿＿＿＿＿＿＿＿。

（四）……被视为……／ A 被 B 视为…… (to be considered)

> ✍ 被视为, "to be considered", forms a passive sentence which lacks the adverse or negative tone associated with most 被 structures. It can be used with or without an agent. If the agent is used, it must be placed after 被 and before the verb 视为. Example: 现在找工作被年青人视为一生中的头等大事. (For young people, finding a job is now considered the first priority in life.) This pattern is often used in both spoken and written Chinese. A more colloquial version is 把……看成是……. Example: 他把找工作看成是头等重要的事. (He thinks finding a job is an extremely important thing.)

☞ 结婚历来被视为中国人一生中的头等大事。

1、以前下海干个体户被视为让人吃惊的举动。

In the past, to become an entrepreneur was considered shocking.

2、結婚以後攢錢買房子被老百姓視為頭等大事。

After marriage, saving money to buy a house is considered the most important thing.

問：現在甚麼問題被美國政府視為頭等大事？

答：＿＿＿＿＿＿＿＿＿＿＿＿＿＿＿＿＿＿＿＿。

（五）加重／減輕（工作／生活／學習）負擔 (to add/reduce burden)

> ✍ 加重 means "to add weight"; 減輕 means "to reduce". Unlike the English verb "to add", which often takes objects such as "pressure", "stress", "work", etc., 加重 most often takes 負擔 or 任務 as its object. Modifying elements 工作, 學習, 經濟, and 生活 can be placed before 負擔 to specify the type of burden. Negative particles 不 and 沒 must be placed before the verb 加重。

☞ 可是要挑上一件既不加重經濟負擔，又拿得出手的禮品還真挺傷腦筋。

1、為了不加重學生的負擔，老師把考試改在下星期三了。

In order not to put added pressure on students, the professor changed the exam to next Wednesday.

2、我們都知道中國家庭的收入情況，所以不能總去他們那兒吃飯，加重他們的經濟負擔。

We all know about the financial situation of Chinese families, so we can't add to their economic burden by always going to their house to eat.

問：像你這樣出國留學來北京，會不會加重你父母的經濟負擔？

答：＿＿＿＿＿＿＿＿＿＿＿＿＿＿＿＿＿＿＿＿。

（六）很難說…… (it's hard for me to say, it's hard to tell)

> ✍ 很難說, "it's hard for me to say" or "it's hard to tell", is a structure in which the subject is the speaker, which is often omitted. 很難說 may be positioned either before or after the subject. This expression is used in both spoken and written Chinese.

☞ 作為新人的親朋好友，有幸被邀請參加婚禮竟很難說是好事還是壞事。

1、被親朋好友邀請參加婚禮，很難說是好事還是壞事。因為一個婚禮你最少得出100元。

It is hard to say whether it is a good or bad thing to be invited to a wedding by friends and relatives, because you will spend at least 100 *yuan* at the wedding ceremony.

165

2、结婚以后攒钱买房子被老百姓视为头等大事。

After marriage, saving money to buy a house is considered the most important thing.

问：现在什么问题被美国政府视为头等大事？

答：＿＿＿＿＿＿＿＿＿＿＿＿＿＿＿＿＿＿＿。

（五）加重／减轻（工作／生活／学习）负担 (to add/reduce burden)

> ✍ 加重 means "to add weight"; 减轻 means "to reduce". Unlike the English verb "to add", which often takes objects such as "pressure", "stress", "work", etc., 加重 most often takes 负担 or 任务 as its object. Modifying elements 工作, 学习, 经济, and 生活 can be placed before 负担 to specify the type of burden. Negative particles 不 and 没 must be placed before the verb 加重.

☞ 可是要挑上一件既不加重经济负担，又拿得出手的礼品还真挺伤脑筋。

1、为了不加重学生的负担，老师把考试改在下星期三了。

In order not to put added pressure on students, the professor changed the exam to next Wednesday.

2、我们都知道中国家庭的收入情况，所以不能总去他们那儿吃饭，加重他们的经济负担。

We all know about the financial situation of Chinese families, so we can't add to their economic burden by always going to their house to eat.

问：象你这样出国留学来北京，会不会加重你父母的经济负担？

答：＿＿＿＿＿＿＿＿＿＿＿＿＿＿＿＿＿＿＿。

（六）很难说…… (it's hard for me to say, it's hard to tell)

> ✍ 很难说, "it's hard for me to say" or "it's hard to tell", is a structure in which the subject is the speaker, which is often omitted. 很难说 may be positioned either before or after the subject. This expression is used in both spoken and written Chinese.

☞ 作为新人的亲朋好友，有幸被邀请参加婚礼竟很难说是好事还是坏事。

1、被亲朋好友邀请参加婚礼，很难说是好事还是坏事。因为一个婚礼你最少得出100元。

It is hard to say whether it is a good or bad thing to be invited to a wedding by friends and relatives, because you will spend at least 100 *yuan* at the wedding ceremony.

2、很難説甚麼樣的結婚禮品最拿得出手。

It is hard to say what type of wedding gift is most presentable.

問：你認為買住房保險會加重老百姓的生活負擔嗎？
答：＿＿＿＿＿＿＿＿＿＿＿＿＿＿＿＿＿＿＿。

（七）開設 (to establish, to open up)

> ✍ 開設 is a verb meaning "to establish", "to open up". Unlike its English counterpart, which can take many different types of objects, 開設 usually takes nouns that indicate a subdivision or a program within an institution or establishment, e.g., 開設業務 (to establish a business), 開設項目 (to open a new product line), 開設課程 (to establish a curriculum), 開設分公司 (to establish a branch company). 開設 is rarely used with objects such as 大學 and 大飯店. The verb 開辦 is similar to 開設, but 開辦 can take a wider range of objects, including all objects taken by 開設 as well as nouns which refer to larger establishments or complete institutions, such as 大學 and 大公司.

☞ 梁為民送給朋友的結婚禮品是北京市人民保險公司新近開設的結婚紀念保險。

1、這個保險公司開設的項目有汽車保險、房子保險和人壽保險等。

This insurance company offers automobile, home owner's, and life insurance.

2、這個結婚禮品店最近開設了三個分店。可想而知，這個結婚禮品店的生意很好。

This bridal shop recently opened up three branch stores. It is not hard to figure out that business is very good.

問：這家大飯店都開設哪些服務項目？
答：＿＿＿＿＿＿＿＿＿＿＿＿＿＿＿＿＿。

（八）分為……種（／類／樣） (to be divided into, to be apportioned into)

> ✍ 分為, "to be divided into" or "to be apportioned into", must be followed either by a number and a measure word or a question word asking about a number. An alternate way of saying 分為 is 分成, which is preferred in colloquial Chinese. 分為 is more formal than 分成 and is used mostly in formal and written contexts. 種 can be replaced by either 類 or 樣.

☞ 保險費分為66元，88元和100元三種。

1、中國經濟制度大致可以分為兩種：一種是市場經濟，一種是計劃經濟。

The economic system in China can generally be divided into two categories: market economy and planned economy.

2、很难说什么样的结婚礼品最拿得出手。

It is hard to say what type of wedding gift is most presentable.

问：你认为买住房保险会加重老百姓的生活负担吗？

答：_____。

（七）开设 (to establish, to open up)

> ✍ 开设 is a verb meaning "to establish", "to open up". Unlike its English counterpart, which can take many different types of objects, 开设 usually takes nouns that indicate a subdivision or a program within an institution or establishment, e.g., 开设业务 (to establish a business), 开设项目 (to open a new product line), 开设课程 (to establish a curriculum), 开设分公司 (to establish a branch company). 开设 is rarely used with objects such as 大学 and 大饭店. The verb 开办 is similar to 开设, but 开办 can take a wider range of objects, including all objects taken by 开设 as well as nouns which refer to larger establishments or complete institutions, such as 大学 and 大公司.

☞ 梁为民送给朋友的结婚礼品是北京市人民保险公司新近开设的结婚纪念保险。

1、这个保险公司开设的项目有汽车保险、房子保险和人寿保险等。

This insurance company offers automobile, home owner's, and life insurance.

2、这个结婚礼品店最近开设了三个分店。可想而知，这个结婚礼品店的生意很好。

This bridal shop recently opened up three branch stores. It is not hard to figure out that business is very good.

问：这家大饭店都开设哪些服务项目？

答：_____。

（八）分为……种（／类／样）(to be divided into, to be apportioned into)

> ✍ 分为, "to be divided into" or "to be apportioned into", must be followed either by a number and a measure word or a question word asking about a number. An alternate way of saying 分为 is 分成, which is preferred in colloquial Chinese. 分为 is more formal than 分成 and is used mostly in formal and written contexts. 种 can be replaced by either 类 or 样.

☞ 保险费分为66元，88元和100元三种。

1、中国经济制度大致可以分为两种：一种是市场经济，一种是计划经济。

The economic system in China can generally be divided into two categories: market economy and planned economy.

2、午餐可以分為如下幾種：中式快餐、洋快餐、盒飯、工作午餐等。

Lunch can be divided into the following categories: Chinese-style fast food, Western fast food, boxed meals, and lunch on the job.

問：美國的大學一般可以分為幾種？你上的是哪種？

答：＿＿＿＿＿＿＿＿＿＿＿＿＿＿＿＿＿＿＿＿＿＿。

（九）考慮（到）……的因素 (considering the factor of)

> 考慮（到）……的因素, "considering the factor of", can function either as a verb phrase in a main clause, or as an adverbial phrase which usually indicates a reason for doing something. When used as an adverbial phrase, 考慮（到）……的因素 must be placed at the beginning of the sentence. 到 can be omitted if completion of the action is not emphasized. Example: 我們應該不應該考慮這些意外的因素呢？ (Should we consider these unforeseen factors?) The negative particles 不 and 沒 are placed immediately before the verb 考慮.

☞ 如果考慮到物價上漲的因素，幾百幾千元保險金或許算不了甚麼。

1、買甚麼東西都要考慮到物價上漲的因素。

Whatever you want to buy, you have to consider inflation.

2、就是因為考慮到時間的因素，很多人現在更喜歡吃快餐。

Because of the time factor, many people nowadays prefer fast food.

問：你為甚麼要放棄大學三年級時出國留學的機會？

答：＿＿＿＿＿＿＿＿＿＿＿＿＿＿＿＿＿＿＿＿＿＿。

（十）出於……（的）目的 (stemming from the motive of, for the purpose of)

> 出於……（的）目的 is often used as an adverbial phrase indicating the purpose of the main clause. Originally, it indicated a speaker's criticism of the subject's ill intentions, but it has since lost much of its negative connotation. The structure is often used in formal and written contexts, but is quite different from the structure 為了……, which does not carry a critical tone. When used as an adverbial phrase, 出於……（的）目的 must be placed before the main clause. Example: 出於一種自私的目的，他決定拋棄自己的家庭. (Stemming from some selfish purpose, he decided to abandon his own family.) Although this pattern can be negated by 不, it often takes 不是 instead. Example: 他離開該公司並不是出於一種個人的目的. (His leaving the company was not for personal reasons.)

☞ 那你們出於甚麼目的來辦這個結婚保險？

2、午餐可以分为如下几种：中式快餐、洋快餐、盒饭、工作午餐等。

Lunch can be divided into the following categories: Chinese-style fast food, Western fast food, boxed meals, and lunch on the job.

问：美国的大学一般可以分为几种？你上的是哪种？

答：＿＿＿＿＿＿＿＿＿＿＿＿＿＿＿＿＿＿＿＿＿＿。

（九）考虑（到）……的因素 (considering the factor of)

> ✍ 考虑（到）……的因素, "considering the factor of", can function either as a verb phrase in a main clause, or as an adverbial phrase which usually indicates a reason for doing something. When used as an adverbial phrase, 考虑（到）……的因素 must be placed at the beginning of the sentence. 到 can be omitted if completion of the action is not emphasized. Example: 我们应该不应该考虑这些意外的因素呢？(Should we consider these unforeseen factors?) The negative particles 不 and 没 are placed immediately before the verb 考虑.

☞ 如果考虑到物价上涨的因素，几百几千元保险金或许算不了什么。

1、买什么东西都要考虑到物价上涨的因素。

Whatever you want to buy, you have to consider inflation.

2、就是因为考虑到时间的因素，很多人现在更喜欢吃快餐。

Because of the time factor, many people nowadays prefer fast food.

问：你为什么要放弃大学三年级时出国留学的机会？

答：＿＿＿＿＿＿＿＿＿＿＿＿＿＿＿＿＿＿＿＿＿＿。

（十）出于……（的）目的 (stemming from the motive of, for the purpose of)

> ✍ 出于……（的）目的 is often used as an adverbial phrase indicating the purpose of the main clause. Originally, it indicated a speaker's criticism of the subject's ill intentions, but it has since lost much of its negative connotation. The structure is often used in formal and written contexts, but is quite different from the structure 为了……, which does not carry a critical tone. When used as an adverbial phrase, 出于……（的）目的 must be placed before the main clause. Example: 出于一种自私的目的，他决定抛弃自己的家庭. (Stemming from some selfish purpose, he decided to abandon his own family.) Although this pattern can be negated by 不, it often takes 不是 instead. Example: 他离开该公司并不是出于一种个人的目的. (His leaving the company was not for personal reasons.)

☞ 那你们出于什么目的来办这个结婚保险？

1、你是出於甚麼目的跑來我們公司申請工作的？

Why did you come to our company to apply for a job?

2、你來辦這個保險是出於甚麼目的？

Why did you buy this insurance?

問：出於甚麼目的政府現在實行新的買房政策？

答：＿＿＿＿＿＿＿＿＿＿＿＿＿＿＿＿＿＿。

（十一）圖的是／圖……(what one pursues is, the purpose of doing something is; to pursue, to seek)

> ✍ 圖的是, "what one pursues is" or "the purpose of doing something is", is used most often in colloquial Chinese to emphasize the purpose or goal of one's action. Example: 買車圖的是方便. (People buy cars for convenience.) 圖 can also be used alone as a verb, as in 在北京買自行車就圖了方便. (In Beijing you purchase a bicycle for convenience.) 圖 and 圖的是 can only take abstract nouns and adjectives such as 簡單 (simplicity), 便宜 (cheap), and 痛快 (carefree) as their objects. The negative form of 圖的是 is either 圖的不是 or 不是圖; for 圖 it is 不圖. A more formal version of 圖的是 is 為了.

☞ 雖然這個東西不起法律的約束作用，但是來登記結婚的人都有一個心理需求，就是願意白頭偕老，地久天長，圖一種吉利。

1、很多人選擇做個體戶，圖的就是有自由。

What many people are seeking when they become entrepreneurs is freedom.

2、我認為給新人買結婚保險並不是圖吉利，而是圖省事。

I believe that you buy marriage insurance for newlyweds not to bring good fortune, but rather because they are looking to save themselves trouble.

問：你來北京六個月到底圖甚麼？

答：＿＿＿＿＿＿＿＿＿＿＿＿＿＿＿＿＿＿＿。

（十二）受……的委託 (to be entrusted by)

> ✍ B 受 A 的委託, "B is entrusted by A", is a passive structure that does not carry any negative overtones. 受 here cannot be replaced by 被. The active form of this structure is A 委託 B. 受 ……委託 can be used as an adverbial phrase before a main clause, or as a verb in a main clause. Examples: 受政府的委託，這兒的地方政府開辦了十家合資公司. (Entrusted by the government, the local government opened ten joint-venture companies.) 這樣的大保險公司都不是個人的，都是受政府委託開辦的. (None of these types of large insurance companies are individually owned; all have been established by government mandate.)

168

1、你是出于什么目的跑来我们公司申请工作的？

Why did you come to our company to apply for a job?

2、你来办这个保险是出于什么目的？

Why did you buy this insurance?

问：出于什么目的政府现在实行新的买房政策？

答：_____。

（十一）图的是／图⋯⋯ (what one pursues is, the purpose of doing something is; to pursue, to seek)

> ✍ 图的是, "what one pursues is" or "the purpose of doing something is", is used most often in colloquial Chinese to emphasize the purpose or goal of one's action. Example: 买车图的是方便. (People buy cars for convenience.) 图 can also be used alone as a verb, as in 在北京买自行车就图了方便. (In Beijing you purchase a bicycle for convenience.) 图 and 图的是 can only take abstract nouns and adjectives such as 简单 (simplicity), 便宜 (cheap), and 痛快 (carefree) as their objects. The negative form of 图的是 is either 图的不是 or 不是图; for 图 it is 不图. A more formal version of 图的是 is 为了.

☞ 虽然这个东西不起法律的约束作用，但是来登记结婚的人都有一个心理需求，就是愿意白头偕老，地久天长，图一种吉利。

1、很多人选择做个体户，图的就是有自由。

What many people are seeking when they become entrepreneurs is freedom.

2、我认为给新人买结婚保险并不是图吉利，而是图省事。

I believe that you buy marriage insurance for newlyweds not to bring good fortune, but rather because they are looking to save themselves trouble.

问：你来北京六个月到底图什么？

答：_____。

（十二）受⋯⋯的委托 (to be entrusted by)

> ✍ B 受 A 的委托, "B is entrusted by A", is a passive structure that does not carry any negative overtones. 受 here cannot be replaced by 被. The active form of this structure is A 委托 B. 受⋯⋯委托 can be used as an adverbial phrase before a main clause, or as a verb in a main clause. Examples: 受政府的委托，这儿的地方政府开办了十家合资公司. (Entrusted by the government, the local government opened ten joint-venture companies.) 这样的大保险公司都不是个人的，都是受政府委托开办的. (None of these types of large insurance companies are individually owned; all have been established by government mandate.)

168

☞ 我們北京婚姻登記處自從92年的9月份，受人民保險公司的委託，開辦這種結婚紀念保險業務以來，受到新婚夫婦熱烈歡迎。

1、受婦女聯合會的委託，北京舉辦了一次"假日父母"活動。

At the request of the Women's Federation, the city of Beijing sponsored a "holiday parents" activity.

2、受保險總公司的委託，我們最近開設了一個新的保險業務。

The head of the insurance company has entrusted us with establishing a new insurance service.

問：_____?

答：我們受教育局的委託舉辦這次義務勞動的活動。

四、文化背景知識 Cultural Notes

1. The numbers 6 and 8 are auspicious numbers in China. "Six" represents smoothness, success, favorable circumstances (順利); "eight" represents the idea of 發, in this context meaning 發財, or or "strike it rich".

2. 拿得出手 (referring here to a gift that is presentable) is related to the idea of "face" (面子). When presenting a gift it is essential that the presenter deliver a suitable gift for the occasion. If an inexpensive, inappropriate gift is selected, then the presenter will lose "face" for appearing to be cheap (小氣).

3. When presenting wedding gifts in China, some items are to be avoided. One obvious example is a clock (鐘). This is because the sound for the word for clock (鐘) sounds the same as the word 終 meaning "to die" (the characters for "clock" and "to die" are of course different). Note also that if one were to say 送鐘 ("send or present a clock as a gift"), this would sound the same as saying "send someone off to die" (送終).

4. 白頭偕老 (偕 means "together") and 地久天長 are common wedding salutations. They can be spoken directly to the bride and groom, or they can be written on a wedding card.

☞ 我们北京婚姻登记处自从92年的9月份，受人民保险公司的委托，开办这种结婚纪念保险业务以来，受到新婚夫妇热烈欢迎。

1、受妇女联合会的委托，北京举办了一次 "假日父母" 活动。

At the request of the Women's Federation, the city of Beijing sponsored a "holiday parents" activity.

2、受保险总公司的委托，我们最近开设了一个新的保险业务。

The head of the insurance company has entrusted us with establishing a new insurance service.

问: _____?
答: 我们受教育局的委托举办这次义务劳动的活动。

四、文化背景知识 Cultural Notes

1. The numbers 6 and 8 are auspicious numbers in China. "Six" represents smoothness, success, favorable circumstances (顺利); "eight" represents the idea of 发, in this context meaning 发财, or "strike it rich".

2. 拿得出手 (referring here to a gift that is presentable) is related to the idea of "face" (面子). When presenting a gift it is essential that the presenter deliver a suitable gift for the occasion. If an inexpensive, inappropriate gift is selected, then the presenter will lose "face" for appearing to be cheap (小气).

3. When presenting wedding gifts in China, some items are to be avoided. One obvious example is a clock (钟). This is because the sound for the word for clock (钟) sounds the same as the word 终 meaning "to die" (the characters for "clock" and "to die" are of course different). Note also that if one were to say 送钟 ("send or present a clock as a gift"), this would sound the same as saying "send someone off to die" (送终).

4. 白头偕老 (偕 means "together") and 地久天长 are common wedding salutations. They can be spoken directly to the bride and groom, or they can be written on a wedding card.

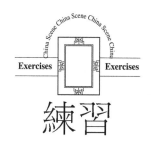

練習

語言結構 Structures

一、短語翻譯 (Phrase translation)

1. to insure one's marriage
2. the most important matter in one's life
3. friends and relatives of the newlyweds
4. an extravagant and fancy wedding
5. conditions of the materialistic life
6. to shop for a wedding gift at a store
7. a family's economic burden
8. lucky number and lucky symbol
9. the insurance fee for a car
10. silver and golden anniversaries
11. serious price inflation
12. the cultural atmosphere
13. to spend one's life together (to be together until one's hair is white)
14. to seek for an auspicious sign and to satisfy one's psychological needs

二、聽力練習 (Listening comprehension)

1、聽寫 (Dictation)

2、聽錄音並回答問題 (Answering questions while listening to the audio CD)
　　(1) 中國人為甚麼開始談論 "保險" 了？
　　(2) 用書上的話說說中國的保險業。
　　(3) 用你自己的話說說美國的一種保險業。（汽車、人壽、醫療、住房等等）

练习

语言结构 Structures

一、短语翻译 (Phrase translation)

1. to insure one's marriage
2. the most important matter in one's life
3. friends and relatives of the newlyweds
4. an extravagant and fancy wedding
5. conditions of the materialistic life
6. to shop for a wedding gift at a store
7. a family's economic burden
8. lucky number and lucky symbol
9. the insurance fee for a car
10. silver and golden anniversaries
11. serious price inflation
12. the cultural atmosphere
13. to spend one's life together (to be together until one's hair is white)
14. to seek for an auspicious sign and to satisfy one's psychological needs

二、听力练习 (Listening comprehension)

1、听写 (Dictation)

2、听录音并回答问题 (Answering questions while listening to the audio CD)
  (1) 中国人为什么开始谈论"保险"了？
  (2) 用书上的话说说中国的保险业。
  (3) 用你自己的话说说美国的一种保险业。（汽车、人寿、医疗、住房等等）

三、填空 (Fill in the blanks)

流動人口、自食其力、日新月異、固定人口

這個城市的經濟發展＿＿＿＿＿＿＿，吸引了很多外地人。以前＿＿＿＿＿＿＿五萬，根本沒有＿＿＿＿＿＿＿。可是現在固定人口和流動人口一共二十萬。雖然城裡人很多，可是人人都有工作，都能＿＿＿＿＿＿＿。

親朋好友、地久天長、經濟負擔、白頭偕老

這個婚禮雖然十分排場，可是並沒有加重＿＿＿＿＿＿＿。新婚夫婦請來了很多＿＿＿＿＿＿＿。每個人都祝福新婚夫婦＿＿＿＿＿＿＿，＿＿＿＿＿＿＿。

四、完成句子 (Complete the sentences)

1、　　Ａ：現在中國學鋼琴的孩子越來越多嗎？
　　　　Ｂ：對。＿＿＿＿＿＿＿＿＿＿＿＿＿＿＿＿＿＿＿＿＿＿＿＿＿＿＿＿＿＿
　　　　（隨著……的改善；……越來越多；很難說……）

2、　　Ａ：你們這個保險公司開設甚麼業務？
　　　　Ｂ：我們＿＿＿＿＿＿＿＿＿＿＿＿＿＿＿＿＿＿＿＿＿＿＿＿＿＿＿＿＿＿
　　　　（受……的委託；給……辦……保險；分為……種）

3、　　Ａ：＿＿＿＿＿＿＿＿＿＿＿＿＿＿＿＿＿＿＿＿＿＿＿＿＿＿＿＿＿＿＿＿
　　　　Ｂ：你知道現在的社會競爭很激烈，為了培養孩子的競爭意識，我們決定送孩子去學鋼琴。
　　　　（出於……的目的；考慮到……的因素）

五、閱讀短文、回答問題 (Answering questions based on the reading passages)

孩子的生日歷來[10]被美國人視為一年中的幾件頭等大事之一。對於大多數的家長來說，安排一個熱熱鬧鬧，有模有樣，有氣派的生日晚會是少不了的事情。生日前，

✎ Notes　[10]In most cases, 歷來, 向來 and 一向, meaning "all along", are interchangeable. They can precede a verb or a negative particle + verb. Examples: 我歷來不主張婚禮太排場. (I have never been in favor of overly fancy weddings.) 他向來不認為這是一個問題. (He never recognized this as a problem.) 這位老師一向上課遲到三分鐘. (This teacher is always three minutes late for class.)

三、填空 (Fill in the blanks)

流动人口、自食其力、日新月异、固定人口

这个城市的经济发展＿＿＿＿＿＿，吸引了很多外地人。以前＿＿＿＿＿＿五万，根本没有＿＿＿＿＿＿。可是现在固定人口和流动人口一共二十万。虽然城里人很多，可是人人都有工作，都能＿＿＿＿＿＿。

亲朋好友、地久天长、经济负担、白头偕老

这个婚礼虽然十分排场，可是并没有加重＿＿＿＿＿＿。新婚夫妇请来了很多＿＿＿＿＿＿。每个人都祝福新婚夫妇＿＿＿＿＿＿，＿＿＿＿＿＿。

四、完成句子 (Complete the sentences)

1、　A：现在中国学钢琴的孩子越来越多吗？
　　B：对。＿＿＿＿＿＿＿＿＿＿＿＿＿＿＿＿＿＿＿＿＿＿＿＿＿＿
　　（随着……的改善；……越来越多；很难说……）

2、　A：你们这个保险公司开设什么业务？
　　B：我们＿＿＿＿＿＿＿＿＿＿＿＿＿＿＿＿＿＿＿＿＿＿＿＿＿＿
　　（受……的委托；给……办……保险；分为……种）

3、　A：＿＿＿＿＿＿＿＿＿＿＿＿＿＿＿＿＿＿＿＿＿＿＿＿＿＿
　　B：你知道现在的社会竞争很激烈，为了培养孩子的竞争意识，我们决定送孩子去学钢琴。
　　（出于……的目的；考虑到……的因素）

五、阅读短文、回答问题 (Answering questions based on the reading passages)

　　孩子的生日历来[10]被美国人视为一年中的几件头等大事之一。对于大多数的家长来说，安排一个热热闹闹，有模有样，有气派的生日晚会是少不了的事情。生日前，

Notes [10]In most cases, 历来, 向来 and 一向, meaning "all along", are interchangeable. They can precede a verb or a negative particle + verb. Examples: 我历来不主张婚礼太排场. (I have never been in favor of overly fancy weddings.) 他向来不认为这是一个问题. (He never recognized this as a problem.) 这位老师一向上课迟到三分钟. (This teacher is always three minutes late for class.)

家長會讓孩子開出一個邀請名單。作為被邀請的小朋友，少不了要父母帶他們去禮品店或者玩具店挑上一件既不加重經濟負擔，又拿得出手的禮品送給自己的朋友。生日那天，很多父母也會委託一些生日晚會公司登台演出，或者自己編節目為孩子們演出。晚會多數都提供晚餐，晚餐的最後一個節目是吃蛋糕，唱生日歌。過去在中國可以說是根本沒有給小孩子過生日的習俗。人要到六十歲才開始過生日，可是現在國門開了，西方的影響越來越大，孩子的生日晚會也開始在中國流行起來。

問題

　　(1) 用五句話敍述生日晚會有哪些節目？

　　(2) 敍述一個你印象最深的生日晚會，或者婚禮。

　　　“生男好聽，生女好命”，眼下這句話正在廣州流行。這種變化的主要特點是，年齡越大，“重男輕女”的現象越嚴重；年齡越輕，喜歡生女孩的越多，據分析，導致這種變化的主要原因是：

(1) 隨著廣州市婦女步入社會生產的行列，她們的社會經濟地位和作用有了很大的提高，這就為打破“重男輕女”的傳統觀念提供了一定的社會條件。

(2) 我國的退休養老制度和醫療保健制度使老百姓不必過分考慮今後的養老問題。

(3) 隨著大家庭的衰落，城市裡的小家庭的日益增多，使得生兒育女的目的從傳宗接代轉到了夫妻間的“私事”。

(4) 男女平等的觀念被大多數的人所接受。

(5) 與男孩相比較，女孩好養好帶，並且女孩心細、體貼人，容易和父母一條心，這也是多數年輕夫婦希望生女孩的重要心理動機。

　　廣州人的這種心理變化，對全國無疑有重要的參考價值。

問題

　　(1) “生男好聽，生女好命”到底有甚麼意思？

　　(2) 翻譯廣州人喜歡生女孩的五個原因。

六、翻譯 (Translate sentences)

1. With the improvement of people's material lives, many are also seeking a new spiritual life or a new cultural atmosphere.

2. Because of the increasing tendency for extravagant weddings nowadays, it is not easy to find a gift which does not add to the family's economic burden and is presentable.

家长会让孩子开出一个邀请名单。作为被邀请的小朋友，少不了要父母带他们去礼品店或者玩具店挑上一件既不加重经济负担，又拿得出手的礼品送给自己的朋友。生日那天，很多父母也会委托一些生日晚会公司登台演出，或者自己编节目为孩子们演出。晚会多数都提供晚餐，晚餐的最后一个节目是吃蛋糕，唱生日歌。过去在中国可以说是根本没给小孩子过生日的习俗。人要到六十岁才开始过生日，可是现在国门开了，西方的影响越来越大，孩子的生日晚会也开始在中国流行起来。

问题

    (1) 用五句话叙述生日晚会有哪些节目？

    (2) 叙述一个你印象最深的生日晚会，或者婚礼。

        "生男好听，生女好命"，眼下这句话正在广州流行。这种变化的主要特点是，年龄越大，"重男轻女"的现象越严重；年龄越轻，喜欢生女孩的越多，据分析，导致这种变化的主要原因是：

    (1) 随着广州市妇女步入社会生产的行列，她们的社会经济地位和作用有了很大的提高，这就为打破"重男轻女"的传统观念提供了一定的社会条件。

    (2) 我国的退休养老制度和医疗保健制度使老百姓不必过分考虑今后的养老问题。

    (3) 随着大家庭的衰落，城市里的小家庭的日益增多，使得生儿育女的目的从传宗接代转到了夫妻间的"私事"。

    (4) 男女平等的观念被大多数的人所接受。

    (5) 与男孩相比较，女孩好养好带，并且女孩心细、体贴人，容易和父母一条心，这也是多数年轻夫妇希望生女孩的重要心理动机。

        广州人的这种心理变化，对全国无疑有重要的参考价值。

问题

    (1) "生男好听，生女好命"到底有什么意思？

    (2) 翻译广州人喜欢生女孩的五个原因。

六、翻译 (Translate sentences)

1. With the improvement of people's material lives, many are also seeking a new spiritual life or a new cultural atmosphere.

2. Because of the increasing tendency for extravagant weddings nowadays, it is not easy to find a gift which does not add to the family's economic burden and is presentable.

3. A: Why did this company start (offering) this new type of business insurance?

   B: Because of the competition among small and big companies and because of price inflation in this country, people need this kind of insurance to satisfy their psychological needs.

4. On behalf of the company and working staff, I give you this small gift to express our wish that you (the newlyweds) will spend your entire lifetime together until death.

3. A: Why did this company start (offering) this new type of business insurance?

   B: Because of the competition among small and big companies and because of price inflation in this country, people need this kind of insurance to satisfy their psychological needs.

4. On behalf of the company and working staff, I give you this small gift to express our wish that you (the newlyweds) will spend your entire lifetime together until death.

語言實踐：Practice

一、根據課文回答問題 (Answering questions based on the dialogue)

1、舉例說明為甚麼結婚被中國人視為一生的頭等大事？
2、為甚麼記者說"有幸被邀請參加婚禮很難說是好事還是壞事"？
3、為甚麼結婚保險是一種不加重經濟負擔，又拿得出手的結婚禮品？
4、"拿得出手"反映了中國人的一種甚麼文化心理？
5、梁為民對結婚紀念保險的看法是甚麼？
6、請你介紹一下結婚紀念保險（保險費、返還金、意義）。
7、很多人出於甚麼目的來辦結婚保險？
8、根據結婚登記處趙秀梅的說法，結婚紀念保險起甚麼作用？

二、活動 (Activities)

　　參加一個中國的婚禮。採訪一下人們送的禮品有些甚麼？婚禮有哪些儀式？它們都象徵甚麼？中國的婚禮和美國的婚禮有甚麼不同？

三、討論題 (Topics for discussion)

1、你認為開設結婚保險業務反映了一個甚麼社會問題？反映了老百姓的甚麼心理需求？
2、66元和88元的數字反映了一種甚麼文化心理？甚麼叫"圖個吉利"？美國文化中的吉祥數字是甚麼？還有甚麼其它吉祥和不吉祥的象征？
3、你認為保險公司或者政府應該不應該賣這種保險，這是不是一種賺錢的方式？

四、報告 (Presentation)

　　《從結婚保險看中國現在的婚姻關係》

语言实践 Practice

一、根据课文回答问题 (Answering questions based on the dialogue)

1、举例说明为什么结婚被中国人视为一生的头等大事？
2、为什么记者说"有幸被邀请参加婚礼很难说是好事还是坏事"？
3、为什么结婚保险是一种不加重经济负担，又拿得出手的结婚礼品？
4、"拿得出手"反映了中国人的一种什么文化心理？
5、梁为民对结婚纪念保险的看法是什么？
6、请你介绍一下结婚纪念保险（保险费、返还金、意义）。
7、很多人出于什么目的来办结婚保险？
8、根据结婚登记处赵秀梅的说法，结婚纪念保险起什么作用？

二、活动 (Activities)

参加一个中国的婚礼。采访一下人们送的礼品有些什么？婚礼有哪些仪式？它们都象征什么？中国的婚礼和美国的婚礼有什么不同？

三、讨论题 (Topics for discussion)

1、你认为开设结婚保险业务反映了一个什么社会问题？反映了老百姓的什么心理需求？
2、66元和88元的数字反映了一种什么文化心理？什么叫"图个吉利"？美国文化中的吉祥数字是什么？还有什么其它吉祥和不吉祥的象征？
3、你认为保险公司或者政府应该不应该卖这种保险，这是不是一种赚钱的方式？

四、报告 (Presentation)

《从结婚保险看中国现在的婚姻关系》

五、看圖討論 (Picto-discussion)

1

2

3

4

5

6

五、看图讨论 (Picto-discussion)

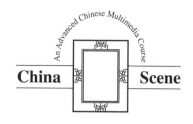

第九課

最後的歸宿

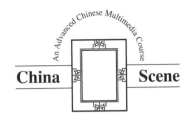

第九课

最后的归宿

課文

一、對話  Dialogs

> 梁為民：這幾天沒看到你，去哪兒了？
>
> 艾利：　別提了[1]。我叔叔過世[2]了，我們都去幫忙送葬，忙了整整兩天。
>
> 梁為民：是嗎？那你一定很難過了。
>
> 艾利：　很難過，尤其是我叔叔在過世前要求他的家屬給他舉行海葬，所以我們全家帶著他的骨灰坐輪船到海上進行了拋撒儀式。這一點讓我的叔母很難接受，老人哭了一路。
>
> 梁為民：甚麼？你叔叔是海葬的？中國人不都習慣土葬嗎？
>
> 艾利：　對，中國人是有土葬的習俗。但是由於中國人多地少的問題越來越嚴重，土葬的習俗也發生了變化。有很多人為了不跟活人爭地，要求家人把他們死後的骨灰拋撒在江河湖海裡，或者森林高山上，以表示回歸[3]大自然。我叔叔就是一個很好的例子。
>
> 梁為民：我也很佩服你叔叔的這種做法。

Notes [1]別提了 means "Ugh! Don't ask"! Use of this phrase usually signals that the speaker recently had a bad or complicated experience and would rather not talk about it. Example: Person A: 你今天沒來上課，發生了甚麼事？ (You didn't come to class today. What happened?) Person B: 別提了，我的車在半路上出毛病了. (Don't ask! I had car trouble on the way here.)

[2]過世, 去世, and 逝世 or 逝去: The verb 死 should be avoided when referring to the death of a person, especially a relative, friend, or person who holds a respected social, political, or professional position. Euphemisms such as 過世, 去世, 逝世, or 逝去 (to pass away) are often used instead, but only when referring to adults. Of these, 逝世 and 逝去 are the most formal, followed by 去世, which can be used in written or spoken settings. 過世 is only used in colloquial Chinese.

[3]Both 回歸 and 回 can serve as verbs meaning "to return". 回歸 is a formal expression indicating the return of a person or thing to its original place, as in 回歸大自然 (to return to nature); 回歸祖國 (to return to the Motherland). 回歸 can also function as a noun, as in 香港的回歸 (the return of Hong Kong to China). 回, "to return", "to go back", can only function as a verb, but is more widely used. Examples: 回到原地 (to return to where one came from). 她已經回來了. (She has already come back.)

课文

一、对话 Dialogs

梁为民：这几天没看到你，去哪儿了？

艾利：　别提了⁽¹⁾。我叔叔过世⁽²⁾了，我们都去帮忙送葬，忙了整整两天。

梁为民：是吗？那你一定很难过了。

艾利：　很难过，尤其是我叔叔在过世前要求他的家属给他举行海葬，所以我们全家带着他的骨灰坐轮船到海上进行了抛撒仪式。这一点让我的叔母很难接受，老人哭了一路。

梁为民：什么？你叔叔是海葬的？中国人不都习惯土葬吗？

艾利：　对，中国人是有土葬的习俗。但是由于中国人多地少的问题越来越严重，土葬的习俗也发生了变化。有很多人为了不跟活人争地，要求家人把他们死后的骨灰抛撒在江河湖海里，或者森林高山上，以表示回归⁽³⁾大自然。我叔叔就是一个很好的例子。

梁为民：我也很佩服你叔叔的这种做法。

Notes ⁽¹⁾别提了 means "Ugh! Don't ask"! Use of this phrase usually signals that the speaker recently had a bad or complicated experience and would rather not talk about it. Example: Person A: 你今天没来上课，发生了什么事？(You didn't come to class today. What happened?) Person B: 别提了，我的车在半路上出毛病了. (Don't ask! I had car trouble on the way here.)

⁽²⁾过世, 去世, and 逝世 or 逝去: The verb 死 should be avoided when referring to the death of a person, especially a relative, friend, or person who holds a respected social, political, or professional position. Euphemisms such as 过世, 去世, 逝世, or 逝去 (to pass away) are often used instead, but only when referring to adults. Of these, 逝世 and 逝去 are the most formal, followed by 去世, which can be used in written or spoken settings. 过世 is only used in colloquial Chinese.

⁽³⁾Both 回归 and 回 can serve as verbs meaning "to return". 回归 is a formal expression indicating the return of a person or thing to its original place, as in 回归大自然 (to return to nature); 回归祖国 (to return to the Motherland). 回归 can also function as a noun, as in 香港的回归 (the return of Hong Kong to China). 回, "to return", "to go back", can only function as a verb, but is more widely used. Examples: 回到原地 (to return to where one came from). 她已经回来了. (She has already come back.)

艾利：　是啊，叔叔活著的時候就常說，人類從自然來，最後還應該重返自然，留出
更多的土地來為活著的人服務。

生詞

歸宿	(guī sù)	N.	final resting place
艾利	(ài lì)	N.	Ai Li, name of a person 人名
別提了	(bié tí le)	VP.	don't ask me
叔叔	(shū shū)	N.	uncle
過世	(guò shì)	VO.	to pass away
送葬	(sòng zàng)	VO.	to attend a funeral
整整	(zhěng zhěng)	Adj.	entire, the whole
難過	(nán guò)	Adj.	sad, sorrowful, difficult to bear
海葬	(hǎi zàng)	NP.	burial at sea
骨灰	(gǔ huī)	N.	ashes of a person
輪船	(lún chuán)	N.	steamship, steamboat
拋撒	(pāo sǎ)	V.	to throw, to scatter
叔母	(shū mǔ)	N.	aunt
一路	(yī lù)	Adv.	the whole way
土葬	(tǔ zàng)	NP.	earth burial, internment
習俗	(xí sú)	N.	custom, convention
活人	(huó rén)	N.	the living, people with life
爭	(zhēng)	V.	to fight for, to compete for
江	(jiāng)	N.	river
河	(hé)	N.	river
湖	(hú)	N.	lake
海	(hǎi)	N.	sea
森林	(sēn lín)	N.	forest
高山	(gāo shān)	N.	mountain
表示	(biǎo shì)	V.	to express
回歸	(huí guī)	V.	to return
重返	(chóng fǎn)	V.	to go back, to return
自然	(zì rán)	N.	nature
佩服	(pèi fú)	V.	to admire
人類	(rén lèi)	N.	human being

艾利： 是啊，叔叔活着的时候就常说，人类从自然来，最后还应该重返自然，留出更多的土地来为活着的人服务。

生词

归宿	(guī sù)	N.	final resting place
艾利	(ài lì)	N.	Ai Li, name of a person 人名
别提了	(bié tí le)	VP.	don't ask me
叔叔	(shū shū)	N.	uncle
过世	(guò shì)	VO.	to pass away
送葬	(sòng zàng)	VO.	to attend a funeral
整整	(zhěng zhěng)	Adj.	entire, the whole
难过	(nán guò)	Adj.	sad, sorrowful, difficult to bear
海葬	(hǎi zàng)	NP.	burial at sea
骨灰	(gǔ huī)	N.	ashes of a person
轮船	(lún chuán)	N.	steamship, steamboat
抛撒	(pāo sǎ)	V.	to throw, to scatter
叔母	(shū mǔ)	N.	aunt
一路	(yī lù)	Adv.	the whole way
土葬	(tǔ zàng)	NP.	earth burial, internment
习俗	(xí sú)	N.	custom, convention
活人	(huó rén)	N.	the living, people with life
争	(zhēng)	V.	to fight for, to compete for
江	(jiāng)	N.	river
河	(hé)	N.	river
湖	(hú)	N.	lake
海	(hǎi)	N.	sea
森林	(sēn lín)	N.	forest
高山	(gāo shān)	N.	mountain
表示	(biǎo shì)	V.	to express
回归	(huí guī)	V.	to return
重返	(chóng fǎn)	V.	to go back, to return
自然	(zì rán)	N.	nature
佩服	(pèi fú)	V.	to admire
人类	(rén lèi)	N.	human being

二、廣告

北京民政部將於3月15日舉行第四次海上骨灰拋撒儀式。

儀式共分三部分：第一，由中國歌劇院交響樂團演奏安靈交響曲；第二，親屬與逝者告別五分鐘；最後，拋撒骨灰同時聆聽安魂曲。

所有的活動均在海上進行，"東方一號"將為此次撒葬儀式的輪船。

參加者請與北京民政部聯繫，電話6202—5477。

生詞

民政	(mín zhèng)	N.	public affairs, civil affairs
歌劇院	(gē jù yuàn)	NP.	opera house
交響樂團	(jiāo xiǎng yuè tuán)	NP.	symphony orchestra
安靈	(ān líng)	VO.	to rest in peace
交響曲	(jiāo xiǎng qǔ)	N.	symphony
逝者	(shì zhě)	N.	the deceased, the dead
告別	(gào bié)	V.	to say good-bye, to pay one's last respects
聆聽	(líng tīng)	V.	to listen
安魂曲	(ān hún qǔ)	NP.	music played in a burial ceremony
參加者	(cān jiā zhě)	N.	participant
聯系	(lián xì)	V/N.	to contact, to get in touch with; contact, connection

三、電視原文 📺 **TV original**

最後的歸宿—海葬

（根據原文改編）

人們常說落葉歸根，無論離家多遠，每一個人都希望最終能夠回到自己熱戀著的故土。其實啊，人從自然中來，他的最美好的歸宿也莫過於重返自然。

二、广告

北京民政部将于3月15日举行第四次海上骨灰抛撒仪式。

仪式共分三部分：第一，由中国歌剧院交响乐团演奏安灵交响曲；第二，亲属与逝者告别五分钟；最后，抛撒骨灰同时聆听安魂曲。

所有的活动均在海上进行，"东方一号"将为此次撒葬仪式的轮船。

参加者请与北京民政部联系，电话6202－5477。

生词

民政	(mín zhèng)	N.	public affairs, civil affairs
歌剧院	(gē jù yuàn)	NP.	opera house
交响乐团	(jiāo xiǎng yuè tuán)	NP.	symphony orchestra
安灵	(ān líng)	VO.	to rest in peace
交响曲	(jiāo xiǎng qǔ)	N.	symphony
逝者	(shì zhě)	N.	the deceased, the dead
告别	(gào bié)	V.	to say good-bye, to pay one's last respects
聆听	(líng tīng)	V.	to listen
安魂曲	(ān hún qǔ)	NP.	music played in a burial ceremony
参加者	(cān jiā zhě)	N.	participant
联系	(lián xì)	V/N.	to contact, to get in touch with; contact, connection

三、电视原文 🖥 TV original

最后的归宿—海葬

（根据原文改编）

人们常说落叶归根，无论离家多远，每一个人都希望最终能够回到自己热恋着的故土。其实啊，人从自然中来，他的最美好的归宿也莫过于重返自然。

1994年3月的一天，一艘⁽⁴⁾具有特殊意義的輪船行駛在中國的渤海海域。有一家叫安靈公司的工作人員，伴隨著肅穆的音樂，做著這樣一件事：將86位逝者的骨灰與鮮花一起拋向大海，重新歸於自然。

現場播音："北京安靈公司第三次骨灰撒葬儀式現在開始。我們請中國歌劇舞劇院交響樂團為我們演奏安靈交響曲。" 在海上拋撒之前，親屬與逝者的骨灰最後告別，共同聆聽由中國著名作曲家譜寫的安魂曲。

參加海撒儀式的家屬給予了他們自己的評價。

（採訪）

被採訪者A："我認為組織這個活動是非常好的，非常有意義。因為人總是最後要走這一條路，應該回歸大自然，留出更多的土地來為活著的人服務。"

被採訪者B："打這以後，我從心底裡覺得踏實了，因為徹底地回歸大自然了。"

被採訪者C："完成老人的遺願'回歸大自然'。我在海邊長大的，海都是相連的，我對母親的愛也有了寄託。"

被採訪者D："這是個自然的回歸。人從自然來，為社會做出了奉獻，自己也享受⁽⁵⁾了他（她）自己應當享受的。'Enjoy life'，然後又回歸自然。不要與活人爭地、爭財富。活人真正的哀思應當促進社會的文明發達和富裕，這才是對死者和亡者最好的奠念。是不是？"

骨灰撒向江河湖海，森林高山，在不少老百姓眼裡這是過去只有偉人才有資格做

Notes ⁽⁴⁾艘 is a classifier for ships and large vessels, as in 一艘輪船 (a steamship). For smaller craft, especially boats made of wood, either 隻 or 條 may be used, as in 一隻小船 (a small boat, a dingy).

⁽⁵⁾享受 vs. 欣賞: 享受 and 欣賞 may both be translated as "to enjoy", but they take different categories of nouns as objects. 享受 refers to enjoying material objects or awards and privileges, as in 享受高檔消費品 (to enjoy high-quality consumer goods), 享受獎學金 (to enjoy a scholarship), 享受生活 (to enjoy life). 享受 can also function as a noun meaning "enjoyment", "fun". Example: 彈鋼琴對她來說不但是工作而且是享受. (For her, playing the piano is not only work; it's also fun.) 欣賞 is often used to refer to enjoying works of art, music, movies, or literature, and carries the meanings "to appreciate" and "to admire". Examples: 欣賞音樂 (to enjoy music, to appreciate music). 我欣賞不了這種詩. (I cannot appreciate this type of poetry.) 他站在畫前，欣賞了半天. (He stood in front of the painting, admiring it for a long time.)

1994年3月的一天，一艘[4]具有特殊意义的轮船行驶在中国的渤海海域。有一家叫安灵公司的工作人员，伴随着肃穆的音乐，做着这样一件事：将86位逝者的骨灰与鲜花一起抛向大海，重新归于自然。

现场播音："北京安灵公司第三次骨灰撒葬仪式现在开始。我们请中国歌剧舞剧院交响乐团为我们演奏安灵交响曲。" 在海上抛撒之前，亲属与逝者的骨灰最后告别，共同聆听由中国著名作曲家谱写的安魂曲。

参加海撒仪式的家属给予了他们自己的评价。

（采访）

被采访者A："我认为组织这个活动是非常好的，非常有意义。因为人总是最后要走这一条路，应该回归大自然，留出更多的土地来为活着的人服务。"

被采访者B："打这以后，我从心底里觉得踏实了，因为彻底地回归大自然了。"

被采访者C："完成老人的遗愿'回归大自然'。我在海边长大的，海都是相连的，我对母亲的爱也有了寄托。"

被采访者D："这是个自然的回归。人从自然来，为社会做出了奉献，自己也享受[5]了他（她）自己应当享受的。'Enjoy life'，然后又回归自然。不要与活人争地、争财富。活人真正的哀思应当促进社会的文明发达和富裕，这才是对死者和亡者最好的奠念。是不是？"

骨灰撒向江河湖海，森林高山，在不少老百姓眼里这是过去只有伟人才有资格做

Notes [4]艘 is a classifier for ships and large vessels, as in 一艘轮船 (a steamship). For smaller craft, especially boats made of wood, either 只 or 条 may be used, as in 一只小船 (a small boat, a dingy).

[5]享受 vs. 欣赏：享受 and 欣赏 may both be translated as "to enjoy", but they take different categories of nouns as objects. 享受 refers to enjoying material objects or awards and privileges, as in 享受高档消费品 (to enjoy high-quality consumer goods), 享受奖学金 (to enjoy a scholarship), 享受生活 (to enjoy life). 享受 can also function as a noun meaning "enjoyment", "fun". Example: 弹钢琴对她来说不但是工作而且是享受. (For her, playing the piano is not only work; it's also fun.) 欣赏 is often used to refer to enjoying works of art, music, movies, or literature, and carries the meanings "to appreciate" and "to admire". Examples: 欣赏音乐 (to enjoy music, to appreciate music). 我欣赏不了这种诗. (I cannot appreciate this type of poetry.) 他站在画前，欣赏了半天. (He stood in front of the painting, admiring it for a long time.)

的事情，讓普通人也接受這樣的觀念，從而[6]改變那種入土為安的觀念，他們能否理解呢？

（採訪）

記者：　　　"你覺得你能接受這種拋撒骨灰的形式嗎？"

被採訪者E：　"我覺得我能。"

被採訪者F：　"我覺得挺進步的。"

被採訪者G：　"對那些老傳統的人可能不能接受。"

記者：　　　"那就你來說，您能接受嗎？"

被採訪者G：　"我本人沒問題，恐怕家屬裡面，可能兩種人都有。"

　　　有消息說，繼安靈公司之後，北京市民政部門也將進行一次海上骨灰拋撒儀式，參加儀式的申請已超過百份以上。

生詞

落葉歸根	(luò yè guī gēn)	Idiom.	leaves settle on their own roots
最終	(zuì zhōng)	Adv.	eventually, finally
熱戀	(rè liàn)	VP.	to love passionately
故土	(gù tǔ)	N.	home land, native land
莫過於	(mò guò yú)	VP.	nothing is better than
艘	(sōu)	Classifier.	classifier for ships
具有	(jù yǒu)	V.	to have, to possess
行駛	(xíng shǐ)	V.	to travel
渤海	(bó hǎi)	N.	name of the sea near East China
海域	(hǎi yù)	N.	sea area, maritime space
伴隨	(bàn suí)	V.	to accompany
肅穆	(sù mù)	Adj.	solemn

Notes [6]從而, "thus" or "therefore", an adverb drawn from Classical Chinese, links two clauses that have the same subject. The clause in front of 從而 describes a particular situation; the clause following 從而 indicates the result of that situation. Example: 通過對外開放，搞活了經濟，從而提高了人民的 生活水平. (Opening up to the outside world made the economy more active, thereby improving the people's standard of living.)

的事情，让普通人也接受这样的观念，从而⁽⁶⁾改变那种入土为安的观念，他们能否理解呢？

（采访）

记者：　　　　"你觉得你能接受这种抛撒骨灰的形式吗？"

被采访者E：　"我觉得我能。"

被采访者F：　"我觉得挺进步的。"

被采访者G：　"对那些老传统的人可能不能接受。"

记者：　　　　"那就你来说，您能接受吗？"

被采访者G：　"我本人没问题，恐怕家属里面，可能两种人都有。"

　　有消息说，继安灵公司之后，北京市民政部门也将进行一次海上骨灰抛撒仪式，参加仪式的申请已超过百份以上。

生词

落叶归根	(luò yè guī gēn)	Idiom.	leaves settle on their own roots
最终	(zuì zhōng)	Adv.	eventually, finally
热恋	(rè liàn)	VP.	to love passionately
故土	(gù tǔ)	N.	home land, native land
莫过于	(mò guò yú)	VP.	nothing is better than
艘	(sōu)	Classifier.	classifier for ships
具有	(jù yǒu)	V.	to have, to possess
行驶	(xíng shǐ)	V.	to travel
渤海	(bó hǎi)	N.	name of the sea near East China
海域	(hǎi yù)	N.	sea area, maritime space
伴随	(bàn suí)	V.	to accompany
肃穆	(sù mù)	Adj.	solemn

Notes ⁽⁶⁾从而, "thus" or "therefore", an adverb drawn from Classical Chinese, links two clauses that have the same subject. The clause in front of 从而 describes a particular situation; the clause following 从而 indicates the result of that situation. Example: 通过对外开放，搞活了经济，从而提高了人民的 生活水平. (Opening up to the outside world made the economy more active, thereby improving the people's standard of living.)

鮮花	(xiān huā)	N.	fresh flower
重新	(chóng xīn)	Adv/V.	again, to start anew
現場	(xiàn chǎng)	Adv.	on the site, on the spot, live
播音	(bō yīn)	V.	to broadcast
撒葬	(sǎ zàng)	VP.	to bury by scattering ashes in the sea
舞劇	(wǔ jù)	N.	musical dance
作曲家	(zuò qǔ jiā)	N.	composer
譜寫	(pǔ xiě)	V.	to compose (music)
海撒	(hǎi sǎ)	VP.	to scatter (ashes) in the sea
給予	(gěi yǔ)	V.	to give
評價	(píng jià)	N/V.	evaluation, to evaluate
有意義	(yǒu yì yì)	Adj.	meaningful, significant
踏實	(tā shí)	Adj.	to feel settled, steady and sure
徹底	(chè dǐ)	Adv.	thoroughly, completely
遺願	(yí yuàn)	N.	will
相連	(xiāng lián)	V.	to be connected
寄託	(jì tuō)	V/N.	to send to the care of someone, to leave in the care of
財富	(cái fù)	N.	property
哀思	(āi sī)	N.	grief, sad memories
文明	(wén míng)	N.	civilization
發達	(fā dá)	N.	advancement, development
奠念	(diàn niàn)	V/N.	to commemorate, commemoration
偉人	(wěi rén)	NP.	a great person
資格	(zī gé)	N.	qualifications, credentials
從而	(cóng ér)	Adv.	thus, therefore
入土為安	(rù tǔ wéi ān)	Idiom.	to settle in the earth
能否	(néng fǒu)	V.	can or cannot
形式	(xíngshì)	N.	form
繼……之後	(jì...zhī hòu)	V.	to follow
部門	(bù mén)	N.	department
超過	(chāo guò)	V.	to pass, to surpass
份	(fèn)	Classifier.	classifier for reports, applications, etc.

鲜花	(xiān huā)	*N.*	fresh flower
重新	(chóng xīn)	*Adv/V.*	again, to start anew
现场	(xiàn chǎng)	*Adv.*	on the site, on the spot, live
播音	(bō yīn)	*V.*	to broadcast
撒葬	(sǎ zàng)	*VP.*	to bury by scattering ashes in the sea
舞剧	(wǔ jù)	*N.*	musical dance
作曲家	(zuò qǔ jiā)	*N.*	composer
谱写	(pǔ xiě)	*V.*	to compose (music)
海撒	(hǎi sǎ)	*VP.*	to scatter (ashes) in the sea
给予	(gěi yǔ)	*V.*	to give
评价	(píng jià)	*N/V.*	evaluation, to evaluate
有意义	(yǒu yì yì)	*Adj.*	meaningful, significant
踏实	(tā shí)	*Adj.*	to feel settled, steady and sure
彻底	(chè dǐ)	*Adv.*	thoroughly, completely
遗愿	(yí yuàn)	*N.*	will
相连	(xiāng lián)	*V.*	to be connected
寄托	(jì tuō)	*V/N.*	to send to the care of someone, to leave in the care of
财富	(cái fù)	*N.*	property
哀思	(āi sī)	*N.*	grief, sad memories
文明	(wén míng)	*N.*	civilization
发达	(fā dá)	*N.*	advancement, development
奠念	(diàn niàn)	*V/N.*	to commemorate, commemoration
伟人	(wěi rén)	*NP.*	a great person
资格	(zī gé)	*N.*	qualifications, credentials
从而	(cóng ér)	*Adv.*	thus, therefore
入土为安	(rù tǔ wéi ān)	*Idiom.*	to settle in the earth
能否	(néng fǒu)	*V.*	can or cannot
形式	(xíngshì)	*N.*	form
继……之后	(jì...zhī hòu)	*V.*	to follow
部门	(bù mén)	*N.*	department
超过	(chāo guò)	*V.*	to pass, to surpass
份	(fèn)	*Classifier.*	classifier for reports, applications, etc.

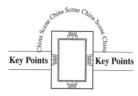

課文要點

一、詞語解釋 Words and Phrases

（一）文言詞、慣用詞 (Classical Chinese and idiomatic expressions)

1、莫＝沒有一個
☞ 他的最美好的歸宿也莫過於重返自然。

2、於＝比
☞ 他的最大的願望也莫過於在飯店大吃一頓。

3、將＝把
☞ 將86位逝者的骨灰與鮮花一起拋向大海。

4、繼＝接著
☞ 繼安靈公司之後，北京市民政部門也將進行一次海上骨灰拋撒儀式。

5、能（否）＝能（不能）
☞ 他們能否理解呢？

（二）成語、慣用語 (idioms and fixed expressions)

◆ 落葉歸根: falling leaves settle on their own roots

◆ 重返自然: to go back to nature

◆ 江河湖海: lakes and rivers

◆ 森林高山: forests and mountains

◆ 入土為安: to find peace when one is buried in the earth

课文要点

一、词语解释 Words and Phrases

（一）文言词、惯用词 (Classical Chinese and idiomatic expressions)

1、莫 = 没有一个
　☞ 他的最美好的归宿也莫过于重返自然。

2、于 = 比
　☞ 他的最大的愿望也莫过于在饭店大吃一顿。

3、将 = 把
　☞ 将86位逝者的骨灰与鲜花一起抛向大海。

4、继 = 接着
　☞ 继安灵公司之后，北京市民政部门也将进行一次海上骨灰抛撒仪式。

5、能（否）= 能（不能）
　☞ 他们能否理解呢？

（二）成语、惯用语 (idioms and fixed expressions)

◆ 落叶归根: falling leaves settle on their own roots

◆ 重返自然: to go back to nature

◆ 江河湖海: lakes and rivers

◆ 森林高山: forests and mountains

◆ 入土为安: to find peace when one is buried in the earth

二、書面語、正式語、口語對照表 📊 Written/formal/colloquial Comparison

	書面／正式語	口語		書面／正式語	口語
1	拋撒	扔／撒	12	行駛在…	在…開／走
2	告別	再見	13	將	把
3	聆聽	聽	14	拋	扔
4	均	都	15	之前／後	以前／以後
5	為	是	16	譜寫	寫
6	此次	這次	17	給予	給
7	最終	最後	18	偉人	偉大的人
8	熱戀	很愛	19	從而	因此
9	故土／家鄉	老家	20	能否	能不能
10	莫過於	沒有甚麼可以超過	21	繼	接著
11	艘	隻			

三、句型 ⬡ Sentence Structures

（一）為……服務 (to serve)

> ✍ 為……服務 is a verb phrase meaning "to serve". 服務 is an intransitive verb which cannot take a direct object. The object of 服務 therefore must be introduced by the preposition 為, meaning "for" or "on behalf of", and must be placed before the verb. To construct the negative form of this structure, 不 or 沒 should be positioned before 為 rather than in front of 服務. All other adverbs or auxiliary verbs should also be placed before 為. Example: 政府一定要為大多數的老百姓服務. (Government should certainly serve the great majority of the common people.)

☞ 因為人總是最後要走這一條路，應該回歸大自然，留出更多的土地來為活著的人服務。

1、無論個體戶還是國營企業的工作人員都是為老百姓服務的。

Whether as private or state employees, all workers still serve the people.

2、現在人們選擇海葬，就是為了把土地留出來為活人服務。

People choose to be buried at sea so that the land can serve the living.

問：你這是甚麼態度？你們的餐館是為誰服務的？

答：＿＿＿＿＿＿＿＿＿＿＿＿＿＿＿＿＿＿＿＿。

二、书面语、正式语、口语对照表 Written/formal/colloquial Comparison

	书面／正式语	口语		书面／正式语	口语
1	抛撒	扔／撒	12	行驶在…	在…开／走
2	告别	再见	13	将	把
3	聆听	听	14	抛	扔
4	均	都	15	之前／后	以前／以后
5	为	是	16	谱写	写
6	此次	这次	17	给予	给
7	最终	最后	18	伟人	伟大的人
8	热恋	很爱	19	从而	因此
9	故土／家乡	老家	20	能否	能不能
10	莫过于	没有什么可以超过	21	继	接着
11	艘	只			

三、句型 Sentence Structures
（一）为……服务 (to serve)

> ✍ 为……服务 is a verb phrase meaning "to serve". 服务 is an intransitive verb which cannot take a direct object. The object of 服务 therefore must be introduced by the preposition 为, meaning "for" or "on behalf of", and must be placed before the verb. To construct the negative form of this structure, 不 or 没 should be positioned before 为 rather than in front of 服务. All other adverbs or auxiliary verbs should also be placed before 为. Example: 政府一定要为大多数的老百姓服务. (Government should certainly serve the great majority of the common people.)

☞ 因为人总是最后要走这一条路，应该回归大自然，留出更多的土地来为活着的人服务。

1、无论个体户还是国营企业的工作人员都是为老百姓服务的。
Whether as private or state employees, all workers still serve the people.

2、现在人们选择海葬，就是为了把土地留出来为活人服务。
People choose to be buried at sea so that the land can serve the living.

问：你这是什么态度？你们的餐馆是为谁服务的？
答：_____。

（二）無論……都…… (regardless of, no matter what)

> ✍ 無論……都……, "regardless of", "no matter what", indicates that the result or conclusion of a situation remains the same under all circumstances. 無論 must be followed by an interrogative pronoun （誰, 甚麼, 哪兒, 怎麼） or a phrase indicating choice between two options (A 還是 B). In the main clause, 都 or 也 must be present before the verb. If the subject of the 無論 clause is the same as that of the main clause, it should not be repeated in the main clause. Examples: 無論你走到哪兒，都應該最終回到自己的家鄉. (No matter where your travels take you, ultimately you should return to your hometown.) 無論你吃不吃快餐，都可以體會到生活節奏 的變化. (No matter whether you eat fast food or not, you can tell that there have been changes in the pace of life.) 無論是中國的婚禮還是外國的婚禮，拿得出手的禮品都是必要的. (Whether you're attending a Chinese wedding ceremony or a foreign wedding ceremony, a presentable gift is a must.)

☞ 人們常說落葉歸根，無論離家多遠，每一個人都希望最終能夠回到自己熱戀著的故土。

1、無論在北京的哪兒，你都能買到一碗牛肉麵。

Wherever you are in Beijing, you can always buy a bowl of beef noodles.

2、無論你有錢沒錢，婚禮都得很排場。

No matter whether you have money or not, wedding ceremonies must be very extravagant.

問：你甚麼時候有空？我想跟你談點事。

答：＿＿＿＿＿＿＿＿＿＿＿＿＿＿＿＿＿。

（三）莫過於 = 沒有一個比得上 (nothing surpasses, nothing is better than)

> ✍ 莫過於, "nothing surpasses" or "nothing is better than", is used mostly in written and formal Chinese. The equivalent spoken form is 沒有一個比得上. Since there is no affirmative form for this structure, it always appears in negative form.

☞ 其實啊，人從自然中來，他的最美好的歸宿也莫過於重返自然。

1、最好的結婚禮品莫過於一份結婚保險。

There is no wedding gift better than a marriage insurance.

2、我認為學中文的最好的地方莫過於中國。

I believe there is no better place to study Chinese than in China.

（四）行駛在……／在……上行駛…… (to travel on, to drive on)

> ✍ 行駛在……, "to travel on" or "to drive on", is a phrase used mostly in written or formal settings. The spoken version is 在……上開／車／船. 行駛在…… and 在……行駛 are almost identical, but 行駛在…… focuses on the action itself, while 在……上行駛 stresses where the action is taking place. The negative form of the pattern is 不在…… 上行駛; 不 cannot be placed before 行駛.

（二）无论……都…… (regardless of, no matter what)

> ✍ 无论……都……, "regardless of", "no matter what", indicates that the result or conclusion of a situation remains the same under all circumstances. 无论 must be followed by an interrogative pronoun（谁,什么,哪儿,怎么）or a phrase indicating choice between two options (A 还是 B). In the main clause, 都 or 也 must be present before the verb. If the subject of the 无论 clause is the same as that of the main clause, it should not be repeated in the main clause. Examples: 无论你走到哪儿，都应该最终回到自己的家乡. (No matter where your travels take you, ultimately you should return to your hometown.) 无论你吃不吃快餐，都可以体会到生活节奏的变化. (No matter whether you eat fast food or not, you can tell that there have been changes in the pace of life.) 无论是中国的婚礼还是外国的婚礼，拿得出手的礼品都是必要的. (Whether you're attending a Chinese wedding ceremony or a foreign wedding ceremony, a presentable gift is a must.)

☞ 人们常说落叶归根，无论离家多远，每一个人都希望最终能够回到自己热恋着的故土。

1、无论在北京的哪儿，你都能买到一碗牛肉面。
Wherever you are in Beijing, you can always buy a bowl of beef noodles.

2、无论你有钱没钱，婚礼都得很排场。
No matter whether you have money or not, wedding ceremonies must be very extravagant.

问：你什么时候有空？我想跟你谈点事。
答：＿＿＿＿＿＿＿＿＿＿＿＿＿＿＿＿。

（三）莫过于＝没有一个比得上 (nothing surpasses, nothing is better than)

> ✍ 莫过于, "nothing surpasses" or "nothing is better than", is used mostly in written and formal Chinese. The equivalent spoken form is 没有一个比得上. Since there is no affirmative form for this structure, it always appears in negative form.

☞ 其实啊，人从自然中来，他的最美好的归宿也莫过于重返自然。

1、最好的结婚礼品莫过于一份结婚保险。
There is no wedding gift better than a marriage insurance.

2、我认为学中文的最好的地方莫过于中国。
I believe there is no better place to study Chinese than in China.

（四）行驶在…… ／ 在……上行驶…… (to travel on, to drive on)

> ✍ 行驶在……, "to travel on" or "to drive on", is a phrase used mostly in written or formal settings. The spoken version is 在……上开／车／船. 行驶在…… and 在……行驶 are almost identical, but 行驶在…… focuses on the action itself, while 在……上行驶 stresses where the action is taking place. The negative form of the pattern is 不在……上行驶; 不 cannot be placed before 行驶.

☞ 1994年3月的一天，一艘具有特殊意義的輪船行駛在中國的渤海海域，

1、這艘輪船常常在渤海灣上行駛

This steamship often travels to Bohai Bay.

2、開車行駛在熱鬧繁華的大街上總是讓我很高興。

To travel by car down a busy and bustling street always makes me happy.

問：常常在三環上行駛的車用不用交城市管理費？

答：＿＿＿＿＿＿＿＿＿＿＿＿＿＿＿＿＿＿＿。

（五）伴隨（著）(accompanying, along with)

> ✍ The verb 伴隨 means "to accompany". It is often followed either by a musical term or by a person, as in 伴隨著歌聲 (to accompany a song), 伴隨一個老朋友去上海 (to accompany an old friend to Shanghai). The use of 著 is optional in this case. When used, 著 stresses that the action of the verb 伴隨 is ongoing; the resulting English translation is often a gerund, such as "accompanying". Example: 伴隨著音樂聲，他開始回憶三十年代的往事. (Following the music, he began to reminisce about events in Shanghai in the 1930s.) The verb 陪 should be distinguished in usage from 伴隨. 陪 is only used to describe accompanying a person, while 伴隨 is most often used for music and occasionally for people.

☞ 有一家叫安靈公司的工作人員，伴隨著肅穆的音樂，做著這樣一件事：將86位逝者的骨灰與鮮花一起拋向大海，重新歸於自然。

1、我的車伴隨著我度過了十年的光陰。

My car has been with me for the past ten years.

2、伴隨著鋼琴聲，他唱起了一隻中國歌。

He sang a Chinese song accompanied by the piano.

問：你父親過世後這幾年誰一直伴隨你母親生活？

答：＿＿＿＿＿＿＿＿＿＿＿＿＿＿＿＿＿＿。

（六）與（／和／跟）……告別 (to say good-bye to someone, to bid someone farewell)

> ✍ 告別 means "to say good-bye", "to bid farewell" (literally, "to announce one's departure"). This structure is exclusively used in descriptive sentences where one person is parting with another. Example: 我跟他在公司的辦公室告別後就去了飛機場. (After we said our good-byes at the company office, I left for the airport.) This expression is not used like 再見 to describe face-to-face partings. 與, 和, or 跟 may all be used with 告別, but 與 is more formal than 和 and 跟. The negative particle 不 or 沒 should be placed before the prepositions 和 and 跟.

☞ 1994年3月的一天，一艘具有特殊意义的轮船行驶在中国的渤海海域，

1、这艘轮船常常在渤海湾上行驶
This steamship often travels to Bohai Bay.

2、开车行驶在热闹繁华的大街上总是让我很高兴。
To travel by car down a busy and bustling street always makes me happy.

问：常常在三环上行驶的车用不用交城市管理费？
答：_____。

（五）伴随（着）(accompanying, along with)

✑ The verb 伴随 means "to accompany". It is often followed either by a musical term or by a person, as in 伴随着歌声 (to accompany a song), 伴随一个老朋友去上海 (to accompany an old friend to Shanghai). The use of 着 is optional in this case. When used, 着 stresses that the action of the verb 伴随 is ongoing; the resulting English translation is often a gerund, such as "accompanying". Example: 伴随着音乐声，他开始回忆三十年代的往事. (Following the music, he began to reminisce about events in Shanghai in the 1930s.) The verb 陪 should be distinguished in usage from 伴随. 陪 is only used to describe accompanying a person, while 伴随 is most often used for music and occasionally for people.

☞ 有一家叫安灵公司的工作人员，伴随着肃穆的音乐，做着这样一件事：将86位逝者的骨灰与鲜花一起抛向大海，重新归于自然。

1、我的车伴随着我度过了十年的光阴。
My car has been with me for the past ten years.

2、伴随着钢琴声，他唱起了一支中国歌。
He sang a Chinese song accompanied by the piano.

问：你父亲过世后这几年谁一直伴随你母亲生活？
答：_____。

（六）与（／和／跟）……告别 (to say good-bye to someone, to bid someone farewell)

✑ 告别 means "to say good-bye", "to bid farewell" (literally, "to announce one's departure"). This structure is exclusively used in descriptive sentences where one person is parting with another. Example: 我跟他在公司的办公室告别后就去了飞机场. (After we said our good-byes at the company office, I left for the airport.) This expression is not used like 再见 to describe face-to-face partings. 与, 和, or 跟 may all be used with 告别, but 与 is more formal than 和 and 跟. The negative particle 不 or 没 should be placed before the prepositions 和 and 跟.

☞ 在海上拋撒之前，親屬與逝者的骨灰最後告別，共同聆聽由中國著名作曲家譜寫的安魂曲。

1、海葬中最重要的一部分就是與死者告別，將骨灰撒向大海。

The most important part of a sea burial is saying good-bye to the deceased and scattering the ashes into the sea.

2、吃過午餐，他與公司的人告別，就回通訊處了。

After eating lunch, he said good-bye to everyone at the company and returned to the communications office.

問：＿＿＿＿＿＿＿＿＿＿＿＿＿＿＿＿＿＿＿＿＿？

答：我跟小王是在船上告別的，沒想到我們一別就是十年。

（七）由／為……譜寫的 (to be composed by/for someone or something)

> ✎ 由／為……譜寫（的）is a structure used to describe a musical piece or verse written（譜寫）either by（由）someone or for（為）someone. 由 indicates the agent of the action and makes the pattern passive, while 為 indicates the object of the action and forms an active sentence. 的 may be placed after 譜寫 to emphasize either the agent or object of the verb. Since 譜寫 can only be used for musical compositions or poetry, its range of possible objects is limited to 曲子, 歌曲, 詩篇, etc.

☞ 在海上拋撒之前，親屬與逝者的骨灰最後告別，共同聆聽由中國著名作曲家譜寫的魂曲。

1、這首鋼琴曲是由著名音樂家貝多芬譜寫的。

This piano concerto was composed by the famous musician Beethoven.

2、這個曲子是為小能手活動譜寫的。

This song was composed for the skills campaign.

問：＿＿＿＿＿＿＿＿＿＿＿＿＿＿＿＿？

答：這首歌是專門為他的妻子譜寫的。

（八）對……給予……的評價 (to offer an evaluation of someone or something)

> ✎ 對……給予……的評價, "to offer an evaluation of someone or something", is often used in written or formal Chinese. The spoken form is A 評價 B. The 對 phrase introduces the person or thing that is being given（給予）an evaluation and can be placed either before or after the subject. Examples: 很多人對他們的就餐制度給予了很高的評價 or 對他們的就餐制度，很多人給予了很高的評價. (Many people have given their dining system a high rating.) Sometimes the 對 phrase is omitted altogether, as in 政府給予了很高的評價. (The government gave it a high evaluation.)

☞ 在海上抛撒之前，亲属与逝者的骨灰最后告别，共同聆听由中国著名作曲家谱写的安魂曲。

1、海葬中最重要的一部分就是与死者告别，将骨灰撒向大海。
The most important part of a sea burial is saying good-bye to the deceased and scattering the ashes into the sea.

2、吃过午餐，他与公司的人告别，就回通讯处了。
After eating lunch, he said good-bye to everyone at the company and returned to the communications office.

问：_____?
答：我跟小王是在船上告别的，没想到我们一别就是十年。

（七）由／为……谱写的 (to be composed by/for someone or something)

> ✍ 由／为……谱写（的）is a structure used to describe a musical piece or verse written（谱写）either by（由）someone or for（为）someone. 由 indicates the agent of the action and makes the pattern passive, while 为 indicates the object of the action and forms an active sentence. 的 may be placed after 谱写 to emphasize either the agent or object of the verb. Since 谱写 can only be used for musical compositions or poetry, its range of possible objects is limited to 曲子, 歌曲, 诗篇, etc.

☞ 在海上抛撒之前，亲属与逝者的骨灰最后告别，共同聆听由中国著名作曲家谱写的安魂曲。

1、这首钢琴曲是由著名音乐家贝多芬谱写的。
This piano concerto was composed by the famous musician Beethoven.

2、这个曲子是为小能手活动谱写的。
This song was composed for the skills campaign.

问：_____?
答：这首歌是专门为他的妻子谱写的。

（八）对……给予……的评价 (to offer an evaluation of someone or something)

> ✍ 对……给予……的评价, "to offer an evaluation of someone or something", is often used in written or formal Chinese. The spoken form is A 评价 B. The 对 phrase introduces the person or thing that is being given（给予）an evaluation and can be placed either before or after the subject. Examples: 很多人对他们的就餐制度给予了很高的评价 or 对他们的就餐制度，很多人给予了很高的评价. (Many people have given their dining system a high rating.) Sometimes the 对 phrase is omitted altogether, as in 政府给予了很高的评价. (The government gave it a high evaluation.)

☞ 參加海撒儀式的家屬給予了他們自己的評價。

1、對像他這樣的人你給予甚麼樣的評價？

What is your evaluation of a person like him?

2、對張藝謀的電影《活著》，世界影壇給予了很高的評價。

World film circles gave Zhang Yimou's movie *To Live* a high evaluation.

問：對這樣的義務活動，學校怎麼評價？

答：＿＿＿＿＿＿＿＿＿＿＿＿＿＿＿＿＿。

（九）打這以後……(from now on)

> ✍ 打這以後, "from now on", is used most often in colloquial Chinese. The equivalent written form is 從此以後, which was introduced in Lesson 1. 打 is interchangeable with 從. This structure is usually placed at the beginning of a sentence to indicate the beginning of an event or action. 這 can be replaced with 那, yielding the pattern 打那以後, "from then on", to be discussed in Lesson 13.

☞ 打這以後，我從心底裡覺得踏實了，因為徹底地回歸大自然了。

1、打這以後，我時時想回到自己熱戀的故土。

From that time on, I often thought of returning to my own beloved homeland.

2、打這（那）以後，我就不再有那種入土為安的觀念了。

Ever since, I have never again believed that one finds peace where one is buried.

問：你是甚麼時候開始起吃素的？

答：＿＿＿＿＿＿＿＿＿＿＿＿＿＿＿。

（十）從心底裡 (from the bottom of one's heart)

> ✍ 從心底裡 means "from the bottom of one's heart". This expression is used both in spoken and written settings. Its spoken equivalence is 從心眼兒裡. Its written counterpart is 發自內心地. 從心底裡 can be used either before or after the subject of a sentence. Examples: 從心底裡我認為人應該回歸大自然. (From the bottom of my heart I believe that man should return to nature.) 我從心底裡認為人應該回歸大自然. (I believe from the bottom of my heart that man should return to nature.)

☞ 打這以後，我從心底裡覺得踏實了，因為徹底地回歸大自然了。

1、我從心底裡覺得買禮品真是一件很傷腦筋的事。

From the bottom of my heart, I feel that buying a gift is a troublesome thing.

2、我從心底裡覺得人回歸自然這個觀念是很進步的。

189

☞ 参加海撒仪式的家属给予了他们自己的评价。

1、对象他这样的人你给予什么样的评价？
What is your evaluation of a person like him?
2、对张艺谋的电影《活着》，世界影坛给予了很高的评价。
World film circles gave Zhang Yimou's movie *To Live* a high evaluation.

问：对这样的义务活动，学校怎么评价？
答：＿＿＿＿＿＿＿＿＿＿＿＿＿＿＿。

（九）打这以后……(from now on)

> ✍ 打这以后，"from now on", is used most often in colloquial Chinese. The equivalent written form is 从此以后, which was introduced in Lesson 1. 打 is interchangeable with 从. This structure is usually placed at the beginning of a sentence to indicate the beginning of an event or action. 这 can be replaced with 那, yielding the pattern 打那以后，"from then on", to be discussed in Lesson 13.

☞ 打这以后，我从心底里觉得踏实了，因为彻底地回归大自然了。

1、打这以后，我时时想回到自己热恋的故土。
From that time on, I often thought of returning to my own beloved homeland.
2、打这（那）以后，我就不再有那种入土为安的观念了。
Ever since, I have never again believed that one finds peace where one is buried.

问：你是什么时候开始起吃素的？
答：＿＿＿＿＿＿＿＿＿＿＿＿＿＿＿。

（十）从心底里 (from the bottom of one's heart)

> ✍ 从心底里 means "from the bottom of one's heart". This expression is used both in spoken and written settings. Its spoken equivalence is 从心眼儿里. Its written counterpart is 发自内心地. 从心底里 can be used either before or after the subject of a sentence. Examples: 从心底里我认为人应该回归大自然. (From the bottom of my heart I believe that man should return to nature.) 我从心底里认为人应该回归大自然. (I believe from the bottom of my heart that man should return to nature.)

☞ 打这以后，我从心底里觉得踏实了，因为彻底地回归大自然了。

1、我从心底里觉得买礼品真是一件很伤脑筋的事。
From the bottom of my heart, I feel that buying a gift is a troublesome thing.
2、我从心底里觉得人回归自然这个观念是很进步的。

From the bottom of my heart, I feel that the idea of man returning to nature is a progressive concept.

問：你真的認為彈琴是一件很苦的事嗎？
答：＿＿＿＿＿＿＿＿＿＿＿＿＿＿＿＿＿。

（十一）對……的奠念 (to honor someone, to commemorate someone)（多用在書面／正式語體）

> ✍ 對……的奠念, "to honor someone" or "to commemorate someone", is used most often in formal and written settings. The spoken form is 對……的紀念. 奠念 (or 紀念) can be used either as a verb (to commemorate) or a noun (commemoration). Examples: 奠念逝去的親人 (to honor dear ones who have passed away). 葬禮是對逝者的奠念. (Funeral ceremonies are commemorations for those who have passed away.)

☞ 活人真正的哀思應當促進社會的文明發達和富裕，這才是對死者和亡者最好的奠念。

1、無論土葬、海葬、還是天葬，都是活著的人對死者的一種奠念。
No matter whether on land, sea, or sky, all burials are commemorations of the deceased by the living.

2、做一些事情促進社會的文明和發達才是對死去的父親的最好的奠念。
The best commemoration that one can give one's deceased father is to do something good for civilization and the advancement of society.

（十二）在……的眼裡 (in the eyes of)

> ✍ …的眼裡, "in the eyes of", is used mostly in colloquial Chinese. Its written form is 在……的目光中. Both structures are usually placed before the subject of a sentence, although they can also appear after the subject. Examples: 他在學生的眼裡是一個英雄. (He is a hero in the eyes of the students.) 在學生的目光中，他是一個英雄. (In the eyes of the students, he is a hero.)

☞ 骨灰撒向江河湖海，森林高山，在不少老百姓眼裡這是過去只有偉人才有資格做的事情，

1、在老百姓的眼裡，結婚是一生中的頭等大事。
In the eyes of ordinary people, marriage is the most important thing in life.

2、在一般人的眼裡，買得起汽車的人都是有錢的人。
To a common person, anyone who can afford to buy a car is rich.

From the bottom of my heart, I feel that the idea of man returning to nature is a progressive concept.

问：你真的认为弹琴是一件很苦的事吗？

答：_____。

（十一）对……的奠念 (to honor someone, to commemorate someone)（多用在书面／正式语体）

> ✍ 对……的奠念, "to honor someone" or "to commemorate someone", is used most often in formal and written settings. The spoken form is 对……的纪念. 奠念 (or 纪念) can be used either as a verb (to commemorate) or a noun (commemoration). Examples: 奠念逝去的亲人 (to honor dear ones who have passed away). 葬礼是对逝者的奠念. (Funeral ceremonies are commemorations for those who have passed away.)

☞ 活人真正的哀思应当促进社会的文明发达和富裕，这才是对死者和亡者最好的奠念。

1、无论土葬、海葬、还是天葬，都是活着的人对死者的一种奠念。

No matter whether on land, sea, or sky, all burials are commemorations of the deceased by the living.

2、做一些事情促进社会的文明和发达才是对死去的父亲的最好的奠念。

The best commemoration that one can give one's deceased father is to do something good for civilization and the advancement of society.

（十二）在……的眼里 (in the eyes of)

> ✍ 在……的眼里, "in the eyes of", is used mostly in colloquial Chinese. Its written form is 在……的目光中. Both structures are usually placed before the subject of a sentence, although they can also appear after the subject. Examples: 他在学生的眼里是一个英雄. (He is a hero in the eyes of the students.) 在学生的目光中，他是一个英雄. (In the eyes of the students, he is a hero.)

☞ 骨灰撒向江河湖海，森林高山，在不少老百姓眼里这是过去只有伟人才有资格做的事情，

1、在老百姓的眼里，结婚是一生中的头等大事。

In the eyes of ordinary people, marriage is the most important thing in life.

2、在一般人的眼里，买得起汽车的人都是有钱的人。

To a common person, anyone who can afford to buy a car is rich.

問：麥當勞對中國人來說算是一家比較講究的飯館嗎？

答：＿＿＿＿＿＿＿＿＿＿＿＿＿＿＿＿＿＿＿＿＿＿。

（十三）有消息說 (it is said that, the news says that, word has it that)

> ✍ 有消息說, "it is said that", "the news says that" or "word has it that", is used most often in colloquial Chinese. Equivalent written forms include 據説, 據悉, 據稱, and 據報導. This phrase can only be placed at the beginning of a sentence, never after the subject.

☞ 有消息說，繼安靈公司之後，北京市民政部門也將進行一次海上骨灰拋撒儀式，參加儀式的申請已超過百份以上。

1、有消息說，這家公司要開設汽車保險的業務。

It is said that this company wants to establish an automobile insurance service.

2、有消息說，現在中國花上萬元去土葬的人越來越少。

It is said that fewer Chinese people are spending tens of thousands of *yuan* on funerals these days.

問：現在用旅行支票換錢還要護照嗎？

答：不要了，＿＿＿＿＿＿＿＿＿＿＿＿。

（十四）繼⋯⋯之後，⋯⋯ (after, following)（多用在書面／正式語體）

> ✍ 繼⋯⋯之後, "after" or "following", is used to indicate a time frame for an event or action. This pattern is used mostly in written settings; its equivalent spoken form is 在⋯⋯以後 or ⋯⋯以後. 繼⋯⋯之後 is usually placed at the beginning of a sentence, before the subject. 繼 can be replaced with 在. Example: 繼（在）領養秋雲之後，日報社又義務領養了一個男孩. (Following Qiu Yun's adoption, the newspaper volunteered again to adopt a baby boy.)

☞ 有消息說，繼安靈公司之後，北京市民政部門也將進行一次海上骨灰拋撒儀式，參加儀式的申請已超過百份以上。

1、繼人民保險公司之後，又有很多家公司賣這種保險。

Following the lead of the People's Insurance Company, many companies provide this type of insurance.

2、繼安靈公司之後，北京市民政部門也要舉行一次海葬儀式。

Following the practice of the Rest In Peace Company, the Beijing Civil Service Department also wanted to organize a sea burial ceremony.

问: 麦当劳对中国人来说算是一家比较讲究的饭馆吗？

答: ＿＿＿＿＿＿＿＿＿＿＿＿＿＿＿＿＿＿＿＿＿＿。

（十三）有消息说 (it is said that, the news says that, word has it that)

> ✍ 有消息说, "it is said that", "the news says that" or "word has it that", is used most often in colloquial Chinese. Equivalent written forms include 据说, 据悉, 据称, and 据报道. This phrase can only be placed at the beginning of a sentence, never after the subject.

☞ 有消息说，继安灵公司之后，北京市民政部门也将进行一次海上骨灰抛撒仪式，参加仪式的申请已超过百份以上。

1、有消息说，这家公司要开设汽车保险的业务。

It is said that this company wants to establish an automobile insurance service.

2、有消息说，现在中国花上万元去土葬的人越来越少。

It is said that fewer Chinese people are spending tens of thousands of *yuan* on funerals these days.

问: 现在用旅行支票换钱还要护照吗？

答: 不要了，＿＿＿＿＿＿＿＿＿＿＿＿＿。

（十四）继⋯⋯之后，⋯⋯ (after, following)（多用在书面／正式语体）

> ✍ 继⋯⋯之后, "after" or "following", is used to indicate a time frame for an event or action. This pattern is used mostly in written settings; its equivalent spoken form is 在⋯⋯以后 or ⋯⋯以后. 继⋯⋯之后 is usually placed at the beginning of a sentence, before the subject. 继 can be replaced with 在. Example: 继（在）领养秋云之后，日报社又义务领养了一个男孩. (Following Qiu Yun's adoption, the newspaper volunteered again to adopt a baby boy.)

☞ 有消息说，继安灵公司之后，北京市民政部门也将进行一次海上骨灰抛撒仪式，参加仪式的申请已超过百份以上。

1、继人民保险公司之后，又有很多家公司卖这种保险。

Following the lead of the People's Insurance Company, many companies provide this type of insurance.

2、继安灵公司之后，北京市民政部门也要举行一次海葬仪式。

Following the practice of the Rest In Peace Company, the Beijing Civil Service Department also wanted to organize a sea burial ceremony.

四、文化背景知識 Cultural Notes

1. In traditional times people were usually buried in family burial grounds. China's ever-rising population, however, has strained this practice. There is simply less and less land available for burial. Burial at sea (海葬) is a recent development in China and is still not common. As mentioned in our text, arrangements for sea burial are made through the Civil Administration Office (民政部). Most people in China these days are cremated. After cremation, a person's ashes (骨灰) are put into an ash urn (骨灰盒). Sometimes these urns will be buried in a public cemetery (公墓). Alternately, they can be stored at a crematorium.

2. Chinese customarily wear white (素) clothing at funeral ceremonies. To be precise, they don a kind of unbleached sackcloth for mourning apparel, which is a brownish-yellow rather than white. In general, white is the color of autumn and hence is associated with old age and death (hence, it is very unlucky in China to wear anything white in one's hair!). The deceased is regarded to be at "peace"(安) only after the body has been buried (入土為安).

3. The reference to "matters only great persons are qualified to undertake" (偉人才有資格做的事) refers to the late Premier Zhou Enlai (1898-1976), who in fact was buried at sea.

四、文化背景知识 Cultural Notes

1. In traditional times people were usually buried in family burial grounds. China's ever-rising population, however, has strained this practice. There is simply less and less land available for burial. Burial at sea (海葬) is a recent development in China and is still not common. As mentioned in our text, arrangements for sea burial are made through the Civil Administration Office (民政部). Most people in China these days are cremated. After cremation, a person's ashes (骨灰) are put into an ash urn (骨灰盒). Sometimes these urns will be buried in a public cemetery (公墓). Alternately, they can be stored at a crematorium.

2. Chinese customarily wear white (素) clothing at funeral ceremonies. To be precise, they don a kind of unbleached sackcloth for mourning apparel, which is a brownish-yellow rather than white. In general, white is the color of autumn and hence is associated with old age and death (hence, it is very unlucky in China to wear anything white in one's hair!). The deceased is regarded to be at "peace" (安) only after the body has been buried (入土为安).

3. The reference to "matters only great persons are qualified to undertake" (伟人才有资格做的事) refers to the late Premier Zhou Enlai (1898-1976), who in fact was buried at sea.

練習

語言結構 Structures

一、短語翻譯 (Phrase translation)

1. final resting place
2. to believe in going back to nature
3. to have a special meaning
4. to throw ashes while listening to the solemn music
5. the working staff of this company
6. the opera house and the dance company
7. to perform the symphony
8. to spare the land for the living people
9. oceans and rivers, mountains and forests
10. to evaluate the performance
11. to accept the concept of an ocean burial
12. to qualify for such a choice

二、聽力練習 (Listening comprehension)

1、聽寫 (Dictation)

2、聽錄音並回答問題 (Answering questions while listening to the audio CD)

(1) 寫出聽力原文。

(2) 由於美國的情況是地多人少，土葬是一件很平常的事情。但是火葬和海葬倒不太常見。你可以不可以根據你的了解，談談你認識的人對火葬、海葬或者回歸大自然的看法？

练习

语言结构 Structures

一、短语翻译 (Phrase translation)

1. final resting place
2. to believe in going back to nature
3. to have a special meaning
4. to throw ashes while listening to the solemn music
5. the working staff of this company
6. the opera house and the dance company
7. to perform the symphony
8. to spare the land for the living people
9. oceans and rivers, mountains and forests
10. to evaluate the performance
11. to accept the concept of an ocean burial
12. to qualify for such a choice

二、听力练习 (Listening comprehension)

1、听写 (Dictation)

2、听录音并回答问题 (Answering questions while listening to the audio CD)

(1) 写出听力原文。
(2) 由于美国的情况是地多人少，土葬是一件很平常的事情。但是火葬和海葬倒不太常见。你可以不可以根据你的了解，谈谈你认识的人对火葬、海葬或者回归大自然的看法？

三、填空 (Fill in the blanks)

落葉歸根、重返自然、安靈曲、江河湖海、森林高山、入土為安

　　中國人的傳統觀念是老了以後＿＿＿＿＿＿，人死以後＿＿＿＿＿＿。現在呢，很多人的觀念發生了變化，他們開始相信人應該＿＿＿＿＿＿，他們要求家人火葬他們，並把他們的骨灰撒向＿＿＿＿＿、＿＿＿＿＿＿。這跟以前的觀念是完全不同的。

四、完成句子 (Complete the sentences)

1、　　A：你喜歡這個曲子嗎？
　　　　B：喜歡。這個曲子＿＿＿＿＿＿＿＿＿＿＿＿＿＿＿＿＿＿＿＿
　　　　（由……譜寫的；對……給予……的評價）

2、　　A：你覺得這頓午餐是不是有點兒過分排場？
　　　　B：＿＿＿＿＿＿＿＿＿＿＿＿＿＿＿＿＿＿＿＿＿＿＿＿＿＿＿
　　　　（在……的眼裡；莫過於……）

3、　　A：＿＿＿＿＿＿＿＿＿＿＿＿＿＿＿＿＿＿＿＿＿＿＿＿＿＿＿
　　　　B：是嗎？那我以後要天天帶上我的卡。要不然我不能吃飯了。
　　　　（有消息說；無論……都……）

4、　　A：你甚麼時候開始為你的同學服務的？
　　　　B：我自從跟他們吵架以後，＿＿＿＿＿＿＿＿＿＿＿＿＿＿＿＿
　　　　（從心底裡……；打這兒以後）

五、閱讀短文、回答問題 (Answering questions based on the reading passages)

　　過去，中國人喜歡說一句話叫"落葉歸根"。就是說，不管你到哪個國家，不管你離家多遠，最終都要返回到自己的故土養老，然後再在自己的故土找到歸宿，重返自然。有些人出國幾十年，到老了，還要回到自己的老家度過晚年。但是這幾十年來，人們的想法似乎也改變了。尤其是一些在海外有兒女的老人，不但年老了還要出國、出門，而且還要永遠留在國外，不要回到自己的故土"落葉歸根"。這種情況在北美和歐洲尤其多。很多人說，反正是回歸大自然，在外國在中國都一樣。留在外國也可以入土為安，還不必和中國的活人爭地，這也算是對中國社會的一點兒貢獻吧！

194

三、填空 (Fill in the blanks)

落叶归根、重返自然、安灵曲、江河湖海、森林高山、入土为安

中国人的传统观念是老了以后_____，人死以后_____。现在呢，很多人的观念发生了变化，他们开始相信人应该_____，他们要求家人火葬他们，并把他们的骨灰撒向_____、_____。这跟以前的观念是完全不同的。

四、完成句子 (Complete the sentences)

1、　A：你喜欢这个曲子吗？
　　B：喜欢。这个曲子_____
　　（由……谱写的；对……给予……的评价）

2、　A：你觉得这顿午餐是不是有点儿过分排场？
　　B：_____
　　（在……的眼里；莫过于……）

3、　A：_____
　　B：是吗？那我以后要天天带上我的卡。要不然我不能吃饭了。
　　（有消息说；无论……都……）

4、　A：你什么时候开始为你的同学服务的？
　　B：我自从跟他们吵架以后，_____
　　（从心底里……；打这儿以后）

五、阅读短文、回答问题 (Answering questions based on the reading passages)

过去，中国人喜欢说一句话叫"落叶归根"。就是说，不管你到哪个国家，不管你离家多远，最终都要返回到自己的故土养老，然后再在自己的故土找到归宿，重返自然。有些人出国几十年，到老了，还要回到自己的老家度过晚年。但是这几十年来，人们的想法似乎也改变了。尤其是一些在海外有儿女的老人，不但年老了还要出国、出门，而且还要永远留在国外，不要回到自己的故土"落叶归根"。这种情况在北美和欧洲尤其多。很多人说，反正是回归大自然，在外国在中国都一样。留在外国也可以入土为安，还不必和中国的活人争地，这也算是对中国社会的一点儿贡献吧！

問題

　　(1) 中國人過去對自己的最後的歸宿有甚麼看法？

　　(2) 現在的看法呢？為甚麼？

　　(3) 請你談談美國人怎麼看自己"最後的歸宿"。多數美國人在晚年時為自己做甚麼安排？

　　北京人對排隊的現象並不陌生。如今，北京人為甚麼而排隊？

(1) 出國領護照

　　隨著中國改革開放的進一步發展，現在有越來越多的北京人出國留學、觀光旅遊、探親訪友。每天前往北京市公安局管理處辦理出國護照的人數不勝數。儘管難以得到北京每天、每年有多少個人出國的數字，但可以肯定是越來越多。

(2) 公共交通〔公交〕月票

　　每月最有規律的排隊現象，莫過於購買公交月票。北京市公交總公司平均每月出售月票一百一十萬張，近十分之一的北京市民是公交車的乘客。這個數字還不包括每月坐地鐵的人。九十年代初，北京市公交月票價格做過一次調整：市內職工月票為七元，學生月票為二元；郊區職工月票為八元，學生月票為三元；市、郊職工通用月票為十元，學生月票為四元；與大陸其它城市相比，北京市公交月票價格是最低的，當然排隊買票的人也最多。

問題

　　(1) 從北京人的"排隊"你看到如今的中國的社會有甚麼變化？這些變化跟甚麼社會發展有關係？

　　(2) 除了"排隊"以外，你還可以從哪些方面了解一個社會的變化？

六、翻譯 (Translate sentences)

1. As the saying goes, "The falling leaves settle on their own roots". This means that for one's last place of rest, nothing is better than returning to nature.

2. In the eyes of common people, only great people are qualified for this kind of extravagant ceremony. Even the symphony orchestra in the city came to play at the ceremony.

3. We advocate that people should change their traditional concept of "peace being found when one is buried in the earth". They should go back to nature and spare more land for the living people.

4. The best commemoration for the dead is for the living to promote the civilization and prosperity of human society.

问题

    (1) 中国人过去对自己的最后的归宿有什么看法？

    (2) 现在的看法呢？为什么？

    (3) 请你谈谈美国人怎么看自己"最后的归宿"。多数美国人在晚年时为自己做什么安排？

北京人对排队的现象并不陌生。如今，北京人为什么而排队？

(1) 出国领护照

    随着中国改革开放的进一步发展，现在有越来越多的北京人出国留学、观光旅游、探亲访友。每天前往北京市公安局管理处办理出国护照的人数不胜数。尽管难以得到北京每天、每年有多少个人出国的数字，但可以肯定是越来越多。

(2) 公共交通（公交）月票

    每月最有规律的排队现象，莫过于购买公交月票。北京市公交总公司平均每月出售月票一百一十万张，近十分之一的北京市民是公交车的乘客。这个数字还不包括每月坐地铁的人。九十年代初，北京市公交月票价格做过一次调整：市内职工月票为七元，学生月票为二元；郊区职工月票为八元，学生月票为三元；市、郊职工通用月票为十元，学生月票为四元；与大陆其它城市相比，北京市公交月票价格是最低的，当然排队买票的人也最多。

问题

    (1) 从北京人的"排队"你看到如今的中国的社会有什么变化？这些变化跟什么社会发展有关系？

    (2) 除了"排队"以外，你还可以从哪些方面了解一个社会的变化？

六、翻译 (Translate sentences)

1. As the saying goes, "The falling leaves settle on their own roots". This means that for one's last place of rest, nothing is better than returning to nature.

2. In the eyes of common people, only great people are qualified for this kind of extravagant ceremony. Even the symphony orchestra in the city came to play at the ceremony.

3. We advocate that people should change their traditional concept of "peace being found when one is buried in the earth". They should go back to nature and spare more land for the living people.

4. The best commemoration for the dead is for the living to promote the civilization and prosperity of human society.

語言實踐 : Practice

一、根據課文回答問題 (Answering questions based on the dialogue)

1、中國人說 "落葉歸根" 的意思是甚麼？
2、1994年3月在中國渤海灣上有甚麼事情發生？
3、在你看來，用交響樂奏安魂曲與骨灰告別，是不是西方人的送葬的習慣？
4、中國人對海撒儀式的看法是甚麼？你最同意哪個人的看法？
5、你覺得多數中國人對海葬的看法有這麼進步嗎？
6、為甚麼記者說 "骨灰撒向江河湖海、森林高山，在不少老百姓眼裡是只有偉人才有資格做的事情？"
7、甚麼叫 "入土為安" ？
8、請你報導一下北京民政部門最近要舉行的一個活動。

二、活動 (Activities)

去你的中國朋友家或中國家庭採訪一下他們對海撒儀式的看法。跟你的中國爸爸媽媽討論一下甚麼是 "入土為安" ， "落葉歸根" ，對他們來說這有甚麼意義？

三、討論題 (Topics for discussion)

1、中國人的 "回歸自然" 或者 "歸天" 跟西方人的 "上天堂" 的說法有甚麼區別？中西方對人的 "最後的歸宿" 有沒有不同的看法？
2、你知道為甚麼骨灰撒向江河湖海是過去只有偉人才可以做的事情？
3、甚麼是中國 "入土為安" 的觀念？你覺得海葬對中國的國情有沒有影響？

四、報告 (Presentation)

《我對 "回歸大自然" 的看法》

语言实践 ⋮ **Practice**

一、根据课文回答问题 (Answering questions based on the dialogue)

1、中国人说"落叶归根"的意思是什么？
2、1994年3月在中国渤海湾上有什么事情发生？
3、在你看来，用交响乐奏安魂曲与骨灰告别，是不是西方人的送葬的习惯？
4、中国人对海撒仪式的看法是什么？你最同意哪个人的看法？
5、你觉得多数中国人对海葬的看法有这么进步吗？
6、为什么记者说"骨灰撒向江河湖海、森林高山，在不少老百姓眼里是只有伟人才有资格做的事情？"
7、什么叫"入土为安"？
8、请你报道一下北京民政部门最近要举行的一个活动。

二、活动 (Activities)

　　去你的中国朋友家或中国家庭采访一下他们对海撒仪式的看法。跟你的中国爸爸妈妈讨论一下什么是"入土为安"，"落叶归根"，对他们来说这有什么意义？

三、讨论题 (Topics for discussion)

1、中国人的"回归自然"或者"归天"跟西方人的"上天堂"的说法有什么区别？中西方对人的"最后的归宿"有没有不同的看法？
2、你知道为什么骨灰撒向江河湖海是过去只有伟人才可以做的事情？
3、什么是中国"入土为安"的观念？你觉得海葬对中国的国情有没有影响？

四、报告 (Presentation)

　　《我对"回归大自然"的看法》

五、看圖討論 (Picto-discussion)

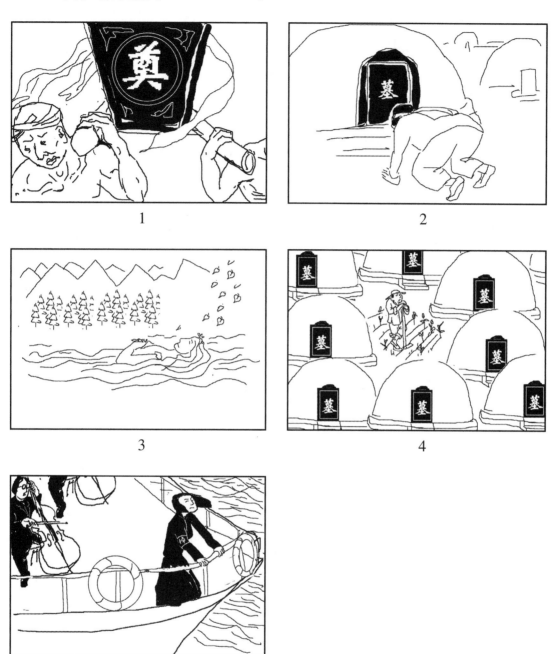

五、看图讨论 (Picto-discussion)

1

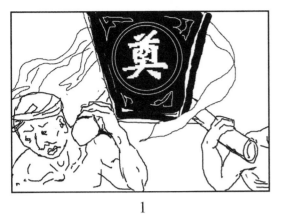

3

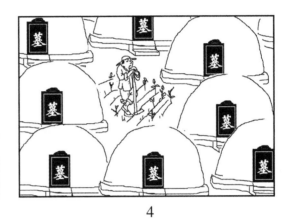

4

5

第十課

下海

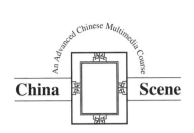

第十课

下海

課文

一、對話 Dialogs

（一）

安麗沙：現在中國人私人買車算不算一件大事？

張師傅：現在已經不算一件很讓人吃驚[1]的大事了。據統計，中國北京的個體出租車占全市汽車的百分之四十。這還不算，現在還有很多人買了車上不了汽車牌照[2]，有的人有了牌照還得排隊領取客運資格證，你說難不難？

安麗沙：看來中國人的私人汽車越來越多了。

生詞

安麗沙	(ān lì shā)	*N.*	An Lisha, name of a person 人名
吃驚	(chī jīng)	*V.*	to be surprised, to be startled
據統計	(jù tǒng jì)	*Adv.*	according to statistics
出租汽車	(chū zū qì chē)	*N.*	taxi
牌照	(pái zhào)	*N.*	license plate
客運	(kè yùn)	*N.*	passenger transport
資格證	(zī gé zhèng)	*N.*	certificate

Notes [1]讓人吃驚 vs. 吃了一驚：吃驚, or 吃了一驚, is a VO structure that means "to be startled", "to be shocked". Example: 聽到這個消息，他吃了一驚. (He was shocked when he heard this news.) 讓人吃驚 means "to startle someone", "to surprise someone". This expression can modify other nouns, as in 讓人吃驚的大事 (important and shocking matters), or can function as a verb, as in 這件事情真讓人吃驚！ (This is really surprising!) When used with 驚 or other nouns with negative connotations, 吃 means "to suffer", as in 吃苦 (to experience bitterness), 吃虧 (to suffer loss).

[2]上牌照：When used with 牌照, 上 is a verb meaning "to go through a registration process". While 牌照 means "license plate", when referring to cabs in China it also connotes the idea of "medallion" or "registration", that is, official permission from a local government office to operate a taxi.

课文

一、对话  Dialogs

（一）

安丽沙： 现在中国人私人买车算不算一件大事？

张师傅： 现在已经不算一件很让人吃惊[1]的大事了。据统计，中国北京的个体出租车占全市汽车的百分之四十。这还不算，现在还有很多人买了车上不了汽车牌照[2]，有的人有了牌照还得排队领取客运资格证，你说难不难？

安丽沙： 看来中国人的私人汽车越来越多了。

生词

安丽沙	(ān lì shā)	*N.*	An Lisha, name of a person 人名
吃惊	(chī jīng)	*V.*	to be surprised, to be startled
据统计	(jù tǒng jì)	*Adv.*	according to statistics
出租汽车	(chū zū qì chē)	*N.*	taxi
牌照	(pái zhào)	*N.*	license plate
客运	(kè yùn)	*N.*	passenger transport
资格证	(zī gé zhèng)	*N.*	certificate

Notes [1]让人吃惊 vs. 吃了一惊: 吃惊, or 吃了一惊, is a VO structure that means "to be startled", "to be shocked". Example: 听到这个消息，他吃了一惊. (He was shocked when he heard this news.) 让人吃惊 means "to startle someone", "to surprise someone". This expression can modify other nouns, as in 让人吃惊的大事 (important and shocking matters), or can function as a verb, as in 这件事情真让人吃惊！ (This is really surprising!) When used with 惊 or other nouns with negative connotations, 吃 means "to suffer", as in 吃苦 (to experience bitterness), 吃亏 (to suffer loss).

[2]上牌照: When used with 牌照, 上 is a verb meaning "to go through a registration process". While 牌照 means "license plate", when referring to cabs in China it also connotes the idea of "medallion" or "registration", that is, official permission from a local government office to operate a taxi.

（二）

出租車司機：喂，請上車，去哪兒？

安麗沙：　　謝謝師傅。去首都經貿大學。

（After a while）

安麗沙　　　師傅，我想問問，您是甚麼時候開始開出租車的？

出租車司機：那還是前幾年的事了。我那時候在國營單位當工人，工作不但單調枯燥，
　　　　　　而且沒有技術，一個月就那麼三、四十塊錢。

安麗沙：　　是嗎？那後來呢？

出租車司機：後來，大家都開始下海，我的腦子也活了，就跟我太太商量買輛出租車。

安麗沙：　　那你太太說甚麼呢？

出租車司機：她一聽就吃了一驚[3]。她說：“我們連小汽車都很少坐，怎麼能拿得出幾
　　　　　　十萬塊錢買車呢？”

安麗沙：　　那後來你怎麼辦呢？

出租車司機：我東借西借終於買了輛出租車跑起出租來了。現在人們看到開出租很賺
　　　　　　錢，所以買車的人越來越多。連牌照也上不上，客運資格證也領不上。

安麗沙：　　可是這些出租車真方便了老百姓。在街上招手就可以上車，十幾塊、十
　　　　　　幾分鐘就可以去想去的地方。

出租車司機：到首經大了。十五公里，十五塊。

安麗沙：　　這是十五塊錢。請您給開張發票。

生詞

司機	(sī jī)	N.	driver
首都經貿大學	(shǒu dū jīng mào dà xué)	NP.	Capital University of Economics and Business
首經大	(shǒu jīng dà)	NP.	首都經貿大學

✎ **Notes** [3]See Note (1).

（二）

出租车司机： 喂，请上车，去哪儿？

安丽沙： 谢谢师傅。去首都经贸大学。

（After a while）

安丽沙 师傅，我想问问，您是什么时候开始开出租车的？

出租车司机：那还是前几年的事了。我那时候在国营单位当工人，工作不但单调枯
燥，而且没有技术，一个月就那么三、四十块钱。

安丽沙： 是吗？那后来呢？

出租车司机：后来，大家都开始下海，我的脑子也活了，就跟我太太商量买辆出租
车。

安丽沙： 那你太太说什么呢？

出租车司机：她一听就吃了一惊(3)。她说："我们连小汽车都很少坐，怎么能拿得出几
十万块钱买车呢？"

安丽沙： 那后来你怎么办呢？

出租车司机：我东借西借终于买了辆出租车跑起出租来了。现在人们看到开出租很赚
钱，所以买车的人越来越多。连牌照也上不上，客运资格证也领不上。

安丽沙： 可是这些出租车真方便了老百姓。在街上招手就可以上车，十几块、十
几分钟就可以去想去的地方。

出租车司机：到首经大了。十五公里，十五块。

安丽沙： 这是十五块钱。请您给开张发票。

生词

司机	(sī jī)	N.	driver
首都经贸大学	(shǒu dū jīng mào dà xué)	NP.	Capital University of Economics and Business
首经大	(shǒu jīng dà)	NP.	首都经贸大学

✏️ **Notes** (3)See Note (1).

單調	(dān diào)	*Adj.*	monotonous
枯燥	(kū zào)	*Adj.*	dull and dry, boring
腦子	(nǎo zi)	*N.*	brain
招手	(zhāo shǒu)	*V.*	to wave at
發票	(fā piào)	*N.*	receipt

二、電視原文 💻 TV original

攢錢[4]買輛出租車

（根據原文改編）

　　早晨七點二十分是周師傅自己給自己定下的上班時間。在家門口細細地擦上一遍已經是一塵不染的車身，周師傅心裡有一種說不出的舒坦。

　　三十出頭[5]的周師傅，曾經幹過不少的工作，四年前終於不滿足原先每天單調枯燥又毫無技術的工作，而辭職不幹了，湊錢[6]買了輛微型[7]麵包車，跑起了個體運輸。這在當時是讓朋友和親戚們看了都吃驚的舉動，因為在那時，私人買車在中國並不多，外出坐車的人那就更少了。

（採訪一）

記者：　“剛才你說你開了四年了，是嗎？開了四年你怎麼安排休息和工作的時間？”

✏️ **Notes** [4]湊錢 vs. 攢錢: 湊錢 and 攢錢 are both VO structures related to money. 湊錢 means "to collect money" or "to raise funds" and suggests a goal or purpose for the money. 攢錢 means "to save money", either with or without a particular goal in mind. Two related terms, both of which mean "to earn money", are 賺錢 and 掙錢.

[5]出頭, meaning "more than" or "over", is a colloquial expression used to refer to an indefinite age or number. Example: 李先生已經六十出頭了. (Mr. Li is already over 60.) 出頭 must follow a round number (30, 40, 50, etc.). Another expression, similar in meaning and usage to 出頭, is 以上. Both terms can be used to express the idea "an annual salary of over 4,000": 年薪 4,000 以上 or 年薪 4,000 出頭.

[6]See Note (4).

[7]微型: The prefix 微型 means "miniature", as in 微型麵包車 (minivan), 微型電腦 (microcomputer), 微型詞典 (pocket dictionary).

单调	(dān diào)	*Adj.*	monotonous
枯燥	(kū zào)	*Adj.*	dull and dry, boring
脑子	(nǎo zi)	*N.*	brain
招手	(zhāo shǒu)	*V.*	to wave at
发票	(fā piào)	*N.*	receipt

二、电视原文　💻 TV original

攒钱⁽⁴⁾买辆出租车

（根据原文改编）

　　早晨七点二十分是周师傅自己给自己定下的上班时间。在家门口细细地擦上一遍已经是一尘不染的车身，周师傅心里有一种说不出的舒坦。

　　三十出头⁽⁵⁾的周师傅，曾经干过不少的工作，四年前终于不满足原先每天单调枯燥又毫无技术的工作，而辞职不干了，凑钱⁽⁶⁾买了辆微型⁽⁷⁾面包车，跑起了个体运输。这在当时是让朋友和亲戚们看了都吃惊的举动，因为在那时，私人买车在中国并不多，外出坐车的人那就更少了。

（采访一）

记者：　　"刚才你说你开了四年了，是吗？开了四年你怎么安排休息和工作的时间？"

✎ **Notes** ⁽⁴⁾凑钱 vs. 攒钱: 凑钱 and 攒钱 are both VO structures related to money. 凑钱 means "to collect money" or "to raise funds" and suggests a goal or purpose for the money. 攒钱 means "to save money", either with or without a particular goal in mind. Two related terms, both of which mean "to earn money", are 赚钱 and 挣钱.

⁽⁵⁾出头, meaning "more than" or "over", is a colloquial expression used to refer to an indefinite age or number. Example: 李先生已经六十出头了. (Mr. Li is already over 60.) 出头 must follow a round number (30, 40, 50, etc.). Another expression, similar in meaning and usage to出头, is 以上. Both terms can be used to express the idea "an annual salary of over 4,000": 年薪 4,000 以上 or 年薪 4,000 出头.

⁽⁶⁾See Note (4).

⁽⁷⁾微型: The prefix 微型 means "miniature", as in 微型面包车 (minivan), 微型电脑 (microcomputer), 微型词典 (pocket dictionary).

周師傅："我以前開麵包車，一般在夏天中午休息兩個小時，晚上一般上到十二點左右。早晨是七點半出發，午飯一般都在外面吃一點，晚上回家吃。"

記者："你有沒有星期天？"

周師傅："沒有，像我的這車，本錢還沒還，總想多賺一點。在節假日，單位放假，對我們來講，是最好的生意。像春節、國慶節這些節日，尤其要幹。"

記者："就不能休息了？"

周師傅："對。在這四年當中我休息得最痛快的就是在92年的7月份，我以前的那輛麵包車在7月份的時候賣掉了，在這個車還沒買進的時候，我休息了一個多月，最暢快了。"

記者："想幹甚麼幹甚麼？"

周師傅："對，這個車買了以後，就基本上沒有休息過。"

記者："如果你生病了怎麼辦？"

周師傅："像我呢，身體應該說很好！平時感冒了，最多一、兩天就好了。"

（採訪二）

記者："你這個車是你自己買的？"

張師傅："自己買的。"

記者："那要很貴了？多少錢？"

張師傅："二十多萬。"

記者："買了多長時間？"

張師傅："一年多一點。"

記者："那這車全部是你自己的錢買的，還是要借一部分？"

張師傅："稍微不夠一點麼，要借一點。"

記者："車的本錢應該賺回來了吧？"

張師傅："還沒有，才一年。"

記者："對不起，我問一下，你原來幹甚麼工作？"

周师傅： "我以前开面包车，一般在夏天中午休息两个小时，晚上一般上到十二点左右。早晨是七点半出发，午饭一般都在外面吃一点，晚上回家吃。"

记者： "你有没有星期天？"

周师傅： "没有，象我的这车，本钱还没还，总想多赚一点。在节假日，单位放假，对我们来讲，是最好的生意。象春节、国庆节这些节日，尤其要干。"

记者： "就不能休息了？"

周师傅： "对。在这四年当中我休息得最痛快的就是在92年的7月份，我以前的那辆面包车在7月份的时候卖掉了，在这个车还没买进的时候，我休息了一个多月，最畅快了。"

记者： "想干什么干什么？"

周师傅： "对，这个车买了以后，就基本上没有休息过。"

记者： "如果你生病了怎么办？"

周师傅： "象我呢，身体应该说很好！平时感冒了，最多一、两天就好了。"

（采访二）

记者： "你这个车是你自己买的？"

张师傅： "自己买的。"

记者： "那要很贵了？多少钱？"

张师傅： "二十多万。"

记者： "买了多长时间？"

张师傅： "一年多一点。"

记者： "那这车全部是你自己的钱买的，还是要借一部分？"

张师傅： "稍微不够一点么，要借一点。"

记者： "车的本钱应该赚回来了吧？"

张师傅： "还没有，才一年。"

记者： "对不起，我问一下，你原来干什么工作？"

張師傅：　"原來做生意的。"

記者：　　"我覺得總是做生意好輕鬆，錢來得快。"

張師傅：　"本來是這樣想，可是做生意也很辛苦。他們說開出租車很好，但現在感覺開出租好像 wandang。"

記者：　　"wandang 用普通話說，應該怎麼說？"

張師傅：　"就好像跳進泥坑一樣。"

　　閒聊之中，似乎司機們對自己所從事的職業都深惡痛絕。但據我了解，眼下本市還有近八千名司機等著領取客運資格證。有人想進，有人想出，簡直就是一座圍城。

　　下午四點，周師傅和往常一樣去接下班的妻子回家。我們到了廠門口，他妻子已經在那兒等了一會了。見到攝像機，她有些不自然，低著頭不看我們，默默享受丈夫給予的貴賓級[8]的禮遇。妻子在旁邊，原先挺能說的周師傅，也關上了話匣子，一路上只是"呵呵"地笑。

　　小倆口[9]在非常默契的合作中把晚飯做好了，晚飯總是三個人吃的，除了小倆口外，還有周師傅的母親。約六點鐘的時候，周師傅又要出車了，母親和妻子總是送到車門口，每天都這樣。

　　夜，已經很深了，奔忙一天的司機們都紛紛回家了。但周師傅還不想收車，也許前方街道拐角處還會站著一位要車的人，去醫院，還是去車站。嗨！管他呢？反正送他去他要去的地方，不能讓人家在黑夜裡總站在大街上等啊！只有在這個時候，周師傅才騰出空來，想一想自己的過去、今天和未來，此刻他並不寂寞。

生詞

攢錢	(zǎn qián)	*VO.*	to save money
細細地	(xì xì de)	*Adv.*	carefully

✎ **Notes** [8]貴賓級 means "VIP rank" or "VIP status". 貴賓 means "honored guest" or "VIP", and 級 means "grade", "rank", "level". In the dialogue, 貴賓級 is used as an adjective: 貴賓級的禮遇 (VIP treatment).

　　[9]小倆口: 小倆口, meaning "the two of us" or "the two of them", is a common expression for young couples. 口 can function as a classifier for members of a family. Example: 我家裡有四口人. (There are four people in my family.)

张师傅：　"原来做生意的。"

记者：　　"我觉得总是做生意好轻松，钱来得快。"

张师傅：　"本来是这样想，可是做生意也很辛苦。他们说开出租车很好，但现在感觉
　　　　　开出租好象 wandang。"

记者：　　"wandang 用普通话说，应该怎么说？"

张师傅：　"就好象跳进泥坑一样。"

　　闲聊之中，似乎司机们对自己所从事的职业都深恶痛绝。但据我了解，眼下本市还有近八千名司机等着领取客运资格证。有人想进，有人想出，简直就是一座围城。

　　下午四点，周师傅和往常一样去接下班的妻子回家。我们到了厂门口，他妻子已经在那儿等了一会了。见到摄像机，她有些不自然，低着头不看我们，默默享受丈夫给予的贵宾级[8]的礼遇。妻子在旁边，原先挺能说的周师傅，也关上了话匣子，一路上只是"呵呵"地笑。

　　小俩口[9]在非常默契的合作中把晚饭做好了，晚饭总是三个人吃的，除了小俩口外，还有周师傅的母亲。约六点钟的时候，周师傅又要出车了，母亲和妻子总是送到车门口，每天都这样。

　　夜，已经很深了，奔忙一天的司机们都纷纷回家了。但周师傅还不想收车，也许前方街道拐角处还会站着一位要车的人，去医院，还是去车站。嗨！管他呢？反正送他去他要去的地方，不能让人家在黑夜里总站在大街上等啊！只有在这个时候，周师傅才腾出空来，想一想自己的过去、今天和未来，此刻他并不寂寞。

生词

攒钱	(zǎn qián)	*VO.*	to save money
细细地	(xì xì de)	*Adv.*	carefully

✎ **Notes** [8]贵宾级 means "VIP rank" or "VIP status". 贵宾 means "honored guest" or "VIP", and 级 means "grade", "rank", "level". In the dialogue, 贵宾级 is used as an adjective: 贵宾级的礼遇 (VIP treatment).

[9]小俩口: 小俩口, meaning "the two of us" or "the two of them", is a common expression for young couples. 口 can function as a classifier for members of a family. Example: 我家里有四口人. (There are four people in my family.)

一塵不染	(yī chén bù rǎn)	*Idiom.*	dustless
車身	(chē shēn)	*N.*	car body
舒坦	(shū tǎn)	*Adj.*	comfortable
終於	(zhōng yú)	*Adv.*	eventually, finally
不滿足	(bù mǎn zú)	*Adj.*	not satisfied with
毫無	(háo wú)	*Adv.*	not at all
辭職	(cí zhí)	*V.*	to resign
湊錢	(còu qián)	*V.*	to collect money, to raise funds
微型	(wēi xíng)	*Adj.*	mini, miniature
運輸	(yùn shū)	*N.*	transportation
舉動	(jǔ dòng)	*N.*	action
外出	(wài chū)	*V.*	to go out
國慶節	(guó qìng jié)	*NP.*	National Day
痛快	(tòng kuài)	*Adj.*	happy, delighted
暢快	(chàng kuài)	*Adj.*	joyful, carefree
感冒	(gǎn mào)	*VO.*	to catch a cold
稍微	(shāo wēi)	*Adj.*	a little bit, slightly
輕鬆	(qīng sōng)	*Adj.*	light and relaxed
普通話	(pǔ tōng huà)	*NP.*	Mandarin, standard Chinese language
泥坑	(ní kēng)	*N.*	mud pit
閒聊	(xián liáo)	*V.*	to chat casually
深惡痛絕	(shēn wù tòng jué)	*V.*	to hate bitterly, to detest
圍城	(wéi chéng)	*NP.*	surrounded town, besieged town
攝像機	(shè xiàng jī)	*N.*	video camera
低頭	(dī tóu)	*VO.*	to lower one's head
默默	(mò mò)	*Adv.*	quietly, silently
貴賓級	(guì bīn jí)	*NP.*	the rank of VIP
禮遇	(lǐ yù)	*N.*	courteous treatment
話匣子	(huà xiá zi)	*N.*	chatterbox
呵呵	(hē hē)	*N.*	sound of laughter
默契	(mò qì)	*N.*	tacit agreement
合作	(hé zuò)	*N/V.*	cooperation; to cooperate, to collaborate
收車	(shōu chē)	*VO.*	to stop driving around

一尘不染	(yī chén bù rǎn)	Idiom.	dustless
车身	(chē shēn)	N.	car body
舒坦	(shū tǎn)	Adj.	comfortable
终于	(zhōng yú)	Adv.	eventually, finally
不满足	(bù mǎn zú)	Adj.	not satisfied with
毫无	(háo wú)	Adv.	not at all
辞职	(cí zhí)	V.	to resign
凑钱	(còu qián)	V.	to collect money, to raise funds
微型	(wēi xíng)	Adj.	mini, miniature
运输	(yùn shū)	N.	transportation
举动	(jǔ dòng)	N.	action
外出	(wài chū)	V.	to go out
国庆节	(guó qìng jié)	NP.	National Day
痛快	(tòng kuài)	Adj.	happy, delighted
畅快	(chàng kuài)	Adj.	joyful, carefree
感冒	(gǎn mào)	VO.	to catch a cold
稍微	(shāo wēi)	Adj.	a little bit, slightly
轻松	(qīng sōng)	Adj.	light and relaxed
普通话	(pǔ tōng huà)	NP.	Mandarin, standard Chinese language
泥坑	(ní kēng)	N.	mud pit
闲聊	(xián liáo)	V.	to chat casually
深恶痛绝	(shēn wù tòng jué)	V.	to hate bitterly, to detest
围城	(wéi chéng)	NP.	surrounded town, besieged town
摄像机	(shè xiàng jī)	N.	video camera
低头	(dī tóu)	VO.	to lower one's head
默默	(mò mò)	Adv.	quietly, silently
贵宾级	(guì bīn jí)	NP.	the rank of VIP
礼遇	(lǐ yù)	N.	courteous treatment
话匣子	(huà xiá zi)	N.	chatterbox
呵呵	(hē hē)	N.	sound of laughter
默契	(mò qì)	N.	tacit agreement
合作	(hé zuò)	N/V.	cooperation; to cooperate, to collaborate
收车	(shōu chē)	VO.	to stop driving around

奔忙	(bēn máng)	*VP.*	to hurry around, to be busy doing something
拐角	(guǎi jiǎo)	*N.*	corner
嗨	(hài)	*Interj.*	hey!
騰出	(téng chū)	*V.*	to spare
此刻	(cǐ kè)	*Adv.*	at this time, now
寂寞	(jì mò)	*Adj.*	lonely

奔忙	(bēn máng)	*VP.*	to hurry around, to be busy doing something
拐角	(guǎi jiǎo)	*N.*	corner
嗨	(hài)	*Interj.*	hey!
腾出	(téng chū)	*V.*	to spare
此刻	(cǐ kè)	*Adv.*	at this time, now
寂寞	(jì mò)	*Adj.*	lonely

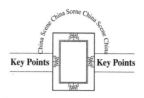

課文要點

一、詞語解釋 Words and Phrases

（一）慣用詞 (idiomatic expressions)

1、曾經＝以前有過經驗
☞ 曾經幹過不少的工作。

2、外出＝去外頭
☞ 外出坐車的人很少。

3、暢快＝痛快、舒服
☞ 我休息了一個多月，最暢快了。

4、眼下＝現在
☞ 眼下，本市還有近八千名司機等著領取客運資格證。

5、此刻＝這個時候
☞ 此刻他並不寂寞。

（二）成語、方言詞 (idioms and dialect)

◆ 一塵不染: dustless
◆ 單純枯燥: simple and boring
◆ 閒聊之中: while chatting
◆ 話匣子: chatter box, talking

二、書面語、正式語、口語對照表 Written/formal/colloquial Comparison

	書面／正式語	口語		書面／正式語	口語
1	一塵不染	一點灰塵都沒有	8	深惡痛絕	非常不喜歡
2	毫無	一點兒也不／沒	9	本市	我們這個市
3	辭職	辭掉工作	10	近八千名	差不多八千個
4	舉動	作法	11	領取	領
5	那時	那個時候	12	默默	不說一句話
6	外出	到外邊去	13	奔忙	忙
7	之中	當中	14	此刻	這時候

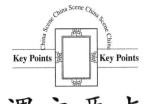

课文要点

一、词语解释 Words and Phrases

（一）惯用词 (idiomatic expressions)

1、曾经 = 以前有过经验
☞ 曾经干过不少的工作。

2、外出 = 去外头
☞ 外出坐车的人很少。

3、畅快 = 痛快、舒服
☞ 我休息了一个多月，最畅快了。

4、眼下 = 现在
☞ 眼下，本市还有近八千名司机等着领取客运资格证。

5、此刻 = 这个时候
☞ 此刻他并不寂寞。

（二）成语、方言词 (idioms and dialect)

◆ 一尘不染: dustless
◆ 单纯枯燥: simple and boring
◆ 闲聊之中: while chatting
◆ 话匣子: chatter box, talking

二、书面语、正式语、口语对照表 Written/formal/colloquial Comparison

	书面／正式语	口语		书面／正式语	口语
1	一尘不染	一点灰尘都没有	8	深恶痛绝	非常不喜欢
2	毫无	一点儿也不／没	9	本市	我们这个市
3	辞职	辞掉工作	10	近八千名	差不多八千个
4	举动	作法	11	领取	领
5	那时	那个时候	12	默默	不说一句话
6	外出	到外边去	13	奔忙	忙
7	之中	当中	14	此刻	这时候

三、句型 Sentence Structures

（一）據統計 (according to statistics)

> ✍ 據統計, "according to statistics", is placed at the beginning of a sentence, before the subject. It cannot appear after the subject. Similar versions of the same expression include 據有關數字顯示 (according to related figures) and 據統計資料顯示 (according to statistical materials). 據統計 is most often used in written and formal contexts, and the subject of the verb 統計 is frequently omitted.

☞ 據統計，中國北京的個體出租車占全市汽車的百分之四十。

1、據統計，中國現在的女嬰比男嬰多百分之一。

According to statistics, China now has 1% more baby girls than baby boys.

2、據統計，中國人可以買車的人占全國人口的百分之零點四。

According to statistics, 0.4% of the Chinese population can afford to buy cars.

問：請問，美國人中買不起醫療保險的人占全國人數的百分之多少？

答：＿＿＿＿＿＿＿＿＿＿＿＿＿＿＿＿＿＿。

（二）滿足／不滿足；對……滿足／對……不滿足…… (to be satisfied/dissatisfied with)

> ✍ 滿足／不滿足 is used to describe satisfaction（滿足）or dissatisfaction（不滿足）toward something. 滿足 can function either as a verb (A 滿足 B) or an adjective (A 對 B 很滿足). The verb structure appears most frequently in written Chinese and is often accompanied by 於, resulting in the expression 滿足於…… (satisfied with respect to). Examples: 政府現在的住房政策並不能滿足老百姓的需要. (The government's present housing policy cannot satisfy the demands of the common people.) 我對我現在的收入很滿足. (I am very satisfied with my present salary.)

☞ 三十出頭的周師傅，曾經幹過不少的工作，四年前終於不滿足原先每天單調枯燥又毫無技術的工作，而辭職不幹了，湊錢買了輛微型麵包車，跑起了個體運輸。

1、無疑他是因為不滿足農村的生活條件才跑到城裡來的。

Undoubtedly, it was because he was dissatisfied with the living conditions in the countryside that he came to the city.

2、出租車司機似乎都對自己的工作不滿足。

Almost all cab drivers seem dissatisfied with their jobs.

問：你覺得最近找到的這個新工作怎麼樣？

答：＿＿＿＿＿＿＿＿＿＿＿＿＿＿＿＿＿＿。

三、句型 Sentence Structures

（一）据统计 (according to statistics)

> 据统计, "according to statistics", is placed at the beginning of a sentence, before the subject. It cannot appear after the subject. Similar versions of the same expression include 据有关数字显示 (according to related figures) and 据统计资料显示 (according to statistical materials). 据统计 is most often used in written and formal contexts, and the subject of the verb 统计 is frequently omitted.

☞ 据统计，中国北京的个体出租车占全市汽车的百分之四十。

1、据统计，中国现在的女婴比男婴多百分之一。
According to statistics, China now has 1% more baby girls than baby boys.

2、据统计，中国人可以买车的人占全国人口的百分之零点四。
According to statistics, 0.4% of the Chinese population can afford to buy cars.

问：请问，美国人中买不起医疗保险的人占全国人数的百分之多少？
答：_____。

（二）满足／不满足；对……满足／对……不满足…… (to be satisfied/dissatisfied with)

> 满足／不满足 is used to describe satisfaction（满足）or dissatisfaction（不满足）toward something. 满足 can function either as a verb (A 满足 B) or an adjective (A 对 B 很满足). The verb structure appears most frequently in written Chinese and is often accompanied by 于, resulting in the expression 满足于…… (satisfied with respect to). Examples: 政府现在的住房政策并不能满足老百姓的需要. (The government's present housing policy cannot satisfy the demands of the common people.) 我对我现在的收入很满足. (I am very satisfied with my present salary.)

☞ 三十出头的周师傅，曾经干过不少的工作，四年前终于不满足原先每天单调枯燥又毫无技术的工作，而辞职不干了，凑钱买了辆微型面包车，跑起了个体运输。

1、无疑他是因为不满足农村的生活条件才跑到城里来的。
Undoubtedly, it was because he was dissatisfied with the living conditions in the countryside that he came to the city.

2、出租车司机似乎都对自己的工作不满足。
Almost all cab drivers seem dissatisfied with their jobs.

问：你觉得最近找到的这个新工作怎么样？
答：_____。

（三）毫無技術（／能力／自信心）(to lack the slightest amount of)

> ✍ 毫無, "to lack the slightest amount of", is a Classical Chinese phrase which often carries a formal tone. Its spoken counterpart is 一點N也沒有. There is no affirmative version of this expression; it only appears in negative form. 毫無 is usually followed by a disyllabic, non-countable, abstract noun, such as 能力, 技術, 信心.

☞ 三十出頭的周師傅，曾經幹過不少的工作，四年前終於不滿足原先每天單調枯燥又毫無技術的工作，而辭職不幹了。

1、有些獨生子女毫無獨立生活的能力。

Some single children don't have the slightest ability to do anything for themselves.

2、據統計，這種毫無自由的國營單位的工作已經越來越少了。

According to statistics, there are fewer and fewer jobs with no freedom at state-owned companies.

問：真沒想到你已經辭去這個經理的工作了，為甚麼？

答：＿＿＿＿＿＿＿＿＿＿＿＿＿＿＿＿＿＿＿。

（四）跑（起）……＋N （運輸／買賣／批發）來 (to run around doing business, to do business, to run a business)

> ✍ This expression is used both in the figurative sense ("doing business", "running a business") and the literal sense ("to run around"), and is most commonly used in casual, spoken settings. This pattern is used to describe the kind of business that requires transactions in different places, or requires that a person travel a great deal. Example: 他這幾年一直在跑關係以便創辦個體運輸公司. (For the last few years, he has constantly been building his connections so that he can start up his own shipping company.)

☞ 三十出頭的周師傅，曾經幹過不少的工作，四年前終於不滿足原先每天單調枯燥又毫無技術的工作，而辭職不幹了，湊錢買了輛微型麵包車，跑起了個體運輸。

1、現在最賺錢的法子就是買輛麵包車跑批發運輸。

The fastest way to earn money nowadays is to buy a minivan and transport goods for wholesale businesses.

2、這裡的農民現在都自己攢錢買車跑起個體買賣來了。

Now all the farmers here are saving their money to buy cars and start private businesses.

問：最近一段時間沒看到你，在跑甚麼事情？

答：＿＿＿＿＿＿＿＿＿＿＿＿＿＿＿＿。

（三）毫无技术（／能力／自信心）(to lack the slightest amount of)

> ✍ 毫无, "to lack the slightest amount of", is a Classical Chinese phrase which often carries a formal tone. Its spoken counterpart is 一点N也没有. There is no affirmative version of this expression; it only appears in negative form. 毫无 is usually followed by a disyllabic, non-countable, abstract noun, such as 能力, 技术, 信心.

☞ 三十出头的周师傅，曾经干过不少的工作，四年前终于不满足原先每天单调枯燥又毫无技术的工作，而辞职不干了。

1、有些独生子女毫无独立生活的能力。

Some single children don't have the slightest ability to do anything for themselves.

2、据统计，这种毫无自由的国营单位的工作已经越来越少了。

According to statistics, there are fewer and fewer jobs with no freedom at state-owned companies.

问：真没想到你已经辞去这个经理的工作了，为什么？

答：_____。

（四）跑（起）……+N（运输／买卖／批发）来 (to run around doing business, to do business, to run a business)

> ✍ This expression is used both in the figurative sense ("doing business", "running a business") and the literal sense ("to run around"), and is most commonly used in casual, spoken settings. This pattern is used to describe the kind of business that requires transactions in different places, or requires that a person travel a great deal. Example: 他这几年一直在跑关系以便创办个体运输公司. (For the last few years, he has constantly been building his connections so that he can start up his own shipping company.)

☞ 三十出头的周师傅，曾经干过不少的工作，四年前终于不满足原先每天单调枯燥又毫无技术的工作，而辞职不干了，凑钱买了辆微型面包车，跑起了个体运输。

1、现在最赚钱的法子就是买辆面包车跑批发运输。

The fastest way to earn money nowadays is to buy a minivan and transport goods for wholesale businesses.

2、这里的农民现在都自己攒钱买车跑起个体买卖来了。

Now all the farmers here are saving their money to buy cars and start private businesses.

问：最近一段时间没看到你，在跑什么事情？

答：_____。

（五）讓……吃驚 (to surprise someone)

> ✍ 吃驚, "to surprise", is used as a verb in causative sentences. Example: 私人攢錢買飛機太讓人吃驚了. (An individual saving money to buy an airplane would really surprise people.) 吃驚 can also function as an adjective, as in 我很吃驚 or 我吃驚極了. (I was very surprised.) The negative form of this structure normally requires that 不 or 沒 be placed before 讓.

☞ 現在已經不算一件很讓人吃驚的大事了。

1、幾十年前，辭去公職是一件讓人聽了十分吃驚的舉動。
Several decades ago, resigning from a public post would really have surprised people.

2、五歲的孩子彈鋼琴彈得這麼好，真讓我吃驚。
I was so surprised that a 5-year-old could play the piano so well.

問：你知道嗎？小李已經買房了。
答：是嗎？他才工作三年就有錢買房，＿＿＿＿＿＿＿＿＿＿。

（六）對……深惡痛絕 (to detest, to abhor, to hate)

> ✍ 對……深惡痛絕 expresses extreme dislike or hatred of something. It is used mostly in written and formal Chinese. When used in spoken settings, it sounds slightly bookish. Spoken equivalents include 非常厭惡 and 討厭. Example: 老百姓對這種騙錢的禮品公司深惡痛絕. (The common people detest gift companies that cheat them out of their money.)

☞ 閒聊之中，似乎司機們對自己所從事的職業都深惡痛絕。

1、沒想到他對他自己從事的職業這麼深惡痛絕。
I never imagined that he hated his job so bitterly.

2、我對那些狠心拋棄自己子女的父母深惡痛絕。
I detest those cruel parents who abandon their own sons and daughters.

問：為甚麼你一看到地上的紙就很不高興？
答：＿＿＿＿＿＿＿＿＿＿＿＿＿＿＿＿＿＿。

（七）據……了解 (according to or based on someone's understanding)

> ✍ 據……了解, "according to or based on someone's understanding", can be used in both written and spoken settings. Although in English it is customary to say, "it is my understanding that", in Chinese it is preferable to add the word 據 (according to, based on) at the beginning of the phrase, as in 據當地政府了解 (according to the understanding of the local government). The 據……了解 phrase usually appears at the beginning of a sentence, though at times it may appear after the subject. 據……了解 should be distinguished from 據……調查. 調查 indicates a formal investigation or survey of some sort, whereas 了解 implies a more informal understanding of a matter or situation.

（五）让……吃惊 (to surprise someone)

> ✍ 吃惊, "to surprise", is used as a verb in causative sentences. Example: 私人攒钱买飞机太让人吃惊了. (An individual saving money to buy an airplane would really surprise people.) 吃惊 can also function as an adjective, as in 我很吃惊 or 我吃惊极了. (I was very surprised.) The negative form of this structure normally requires that 不 or 没 be placed before 让.

☞ 现在已经不算一件很让人吃惊的大事了。

1、几十年前，辞去公职是一件让人听了十分吃惊的举动。
Several decades ago, resigning from a public post would really have surprised people.

2、五岁的孩子弹钢琴弹得这么好，真让我吃惊。
I was so surprised that a 5-year-old could play the piano so well.

问：你知道吗？小李已经买房了。
答：是吗？他才工作三年就有钱买房，＿＿＿＿＿＿＿＿＿＿＿＿。

（六）对……深恶痛绝 (to detest, to abhor, to hate)

> ✍ 对……深恶痛绝 expresses extreme dislike or hatred of something. It is used mostly in written and formal Chinese. When used in spoken settings, it sounds slightly bookish. Spoken equivalents include 非常厌恶 and 讨厌. Example: 老百姓对这种骗钱的礼品公司深恶痛绝. (The common people detest gift companies that cheat them out of their money.)

☞ 闲聊之中，似乎司机们对自己所从事的职业都深恶痛绝。

1、没想到他对他自己从事的职业这么深恶痛绝。
I never imagined that he hated his job so bitterly.

2、我对那些狠心抛弃自己子女的父母深恶痛绝。
I detest those cruel parents who abandon their own sons and daughters.

问：为什么你一看到地上的纸就很不高兴？
答：＿＿＿＿＿＿＿＿＿＿＿＿＿＿＿＿＿＿＿。

（七）据……了解 (according to or based on someone's understanding)

> ✍ 据……了解, "according to or based on someone's understanding", can be used in both written and spoken settings. Although in English it is customary to say, "it is my understanding that", in Chinese it is preferable to add the word 据 (according to, based on) at the beginning of the phrase, as in 据当地政府了解 (according to the understanding of the local government). The 据……了解 phrase usually appears at the beginning of a sentence, though at times it may appear after the subject. 据……了解 should be distinguished from 据……调查. 调查 indicates a formal investigation or survey of some sort, whereas 了解 implies a more informal understanding of a matter or situation.

☞ 但據我了解，眼下，本市還有近八千名司機等著領取客運資格證。

1、據他了解，現在跑運輸的人都不滿足他們的工作，都想辭職不幹。

According to his understanding, all of the transportation workers are dissatisfied with their jobs. They all want to resign.

2、據我了解，這個人很沉默怪僻，常常一個人待在家裡不出門。

As I understand it, this person is very quiet and eccentric. He often stays in his house and never goes outside.

問：美國人每年交的稅占工資的百分之多少？
答：＿＿＿＿＿＿＿＿＿＿＿＿＿＿＿＿。

（八）和往常一樣 (as usual)

✍ 和往常一樣, "as usual", can be used in both spoken and written contexts. A more formal version is 與往日相同. 和往常一樣 usually appears at the beginning of a sentence, either before or after the subject. Examples: 和往常一樣，老李一大早就去跑出租了. (As usual, Lao Li goes out to start driving his cab at dawn.) 老李和往常一樣，一大早就去跑出租了. (Lao Li, as usual, goes out to start driving his cab at dawn.)

☞ 下午四點，周師傅和往常一樣去接下班的妻子回家。

1、和往常一樣，我要在7點20分上班，下午4點下班，然後接孩子去練鋼琴。

As usual, I will start work at 7:20 A.M. and get off work at 4:00 P.M., and then take my child to piano lessons.

2、小麗和往常一樣要到街頭快餐店買午飯。

As usual, Xiao Li wants to go to the fast food place on the corner to buy a boxed lunch.

問：你今天打算去甚麼地方"解決"晚飯？
答：＿＿＿＿＿＿＿＿＿＿＿＿＿＿＿＿。

（九）享受……的禮遇（／生活／待遇／條件）(to enjoy)

✍ 享受 functions as both a transitive verb and a noun. As a transitive verb, it means "to enjoy" and takes objects such as 禮遇 (courteous reception), 生活 (life), 待遇 (salary), and 條件 (conditions). As a noun, it means "enjoyment", as in 去海邊是一種享受. (Going to the beach is a pleasant experience.) 享受 does not function like the salutation "enjoy" in English. For instance, when a friend is going on vacation, an English speaker might say "Enjoy yourself!" But in Chinese, 享受 cannot be used in this way. To express the idea "Enjoy yourself!" in Chinese, one should say 好好玩; to say "Enjoy your meal!" one would say 好好吃.

☞ 但据我了解，眼下，本市还有近八千名司机等着领取客运资格证。

1、据他了解，现在跑运输的人都不满足他们的工作，都想辞职不干。

According to his understanding, all of the transportation workers are dissatisfied with their jobs. They all want to resign.

2、据我了解，这个人很沉默怪僻，常常一个人待在家里不出门。

As I understand it, this person is very quiet and eccentric. He often stays in his house and never goes outside.

问：美国人每年交的税占工资的百分之多少？

答：＿＿＿＿＿＿＿＿＿＿＿＿＿＿＿＿＿＿＿。

（八）和往常一样 (as usual)

> ✍ 和往常一样, "as usual", can be used in both spoken and written contexts. A more formal version is 与往日相同. 和往常一样 usually appears at the beginning of a sentence, either before or after the subject. Examples: 和往常一样，老李一大早就去跑出租了. (As usual, Lao Li goes out to start driving his cab at dawn.) 老李和往常一样，一大早就去跑出租了. (Lao Li, as usual, goes out to start driving his cab at dawn.)

☞ 下午四点，周师傅和往常一样去接下班的妻子回家。

1、和往常一样，我要在7点20分上班，下午4点下班，然后接孩子去练钢琴。

As usual, I will start work at 7:20 A.M. and get off work at 4:00 P.M., and then take my child to piano lessons.

2、小丽和往常一样要到街头快餐店买午饭。

As usual, Xiao Li wants to go to the fast food place on the corner to buy a boxed lunch.

问：你今天打算去什么地方"解决"晚饭？

答：＿＿＿＿＿＿＿＿＿＿＿＿＿＿＿＿＿＿＿。

（九）享受……的礼遇（／生活／待遇／条件）(to enjoy)

> ✍ 享受 functions as both a transitive verb and a noun. As a transitive verb, it means "to enjoy" and takes objects such as 礼遇 (courteous reception), 生活 (life), 待遇 (salary), and 条件 (conditions). As a noun, it means "enjoyment", as in 去海边是一种享受. (Going to the beach is a pleasant experience.) 享受 does not function like the salutation "enjoy" in English. For instance, when a friend is going on vacation, an English speaker might say "Enjoy yourself!" But in Chinese, 享受 cannot be used in this way. To express the idea "Enjoy yourself!" in Chinese, one should say 好好玩; to say "Enjoy your meal!" one would say 好好吃.

☞ 她有些不自然，低著頭不看我們，默默享受丈夫給予的貴賓級的禮遇。

1、以前中國人覺得坐小汽車就是享受最高的禮遇了。現在有車的人很多，人們的想法也變了。

In the past, Chinese people believed that to ride in a car was to enjoy the highest prestige. Now, because many people have cars, the way people think has changed.

2、隨著經濟條件的改善，只要你有錢，到處都可以享受貴賓級的禮遇。

As a result of improved economic conditions, as long as you have money, you can enjoy VIP treatment wherever you go.

問：一般在公司工作的人要到多大歲數才能享受公司的退休金？

答：＿＿＿＿＿＿＿＿＿＿＿＿＿＿＿＿＿＿＿＿＿。

（十）（大）約……的時候……(it is about)

> ✍ In the pattern （大）約……的時候……, 約 means the same as 差不多. Use of 大 is optional; when used, it softens the formal tone of 約. The noun inserted between 大約 and 的時候 can be a time expression or a verb-object structure indicating a time. When the element after 約 is a term indicating a specific time, such as 十二點 or 晚上五點, ……的時候 can be omitted, as in 大約四點半 (around 4:30); 大約吃飯的時候 (around mealtime). This pattern appears most often in written and formal Chinese. The equivalent spoken form is 差不多……的時候.

☞ 約六點鐘的時候，周師傅又要出車了，母親和妻子總是送到車門口，每天都這樣。

1、（大）約下午5點的時候，司機們都還在外面等著領取客運資格證。

It is about 5:00 in the afternoon, but the drivers are still outside waiting to receive their passenger transport permits.

2、（大）約下午2點的時候，我看見他去了車站。

At around 2:00 in the afternoon, I saw him going to the train station.

問：你們是甚麼時候開始攢錢買房的？

答：＿＿＿＿＿＿＿＿＿＿＿＿＿＿＿＿＿＿＿＿＿。

（十一）騰出空兒 + V (to spare the time or space to do something)

> ✍ 騰出空兒 + V, "to spare the time or space to do something", is used mostly in colloquial Chinese. 騰 literally means "to mount" or "to ascend", and the noun 空兒 can refer to either time or space. 騰出空兒 is usually followed by a verb to indicate its purpose. It can also be used in the potential form to indicate possibility, as in 騰得出空兒 (able to spare time or space); 騰不出空兒 (unable to spare time or space). Example: 最近幾年我一直騰不出空來去看望我的老朋友. (Over the last few years I have not been able to spare the time to go visit old friends.)

☞ 她有些不自然，低着头不看我们，默默享受丈夫给予的贵宾级的礼遇。

1、以前中国人觉得坐小汽车就是享受最高的礼遇了。现在有车的人很多，人们的想法也变了。

In the past, Chinese people believed that to ride in a car was to enjoy the highest prestige. Now, because many people have cars, the way people think has changed.

2、随着经济条件的改善，只要你有钱，到处都可以享受贵宾级的礼遇。

As a result of improved economic conditions, as long as you have money, you can enjoy VIP treatment wherever you go.

问：一般在公司工作的人要到多大岁数才能享受公司的退休金？

答：＿＿＿＿＿＿＿＿＿＿＿＿＿＿＿＿＿＿＿＿＿＿。

（十）（大）约……的时候…… (it is about)

> ✎ In the pattern （大）约……的时候……, 约 means the same as 差不多. Use of 大 is optional; when used, it softens the formal tone of 约. The noun inserted between 大约 and 的时候 can be a time expression or a verb-object structure indicating a time. When the element after 约 is a term indicating a specific time, such as 十二点 or 晚上五点, ……的时候 can be omitted, as in 大约四点半 (around 4:30); 大约吃饭的时候 (around mealtime). This pattern appears most often in written and formal Chinese. The equivalent spoken form is 差不多……的时候.

☞ 约六点钟的时候，周师傅又要出车了，母亲和妻子总是送到车门口，每天都这样。

1、（大）约下午5点的时候，司机们都还在外面等着领取客运资格证。

It is about 5:00 in the afternoon, but the drivers are still outside waiting to receive their passenger transport permits.

2、（大）约下午2点的时候，我看见他去了车站。

At around 2:00 in the afternoon, I saw him going to the train station.

问：你们是什么时候开始攒钱买房的？

答：＿＿＿＿＿＿＿＿＿＿＿＿＿＿＿＿＿＿。

（十一）腾出空儿 + V (to spare the time or space to do something)

> ✎ 腾出空儿 + V, "to spare the time or space to do something", is used mostly in colloquial Chinese. 腾 literally means "to mount" or "to ascend", and the noun 空儿 can refer to either time or space. 腾出空儿 is usually followed by a verb to indicate its purpose. It can also be used in the potential form to indicate possibility, as in 腾得出空儿 (able to spare time or space); 腾不出空儿 (unable to spare time or space). Example: 最近几年我一直腾不出空来去看望我的老朋友. (Over the last few years I have not been able to spare the time to go visit old friends.)

☞ 只有在這個時候，周師傅才騰出空兒來，想一想自己的過去、今天和未來，此刻他並不寂寞。

1、很多人奔忙了一天，還要騰出空兒再去街頭做小買賣。

Many people have to find some spare time to sell items on the street after a busy day.

2、剛才你的父親來了個電話，要你騰出空兒給他回個電話。

Your father just called. He wants you to spare a minute to call him back.

3、我的桌子不大，我得想法騰出空兒來放我的電腦。

My desk is not very big, so I have to make some room to put my computer on it.

問：你大約甚麼時候能幫我修一下車？

答：明天下午，我會＿＿＿＿＿＿＿＿＿＿＿＿。

四、文化背景知識 Cultural Notes

1. As is the case in the United States, taxi drivers who go into business for themselves in China must invest a great amount of money, time, and labor. First, they need to apply for a special license plate (or "medallion", as they are called in New York City, 牌照) for taxis. Next they need to undergo special training and take an examination, after which they can apply for a "passenger transport certificate" (客運資格證). As mentioned in our lesson, those who apply for these certificates must wait a long time to get one.

2. The expression "besieged city"(圍城) is used here as a metaphor to describe the "world" of the taxi driver. In other words, it is very difficult to penetrate that world. But once inside, it is equally difficult to get out. This expression is taken from the well-known novel *Weicheng* (1947), penned by the famous writer Qian Zhongshu (錢鍾書), where it is used as a metaphor for marriage (everyone wants to get "in", but once "in", many want to get "out").

☞ 只有在这个时候，周师傅才腾出空儿来，想一想自己的过去、今天和未来，此刻他并不寂寞。

1、很多人奔忙了一天，还要腾出空儿再去街头做小买卖。

Many people have to find some spare time to sell items on the street after a busy day.

2、刚才你的父亲来了个电话，要你腾出空儿给他回个电话。

Your father just called. He wants you to spare a minute to call him back.

3、我的桌子不大，我得想法腾出空儿来放我的电脑。

My desk is not very big, so I have to make some room to put my computer on it.

问：你大约什么时候能帮我修一下车？
答：明天下午，我会_____。

四、文化背景知识 ⚇⚇⚇⚇ Cultural Notes

1. As is the case in the United States, taxi drivers who go into business for themselves in China must invest a great amount of money, time, and labor. First, they need to apply for a special license plate (or "medallion", as they are called in New York City, 牌照) for taxis. Next they need to undergo special training and take an examination, after which they can apply for a "passenger transport certificate" (客运资格证). As mentioned in our lesson, those who apply for these certificates must wait a long time to get one.

2. The expression "besieged city" (围城) is used here as a metaphor to describe the "world" of the taxi driver. In other words, it is very difficult to penetrate that world. But once inside, it is equally difficult to get out. This expression is taken from the well-known novel *Weicheng* (1947), penned by the famous writer Qian Zhongshu (钱锺书), where it is used as a metaphor for marriage (everyone wants to get "in", but once "in", many want to get "out").

練習

語言結構 Structures

一、短語翻譯 (Phrase translation)

1. taxi driver
2. a spotless van
3. a simple and boring job
4. to resign from one's job to become a manager
5. Spring Festival and National Day
6. to catch the flu
7. in the midst of chatting
8. to hate bitterly the profession that one is engaged in
9. to quietly enjoy the treatment of a special guest
10. to work in tacit cooperation

二、聽力練習 (Listening comprehension)

1、聽寫 (Dictation)

2、聽錄音並回答問題 (Answering questions while listening to the audio CD)
    (1) 甚麼是 "下海" ？
    (2) "下海" 的結果是甚麼？
    (3) 既然下海有點兒冒險？為甚麼還有很多人下海？

三、改寫下面劃線的詞 (Replace the underlined words)

1、他的汽車<u>一點兒塵土</u>都沒有。
2、他的工作<u>既沒有意思，又很無聊</u>。所以他辭職不幹了。
3、在我們聊天當中，我知道他<u>非常不喜歡他的工作</u>。
4、今天不知道為甚麼他<u>一句話也不說</u>。

练习

语言结构 Structures

一、短语翻译 (Phrase translation)

1. taxi driver
2. a spotless van
3. a simple and boring job
4. to resign from one's job to become a manager
5. Spring Festival and National Day
6. to catch the flu
7. in the midst of chatting
8. to hate bitterly the profession that one is engaged in
9. to quietly enjoy the treatment of a special guest
10. to work in tacit cooperation

二、听力练习 (Listening comprehension)

1、听写 (Dictation)

2、听录音并回答问题 (Answering questions while listening to the audio CD)
　　(1) 什么是"下海"？
　　(2)"下海"的结果是什么？
　　(3) 既然下海有点儿冒险？为什么还有很多人下海？

三、改写下面划线的词 (Replace the underlined words)

1、他的汽车一点儿尘土都没有。
2、他的工作既没有意思，又很无聊。所以他辞职不干了。
3、在我们聊天当中，我知道他非常不喜欢他的工作。
4、今天不知道为什么他一句话也不说。

四、完成句子 (Complete the sentences)

1、　　A：他每天甚麼時候去見他的女朋友？
　　　　B：_____
　　　　　（據……了解；和往常一樣；約……的時候）

2、　　A：你覺得現在的生活怎麼樣？老百姓滿意不滿意現在的生活？
　　　　B：_____
　　　　　（不滿足……；對……深惡痛絕）

五、閱讀短文、回答問題 (Answering questions based on the reading passages)

　　這幾年在中國私人買車已經不算一件令人吃驚的舉動了。就拿二十出頭的劉小姐來說，幾年以前她從北京大學英語系畢業，一畢業就在一家合資企業找到了工作，工作剛五年，就攢錢買了輛三十萬的新車，走了很多後門才領到了牌照。因為北京的交通太擁擠，平時上下班劉小姐都是打“的”去，從來都不開車。可是到了節假日或者公休日，單位一放假，劉小姐就和朋友一塊兒開著一塵不染的汽車到外地去旅遊。她說每次開車出去心裡都有一種說不出的舒坦和快樂。十年前，這種私人車還是政府控制的，就是你攢夠了錢也沒地方買，但是十年後連一個二十多歲，工作只有五年的人也能夠買得起，你不能不承認中國這幾年的發展變化實在太快了。

問題
　　(1) 談談劉小姐買車是為了甚麼？
　　(2) 過去中國人買車受到甚麼限制？錢能不能讓人們擺脫這種限制？
　　(3) 從劉小姐買車，你看到了中國的甚麼變化？

　　對於中國老百姓來說，像發達國家普通老百姓一樣擁有私人轎車，不再是一件不可想像的事情。而十幾年前，人們想擁有的還僅是自行車。
據統計，1978年中國家庭私人汽車數量幾乎為零，現今私人汽車已達千萬輛，其中私人轎車近10萬輛。轎車、住房和電腦一起，成為九十年代中國家庭最熱門的話題。
對於中國這個巨大的汽車市場來說，幾萬輛私人轎車根本算不上一個大數字。據上海市對200名高薪階層人士的調查，一半多的人想在2000年前擁有轎車。

問題
　　(1) 用兩個例子說明中國人的轎車夢
　　(2) 你認為現在中國應該怎麼發展私人轎車？如果管理不合理會給社會造成一些甚麼問題？

四、完成句子 (Complete the sentences)

1、　A：他每天什么时候去见他的女朋友？

　　B：_____

　　（据……了解；和往常一样；约……的时候）

2、　A：你觉得现在的生活怎么样？老百姓满意不满意现在的生活？

　　B：_____

　　（不满足……；对……深恶痛绝）

五、阅读短文、回答问题 (Answering questions based on the reading passages)

　　这几年在中国私人买车已经不算一件令人吃惊的举动了。就拿二十出头的刘小姐来说，几年以前她从北京大学英语系毕业，一毕业就在一家合资企业找到了工作，工作刚五年，就攒钱买了辆三十万的新车，走了很多后门才领到了牌照。因为北京的交通太拥挤，平时上下班刘小姐都是打"的"去，从来都不开车。可是到了节假日或者公休日，单位一放假，刘小姐就和朋友一块儿开着一尘不染的汽车到外地去旅游。她说每次开车出去心里都有一种说不出的舒坦和快乐。十年前，这种私人车还是政府控制的，就是你攒够了钱也没地方买，但是十年后连一个二十多岁，工作只有五年的人也能够买得起，你不能不承认中国这几年的发展变化实在太快了。

问题

(1) 谈谈刘小姐买车是为了什么？

(2) 过去中国人买车受到什么限制？钱能不能让人们摆脱这种限制？

(3) 从刘小姐买车，你看到了中国的什么变化？

　　对于中国老百姓来说，象发达国家普通老百姓一样拥有私人轿车，不再是一件不可想象的事情。而十几年前，人们想拥有的还仅是自行车。

据统计，1978年中国家庭私人汽车数量几乎为零，现今私人汽车已达千万辆，其中私人轿车近10万辆。轿车、住房和电脑一起，成为九十年代中国家庭最热门的话题。

对于中国这个巨大的汽车市场来说，几万辆私人轿车根本算不上一个大数字。据上海市对200名高薪阶层人士的调查，一半多的人想在2000年前拥有轿车。

问题

(1) 用两个例子说明中国人的轿车梦

(2) 你认为现在中国应该怎么发展私人轿车？如果管理不合理会给社会造成一些什么问题？

六、翻譯 (Translate sentences)

1. Because of economic reform and the open door policy, people are no longer satisfied with their jobs in the state-owned factory. Many of them resigned from their jobs and began to work as a taxi drivers.

2. As private business owners, we are at risk all the time. We have to work especially hard during national holidays such as the Spring Festival and Labor Day.

3. Because he is a celebrity in the city, he is always treated as a VIP. His becoming a driver surprised many people here.

4. It is quite convenient to take a taxi in Beijing. One can get a taxi by waving at the driver and can reach his or her destination in a few minutes for a couple of dollars.

六、翻译 (Translate sentences)

1. Because of economic reform and the open door policy, people are no longer satisfied with their jobs in the state-owned factory. Many of them resigned from their jobs and began to work as a taxi drivers.

2. As private business owners, we are at risk all the time. We have to work especially hard during national holidays such as the Spring Festival and Labor Day.

3. Because he is a celebrity in the city, he is always treated as a VIP. His becoming a driver surprised many people here.

4. It is quite convenient to take a taxi in Beijing. One can get a taxi by waving at the driver and can reach his or her destination in a few minutes for a couple of dollars.

語言實踐 ⋮ Practice

一、根據課文回答問題 (Answering questions based on the dialogue)

1、為甚麼周師傅自己給自己定上下班時間，自己擦車可是心裡還是很舒坦？
2、談談周師傅以前的經歷。
3、為甚麼買麵包車是讓人吃驚的舉動？
4、周師傅開車四年是怎麼安排他的休息和工作的？
5、周師傅甚麼時候尤其要出去上班？
6、從談話中你知道周師傅有沒有醫療保險？
7、買一輛出租車要多少錢？錢不夠怎麼辦？
8、為甚麼張師傅說開出租車好像是跳進泥坑？
9、下午四點以後周師傅做甚麼？晚上呢？

二、活動 (Activities)

出去打個的，問問下面幾個問題：

1、以前司機是做甚麼工作的？
2、買一輛車要多少錢？上牌照、領取客運資格證要多長時間？
3、現在車錢還完了沒有？還要還多久？
4、司機一天的工作時間。
5、工資和福利待遇、醫療保險。
6、當出租汽車司機的好處和壞處。
7、以後打算做甚麼？

三、討論題 (Topics for discussion)

1、談談你所知道的出租汽車司機和他們的工作、生活情況。
2、中國的出租個體戶對中國經濟有甚麼貢獻？
3、中國的出租汽車司機跟紐約的有甚麼不同？

四、報告 (Presentation)

《北京的出租汽車司機》

语言实践 ⋮ Practice

一、根据课文回答问题 (Answering questions based on the dialogue)

1、为什么周师傅自己给自己定上下班时间，自己擦车可是心里还是很舒坦？
2、谈谈周师傅以前的经历。
3、为什么买面包车是让人吃惊的举动？
4、周师傅开车四年是怎么安排他的休息和工作的？
5、周师傅什么时候尤其要出去上班？
6、从谈话中你知道周师傅有没有医疗保险？
7、买一辆出租车要多少钱？钱不够怎么办？
8、为什么张师傅说开出租车好象是跳进泥坑？
9、下午四点以后周师傅做什么？晚上呢？

二、活动 (Activities)

出去打个的，问问下面几个问题:

1、以前司机是做什么工作的？
2、买一辆车要多少钱？上牌照、领取客运资格证要多长时间？
3、现在车钱还完了没有？还要还多久？
4、司机一天的工作时间。
5、工资和福利待遇、医疗保险。
6、当出租汽车司机的好处和坏处。
7、以后打算做什么？

三、讨论题 (Topics for discussion)

1、谈谈你所知道的出租汽车司机和他们的工作、生活情况。
2、中国的出租个体户对中国经济有什么贡献？
3、中国的出租汽车司机跟纽约的有什么不同？

四、报告 (Presentation)

《北京的出租汽车司机》

五、看圖討論 (Picto-discussion)

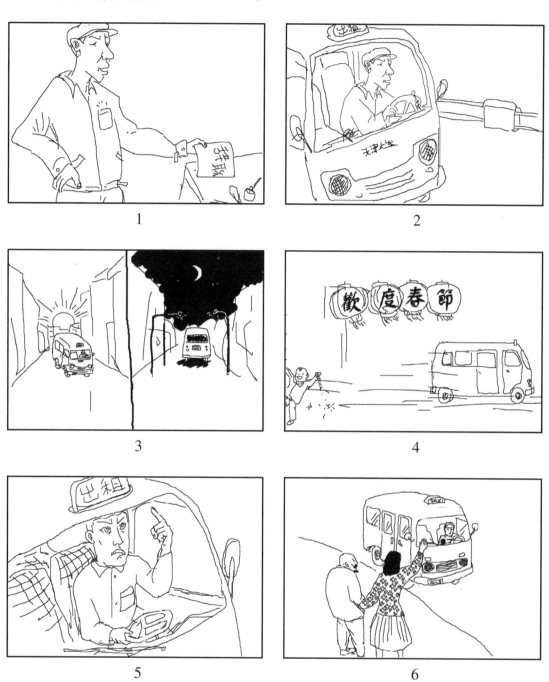

五、看图讨论 (Picto-discussion)

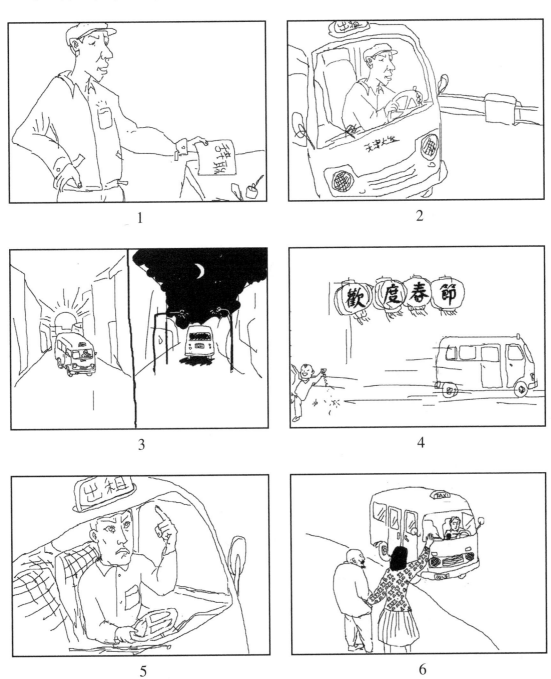

1

2

3

4

5

6

第十一課

市場經濟

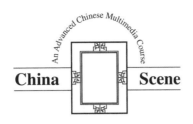

第十一课

市场经济

課文

一、對話 Dialogs

（一）

王鐵生：我們學了幾課課文都是談農民企業家以做批發起家，經商⁽¹⁾致富的問題，"白溝市場" 也跟這個問題有關。

湯目：　是啊，學完了這幾課，讓我有個感覺，就是中國的農民真了不起。中國搞市場經濟，最初是從農民那兒開始的。

王鐵生：對呀！這些農民既沒有經商的學歷，也沒有經商的經驗，全靠他們對市場行情⁽²⁾的分析去進貨⁽³⁾和批發。

湯目：　就是這樣的經營方式讓千千萬萬的中國農民擺脫了貧困，當上了萬元戶。

王鐵生：中國的農民在中國經濟改革中真是起了很大的作用。

生詞

經商	(jīng shāng)	*VO.*	to do business
王鐵生	(wáng tiě shēng)	*N.*	Wang Tiesheng, name of a person 人名
白溝	(bái gōu)	*PlaceP.*	Bai Gou, White Gully 地名
起家	(qǐ jiā)	*VO.*	to build up, to grow and thrive
湯目	(tāng mù)	*N.*	Tang Mu, name of a person 人名
了不起	(liǎo bù qǐ)	*Adj.*	extraordinary, amazing

Notes ⁽¹⁾經商 vs. 做生意: 經商 is a more formal VO that has the same meaning. 經 here means 經營 (to engage in, to do); 商 means 商業 (business). 經 is used here to describe an economic or business transaction. The VO structure 做生意, introduced in Lesson 4, Note 1, is a colloquial expression meaning "to do business".

⁽²⁾行 (háng) 情 means "price situation" or "prices" and almost always refers to the prices on a particular market, such as 市場行情 (market prices), 小麥行情 (wheat prices), 黃金行情 (gold prices), 股市行情 (stock market prices). 情形 and 情況 are more general terms meaning "situation", "circumstances", "conditions", as in 當時的情形 (the situation at that time), 工作情況 (working conditions).

⁽³⁾The verb 進 in the expression 進貨 literally means 買進, "to stock" or "to keep in stock". 貨 means "goods" or "commodities offered for sale". Other expressions using 進 include 進口 (to import) and 進款 (to collect revenue).

220

课文

一、对话 Dialogs

（一）

王铁生：　我们学了几课课文都是谈农民企业家以做批发起家，经商[1]致富的问题，"白沟市场"也跟这个问题有关。

汤目：　　是啊，学完了这几课，让我有个感觉，就是中国的农民真了不起。中国搞市场经济，最初是从农民那儿开始的。

王铁生：　对呀！这些农民既没有经商的学历，也没有经商的经验，全靠他们对市场行情[2]的分析去进货[3]和批发。

汤目：　　就是这样的经营方式让千千万万的中国农民摆脱了贫困，当上了万元户。

王铁生：　中国的农民在中国经济改革中真是起了很大的作用。

生词

经商	(jīng shāng)	VO.	to do business
王铁生	(wáng tiě shēng)	N.	Wang Tiesheng, name of a person 人名
白沟	(bái gōu)	PlaceP.	Bai Gou, White Gully 地名
起家	(qǐ jiā)	VO.	to build up, to grow and thrive
汤目	(tāng mù)	N.	Tang Mu, name of a person 人名
了不起	(liǎo bù qǐ)	Adj.	extraordinary, amazing

Notes [1]经商 vs. 做生意: 经商 is a more formal VO that has the same meaning. 经 here means 经营 (to engage in, to do); 商 means 商业 (business). 经 is used here to describe an economic or business transaction. The VO structure 做生意, introduced in Lesson 4, Note 1, is a colloquial expression meaning "to do business".

[2]行 (háng) 情 means "price situation" or "prices" and almost always refers to the prices on a particular market, such as 市场行情 (market prices), 小麦行情 (wheat prices), 黄金行情 (gold prices), 股市行情 (stock market prices). 情形 and 情况 are more general terms meaning "situation", "circumstances", "conditions", as in 当时的情形 (the situation at that time), 工作情况 (working conditions).

[3]The verb 进 in the expression 进货 literally means 买进, "to stock" or "to keep in stock". 货 means "goods" or "commodities offered for sale". Other expressions using 进 include 进口 (to import) and 进款 (to collect revenue).

行情	(háng qíng)	*N.*	general price situation
分析	(fēn xī)	*V.*	to analyze
進貨	(jìn huò)	*VO.*	to buy goods wholesale
經營方式	(jīng yíng fāng shì)	*NP.*	managerial style
貧困	(pín kùn)	*Adj/N.*	poor; poverty
萬元戶	(wàn yuán hù)	*N.*	millionaire

（二）

湯目：老王，今天是星期一，你怎麼還要去白溝？

老王：雖然人們都說"星期一，生意稀"，可是白溝市場的星期一例外[4]，不休息，照
常紅火[5]熱鬧，所以我得去那兒進一批箱子來。

湯目：為甚麼你要去白溝進箱子呢？

老王：那兒的箱子是當地生產的，所以批發價很低，稅收[6]也少，買進來一定賠不了錢，
而且還能得到不少的利潤。

湯目：那我跟你一塊兒去白溝看看，行嗎？

生詞

生意稀	(shēng yì xī)	*Idiom.*	slow business
例外	(lì wài)	*Adj/N.*	exception
照常	(zhào cháng)	*Adv.*	as usual
紅火	(hóng huǒ)	*Adj.*	busy and bustling
進	(jìn)	*V.*	to buy
箱子	(xiāng zi)	*N.*	suitcase
稅收	(shuì shōu)	*N.*	taxation
利潤	(lì rùn)	*N.*	profit

Notes [4]例外 can function either as a verb (to be an exception) or as a noun (exception). Examples: 所有的人都要遵守國家法律，誰也不能例外. (All citizens must abide by the nation's laws; there are no exceptions.) 我每天都去運動場鍛煉，今天是一個例外. (I work out at the athletic field every day, but today is an exception.)

[5]紅火 vs. a verb meaning "busy and bustling", "lively", "prosperous", "flourishing". Examples: 晚會開得很紅火. (The party was lively.) 她家的日子越過越紅火. (Her family becomes more prosperous each day.) 市中心的生意都很紅火 (Business is booming in the city.) 紅火 is usually used in colloquial Chinese. 火 is pronounced with a neutral tone.

[6]稅, 稅收, and 交稅: 稅收 means "taxes" or "tax revenue". It refers specifically to money accumulated by a government through taxation. The character 稅 means "tax" or "tax money", indicating the money itself; 收, short for 收入, means "income". 交稅 is a verb meaning "to pay taxes", and refers to individuals paying taxes to the government.

221

行情	(háng qíng)	N.	general price situation
分析	(fēn xī)	V.	to analyze
进货	(jìn huò)	VO.	to buy goods wholesale
经营方式	(jīng yíng fāng shì)	NP.	managerial style
贫困	(pín kùn)	Adj/N.	poor; poverty
万元户	(wàn yuán hù)	N.	millionaire

（二）

汤目：老王，今天是星期一，你怎么还要去白沟？

老王：虽然人们都说"星期一，生意稀"，可是白沟市场的星期一例外⁽⁴⁾，不休息，照常红火⁽⁵⁾热闹，所以我得去那儿进一批箱子来。

汤目：为什么你要去白沟进箱子呢？

老王：那儿的箱子是当地生产的，所以批发价很低，税收⁽⁶⁾也少，买进来一定赔不了钱，而且还能得到不少的利润。

汤目：那我跟你一块儿去白沟看看，行吗？

生词

生意稀	(shēng yì xī)	Idiom.	slow business
例外	(lì wài)	Adj/N.	exception
照常	(zhào cháng)	Adv.	as usual
红火	(hóng huǒ)	Adj.	busy and bustling
进	(jìn)	V.	to buy
箱子	(xiāng zi)	N.	suitcase
税收	(shuì shōu)	N.	taxation
利润	(lì rùn)	N.	profit

Notes ⁽⁴⁾例外 can function either as a verb (to be an exception) or as a noun (exception). Examples: 所有的人都要遵守国家法律，谁也不能例外. (All citizens must abide by the nation's laws; there are no exceptions.) 我每天都去运动场锻炼，今天是一个例外. (I work out at the athletic field every day, but today is an exception.)

⁽⁵⁾红火 is a verb meaning "busy and bustling", "lively", "prosperous", "flourishing". Examples: 晚会开得很红火. (The party was lively.) 她家的日子越过越红火. (Her family becomes more prosperous each day.) 市中心的生意都很红火 (Business is booming in the city.) 红火 is usually used in colloquial Chinese. 火 is pronounced with a neutral tone.

⁽⁶⁾税, 税收, and 交税: 税收 means "taxes" or "tax revenue". It refers specifically to money accumulated by a government through taxation. The character 税 means "tax" or "tax money", indicating the money itself; 收, short for 收入, means "income". 交税 is a verb meaning "to pay taxes", and refers to individuals paying taxes to the government.

二、電視原文 🖥️ TV original

白溝市場
（根據原文改編）

　　人們常說"星期一，生意稀"。可白溝市場的星期一卻仍舊是車水馬龍，購銷兩旺。白溝市場非常的大，走兩個小時也只走了市場的一半。這個市場以日用小商品批發為主，除了箱包自產以外，其它商品大多是從南方購進來的。市場內有固定的攤位17,000多個，每天的客流量大約在15萬人次左右，在這裡操外地口音的顧客隨處可見。據說白溝市場真正紅火起來是在近幾年，經銷額不斷上升，去年上交的稅收比率占到了整個新城縣的十分之一，經濟地位日趨重要。白溝鎮的農民幾乎家家戶戶都搞批發，在這裡手頭⁽⁷⁾有十幾萬的被稱為貧困戶。可想而知白溝人的富裕程度了。

　　白溝市場確實是適應了市場經濟的客觀規律，在這裡幾乎找不到指令性計劃的影子。生產甚麼、經銷甚麼、批量大小，全由農民自己定，⁽⁸⁾賠錢的生意他們絕對⁽⁹⁾不去做。他們決策的依據⁽¹⁰⁾只有一個，那就是市場行情。這種以市場經濟調節為主的農村經濟方式，為白溝市場的超前發展提供了先決條件。

　　與國營經濟相比，個體經濟所特有的利益機制和靈活的經營方法為白溝市場的壯大注入生機。

✏️ **Notes** ⁽⁷⁾The colloquial expression 手頭 usually translates as "at hand", "on hand", "within reach". Example: 你要的那本雜誌，現在不在我手頭. (The magazine you want is not on me right now.) 手頭 can also mean "one's current financial situation", as in the text. Example: 他剛買了電視機，所以手頭比較緊. (He just bought a TV, so he's a little short on cash.)

⁽⁸⁾賠錢 is a VO structure meaning "to lose money". This term is most often used in reference to money or property lost in a business transaction. Example: 他把家底都賠光了. (He lost all of his family's money.) 賠錢 is also used for situations where a person loses someone else's property and must pay damages. Example: 他丟了圖書館的書所以要賠錢. (He has to pay for the library books he lost.)

⁽⁹⁾絕對 can function as an adverb meaning "absolutely", "unconditionally", or as an adjective meaning "absolute" or "extreme". Examples: 絕對正確 (absolutely correct); 有絕對把握 (with complete confidence); 你絕對想不到他會做甚麼. (You'd never think she could do anything at all.) 你的看法太絕對了. (Your opinion is too extreme.)

⁽¹⁰⁾依據 vs. 根據: 依據 and 根據 can both function as nouns meaning "deciding factor" or "basis". Example: 他們決策的依據只有一個. (There was one only one deciding factor in their decision.) As prepositions, 依據 and 根據 both mean "on the basis of" or "according to". They can precede a noun to form an adverbial phrase before a main verb, as in 依據合同條件辦事 (to do something according to the conditions of a contract). 依據, however, can only be used in formal settings with nouns such as 法律, 規定, 協議, or 政策, never with nouns such as 情況 or 他說的話. 根據, on the other hand, can be used in either formal or colloquial Chinese with any type of noun, as in 根據她現在的情況 (in keeping with her present situation), 根據協議 (according to the agreement).

二、电视原文 　🖥 TV original

白沟市场

（根据原文改编）

　　人们常说"星期一，生意稀"。可白沟市场的星期一却仍旧是车水马龙，购销两旺。白沟市场非常的大，走两个小时也只走了市场的一半。这个市场以日用小商品批发为主，除了箱包自产以外，其它商品大多是从南方购进来的。市场内有固定的摊位17,000多个，每天的客流量大约在15万人次左右，在这里操外地口音的顾客随处可见。据说白沟市场真正红火起来是在近几年，经销额不断上升，去年上交的税收比率占到了整个新城县的十分之一，经济地位日趋重要。白沟镇的农民几乎家家户户都搞批发，在这里手头⁽⁷⁾有十几万的被称为贫困户。可想而知白沟人的富裕程度了。

　　白沟市场确实是适应了市场经济的客观规律，在这里几乎找不到指令性计划的影子。生产什么、经销什么、批量大小，全由农民自己定，⁽⁸⁾赔钱的生意他们绝对⁽⁹⁾不去做。他们决策的依据⁽¹⁰⁾只有一个，那就是市场行情。这种以市场经济调节为主的农村经济方式，为白沟市场的超前发展提供了先决条件。

　　与国营经济相比，个体经济所特有的利益机制和灵活的经营方法为白沟市场的壮大注入生机。

Notes　⁽⁷⁾The colloquial expression 手头 usually translates as "at hand", "on hand", "within reach". Example: 你要的那本杂志，现在不在我手头. (The magazine you want is not on me right now.) 手头 can also mean "one's current financial situation", as in the text. Example: 他刚买了电视机，所以手头比较紧. (He just bought a TV, so he's a little short on cash.)

　　⁽⁸⁾赔钱 is a VO structure meaning "to lose money". This term is most often used in reference to money or property lost in a business transaction. Example: 他把家底都赔光了. (He lost all of his family's money.) 赔钱 is also used for situations where a person loses someone else's property and must pay damages. Example: 他丢了图书馆的书所以要赔钱. (He has to pay for the library books he lost.)

　　⁽⁹⁾绝对 can function as an adverb meaning "absolutely", "unconditionally", or as an adjective meaning "absolute" or "extreme". Examples: 绝对正确 (absolutely correct); 有绝对把握 (with complete confidence); 你绝对想不到他会做什么. (You'd never think she could do anything at all.) 你的看法太绝对了. (Your opinion is too extreme.)

　　⁽¹⁰⁾依据 vs. 根据: 依据 and 根据 can both function as nouns meaning "deciding factor" or "basis". Example: 他们决策的依据只有一个. (There was one only one deciding factor in their decision.) As prepositions, 依据 and 根据 both mean "on the basis of" or "according to". They can precede a noun to form an adverbial phrase before a main verb, as in 依据合同条件办事 (to do something according to the conditions of a contract). 依据, however, can only be used in formal settings with nouns such as 法律、规定、协议、or 政策, never with nouns such as 情况 or 他说的话. 根据, on the other hand, can be used in either formal or colloquial Chinese with any type of noun, as in 根据她现在的情况 (in keeping with her present situation), 根据协议 (according to the agreement).

（採訪）

記者： "（你）從吉林來，為甚麼特意跑到白溝來呢？"

被採訪者："白溝最便宜了，我聽說的。"

記者： "你們那邊的人是不是都知道白溝的東西便宜？"

被採訪者："對。"

記者： "這次買了多少？"

被採訪者："這次買了四千多塊錢的。"

記者： "回去能有利潤嗎？"

被採訪者："有。"

　　競爭是挑戰，更是機遇[11]。願自發成長起來的白溝市場在未來的競爭中能迎接起挑戰，一步步走向成熟。

生詞

仍舊	(réng jiù)	Adv.	still, yet
車水馬龍	(chē shuǐ mǎ lóng)	Idiom.	incessant stream of horses and carriages, heavy traffic
購銷兩旺	(gòu xiāo liǎng wàng)	Idiom.	active buying and selling
日用小商品	(rì yòng xiǎo shāng pǐn)	NP.	everyday goods
箱包	(xiāng bāo)	NP.	bags and suitcases
自產	(zì chǎn)	N.	self-production
大多	(dà duō)	Adv.	mostly
攤位	(tān wèi)	N.	vendor's stand
客流量	(kè liú liàng)	N.	number of customers
大約	(dà yuē)	Adv.	approximately
人次	(rén cì)	N.	number of people
左右	(zuǒ yòu)	Adv.	around, approximately

Notes [11]機會 vs. 機遇: 機會 means "chance" or "opportunity" and is used in both spoken and written Chinese. It can refer to almost any sort of opportunity, large or small. Example: 這種機會很難得，不要錯過！ (Opportunities like this are hard to come by. Don't mess up!) 機遇 also means "opportunity", but is more commonly used in written settings. The referent of 機遇 is usually something abstract or of major significance, as in 發展機遇 (opportunity for development), 人生的機遇 (the opportunity of a lifetime).

（采访）

记者：　　　　"（你）从吉林来，为什么特意跑到白沟来呢？"

被采访者：　　"白沟最便宜了，我听说的。"

记者：　　　　"你们那边的人是不是都知道白沟的东西便宜？"

被采访者：　　"对。"

记者：　　　　"这次买了多少？"

被采访者：　　"这次买了四千多块钱的。"

记者：　　　　"回去能有利润吗？"

被采访者：　　"有。"

　　竞争是挑战，更是机遇[11]。愿自发成长起来的白沟市场在未来的竞争中能迎接起挑战，一步步走向成熟。

生词

仍旧	(réng jiù)	Adv.	still, yet
车水马龙	(chē shuǐ mǎ lóng)	Idiom.	incessant stream of horses and carriages, heavy traffic
购销两旺	(gòu xiāo liǎng wàng)	Idiom.	active buying and selling
日用小商品	(rì yòng xiǎo shāng pǐn)	NP.	everyday goods
箱包	(xiāng bāo)	NP.	bags and suitcases
自产	(zì chǎn)	N.	self-production
大多	(dà duō)	Adv.	mostly
摊位	(tān wèi)	N.	vendor's stand
客流量	(kè liú liàng)	N.	number of customers
大约	(dà yuē)	Adv.	approximately
人次	(rén cì)	N.	number of people
左右	(zuǒ yòu)	Adv.	around, approximately

Notes [11]机会 vs. 机遇: 机会 means "chance" or "opportunity" and is used in both spoken and written Chinese. It can refer to almost any sort of opportunity, large or small. Example: 这种机会很难得，不要错过！(Opportunities like this are hard to come by. Don't mess up!) 机遇 also means "opportunity", but is more commonly used in written settings. The referent of 机遇 is usually something abstract or of major significance, as in 发展机遇 (opportunity for development), 人生的机遇 (the opportunity of a lifetime).

操……口音	(cāo...kǒu yīn)	*VO.*	with an accent of
隨處可見	(suí chù kě jiàn)	*Idiom.*	to be seen everywhere
經銷額	(jīng xiāo é)	*NP.*	amount sold
不斷	(bù duàn)	*Adv.*	continuous, constant, ceaseless
比率	(bǐ lǜ)	*N.*	rate
縣	(xiàn)	*N.*	county
日趨重要	(rì qū zhòng yào)	*VP.*	to become more important day by day
手頭	(shǒu tóu)	*N.*	(at) hand
被稱為	(bèi chēng wéi)	*VP.*	to be called
貧困戶	(pín kùn hù)	*NP.*	poor household
可想而知	(kě xiǎng ér zhī)	*Idiom.*	to know through imagination, to easily figure out
賠錢	(péi qián)	*V.*	to lose money
客觀規律	(kè guān guī lǜ)	*NP.*	objective principle
指令性	(zhǐ lìng xìng)	*N.*	quota system
影子	(yǐng zi)	*N.*	shadow
批量	(pī liàng)	*N.*	amount
絕對	(jué duì)	*Adv.*	absolutely
決策	(jué cè)	*VO.*	decision making
依據	(yī jù)	*N.*	basis, deciding factor
調節	(tiáo jié)	*V.*	to adjust, to regulate
超前	(chāo qián)	*V.*	ahead of time
先決	(xiān jué)	*Adj.*	predetermined
特有的	(tè yǒu de)	*Adj.*	specially possess
利益	(lì yì)	*N.*	interest
靈活	(líng huó)	*Adj.*	flexible
壯大	(zhuàng dà)	*V.*	to strengthen
注入	(zhù rù)	*V.*	to pour into
生機	(shēng jī)	*N.*	vitality
挑戰	(tiǎo zhàn)	*V/N.*	to challenge; challenge
機遇	(jī yù)	*N.*	the opportunity of a lifetime
自發成長	(zì fā chéng zhǎng)	*VP.*	to grow spontaneously
未來	(wèi lái)	*N.*	future
迎接	(yíng jiē)	*V.*	to welcome
走向	(zǒu xiàng)	*VP.*	to march toward

操……口音	(cāo...kǒu yīn)	VO.	with an accent of
随处可见	(suí chù kě jiàn)	Idiom.	to be seen everywhere
经销额	(jīng xiāo é)	NP.	amount sold
不断	(bù duàn)	Adv.	continuous, constant, ceaseless
比率	(bǐ lǜ)	N.	rate
县	(xiàn)	N.	county
日趋重要	(rì qū zhòng yào)	VP.	to become more important day by day
手头	(shǒu tóu)	N.	(at) hand
被称为	(bèi chēng wéi)	VP.	to be called
贫困户	(pín kùn hù)	NP.	poor household
可想而知	(kě xiǎng ér zhī)	Idiom.	to know through imagination, to easily figure out
赔钱	(péi qián)	V.	to lose money
客观规律	(kè guān guī lǜ)	NP.	objective principle
指令性	(zhǐ lìng xìng)	N.	quota system
影子	(yǐng zi)	N.	shadow
批量	(pī liàng)	N.	amount
绝对	(jué duì)	Adv.	absolutely
决策	(jué cè)	VO.	decision making
依据	(yī jù)	N.	basis, deciding factor
调节	(tiáo jié)	V.	to adjust, to regulate
超前	(chāo qián)	V.	ahead of time
先决	(xiān jué)	Adj.	predetermined
特有的	(tè yǒu de)	Adj.	specially possess
利益	(lì yì)	N.	interest
灵活	(líng huó)	Adj.	flexible
壮大	(zhuàng dà)	V.	to strengthen
注入	(zhù rù)	V.	to pour into
生机	(shēng jī)	N.	vitality
挑战	(tiǎo zhàn)	V/N.	to challenge; challenge
机遇	(jī yù)	N.	the opportunity of a lifetime
自发成长	(zì fā chéng zhǎng)	VP.	to grow spontaneously
未来	(wèi lái)	N.	future
迎接	(yíng jiē)	V.	to welcome
走向	(zǒu xiàng)	VP.	to march toward

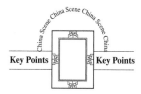

課文要點

一、詞語解釋 Words and Phrases

（一）文言詞、慣用詞 (Classical Chinese and idiomatic expressions)

1、大多＝多半、多數
　　☞ 除了箱包自產以外，其它商品大多是從南方購進來的。
2、內＝裡
　　☞ 市場內有固定的攤位17,000多個。
3、日趨＝一天比一天
　　☞ 經濟地位日趨重要。
4、幾乎＝差不多
　　☞ 白溝鎮的農民幾乎家家戶戶都搞批發。
5、入＝進
　　☞ 個體經濟所特有的利益機制和靈活的經營方法為白溝市場的壯大注入生機。

（二）成語、慣用語 (idioms and fixed expressions)

◆ 車水馬龍: heavy traffic
◆ 購銷兩旺: active selling and buying
◆ 隨處可見: ubiquitous
◆ 日趨重要: getting more important every day
◆ 可想而知: one can easily figure out
◆ 市場行情: market price trends
◆ 注入生機: to add vitality

课文要点

一、词语解释 Words and Phrases

（一）文言词、惯用词 (Classical Chinese and idiomatic expressions)

1、大多 = 多半、多数
☞ 除了箱包自产以外，其它商品大多是从南方购进来的。

2、内 = 里
☞ 市场内有固定的摊位17,000多个。

3、日趋 = 一天比一天
☞ 经济地位日趋重要。

4、几乎 = 差不多
☞ 白沟镇的农民几乎家家户户都搞批发。

5、入 = 进
☞ 个体经济所特有的利益机制和灵活的经营方法为白沟市场的壮大注入生机。

（二）成语、惯用语 (idioms and fixed expressions)

◆ 车水马龙: heavy traffic

◆ 购销两旺: active selling and buying

◆ 随处可见: ubiquitous

◆ 日趋重要: getting more important every day

◆ 可想而知: one can easily figure out

◆ 市场行情: market price trends

◆ 注入生机: to add vitality

二、書面語、正式語、口語對照表 Written/formal/colloquial Comparison

	書面／正式語	口語		書面／正式語	口語
1	以⋯起家	從⋯開始	7	大約	差不多
2	仍舊／仍然	還是	8	隨處可見	到處都看得見
3	車水馬龍	車和人來來往往	9	日趨	一天比一天
4	購銷兩旺	買賣很好／很興旺	10	可想而知	一想就明白
5	以⋯為主	主要是	11	決策	決定
6	自產	自己產生	12	愿／祝愿	希望

三、句型 Sentence Structures

（一）以⋯⋯起家 (to start out as)

> ✍ 以⋯⋯起家, "to start out as", is often used to describe the early state or condition of a business, enterprise, or career. It can be replaced by 從⋯⋯開始 or 從⋯⋯開始做起. 以⋯⋯起家 is often followed by a statement indicating change, expansion, or growth of some sort. Verbs that often follow 以⋯⋯起家 include 發展成, 變成, and 已經有. Example: 這個公司最早以賣茶葉起家，現在已經發展成有十個分公司的大企業. (This company started out selling tea; now it has developed into a large corporation with ten branch companies.)

☞ 我們學了幾課課文都是談農民企業家以做批發起家，經商致富的問題。"白溝市場"也跟這個問題有關。

1、這家店最早以賣日用品起家，現在已經發展到電器批發了。

This store started out selling articles for daily use. Now it sells electronic equipment wholesale.

2、這個人從小是"神童"，以鋼琴起家，現在已經是有名的指揮家了。

He was a child prodigy when he was young. He started as a pianist, and now he is a famous conductor.

問：瓜市村的農民是怎麼走上致富之路的？
答：＿＿＿＿＿＿＿＿＿＿＿＿＿＿＿＿＿＿＿。

（二）以⋯⋯為主 (to focus primarily on something)

> ✍ 以⋯⋯為主, "to focus primarily on something", is a structure derived from Classical Chinese. 以 means "to take up" or "to use"; 为 (wéi) means "as" or "to be". The phrase that appears between 以 and 為主 can be a noun, as in 上課應該以學生對話為主. (Class should focus primarily on student conversation.) Or it can be a VO structure, as in 這兒的箱包個體戶以做批發為主. (Vendors selling purses and suitcases here do mainly wholesale business.)

226

二、书面语、正式语、口语对照表 ▥▥Written/formal/colloquial Comparison

	书面／正式语	口语		书面／正式语	口语
1	以…起家	从…开始	7	大约	差不多
2	仍旧／仍然	还是	8	随处可见	到处都见得到
3	车水马龙	车和人来来往往	9	日趋	一天比一天
4	购销两旺	买卖很好／很兴旺	10	可想而知	一想就明白
5	以…为主	主要是	11	决策	决定
6	自产	自己生产	12	愿／祝愿	希望

三、句型 ✦✦✦ Sentence Structures

（一）以……起家 (to start out as)

> ✍ 以……起家, "to start out as", is often used to describe the early state or condition of a business, enterprise, or career. It can be replaced by 从……开始 or 从……开始做起. 以……起家 is often followed by a statement indicating change, expansion, or growth of some sort. Verbs that often follow 以……起家 include 发展成, 变成, and 已经有. Example: 这个公司最早以卖茶叶起家, 现在已经发展成有十个分公司的大企业. (This company started out selling tea; now it has developed into a large corporation with ten branch companies.)

☞ 我们学了几课课文都是谈农民企业家以做批发起家，经商致富的问题。 "白沟市场"也跟这个问题有关。

1、这家店最早以卖日用品起家，现在已经发展到电器批发了。
This store started out selling articles for daily use. Now it sells electronic equipment wholesale.

2、这个人从小是"神童"，以钢琴起家，现在已经是有名的指挥家了。
He was a child prodigy when he was young. He started as a pianist, and now he is a famous conductor.

问：瓜市村的农民是怎么走上致富之路的？
答：＿＿＿＿＿＿＿＿＿＿＿＿＿＿＿＿＿＿。

（二）以……为主 (to focus primarily on something)

> ✍ 以……为主, "to focus primarily on something", is a structure derived from Classical Chinese. 以 means "to take up" or "to use"; 为 (wéi) means "as" or "to be". The phrase that appears between 以 and 为主 can be a noun, as in 上课应该以学生对话为主. (Class should focus primarily on student conversation.) Or it can be a VO structure, as in 这儿的箱包个体户以做批发为主. (Vendors selling purses and suitcases here do mainly wholesale business.)

☞ 這個市場以日用小商品批發為主，除了箱包自產以外，其它商品大多是從南方購進來的。

1、中國以出口茶葉、日用品為主。

China mainly exports tea and products for daily use.

2、這裡的農民以前多數是以種地為主，有的也做些小生意。

In the past, most of the farmers here mainly did farmwork. Some of them also did some business on the side.

問：多數東亞研究的學生以學甚麼課程為主？

答：_____。

（三）（在）……左右 (approximately, about)

✍ （在）……左右, "approximately", "about", is used mostly in colloquial Chinese. Its written and formal counterpart is 大約 (see Lesson 10, Pattern 10), but the two differ significantly in usage. While 大約 must be placed before a number, 左右 must be placed after a number and measure word. 左右 and 大約 can sometimes appear in the same sentence. Example: 這所大學的教職工大約 500 人左右. (The teaching and administrative staff at this university number approximately 500.)

☞ 市場內有固定的攤位17,000多個，每天的客流量大約在15萬人次左右，在這裡操外地口音的顧客隨處可見。

1、北京火車站的客流量每天都在15萬人次左右。

Every day the passengers at the Beijing Train Station number approximately 150,000.

2、你知道他家的收入每年在5萬左右，流動資金在10萬左右。

You know, his family's annual income is approximately 50,000 *yuan*, and their floating capital is around 100,000.

問：每年來紐約的移民有多少？多數來自甚麼地方？

答：_____。

（四）操（／帶）……口音 (to speak with an accent)

✍ The verb 操 here means 用 and can be replaced by 帶 and 有. Place words are often used before 口音, as in 外地口音 (non-local accent), 北京口音 (Beijing accent). Examples: 他說話帶外地口音. (He speaks with a non-local accent.) 這兒操美國口音的人越來越多. (People with American accents are becoming more and more numerous around here.)

☞ 这个市场以日用小商品批发为主，除了箱包自产以外，其它商品大多是从南方购进来的。

1、中国以出口茶叶、日用品为主。

China mainly exports tea and products for daily use.

2、这里的农民以前多数是以种地为主，有的也做些小生意。

In the past, most of the farmers here mainly did farmwork. Some of them also did some business on the side.

问：多数东亚研究的学生以学什么课程为主？

答：_____。

（三）（在）……左右 (approximately, about)

> ✎ （在）……左右, "approximately", "about", is used mostly in colloquial Chinese. Its written and formal counterpart is 大约 (see Lesson 10, Pattern 10), but the two differ significantly in usage. While 大约 must be placed before a number, 左右 must be placed after a number and measure word. 左右 and 大约 can sometimes appear in the same sentence. Example: 这所大学的教职工大约 500 人左右. (The teaching and administrative staff at this university number approximately 500.)

☞ 市场内有固定的摊位17,000多个，每天的客流量大约在15万人次左右，在这里操外地口音的顾客随处可见。

1、北京火车站的客流量每天都在15万人次左右。

Every day the passengers at the Beijing Train Station number approximately 150,000.

2、你知道他家的收入每年在5万左右，流动资金在10万左右。

You know, his family's annual income is approximately 50,000 *yuan*, and their floating capital is around 100,000.

问：每年来纽约的移民有多少？多数来自什么地方？

答：_____。

（四）操（／带）……口音 (to speak with an accent)

> ✎ The verb 操 here means 用 and can be replaced by 带 and 有. Place words are often used before 口音, as in 外地口音 (non-local accent), 北京口音 (Beijing accent). Examples: 他说话带外地口音. (He speaks with a non-local accent.) 这儿操美国口音的人越来越多. (People with American accents are becoming more and more numerous around here.)

☞ 市場內有固定的攤位17,000多個，每天的客流量大約在15萬人次左右，在這裡操外地口音的顧客隨處可見。

1、每天在這兒你都能看到操外地口音的人買東西。

Every day you can find people with non-local accents buying things here.

2、隨著市場的規模越來越大，帶南方口音的顧客也越來越多。

As a result of market expansion, there are more and more customers with Southern accents.

問：你怎麼知道他是新疆人，現在住在北京的新疆村？

答：_____。

（五）被稱為 (to be referred to as, to be called)

✍　稱為, "to be referred to as", "to be called", is a pattern in which the 被 passive structure carries a neutral meaning. To indicate the agent of the verb, the form 被……稱為 is used and the agent placed after 被, although the structure is often used without it. Both variations of this form are commonly used in written and formal Chinese. When constructing an active sentence, the form 稱……為…… is used. Example: 因為他剛六歲就會做很多事，我們稱他為小能手. (He is only six years old and can already do a lot of things, so we call him the Little Crackerjack.) To negate either structure, the negative particle 不 or 沒 should be placed before 被. Example: 他們沒有被人們稱為怪僻的兩兄弟. (No one refers to them as a couple of eccentric brothers.)

☞ 白溝鎮的農民幾乎家家戶戶都搞批發，在這裡手頭有十幾萬的被稱為貧困戶。

1、中國兒童受到父母的溺愛，被稱為"小皇帝"。

Because Chinese children are spoiled by their parents, they are called "Little Emperors".

2、這裡手頭有10萬元的人就被人們稱為"富裕戶"。

Here, people who have 100,000 *yuan* at hand are called millionaires.

問：像何茹這樣跟母親生活的孩子，你們把他們稱為甚麼樣的孩子？

答：_____。

（六）可想而知…… (one can imagine, it is not hard to imagine)

✍ 可想而知, "one can imagine", "it is not hard to imagine", appears most often in written and formal Chinese. It is positioned at the beginning of a sentence, either before or after the subject. It can also be used as a predicate, as in 如果年輕人在那兒工作都很累，老年人就可想而知了. (If all the young people working there are tired, imagine what it's like for the older folks.)

☞ 可想而知白溝人的富裕程度了。

☞ 市场内有固定的摊位17,000多个，每天的客流量大约在15万人次左右，在这里操外地口音的顾客随处可见。

1、每天在这儿你都能看到操外地口音的人买东西。

Every day you can find people with non-local accents buying things here.

2、随着市场的规模越来越大，带南方口音的顾客也越来越多。

As a result of market expansion, there are more and more customers with Southern accents.

问：你怎么知道他是新疆人，现在住在北京的新疆村？

答：_____。

（五）被称为 (to be referred to as, to be called)

> ✍ 被称为, "to be referred to as", "to be called", is a pattern in which the 被 passive structure carries a neutral meaning. To indicate the agent of the verb, the form 被……称为 is used and the agent placed after 被, although the structure is often used without it. Both variations of this form are commonly used in written and formal Chinese. When constructing an active sentence, the form 称 ……为…… is used. Example: 因为他刚六岁就会做很多事，我们称他为小能手. (He is only six years old and can already do a lot of things, so we call him the Little Crackerjack.) To negate either structure, the negative particle 不 or 没 should be placed before 被. Example: 他们没有被人们称为怪僻的两兄弟. (No one refers to them as a couple of eccentric brothers.)

☞ 白沟镇的农民几乎家家户户都搞批发，在这里手头有十几万的被称为贫困户。

1、中国儿童受到父母的溺爱，被称为"小皇帝"。

Because Chinese children are spoiled by their parents, they are called "Little Emperors".

2、这里手头有10万元的人就被人们称为"富裕户"。

Here, people who have 100,000 *yuan* at hand are called millionaires.

问：像何茹这样跟母亲生活的孩子，你们把他们称为什么样的孩子？

答：_____。

（六）可想而知…… (one can imagine, it is not hard to imagine)

> ✍ 可想而知, "one can imagine", "it is not hard to imagine", appears most often in written and formal Chinese. It is positioned at the beginning of a sentence, either before or after the subject. It can also be used as a predicate, as in 如果年轻人在那儿工作都很累，老年人就可想而知了. (If all the young people working there are tired, imagine what it's like for the older folks.)

☞ 可想而知白沟人的富裕程度了。

1、從何茹的故事裡我們知道了單親家庭孩子的遭遇，那孤兒的遭遇就更可想而知了。

He Ru's story showed us the bitter experience of a child from a single-parent family; you can imagine how much worse it must be for an orphan.

2、可想而知，在中國搞市場經濟前景很好。

It's not hard to imagine that the prospects for China's market economy are good.

問：你怎麼知到秋雲被集體領養後一定會幸福呢？

答：＿＿＿＿＿＿＿＿＿＿＿＿＿＿＿＿＿＿＿。

（七）由……（決）定 (to be decided by someone)

> ✍ 由……（決）定 is a passive construction used in both written and spoken Chinese. Unlike 被, however, 由 does not indicate adversity. The agent must be present and positioned after the preposition 由. 定 here is a shortened form of 決定.

☞ 生產甚麼、經銷甚麼、批量大小，全由農民自己定，賠錢的生意他們絕對不去做。

1、這件事我不能決定，得由經理定。

I cannot make a decision in this matter. It is for the manager to decide.

2、學習計劃，別人不能幫忙，得由你自己定。

No one can help you make your study plans; you have to make your own decision.

問：在美國大學，選甚麼專業是由誰決定的？學生、老師、還是學校？

答：＿＿＿＿＿＿＿＿＿＿＿＿＿＿＿＿＿＿＿。

（八）與（／跟／和）……相比 (as compared with)

> ✍ 與（／跟／和）……相比, "as compared with", is often used as an adverbial phrase before a main clause or main verb. The conjunction 與 is more formal than 跟 and 和. Example: 與美國的進口相比，這種電腦要慢一些. (Compared to American imports, this kind of computer is somewhat slower.) If the two things to be compared must be spelled out, the pattern 拿 A 與 B 相比 should be used. Example: 拿計劃經濟和市場經濟相比，市場經濟對經濟的發展有不少好處. (Comparing planned economies to market economies, market economies offer many advantages for economic development.) In colloquial Chinese, the word 相 in 相比 can be omitted. Example: 拿他跟你比，那顯然是比不過. (Compared to you, he is obviously inferior).

☞ 與國營經濟相比，個體經濟所特有的利益機制和靈活的經營方法為白溝市場的壯大注入生機。

229

1、从何茹的故事里我们知道了单亲家庭孩子的遭遇，那孤儿的遭遇就更可想而知了。

He Ru's story showed us the bitter experience of a child from a single-parent family; you can imagine how much worse it must be for an orphan.

2、可想而知，在中国搞市场经济前景很好。

It's not hard to imagine that the prospects for China's market economy are good.

问：你怎么知到秋云被集体领养后一定会幸福呢？

答：＿＿＿＿＿＿＿＿＿＿＿＿＿＿＿＿＿＿＿＿＿。

（七）由⋯⋯（决）定 (to be decided by someone)

> 由⋯⋯（决）定 is a passive construction used in both written and spoken Chinese. Unlike 被, however, 由 does not indicate adversity. The agent must be present and positioned after the preposition 由. 定 here is a shortened form of 决定.

☞ 生产什么、经销什么、批量大小，全由农民自己定，赔钱的生意他们绝对不去做。

1、这件事我不能决定，得由经理定。

I cannot make a decision in this matter. It is for the manager to decide.

2、学习计划，别人不能帮忙，得由你自己定。

No one can help you make your study plans; you have to make your own decision.

问：在美国大学，选什么专业是由谁决定的？学生、老师、还是学校？

答：＿＿＿＿＿＿＿＿＿＿＿＿＿＿＿＿＿＿＿＿＿。

（八）与（／跟／和）⋯⋯相比 (as compared with)

> 与（／跟／和）⋯⋯相比, "as compared with", is often used as an adverbial phrase before a main clause or main verb. The conjunction 与 is more formal than 跟 and 和. Example: 与美国的进口相比，这种电脑要慢一些. (Compared to American imports, this kind of computer is somewhat slower.) If the two things to be compared must be spelled out, the pattern 拿 A 与 B 相比 should be used. Example: 拿计划经济和市场经济相比，市场经济对经济的发展有不少好处. (Comparing planned economies to market economies, market economies offer many advantages for economic development.) In colloquial Chinese, the word 相 in 相比 can be omitted. Example: 拿他跟你比，那显然是比不过. (Compared to you, he is obviously inferior).

☞ 与国营经济相比，个体经济所特有的利益机制和灵活的经营方法为白沟市场的壮大注入生机。

1、可想而知，這裡的條件與大城市相比，還差得很多。

It is not hard to imagine that conditions here are poor compared to conditions in the city.

2、與國營企業相比，私營企業的流動資金還是很少的。

Compared with state-owned businesses, private businesses have fewer floating funds.

問：計劃經濟和市場經濟各有甚麼好處？

答：＿＿＿＿＿＿＿＿＿＿＿＿＿＿＿＿＿＿ 。

四、文化背景知識 Cultural Notes

1. The economic reforms that began in 1979 and the market economy that has flourished ever since have changed the face of China's work force. As seen in Lesson 3, many persons, including farmers, have gone into business for themselves. Their hope, of course, is to have increased opportunities to make higher incomes. Many have succeeded and become rich, and this has led to great income disparity in China. China's newspapers almost daily carry "Horatio Alger Stories"--accounts of how an uneducated, poor peasant out in some remote province, through his own ingenuity and hard work, became a millionaire. (Note that the Chinese expression for "millionaire" (萬元戶) literally means a "ten-thousand *yuan* household".)

2. The expression 指令性的計劃 refers to economic plans or goals that are set and determined by the central government (that is, a quota system). The opposite is 市場調節, where policies and goals are determined and adjusted by market conditions.

1、可想而知，这里的条件与大城市相比，还差得很多。

It is not hard to imagine that conditions here are poor compared to conditions in the city.

2、与国营企业相比，私营企业的流动资金还是很少的。

Compared with state-owned businesses, private businesses have fewer floating funds.

问：计划经济和市场经济各有什么好处？

答：＿＿＿＿＿＿＿＿＿＿＿＿＿＿＿＿。

四、文化背景知识 Cultural Notes

1. The economic reforms that began in 1979 and the market economy that has flourished ever since have changed the face of China's work force. As seen in Lesson 3, many persons, including farmers, have gone into business for themselves. Their hope, of course, is to have increased opportunities to make higher incomes. Many have succeeded and become rich, and this has led to great income disparity in China. China's newspapers almost daily carry "Horatio Alger Stories"--accounts of how an uneducated, poor peasant out in some remote province, through his own ingenuity and hard work, became a millionaire. (Note that the Chinese expression for "millionaire" (万元户) literally means a "ten-thousand *yuan* household".)

2. The expression 指令性的计划 refers to economic plans or goals that are set and determined by the central government (that is, a quota system). The opposite is 市场调节, where policies and goals are determined and adjusted by market conditions.

練習

語言結構 Structures

一、短語翻譯 (Phrase translation)

1. heavy traffic
2. active trade in this county
3. to do wholesale trade in daily necessities
4. the daily number of customers
5. customers with different local accents
6. constantly in high demand
7. the tax rate of this place
8. to become more important day by day
9. the degree of richness
10. to adjust according to market conditions
11. the natural law of the market
12. the flexibility of the management system

二、聽力練習 (Listening comprehension)

1、聽寫 (Dictation)

2、聽錄音並回答問題 (Answering questions while listening to the audio CD)
   (1) 說出新疆村跟一般農村不一樣的四個方面。
   (2) 用你自己的話談談美國典型的農民市場 (farmer's market)。

三、改寫下面劃線的詞 (Replace the underlined words)

這個市場的經營者<u>大多</u>是批發商，他們的生意遠近幾百里<u>內</u>無人不知。<u>據</u>有關消息報導，這個市場的經濟地位<u>日趨</u>重要，引起了市政府的重視。

练习

语言结构 Structures

一、短语翻译 (Phrase translation)

1. heavy traffic
2. active trade in this county
3. to do wholesale trade in daily necessities
4. the daily number of customers
5. customers with different local accents
6. constantly in high demand
7. the tax rate of this place
8. to become more important day by day
9. the degree of richness
10. to adjust according to market conditions
11. the natural law of the market
12. the flexibility of the management system

二、听力练习 (Listening comprehension)

1、听写 (Dictation)

2、听录音并回答问题 (Answering questions while listening to the audio CD)
   (1) 说出新疆村跟一般农村不一样的四个方面。
   (2) 用你自己的话谈谈美国典型的农民市场 (farmer's market)。

三、改写下面划线的词 (Replace the underlined words)

　　这个市场的经营者大多是批发商，他们的生意远近几百里内无人不知。据有关消息报道，这个市场的经济地位日趋重要，引起了市政府的重视。

四、填空 (Fill in the blanks)

隨處可見、可想而知、市場行情、車水馬龍、購銷兩旺

　　要是你去瓜市村看看，那兒天天都是_____，_____。買東西的，賣東西的_____。這兒的個體戶不做賠本的生意，所以他們對_____十分了解。_____，他們的生意有多好了。

五、完成句子 (Complete the sentences)

1、　　Ａ：請你告訴我你這個公司是怎麼發展起來的？
　　　　Ｂ：_____。現在我的店已經賣了，副食品生意也不做了，我們幹起大買賣來了。
　　　　（以……起家；以……為主）

2、　　Ａ：你認為中國的開放政策對中國人有甚麼好處？
　　　　Ｂ：_____
　　　　（為……提供……條件；與……相比）

3、　　Ａ：聽說這個地方的流動人口很多，尤其是上海人。
　　　　Ｂ：可不是嗎。這個地方_____
　　　　（被稱為……；操……口音；隨處可見）

六、閱讀短文、回答問題 (Answering questions based on the reading passages)

　　　　瓜市村和白溝一樣也是一個小商品批發市場。這個市場天天車水馬龍，人來人往，有八千多個固定攤位，客流量每天大約在十萬人左右。這裡除了本村的村民搞批發外，很多操南方口音的外地人也來這兒做批發或者購貨。這裡沒有甚麼政府的指令性計劃。生產甚麼，銷售甚麼，批量大小全靠農民分析市場行情，再自己決定。這裡貧困戶的概念就是有十幾萬塊錢，上百萬塊錢也不算富裕戶。

問題
　　從五個方面寫出瓜市村的特點來。

　　　　離開家五年半，最想念的人是我姐姐。她雖然比我大七歲，可我從來就認為她性格太軟弱，為人太善良，分不清好人壞人。這幾年她離了婚又結婚，聽說沒見過面的姐夫有兩個孩子，這兩個孩子還不是一個媽，越聽越讓我擔心。

232

四、填空 (Fill in the blanks)

随处可见、可想而知、市场行情、车水马龙、购销两旺

要是你去瓜市村看看，那儿天天都是_____，_____。买东西的，卖东西的_____。这儿的个体户不做赔本的生意，所以他们对_____十分了解。_____，他们的生意有多好了。

五、完成句子 (Complete the sentences)

1、　　A：请你告诉我你这个公司是怎么发展起来的？
　　　　B：_____。现在我的店
　　　　　　已经卖了，副食品生意也不做了，我们干起大买卖来了。
　　　　（以……起家；以……为主）

2、　　A：你认为中国的开放政策对中国人有什么好处？
　　　　B：_____
　　　　　　（为……提供……条件；与……相比）

3、　　A：听说这个地方的流动人口很多，尤其是上海人。
　　　　B：可不是吗。这个地方_____
　　　　　　（被称为……；操……口音；随处可见）

六、阅读短文、回答问题 (Answering questions based on the reading passages)

瓜市村和白沟一样也是一个小商品批发市场。这个市场天天车水马龙，人来人往，有八千多个固定摊位，客流量每天大约在十万人左右。这里除了本村的村民搞批发外，很多操南方口音的外地人也来这儿做批发或者购货。这里没有什么政府的指令性计划。生产什么，销售什么，批量大小全靠农民分析市场行情，再自己决定。这里贫困户的概念就是有十几万块钱，上百万块钱也不算富裕户。

问题

从五个方面写出瓜市村的特点来。

离开家五年半，最想念的人是我姐姐。她虽然比我大七岁，可我从来就认为她性格太软弱，为人太善良，分不清好人坏人。这几年她离了婚又结婚，听说没有见过面的姐夫有两个孩子，这两个孩子还不是一个妈，越听越让我担心。

在深圳海關見到了我姐姐，我們兩個人一見面就聊個不停。我跟姐姐談她生意上的事情並不多，大部分時間是在談我媽，因為我媽對她新家庭的這種複雜的關係一直非常不滿意，　可她又不得不和我媽住在一起。他們是個體戶，沒有單位給他們分房子，暫時又拿不出閒錢買商品房，我媽一個人住四室一廳，她身體不好也需要人照顧。

我姐姐告訴我生意不好做，一個女人做生意就更難。出去做事，事事要求人。她有一個箱包公司，在外縣，甚至外省都有經銷點。最近又開了一個箱包工廠，有時候要請二三十個工人。來深圳接我的前幾天，我姐姐剛從新疆回來。她帶著箱子去新疆交貨。對方說好貨到交錢，可到貨一個星期連人都沒有見到。對方一再找藉口拖延時間，我姐只好在那兒等著。一個星期兩個星期，最後因為著急、生氣、水土不服而病倒。她說她覺得她要死在那兒了。最後錢是拿到了，她決定再不做這種賠錢的事了。

我老是說她傻人有傻福，她好像從來都是我們家最有錢的一個。現在還是，是我們家裡下海的人當中生意做得最大的一個。

問題

    (1)“姐姐”有甚麼複雜的家庭關係？

    (2) 用你的話說說“姐姐”的生活經歷。

七、翻譯 (Translate sentences)

1. These peasants who got rich initially did not have any credentials or background in business management. They rely solely upon their analysis of market trends to manage their business.

2. This train station provides trains to destinations all over the country. Their capacity is about 20,000 passengers daily. One can easily run into someone with a different accent.

3. The economic standing of China is getting crucial in the world due to the implementation of market economy. The country has become economically mature step by step.

4. One can imagine what living and learning environment parents have to provide for their children in order to make them prodigies.

在深圳海关见到了我姐姐，我们两个人一见面就聊个不停。我跟姐姐谈她生意上的事情并不多，大部分时间是在谈我妈，因为我妈对她新家庭的这种复杂的关系一直非常不满意， 可她又不得不和我妈住在一起。他们是个体户，没有单位给他们分房子，暂时又拿不出闲钱买商品房，我妈一个人住四室一厅，她身体不好也需要人照顾。

我姐姐告诉我生意不好做，一个女人做生意就更难。出去做事，事事要求人。她有一个箱包公司，在外县，甚至外省都有经销点。最近又开了一个箱包工厂，有时候要请二三十个工人。来深圳接我的前几天，我姐姐刚从新疆回来。她带着箱子去新疆交货。对方说好货到交钱，可到货一个星期连人都没有见到。对方一再找借口拖延时间，我姐只好在那儿等着。一个星期两个星期，最后因为着急、生气、水土不服而病倒。她说她觉得她要死在那儿了。最后钱是拿到了，她决定再不做这种赔钱的事了。

我老是说她傻人有傻福，她好象从来都是我们家最有钱的一个。现在还是，是我们家里下海的人当中生意做得最大的一个。

问题

    (1) "姐姐" 有什么复杂的家庭关系？

    (2) 用你的话说说 "姐姐" 的生活经历。

七、翻译 (Translate sentences)

1. These peasants who got rich initially did not have any credentials or background in business management. They rely solely upon their analysis of market trends to manage their business.

2. This train station provides trains to destinations all over the country. Their capacity is about 20,000 passengers daily. One can easily run into someone with a different accent.

3. The economic standing of China is getting crucial in the world due to the implementation of market economy. The country has become economically mature step by step.

4. One can imagine what living and learning environment parents have to provide for their children in order to make them prodigies.

語言實踐 ⋮ Practice

一、根據課文回答問題 (Answering questions based on the dialogue)

1、"星期一，生意稀"是甚麼意思？白溝的星期一呢？
2、白溝市場以做甚麼為主？商品從哪兒來？
3、談談白溝市場的攤位有多少？客流量有多大？都從哪來？
4、為甚麼白溝的經濟地位日趨重要？
5、白溝鎮的人都做甚麼？貧困戶是甚麼樣的？富裕戶呢？
6、農民決策的依據是甚麼？他們每天用甚麼規律決定他們的生產、經銷和批量？
7、個體經濟有甚麼特點？
8、從採訪中你知道為甚麼很多人來白溝？

二、活動 (Activities)

去北京的一個小商品批發市場了解一下那裡的市場行情。

1、做甚麼批發生意？
2、攤位多少、客流量多大？
3、做生意的人都是從哪兒來的？收入多少？流動資金多少？
4、買東西的人都從哪兒來？為甚麼來？
5、跟美國的市場比，中國的市場有甚麼不同？

三、討論題 (Topics for discussion)

1、像白溝這樣的市場以後有沒有發展的前途？為甚麼？
2、利用"市場行情"去決策的好處是甚麼？
3、"指令性計劃"和"市場調節"有甚麼不同？你覺得在中國應該用甚麼方式？

四、報告 (Presentation)

《介紹中國的市場經濟》

语言实践 : Practice

一、根据课文回答问题 (Answering questions based on the dialogue)

1、"星期一，生意稀"是什么意思？白沟的星期一呢？
2、白沟市场以做什么为主？商品从哪儿来？
3、谈谈白沟市场的摊位有多少？客流量有多大？都从哪来？
4、为什么白沟的经济地位日趋重要？
5、白沟镇的人都做什么？贫困户是什么样的？富裕户呢？
6、农民决策的依据是什么？他们每天用什么规律决定他们的生产、经销和批量？
7、个体经济有什么特点？
8、从采访中你知道为什么很多人来白沟？

二、活动 (Activities)

去北京的一个小商品批发市场了解一下那里的市场行情。

1、做什么批发生意？
2、摊位多少、客流量多大？
3、做生意的人都是从哪儿来的？收入多少？流动资金多少？
4、买东西的人都从哪儿来？为什么来？
5、跟美国的市场比，中国的市场有什么不同？

三、讨论题 (Topics for discussion)

1、象白沟这样的市场以后有没有发展的前途？为什么？
2、利用"市场行情"去决策的好处是什么？
3、"指令性计划"和"市场调节"有什么不同？你觉得在中国应该用什么方式？

四、报告 (Presentation)

《介绍中国的市场经济》

五、看圖討論 (Picto-discussion)

五、看图讨论 (Picto-discussion)

第十二課

舞台藝術家譚宗堯

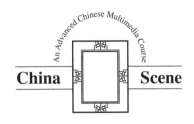

第十二课

舞台艺术家谭宗尧

237

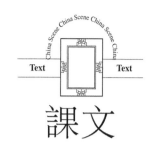

課文

一、對話  Dialogs

（一）

劉海明：老張，真奇怪，一般老百姓家現在好像都是三口人，你家怎麼有四口人呢？

老張：　說來也巧，我們建立家庭的那時候，正好政府提倡"一個不少，兩個正好"，那我們老二就擠進來了，成了四口之家。

劉海明：那現在你的孩子們都不小了吧？

老張：　對了。老大[1]已經在麥當勞當公關部[2]的經理，老二在戲劇學院學表演。說來有點慚愧，這幾十年來，我光顧忙自己的事，把整個家庭的重擔都卸給了我太太[3]，根本沒照顧家。我的孩子、家庭這麼好，多虧了我太太。

生詞

譚宗堯	(tán zōng yáo)	N.	Tan Zongyao, name of a person, a famous performer of Chinese modern plays 人名
劉海明	(liú hǎi míng)	N.	Liu Haiming, name of a person 人名
麥當勞	(mài dāng láo)	N.	McDonald's
巧	(qiǎo)	Adj/Adv.	coincidental, fortuitous
擠進	(jǐ jìn)	VP.	to force oneself in, to squeeze oneself in
公關部	(gōng guān bù)	N.	public relations department
經理	(jīng lǐ)	N.	manager

Notes [1]老大: Chinese families with more than one child use casual terms of address, usually based on age, to refer to their children. The oldest child is often called 老大, the second oldest is 老二, the third oldest is 老三, etc. Examples: 我們家老大長得最高. (Our oldest child is the tallest.) 你們家老二的學習成績怎麼樣？ (How are your second child's grades in school?) Because of the one-child policy, such terms are now heard less frequently in Mainland China.

[2]公關部 means "public relations department". 公關 is an abbreviated form of 公共 (public) 關系 (relations). Businesses in China began creating such departments after the economic reforms initiated in 1979.

[3]See Note (8).

课文

一、对话

（一）

刘海明：老张，真奇怪，一般老百姓家现在好象都是三口人，你家怎么有四口人呢？

老张：　说来也巧，我们建立家庭的那时候，正好政府提倡"一个不少，两个正好"，那我们老二就挤进来了，成了四口之家。

刘海明：那现在你的孩子们都不小了吧？

老张：　对了。老大[1]已经在麦当劳当公关部[2]的经理，老二在戏剧学院学表演。说来有点惭愧，这几十年来，我光顾忙自己的事，把整个家庭的重担都卸给了我太太[3]，根本没照顾家。我的孩子、家庭这么好，多亏了我太太。

生词

谭宗尧	(tán zōng yáo)	N.	Tan Zongyao, name of a person, a famous performer of Chinese modern plays 人名
刘海明	(liú hǎi míng)	N.	Liu Haiming, name of a person 人名
麦当劳	(mài dāng láo)	N.	McDonald's
巧	(qiǎo)	Adj/Adv.	coincidental, fortuitous
挤进	(jǐ jìn)	VP.	to force oneself in, to squeeze oneself in
公关部	(gōng guān bù)	N.	public relations department
经理	(jīng lǐ)	N.	manager

Notes [1]老大: Chinese families with more than one child use casual terms of address, usually based on age, to refer to their children. The oldest child is often called 老大, the second oldest is 老二, the third oldest is 老三, etc. Examples: 我们家老大长得最高. (Our oldest child is the tallest.) 你们家老二的学习成绩怎么样？ (How are your second child's grades in school?) Because of the one-child policy, such terms are now heard less frequently in Mainland China.

[2]公关部 means "public relations department". 公关 is an abbreviated form of 公共 (public) 关系 (relations). Businesses in China began creating such departments after the economic reforms initiated in 1979.

[3]See Note (8).

戲劇	(xì jù)	N.	drama and opera, theater
表演	(biǎo yǎn)	V.	to perform, to act
慚愧	(cán kuì)	Adj.	to feel ashamed (of)
光顧	(guāng gù)	V.	to pay attention to, to focus solely on
整個	(zhěng gè)	Adj.	entire, whole
卸給	(xiè gěi)	VP.	to shift to, to push to
多虧	(duō kuī)	V/Adv.	thanks to, luckily

（二）

劉海明：譚波，聽説你辭去了國際飯店前台的工作，跑去開"憶苦思甜"飯莊了，是
真的嗎？

譚波：　是的。我的朋友關雲峰的腦子很活，是他想到的這個主意。

劉海明：你們開的這"憶苦思甜"大雜院到底是做甚麼的？

譚波：　是個飯店，可是這個飯店除了提供飯菜以外，還讓人們在吃飯的時候享受一
下老北京的舊情。你別説⁽⁴⁾這種氣氛還真吸引了不少人來，從開張⁽⁵⁾到現在，
來的人越來越多，飯店越辦越紅火。

劉海明：看來還是年輕人⁽⁶⁾敢闖敢幹哪！

生詞

譚波	(tán bō)	N.	Tan Bo, name of a person 人名
前台	(qián tái)	N.	front desk
憶苦思甜	(yì kǔ sī tián)	Idiom.	to recall one's bitterness in order to

Notes [4]你別説, "I tell you" or "what do you know", is an inserted element often used in colloquial Chinese. It indicates the speaker's surprise at the result or outcome of a situation. Its use in the text indicates that the speaker did not expect the restaurant to succeed, but to his surprise, it did. Example: 你別説，這次去農村還真學了不少東西！(What do you know, I learned a lot on my visit to the countryside!)

[5]開張 can function either as verb (to open a new store or business) or as a noun (grand opening). 開張 typically refers to the first day of business at a new store. Examples: 他們的百貨商店今天開張. (Their department store opens today.) 三友百貨公司的開張很熱鬧！(The grand opening of the Three Friends Department Store was exciting!) Another verb similar to 開張 is 開始營業 (to start a business).

[6]年輕人: In China, people are classified into four general age categories: 少 (shào) 年人 (early youth, boys and girls between 10 and 16), 年輕人 or 青年人 (young people, from mid-teens to about 30), 中年人 or 壯年人 (middle-aged people in their 30s and 40s), and 老年人 (seniors over 50). Sometimes 年輕 functions as an adjective, as in 年輕的老師 (young teachers), 年輕的鋼琴家 (young pianist).

戏剧	(xì jù)	*N.*	drama and opera, theater
表演	(biǎo yǎn)	*V.*	to perform, to act
惭愧	(cán kuì)	*Adj.*	to feel ashamed (of)
光顾	(guāng gù)	*V.*	to pay attention to, to focus solely on
整个	(zhěng gè)	*Adj.*	entire, whole
卸给	(xiè gěi)	*VP.*	to shift to, to push to
多亏	(duō kuī)	*V/Adv.*	thanks to, luckily

（二）

刘海明：谭波，听说你辞去了国际饭店前台的工作，跑去开"忆苦思甜"饭庄了，是真的吗？

谭波：　是的。我的朋友关云峰的脑子很活，是他想到的这个主意。

刘海明：你们开的这"忆苦思甜"大杂院到底是做什么的？

谭波：　是个饭店，可是这个饭店除了提供饭菜以外，还让人们在吃饭的时候享受一下老北京的旧情。你别说⁽⁴⁾这种气氛还真吸引了不少人来，从开张⁽⁵⁾到现在，来的人越来越多，饭店越办越红火。

刘海明：看来还是年轻人⁽⁶⁾敢闯敢干哪！

生词

谭波	(tán bō)	*N.*	Tan Bo, name of a person 人名
前台	(qián tái)	*N.*	front desk
忆苦思甜	(yì kǔ sī tián)	*Idiom.*	to recall one's bitterness in order to

Notes (4)你别说, "I tell you" or "what do you know", is an inserted element often used in colloquial Chinese. It indicates the speaker's surprise at the result or outcome of a situation. Its use in the text indicates that the speaker did not expect the restaurant to succeed, but to his surprise, it did. Example: 你别说，这次去农村还真学了不少东西!) (What do you know, I learned a lot on my visit to the countryside!)

(5)开张 can function either as verb (to open a new store or business) or as a noun (grand opening). 开张 typically refers to the first day of business at a new store. Examples: 他们的百货商店今天开张. (Their department store opens today.) 三友百货公司的开张很热闹！ (The grand opening of the Three Friends Department Store was exciting!) Another verb similar to 开张 is 开始营业 (to start a business).

(6)年轻人: In China, people are classified into four general age categories: 少 (shào) 年人 (early youth, boys and girls between 10 and 16), 年轻人 or 青年人 (young people, from mid-teens to about 30), 中年人 or 壮年人 (middle-aged people in their 30s and 40s), and 老年人 (seniors over 50). Sometimes 年轻 functions as an adjective, as in 年轻的老师 (young teachers), 年轻的钢琴家 (young pianist).

			appreciate the present sweet reality
飯莊	(fàn zhuāng)	*N.*	restaurant
關雲峰	(guān yún fēng)	*N.*	Guan Yunfeng, name of a person 人名
腦子活	(nǎo zi huó)	*Idiom.*	smart, flexible way of thinking
主意	(zhǔ yì)	*N.*	idea
大雜院	(dà zá yuàn)	*N.*	an enclosed compound occupied by several households
舊情	(jiù qíng)	*NP.*	old feelings, recollections of the past
吸引	(xī yǐn)	*V.*	to attract
開張	(kāi zhāng)	*V.*	grand opening
敢闖敢幹	(gǎn chuǎng gǎn gàn)	*Idiom.*	to bravely explore and bravely engage in

---

（三）

劉海明：你聽說過譚宗堯嗎？他是誰？

白蘭：　聽說過。他是我們北京城裡的名人。早先是北京人民藝術劇院（北京人藝）的話劇演員，演出過很多部話劇、電影、和電視劇。

劉海明：現在呢？他還登台演出嗎？

白蘭：　他有時候也上台。但是，自從他當了北京人藝的副院長以後，演出就越來越少了，因為工作太忙了。

劉海明：那老百姓知道的譚宗堯是舞台上的譚宗堯，他在真正的生活中又是甚麼樣的呢？

白蘭：　他也是一個普普通通的人，有一個四口之家。太太是北京藝術學校的老師，工作十分努力；女兒敢闖敢幹，在合資公司和飯店當過公關部經理；小兒子雖然是高中生，但興趣廣泛，也熱愛藝術。

劉海明：嘿，這一家過得還挺紅火的。

生詞

白蘭	(bái lán)	*N.*	Bai Lan, name of a person 人名
早先	(zǎo xiān)	*Adj.*	earlier
藝術	(yì shù)	*N.*	art

			appreciate the present sweet reality
饭庄	(fàn zhuāng)	N.	restaurant
关云峰	(guān yún fēng)	N.	Guan Yunfeng, name of a person 人名
脑子活	(nǎo zi huó)	Idiom.	smart, flexible way of thinking
主意	(zhǔ yì)	N.	idea
大杂院	(dà zá yuàn)	N.	an enclosed compound occupied by several households
旧情	(jiù qíng)	NP.	old feelings, recollections of the past
吸引	(xī yǐn)	V.	to attract
开张	(kāi zhāng)	V.	grand opening
敢闯敢干	(gǎn chuǎng gǎn gàn)	Idiom.	to bravely explore and bravely engage in

（三）

刘海明：　你听说过谭宗尧吗？他是谁？

白兰：　　听说过。他是我们北京城里的名人。早先是北京人民艺术剧院（北京人艺）的话剧演员，演出过很多部话剧、电影、和电视剧。

刘海明：　现在呢？他还登台演出吗？

白兰：　　他有时候也上台。但是，自从他当了北京人艺的副院长以后，演出就越来越少了，因为工作太忙了。

刘海明：　那老百姓知道的谭宗尧是舞台上的谭宗尧，他在真正的生活中又是什么样的呢？

白兰：　　他也是一个普普通通的人，有一个四口之家。太太是北京艺术学校的老师，工作十分努力；女儿敢闯敢干，在合资公司和饭店当过公关部经理；小儿子虽然是高中生，但兴趣广泛，也热爱艺术。

刘海明：　嘿，这一家过得还挺红火的。

生词

白兰	(bái lán)	N.	Bai Lan, name of a person 人名
早先	(zǎo xiān)	Adj.	earlier
艺术	(yì shù)	N.	art

劇院	(jù yuàn)	*N.*	opera house
話劇	(huà jù)	*N.*	play
電視劇	(diàn shì jù)	*N.*	TV play, TV series
普普通通	(pǔ pǔ tōng tōng)	*Adj.*	common, ordinary
廣泛	(guǎng fàn)	*Adj.*	wide ranging, extensive
熱愛	(rè ài)	*V.*	to love passionately
嘿	(hèi)	*Interj.*	hey!

二、電視原文 💻 TV original

譚宗堯一家

（根據原文改編）

　　我這個家庭啊，是個普普通通的家庭，也很一般。如果説要認真地想一想，倒是還有幾個特點。你比如説我是個回族家庭，這個家庭從建立以來到現在二十五年了。那麼我這個家庭是四口之家，現在年輕人組織家庭就三口人。那我得益於甚麼呢？我得益於提倡"一個不少，兩個正好"的時候，那我的老二就擠進來了，成了四口之家。還有呢，就是我跟我的太太都是從事藝術教育的或是藝術活動的，這也算個特點哪。我們這個家庭四口人，都在做著自己喜歡做的事情，而且做得我覺得還可以。

　　我們家四口人都有自己的一攤子[7]事，所以都很忙。哎，這個家裡沒個閒人，也算是個特點吧。我[8]媳婦馬桂茹，"媳婦"這兩個字是我們北京人藝的人對自己妻子的稱謂，我媳婦真不簡單，説來呢，我還真有點慚愧。二十多年來，我光顧忙自己的

✏️ **Notes** [7]一攤子 is a colloquial expression meaning "a pile of" or "whole bunch of". Example: 我們家四口人都有他們自己一攤子事. (All four members of our family have a whole bunch of things to do.)

[8]媳婦, 太太, and 愛人: 媳婦 and 太太 are both terms of address used for one's own wife or the wife of someone else. 媳婦 originally meant "daughter-in-law", and came to mean "wife" through colloquial Beijing dialect. The term 太太 was originally used an honorific form of address for the matriarch of a rich family. For many years the term 太太 was out of vogue in Mainland China because of its "feudal" （封建） overtone, but now is being used once again. It is used extensively in Taiwan. Since 愛人 can be used for a husband or wife, it is perhaps best translated as "spouse". 愛人 dates from the revolutionary period of the early 20th century. Generally speaking, it is only used by people over fifty. Occasionally, 愛人 is also used to mean "sweetheart".

剧院	(jù yuàn)	*N.*	opera house
话剧	(huà jù)	*N.*	play
电视剧	(diàn shì jù)	*N.*	TV play, TV series
普普通通	(pǔ pǔ tōng tōng)	*Adj.*	common, ordinary
广泛	(guǎng fàn)	*Adj.*	wide ranging, extensive
热爱	(rè ài)	*V.*	to love passionately
嘿	(hèi)	*Interj.*	hey!

二、电视原文 TV original

谭宗尧一家
（根据原文改编）

　　我这个家庭啊，是个普普通通的家庭，也很一般。如果说要认真地想一想，倒是还有几个特点。你比如说我是个回族家庭，这个家庭从建立以来到现在二十五年了。那么我这个家庭是四口之家，现在年轻人组织家庭就三口人。那我得益于什么呢？我得益于提倡"一个不少，两个正好"的时候，那我的老二就挤进来了，成了四口之家。还有呢，就是我跟我的太太都是从事艺术教育的或是艺术活动的，这也算个特点哪。我们这个家庭四口人，都在做着自己喜欢做的事情，而且做得我觉得还可以。

　　我们家四口人都有自己的一摊子[7]事，所以都很忙。哎，这个家里没个闲人，也算是个特点吧。我[8]媳妇马桂茹，"媳妇"这两个字是我们北京人艺的人对自己妻子的称谓，我媳妇真不简单，说来呢，我还真有点惭愧。二十多年来，我光顾忙自己的

Notes [7]一摊子 is a colloquial expression meaning "a pile of" or "whole bunch of". Example: 我们家四口人都有他们自己一摊子事. (All four members of our family have a whole bunch of things to do.)

[8]媳妇, 太太, and 爱人: 媳妇 and 太太 are both terms of address used for one's own wife or the wife of someone else. 媳妇 originally meant "daughter-in-law", and came to mean "wife" through colloquial Beijing dialect. The term 太太 was originally used an honorific form of address for the matriarch of a rich family. For many years the term 太太 was out of vogue in Mainland China because of its "feudal" （封建） overtone, but now is being used once again. It is used extensively in Taiwan. Since 爱人 can be used for a husband or wife, it is perhaps best translated as "spouse". 爱人 dates from the revolutionary period of the early 20th century. Generally speaking, it is only used by people over fifty. Occasionally, 爱人 is also used to mean "sweetheart".

事了，把整個家庭的重擔都卸給她了。但是她有她自己的事業和追求，她是解放軍藝術學院戲劇系的形體教員。在她上課之餘，覺得自己應當對社會上儀表美的教育也負有責任，所以她在校內校外都有課，回家還有一大堆的家務事。可她就在這裡裡外外的一片忙碌中，竟然還寫了一本叫《儀表美與訓練》的書。這本書的銷路還挺好，幾個月裡就印了兩次。

忙，我確實挺忙。我每天在家的時間很少。用家裡人的話說，你只有閉著眼睛的時候才算和家裡人在一起，早上睜開眼你又該走了。可是不忙又能怎麼著呢[9]？我72年到人藝。從72年到現在，我在人藝演了30來部戲，拍過十幾部電影或者電視劇，可我覺得今天我的事業才真正剛剛開始。人藝的舞台，說老實話，我覺得是我生命的一部分。

我的女兒叫譚波，就是波浪的波。在這起名的時候，也掀起一層波浪。就是我父親反對－覺得這個波字不好，去掉三點水就是個皮字，那麼這孩子就會調皮搗蛋。二十幾年來，確實是幹了不少調皮搗蛋的事。王府飯店她在前台搞得很好，辭了。又跑到那個新洋國際貿易集團。現在呢，又跟她的朋友關雲峰折騰了一個大雜院。當初我一聽她到憶苦思甜大雜院飯莊做公關部經理，我就想你小孩子們經過甚麼，你們知道甚麼憶苦思甜？哎，你還別說，這憶苦思甜大雜院一開張，還越來越火，還真弄了不少老北京的東西。電台、電視台，報紙都報導了。看來還是年輕人敢闖敢幹，腦子活。

我的老二是個兒子，叫譚濤。哎，這個濤字我父親也反對，濤，淘氣，這是諧音。"太淘氣，這孩子。你起這麼個名兒幹嗎？"就是覺得淘氣。這孩子淘來淘去的，現在也大了。他正在念高中，興趣廣泛，也熱愛藝術，他還是金帆交響樂團的巴松演奏員呢。哎，對了，讓我驚喜的是他前些日子在學校裡給同學導演過話劇《白毛女》，

Notes [9] （又能）怎麼著 (zhāo) 呢？is a very colloquial expression meaning "what can you do about something", "what's to be done", or "there's nothing else you can do about it". English translations vary according to the context of the Chinese sentence. Examples: 他不同意又能怎麼著呢？(What are we going to do if he doesn't agree?) 他不交稅政府又能怎麼著呢？(If he doesn't pay his taxes, what can the government do about it?)

事了，把整个家庭的重担都卸给她了。但是她有她自己的事业和追求，她是解放军艺术学院戏剧系的形体教员。在她上课之余，觉得自己应当对社会上仪表美的教育也负有责任，所以她在校内校外都有课，回家还有一大堆的家务事。可她就在这里里外外的一片忙碌中，竟然还写了一本叫《仪表美与训练》的书。这本书的销路还挺好，几个月里就印了两次。

忙，我确实挺忙。我每天在家的时间很少。用家里人的话说，你只有闭着眼睛的时候才算和家里人在一起，早上睁开眼你又该走了。可是不忙又能怎么着呢[9]？我72年到人艺。从72年到现在，我在人艺演了30来部戏，拍过十几部电影或者电视剧，可我觉得今天我的事业才真正刚刚开始。人艺的舞台，说老实话，我觉得是我生命的一部分。

我的女儿叫谭波，就是波浪的波。在这起名的时候，也掀起一层波浪。就是我父亲反对——觉得这个波字不好，去掉三点水就是个皮字，那么这孩子就会调皮捣蛋。二十几年来，确实是干了不少调皮捣蛋的事。王府饭店她在前台搞得很好，辞了。又跑到那个新洋国际贸易集团。现在呢，又跟她的朋友关云峰折腾了一个大杂院。当初我一听她到忆苦思甜大杂院饭庄做公关部经理，我就想你小孩子们经过什么，你们知道什么忆苦思甜？哎，你还别说，这忆苦思甜大杂院一开张，还越来越火，还真弄了不少老北京的东西。电台、电视台，报纸都报道了。看来还是年轻人敢闯敢干，脑子活。

我的老二是个儿子，叫谭涛。哎，这个涛字我父亲也反对，涛，淘气，这是谐音。"太淘气，这孩子。你起这么个名儿干吗？"就是觉得淘气。这孩子淘来淘去的，现在也大了。他正在念高中，兴趣广泛，也热爱艺术，他还是金帆交响乐团的巴松演奏员呢。哎，对了，让我惊喜的是他前些日子在学校里给同学导演过话剧《白毛

Notes [9]（又能）怎么着 (zhāo) 呢？is a very colloquial expression meaning "what can you do about something", "what's to be done", or "there's nothing else you can do about it". English translations vary according to the context of the Chinese sentence. Examples: 他不同意又能怎么着呢？(What are we going to do if he doesn't agree?) 他不交税政府又能怎么着呢？(If he doesn't pay his taxes, what can the government do about it?)

和《駱駝祥子》的片段，居然還得了個一等獎。這事我和他媽原本[10]可一點也不知道。

譚濤："我小時候受藝術薰陶，非常喜歡戲劇，我覺得我的條件比我爸好，我希望[11]將來能在這方面超過我爸。"哈哈，真是後生可畏[12]，不盡長江滾滾來[13]啊！但願[14]他將來能超過他老爸[15]。

瞧，我的家就像北京城一樣，在發展變化，我覺著它會越來越紅火。

生詞

認真	(rèn zhēn)	Adj.	conscientious, earnest
回族	(huí zú)	N.	Islamic nationality in China
得益於	(dé yì yú)	VP.	to benefit from
一攤子	(yī tān zi)	NP.	a pile of
閑人	(xián rén)	N.	idle person, loafer
媳婦	(xí fù)	N.	wife
馬桂茹	(mǎ guì rú)	N.	Ma Guiru, name of a person 人名
稱謂	(chēng wèi)	N.	term of address
追求	(zhuī qiú)	V.	to seek for
解放軍	(jiě fàng jūn)	NP.	People's Liberation Army
形體	(xíng tǐ)	N.	shape, physique

Notes [10]原本, meaning "originally", is derived from combining the first characters of 原來 and 本來. All three of these terms have the same meaning, but 原本 is the most formal. Example: 我原本是學醫的，後來改學電腦了. (Originally, I studied medicine, but later changed to computers.)

[11]See Note (14).

[12]後生可畏 literally means "the later generation can be feared". It suggests that the younger generation is making such great accomplishments (in education, careers, etc.) that they will come to be respected above the older generation.

[13]The line 不盡長江滾滾來 is drawn from a lyric-verse （詞） by the eleventh-century poet Liu Yong （柳永）. 不盡 means "never-ending" or "endlessly"; 長江 is the Great River (or Yangzi River, as it is known in the West); 滾滾 is an onomatopoeic representation of the sound of rushing water; 來 means "comes" or "approaches". The entire line might be rendered: "Endlessly, the Great River rips and roars as it approaches". This line is invoked to emphasize the inevitability of the younger generation endlessly surpassing the older.

[14]但願 vs. 希望: 但願, or 願 for short, means "to wish", "to hope". The character 但 in 但願 means 只 (only); strictly speaking, then, 但願 means "if only" or "my only hope is that" and indicates a strong wish or desire. It may only be used at the beginning of a sentence. Since the first-person pronoun "I" is understood as the subject of 但願, 我 must always be omitted before 但願. Examples: 但願她能平安地回來. (I hope she can come home safely.) 但願這只是謠傳！ (My only wish is that this is a rumor!) 希望 refers to any wish or hope. Unlike 但願, the subject of 希望 may be present or absent, depending on context. Examples: 我希望他早點找工作. (I hope he finds a job soon.) 希望這事能成功！ (I hope this works!)

[15]老爸 (dad, daddy, dear old dad) is an affectionate, intimate term used to refer to one's own father.

女》，和《骆驼祥子》的片段，居然还得了个一等奖。这事我和他妈原本⁽¹⁰⁾可一点也不知道。

谭涛： "我小时候受艺术熏陶，非常喜欢戏剧，我觉得我的条件比我爸好，我希望⁽¹¹⁾将来能在这方面超过我爸。" 哈哈，真是后生可畏⁽¹²⁾，不尽长江滚滚来⁽¹³⁾啊！但愿⁽¹⁴⁾他将来能超过他老爸⁽¹⁵⁾。

瞧，我的家就象北京城一样，在发展变化，我觉着它会越来越红火。

生词

认真	(rèn zhēn)	Adj.	conscientious, earnest
回族	(huí zú)	N.	Islamic nationality in China
得益于	(dé yì yú)	VP.	to benefit from
一摊子	(yī tān zi)	NP.	a pile of
闲人	(xián rén)	N.	idle person, loafer
媳妇	(xí fù)	N.	wife
马桂茹	(mǎ guì rú)	N.	Ma Guiru, name of a person 人名
称谓	(chēng wèi)	N.	term of address
追求	(zhuī qiú)	V.	to seek for
解放军	(jiě fàng jūn)	NP.	People's Liberation Army
形体	(xíng tǐ)	N.	shape, physique

Notes ⁽¹⁰⁾原本, meaning "originally", is derived from combining the first characters of 原来 and 本来. All three of these terms have the same meaning, but 原本 is the most formal. Example: 我原本是学医的，后来改学电脑了. (Originally, I studied medicine, but later changed to computers.)

⁽¹¹⁾See Note (14).

⁽¹²⁾后生可畏 literally means "the later generation can be feared". It suggests that the younger generation is making such great accomplishments (in education, careers, etc.) that they will come to be respected above the older generation.

⁽¹³⁾The line 不尽长江滚滚来 is drawn from a lyric-verse （词） by the eleventh-century poet Liu Yong （柳永）. 不尽 means "never-ending" or "endlessly"; 长江 is the Great River (or Yangzi River, as it is known in the West); 滚滚 is an onomatopoeic representation of the sound of rushing water; 来 means "comes" or "approaches". The entire line might be rendered: "Endlessly, the Great River rips and roars as it approaches". This line is invoked to emphasize the inevitability of the younger generation endlessly surpassing the older.

⁽¹⁴⁾但愿 vs. 希望: 但愿, or 愿 for short, means "to wish", "to hope". The character 但 in 但愿 means 只 (only); strictly speaking, then, 但愿 means "if only" or "my only hope is that" and indicates a strong wish or desire. It may only be used at the beginning of a sentence. Since the first-person pronoun "I" is understood as the subject of 但愿, 我 must always be omitted before 但愿. Examples: 但愿她能平安地回来. (I hope she can come home safely.) 但愿这只是谣传！ (My only wish is that this is a rumor!) 希望 refers to any wish or hope. Unlike 但愿, the subject of 希望 may be present or absent, depending on context. Examples: 我希望他早点找工作. (I hope he finds a job soon.) 希望这事能成功！ (I hope this works!)

⁽¹⁵⁾老爸 (dad, daddy, dear old dad) is an affectionate, intimate term used to refer to one's own father.

在……之餘	(zài zhī yú)	*PrepP.*	in the spare time of
儀表	(yí biǎo)	*N.*	appearance, bearing
忙碌	(máng lù)	*Adj.*	busy
竟然	(jìng rán)	*Adv.*	unexpectedly, surprisingly, even
訓練	(xùn liàn)	*V/N.*	to train, to drill
銷路	(xiāo lù)	*N.*	market, sale
印	(yìn)	*V.*	to print
閉	(bì)	*V.*	to close (eyes)
睜	(zhēng)	*V.*	to open (eyes)
部	(bù)	*Classifier.*	classifier for movies, TV plays, etc.
拍	(pāi)	*V.*	to produce
舞台	(wǔ tái)	*N.*	stage, arena
波浪	(bō làng)	*N.*	wave
掀起	(xiān qǐ)	*V.*	to stir up, to start
三點水	(sān diǎn shuǐ)	*N.*	water radical for Chinese characters
調皮	(tiáo pí)	*Adj.*	naughty, mischievous
搗蛋	(dǎo dàn)	*Idiom.*	to make trouble, trouble making
王府飯店	(wáng fǔ fàn diàn)	*N.*	Palace Hotel
集團	(jí tuán)	*N.*	incorporation, group
折騰	(zhē téng)	*V.*	to do
火	(huǒ)	*Adj.*	popular
弄	(nòng)	*V.*	to make
譚濤	(tán tāo)	*N.*	Tan Tao, name of a person 人名
淘氣	(táo qì)	*Adj.*	mischievous
諧音	(xié yīn)	*V.*	to be homophonic
金帆	(jīn fān)	*N.*	gold sail
巴松	(bā sōng)	*N.*	bassoon
演奏員	(yǎn zòu yuán)	*N.*	player of a musical instrument
驚喜	(jīng xǐ)	*V.*	to be happily surprised at
導演	(dǎo yǎn)	*V/N.*	to direct; director
白毛女	(bái máo nǚ)	*N.*	*White-Haired Girl* (a popular play in China)
駱駝祥子	(luò tuó xiáng zi)	*N.*	*Camel Xiangzi* (a play written by Lao She)
片段	(piàn duàn)	*N.*	excerpt
一等獎	(yī děng jiǎng)	*N.*	first prize
原本	(yuán běn)	*Adv.*	originally

在……之余	(zài zhī yú)	*PrepP.*	in the spare time of
仪表	(yí biǎo)	*N.*	appearance, bearing
忙碌	(máng lù)	*Adj.*	busy
竟然	(jìng rán)	*Adv.*	unexpectedly, surprisingly, even
训练	(xùn liàn)	*V/N.*	to train, to drill
销路	(xiāo lù)	*N.*	market, sale
印	(yìn)	*V.*	to print
闭	(bì)	*V.*	to close (eyes)
睁	(zhēng)	*V.*	to open (eyes)
部	(bù)	*Classifier.*	classifier for movies, TV plays, etc.
拍	(pāi)	*V.*	to produce
舞台	(wǔ tái)	*N.*	stage, arena
波浪	(bō làng)	*N.*	wave
掀起	(xiān qǐ)	*V.*	to stir up, to start
三点水	(sān diǎn shuǐ)	*N.*	water radical for Chinese characters
调皮	(tiáo pí)	*Adj.*	naughty, mischievous
捣蛋	(dǎo dàn)	*Idiom.*	to make trouble, trouble making
王府饭店	(wáng fǔ fàn diàn)	*N.*	Palace Hotel
集团	(jí tuán)	*N.*	incorporation, group
折腾	(zhē téng)	*V.*	to do
火	(huǒ)	*Adj.*	popular
弄	(nòng)	*V.*	to make
谭涛	(tán tāo)	*N.*	Tan Tao, name of a person 人名
淘气	(táo qì)	*Adj.*	mischievous
谐音	(xié yīn)	*V.*	to be homophonic
金帆	(jīn fān)	*N.*	gold sail
巴松	(bā sōng)	*N.*	bassoon
演奏员	(yǎn zòu yuán)	*N.*	player of a musical instrument
惊喜	(jīng xǐ)	*V.*	to be happily surprised at
导演	(dǎo yǎn)	*V/N.*	to direct; director
白毛女	(bái máo nǚ)	*N.*	*White-Haired Girl* (a popular play in China)
骆驼祥子	(luò tuó xiáng zi)	*N.*	*Camel Xiangzi* (a play written by Lao She)
片段	(piàn duàn)	*N.*	excerpt
一等奖	(yī děng jiǎng)	*N.*	first prize
原本	(yuán běn)	*Adv.*	originally

薰陶	(xūn táo)	*N/V.*	cultivation, to cultivate, to influence
後生可畏	(hòu shēng kě wèi)	*Idiom.*	a youth is to be regarded with respect–the younger generation will surpass the older
不盡	(bù jìn)	*VP.*	unrest, always flowing
長江	(cháng jiāng)	*N.*	Yangzi River
滾滾來	(gǔn gǔn lái)	*VP.*	roaring over, gurgling over
但願	(dàn yuàn)	*V.*	to wish
老爸	(lǎo bà)	*NP.*	my old man

熏陶	(xūn táo)	*N/V.*	cultivation, to cultivate, to influence
后生可畏	(hòu shēng kě wèi)	*Idiom.*	a youth is to be regarded with respect–the younger generation will surpass the older
不尽	(bù jìn)	*VP.*	unrest, always flowing
长江	(cháng jiāng)	*N.*	Yangzi River
滚滚来	(gǔn gǔn lái)	*VP.*	roaring over, gurgling over
但愿	(dàn yuàn)	*V.*	to wish
老爸	(lǎo bà)	*NP.*	my old man

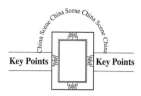

Key Points　Key Points

課文要點

一、詞語解釋 Words and Phrases

（一）文言詞 (Classical Chinese)

於＝從
☞ 那我得益於甚麼呢？

（二）成語、慣用語 (idioms and fixed expressions)

◆ 普普通通: ordinary, common
◆ 調皮搗蛋: naughty and mischievous
◆ 憶苦思甜: to recall one's bitterness in order to appreciate the present sweet reality
◆ 敢闖敢幹: to bravely explore and bravely engage in
◆ 後生可畏: youth is regarded with respect
◆ 不盡長江滾滾來: as in the Changjiang River, the waves behind drive on those before

二、書面語、正式語、口語對照表 Written/formal/colloquial Comparison

	書面／正式語	口語		書面／正式語	口語
1	只／僅	光	8	校內	學校裡邊
2	注意	顧	9	校外	學校外邊
3	把…卸給	把…推給	10	竟然／居然	還
4	得益於…	從…得到好處	11	銷路	賣得
5	敢闖敢幹	敢做自己想做的事	12	憶苦思甜	回憶過去的苦日子，想想現在的好生活
6	從事…工作	作…工作	13	當初	那個時候
7	在…之餘	在…以外的時間裡	14	可畏	讓人害怕

课文要点

一、词语解释 Words and Phrases

（一）文言词 (Classical Chinese)

> 于 = 从
>
> ☞ 那我得益于什么呢？

（二）成语、惯用语 (idioms and fixed expressions)

- ◆ 普普通通: ordinary, common
- ◆ 调皮捣蛋: naughty and mischievous
- ◆ 忆苦思甜: to recall one's bitterness in order to appreciate the present sweet reality
- ◆ 敢闯敢干: to bravely explore and bravely engage in
- ◆ 后生可畏: youth is regarded with respect
- ◆ 不尽长江滚滚来: as in the Changjiang River, the waves behind drive on those before

二、书面语、正式语、口语对照表 Written/formal/colloquial Comparison

	书面／正式语	口语		书面／正式语	口语
1	只／仅	光	8	校内	学校里边
2	注意	顾	9	校外	学校外边
3	把…卸给…	把…推给…	10	竟然／居然	还
4	得益于…	从…得到好处	11	销路	卖得
5	敢闯敢干	敢做自己想做的事	12	忆苦思甜	回忆过去的苦日子，想想现在的好生活
6	从事…工作	做…工作	13	当初	那个时候
7	在…之余	在…以外的时间里	14	可畏	让人害怕

三、句型 ✦ Sentence Structures

（一）說來也巧 (it just so happened that)

> ✐ 說來也巧, "it just so happened that", often functions as a topic starter. Usually it appears at the beginning of a sentence, before the subject. This expression is used most often in colloquial Chinese.

☞ 說來也巧，我們建立家庭的那時候，正好是政府提倡“一個不少，兩個正好”的時候，那我們老二就擠進來了，成了四口之家。

1、說來也巧， 我去禮品店的時候正好碰上他們小倆口也在那兒買東西。
I happened to bump into that young couple in the gift shop while they were shopping.

2、說來也巧，我正要去買啤酒的時候他就給我送來了一打。
It just so happened that he brought me a dozen bottles of beer just as I was about to go buy some.

問：你怎麼知道老王昨天買了新車？
答：＿＿＿＿＿＿＿＿＿＿＿＿＿＿＿＿。

（二）說來有點兒（／些）慚愧（／不好意思／讓我臉紅）……(I'm a little...to say)

> ✐ 說來有點兒（／些）…… means "I'm a little...to say". It is similar to 說來也巧 in that it functions as a topic starter to warn or prepare the listener for what follows. Adjectives and phrases that can follow 有點兒（／些）include 慚愧 (ashamed), 不好意思 (embarrassing), and 讓我臉紅 (to make me blush). This structure usually appears at the beginning of a sentence, before the subject, and is used primarily in spoken settings.

☞ 說來有點兒慚愧，這幾十年來，我光顧忙自己的事，把整個家庭的重擔都卸給了我太太。根本沒照顧家。

1、說來有些不好意思，我忘了這裡是憑卡吃飯，忘了帶卡了。
I am a little embarrassed to say it, but I forgot that you need a card to eat here, and I forgot to bring my card.

2、說來有點兒慚愧，我媳婦生孩子的時候我都沒在家。
I am a little ashamed to say that when my wife gave birth to our child I wasn't even at home.

問：今天開會我怎麼沒有看見你？
答：＿＿＿＿＿＿＿＿＿＿＿＿＿＿＿＿。

三、句型 Sentence Structures

（一）说来也巧 (it just so happened that)

> ✍ 说来也巧, "it just so happened that", often functions as a topic starter. Usually it appears at the beginning of a sentence, before the subject. This expression is used most often in colloquial Chinese.

☞ 说来也巧, 我们建立家庭的那时候, 正好是政府提倡"一个不少, 两个正好"的时候, 那我们老二就挤进来了, 成了四口之家。

1、说来也巧, 我去礼品店的时候正好碰上他们小两口也在那儿买东西。
I happened to bump into that young couple in the gift shop while they were shopping.

2、说来也巧, 我正要去买啤酒的时候他就给我送来了一打。
It just so happened that he brought me a dozen bottles of beer just as I was about to go buy some.

问：你怎么知道老王昨天买了新车？
答：_____。

（二）说来有点儿（/些）惭愧（/不好意思/让我脸红）……… (I'm a little...to say)

> ✍ 说来有点儿（/些）……… means "I'm a little...to say". It is similar to 说来也巧 in that it functions as a topic starter to warn or prepare the listener for what follows. Adjectives and phrases that can follow 有点儿（/些）include 惭愧 (ashamed), 不好意思 (embarrassing), and 让我脸红 (to make me blush). This structure usually appears at the beginning of a sentence, before the subject, and is used primarily in spoken settings.

☞ 说来有点儿惭愧, 这几十年来, 我光顾忙自己的事, 把整个家庭的重担都卸给了我太太。根本没照顾家。

1、说来有些不好意思, 我忘了这里是凭卡吃饭, 忘了带卡了。
I am a little embarrassed to say it, but I forgot that you need a card to eat here, and I forgot to bring my card.

2、说来有点儿惭愧, 我媳妇生孩子的时候我都没在家。
I am a little ashamed to say that when my wife gave birth to our child I wasn't even at home.

问：今天开会我怎么没有看见你？
答：_____。

（三）多虧（了）(thanks to, owing to, luckily)

> ✍ 多虧（了）, "thanks to", "owing to", "luckily", can be used either before or after a main clause. Use of 了 is optional in this structure. Examples: 多虧了改革開放，我們的生活才這麼好. (Thanks to the open door policy, our life is now so good!) 我能來中國，多虧了父母的支持. (Thanks to the support of my parents, I've been able to come to China.)

☞ 我的孩子、家庭這麼好，多虧了我太太。

1、多虧了新的住房政策，我們今天才能買得起新房。

Thanks to the new housing policy, we can now afford to buy a new house.

2、我們老二能上這麼好的大學，多虧了學校的幫助。

Thanks to help from the school, our second child can attend an excellent university.

問：你怎麼從機場來學校的？

答：＿＿＿＿＿＿＿＿＿＿＿＿＿＿＿。

（四）得益於 (to benefit from)

> ✍ Literally, 得益於 means "to derive benefit from". Drawn from Classical Chinese, this structure is used mostly in written and formal settings. The noun phrase before the verb can be either a person or a thing and often identifies the benefactor; the noun phrase after the verb identifies the source or cause of the benefit. This pattern rarely appears in negative form. When so used, however, the Classical Chinese negative particle 非, meaning 不是, is usually employed. Example: 他如此成功，並非得益於政府的資助. (His success is not attributable to government funding.)

☞ 我得益於提倡"一個不少，兩個正好"的時候，那我的老二就擠進來了，

1、個體戶今天的富裕得益於政策的開放。

The prosperity of today's entrepreneurs is due to the open door policy.

2、他的中文說得這麼好，完全得益於中國這個好的語言環境。

He speaks Chinese so well because of the wonderful language environment in China.

問：像你這樣一個地地道道的農民的兒子今天能考上大學得益於甚麼？

答：＿＿＿＿＿＿＿＿＿＿＿＿＿＿＿＿＿＿＿。

（三）多亏（了）(thanks to, owing to, luckily)

> ✍ 多亏（了），"thanks to", "owing to", "luckily", can be used either before or after a main clause. Use of 了 is optional in this structure. Examples: 多亏了改革开放，我们的生活才这么好. (Thanks to the open door policy, our life is now so good!) 我能来中国，多亏了父母的支持. (Thanks to the support of my parents, I've been able to come to China.)

☞ 我的孩子、家庭这么好，多亏了我太太。

1、多亏了新的住房政策，我们今天才能买得起新房。

　　Thanks to the new housing policy, we can now afford to buy a new house.

2、我们老二能上这么好的大学，多亏了学校的帮助。

　　Thanks to help from the school, our second child can attend an excellent university.

　　问：你怎么从机场来学校的？

　　答：＿＿＿＿＿＿＿＿＿＿＿＿＿＿＿＿＿。

（四）得益于 (to benefit from)

> ✍ Literally, 得益于 means "to derive benefit from". Drawn from Classical Chinese, this structure is used mostly in written and formal settings. The noun phrase before the verb can be either a person or a thing and often identifies the benefactor; the noun phrase after the verb identifies the source or cause of the benefit. This pattern rarely appears in negative form. When so used, however, the Classical Chinese negative particle 非, meaning 不是, is usually employed. Example: 他如此成功，并非得益于政府的资助. (His success is not attributable to government funding.)

☞ 我得益于提倡"一个不少，两个正好"的时候，那我的老二就挤进来了，

1、个体户今天的富裕得益于政策的开放。

　　The prosperity of today's entrepreneurs is due to the open door policy.

2、他的中文说得这么好，完全得益于中国这个好的语言环境。

　　He speaks Chinese so well because of the wonderful language environment in China.

　　问：象你这样一个地地道道的农民的儿子今天能考上大学得益于什么？

　　答：＿＿＿＿＿＿＿＿＿＿＿＿＿＿＿＿＿。

（五）……是 A 對 B 的稱謂 (to be the term of address used by A for B, is what A calls B)

> ✍ ……是 A 對 B 的稱謂, "to be the term of address used by A for B", "is what A calls B", is used to identify and explain terms of address, especially when two different terms refer to the same position or relationship. 稱謂 can be used interchangeably with 稱呼, but 稱謂 is more formal.

☞ "媳婦"這兩個字是我們北京人藝的人對自己妻子的稱謂，

1、"老爸"是一般孩子對他父親的稱謂。
Lao ba is most children's term of address for their fathers.
2、"姑娘"是對沒結婚的女性的一般稱謂。
Guniang is a general term of address for young unmarried women.

問：你怎麼叫你的先生是"老公"？
答：＿＿＿＿＿＿＿＿＿＿＿＿＿＿＿＿。

（六）從事……（工作／事業／研究／活動）(to engage in a particular kind of work or cause)

> ✍ 從事, "to engage in", is a more formal verb than 做. This structure, introduced in Lesson 3, often refers to a serious undertaking such as a career, professional activity, or research endeavor. Typical objects for 從事 include 工作 (work), 事業 (cause, undertaking), and 研究 (research), etc.

☞ 還有呢，就是我跟我的太太都是從事藝術教育的或是藝術活動的，這也算個特點哪。

1、他從事鋼琴教學差不多十年了。
He has taught piano for about 10 years.
2、從事電腦研究在中國越來越普遍。
Engaging in computer research is getting more and more common in China.

問：為甚麼他對文學研究那麼有興趣？
答：因為＿＿＿＿＿＿＿＿＿＿＿＿＿＿＿。

（七）（在）……之餘 (in one's spare time, when not doing something)

> ✍ 在……之餘, "in one's spare time", "when not doing something", is usually used in written or Chinese to indicate a time frame for an event or action. The phrase inserted between 在 and 之餘 is often an action verb such as 工作, 上課, or 學習. 在……之餘 can be placed either before or after the subject of the main clause. Use of 在 is optional. Example: 練琴之餘，他常常作曲. (When not playing the piano, he often composes music.)

（五）……是 A 对 B 的称谓 (to be the term of address used by A for B, is what A calls B)

> ✍ ……是 A 对 B 的称谓, "to be the term of address used by A for B", "is what A calls B", is used to identify and explain terms of address, especially when two different terms refer to the same position or relationship. 称谓 can be used interchangeably with 称呼, but 称谓 is more formal.

☞ "媳妇"这两个字是我们北京人艺的人对自己妻子的称谓,

1、"老爸"是一般孩子对他父亲的称谓。
   Lao ba is most children's term of address for their fathers.
2、"姑娘"是对没结婚的女性的一般称谓。
   Guniang is a general term of address for young unmarried women.

问：你怎么叫你的先生是"老公"?
答：＿＿＿＿＿＿＿＿＿＿＿＿＿＿。

（六）从事……（工作／事业／研究／活动）(to engage in a particular kind of work or cause)

> ✍ 从事, "to engage in", is a more formal verb than 做. This structure, introduced in Lesson 3, often refers to a serious undertaking such as a career, professional activity, or research endeavor. Typical objects for 从事 include 工作 (work), 事业 (cause, undertaking), and 研究 (research), etc.

☞ 还有呢，就是我跟我的太太都是从事艺术教育的或是艺术活动的，这也算个特点哪。

1、他从事钢琴教学差不多十年了。
   He has taught piano for about 10 years.
2、从事电脑研究在中国越来越普遍。
   Engaging in computer research is getting more and more common in China.

问：为什么他对文学研究那么有兴趣？
答：因为＿＿＿＿＿＿＿＿＿＿＿＿＿。

（七）（在）……之余 (in one's spare time, when not doing something)

> ✍ 在……之余, "in one's spare time", "when not doing something", is usually used in written or formal Chinese to indicate a time frame for an event or action. The phrase inserted between 在 and 之余 is often an action verb such as 工作, 上课, or 学习. 在……之余 can be placed either before or after the subject of the main clause. Use of 在 is optional. Example: 练琴之余，他常常作曲. (When not playing the piano, he often composes music.)

☞ 在她上課之餘，覺得自己應當對社會上儀表美的教育也負有責任，所以她在校內校外都有課，回家還有一大堆的家務事。

1、在上課之餘，他還寫了五本書。

He was able to write five books in his spare time after classes.

2、在工作之餘，他常常去街上幫他媳婦賣快餐。

When not working, he often helps his wife sell fast food on the street.

問：現在中國人的工作日從六天改成了五天，工作之餘，人們都做些甚麼？

答：據我了解，＿＿＿＿＿＿＿＿＿＿＿＿＿＿＿＿＿＿＿＿。

（八）説老實話 (to tell you the truth)

> ✍ 説老實話 is a topic starter meaning "to tell you the truth". It is most often used in spoken contexts and is positioned either before or after the subject of the main clause. This phrase is interchangeable with 老實説. Example: 説老實話，我對這種情況並不了解. (To be honest, I really don't understand these kinds of situations.)

☞ 人藝的舞台，説老實話，我覺得是我生命的一部分。

1、説老實話，土葬對環境並不好。

To tell you the truth, earth burial is not actually good for the environment.

2、説老實話，人從自然來，當然應該回到自然裡去。

When you think about it, people come from nature and should certainly return to nature.

問：你為甚麼讓你的父母海葬？

答：＿＿＿＿＿＿＿＿＿＿＿＿＿＿＿＿。

（九）讓……驚喜（／吃驚）的是…… (what amazes someone is, what is surprising is)

> ✍ 讓……驚喜（／吃驚）的是, "what amazes someone is" or "what is surprising is", is a causative structure. It is a clause which modifies a noun, 事情, but 事情 is usually omitted from this pattern. Example: 讓我驚喜的（事情）是他昨天就來了. (What amazes me is that he just showed up yesterday.) Other adjectives can also be used instead of 驚喜 or 吃驚, as in 讓我高興的是…… (what makes me happy is), 讓我興奮的是…… (what excites me is). Unlike in English, no subject can be placed before 讓.

☞ 哎，對了，讓我驚喜的是他前些日子在學校裡給同學導演過話劇《白毛女》，和《駱駝祥子》的片段，居然還得了個一等獎。這事我和他媽原本可一點也不知道。

250

☞ 在她上课之余，觉得自己应当对社会上仪表美的教育也负有责任，所以她在校内校外都有课，回家还有一大堆的家务事。

1、在上课之余，他还写了五本书。

He was able to write five books in his spare time after classes.

2、在工作之余，他常常去街上帮他媳妇卖快餐。

When not working, he often helps his wife sell fast food on the street.

问：现在中国人的工作日从六天改成了五天，工作之余，人们都做些什么？
答：据我了解，_____。

（八）说老实话 (to tell you the truth)

> ✍ 说老实话 is a topic starter meaning "to tell you the truth". It is most often used in spoken contexts and is positioned either before or after the subject of the main clause. This phrase is interchangeable with 老实说. Example: 说老实话，我对这种情况并不了解. (To be honest, I really don't understand these kinds of situations.)

☞ 人艺的舞台，说老实话，我觉得是我生命的一部分。

1、说老实话，土葬对环境并不好。

To tell you the truth, earth burial is not actually good for the environment.

2、说老实话，人从自然来，当然应该回到自然里去。

When you think about it, people come from nature and should certainly return to nature.

问：你为什么让你的父母海葬？
答：_____。

（九）让……惊喜（／吃惊）的是…… (what amazes someone is, what is surprising is)

> ✍ 让……惊喜（／吃惊）的是, "what amazes someone is" or "what is surprising is", is a causative structure. It is a clause which modifies a noun, 事情, but 事情 is usually omitted from this pattern. Example: 让我惊喜的（事情）是他昨天就来了. (What amazes me is that he just showed up yesterday.) Other adjectives can also be used instead of 惊喜 or 吃惊, as in 让我高兴的是…… (what makes me happy is), 让我兴奋的是…… (what excites me is). Unlike in English, no subject can be placed before 让.

☞ 哎，对了，让我惊喜的是他前些日子在学校里给同学导演过话剧《白毛女》，和《骆驼祥子》的片段，居然还得了个一等奖。这事我和他妈原本可一点也不知道。

1、讓我們驚喜的是這個殘疾孩子居然成了有名的企業家。

What surprises us is that this handicapped child has become such a famous entrepreneur.

2、讓他的父母驚喜的是這個孩子能自食其力了。

What surprises his parents is that the child is so self-reliant.

問：你們難道不知道老張的女兒去日本參加鋼琴比賽了？

答：我知道，她不但去了日本，＿＿＿＿＿＿＿＿＿＿＿＿＿＿。

（十）受（到）……（的）薰陶 (to be cultivated by, to be nurtured by)

✍ 受（到）……的薰陶, "to be cultivated by" or "to be nurtured by", is generally translated as a passive sentence in English. Use of 到 after 受 indicates completion. 薰陶 is usually modified by nouns related to art, culture, or family tradition, which must be positive or special in meaning, as in 受到父母的薰陶 (nurtured by one's father and mother), 受到音樂的薰陶 (trained in music), 受到傳統文化的薰陶 (instructed in traditional culture). This pattern differs from 受到……影響 in the sense that 影響 can be either positive or negative.

☞ 我小時候受藝術薰陶，非常喜歡戲劇，我覺得我的條件比我爸好，我希望將來能在這方面超過我爸。

1、他從小受父母的薰陶，特別喜愛電影和電視劇藝術。

His parents have encouraged his talents since he was little, so he especially likes the art of film and television.

2、他的孩子們從小就受到中國文化的薰陶，特別崇拜中國文化。

His children have been exposed to traditional Chinese culture since they were little, so now they adore it.

問：你怎麼這麼熱愛中國的文化，而且這麼努力地學中文？

答：＿＿＿＿＿＿＿＿＿＿＿＿＿＿＿＿＿＿＿。

（十一）（在……方面）超過 (to surpass someone or something in the area or field of)

✍ 超過, "to surpass", is a verb which can either be used alone or take 在……方面 to indicate a specific aspect in which someone or something is surpassed. Examples: 在電腦方面，日本的發展要超過美國。 (Japan is going to surpass the United States in the computer field.) 你想超過你的老師嗎？ (Do you want to surpass your teacher?) 方面 can be used interchangeably with 上, e.g., 在藝術方面 can also be 在藝術上. The verb 超過 is rarely negated with 不. It is more common to use 不能 or 沒有 for negation. Example: 在經濟方面，中國的發展還沒有超過美國。 (In the area of economics, China's development still has not surpassed that of the United States.)

☞ 我小時候受藝術薰陶，非常喜歡戲劇，我覺得我的條件比我爸好，我希望將來能在這方面超過我爸。

1、让我们惊喜的是这个残疾孩子居然成了有名的企业家。
What surprises us is that this handicapped child has become such a famous entrepreneur.

2、让他的父母惊喜的是这个孩子能自食其力了。
What surprises his parents is that the child is so self-reliant.

问：你们难道不知道老张的女儿去日本参加钢琴比赛了？
答：我知道，她不但去了日本，＿＿＿＿＿＿＿＿＿＿＿＿＿＿＿＿。

（十）受（到）……（的）熏陶 (to be cultivated by, to be nurtured by)

✍ 受（到）……的熏陶, "to be cultivated by" or "to be nurtured by", is generally translated as a passive sentence in English. Use of 到 after 受 indicates completion. 熏陶 is usually modified by nouns related to art, culture, or family tradition, which must be positive or special in meaning, as in 受到父母的熏陶 (nurtured by one's father and mother), 受到音乐的熏陶 (trained in music), 受到传统文化的熏陶 (instructed in traditional culture). This pattern differs from 受到……影响 in the sense that 影响 can be either positive or negative.

☞ 我小时候受艺术熏陶，非常喜欢戏剧，我觉得我的条件比我爸好，我希望将来能在这方面超过我爸。

1、他从小受父母的熏陶，特别喜爱电影和电视剧艺术。
His parents have encouraged his talents since he was little, so he especially likes the art of film and television.

2、他的孩子们从小就受到中国文化的熏陶，特别崇拜中国文化。
His children have been exposed to traditional Chinese culture since they were little, so now they adore it.

问：你怎么这么热爱中国的文化，而且这么努力地学中文？
答：＿＿＿＿＿＿＿＿＿＿＿＿＿＿＿＿＿＿＿＿＿。

（十一）（在……方面）超过 (to surpass someone or something in the area or field of)

✍ 超过, "to surpass", is a verb which can either be used alone or take 在……方面 to indicate a specific aspect in which someone or something is surpassed. Examples: 在电脑方面，日本的发展要超过美国。 (Japan is going to surpass the United States in the computer field.) 你想超过你的老师吗？ (Do you want to surpass your teacher?) 方面 can be used interchangeably with 上, e.g., 在艺术方面 can also be 在艺术上. The verb 超过 is rarely negated with 不. It is more common to use 不能 or 没有 for negation. Example: 在经济方面，中国的发展还没有超过美国。 (In the area of economics, China's development still has not surpassed that of the United States.)

☞ 我小时候受艺术熏陶，非常喜欢戏剧，我觉得我的条件比我爸好，我希望将来能在这方面超过我爸。

251

1、我想在藝術方面超過我的老師。

I want to surpass my teacher in the arts.

2、在科學技術方面，你覺得中國能超過美國嗎？

Do you believe that China can surpass the United States with respect to science and technology?

問：你認為在科學技術的發展方面，哪個國家有機會超過美國？

答：＿＿＿＿＿＿＿＿＿＿＿＿＿＿＿＿＿＿＿。

（十二）但願 (to wish, to hope, if only)

> ✍ 但願, "to wish", "to hope", "if only", always appears at the beginning of a sentence, before the subject, and indicates the speaker's silent or secret wish. Unlike "to wish" and "to hope" in English, 但願 cannot be preceded by a subject. Even when 但願 clearly reflects the speaker's wish, 我 is not used.

☞ 但願他將來能超過他老爸。

1、但願你能像你老爸那樣不簡單。

I hope you can become as accomplished as your father.

2、但願你們的生意越來越紅火。

I hope your business becomes more and more prosperous.

問：聽説你父親的公司最近幾年有一些問題，一直發展不起來。你很擔心嗎？

答：＿＿＿＿＿＿＿＿＿＿＿＿＿＿＿＿＿。

1、我想在艺术方面超过我的老师。

I want to surpass my teacher in the arts.

2、在科学技术方面，你觉得中国能超过美国吗？

Do you believe that China can surpass the United States with respect to science and technology?

问：你认为在科学技术的发展方面，哪个国家有机会超过美国？

答：＿＿＿＿＿＿＿＿＿＿＿＿＿＿＿＿＿＿＿。

（十二）但愿 (to wish, to hope, if only)

> ✍ 但愿, "to wish", "to hope", "if only", always appears at the beginning of a sentence, before the subject, and indicates the speaker's silent or secret wish. Unlike "to wish" and "to hope" in English, 但愿 cannot be preceded by a subject. Even when 但愿 clearly reflects the speaker's wish, 我 is not used.

☞ 但愿他将来能超过他老爸。

1、但愿你能象你老爸那样不简单。

I hope you can become as accomplished as your father.

2、但愿你们的生意越来越红火。

I hope your business becomes more and more prosperous.

问：听说你父亲的公司最近几年有一些问题，一直发展不起来。你很担心吗？

答：＿＿＿＿＿＿＿＿＿＿＿＿＿＿＿＿＿＿＿。

四、文化背景知識 Cultural Notes

1. 一個不少，兩個正好. This phrase dates back to the 1970s, perhaps earlier, when it was used to describe the most appropriate number of children a family should have. In other words, having one child was pretty good (不少), but having two was considered ideal (正好). China's more recent one-child policy has rendered this phase obsolete.

2. Almost all homes in traditional China had a central courtyard (院), around which (on all four sides) were placed various rooms and halls. The "compounds"(大雜院) mentioned in this lesson refer to such homes with courtyards. The difference is that several families (not just one) would share the rooms and halls around the courtyard.

3. Many Chinese share the idea that one has to remember or recall (憶) the bitter (苦) times of China's past before he or she can consider or appreciate (思) the good or "sweet" times of the present (甜). Hence the phrase 憶苦思甜. Note the parallel structure of the idiom: V + O, V + O.

4. 北京人藝 is an abbreviation of 北京人民藝術劇院, one of China's most famous opera houses. Plays (話劇) are considered an art form (藝術) in China, hence 藝術 appears in the name. Two famous plays performed there since the 1950s are 老舍's (1899-1966) *Teahouse* (茶館) and *Camel Xiangzi* (駱駝祥子).

5. *The White-Haired Girl* (白毛女) is a famous opera that was popular during the Cultural Revolution (1966-1976) in China. The play takes place during the Anti-Japanese War in China (1937-1945) and concerns the cruelty and exploitation of rich landlords in North China.

6. *Camel Xiangzi* (駱駝祥子), mentioned earlier, is a famous novel by 老舍. Published in 1938 and set in Beijing, the novel concerns a rickshaw puller's struggle, failure, and corruption.

四、文化背景知识 Cultural Notes

1. 一个不少，两个正好. This phrase dates back to the 1970s, perhaps earlier, when it was used to describe the most appropriate number of children a family should have. In other words, having one child was pretty good (不少), but having two was considered ideal (正好). China's more recent one-child policy has rendered this phase obsolete.

2. Almost all homes in traditional China had a central courtyard (院), around which (on all four sides) were placed various rooms and halls. The "compounds" (大杂院) mentioned in this lesson refer to such homes with courtyards. The difference is that several families (not just one) would share the rooms and halls around the courtyard.

3. Many Chinese share the idea that one has to remember or recall (忆) the bitter (苦) times of China's past before he or she can consider or appreciate (思) the good or "sweet" times of the present (甜). Hence the phrase 忆苦思甜. Note the parallel structure of the idiom: V + O, V + O.

4. 北京人艺 is an abbreviation of 北京人民艺术剧院, one of China's most famous opera houses. Plays (话剧) are considered an art form (艺术) in China, hence 艺术 appears in the name. Two famous plays performed there since the 1950s are 老舍's (1899-1966) *Teahouse* (茶馆) and *Camel Xiangzi* (骆驼祥子).

5. *The White-Haired Girl* (白毛女) is a famous opera that was popular during the Cultural Revolution (1966-1976) in China. The play takes place during the Anti-Japanese War in China (1937-1945) and concerns the cruelty and exploitation of rich landlords in North China.

6. *Camel Xiangzi* (骆驼祥子), mentioned earlier, is a famous novel by 老舍. Published in 1938 and set in Beijing, the novel concerns a rickshaw puller's struggle, failure, and corruption.

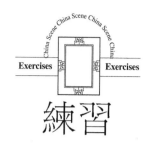

練習

語言結構 Structures

一、短語翻譯 (Phrase translation)

1. the characteristics of this family
2. to engage in art education
3. a term of address for husband and wife
4. the family burden
5. to work in the theater department
6. a Muslim family
7. TV plays and films
8. an important part of one's life
9. the front desk of the hotel
10. international trade company
11. the manager of public relations
12. to bravely explore and engage in things
13. a wide range of interests
14. to give the bassoon player first prize

二、聽力練習 (Listening comprehension)

1、聽寫 (Dictation)

2、聽錄音並回答問題 (Answering questions while listening to the audio CD)
  (1) 現在的年輕人有甚麼特點？
  (2) 談談小李畢業後做了些甚麼事情？為甚麼説他能代表中國的新一代年輕人？
  (3) 在美國有很多人靠自己的本事創辦公司，你認識或者聽説過這樣的人嗎？請你用自己的話談談他（她）的故事。

练习

语言结构 Structures

一、短语翻译 (Phrase translation)

1. the characteristics of this family
2. to engage in art education
3. a term of address for husband and wife
4. the family burden
5. to work in the theater department
6. a Muslim family
7. TV plays and films
8. an important part of one's life
9. the front desk of the hotel
10. international trade company
11. the manager of public relations
12. to bravely explore and engage in things
13. a wide range of interests
14. to give the bassoon player first prize

二、听力练习 (Listening comprehension)

1、听写 (Dictation)

2、听录音并回答问题 (Answering questions while listening to the audio CD)
   (1) 现在的年轻人有什么特点？
   (2) 谈谈小李毕业后做了些什么事情？为什么说他能代表中国的新一代年轻人？
   (3) 在美国有很多人靠自己的本事创办公司，你认识或者听说过这样的人吗？请你用自己的话谈谈他（她）的故事。

三、填空 (Fill in the blanks)

憶苦思甜、敢闖敢幹、普普通通、調皮搗蛋

　　我出生在一個＿＿＿＿＿＿的家庭，每次我不聽話，＿＿＿＿＿＿的時候，爸爸總要給我＿＿＿＿＿＿，說他小時侯多苦多不好，哪能像我這樣想幹甚麼就幹甚麼。我說：“只有這樣，長大才能＿＿＿＿＿＿！”

四、完成句子 (Complete the sentences)

1、　　Ａ：我問你“老公”到底是甚麼意思？
　　　　Ｂ：＿＿＿＿＿＿＿＿＿＿＿＿＿＿＿＿＿＿
　　　　（説起來……；對……的稱謂）

2、　　Ａ：你出身在一個甚麼家庭？
　　　　Ｂ：一個藝術家庭。＿＿＿＿＿＿＿＿＿＿＿＿＿
　　　　（受……的薰陶；在……超過……）

3、　　Ａ：你除了工作以外，還做些甚麼？
　　　　Ｂ：＿＿＿＿＿＿＿＿＿＿＿＿＿＿＿＿＿＿＿
　　　　（説老實話；在……之餘）

4、　　Ａ：為甚麼你彈鋼琴彈得這麼好？
　　　　Ｂ：因為＿＿＿＿＿＿＿＿＿＿＿＿＿＿＿＿＿
　　　　（得益於……；但願……）

五、閱讀短文、回答問題 (Answering questions based on the reading passages)

　　　　我的家庭是一個普普通通的三口之家。這種“小家庭”得益於甚麼呢？用大家的話説，是得益於政府一家一個孩子的政策。説來呢，還真有意思，七十年代我們剛想生老二，組織一個四口之家，政府就開始提倡一家一個孩子。當時我們想，中國的人口問題的確太嚴重了，要是現在不控制，以後還了得嗎？我和我內人都是從事教育事業的人，我們對社會的人口控制也應該負有責任。順便説一下，“內人”是我們對太太的稱謂。再説我們在校內校外都有一大堆的責任，回家要操持的家務也不少，再要一個孩子，家裡家外的事會讓我們更忙碌。就這樣，我們就決定不要老二了，我不用説，你也可以想像我們做了甚麼才不要的老二。説實話，現在想起來還覺得有點遺憾呢。

三、填空 (Fill in the blanks)

忆苦思甜、敢闯敢干、普普通通、调皮捣蛋

我出生在一个_____的家庭，每次我不听话，_____的时候，爸爸总要给我_____，说他小时侯多苦多不好，哪能象我这样想干什么就干什么。我说："只有这样，长大才能_____！"

四、完成句子 (Complete the sentences)

1、 A：我问你"老公"到底是什么意思？
   B：_____
   （说起来……；对……的称谓）

2、 A：你出身在一个什么家庭？
   B：一个艺术家庭。_____
   （受……的熏陶；在……超过……）

3、 A：你除了工作以外，还做些什么？
   B：_____
   （说老实话；在……之余）

4、 A：为什么你弹钢琴弹得这么好？
   B：因为_____
   （得益于……；但愿……）

五、阅读短文、回答问题 (Answering questions based on the reading passages)

我的家庭是一个普普通通的三口之家。这种"小家庭"得益于什么呢？用大家的话说，是得益于政府一家一个孩子的政策。说来呢，还真有意思，七十年代我们刚想生老二，组织一个四口之家，政府就开始提倡一家一个孩子。当时我们想，中国的人口问题的确太严重了，要是现在不控制，以后还了得吗？我和我内人都是从事教育事业的人，我们对社会的人口控制也应该负有责任。顺便说一下，"内人"是我们对太太的称谓。再说我们在校内校外都有一大堆的责任，回家要操持的家务也不少，再要一个孩子，家里家外的事会让我们更忙碌。就这样，我们就决定不要老二了，我不用说，你也可以想象我们做了什么才不要的老二。说实话，现在想起来还觉得有点遗憾呢。

問題
　　(1)用兩個方面的原因説明為甚麼作者有一個三口之家。
　　(2)你對自己將來的小家庭有甚麼安排和打算？

　　　　周裕鍇是四川大學自己培養出來的教授。1984年他研究生畢業後就留在學校當教師，專門研究古典文學。從事教學科研工作十一年來，他出版了兩本書，其中由上海人民出版社出版的《中國禪宗與詩歌》，被評為華東地區優秀圖書獎，四川省社會科學優秀成果三等獎，並一版再版。
　　　　周裕鍇教授的生活很簡單，五年前他搬進現在的住房，屋子很小，一間廚房用布帘子一拉改做保姆的臥室。他不好意思地向記者説："去年我是又做飯又帶小孩，現在小孩上幼兒園，我又要讀書教書，實在忙不過來，只好咬著牙請了保姆。"
　　　　不用説，周裕鍇的家在這個大城市算不上富有，但他願意在寂寞和清貧中默默地追求著他所熱愛的專業。

問題
　　翻譯全文

六、翻譯 (Translate sentences)

1. Ever since the establishment of the flower shop, he and his wife have been busy working with customers. He had to shift the burden of taking care of the house and educating the children to his mother.

2. He felt that he is responsible for the art education and artistic activities of the country, so he wrote a book on the art of Chinese plays in his spare time after work.

3. To tell you the truth, his younger brother has done quite a lot of mischievous things at his school. This younger brother said he wanted to surpass his "dear old dad" in this respect.

4. What surprises me is that his girlfriend has a wide range of interests and a passion for art. She was awarded first prize for directing a famous play in Beijing.

问题

    (1) 用两个方面的原因说明为什么作者有一个三口之家。

    (2) 你对自己将来的小家庭有什么安排和打算？

        周裕锴是四川大学自己培养出来的教授。1984年他研究生毕业后就留在学校当教师，专门研究古典文学。从事教学科研工作十一年来，他出版了两本书，其中由上海人民出版社出版的《中国禅宗与诗歌》，被评为华东地区优秀图书奖，四川省社会科学优秀成果三等奖，并一版再版。

        周裕锴教授的生活很简单，五年前他搬进现在的住房，屋子很小，一间厨房用布帘子一拉改做保姆的卧室。他不好意思地向记者说：“去年我是又做饭又带小孩，现在小孩上幼儿园，我又要读书教书，实在忙不过来，只好咬着牙请了保姆。”

        不用说，周裕锴的家在这个大城市算不上富有，但他愿意在寂寞和清贫中默默地追求着他所热爱的专业。

问题

    翻译全文

六、翻译 (Translate sentences)

1. Ever since the establishment of the flower shop, he and his wife have been busy working with customers. He had to shift the burden of taking care of the house and educating the children to his mother.

2. He felt that he is responsible for the art education and artistic activities of the country, so he wrote a book on the art of Chinese plays in his spare time after work.

3. To tell you the truth, his younger brother has done quite a lot of mischievous things at his school. This younger brother said he wanted to surpass his "dear old dad" in this respect.

4. What surprises me is that his girlfriend has a wide range of interests and a passion for art. She was awarded first prize for directing a famous play in Beijing.

語言實踐 ⋮ Practice

一、根據課文回答問題 (Answering questions based on the dialogue)

1、譚宗堯的家建立多少年了？有甚麼特點？
2、譚宗堯的太太是做甚麼的？談談她的工作和生活。
3、譚宗堯自己的工作、生活經歷是甚麼？
4、譚波是誰？她有些甚麼經歷？她是一個甚麼樣的人？
5、譚宗堯的老二叫甚麼？他現在怎麼樣？有甚麼愛好？
6、譚濤說他比他爸條件好，是甚麼意思？
7、甚麼是“後生可畏”、“不盡長江滾滾來”？

二、活動 (Activities)

談談你的中國家庭，或者朋友家。

1、幾口人？
2、每個人都從事甚麼？熱愛甚麼？
3、每個人都有甚麼工作和生活經歷？
4、這個家有甚麼特點？

三、討論題 (Topics for discussion)

1、你所知道的中國家庭跟美國家庭有甚麼不同？
2、譚宗堯一家是不是典型的中國家庭？他們家的生活能不能反映現在中國人的生活？為甚麼？

四、報告 (Presentation)

《我的中國爸爸（媽媽）》

语言实践 Practice

一、根据课文回答问题 (Answering questions based on the dialogue)

1、谭宗尧的家建立多少年了？有什么特点？
2、谭宗尧的太太是做什么的？谈谈她的工作和生活。
3、谭宗尧自己的工作、生活经历是什么？
4、谭波是谁？她有些什么经历？她是一个什么样的人？
5、谭宗尧的老二叫什么？他现在怎么样？有什么爱好？
6、谭涛说他比他爸条件好，是什么意思？
7、什么是"后生可畏"、"不尽长江滚滚来"？

二、活动 (Activities)

谈谈你的中国家庭，或者朋友家。

1、几口人？
2、每个人都从事什么？热爱什么？
3、每个人都有什么工作和生活经历？
4、这个家有什么特点？

三、讨论题 (Topics for discussion)

1、你所知道的中国家庭跟美国家庭有什么不同？
2、谭宗尧一家是不是典型的中国家庭？他们家的生活能不能反映现在中国人的生活？为什么？

四、报告 (Presentation)

《我的中国爸爸（妈妈）》

五、看圖討論 (Picto-discussion)

五、看图讨论 (Picto-discussion)

1

2

3

4

5

第十三課

電影導演張藝謀

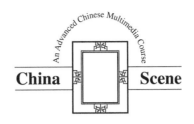

第十三课

电影导演张艺谋

RED SORGHUM

課文

一、對話 Dialogs

趙明：白石，你在學甚麼？

白石：我在練習我的中國字，明天有一個考試。

趙明：我看現在刮起了一股中國風。很多人在談中國，也有很多人在學中文。

白石：是啊，很多人開始對中國的文化、藝術、政治、經濟有了興趣，我就是其中的
一個。

趙明：這種中國熱是不是從中國電影熱開始的？

白石：我想有一定的關係。中國電影從88年以來，連連在國際電影節上提名、獲獎，
比如《紅高粱》、《菊豆》等，中國電影從來沒有像今天這樣受到海外人士的
矚目。

趙明：這是不是都應該歸功於中國的第五代導演，比如張藝謀、陳凱歌、田壯壯等？

白石：對。他們這批導演都是文化大革命以後電影學院畢業的大學生。他們追求自然、
真實，從新的角度反映社會。但是正是因為這些，他們在國內受到很多人的批
評。

趙明：是嗎？

白石：是啊，從我們今天學的這課電視採訪裡就能知道一些張藝謀的壓力。

生詞

張藝謀	(zhāng yì móu)	*N.*	Zhang Yimou, name of a person, a famous film director in China 人名
白石	(bái shí)	*N.*	Bai Shi, name of a person 人名
刮	(guā)	*V.*	to blow
股	(gǔ)	*Classifier.*	a stream of, a classifier for wind, water, etc.

课文

一、对话  Dialogs

赵明：白石，你在学什么？

白石：我在练习我的中国字，明天有一个考试。

赵明：我看现在刮起了一股中国风。很多人在谈中国，也有很多人在学中文。

白石：是啊，很多人开始对中国的文化、艺术、政治、经济有了兴趣，我就是其中的一个。

赵明：这种中国热是不是从中国电影热开始的？

白石：我想有一定的关系。中国电影从88年以来，连连在国际电影节上提名、获奖，比如《红高粱》、《菊豆》等，中国电影从来没有象今天这样受到海外人士的瞩目。

赵明：这是不是都应该归功于中国的第五代导演，比如张艺谋、陈凯歌、田壮壮等？

白石：对。他们这批导演都是文化大革命以后电影学院毕业的大学生。他们追求自然、真实，从新的角度反映社会。但是正是因为这些，他们在国内受到很多人的批评。

赵明：是吗？

白石：是啊，从我们今天学的这课电视采访里就能知道一些张艺谋的压力。

生词

张艺谋	(zhāng yì móu)	N.	Zhang Yimou, name of a person, a famous film director in China 人名
白石	(bái shí)	N.	Bai Shi, name of a person 人名
刮	(guā)	V.	to blow
股	(gǔ)	Classifier.	a stream of, a classifier for wind, water, etc.

連連	(lián lián)	*Adv.*	one after another, constantly
電影節	(diàn yǐng jié)	*N.*	film festival
提名	(tí míng)	*VO/N.*	to nominate; nomination
獲獎	(huò jiǎng)	*VO.*	to win the award
紅高粱	(hóng gāo liáng)	*NP.*	*Red Sorgham*, the name of a film directed by Zhang Yimou
菊豆	(jú dòu)	*N.*	*Ju Dou*, name of a person, the name of a film directed by Zhang Yimou 人名
海外	(hǎi wài)	*N.*	overseas
人士	(rén shì)	*N.*	people
矚目	(zhǔ mù)	*VO.*	to receive attention, to be focused closely on
歸功於	(guī gōng yú)	*VP.*	to give the credit to, attribute to
代	(dài)	*N.*	generation
陳凱歌	(chén kǎi gē)	*N.*	Chen Kaige, name of a person, a famous film director in China 人名
田壯壯	(tián zhuàng zhuàng)	*N.*	Tian Zhuangzhuang, name of a person, a famous film director in China 人名
批	(pī)	*Classifier.*	classifier for a group
文化大革命	(wén huà dà gé mìng)	*NP.*	the Cultural Revolution
角度	(jiǎo dù)	*N.*	angle, perspective
批評	(pī píng)	*N/V.*	criticism; to criticize

二、電視原文 TV original

訪張藝謀

（根據原文改編）

1988年電影《紅高粱》在西柏林國際電影節上榮獲金熊獎。打那以後，中國電影連連在國際性電影節上提名獲獎，可以説中國電影從來沒有像今天這樣受海外人士所矚目。世界影壇刮起中國風，應該歸功於第五代導演。

在這個導演群中，張藝謀尤其受到觀眾和輿論界的關注。前不久，記者來到電影《活著》劇組的外邊。

在一座小山坡上，這位被譽為影壇奇才的導演接受了我們的採訪。

连连	(lián lián)	*Adv.*	one after another, constantly
电影节	(diàn yǐng jié)	*N.*	film festival
提名	(tí míng)	*VO/N.*	to nominate; nomination
获奖	(huò jiǎng)	*VO.*	to win the award
红高粱	(hóng gāo liáng)	*NP.*	*Red Sorgham*, the name of a film directed by Zhang Yimou
菊豆	(jú dòu)	*N.*	*Ju Dou*, name of a person, the name of a film directed by Zhang Yimou 人名
海外	(hǎi wài)	*N.*	overseas
人士	(rén shì)	*N.*	people
瞩目	(zhǔ mù)	*VO.*	to receive attention, to be focused closely on
归功于	(guī gōng yú)	*VP.*	to give the credit to, attribute to
代	(dài)	*N.*	generation
陈凯歌	(chén kǎi gē)	*N.*	Chen Kaige, name of a person, a famous film director in China 人名
田壮壮	(tián zhuàng zhuàng)	*N.*	Tian Zhuangzhuang, name of a person, a famous film director in China 人名
批	(pī)	*Classifier.*	classifier for a group
文化大革命	(wén huà dà gé mìng)	*NP.*	the Cultural Revolution
角度	(jiǎo dù)	*N.*	angle, perspective
批评	(pī píng)	*N/V.*	criticism; to criticize

二、电视原文 TV original

访张艺谋
（根据原文改编）

　　1988年电影《红高粱》在西柏林国际电影节上荣获金熊奖。打那以后，中国电影连连在国际性电影节上提名获奖，可以说中国电影从来没有象今天这样受海外人士所瞩目。世界影坛刮起中国风，应该归功于第五代导演。

　　在这个导演群中，张艺谋尤其受到观众和舆论界的关注。前不久，记者来到电影《活着》剧组的外边。

　　在一座小山坡上，这位被誉为影坛奇才的导演接受了我们的采访。

（採訪）

記者：　　“有人批評您的電影，是拍給外國人看的。您如何看待⁽¹⁾這種批評？”

張藝謀：　“我從來不接受這種批評。這是因為，我自己認為外國人很多，除了中國人都是外國人。你算哪一個國家？英國、法國、意大利、美國，都不一樣，日本，都不一樣。你就說為外國人拍，你為誰拍呀？而且我認為全世界一百多個國家，他們的口味都不一樣，他們的興趣又都不一樣。當你不知道人家需要甚麼的時候，你怎麼可能說是我去迎合你。所以這很難。你想這樣做也很難。這是一個客觀（原因）；那麼還有一個主觀的，就是我自己心裡頭，從來沒有去想這樣的事情。我們去看一個故事，我們對這個題材發生興趣，你會很自然地去感覺它。實際上⁽²⁾因為我是中國人，我也不會講外語，每年出去的機會也不多，長期在中國生活，我會很自然地從一個中國人的心理去感覺。”

記者：　　“有人說您的電影是悲劇的宿命模式，您同意這樣的說法嗎？”

張藝謀：　“我倒不是很完全同意的。我覺得可能有一兩部作品是這樣子的。但總的來說，像我自己拍電影，我一般沒有一個長期的計劃，也就是說我明年幹甚麼，後年幹甚麼，大後年幹甚麼，這個計劃排滿十年，我要拍這麼些東西，我沒有計劃過。一般我都是讓自己很隨便，看到甚麼喜歡的東西，一有興趣就拍。所以像現在我這部戲《活著》拍完以後，下一步拍甚麼，我現在一時還沒有甚麼目標，所以總是希望有不同的變化，不同的要求，這樣才能刺激你自己，創作上就可以更容易發揮些。所以這樣的話，這種悲劇或宿命的題材不是我一直要堅持的。”

✎ **Notes** ⁽¹⁾看待 vs. 看: 看待 means "to treat", "to deal with", "to regard", as in 你怎麼看待這個問題？(How will you deal with this problem?) 待 in 看待 is drawn from 對待, which means "to treat", "to act toward". In addition to its other meanings, 看 can be used to mean 看待. For example, the above example could also be rendered 你怎麼看這個問題. 看待 carries a more formal tone, while 看 is more colloquial. Context and common sense usually indicate when 看 is being used to mean 看待.

⁽²⁾實際上 means "as a matter of fact", "in fact", "in reality", "actually". It often appears at the beginning of a sentence, as in 實際上因為我是一個中國人…… (In fact, because I'm Chinese, ...) The expression 事實上 can be used interchangeably with 實際上. 實際上 and 事實上 can both be used to modify nouns, as in 事實上的朋友 (true friends), 事實上的承認 (*de facto* recognition).

（采访）

记者：　　“有人批评您的电影，是拍给外国人看的。您如何看待[1]这种批评？”

张艺谋：　“我从来不接受这种批评。这是因为，我自己认为外国人很多，除了中国人都是外国人。你算哪一个国家？英国、法国、意大利、美国，都不一样，日本，都不一样。你就说为外国人拍，你为谁拍呀？而且我认为全世界一百多个国家，他们的口味都不一样，他们的兴趣又都不一样。当你不知道人家需要什么的时候，你怎么可能说是我去迎合你。所以这很难。你想这样做也很难。这是一个客观（原因）；那么还有一个主观的，就是我自己心里头，从来没有去想这样的事情。我们去看一个故事，我们对这个题材发生兴趣，你会很自然地去感觉它。实际上[2]因为我是中国人，我也不会讲外语，每年出去的机会也不多，长期在中国生活，我会很自然地从一个中国人的心理去感觉。”

记者：　　“有人说您的电影是悲剧的宿命模式，您同意这样的说法吗？”

张艺谋：　“我倒不是很完全同意的。我觉得可能有一两部作品是这样子的。但总的来说，象我自己拍电影，我一般没有一个长期的计划，也就是说我明年干什么，后年干什么，大后年干什么，这个计划排满十年，我要拍这么些东西，我没有计划过。一般我都是让自己很随便，看到什么喜欢的东西，一有兴趣就拍。所以象现在我这部戏《活着》拍完以后，下一步拍什么，我现在一时还没有什么目标，所以总是希望有不同的变化，不同的要求，这样才能刺激你自己，创作上就可以更容易发挥些。所以这样的话，这种悲剧或宿命的题材不是我一直要坚持的。”

Notes [1]看待 vs. 看: 看待 means "to treat", "to deal with", "to regard", as in 你怎么看待这个问题？ (How will you deal with this problem?) 待 in 看待 is drawn from 对待, which means "to treat", "to act toward". In addition to its other meanings, 看 can be used to mean 看待. For example, the above example could also be rendered 你怎么看这个问题. 看待 carries a more formal tone, while 看 is more colloquial. Context and common sense usually indicate when 看 is being used to mean 看待.

[2]实际上 means "as a matter of fact", "in fact", "in reality", "actually". It often appears at the beginning of a sentence, as in 实际上因为我是一个中国人…… (In fact, because I'm Chinese, ...) The expression 事实上 can be used interchangeably with 实际上. 实际上 and 事实上 can both be used to modify nouns, as in 事实上的朋友 (true friends), 事实上的承认 (*de facto* recognition).

記者：　　"從您的作品可以看出您盡力使自己的每一部電影都有新的突破[3]，那麼《活著》有甚麼新的嘗試[4]嗎？"

張藝謀：　"我們看到的中國電影，過去的描寫，比如說，描寫文化大革命，描寫過去的五十年代我們所面臨的很多問題和經過的很多困難時候，差不多都是用傳統的、悲劇的方法去描寫，很沉重。那麼我們這一次呢，就試用一個新的角度，比如說我們不斷地[5]有些幽默。另外我們使政治的背景推得很遠。我們使這一家人呢永遠處於一個很溫馨的、很自然的、很可愛的一個情況，然後使他們呢，盡可能[6]地保持生活裡面很輕鬆的東西。這樣呢，試圖[7]用跟過去完全不同的角度來反映這個整個時代的變化。這次我們這樣處理這個題材更多的是基於希望拍出一種不同的感覺來。就是以前所有的中國電影在處理這種題材方面都是從正面角度，很直接的角度去反映。那麼我們就是想很間接地把注意力更多地放在普通人和普通家庭方面，更多的是他們的家庭生活，使他們個人，人和人之間的感情，使他們夫妻之間，父女之間，母子之間，中國人特別有的傳統親情關係，使這個東西作為最主要的部分，所以有必要使政治的東西放得很淡[8]。"

Notes [3]突破 can function either as a noun, as in 醫學上的突破 (medical breakthrough), or as a verb, as in 突破重重困難 (to surmount one difficulty after another).

[4]嘗試, literally "taste and try", is a formal term which functions either as a noun or a verb. As a noun, it means "attempt" or "try", as in 新的嘗試 (a new attempt). As a verb, 嘗試 means "to sample" or "to try". It takes a noun that refers to something significant or formal as its object, as in 嘗試各種方法 (try various approaches), 嘗試人生 (to live life to its fullest).

[5]不斷地 vs. 連連: 不斷地 and 連連 are both adverbial expressions used directly before a verb. 斷 by itself means "to end", "to stop", "to cut off"; 不斷地, "without stopping", "continuously", "endlessly", focuses on the constant occurrence of the same event, usually one that cannot be counted, as in 不斷地學習 (to study continuously), 不斷地加水 (to continuously add water). 連連 means "one after another", "in a row". It indicates the repetitive occurrence of an event or action and is often accompanied by expressions indicating frequency of an action. Example: 雨連連下了三天. (It rained for three days in a row.)

[6]盡可能: The word 盡 means "to exhaust", "to use up completely". It can precede nouns to form new adverbs, such as 盡量 (to the best of one's ability) andd 盡力 (with all one's strength), or 盡可能 "to exhaust all possibilities". Examples: 我要盡力地取得好成績. (I will try my hardest to get good grades.) 外面很冷，要盡可能讓孩子們待在家裡. (It's cold outside, so I will make every effort to keep the children inside.)

[7]試圖, "to try to" or "to attempt to", is a verb which must be followed by another verb. 試圖 is used in written Chinese to refer to someone's serious attempt to do something. Example: 我試圖說服她，但是沒有成功. (I tried to persuade her, but did not succeed.) 試 is a colloquial version of 試圖 and is used in expressions such as 試試看 and 試著. However, neither 試 nor 試圖 should be used as equivalents of the English verb "to try" in sentences such as "I tried to call you yesterday".

[8]When used to describe food, 淡 means "bland" or "tasteless" and usually suggests that a dish is not salty enough. Example: 這個菜太淡了. (This dish has no taste.) 淡 is also used to mean "treat lightly" or "treat with indifference", as in 他把錢看得很淡. (He treats money lightly.)

263

记者： "从您的作品可以看出您尽力使自己的每一部电影都有新的突破[3]，那么《活着》有什么新的尝试[4]吗？"

张艺谋： "我们看到的中国电影，过去的描写，比如说，描写文化大革命，描写过去的五十年代我们所面临的很多问题和经过的很多困难时候，差不多都是用传统的、悲剧的方法去描写，很沉重。那么我们这一次呢，就试用一个新的角度，比如说我们不断地[5]有些幽默。另外我们使政治的背景推得很远。我们使这一家人呢永远处于一个很温馨的、很自然的、很可爱的一个情况，然后使他们呢，尽可能[6]地保持生活里面很轻松的东西。这样呢，试图[7]用跟过去完全不同的角度来反映这个整个时代的变化。这次我们这样处理这个题材更多的是基于希望拍出一种不同的感觉来。就是以前所有的中国电影在处理这种题材方面都是从正面角度，很直接的角度去反映。那么我们就是想很间接地把注意力更多地放在普通人和普通家庭方面，更多的是他们的家庭生活，使他们个人，人和人之间的感情，使他们夫妻之间，父女之间，母子之间，中国人特别有的传统亲情关系，使这个东西作为最主要的部分，所以有必要使政治的东西放得很淡[8]。"

Notes [3]突破 can function either as a noun, as in 医学上的突破 (medical breakthrough), or as a verb, as in 突破重重困难 (to surmount one difficulty after another).

[4]尝试, literally "taste and try", is a formal term which functions either as a noun or a verb. As a noun, it means "attempt" or "try", as in 新的尝试 (a new attempt). As a verb, 尝试 means "to sample" or "to try". It takes a noun that refers to something significant or formal as its object, as in 尝试各种方法 (try various approaches), 尝试人生 (to live life to its fullest).

[5]不断地 vs. 连连: 不断地 and 连连 are both adverbial expressions used directly before a verb. 断 by itself means "to end", "to stop", "to cut off"; 不断地, "without stopping", "continuously", "endlessly", focuses on the constant occurrence of the same event, usually one that cannot be counted, as in 不断地学习 (to study continuously), 不断地加水 (to continuously add water). 连连 means "one after another", "in a row". It indicates the repetitive occurrence of an event or action and is often accompanied by expressions indicating frequency of an action. Example: 雨连连下了三天. (It rained for three days in a row.)

[6]尽可能: The word 尽 means "to exhaust", "to use up completely". It can precede nouns to form new adverbs, such as 尽量 (to the best of one's ability) and 尽力 (with all one's strength), or 尽可能 "to exhaust all possibilities". Examples: 我要尽力地取得好成绩. (I will try my hardest to get good grades.) 外面很冷，要尽可能让孩子们待在家里. (It's cold outside, so I will make every effort to keep the children inside.)

[7]试图, "to try to" or "to attempt to", is a verb which must be followed by another verb. 试图 is used in written Chinese to refer to someone's serious attempt to do something. Example: 我试图说服她，但是没有成功. (I tried to persuade her, but did not succeed.) 试 is a colloquial version of 试图 and is used in expressions such as 试试看 and 试着. However, neither 试 nor 试图 should be used as equivalents of the English verb "to try" in sentences such as "I tried to call you yesterday".

[8]When used to describe food, 淡 means "bland" or "tasteless" and usually suggests that a dish is not salty enough. Example: 这个菜太淡了. (This dish has no taste.) 淡 is also used to mean "treat lightly" or "treat with indifference", as in 他把钱看得很淡. (He treats money lightly.)

生詞

西柏林	(xī bó lín)	N.	West Berlin 地名
榮獲	(róng huò)	V.	to win the award of
金熊獎	(jīn xióng jiǎng)	N.	Golden Bear Award
影壇	(yǐng tán)	N.	film circle
輿論界	(yú lùn jiè)	NP.	opinion poll, public opinion
關注	(guān zhù)	N.	concern, attention
《活著》	(huó zhe)	N.	*To Live*, name of a film by Zhang Yimou
劇組	(jù zǔ)	N.	production team
山坡	(shān pō)	N.	hillside
被譽為	(bèi yù wéi)	VP.	to be honored as
奇才	(qí cái)	N.	unusual talent
口味	(kǒu wèi)	N.	taste
迎合	(yíng hé)	V.	to please, to satisfy
客觀	(kè guān)	Adj.	objective
原因	(yuán yīn)	N.	reason, cause
主觀	(zhǔ guān)	Adj.	subjective
題材	(tí cái)	N.	theme, topic
悲劇	(bēi jù)	N.	tragedy, tragic
宿命	(sù mìng)	Adj.	fatal, fatalistic
模式	(mó shì)	N.	model, pattern
目標	(mù biāo)	N.	goal, aim
刺激	(cì jī)	V/Adj.	to excite, to stimulate; stimulating
創作	(chuàng zuò)	V.	to create, creation
突破	(tū pò)	V.	to break through
嘗試	(cháng shì)	N.	attempt, try
描寫	(miáo xiě)	V.	to describe, description
面臨	(miàn lín)	V.	to face
傳統	(chuán tǒng)	Adj.	traditional
沉重	(chén zhòng)	Adj.	heavy, serious
幽默	(yōu mò)	N/Adj	humor; humorous
背景	(bèi jǐng)	N.	background
推	(tuī)	V.	to push
溫馨	(wēn xīn)	Adj.	warm and pleasant
時代	(shí dài)	N.	era

生词

西柏林	(xī bó lín)	N.	West Berlin 地名
荣获	(róng huò)	V.	to win the award of
金熊奖	(jīn xióng jiǎng)	N.	Golden Bear Award
影坛	(yǐng tán)	N.	film circle
舆论界	(yú lùn jiè)	NP.	opinion poll, public opinion
关注	(guān zhù)	N.	concern, attention
《活着》	(huó zhe)	N.	*To Live*, name of a film by Zhang Yimou
剧组	(jù zǔ)	N.	production team
山坡	(shān pō)	N.	hillside
被誉为	(bèi yù wéi)	VP.	to be honored as
奇才	(qí cái)	N.	unusual talent
口味	(kǒu wèi)	N.	taste
迎合	(yíng hé)	V.	to please, to satisfy
客观	(kè guān)	Adj.	objective
原因	(yuán yīn)	N.	reason, cause
主观	(zhǔ guān)	Adj.	subjective
题材	(tí cái)	N.	theme, topic
悲剧	(bēi jù)	N.	tragedy, tragic
宿命	(sù mìng)	Adj.	fatal, fatalistic
模式	(mó shì)	N.	model, pattern
目标	(mù biāo)	N.	goal, aim
刺激	(cì jī)	V/Adj.	to excite, to stimulate; stimulating
创作	(chuàng zuò)	V.	to create, creation
突破	(tū pò)	V.	to break through
尝试	(cháng shì)	N.	attempt, try
描写	(miáo xiě)	V.	to describe, description
面临	(miàn lín)	V.	to face
传统	(chuán tǒng)	Adj.	traditional
沉重	(chén zhòng)	Adj.	heavy, serious
幽默	(yōu mò)	N/Adj	humor; humorous
背景	(bèi jǐng)	N.	background
推	(tuī)	V.	to push
温馨	(wēn xīn)	Adj.	warm and pleasant
时代	(shí dài)	N.	era

處理	(chǔ lǐ)	*V.*	to handle, to deal with
基於	(jī yú)	*VP.*	to be based on
正面	(zhèng miàn)	*N.*	front side
直接	(zhí jiē)	*Adj.*	direct, immediate
反映	(fǎn yìng)	*V.*	to reflect
間接	(jiàn jiē)	*Adj.*	indirect
親情	(qīn qíng)	*N.*	blood relationship
淡	(dàn)	*Adj.*	light, thin

处理	(chǔ lǐ)	*V.*	to handle, to deal with
基于	(jī yú)	*VP.*	to be based on
正面	(zhèng miàn)	*N.*	front side
直接	(zhí jiē)	*Adj.*	direct, immediate
反映	(fǎn yìng)	*V.*	to reflect
间接	(jiàn jiē)	*Adj.*	indirect
亲情	(qīn qíng)	*N.*	blood relationship
淡	(dàn)	*Adj.*	light, thin

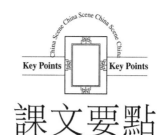

課文要點

一、詞語解釋 Words and Phrases

（一）文言詞、方言詞 (Classical Chinese and dialect)

1、如何＝怎麼樣
　☞ 您如何看待這種批評？
2、打＝從
　☞ 打那以後，中國電影連連在國際性電影節上提名獲獎。
3、於＝到、從、比、在
　☞ 歸功於、得益於、莫過於、位於

（二）慣用語 (fixed expressions)

◆ 影壇奇才: a unusually talented person in film circles

二、書面語、正式語、口語對照表 Written/formal/colloquial Comparison

	書面／正式語	口語		書面／正式語	口語
1	獲獎	得獎	5	影壇	電影界
2	受到矚目	受到注意	6	奇才	少有的天才
3	歸功於	是…的功勞	7	如何	怎麼樣
4	被譽為	人們稱讚…是	8	處於	處在

＊方言、普通話對照表 Putonghua/dialect Comparison

	方言	普通話		方言	普通話
1	打那以後	從那以後			

课文要点

一、词语解释 Words and Phrases

（一）文言词、方言词 (Classical Chinese and dialect)

1、如何 = 怎么样
　　☞ 您如何看待这种批评？
2、打 = 从
　　☞ 打那以后，中国电影连连在国际性电影节上提名获奖。
3、于 = 到、从、比、在
　　☞ 归功于、得益于、莫过于、位于

（二）惯用语 (fixed expressions)

◆ 影坛奇才: a unusually talented person in film circles

二、书面语、正式语、口语对照表 Written/formal/colloquial Comparison

	书面／正式语	口语		书面／正式语	口语
1	获奖	得奖	5	影坛	电影界
2	受到瞩目	受到注意	6	奇才	少有的天才
3	归功于	是…的功劳	7	如何	怎么样
4	被誉为	人们称赞…是	8	处于	处在

＊方言、普通话对照表 Putonghua/dialect Comparison

	方言	普通话		方言	普通话
1	打那以后	从那以后			

三、句型 Sentence Structures

（一）打那以後 (since then)

> ✍ 打那以後 "since then", is used mostly in colloquial Chinese, indicating the beginning of an event or action. A common written or literary version, 從此以後, was introduced in Lesson 1, and a similar colloquial expression, 打這以後, was discussed in Lesson 9, Pattern 9. This expression can be placed either before or after the subject of a main clause. Example: 小林打那以後變得更不愛說話了. (Since then, Xiao Lin has become more reserved.)

☞ 打那以後，中國電影連連在國際性電影節上提名獲獎，可以說中國電影從來沒有像今天這樣受海外人士所矚目。

1、打那以後，中國的鋼琴漸漸進入了老百姓家。

Since then, the piano has been gradually entering Chinese homes.

2、打那以後，他變得越來越怪僻。

Since then, he has become more and more eccentric.

問：從甚麼時候起，何茹的成績一天天好起來了？但是從這以後她對父親有甚麼看法？

答：＿＿＿＿＿＿＿＿＿＿＿＿＿＿＿＿＿＿＿＿＿＿＿＿。

（二）受（到）……的矚目（／關注／批評／重視／歡迎）(to receive attention from)

> ✍ This pattern is a variation on the use of 受 and 受到. Refer to Lesson 12, Pattern 9 for an explanation of how these expressions are used. Possible objects for 受 or 受到 in this pattern are primarily disyllabic verbs, such as 矚目, 關注, 批評, 重視, or 歡迎. This structure often carries a formal tone.

☞ 打那以後，中國電影連連在國際性電影節上提名獲獎，可以說中國電影從來沒有像今天這樣受海外人士所矚目。

1、中國的經濟發展受到全世界的矚目。

China's economic development has received attention from the whole world.

2、香港97回歸大陸問題受到全世界的關注。

The return of Hong Kong to Mainland China in 1997 received attention from the whole world.

問：現在亞洲的經濟情況不太好，其它的國家怎麼看這個問題？

答：＿＿＿＿＿＿＿＿＿＿＿＿＿＿＿＿＿＿＿＿＿＿＿＿。

三、句型 ⊗ Sentence Structures

（一）打那以后 (since then)

> ✍ 打那以后 "since then", is used mostly in colloquial Chinese, indicating the beginning of an event or action. A common written or literary version, 从此以后, was introduced in Lesson 1, and a similar colloquial expression, 打这以后, was discussed in Lesson 9, Pattern 9. This expression can be placed either before or after the subject of a main clause. Example: 小林打那以后变得更不爱说话了. (Since then, Xiao Lin has become more reserved.)

☞ 打那以后，中国电影连连在国际性电影节上提名获奖，可以说中国电影从来没有象今天这样受海外人士所瞩目。

1、打那以后，中国的钢琴渐渐进入了老百姓家。
Since then, the piano has been gradually entering Chinese homes.

2、打那以后，他变得越来越怪僻。
Since then, he has become more and more eccentric.

问：从什么时候起，何茹的成绩一天天好起来了？但是从这以后她对父亲有什么看法？
答：_____。

（二）受（到）……的瞩目（／关注／批评／重视／欢迎）(to receive attention from)

> ✍ This pattern is a variation on the use of 受 and 受到. Refer to Lesson 12, Pattern 9 for an explanation of how these expressions are used. Possible objects for 受 or 受到 in this pattern are primarily disyllabic verbs, such as 瞩目, 关注, 批评, 重视, or 欢迎. This structure often carries a formal tone.

☞ 打那以后，中国电影连连在国际性电影节上提名获奖，可以说中国电影从来没有象今天这样受海外人士所瞩目。

1、中国的经济发展受到全世界的瞩目。
China's economic development has received attention from the whole world.

2、香港97回归大陆问题受到全世界的关注。
The return of Hong Kong to Mainland China in 1997 received attention from the whole world.

问：现在亚洲的经济情况不太好，其它的国家怎么看这个问题？
答：_____。

（三）連連 + V (repeatedly, one after another, again and again)

> ✍ 連連 "repeatedly", "one after another", "again and again", appears most often in spoken settings. Unlike 連續, which can take a time word before the verb, as in 連續三年獲獎 (to win an award for three years in a row), 連連 must immediately precede a verb and cannot be followed by a time word. Example: 他今天下午連連吃了三碗米飯. (He ate three bowls of noodles in a row this afternoon.) Only rarely is 連連 used in a negative structure.

☞ 中國電影從88年以來，連連在國際電影節上提名、獲獎，比如《紅高粱》、《菊豆》等，中國電影從來沒有像今天這樣受到海外人士的矚目。

1、那家出租汽車公司在過去三個月中連連出了五次車禍，所以出現了很大的資金問題。

In the last three months, that cab company has had five successive accidents, so capital has become a big problem.

2、看到老張的時候，他連連說 "真對不起，讓你久等了"。

When he saw Lao Zhang, he kept saying, "I'm really sorry to have made you wait so long!"

問：你男朋友見到你的時候說了甚麼？
答：＿＿＿＿＿＿＿＿＿＿＿＿＿＿。

（四）從來沒（有）像今天這樣…… (something has never been like this before, never like today)

> ✍ 從來沒（有）像今天這樣, "something has never been like this before" or "never like today", is an an adverbial phrase placed between a subject and a predicate. It can precede either a verb or an adjective. Examples: 白溝的經濟從來沒有像今天這樣引人矚目. (White Gully's economy has never attracted people's attention the way it does today.) 這個地方從來沒有像今天這樣繁華熱鬧過. (This place has never been bustling and lively like this before.) The aspect marker 過 is often used after the verb or adjective.

☞ 打那以後，中國電影連連在國際性電影節上提名獲獎，可以說中國電影從來沒有像今天這樣受海外人士所矚目。

1、這位影壇奇才從來沒像今天這樣高興。

This talented movie star has never been as happy as he is today.

2、世界上的中國熱從來沒像今天這樣強烈。

The world never expected a China craze this strong.

問：北京這幾年發展很快，交通情況怎麼樣？
答：說老實話，＿＿＿＿＿＿＿＿＿＿＿＿＿。

（三）连连 + V (repeatedly, one after another, again and again)

> ✍ 连连 "repeatedly", "one after another", "again and again", appears most often in spoken settings. Unlike 连续, which can take a time word before the verb, as in 连续三年获奖 (to win an award for three years in a row), 连连 must immediately precede a verb and cannot be followed by a time word. Example: 他今天下午连连吃了三碗米饭. (He ate three bowls of noodles in a row this afternoon.) Only rarely is 连连 used in a negative structure.

☞ 中国电影从88年以来，连连在国际电影节上提名、获奖，比如《红高粱》、《菊豆》等，中国电影从来没有象今天这样受到海外人士的瞩目。

1、那家出租汽车公司在过去三个月中连连出了五次车祸，所以出现了很大的资金问题。

In the last three months, that cab company has had five successive accidents, so capital has become a big problem.

2、看到老张的时候，他连连说"真对不起，让你久等了"。

When he saw Lao Zhang, he kept saying, "I'm really sorry to have made you wait so long!"

问: 你男朋友见到你的时候说了什么？

答: ＿＿＿＿＿＿＿＿＿＿＿＿＿＿＿＿＿＿＿。

（四）从来没（有）象今天这样…… (something has never been like this before, never like today)

> ✍ 从来没（有）像今天这样, "something has never been like this before" or "never like today", is an adverbial phrase placed between a subject and a predicate. It can precede either a verb or an adjective. Examples: 白沟的经济从来没有像今天这样引人瞩目. (White Gully's economy has never attracted people's attention the way it does today.) 这个地方从来没有像今天这样繁华热闹过. (This place has never been bustling and lively like this before.) The aspect marker 过 is often used after the verb or adjective.

☞ 打那以后，中国电影连连在国际性电影节上提名获奖，可以说中国电影从来没有象今天这样受海外人士所瞩目。

1、这位影坛奇才从来没象今天这样高兴。

This talented movie star has never been as happy as he is today.

2、世界上的中国热从来没象今天这样强烈。

The world never expected a China craze this strong.

问: 北京这几年发展很快，交通情况怎么样？

答: 说老实话，＿＿＿＿＿＿＿＿＿＿＿＿＿＿＿＿。

（五）刮起（一股）……風 (to start a new fad in)

> ✍ 刮起(一股)……風 is used to describe the rise of a new, large-scale "fad" or "trend". Nouns that appear before 刮起 indicate where the trend is influential and are often place words, institution names, brand names, or companies, such as 中國, 中學, 美國大公司, etc.

☞ 世界影壇刮起中國風，應該歸功於第五代導演。

1、現在社會上甚麼風都有，以前有"出國風"，現在又刮起了"退學風"。

There are trends for everything in today's society. First there was the study abroad trend; now quitting school has become popular.

2、現在美國中小學又刮起了"吸毒風"。

Drugs have again become popular in American middle schools.

問：現在有很多人辭去公職，下海當個體戶嗎？

答：＿＿＿＿＿＿＿＿＿＿＿＿＿＿＿＿＿＿＿。

（六）歸功於 (to give credit to, to attribute one's success to)

> ✍ 歸功於, "to give credit to", "to attribute one's success to", is a verb used mostly in formal or written settings. 於, a Classical Chinese word meaning 到, indicates arrival at a place. The subject of 歸功於 must be a description of an accomplishment, achievement, or successful effort. Example: 我的成就歸功於父母的培養。(I credit my success to the upbringing I received from my parents.) Three spoken versions of the 歸功於 pattern are ……是……的功勞, 是因為……, and 是由於 …….

☞ 世界影壇刮起中國風，應該歸功於第五代導演。

1、中國電影現在受到全世界的矚目，應該歸功於中國的好導演。

China's movies have received the whole world's attention. Their popularity should be attributed to China's good directors.

2、孩子學習好，應該歸功於父母的教育。

Students' success in school should be attributed to the education they receive from their parents.

問：現在人們只要用幾秒鐘就可以互相傳送信息，應該歸功於甚麼？

答：＿＿＿＿＿＿＿＿＿＿＿＿＿＿＿＿＿＿＿。

（五）刮起（一股）……风 (to start a new fad in)

> ✍ 刮起(一股)……风 is used to describe the rise of a new, large-scale "fad" or "trend". Nouns that appear before 刮起 indicate where the trend is influential and are often place words, institution names, brand names, or companies, such as 中国, 中学, 美国大公司, etc.

☞ 世界影坛刮起中国风，应该归功于第五代导演。

1、现在社会上什么风都有，以前有"出国风"，现在又刮起了"退学风"。

There are trends for everything in today's society. First there was the study abroad trend; now quitting school has become popular.

2、现在美国中小学又刮起了"吸毒风"。

Drugs have again become popular in American middle schools.

问：现在有很多人辞去公职，下海当个体户吗？

答：_____。

（六）归功于 (to give credit to, to attribute one's success to)

> ✍ 归功于, "to give credit to", "to attribute one's success to", is a verb used mostly in formal or written settings. 于, a Classical Chinese word meaning 到, indicates arrival at a place. The subject of 归功于 must be a description of an accomplishment, achievement, or successful effort. Example: 我的成就归功于父母的培养. (I credit my success to the upbringing I received from my parents.) Three spoken versions of the 归功于 pattern are ……是……的功劳, 是因为……, and 是由于……。

☞ 世界影坛刮起中国风，应该归功于第五代导演。

1、中国电影现在受到全世界的瞩目，应该归功于中国的好导演。

China's movies have received the whole world's attention. Their popularity should be attributed to China's good directors.

2、孩子学习好，应该归功于父母的教育。

Students' success in school should be attributed to the education they receive from their parents.

问：现在人们只要用几秒钟就可以互相传送信息，应该归功于什么？

答：_____。

（七）從……角度＋V（反映／描寫／考慮／表現）(from the perspective of)

> Depending on the context, 角度 can be modified by different elements, such as 新的 (new), 直接的 (directly), 間接的 (indirectly), 客觀的 (objective), 主觀的 (subjective), or 正面的 (straight-on). This pattern is often used to describe a work of art or literary text. For this reason, verbs that follow 從……角度 include 反映, 描寫, 考慮, and 表現. Example: 怎麼樣才能從客觀的角度描寫歷史的發展? (How is it possible to write about the development of history from an objective viewpoint?) To negate this structure, 不 or 沒 should be placed before 從, not before the verb.

☞ 他們追求自然、真實，從新的角度反映社會。

1、她的電影常常從婦女的角度出發來反映當時的社會問題。

Her films often reflect social problems from the perspective of women in those days.

2、我認為政府應該從老百姓的角度來考慮制定新的經濟政策。

I believe that the government should consider things from the perspective of the common people when formulating new economic policies.

問：＿＿＿＿＿＿＿＿＿＿＿＿＿？

答：當然應該從客觀的角度去描寫。

（八）被譽為 (to be honored as)

> 被譽為……, "to be honored as", is a verb phrase which is used in formal and written settings. It is similar to 被稱為 in Pattern 6, Lesson 11, except that 譽 indicates honoring someone, whereas 稱 indicates recognizing someone. Unlike most 被 structures, which express adversity, 被譽為…… is used in a positive sense. If necessary, the agent of the verb can be inserted between 被 and 譽為. Example: 中國導演張藝謀被國際影壇譽為導演天才. (The Chinese director Zhang Yimou has been honored by international film circles as a gifted director.)

☞ 在一座小山坡上，這位被譽為影壇奇才的導演接受了我們的採訪。

1、譚宗堯被譽為有名的中國話劇藝術家。

Tan Zongyao is honored as a famous Chinese stage actor.

2、中國電影導演張藝謀被譽為影壇奇才。

The Chinese movie director Zhang Yimou is honored as an unusual talent in the film industry.

問：像喬丹這樣的籃球手，美國人對他是怎麼評價的？

答：＿＿＿＿＿＿＿＿＿＿＿＿＿＿＿＿＿。

（七）从……角度＋V（反映／描写／考虑／表现）(from the perspective of)

> ✍ Depending on the context, 角度 can be modified by different elements, such as 新的 (new), 直接的 (directly), 间接的 (indirectly), 客观的 (objective), 主观的 (subjective), or 正面的 (straight-on). This pattern is often used to describe a work of art or literary text. For this reason, verbs that follow 从……角度 include 反映, 描写, 考虑, and 表现. Example: 怎麼樣才能从客观的角度描写历史的发展? (How is it possible to write about the development of history from an objective viewpoint?) To negate this structure, 不 or 没 should be placed before 从, not before the verb.

☞ 他们追求自然、真实，从新的角度反映社会。

1、她的电影常常从妇女的角度出发来反映当时的社会问题。

Her films often reflect social problems from the perspective of women in those days.

2、我认为政府应该从老百姓的角度来考虑制定新的经济政策。

I believe that the government should consider things from the perspective of the common people when formulating new economic policies.

问: _____?

答: 当然应该从客观的角度去描写。

（八）被誉为 (to be honored as)

> ✍ 被誉为……, "to be honored as", is a verb phrase which is used in formal and written settings. It is similar to 被称为 in Pattern 6, Lesson 11, except that 誉 indicates honoring someone, whereas 称 indicates recognizing someone. Unlike most 被 structures, which express adversity, 被誉为…… is used in a positive sense. If necessary, the agent of the verb can be inserted between 被 and 誉为. Example: 中国导演张艺谋被国际影坛誉为导演天才. (The Chinese director Zhang Yimou has been honored by international film circles as a gifted director.)

☞ 在一座小山坡上，这位被誉为影坛奇才的导演接受了我们的采访。

1、谭宗尧被誉为有名的中国话剧艺术家。

Tan Zongyao is honored as a famous Chinese stage actor.

2、中国电影导演张艺谋被誉为影坛奇才。

The Chinese movie director Zhang Yimou is honored as an unusual talent in the film industry.

问: 象乔丹这样的篮球手，美国人对他是怎么评价的？

答: _____。

（九）A 迎合 B 的 + N（口味／心理／興趣／需求）(to please, to satisfy)

> ✎ The verb 迎合, "to please" or "to satisfy", carries a negative tone. Nouns that can be used as objects for 迎合 include 口味, 心理, 興趣, and 需求. Unlike the English word "to please" 迎合 cannot be used with nouns that indicate a person.

☞ 當你不知道人家需要甚麼的時候，你怎麼可能說是我去迎合你。

1、我認為這種產品就是為了迎合中學生的口味才做的。

I believe that such products are only designed to appeal to middle school students.

2、他最會迎合老板的心理了，你看他連穿衣服上班都很小心。

He is a master at catering to the boss's preferences. Look, he is even careful about the clothes he wears to work!

問：甚麼樣的中國電影最受美國人的歡迎？

答：＿＿＿＿＿＿＿＿＿＿＿＿＿＿＿。

（十）面臨 (to be faced with)

> ✎ 面臨, "to be faced with", can be used either as a main verb or as part of an adverbial phrase. Unlike 面對 (see Lesson 14, Pattern 8), which can take both concrete and abstract nouns, 面臨 can only take abstract nouns such as 現實 (reality), 困難 (difficulties), 挑戰 (challenges), or 畢業 (graduation). Concrete nouns like a personal name cannot follow 面臨. Examples: 中國面臨很多的挑戰。(China is facing many challenges.) 面臨很大的困難，他決定放棄這份工作。(Faced with great difficulties, he decided to give up this job.)

☞ 我們看到的中國電影，過去的描寫，比如說，描寫文化大革命，描寫過去的五十年代我們所面臨的很多問題和經過的很多困難時候，差不多都是用傳統的、悲劇的方法去描寫，很沉重。

1、面臨考級的緊張氣氛，小神童一點也不緊張。

The child prodigies were not at all nervous when faced with the tense atmosphere of the test.

2、白溝市場雖然發展很快，可是也要面臨新的考驗。

Although the White Gully Market developed fast, it also faces new trials.

問：像日本這樣的大國，經濟發展已經很成熟了，還會面臨些甚麼新的挑戰？

答：＿＿＿＿＿＿＿＿＿＿＿＿＿＿＿＿＿＿。

（九）A 迎合 B 的 + N（口味 / 心理 / 兴趣 / 需求）(to please, to satisfy)

> ✍ The verb 迎合, "to please" or "to satisfy", carries a negative tone. Nouns that can be used as objects for 迎合 include 口味, 心理, 兴趣, and 需求. Unlike the English word "to please", 迎合 cannot be used with nouns that indicate a person.

☞ 当你不知道人家需要什么的时候，你怎么可能说是我去迎合你。

1、我认为这种产品就是为了迎合中学生的口味才做的。

I believe that such products are only designed to appeal to middle school students.

2、他最会迎合老板的心理了，你看他连穿衣服上班都很小心。

He is a master at catering to the boss's preferences. Look, he is even careful about the clothes he wears to work!

问：什么样的中国电影最受美国人的欢迎？

答：_____。

（十）面临 (to be faced with)

> ✍ 面临, "to be faced with", can be used either as a main verb or as part of an adverbial phrase. Unlike 面对 (see Lesson 14, Pattern 8), which can take both concrete and abstract nouns, 面临 can only take abstract nouns such as 现实 (reality), 困难 (difficulties), 挑战 (challenges), or 毕业 (graduation). Concrete nouns like a personal name cannot follow 面临. Examples: 中国面临很多的挑战。(China is facing many challenges.) 面临很大的困难，他决定放弃这份工作。(Faced with great difficulties, he decided to give up this job.)

☞ 我们看到的中国电影，过去的描写，比如说，描写文化大革命，描写过去的五十年代我们所面临的很多问题和经过的很多困难时候，差不多都是用传统的、悲剧的方法去描写，很沉重。

1、面临考级的紧张气氛，小神童一点也不紧张。

The child prodigies were not at all nervous when faced with the tense atmosphere of the test.

2、白沟市场虽然发展很快，可是也要面临新的考验。

Although the White Gully Market developed fast, it also faces new trials.

问：象日本这样的大国，经济发展已经很成熟了，还会面临些什么新的挑战？

答：_____。

（十一）處於⋯⋯的情況 (to be in the situation of)

> ✍ 處於⋯⋯的情況, "to be in the situation of", is used mostly in formal and written Chinese to indicate what is usually an undesirable situation. The verb 處 (chǔ) here means "to put", "to place", "to situate" It often suggests the idea of being trapped in a situation. 處於 can be replaced by 處在, which is less formal.

☞ 我們使這一家人呢永遠處於一個很溫馨的、很自然的、很可愛的一個情況，然後使他們呢，盡可能地保持生活裡面很輕鬆的東西。

1、在學校的時候，我常處於一種不知做甚麼好的情況。

When I was in school, I often found myself in situations where I did not know what to do.

2、處於這種經濟改革的情況，很多人辭去公職，當了個體戶。

During economic reform, many people resigned from public posts and became entrepreneurs.

問：現在你哥哥打算上研究院還是找工作？
答：他很矛盾，＿＿＿＿＿＿＿＿＿＿＿＿＿。

（十二）把注意力放在⋯⋯ (to focus one's attention on)

> ✍ 把注意力放在⋯⋯上, "to focus one's attention on", requires the use of the 把 construction. Example: 他把注意力都放在家庭上了，根本不努力工作. (He focuses his attention on his family and never works hard at his job.) When 注意力 is the subject of the sentence, however, the 把 construction is not used. Example: 他的注意力都放在了學習上. (All of his attention went into his studies.) As is usually the case with sentences using the 把 construction, negative particles 不 and 沒 are placed before 把 rather than before the main verb.

☞ 那麼我們就是想很間接地把注意力更多地放在普通人和普通家庭方面。

1、處理電影人物，應該把注意力放在人的感覺上。

To play a movie character, you must focus all your attention on emotions.

2、學中文應該把注意力放在聽、說上。

To study Chinese, one must focus on listening and speaking.

問：你認為學中文的學生應該把自己的注意力放在甚麼方面？
答：＿＿＿＿＿＿＿＿＿＿＿＿＿＿＿＿＿＿＿。

（十一）处于……的情况 (to be in the situation of)

> ✍ 处于……的情况, "to be in the situation of", is used mostly in formal and written Chinese to indicate what is usually an undesirable situation. The verb 处 (chǔ) here means "to put", "to place", "to situate". It often suggests the idea of being trapped in a situation. 处于 can be replaced by 处在, which is less formal.

☞ 我们使这一家人呢永远处于一个很温馨的、很自然的、很可爱的一个情况，然后使他们呢，尽可能地保持生活里面很轻松的东西。

1、在学校的时候，我常处于一种不知做什么好的情况。

When I was in school, I often found myself in situations where I did not know what to do.

2、处于这种经济改革的情况，很多人辞去公职，当了个体户。

During economic reform, many people resigned from public posts and became entrepreneurs.

问: 现在你哥哥打算上研究院还是找工作？

答: 他很矛盾，＿＿＿＿＿＿＿＿＿＿＿＿＿。

（十二）把注意力放在…… (to focus one's attention on)

> ✍ 把注意力放在……上, "to focus one's attention on", requires the use of the 把 construction. Example: 他把注意力都放在家庭上了，根本不努力工作. (He focuses his attention on his family and never works hard at his job.) When 注意力 is the subject of the sentence, however, the 把 construction is not used. Example: 他的注意力都放在了学习上. (All of his attention went into his studies.) As is usually the case with sentences using the 把 construction, negative particles 不 and 没 are placed before 把 rather than before the main verb.

☞ 那么我们就是想很间接地把注意力更多地放在普通人和普通家庭方面。

1、处理电影人物，应该把注意力放在人的感觉上。

To play a movie character, you must focus all your attention on emotions.

2、学中文应该把注意力放在听、说上。

To study Chinese, one must focus on listening and speaking.

问: 你认为学中文的学生应该把自己的注意力放在什么方面？

答: ＿＿＿＿＿＿＿＿＿＿＿＿＿＿＿＿＿。

四、文化背景知識 Cultural Notes

1. China's "fifth generation of directors" (第五代導演) refers to directors such as 張藝謀, 陳凱歌 (Chén Kǎigē), and 田壯壯 (Tián Zhuàngzhuàng), all of whom graduated from the Beijing Film Academy (北京電影學院).

2. 張藝謀 is one of China's best-known film directors. After graduating from the Beijing Film Academy in 1982, he worked first at the Guangxi Film Studio and then quickly moved to the Xi'an Film Studio in his home province of Shaanxi. In 1984 Zhang Yimou served as a cameraman for 陳凱歌's award-winning film *Yellow Earth*. In the years that followed, Zhang directed several movies that received substantial exposure outside of China, including *Red Sorghum* 《紅高粱》 (1987) and *Judou* 《菊豆》 (1990). *Judou* was nominated for an Oscar, but authorities in China prevented Zhang from attending the ceremonies in Hollywood. Apparently, censors in China deemed the movie unsuitable, both for domestic (the movie was banned in China) and foreign audiences because of its explicit sexual content. Several more successful films followed, including *Raise the Red Lantern* 《大紅燈籠高高掛》 (1991), *The Story of Qiu Ju* 《秋菊打官司》 (1992), *To Live* 《活著》 (1994), and *Shanghai Triad* 《搖啊搖，搖到外婆橋》 (1995). All of these films starred 鞏俐 (Gǒng Lì), China's best-known actress.

四、文化背景知识 Cultural Notes

1. China's "fifth generation of directors" (第五代导演) refers to directors such as 张艺谋, 陈凯歌 (Chén Kǎigē), and 田壮壮 (Tián Zhuàngzhuàng), all of whom graduated from the Beijing Film Academy (北京电影学院).

2. 张艺谋 is one of China's best-known film directors. After graduating from the Beijing Film Academy in 1982, he worked first at the Guangxi Film Studio and then quickly moved to the Xi'an Film Studio in his home province of Shaanxi. In 1984 Zhang Yimou served as a cameraman for 陈凯歌's award-winning film *Yellow Earth*. In the years that followed, Zhang directed several movies that received substantial exposure outside of China, including *Red Sorghum* 红高粱 (1987) and *Judou* 菊豆 (1990). *Judou* was nominated for an Oscar, but authorities in China prevented Zhang from attending the ceremonies in Hollywood. Apparently, censors in China deemed the movie unsuitable, both for domestic (the movie was banned in China) and foreign audiences because of its explicit sexual content. Several more successful films followed, including *Raise the Red Lantern* 大红灯笼高高挂 (1991), *The Story of Qiu Ju* 秋菊打官司 (1992), *To Live* 活着 (1994), and *Shanghai Triad* (摇啊摇，摇到外婆桥) (1995). All of these films starred 巩俐 (Gǒng Lì), China's best-known actress.

練習

語言結構 Structures

一、短語翻譯 (Phrase translation)

1. the film festival in West Berlin
2. to win nominations and awards
3. recognition from people overseas
4. world film industry
5. fifth generation director
6. to feel for things as a Chinese
7. tragic and fatalistic themes
8. to make a film on a hill
9. a new breakthrough
10. to use a traditional method to make a film
11. to push politics far away
12. to take a new perspective
13. to base on different feelings
14. to reflect life from a direct and an indirect angle

二、聽力練習 (Listening comprehension)

1、聽寫 (Dictation)

2、聽錄音並回答問題 (Answering questions while listening to the audio CD)
    (1) 張藝謀的《菊豆》描寫甚麼，反映了甚麼？
    (2) 張藝謀的電影與傳統的中國電影有甚麼不同？
    (3) 你還看過甚麼張藝謀的電影？談談你對這些電影的看法。

练习

语言结构 Structures

一、短语翻译 (Phrase translation)

1. the film festival in West Berlin
2. to win nominations and awards
3. recognition from people overseas
4. world film industry
5. fifth generation director
6. to feel for things as a Chinese
7. tragic and fatalistic themes
8. to make a film on a hill
9. a new breakthrough
10. to use a traditional method to make a film
11. to push politics far away
12. to take a new perspective
13. to base on different feelings
14. to reflect life from a direct and an indirect angle

二、听力练习 (Listening comprehension)

1、听写 (Dictation)

2、听录音并回答问题 (Answering questions while listening to the audio CD)
    (1) 张艺谋的《菊豆》描写什么，反映了什么？
    (2) 张艺谋的电影与传统的中国电影有什么不同？
    (3) 你还看过什么张艺谋的电影？谈谈你对这些电影的看法。

三、完成句子 (Complete the sentences)

1、 　　A：你最近看了一個甚麼中國電影？
　　　　B：張藝謀的《活著》，這部電影＿＿＿＿＿＿＿＿＿＿＿＿＿＿＿＿＿＿＿＿＿＿＿
　　　（受到……矚目；歸功於……）

2、 　　A：昨天美國總統又上電視了。
　　　　B：對了。有很多人對總統不滿意。＿＿＿＿＿＿＿＿＿＿＿＿＿＿＿＿＿＿＿＿
　　　（面臨……；接受……的採訪）

3、 　　A：為甚麼中國人現在人人都在做生意？
　　　　B：你還不知道嗎？現在＿＿＿＿＿＿＿＿＿＿＿＿＿＿＿＿＿＿＿＿＿＿＿＿＿
　　　（刮起……風；把注意力放在……）

四、閱讀短文、回答問題 (Answering questions based on the reading passage)

張藝謀簡介

　　張藝謀是中國第五代最有才華的導演。張藝謀於1952年生於西安附近。1976年文化大革命期間，他上山下鄉到西安北部的農村，後來分配到一家紡織廠當工人。在工廠期間，張藝謀開始學習攝影。1978年，文化大革命結束後，張藝謀報考北京電影學院。由於年齡超過，周折很多，經過教育部及學校特批才正式進入電影學院學習。

　　張藝謀四年學習結束後，由於在學校沒有後門及關係被分配到偏遠的廣西電影制片廠，後來他與中國第四代導演西電影制片廠的吳天明合作拍攝了《黃土地》。1978年他主演《老井》，獲第二屆東京國際電影節最佳男演員。
　　張藝謀後來轉入導演生涯。僅在幾年當中，他就導演出好幾部具有世界水平的電影，並連連在國際電影節上提名獲獎。例如，《菊豆》、《紅高粱》、《活著》、《大紅燈籠高高掛》等。可以說中國電影從來沒有像今天這樣受到海外人士的矚目。很多人說世界影壇刮起的中國風應歸功於張藝謀和其它第五代導演。

問題
　(1) 張藝謀上大學以前有過甚麼樣的經歷？
　(2) 你知道文章中 "由於年齡超過，周折很多，經過教育部及學校特批才正式進入電影學院學習。" 指的是甚麼意思？如果不知道請你問你的老師或者朋友然後把答案寫出。

三、完成句子 (Complete the sentences)

1、　A：你最近看了一个什么中国电影？

　　　B：张艺谋的《活着》，这部电影_____

　　（受到……瞩目；归功于……）

2、　A：昨天美国总统又上电视了。

　　　B：对了。有很多人对总统不满意。_____

　　（面临……；接受……的采访）

3、　A：为什么中国人现在人人都在做生意？

　　　B：你还不知道吗？现在_____

　　（刮起……风；把注意力放在……）

四、阅读短文、回答问题 (Answering questions based on the reading passage)

张艺谋简介

　　张艺谋是中国第五代最有才华的导演。张艺谋于1952年生于西安附近。1976年文化大革命期间，他上山下乡到西安北部的农村，后来分配到一家纺织厂当工人。在工厂期间，张艺谋开始学习摄影。1978年，文化大革命结束后，张艺谋报考北京电影学院。由于年龄超过，周折很多，经过教育部及学校特批才正式进入电影学院学习。

　　张艺谋四年学习结束后，由于在学校没有后门及关系被分配到偏远的广西电影制片厂，后来他与中国第四代导演西电影制片厂的吴天明合作拍摄了《黄土地》。1978年他主演《老井》，获第二届东京国际电影节最佳男演员。

　　张艺谋后来转入导演生涯。仅在几年当中，他就导演出好几部具有世界水平的电影，并连连在国际电影节上提名获奖。例如，《菊豆》、《红高粱》、《活着》、《大红灯笼高高挂》等。可以说中国电影从来没有象今天这样受到海外人士的瞩目。很多人说世界影坛刮起的中国风应归功于张艺谋和其它第五代导演。

问题

　　(1) 张艺谋上大学以前有过什么样的经历？

　　(2) 你知道文章中"由于年龄超过，周折很多，经过教育部及学校特批才正式进入电影学院学习。"指的是什么意思？如果不知道请你问你的老师或者朋友然后把答案写出。

五、翻譯 (Translate sentences)

1. Because its car was nominated for prizes and won several international awards, the world's attention has focused on the company.

2. There are both subjective and objective reasons why he wants to leave politics out of the film he is making.

3. Not long ago, he accepted an interview with our reporter regarding his view on the criticism from the public opinion poll.

4. Based on his intuition about the Chinese family structure, he hopes to make a film which places attention on the relationships between father and son, mother and daughter, and husband and wife.

五、翻译 (Translate sentences)

1. Because its car was nominated for prizes and won several international awards, the world's attention has focused on the company.

2. There are both subjective and objective reasons why he wants to leave politics out of the film he is making.

3. Not long ago, he accepted an interview with our reporter regarding his view on the criticism from the public opinion poll.

4. Based on his intuition about the Chinese family structure, he hopes to make a film which places attention on the relationships between father and son, mother and daughter, and husband and wife.

語言實踐 ∶ Practice

一、根據課文回答問題 (Answering questions based on the dialogue)

1、為甚麼中國電影受到海外人士矚目？

2、甚麼是第五代導演？你知道幾個中國第五代導演？

3、用你的話説説張藝謀是怎麼回答第一個問題的？你同意不同意有些人對張藝謀的批評？

4、甚麼是"悲劇"、"宿命"題材？張藝謀覺得他的作品都是悲劇的模式嗎？

5、張藝謀説他在《活著》中的新的突破和嘗試是甚麼？

二、活動 (Activities)

跟你的中國朋友一塊兒看《活著》，或者《菊豆》，讓他們談談他們對張藝謀電影的看法。

三、討論題 (Topics for discussion)

1、你覺得張藝謀的電影有甚麼特點？你喜歡嗎？

2、你同意不同意有的人對張藝謀的批評，説他拍電影是給外國人看？

3、《活著》這部電影真像張藝謀説的那樣，把政治背景推得很遠嗎？舉例説明為甚麼。

四、報告 (Presentation)

《我所看過的中國電影》

语言实践 ⋮ Practice

一、根据课文回答问题 (Answering questions based on the dialogue)

1、为什么中国电影受到海外人士瞩目？
2、什么是第五代导演？你知道几个中国第五代导演？
3、用你的话说说张艺谋是怎么回答第一个问题的？你同意不同意有些人对张艺谋的批评？
4、什么是"悲剧"、"宿命"题材？张艺谋觉得他的作品都是悲剧的模式吗？
5、张艺谋说他在《活着》中的新的突破和尝试是什么？

二、活动 (Activities)

跟你的中国朋友一块儿看《活着》，或者《菊豆》，让他们谈谈他们对张艺谋电影的看法。

三、讨论题 (Topics for discussion)

1、你觉得张艺谋的电影有什么特点？你喜欢吗？
2、你同意不同意有的人对张艺谋的批评，说他拍电影是给外国人看？
3、《活着》这部电影真象张艺谋说的那样，把政治背景推得很远吗？举例说明为什么。

四、报告 (Presentation)

《我所看过的中国电影》

五、看圖討論 (Picto-discussion)

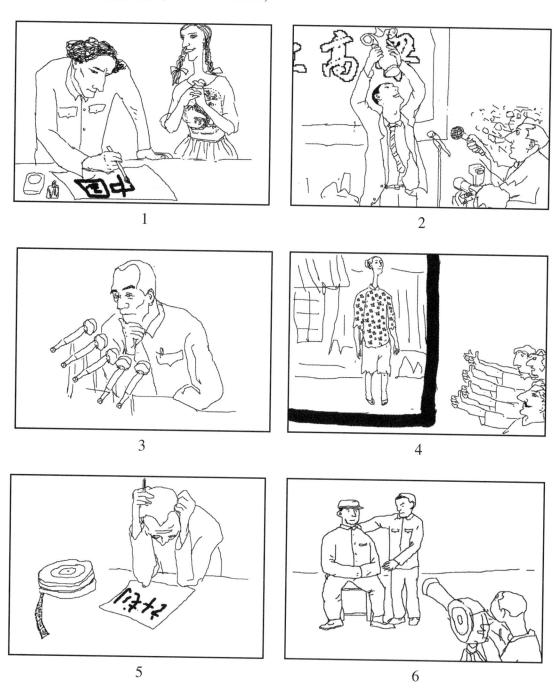

1

2

3

4

5

6

五、看图讨论 (Picto-discussion)

1

2

3

4

5

6

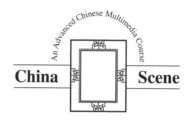

第十四課

中國的體操運動員

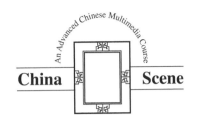

China **Scene**
An Advanced Chinese Multimedia Course

第十四课

中国的体操运动员

課文

一、對話  Dialogs

江民：體操運動中你最喜歡哪種？

李輝：自由體操、平衡木、單槓和雙槓我都喜歡。

江民：那鞍馬呢？這也是一項很好的體操項目。

李輝：對了。我尤其喜歡看中國的鞍馬運動員國林耀。他的動作熟練、漂亮，儘管他
才22歲，可是他已經是中國體操隊的老主力隊員了。

江民：這些體操運動員看上去[1]都很年輕，他們的平均[2]年齡是多大？

李輝：差不多是15歲到23歲。你知道，這些小運動員的生活也不容易。在10歲左右就
離開家去北京國家集訓[3]隊集訓，在單槓或平衡木前度過他們寶貴的青少年時
期。儘管他們的待遇非常好，可是他們都不能象別的孩子那樣有自己的家，在
父母身邊長大。這還不說，從事體操的人都知道，十年以後很多人就得結束[4]

Notes [1]看上去 vs. 看起來: 看上去 and 看起來, sometimes shortened to 看來, are inserted elements meaning "to appear" or "to seem". These phrases are used to express a speaker's assumption based on the outward appearance of someone or something, but they are used differently in a sentence. 看上去 must be inserted between the subject and verb of a sentence, as in 老王看上去四十出頭. (Lao Wang looks to be over 40 years old.) 看起來, on the other hand, may be inserted at the beginning of a sentence or between the subject and verb. Examples: 已經很晚了，看起來他不會來了. (It's already very late. It looks like he is not coming.) 老王看起來四十出頭. (Lao Wang looks to be over 40 years old.)

[2]As an adjective, 平均 functions almost the same as the English adjective "average", as in 平均年齡 (average age). As a predicate, it means "about the same" or "distributed evenly". Example: 現在中國人的收入很不平均. (There are great disparities in the salaries of Chinese people.) 平均 is only used for averages which are related to numbers, never in expressions such as "average person".

[3]集訓, meaning "to assemble for training" or "to conduct group training", is an abbreviation for 集中訓練. 集 in 集中 means "to bring together" or "to assemble"; 訓 in 訓練 means "to teach" or "to train". Example: 運動員在出國比賽以前都要集訓一個月. (Before the athletes leave to compete overseas, they must train together for a month.)

[4]結束, meaning "to end", "to conclude", or "to wrap up", is a verb often used in formal settings. 結 by itself means "to connect" or "to knot together"; 束 means "to bind" or "to tie". The objects of 結束 are often stages in a person's life, official meetings, performances, visitations, and so on. Example: 代表團結束了這次參觀訪問. (The delegation has concluded its current tour.) 結束 is not used to indicate the end of a common or habitual action; instead, a verb plus the complement 完 should be used. Example: 辦完這件事我就到你家裡去. (Once I finish this task I'll go right over to your house.)

课文

一、对话 Dialogs

江民：体操运动中你最喜欢哪种？

李辉：自由体操、平衡木、单杠和双杠我都喜欢。

江民：那鞍马呢？这也是一项很好的体操项目。

李辉：对了。我尤其喜欢看中国的鞍马运动员国林耀。他的动作熟练、漂亮，尽管他才22岁，可是他已经是中国体操队的老主力队员了。

江民：这些体操运动员看上去[(1)]都很年轻，他们的平均[(2)]年龄是多大？

李辉：差不多是15岁到23岁。你知道，这些小运动员的生活也不容易。在10岁左右就离开家去北京国家集训[(3)]队集训，在单杠或平衡木前度过他们宝贵的青少年时期。尽管他们的待遇非常好，可是他们都不能象别的孩子那样有自己的家，在父母身边长大。这还不说，从事体操的人都知道，十年以后很多人就得结束[(4)]

✎ Notes [(1)]看上去 vs. 看起来: 看上去 and 看起来, sometimes shortened to 看来, are inserted elements meaning "to appear" or "to seem". These phrases are used to express a speaker's assumption based on the outward appearance of someone or something, but they are used differently in a sentence. 看上去 must be inserted between the subject and verb of a sentence, as in 老王看上去四十出头. (Lao Wang looks to be over 40 years old.) 看起来, on the other hand, may be inserted at the beginning of a sentence or between the subject and verb. Examples: 已经很晚了，看起来他不会来了. (It's already very late. It looks like he is not coming.) 老王看起来四十出头. (Lao Wang looks to be over 40 years old.)

[(2)]As an adjective, 平均 functions almost the same as the English adjective "average", as in 平均年龄 (average age). As a predicate, it means "about the same" or "distributed evenly". Example: 现在中国人的收入很不平均. (There are great disparities in the salaries of Chinese people.) 平均 is only used for averages which are related to numbers, never in expressions such as "average person".

[(3)]集训, meaning "to assemble for training" or "to conduct group training", is an abbreviation for 集中训练. 集 in 集中 means "to bring together" or "to assemble"; 训 in 训练 means "to teach" or "to train". Example: 运动员在出国比赛以前都要集训一个月. (Before the athletes leave to compete overseas, they must train together for a month.)

[(4)]结束, meaning "to end", "to conclude", or "to wrap up", is a verb often used in formal settings. 结 by itself means "to connect" or "to knot together"; 束 means "to bind" or "to tie". The objects of 结束 are often stages in a person's life, official meetings, performances, visitations, and so on. Example: 代表团结束了这次参观访问. (The delegation has concluded its current tour.) 结束 is not used to indicate the end of a common or habitual action; instead, a verb plus the complement 完 should be used. Example: 办完这件事我就到你家里去. (Once I finish this task I'll go right over to your house.)

他們的體操生涯了。你看楊波才20歲就已經是一員⁽⁵⁾老將了。

江民：看來當一個體操運動員也不容易啊！

生詞

體操	(tǐ cāo)	N.	gymnastics
運動員	(yùn dòng yuán)	N.	athlete
自由體操	(zì yóu tǐ cāo)	NP.	floor exercise
平衡木	(píng héng mù)	N.	balance beam
單槓	(dān gàng)	N.	single bar
雙槓	(shuāng gàng)	N.	double bar
鞍馬	(ān mǎ)	N.	sidehorse
項	(xiàng)	Classifier.	one item of
國林耀	(guó lín yuè/yào)	N.	Guo Linyue/yao, name of a person 人名
動作	(dòng zuò)	N.	movement, action
熟練	(shóu liàn)	Adj.	skilled, proficient
主力隊員	(zhǔ lì duì yuán)	NP.	major player
年輕	(nián qīng)	Adj.	young
平均	(píng jūn)	N/Prep.	average
集訓隊	(jí xùn duì)	N.	training camp
集訓	(jí xùn)	N/V.	to bring people together for training
寶貴	(bǎo guì)	Adj.	precious, valuable
生涯	(shēng yá)	N.	career
楊波	(yáng bō)	N.	Yang Bo, name of a person 人名
老將	(lǎo jiàng)	N.	old-timer, veteran

Notes ⁽⁵⁾員 is a classifier used for members of an organization or institution, especially the military, as in 一員老將 (jiàng) (a veteran) or 一員虎將 (a brave general). 一員 is always followed by a disyllabic noun. When used after a noun that refers to a social organization, 員 means "a member of", as in 家庭的一員 (a member of a family), 社會的一員 (a member of society).

他们的体操生涯了。你看杨波才20岁就已经是一员[5]老将了。

江民：看来当一个体操运动员也不容易啊！

生词

体操	(tǐ cāo)	N.	gymnastics
运动员	(yùn dòng yuán)	N.	athlete
自由体操	(zì yóu tǐ cāo)	NP.	floor exercise
平衡木	(píng héng mù)	N.	balance beam
单杠	(dān gàng)	N.	single bar
双杠	(shuāng gàng)	N.	double bar
鞍马	(ān mǎ)	N.	sidehorse
项	(xiàng)	Classifier.	one item of
国林耀	(guó lín yuè/yào)	N.	Guo Linyue/yao, name of a person 人名
动作	(dòng zuò)	N.	movement, action
熟练	(shóu liàn)	Adj.	skilled, proficient
主力队员	(zhǔ lì duì yuán)	NP.	major player
年轻	(nián qīng)	Adj.	young
平均	(píng jūn)	N/Prep.	average
集训队	(jí xùn duì)	N.	training camp
集训	(jí xùn)	N/V.	to bring people together for training
宝贵	(bǎo guì)	Adj.	precious, valuable
生涯	(shēng yá)	N.	career
杨波	(yáng bō)	N.	Yang Bo, name of a person 人名
老将	(lǎo jiàng)	N.	old-timer, veteran

Notes [5]员 is a classifier used for members of an organization or institution, especially the military, as in 一员老将 (jiàng) (a veteran) or 一员虎将 (a brave general). 一员 is always followed by a disyllabic noun. When used after a noun that refers to a social organization, 员 means "a member of", as in 家庭的一员 (a member of a family), 社会的一员 (a member of society).

二、電視原文 TV original

介紹四個中國體操運動員
（根據原文改編）

李春陽

廣東省運動員李春陽，現年[6]24歲，是中國體操隊中的老大哥，國際級[7]運動健將，兩次單槓世界冠軍的獲得者[8]，　第26屆世界體操錦標賽和第25屆巴塞羅那奧運會男子團體亞軍的主力隊員。李春陽1974年開始練體操，1985年1月進國家集訓隊，有十多年的體操生涯。如今他已成為戰功赫赫的老將。

國林耀

1972年出生的國林耀1987年底[9]進國家集訓隊，是第26屆世界體操錦標賽和第25屆世界奧運會的男子團體亞軍的主力隊員，並多次在中國和世界雙槓、鞍馬兩個單項比賽中有出色的表演。國林耀有個體操之家，他的父母都是出色的老體操工作者，兩個哥哥和一個姐姐都曾是優秀的中國體操選手。他一家六口人為中國體操事業做出了很大貢獻，被中國體操界譽為＂國家隊＂。他們的業績生動地體現了中國體操今天的成就凝聚幾代人的心血，來之不易。

楊波

不滿20歲的楊波已經是一位老將了。這位浙江省姑娘1980年參加體操訓練，1985

Notes [6]現年, "one's present age", is an abbreviation for 現在的年齡. It is often used in an introduction to give someone's age. 現年 is only used in formal settings, especially in the media. Example: 這位漂亮的姑娘是福建省運動員李弈芳現年17歲. (This beautiful girl is the athlete Li Yifang from Fujian province, 17 years old this year.)

[7]級 is a suffix which indicates the level, rank, or grade of someone or something, as in 三年級中文學生 (third-year Chinese language student), 國際級 (international level); 五星級賓館(five-star hotel); 高級幹部 (high-ranking cadres).

[8]者 vs. 家: 者, meaning "one who", "person who", or "-er", is a suffix borrowed from Classical Chinese which indicates the agent of a verb, as in 獲得者 (winner), 革命者 (those who carry out revolution). 家 functions similarly as a suffix, but means "specialist" or "expert in a field", as in 發明家 (inventor), 科學家 (scientist), 作家 (writer).

[9]底 vs. 末: 底 and 末 are both time expression meaning "the end of", as in 月底 or 月末 (end of the month), 年底 or 年末 (the end of the year). 末, however, can be used with 周 or 星期, while 底 cannot.

二、电视原文　🖥 TV original

介绍四个中国体操运动员
（根据原文改编）

李春阳

广东省运动员李春阳，现年[6]24岁，是中国体操队中的老大哥，国际级[7]运动健将，两次单杠世界冠军的获得者[8]，　第26届世界体操锦标赛和第25届巴塞罗那奥运会男子团体亚军的主力队员。李春阳1974年开始练体操，1985年1月进国家集训队，有十多年的体操生涯。如今他已成为战功赫赫的老将。

国林耀

1972年出生的国林耀1987年底[9]进国家集训队，是第26届世界体操锦标赛和第25届世界奥运会的男子团体亚军的主力队员，并多次在中国和世界双杠、鞍马两个单项比赛中有出色的表演。国林耀有个体操之家，他的父母都是出色的老体操工作者，两个哥哥和一个姐姐都曾是优秀的中国体操选手。他一家六口人为中国体操事业做出了很大贡献，被中国体操界誉为"国家队"。他们的业绩生动地体现了中国体操今天的成就凝聚几代人的心血，来之不易。

杨波

不满20岁的杨波已经是一位老将了。这位浙江省姑娘1980年参加体操训练，1985

Notes [6]现年, "one's present age", is an abbreviation for 现在的年龄. It is often used in an introduction to give someone's age. 现年 is only used in formal settings, especially in the media. Example: 这位漂亮的姑娘是福建省运动员李弈芳现年17岁. (This beautiful girl is the athlete Li Yifang from Fujian province, 17 years old this year.)

[7]级 is a suffix which indicates the level, rank, or grade of someone or something, as in 三年级中文学生 (third-year Chinese language student), 国际级 (international level); 五星级宾馆(five-star hotel); 高级干部 (high-ranking cadres).

[8]者 vs. 家: 者, meaning "one who", "person who", or "-er", is a suffix borrowed from Classical Chinese which indicates the agent of a verb, as in 获得者 (winner), 革命者 (those who carry out revolution). 家 functions similarly as a suffix, but means "specialist" or "expert in a field", as in 发明家 (inventor), 科学家 (scientist), 作家 (writer).

[9]底 vs. 末: 底 and 末 are both time expression meaning "the end of", as in 月底 or 月末 (end of the month), 年底 or 年末 (the end of the year). 末, however, can be used with 周 or 星期, while 底 cannot.

年進國家隊，現在是國際級運動健將，中國體操女隊的隊長。她在第八屆世界杯體操賽上獲得平衡木冠軍後，國際體操聯合會正式[10]把她獨創的平衡木跳步命名為"楊波跳"。她也是第26屆世界體操錦標賽和第25屆奧運會女子團體第四名的主力隊員。女隊的姑娘們誇楊波有一副出色的嗓子，舞跳得也好。

李奕芳

　　這位漂亮的姑娘是福建省運動員李奕芳，現在17歲，1982年開始練體操，1988年初到國家集訓隊，是"李家軍"中的又一位女將，第26屆世界體操錦標賽和第25屆奧運會的女子團體第四名的主力隊員。她曾經奪得過中國體操錦標賽全能冠軍，自由體操第一名。在世界體操錦標賽上，她獲得平衡木第二名。婷婷玉立的李奕芳，在奧運會賽場上拇指骨折的情況下以超人的毅力克服傷痛，始終[11]以甜美的微笑面對[12]裁判，面對觀眾。

生詞

李春陽	(lǐ chūn yáng)	N.	Li Chunyang, name of a person 人名
廣東	(guǎng dōng)	PlaceN.	Guangdong (Province)
省	(shěng)	N.	province
老大哥	(lǎo dà gē)	N.	old brother
國際級	(guó jì jí)	Adj/N.	internationally ranked
健將	(jiàn jiàng)	N.	top player
冠軍	(guàn jūn)	N.	championship

Notes [10]正式, functions most often as an adjective meaning "formal" or "regular", as in 正式黨員 (an official member of the Party), 正式訪問 (a formal or official visit). 正式 can also function as an adverb meaning "formally" or "officially", as in 他今天正式宣布中美友好協會成立了. (Today he formally announced the founding of the Sino-American Friendship Association.)

[11]始終 is an adverb eaning "from beginning （始）to end （終）", "throughout", "all along", "always". Example: 我始終熱愛我所從事的工作. (I've always loved my work.) When used in a negative sentence, 始終 must precede the negative particle. Example: 這位有名的運動員始終沒結過婚. (This famous athlete has never married.)

[12]面對 and 面臨 are both used mostly in formal settings. 面對 means "to face" and "to confront". Its objects can be nouns referring to people, things, or situations. Examples: 面對事實 (to face reality); 他不能面對他過去的女朋友. (He cannot face his ex-girlfriend.) 面臨 means "to be confronted with", "to be faced with". Its object is an upcoming event or situation. Examples: 熊貓面臨滅絕. (The panda is confronted with extinction.) 中國社會現在面臨很多問題. (The Chinese society is confronted with many problems.)

年进国家队，现在是国际级运动健将，中国体操女队的队长。她在第八届世界杯体操赛上获得平衡木冠军后，国际体操联合会正式⁽¹⁰⁾把她独创的平衡木跳步命名为"杨波跳"。她也是第26届世界体操锦标赛和第25届奥运会女子团体第四名的主力队员。女队的姑娘们夸杨波有一副出色的嗓子，舞跳得也好。

李奕芳

这位漂亮的姑娘是福建省运动员李奕芳，现在17岁，1982年开始练体操，1988年初到国家集训队，是"李家军"中的又一位女将，第26届世界体操锦标赛和第25届奥运会的女子团体第四名的主力队员。她曾经夺得过中国体操锦标赛全能冠军，自由体操第一名。在世界体操锦标赛上，她获得平衡木第二名。婷婷玉立的李奕芳，在奥运会赛场上拇指骨折的情况下以超人的毅力克服伤痛，始终⁽¹¹⁾以甜美的微笑面对⁽¹²⁾裁判，面对观众。

生词

李春阳	(lǐ chūn yáng)	N.	Li Chunyang, name of a person 人名
广东	(guǎng dōng)	PlaceN.	Guangdong (Province)
省	(shěng)	N.	province
老大哥	(lǎo dà gē)	N.	old brother
国际级	(guó jì jí)	Adj/N.	internationally ranked
健将	(jiàn jiàng)	N.	top player
冠军	(guàn jūn)	N.	championship

Notes ⁽¹⁰⁾正式, functions most often as an adjective meaning "formal" or "regular", as in 正式党员 (an official member of the Party), 正式访问 (a formal or official visit). 正式 can also function as an adverb meaning "formally" or "officially", as in 他今天正式宣布中美友好协会成立了. (Today he formally announced the founding of the Sino-American Friendship Association.)

⁽¹¹⁾始终 is an adverb meaning "from beginning（始）to end（终）", "throughout", "all along", "always". Example: 我始终热爱我所从事的工作. (I've always loved my work.) When used in a negative sentence, 始终 must precede the negative particle. Example: 这位有名的运动员始终没结过婚. (This famous athlete has never married.)

⁽¹²⁾面对 and 面临 are both used mostly in formal settings. 面对 means "to face" and "to confront". Its objects can be nouns referring to people, things, or situations. Examples: 面对事实 (to face reality); 他不能面对他过去的女朋友. (He cannot face his ex-girlfriend.) 面临 means "to be confronted with", "to be faced with". Its object is an upcoming event or situation. Examples: 熊猫面临灭绝. (The panda is confronted with extinction.) 中国社会现在面临很多问题. (The Chinese society is confronted with many problems.)

獲得者	(huò dé zhě)	NP.	winner
錦標賽	(jǐn biāo sài)	N.	championship contest
巴塞羅那	(bā sài luó nà)	N.	Barcelona 地名
奧運會	(ào yùn huì)	N.	Olympic Games
團體	(tuán tǐ)	N.	team
亞軍	(yà jūn)	N.	runner-up
戰功赫赫	(zhàn gōng hè hè)	Idiom.	with excessive awards, winning numerous titles
單項	(dān xiàng)	N.	single item
出色	(chū sè)	Adj.	outstanding, remarkable
工作者	(gōng zuò zhě)	NP.	worker
選手	(xuǎn shǒu)	N.	athlete
貢獻	(gòng xiàn)	N.	contribution
譽為	(yù wéi)	VP.	to be honored as
業績	(yè jī)	N.	achievement
生動地	(shēng dòng de)	Adv.	vividly
成就	(chéng jiù)	N.	accomplishment, success
凝聚	(níng jù)	V.	to embody
心血	(xīn xuè)	N.	heart and blood
來之不易	(lái zhī bù yì)	Idiom.	hard to obtain
隊長	(duì zhǎng)	N.	team leader
世界杯	(shì jiè bēi)	N.	World Cup
正式	(zhèng shì)	Adj/Adv.	formal; formally, officially
獨創	(dú chuàng)	VP.	to be created solely by
跳步	(tiào bù)	N.	jump
命名	(mìng míng)	VO.	to name (after)
誇	(kuā)	V.	to praise
副	(fù)	Classifier.	classifier for voice
嗓子	(sǎng zi)	N.	voice
李奕芳	(lǐ yì fāng)	N.	Li Yifang, name of a person 人名
女將	(nǚ jiàng)	N.	female general
全能	(quán néng)	Adj.	all around
婷婷玉立	(tíng tíng yù lì)	Idiom.	slim and graceful
拇指	(mǔ zhǐ)	N.	thumb

获得者	(huò dé zhě)	*NP.*	winner
锦标赛	(jǐn biāo sài)	*N.*	championship contest
巴塞罗那	(bā sài luó nà)	*N.*	Barcelona 地名
奥运会	(ào yùn huì)	*N.*	Olympic Games
团体	(tuán tǐ)	*N.*	team
亚军	(yà jūn)	*N.*	runner-up
战功赫赫	(zhàn gōng hè hè)	*Idiom.*	with excessive awards, winning numerous titles
单项	(dān xiàng)	*N.*	single item
出色	(chū sè)	*Adj.*	outstanding, remarkable
工作者	(gōng zuò zhě)	*NP.*	worker
选手	(xuǎn shǒu)	*N.*	athlete
贡献	(gòng xiàn)	*N.*	contribution
誉为	(yù wéi)	*VP.*	to be honored as
业绩	(yè jī)	*N.*	achievement
生动地	(shēng dòng de)	*Adv.*	vividly
成就	(chéng jiù)	*N.*	accomplishment, success
凝聚	(níng jù)	*V.*	to embody
心血	(xīn xuè)	*N.*	heart and blood
来之不易	(lái zhī bù yì)	*Idiom.*	hard to obtain
队长	(duì zhǎng)	*N.*	team leader
世界杯	(shì jiè bēi)	*N.*	World Cup
正式	(zhèng shì)	*Adj/Adv.*	formal; formally, officially
独创	(dú chuàng)	*VP.*	to be created solely by
跳步	(tiào bù)	*N.*	jump
命名	(mìng míng)	*VO.*	to name (after)
夸	(kuā)	*V.*	to praise
副	(fù)	*Classifier.*	classifier for voice
嗓子	(sǎng zi)	*N.*	voice
李奕芳	(lǐ yì fāng)	*N.*	Li Yifang, name of a person 人名
女将	(nǚ jiàng)	*N.*	female general
全能	(quán néng)	*Adj.*	all around
婷婷玉立	(tíng tíng yù lì)	*Idiom.*	slim and graceful
拇指	(mǔ zhǐ)	*N.*	thumb

骨折	(gǔ zhé)	*N.*	fracture
超人	(chāo rén)	*N.*	beyond the ability of an ordinary person
毅力	(yì lì)	*N.*	will power
克服	(kè fú)	*V.*	to overcome
傷痛	(shāng tòng)	*N.*	pain
始終	(shǐ zhōng)	*Adv.*	from the beginning to the end, always
甜美	(tián měi)	*Adj.*	sweet and beautiful
面對	(miàn duì)	*V.*	to face, to confront
微笑	(wēi xiào)	*N.*	smile
裁判	(cái pàn)	*N.*	referee

骨折	(gǔ zhé)	*N.*	fracture
超人	(chāo rén)	*N.*	beyond the ability of an ordinary person
毅力	(yì lì)	*N.*	will power
克服	(kè fú)	*V.*	to overcome
伤痛	(shāng tòng)	*N.*	pain
始终	(shǐ zhōng)	*Adv.*	from the beginning to the end, always
甜美	(tián měi)	*Adj.*	sweet and beautiful
面对	(miàn duì)	*V.*	to face, to confront
微笑	(wēi xiào)	*N.*	smile
裁判	(cái pàn)	*N.*	referee

課文要點

一、詞語解釋 Words and Phrases

（一）文言詞、慣用詞 (Classical Chinese and idiomatic expressions)

1、如今＝現在
  ☞ 如今他已成為戰功赫赫的老將。
2、曾＝曾經
  ☞ 兩個哥哥和一個姐姐都曾是優秀的中國體操選手。
3、（命名）為＝（正式定）成
  ☞ 國際體操聯合會正式把她獨創的平衡木跳步命名為"楊波跳"。

（二）成語 (idioms)

◆ 戰功赫赫: with excessive awards, winning numerous titles
◆ 婷婷玉立: slim and graceful

二、書面語、正式語、口語對照表 Written/formal/colloquial Comparison

	書面／正式語	口語		書面／正式語	口語
1	度過	過	7	凝聚	聚
2	生涯	生活	8	來之不易	來得很不容易
3	一員	一個	9	不滿	不到
4	現年	現在的年齡	10	獨創	自己創造
5	…之家	…的家庭	11	始終	從頭到尾
6	業績	成績			

课文要点

一、词语解释 Words and Phrases

（一）文言词、惯用词 (Classical Chinese and idiomatic expressions)

> 1、如今 = 现在
> ☞ 如今他已成为战功赫赫的老将。
> 2、曾 = 曾经
> ☞ 两个哥哥和一个姐姐都曾是优秀的中国体操选手。
> 3、（命名）为 =（正式定）成
> ☞ 国际体操联合会正式把她独创的平衡木跳步命名为"杨波跳"。

（二）成语 (idioms)

> ◆ 战功赫赫: with excessive awards, winning numerous titles
> ◆ 婷婷玉立: slim and graceful

二、书面语、正式语、口语对照表 Written/formal/colloquial Comparison

	书面／正式语	口语		书面／正式语	口语
1	度过	过	7	凝聚	聚
2	生涯	生活	8	来之不易	来得很不容易
3	一员	一个	9	不满	不到
4	现年	现在的年龄	10	独创	自己创造
5	…之家	…的家庭	11	始终	从头到尾
6	业绩	成绩			

三、句型 Sentence Structures

（一）在……度過 + N （假期／時期／時間） (to spend a period of time somewhere)

> 在……度過……時期／時間 is used primarily with terms relating to age and historical periods, such as 少年時期 (the period of one's youth), 晚年 (later years), 戰爭年代 (war era). It often appears in formal and written Chinese. Unlike the English verb "to spend" 度過 cannot be used in the sense of spending time to do something. Moreover, 度過 should not be used to ask questions such as "How do you spend your evenings?" because it would sound bookish. In this kind of sentence, 花 should be used rather than 度過.

☞在10歲左右就離開家去北京國家集訓隊集訓，在單槓或平衡木前度過他們寶貴的青少年時期。

1、他是在戰爭中度過了他的童年時期。

He spent his childhood in wartime.

2、我在北京度過了三個月。雖然生活緊張，但是學到了不少東西。

I spent three months in Beijing. Although life was hectic, I learned a lot.

問：為甚麼張藝謀拍了那麼多反映陝西農村的電影？
答：＿＿＿＿＿＿＿＿＿＿＿＿＿＿＿＿＿＿＿。

（二）開始／結束……生涯 (to begin/end a career in)

> 生涯, literally, the shore or limit (涯) of one's life (生), means "the means of one's livelihood" or "career". Because 生涯 is a formal word, 開始／結束……生涯 often appears in formal and written settings. Nouns used to modify 生涯 are often related to professions, such as 總統生涯 (the career of a President), 體育生涯 (sports career), 音樂生涯 (a career in music). Unlike 事業, 生涯 cannot refer to common or run-of-the-mill careers, but rather must refer to some sort of adventurous or uncommon profession. 生涯 may be used with the verb 從事 to indicate being engaged in a career, as well as with verbs such as 開始 and 結束 to indicate the beginning or end of a career.

☞ 這還不說，從事體操的人都知道，十年以後很多人就得結束他們的體操生涯了。

1、在那個時候，任何一件跟女性有關的事情都能結束他的政治生涯。

At that time, any incident related to a woman could have ended his political career.

2、貝多芬是從甚麼時候開始他的音樂生涯的？

When did Beethoven begin his musical career?

問：你認為＿＿＿＿＿＿＿＿＿＿＿＿＿＿？
答：當然。任何一點小的錯誤都可以導致這樣的結果。

三、句型 Sentence Structures

（一）在……度过 + N （假期／时期／时间） (to spend a period of time somewhere)

> ✍ 在……度过……时期／时间 is used primarily with terms relating to age and historical periods, such as 少年时期 (the period of one's youth), 晚年 (later years), 战争年代 (war era). It often appears in formal and written Chinese. Unlike the English verb "to spend", 度过 cannot be used in the sense of spending time to do something. Moreover, 度过 should not be used to ask questions such as "How do you spend your evenings?", because it would sound bookish. In this kind of sentence, 花 should be used rather than 度过.

☞ 在10岁左右就离开家去北京国家集训队集训，在单杠或平衡木前度过他们宝贵的青少年时期。

1、他是在战争中度过了他的童年时期。

He spent his childhood in wartime.

2、我在北京度过了三个月。虽然生活紧张，但是学到了不少东西。

I spent three months in Beijing. Although life was hectic, I learned a lot.

问：为什么张艺谋拍了那么多反映陕西农村的电影？

答：_____。

（二）开始／结束……生涯 (to begin/end a career in)

> ✍ 生涯, literally, the shore or limit (涯) of one's life (生), means "the means of one's livelihood" or "career". Because 生涯 is a formal word, 开始／结束……生涯 often appears in formal and written settings. Nouns used to modify 生涯 are often related to professions, such as 总统生涯 (the career of a President), 体育生涯 (sports career), 音乐生涯 (a career in music). Unlike 事业, 生涯 cannot refer to common or run-of-the-mill careers, but rather must refer to some sort of adventurous or uncommon profession. 生涯 may be used with the verb 从事 to indicate being engaged in a career, as well as with verbs such as 开始 and 结束 to indicate the beginning or end of a career.

☞ 这还不说，从事体操的人都知道，十年以后很多人就得结束他们的体操生涯了。

1、在那个时候，任何一件跟女性有关的事情都能结束他的政治生涯。

At that time, any incident related to a woman could have ended his political career.

2、贝多芬是从什么时候开始他的音乐生涯的？

When did Beethoven begin his musical career?

问：你认为_____？

答：当然。任何一点小的错误都可以导致这样的结果。

（三）為……作（出）貢獻 (to contribute to, to dedicate to, to make a contribution to)

> ✍ 貢獻 can serve as either a noun (contribution) or a verb (to contribute, to dedicate, to devote). When used as a noun, it often follows the verb 作 or 作出. When used as a verb, it can take an object, as in 貢獻時間 (to contribute time), 貢獻生命 (to dedicate one's life to). The recipient of 貢獻 must appear before the verb and be introduced by 為. Example: 為音樂事業作出貢獻 (to make contributions to the music profession). Placement of 出 after 作 is optional. Negative particles usually appear before the 為 phrase. Example: 你怎麼可以說他沒有為教育事業作過任何貢獻？ (How could you say that he has not contributed to the cause of education?)

☞ 他一家六口人為中國體操事業作出了很大貢獻，被中國體操界譽為"國家隊"。

1、個體經濟為中國的經濟發展作出了很大的貢獻。

Private enterprise has contributed greatly to China's economic growth.

2、他為中國的電影事業作出了很大的貢獻。

He has made an important contribution to China's movie industry.

問：美國政府對科學事業作出很大貢獻的人有甚麼獎勵？
答：＿＿＿＿＿＿＿＿＿＿＿＿＿＿＿＿＿＿＿＿＿＿＿。

（四）……是……的獲得者（／主力隊員） (to be the winner or key player in)

> ✍ 是……的獲得者／主力隊員, "to be the winner or key player in", appears most often in written or formal settings.

☞ 廣東省運動員李春陽，現年24歲，是中國體操隊中的老大哥，國際級運動健將，兩次單槓世界冠軍的獲得者，

1、他連續三年都是體操冠軍的獲得者。

He has been the winner of the gymnastics championship for three consecutive years.

2、喬丹一直是芝加哥公牛隊的主力隊員。

Michael Jordan has always been the dominant player on the Chicago Bulls basketball team.

問：喬丹，你在這十幾年的籃球生活中獲得過甚麼獎？
答：＿＿＿＿＿＿＿＿＿＿＿＿＿＿＿＿＿＿＿＿＿＿＿。

（三）为……作（出）贡献 (to contribute to, to dedicate to, to make a contribution to)

> ✍ 贡献 can serve as either a noun (contribution) or a verb (to contribute, to dedicate, to devote). When used as a noun, it often follows the verb 作 or 作出. When used as a verb, it can take an object, as in 贡献时间 (to contribute time), 贡献生命 (to dedicate one's life to). The recipient of 贡献 must appear before the verb and be introduced by 为. Example: 为音乐事业作出贡献 (to make contributions to the music profession). Placement of 出 after 作 is optional. Negative particles usually appear before the 为 phrase. Example: 你怎么可以说他没有为教育事业作过任何贡献？(How could you say that he has not contributed to the cause of education?)

☞ 他一家六口人为中国体操事业作出了很大贡献，被中国体操界誉为"国家队"。

1、个体经济为中国的经济发展作出了很大的贡献。

Private enterprise has contributed greatly to China's economic growth.

2、他为中国的电影事业作出了很大的贡献。

He has made an important contribution to China's movie industry.

问：美国政府对科学事业作出很大贡献的人有什么奖励？

答：＿＿＿＿＿＿＿＿＿＿＿＿＿＿＿＿＿＿＿＿。

（四）……是……的获得者（／主力队员）(to be the winner or key player in)

> ✍ 是……的获得者／主力队员, "to be the winner or key player in", appears most often in written or formal settings.

☞ 广东省运动员李春阳，现年24岁，是中国体操队中的老大哥，国际级运动健将，两次单杠世界冠军的获得者，

1、他连续三年都是体操冠军的获得者。

He has been the winner of the gymnastics championship for three consecutive years.

2、乔丹一直是芝加哥公牛队的主力队员。

Michael Jordan has always been the dominant player on the Chicago Bulls basketball team.

问：乔丹，你在这十几年的篮球生活中获得过什么奖？

答：＿＿＿＿＿＿＿＿＿＿＿＿＿＿＿＿＿＿＿。

（五）A 把 B 命名為 C; B 被 A 命名為 C (A names B after C)

> These two patterns share the same meaning, but the first is active and focuses on the subject, while the second is passive and places emphasis on the object. The agent of 命名 must be a higher authority with a formal title or position of power, such as 奧委會 (Olympic Committee), 政府 (government), or 校長 (president or headmaster of a school). 被命名為, although passive, does not convey a tone of adversity. Negation of this structure is rare. Example: 為了紀念我們的老師，我們把這個教學樓命名為 "李良" 教學樓. (In order to commemorate our professor, we named this classroom building the Li Liang Building.)

☞ 她在第八屆世界杯體操賽上獲得平衡木冠軍後，國際體操聯合會正式把她獨創的平衡木跳步命名為 "楊波跳"。

1、國際奧委會把他創造的體操動作命名為 "李林"。

The International Olympic Committee named the gymnastics move that he created the 'Li Lin' after him.

2、北京保險公司把這種保險命名為 "國家級保險"。

The Beijing Insurance Company named this type of insurance National Grade Insurance.

問：你知道這條 "毛澤東路" 是怎麼來的嗎？

答：_____。

（六）在……（的）情況下 (under the circumstances of)

> 在……（的）情況下, "under the circumstances of", is an adverbial phrase which is always placed before the main clause. It indicates the conditions under which an event or action takes place.

☞ 婷婷玉立的李奕芳，在奧運會賽場上拇指骨折的情況下以超人的毅力克服傷痛，始終以甜美的微笑面對裁判，面對觀眾。

1、在父母離異的情況下，他以最好的成績考上了南開中學。

Even though his parents were separating, he had the best grades on the entrance exam for Nankai Middle School.

2、在手指受傷的情況下，他仍然堅持比賽。

Even with an injured finger, he still persists in competing.

問：你為甚麼決定出國留學？

答：因為我原來單位的工作_____。

（五）A 把 B 命名为 C；B 被 A 命名为 C (A names B after C)

> ✍ These two patterns share the same meaning, but the first is active and focuses on the subject, while the second is passive and places emphasis on the object. The agent of 命名 must be a higher authority with a formal title or position of power, such as 奥委会 (Olympic Committee), 政府 (government), or 校长 (president or headmaster of a school). 被命名为, although passive, does not convey a tone of adversity. Negation of this structure is rare. Example: 为了记念我们的老师，我们把这个教学楼命名为"李良"教学楼. (In order to commemorate our professor, we named this classroom building the Li Liang Building.)

☞ 她在第八届世界杯体操赛上获得平衡木冠军后，国际体操联合会正式把她独创的平衡木跳步命名为"杨波跳"。

1、国际奥委会把他创造的体操动作命名为"李林"。
The International Olympic Committee named the gymnastics move that he created the 'Li Lin' after him.

2、北京保险公司把这种保险命名为"国家级保险"。
The Beijing Insurance Company named this type of insurance National Grade Insurance.

问：你知道这条"毛泽东路"是怎么来的吗？
答：＿＿＿＿＿＿＿＿＿＿＿＿＿＿＿＿＿＿。

（六）在……（的）情况下 (under the circumstances of)

> ✍ 在……（的）情况下, "under the circumstances of", is an adverbial phrase which is always placed before the main clause. It indicates the conditions under which an event or action takes place.

☞ 婷婷玉立的李奕芳，在奥运会赛场上拇指骨折的情况下以超人的毅力克服伤痛，始终以甜美的微笑面对裁判，面对观众。

1、在父母离异的情况下，他以最好的成绩考上了南开中学。
Even though his parents were separating, he had the best grades on the entrance exam for Nankai Middle School.

2、在手指受伤的情况下，他仍然坚持比赛。
Even with an injured finger, he still persists in competing.

问：你为什么决定出国留学？
答：因为我原来单位的工作＿＿＿＿＿＿＿＿＿＿＿＿＿。

（七）以（／用）……的毅力（／態度／服務）＋V (to use one's willpower)

> ✍ 以……的毅力（／態度／服務）usually appears in formal or written settings to indicate the means by which an action is achieved. 毅力 can be replaced by 態度 or 服務. Modifying elements which commonly appear before 毅力, 態度, and 服務 are mostly disyllabic. 以 can be replaced with 用.

☞ 婷婷玉立的李奕芳，在奧運會賽場上拇指骨折的情況下以超人的毅力克服傷痛，始終以甜美的微笑面對裁判，面對觀眾。

1、你應該以一種肯定的態度來看待人生。

You should take a positive attitude toward life.

2、要想成功，公司必須用最好的服務來吸引顧客。

If a company wants to succeed, it must provide the best service possible in order to attract new customers.

問：你們成功的秘密是甚麼？

答：＿＿＿＿＿＿＿＿＿＿＿＿＿＿＿＿＿＿＿＿＿　。

（八）……面對……＋N（困難／壓力／問題）(to face)

> ✍ 面對 usually takes nouns that indicate problems or difficulties, or someone or something which must be faced with courage. It can be used as a main verb or as part of an adverbial phrase at the beginning of a sentence. Example: 面對殘酷的現實，他決定放棄自己的興趣去做生意。(Faced with the cruel reality, he decided to abandon his own interests and go into business.) 面對 here is interchangeable with 面臨 (see Lesson 13, Pattern 10).

☞ 婷婷玉立的李奕芳，在奧運會賽場上拇指骨折的情況下以超人的毅力克服傷痛，始終以甜美的微笑面對裁判，面對觀眾。

1、她常常以微笑面對顧客。

She often greets customers with a smile.

2、他以堅強的毅力面對體操訓練中的困難。

He faced the difficulties of gymnastics training with strong willpower.

問：在你有很多壓力和困難的時候，你會怎麼鼓勵你自己繼續向前？

答：＿＿＿＿＿＿＿＿＿＿＿＿＿＿＿＿＿＿＿　。

（七）以（／用）……的毅力（／态度／服务）＋ V (to use one's willpower)

> ✍ 以……的毅力（／态度／服务） usually appears in formal or written settings to indicate the means by which an action is achieved. 毅力 can be replaced by 态度 or 服务. Modifying elements which commonly appear before 毅力, 态度, and 服务 are mostly disyllabic. 以 can be replaced with 用.

☞ 婷婷玉立的李奕芳，在奥运会赛场上拇指骨折的情况下以超人的毅力克服伤痛，始终以甜美的微笑面对裁判，面对观众。

1、你应该以一种肯定的态度来看待人生。
   You should take a positive attitude toward life.

2、要想成功，公司必须用最好的服务来吸引顾客。
   If a company wants to succeed, it must provide the best service possible in order to attract new customers.

问：你们成功的秘密是什么？
答：＿＿＿＿＿＿＿＿＿＿＿＿＿＿＿＿＿＿＿＿＿。

（八）……面对……＋ N（困难／压力／问题）(to face)

> ✍ 面对 usually takes nouns that indicate problems or difficulties, or someone or something which must be faced with courage. It can be used as a main verb or as part of an adverbial phrase at the beginning of a sentence. Example: 面对残酷的现实，他决定放弃自己的兴趣去做生意. (Faced with the cruel reality, he decided to abandon his own interests and go into business.) 面对 here is interchangeable with 面临 (see Lesson 13, Pattern 10).

☞ 婷婷玉立的李奕芳，在奥运会赛场上拇指骨折的情况下以超人的毅力克服伤痛，始终以甜美的微笑面对裁判，面对观众。

1、她常常以微笑面对顾客。
   She often greets customers with a smile.

2、他以坚强的毅力面对体操训练中的困难。
   He faced the difficulties of gymnastics training with strong willpower.

问：在你有很多压力和困难的时候，你会怎么鼓励你自己继续向前？
答：＿＿＿＿＿＿＿＿＿＿＿＿＿＿＿＿＿＿＿。

（九）A 誇 B (A praises B)

> ✍ 誇 is a transitive verb meaning "to praise". It is used most often in spoken settings, and its written counterpart is 稱讚. Example: 女運動員都誇楊波有一副出色的嗓子. (All the female athletes on the team praise Yang Bo for her remarkable voice.) The verb 誇 can never be used for inanimate or formal institutions such as 政府, 公司, or 學校.

☞ 女隊的姑娘們誇楊波有一副出色的嗓子，舞跳得也好。

1、所有的教授都誇那個殘疾學生有毅力。

All of the professors praised that handicapped person's strong willpower.

2、很多父母都誇這所大學有很多有經驗的教授和先進的設備。

Many parents praised this college for having many experienced professors and up-to-date facilities.

問：為甚麼你雇那個農民來你的公司工作？

答：＿＿＿＿＿＿＿＿＿＿＿＿＿＿＿＿＿＿＿。

四、文化背景知識 Cultural Notes

> China's National Training Camps (國家集訓隊) are organized similarly to those in the United States. The most talented young athletes are recruited while still very young and brought to the camps, where they attend regular school and train in their sport year round. There are also training camps organized at the provincial level in China.

（九）A 夸 B (A praises B)

✍ 夸 is a transitive verb meaning "to praise". It is used most often in spoken settings, and its written counterpart is 称赞. Example: 女运动员都夸杨波有一副出色的嗓子. (All the female athletes on the team praise Yang Bo for her remarkable voice.) The verb 夸 can never be used for inanimate or formal institutions such as 政府, 公司, or 学校.

☞ 女队的姑娘们夸杨波有一副出色的嗓子，舞跳得也好。

1、所有的教授都夸那个残疾学生有毅力。

All of the professors praised that handicapped person's strong willpower.

2、很多父母都夸这所大学有很多有经验的教授和先进的设备。

Many parents praised this college for having many experienced professors and up-to-date facilities.

问：为什么你雇那个农民来你的公司工作？

答：_____。

四、文化背景知识 Cultural Notes

China's National Training Camps (国家集训队) are organized similarly to those in the United States. The most talented young athletes are recruited while still very young and brought to the camps, where they attend regular school and train in their sport year round. There are also training camps organized at the provincial level in China.

練習

語言結構 Structures

一、短語翻譯 (Phrase translation)

1. gymnastic team
2. an internationally known athlete
3. single bar and balance beam champions
4. world cup meet
5. 26th Olympic Games
6. gymnastic career
7. major player on the team
8. double bar and side horse
9. excellent performance
10. to vividly represent
11. floor exercise
12. all-round champion

二、聽力練習 (Listening comprehension)

1、聽寫 (Dictation)

2、聽錄音並回答問題 (Answering questions while listening to the audio CD)
 (1) 馬羚是一個甚麼樣的人？
 (2) 馬羚在24歲前取得了甚麼樣的成就？
 (3) 用書上的話說說美國的籃球明星喬丹。

三、完成句子 (Complete the sentences)

1、 Ａ：你知道 Dustin Hoffman 嗎？
  Ｂ：誰不知道他？他 _____
   （……獲得者；為……作出貢獻）

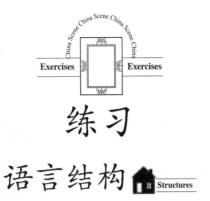

练习

语言结构 Structures

一、短语翻译 (Phrase translation)

1. gymnastic team
2. an internationally known athlete
3. single bar and balance beam champions
4. world cup meet
5. 26th Olympic Games
6. gymnastic career
7. major player on the team
8. double bar and side horse
9. excellent performance
10. to vividly represent
11. floor exercise
12. all-round champion

二、听力练习 (Listening comprehension)

1、听写 (Dictation)

2、听录音并回答问题 (Answering questions while listening to the audio CD)
   (1) 马羚是一个什么样的人？
   (2) 马羚在24岁前取得了什么样的成就？
   (3) 用书上的话说说美国的篮球明星乔丹。

三、完成句子 (Complete the sentences)

1、　　A：你知道 Dustin Hoffman 吗？
　　　　B：谁不知道他？他＿＿＿＿＿＿＿＿＿＿＿＿＿＿＿＿＿＿＿
　　　　（……获得者；为……作出贡献）

2、　　A：為甚麼你常去這家人又多地方又小的店去買東西？

　　　　B：因為這家店_____

　　　　（在……的情況下；以……面對）

四、閱讀短文、回答問題 (Answering questions based on the reading passages)

> 　　四川運動員李舸是中國體操隊"李家軍"中的又一位戰將。現在23歲。十年前進國家隊。他是國際級運動健將，也是第26屆世界體操錦標賽和巴塞羅那第25屆奧運會男子團體亞軍的主力隊員。李舸在巴塞羅那的團體比賽中多次第一個出場。他的技術穩定、全面，為中國男隊奪得銀牌立下了汗馬功勞。

問題

　　(1) 用你自己的話說說李舸

　　(2) 翻譯全文

> 　　這位面孔熟悉的運動員是有名的體操運動員李小雙的孿生哥哥李大雙。小哥倆兒一同開始練體操，1989年底一同來到國家隊。除了體操外，他們的業餘愛好都是跳舞。在多次國內比賽中，性情好動的弟弟李小雙奪第一，稍大一點兒的哥哥緊隨其後。他也是奧運會體操團體賽中國隊的主力隊員。

問題

　　(1) 用你自己的話說說李大雙

　　(2) 翻譯全文

五、翻譯 (Translate sentences)

1. This athlete is only 24 years old, but he has already had an eight-year gymnastic career and has contributed tremendously to Chinese gymnastics.

2. After winning the championship in the World Cup Gymnastics Competition, the International Association of Gymnastics named the balance beam jump created by Yang Bo the "Yang Bo Jump".

3. This first-rate athlete overcame the pain with unusual willpower and presented the audience and referees with a sweet smile from beginning to end.

2、　　A：为什么你常去这家人又多地方又小的店去买东西？
　　　　B：因为这家店_____
　　　　（在……的情况下；以……面对）

四、阅读短文、回答问题 (Answering questions based on the reading passages)

　　　四川运动员李舸是中国体操队"李家军"中的又一位战将。现在23岁。十年前进国家队。他是国际级运动健将，也是第26届世界体操锦标赛和巴塞罗那第25届奥运会男子团体亚军的主力队员。李舸在巴塞罗那的团体比赛中多次第一个出场。他的技术稳定、全面，为中国男队夺得银牌立下了汗马功劳。

问题
　　(1) 用你自己的话说说李舸
　　(2) 翻译全文

　　　这位面孔熟悉的运动员是有名的体操运动员李小双的孪生哥哥李大双。小哥俩儿一同开始练体操，1989年底一同来到国家队。除了体操外，他们的业余爱好都是跳舞。在多次国内比赛中，性情好动的弟弟李小双夺第一，稍大一点儿的哥哥紧随其后。他也是奥运会体操团体赛中国队的主力队员。

问题
　　(1) 用你自己的话说说李大双
　　(2) 翻译全文

五、翻译 (Translate sentences)

1. This athlete is only 24 years old, but he has already had an eight-year gymnastic career and has contributed tremendously to Chinese gymnastics.

2. After winning the championship in the World Cup Gymnastics Competition, the International Association of Gymnastics named the balance beam jump created by Yang Bo the "Yang Bo Jump".

3. This first-rate athlete overcame the pain with unusual willpower and presented the audience and referees with a sweet smile from beginning to end.

語言實踐：Practice

一、根據課文回答問題 (Answering questions based on the dialogue)

1、用你的話說說體操運動員李春陽
2、用你的話說說體操運動員國林耀和他的家庭
3、用你的話說說體操運動員楊波和她的體操成就
4、用你的話說說體操運動員李奕芳和她在賽場上的態度

二、活動 (Activities)

　　　看一場足球、排球、或體操比賽，或者去北京體育學院採訪一下在那裡學習的學生。問問他們：

1、他們是從甚麼時候開始練的？
2、他們在甚麼比賽中得過甚麼獎？
3、他們為甚麼要做這種運動？
4、將來他們打算做甚麼？

三、討論題 (Topics for discussion)

1、你認為練體操的青少年應該不應該有一個正常的青少年生活？他們應該不應該很小就從事專業體操訓練？
2、一個人要在事業上有成就，應該不應該犧牲其它方面的生活？

四、報告 (Presentation)

　　　《我看的一場體育比賽》

语言实践 ⦂ Practice

一、 根据课文回答问题 (Answering questions based on the dialogue)

1、 用你的话说说体操运动员李春阳
2、 用你的话说说体操运动员国林耀和他的家庭
3、 用你的话说说体操运动员杨波和她的体操成就
4、 用你的话说说体操运动员李奕芳和她在赛场上的态度

二、 活动 (Activities)

　　看一场足球、排球、或体操比赛，或者去北京体育学院采访一下在那里学习的学生。问问他们：

1、 他们是从什么时候开始练的？
2、 他们在什么比赛中得过什么奖？
3、 他们为什么要做这种运动？
4、 将来他们打算做什么？

三、 讨论题 (Topics for discussion)

1、 你认为练体操的青少年应该不应该有一个正常的青少年生活？他们应该不应该很小就从事专业体操训练？
2、 一个人要在事业上有成就，应该不应该牺牲其它方面的生活？

四、 报告 (Presentation)

　　《我看的一场体育比赛》

五、看圖討論 (Picto-discussion)

五、看图讨论 (Picto-discussion)

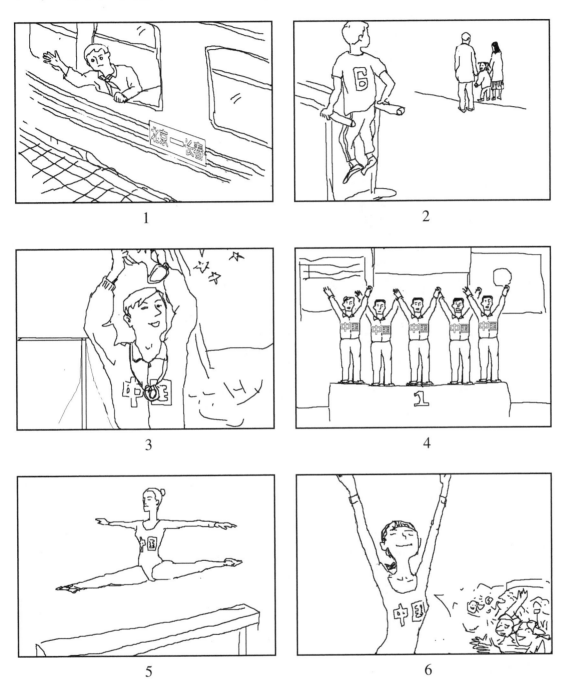

1

2

3

4

5

6

补充课文
Supplementary Texts

補充課文

第十五課

東北風俗

补充课文

第十五课

东北风俗

297

課文

一、對話  Dialogs

---

（一）

裴婉：　為甚麼這兒的男人都抽煙呢？抽煙對人的身體不好。

蔡長安：咱們這兒的人倒不這麼想。很多人在大山和田野裡幹活幹累了，坐在地上抽

一袋煙，又解乏、又解悶兒，冬天能暖和身子，夏天能驅趕蚊蟲。

裴婉：　我可不這麼看，抽煙的好處怎麼也沒有壞處多。

生詞

風俗	(fēng sú)	N.	custom
姑娘	(gū niáng)	N.	unmarried young girl
叼	(diāo)	V.	to hold in the mouth, dangling from one's lips
煙袋	(yān dài)	N.	Chinese tobacco pipe
裴婉	(péi wǎn)	N.	Pei Wan, name of a person 人名
蔡長安	(cài cháng ān)	N.	Cai Changan, name of a person 人名
抽	(chōu)	V.	to smoke
煙	(yān)	N.	tobacco or cigarette
田野	(tián yě)	N.	field
活兒	(huór)	N.	work, job, chore
袋	(dài)	Classifier.	a bag of
解乏	(jiě fá)	VO.	to be refreshing, to recover from fatigue
解悶	(jiě mèn)	VO.	to get rid of loneliness
暖和	(nuǎn huo)	V.	to warm up
身子	(shēn zi)	N.	body
驅趕	(qū gǎn)	V.	to chase away, to get rid of
蚊	(wén)	N.	mosquito
蟲	(chóng)	N.	insects

课文

一、对话 Dialogs

（一）

裴婉： 为什么这儿的男人都抽烟呢？抽烟对人的身体不好。

蔡长安： 咱们这儿的人倒不这么想。很多人在大山和田野里干活干累了，坐在地上抽一袋烟，又解乏、又解闷儿，冬天能暖和身子，夏天能驱赶蚊虫。

裴婉： 我可不这么看，抽烟的好处怎么也没有坏处多。

生词

风俗	(fēng sú)	N.	custom
姑娘	(gū niáng)	N.	unmarried young girl
叼	(diāo)	V.	to hold in the mouth, dangling from one's lips
烟袋	(yān dài)	N.	Chinese tobacco pipe
裴婉	(péi wǎn)	N.	Pei Wan, name of a person 人名
蔡长安	(cài cháng ān)	N.	Cai Changan, name of a person 人名
抽	(chōu)	V.	to smoke
烟	(yān)	N.	tobacco or cigarette
田野	(tián yě)	N.	field
活儿	(huór)	N.	work, job, chore
袋	(dài)	Classifier.	a bag of
解乏	(jiě fá)	VO.	to be refreshing, to recover from fatigue
解闷	(jiě mèn)	VO.	to get rid of loneliness
暖和	(nuǎn huo)	V.	to warm up
身子	(shēn zi)	N.	body
驱赶	(qū gǎn)	V.	to chase away, to get rid of
蚊	(wén)	N.	mosquito
虫	(chóng)	N.	insects

（二）

裴婉： 我聽說山西的姑娘也有自己的習俗。

蔡長安：對了。提起山西的大姑娘，她們可跟東北的大姑娘不一樣。也不知道從甚麼時候開始，在山西就有了這麼一個風俗：姑娘一出嫁，就不能出門了，只能做家裡的活。春種秋收，上山打柴等都是男人的活，女人不能參加。所以山西姑娘的多半生都是在家中做飯、看孩子，自然沒有東北姑娘那麼野氣、豪放。

生詞

山西	(Shān xī)	*PlaceN.*	Shanxi (Province)
提起	(tí qǐ)	*V.*	to mention
出嫁	(chū jià)	*V.*	to marry (for women only)
春種秋收	(chūn zhòng qiū shōu)	*Idiom.*	to plant in spring and harvest in fall
打柴	(dǎ chái)	*VO.*	to collect wood (in the mountains)
野氣	(yě qì)	*N.*	wildness
豪放	(háo fàng)	*Adj.*	unconstrained, bold

二、電視原文 🖥 TV original

大姑娘叼煙袋

（根據原文改編）

在中國的東北有三大怪，其中一怪就是大姑娘叼煙袋。東北的大姑娘為甚麼叼煙袋、從甚麼時候開始興起抽煙的呢？這事兒，老一輩的人也說不清楚。要說男人們叼個煙袋，那沒甚麼奇怪的。幹活累了，心裡煩悶， 抽上一袋關東煙能解解乏，解解悶兒。

提起東北的大姑娘，她們和男人一樣能幹，春種秋收，上山打柴，家裡外頭的活兒，哪一樣兒也拿得起、放得下。早些年，有些女人還要和男人一道兒進山打獵。我想她們大概是為了和男人們比試高低，讓男人們覺得她們哪樣兒也不比男人們差。男

（二）

裴婉： 我听说山西的姑娘也有自己的习俗。

蔡长安： 对了。提起山西的大姑娘，她们可跟东北的大姑娘不一样。也不知道从什么时候开始，在山西就有了这么一个风俗：姑娘一出嫁，就不能出门了，只能做家里的活。春种秋收，上山打柴等都是男人的活，女人不能参加。所以山西姑娘的多半生都是在家中做饭、看孩子，自然没有东北姑娘那么野气、豪放。

生词

山西	(Shān xī)	PlaceN.	Shanxi (Province)
提起	(tí qǐ)	V.	to mention
出嫁	(chū jià)	V.	to marry (for women only)
春种秋收	(chūn zhòng qiū shōu)	Idiom.	to plant in spring and harvest in fall
打柴	(dǎ chái)	VO.	to collect wood (in the mountains)
野气	(yě qì)	N.	wildness
豪放	(háo fàng)	Adj.	unconstrained, bold

二、电视原文 💻 TV original

大姑娘叼烟袋
（根据原文改编）

在中国的东北有三大怪，其中一怪就是大姑娘叼烟袋。东北的大姑娘为什么叼烟袋、从什么时候开始兴起抽烟的呢？这事儿，老一辈的人也说不清楚。要说男人们叼个烟袋，那没什么奇怪的。干活累了，心里烦闷， 抽上一袋关东烟能解解乏，解解闷儿。

提起东北的大姑娘，她们和男人一样能干，春种秋收，上山打柴，家里外头的活儿，哪一样儿也拿得起、放得下。早些年，有些女人还要和男人一道儿进山打猎。我想她们大概是为了和男人们比试高低，让男人们觉得她们哪样儿也不比男人们差。 男人抽煙，所以她們也學了男人的樣兒叼上個煙袋，幹活休息的時候和男人們一起抽上一袋煙，東北的大姑娘就是這麼野氣、豪放。

　　幹活抽袋煙，真能解乏嗎？好象抽煙的人都這麼說。不過據東北人說，抽煙確實有不少好處。東北的大山裡和田野裡甚麼動物都有，而且蛇和蚊子、牛虻特別多。要是你抽煙，這青煙一起，蚊子、牛虻就飛得遠遠兒地，不來叮你。蛇一聞煙味兒，骨頭都酥了，它就不敢上來咬你。冬天在大雪裡抽袋煙，還能暖和暖和身子。這些大概也是東北大姑娘叼煙袋的原因吧。

　　姑娘大了，都要出嫁、結婚。這煙袋也是陪嫁中的東西。新媳婦裝上一袋煙敬給公公婆婆，以表示孝心。您瞧，這老倆口抽到這袋煙，心裡得多美呀！沒錯，現在結婚敬煙的作法也就是從煙袋做陪嫁那個時候傳下來的。

生詞

怪	(guài)	N.	strangeness
興起	(xīng qǐ)	V.	to become popular, to spring up
關東煙	(guān dōng yān)	N.	Northeast Chinese tabacco
煩悶	(fán mèn)	Adj.	restless and lonely
能幹	(néng gàn)	VP.	capable of doing, able
早些	(zǎo xiē)	Adj.	(in) early (years, days)
打獵	(dǎ liè)	V.	to hunt
比試高低	(bǐ shì gāo dī)	Idiom.	to compete
差	(chà)	Adj.	lacking, poor
樣兒	(yàngr)	N.	appearance, style
蛇	(shé)	N.	snake
牛虻	(niú máng)	N.	gadfly
青煙	(qīng yān)	N.	light smoke
叮	(dīng)	V.	to bite
味兒	(wèir)	N.	smell, odor
酥	(sū)	V/Adj.	to be weak, soft
雪	(xuě)	N.	snow
陪嫁	(péi jià)	N.	dowry
敬給	(jìng gěi)	VP.	to present with respect

人抽烟，所以她们也学了男人的样儿叼上个烟袋，干活休息的时候和男人们一起抽上一袋烟，东北的大姑娘就是这么野气、豪放。

干活抽袋烟，真能解乏吗？好象抽烟的人都这么说。不过据东北人说，抽烟确实有不少好处。东北的大山里和田野里什么动物都有，而且蛇和蚊子、牛虻特别多。要是你抽烟，这青烟一起，蚊子、牛虻就飞得远远儿地，不来叮你。蛇一闻烟味儿，骨头都酥了，它就不敢上来咬你。冬天在大雪里抽袋烟，还能暖和暖和身子。这些大概也是东北大姑娘叼烟袋的原因吧。

姑娘大了，都要出嫁、结婚。这烟袋也是陪嫁中的东西。新媳妇装上一袋烟敬给公公婆婆，以表示孝心。您瞧，这老俩口抽到这袋烟，心里得多美呀！没错，现在结婚敬烟的作法也就是从烟袋做陪嫁那个时候传下来的。

生词

怪	(guài)	N.	strangeness
兴起	(xīng qǐ)	V.	to become popular, to spring up
关东烟	(guān dōng yān)	N.	Northeast Chinese tabacco
烦闷	(fán mèn)	Adj.	restless and lonely
能干	(néng gàn)	VP.	capable of doing, able
早些	(zǎo xiē)	Adj.	(in) early (years, days)
打猎	(dǎ liè)	V.	to hunt
比试高低	(bǐ shì gāo dī)	Idiom.	to compete
差	(chà)	Adj.	lacking, poor
样儿	(yàngr)	N.	appearance, style
蛇	(shé)	N.	snake
牛虻	(niú máng)	N.	gadfly
青烟	(qīng yān)	N.	light smoke
叮	(dīng)	V.	to bite
味儿	(wèir)	N.	smell, odor
酥	(sū)	V/Adj.	to be weak, soft
雪	(xuě)	N.	snow
陪嫁	(péi jià)	N.	dowry
敬给	(jìng gěi)	VP.	to present with respect

公公	(gōng gōng)	N.	father-in-law
婆婆	(pó pó)	N.	mother-in-law
孝心	(xiào xīn)	N.	filial piety
老倆口	(lǎo liáng kǒu)	N.	old couple
敬煙	(jìng yān)	VO.	to present the pipe with respect

公公	(gōng gōng)	*N.*	father-in-law
婆婆	(pó pó)	*N.*	mother-in-law
孝心	(xiào xīn)	*N.*	filial piety
老俩口	(lǎo liáng kǒu)	*N.*	old couple
敬烟	(jìng yān)	*VO.*	to present the pipe with respect

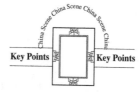

課文要點

一、詞語解釋 Words and Phrases

1、以＝用來
  ☞ 新媳婦裝上一袋煙敬給公公婆婆，以表示孝心。
2、興起＝流行
  ☞ 從甚麼時候開始興起抽煙的呢？
3、要說＝如果說
  ☞ 要說男人們叼個煙袋，那沒甚麼奇怪的。
4、早些年＝以前
  ☞ 早些年，有些女人還要和男人一道兒進山打獵。
5、比試＝比賽
  ☞ 我想她們大概是為了和男人們比試高低。

二、句型 Sentence Structures

（一）興起 (to become popular, to become trendy)
  ☞ 東北的大姑娘為甚麼叼煙袋，從甚麼時候開始興起抽煙的呢？

1、這種風俗習慣誰也不知道是甚麼時候興起的。
  No one knows when this custom became popular.
2、現在中國興起了一股結婚送保險風。
  Marriage insurance has become a popular gift in China.

  問：用電子郵件寄生日卡是從甚麼時候興起的？
  答：誰也說不清＿＿＿＿＿＿＿＿＿＿＿＿＿＿＿＿＿。

（二）要說…… (as for)
  ☞ 要說男人們叼個煙袋，那沒甚麼奇怪的。

1、要說有甚麼計劃，我一點長期計劃也沒有。
  As for plans, I do not have any long-term plans at all.

课文要点

一、词语解释 *Words and Phrases*

> 1、以 = 用来
> ☞ 新媳妇装上一袋烟敬给公公婆婆，以表示孝心。
> 2、兴起 = 流行
> ☞ 从什么时候开始兴起抽烟的呢？
> 3、要说 = 如果说
> ☞ 要说男人们叼个烟袋，那没什么奇怪的。
> 4、早些年 = 以前
> ☞ 早些年，有些女人还要和男人一道儿进山打猎。
> 5、比试 = 比赛
> ☞ 我想她们大概是为了和男人们比试高低。

二、句型 *Sentence Structures*

（一）兴起 (to become popular, to become trendy)
　　☞ 东北的大姑娘为什么叼烟袋，从什么时候开始兴起抽烟的呢？

1、这种风俗习惯谁也不知道是什么时候兴起的。
　　No one knows when this custom became popular.

2、现在中国兴起了一股结婚送保险风。
　　Marriage insurance has become a popular gift in China.

　　问：用电子邮件寄生日卡是从什么时候兴起的？
　　答：谁也说不清＿＿＿＿＿＿＿＿＿＿＿＿＿＿＿＿。

（二）要说…… (as for)
　　☞ 要说男人们叼个烟袋，那没什么奇怪的。

1、要说有什么计划，我一点长期计划也没有。
　　As for plans, I do not have any long-term plans at all.

302

2、要說攢錢買車，我早就想過了，怕不行。

As for saving money to buy a car, I have thought about it, but I'm afraid it's out of the question.

問：中國熱是從甚麼時候興起的？

答：＿＿＿＿＿＿＿＿＿＿＿。

（三）提起……(speaking of)

☞ 提起東北的大姑娘，她們和男人一樣能幹，春種秋收，上山打柴，家裡外頭的活兒，哪一樣兒也拿得起、放得下。

1、提起我媳婦，她可真能幹。

Speaking of my wife, she is really capable.

2、提起張藝謀，愛看電影的人大概都知道。

Speaking of Zhang Yimou, all movie fans have probably heard of him.

問：你現在的男／女朋友還是我前年看見的那個人嗎？

答：＿＿＿＿＿＿＿＿＿＿＿＿＿＿＿。

（四）和……比（試）高低（／能力／錢／……） (to compete with)

☞ 我想她們大概是為了和男人們比試高低，讓男人們覺得她們哪樣兒也不比男人們差。

1、我就喜歡跟好學生比試高低。

I like to compete with my classmates.

2、貧困戶哪裡能跟富裕戶比試錢。

How can poor families compare to prosperous families in terms of wealth?

問：照你現在的彈琴水平，你敢和小神童比試高低嗎？

答：＿＿＿＿＿＿＿＿＿＿＿＿＿＿。

（五）是……的原因 (to be the reason for)

☞ 這些大概也是東北大姑娘叼煙袋的原因吧？

1、這就是他為甚麼辭職不幹的原因。

This is the reason why he quit his job.

2、要说攒钱买车，我早就想过了，怕不行。
As for saving money to buy a car, I have thought about it, but I'm afraid it's out of the question.

问：中国热是从什么时候兴起的？
答：＿＿＿＿＿＿＿＿＿＿＿＿＿＿。

（三）提起……(speaking of)
☞ 提起东北的大姑娘，她们和男人一样能干，春种秋收，上山打柴，家里外头的活儿，哪一样儿也拿得起、放得下。

1、提起我媳妇，她可真能干。
Speaking of my wife, she is really capable.
2、提起张艺谋，爱看电影的人大概都知道。
Speaking of Zhang Yimou, all movie fans have probably heard of him.

问：你现在的男／女朋友还是我前年看见的那个人吗？
答：＿＿＿＿＿＿＿＿＿＿＿＿＿＿＿＿。

（四）和……比（试）高低（／能力／钱／……）(to compete with)
☞ 我想她们大概是为了和男人们比试高低，让男人们觉得她们哪样儿也不比男人们差。

1、我就喜欢跟好学生比试高低。
I like to compete with my classmates.
2、贫困户哪里能跟富裕户比试钱。
How can poor families compare to prosperous families in terms of wealth?

问：照你现在的弹琴水平，你敢和小神童比试高低吗？
答：＿＿＿＿＿＿＿＿＿＿＿＿＿＿＿＿。

（五）是……的原因 (to be the reason for)
☞ 这些大概也是东北大姑娘叼烟袋的原因吧？

1、这就是他为什么辞职不干的原因。
This is the reason why he quit his job.

2、去國家集訓隊是她不能上學的原因。

The reason she couldn't attend school was because she was selected to go to the National Training Camp.

問：你知道現在為甚麼美國政府不能負擔老百姓的醫療保險？

答：我想＿＿＿＿＿＿＿＿＿＿＿＿＿＿＿＿＿＿＿＿＿。

（六）以表示…… (in order to express)

☞ 新媳婦裝上一袋煙敬給公公婆婆，以表示孝心。

1、新婚夫婦買保險以表示結婚人願意長久相處的意願。

For newlyweds, buying insurance expresses the hope that they will be willing to grow old together.

2、給我媽買台電視以表示孝心。

I bought my mother a television to express my respect and love.

問：你為甚麼每年坐輪船去海上悼念你的母親？

答：我這樣做＿＿＿＿＿＿＿＿＿＿＿＿＿＿＿＿。

（七）……的作法 (method, way of doing things)

☞ 現在結婚敬煙的作法也就是從煙袋作陪嫁那個時候傳下來的。

1、這種海葬的作法過去只有偉人才有資格做。

In the past this sort of sea burial was only performed for high officials.

2、用結婚保險代替禮品的作法是這幾年才興起來的。

Within the past few years, it has become popular to give marriage insurance instead of a wedding gift.

問：中國人現在既不睡午覺了，也不回家吃午飯了，這種作法是甚麼時候開始興起的？

答：＿＿＿＿＿＿＿＿＿＿＿＿＿＿＿＿＿＿＿。

2、去国家集训队是她不能上学的原因。

The reason she couldn't attend school was because she was selected to go to the National Training Camp.

问：你知道现在为什么美国政府不能负担老百姓的医疗保险？

答：我想＿＿＿＿＿＿＿＿＿＿＿＿＿＿＿＿＿＿＿＿＿＿＿＿＿。

（六）以表示…… (in order to express)

☞ 新媳妇装上一袋烟敬给公公婆婆，以表示孝心。

1、新婚夫妇买保险以表示结婚人愿意长久相处的意愿。

For newlyweds, buying insurance expresses the hope that they will be willing to grow old together.

2、给我妈买台电视以表示孝心。

I bought my mother a television to express my respect and love.

问：你为什么每年坐轮船去海上悼念你的母亲？

答：我这样做＿＿＿＿＿＿＿＿＿＿＿＿＿＿＿＿＿＿＿。

（七）……的作法 (method, way of doing things)

☞ 现在结婚敬烟的作法也就是从烟袋作陪嫁那个时候传下来的。

1、这种海葬的作法过去只有伟人才有资格做。

In the past this sort of sea burial was only performed for high officials.

2、用结婚保险代替礼品的作法是这几年才兴起来的。

Within the past few years, it has become popular to give marriage insurance instead of a wedding gift.

问：中国人现在既不睡午觉了，也不回家吃午饭了，这种作法是什么时候开始兴起的？

答：＿＿＿＿＿＿＿＿＿＿＿＿＿＿＿＿＿＿＿＿＿＿＿。

（八）從……傳下來 (to pass down, to hand down)

☞ 現在結婚敬煙的作法也就是從煙袋作陪嫁那個時候傳下來的。

1、這個習俗是從甚麼時候、甚麼朝代傳下來的？

From what period and which dynasty was this custom passed down?

2、這種做包子的方法是他家祖輩傳下來的。

His family's method of making steamed buns was handed down from his ancestors.

問：這種每周一次晚會的作法是從誰那兒傳下來的？是不是早期來這裡上學的學生？

答：_____。

三、文化背景知識 Cultural Notes

1. The first of 三大怪 in Northeast China, as mentioned in our text, is that young unmarried women smoke pipes (十八歲的大姑娘，叼個旱煙帶). The other two 三大怪 are (1) covering the outside of windows with paper (窗戶紙，糊在外), and (2) using nets suspended from a ceiling (rather than cradles, or 搖籃 yáolán) for infants (養個小孩，吊起來). Another distinguishing cultural practice of the region is that people sleep on beds called *kang* (炕), which are made of bricks and heatable.

2. Dowries (陪嫁) in China function the same as dowries in the West. The content of the dowry, of course, varies depending on local customs and needs. These days it is not uncommon for a dowry to include practical items such as a refrigerator, television, washing machine, and so on.

（八）从……传下来 (to pass down, to hand down)

☞ 现在结婚敬烟的作法也就是从烟袋作陪嫁那个时候传下来的。

1、这个习俗是从什么时候、什么朝代传下来的？

From what period and which dynasty was this custom passed down?

2、这种做包子的方法是他家祖辈传下来的。

His family's method of making steamed buns was handed down from his ancestors.

问：这种每周一次晚会的作法是从谁那儿传下来的？是不是早期来这里上学的学生？

答：＿＿＿＿＿＿＿＿＿＿＿＿＿＿＿＿＿＿＿。

三、文化背景知识 Cultural Notes

1. The first of 三大怪 in Northeast China, as mentioned in our text, is that young unmarried women smoke pipes (十八岁的大姑娘，叼个旱烟带). The other two 三大怪 are (1) covering the outside of windows with paper (窗户纸，糊在外), and (2) using nets suspended from a ceiling (rather than cradles, or 摇篮 yáolán) for infants (养个小孩，吊起来). Another distinguishing cultural practice of the region is that people sleep on beds called *kang* (炕), which are made of bricks and heatable.

2. Dowries (陪嫁) in China function the same as dowries in the West. The content of the dowry, of course, varies depending on local customs and needs. These days it is not uncommon for a dowry to include practical items such as a refrigerator, television, washing machine, and so on.

練習

語言結構 Structures

一、短語翻譯 (Phrase translation)

1. to smoke a tobacco pipe
2. people from the older generation
3. to release tiredness and depression
4. to plant in spring and harvest in fall
5. to go hunting in the mountains
6. wild and bold
7. snakes and mosquitoes
8. parents-in-law
9. to show one's filial piety
10. to get married (women)

二、聽力練習 (Listening comprehension)

聽寫 (Dictation)

三、完成句子 (Complete the sentences)

1、　A：你聽說過廣東婦女的風俗嗎？　在有的地方女的結婚以後就住在廟裡。
　　B：是嗎？請你告訴我＿＿＿＿＿＿＿＿＿＿＿＿＿＿＿＿＿＿＿＿＿
　　（興起……；從……傳下來）

2、　A：你的男朋友跟你分開了，為甚麼？
　　B：＿＿＿＿＿＿＿＿＿＿＿＿＿＿＿＿＿＿＿＿＿＿＿＿＿＿＿＿＿
　　（提起……；是……的原因）

练习

语言结构 Structures

一、短语翻译 (Phrase translation)

1. to smoke a tobacco pipe
2. people from the older generation
3. to release tiredness and depression
4. to plant in spring and harvest in fall
5. to go hunting in the mountains
6. wild and bold
7. snakes and mosquitoes
8. parents-in-law
9. to show one's filial piety
10. to get married (women)

二、听力练习 (Listening comprehension)

听写 (Dictation)

三、完成句子 (Complete the sentences)

1、　　A：你听说过广东妇女的风俗吗？ 在有的地方女的结婚以后就住在庙里。
　　　　B：是吗？请你告诉我_____
　　　　（兴起……；从……传下来）

2、　　A：你的男朋友跟你分开了，为什么？
　　　　B：_____
　　　　（提起……；是……的原因）

四、閱讀短文、回答問題 (Answering questions based on the reading passages)

> 茶是一種飲料，也代表一種文化。老百姓說得好：“開門七件事，柴、米、油、鹽、醬、醋、茶”。茶跟中國人的生活的確是密切相關的。中國人在原始社會就開始種茶、製茶、飲茶。最初，茶的功用是解毒、治病。到後來飲茶成了一種生活方式，還傳到了國外。因此，有了日本的茶道，南朝鮮的茶禮，到後來，受亞洲人的影響，西方人也漸漸有了用茶的習慣。

問題

    (1) 從三個方面說明茶的功用是甚麼？

    (2) 翻譯全文

> 一晃兒在這兒住了六十年啦，今天是我90歲生日，你看我們全家都來了。我們家是五世同堂。從我這根兒上分出去，是倆兒倆女，三個孫子，三個外孫女兒，一個外孫子。重孫輩兒的十個，再加上玄孫輩兒的兩個，全來齊了啊，滿滿三十六口兒人。
>
> 我二兒媳婦兒真是個孝順媳婦，她也是做奶奶的人啦，每天跟我們住在一起，伺侯公婆，不易，要說我的晚輩兒們，都挺孝敬的，都不錯。
>
> 這是我大孫子瑞林，當著處長。還管著技術，好孩子啊，都說我最喜歡他。嗨，您說　這手心手背不都是自己的肉嗎？這是他兄弟祥林，這哥倆是我們老二的兒子。這是我的外孫賀龍光，大學裡的副教授，說是教數學，有時候我就閉著眼睛想，你說這數學，按我小時候，也就是學一年半年。龍光這孩子當著那麼些人，他怎麼老有教呢？龍生的愛人，就是我這外孫子媳婦兒是中學教師，這倆口子倒也很好，滿恩愛的。
>
> 您瞧瞧，過生日麼，還得吹蠟、吃蛋糕。嘿呀，世事兒變啦，我這麼想，往後的人哪，日子，不一定會怎麼優越哪。

問題

    (1) 從這段話，你可以知道這個老人對自己和自己的家有甚麼感想？舉例說明。

    (2) 用你的話說說老人的後輩都在做甚麼工作？

四、阅读短文、回答问题 (Answering questions based on the reading passages)

茶是一种饮料，也代表一种文化。老百姓说得好："开门七件事，柴、米、油、盐、酱、醋、茶"。茶跟中国人的生活的确是密切相关的。中国人在原始社会就开始种茶、制茶、饮茶。最初，茶的功用是解毒、治病。到后来饮茶成了一种生活方式，还传到了国外。因此，有了日本的茶道，南朝鲜的茶礼，到后来，受亚洲人的影响，西方人也渐渐有了用茶的习惯。

问题

(1) 从三个方面说明茶的功用是什么？

(2) 翻译全文

一晃儿在这儿住了六十年啦，今天是我90岁生日，你看我们全家都来了。我们家是五世同堂。从我这根儿上分出去，是俩儿俩女，三个孙子，三个外孙女儿，一个外孙子。重孙辈儿的十个，再加上玄孙辈儿的两个，全来齐了啊，满满三十六口儿人。

我二儿媳妇儿真是个孝顺媳妇，她也是做奶奶的人啦，每天跟我们住在一起，伺候公婆，不易，要说我的晚辈儿们，都挺孝敬的，都不错。

这是我大孙子瑞林，当着处长。还管着技术，好孩子啊，都说我最喜欢他。嗨，您说　这手心手背不都是自己的肉吗？这是他兄弟祥林，这哥俩是我们老二的儿子。这是我的外孙贺龙光，大学里的副教授，说是教数学，有时候我就闭着眼睛想，你说这数学，按我小时候，也就是学一年半年。龙光这孩子当着那么些人，他怎么老有教呢？龙生的爱人，就是我这外孙子媳妇儿是中学教师，这两口子倒也很好，满恩爱的。

您瞧瞧，过生日么，还得吹蜡、吃蛋糕。嘿呀，世事儿变啦，我这么想，往后的人哪，日子，不一定会怎么优越哪。

问题

(1) 从这段话，你可以知道这个老人对自己和自己的家有什么感想？举例说明。

(2) 用你的话说说老人的后辈都在做什么工作？

語言實踐：Practice

一、根據課文回答問題 (Answering questions based on the dialogue)

1、東北的三大怪是甚麼？
2、為甚麼記者說男人們叼個煙袋沒甚麼奇怪的？
3、抽煙袋和抽煙有甚麼不同？抽煙有甚麼好處？
4、為甚麼東北的大姑娘跟男人一樣抽煙？
5、在東北大山裡抽煙有甚麼好處？
    (1)
    (2)
    (3)
6、在東北姑娘出嫁要用甚麼做陪嫁？
7、新媳婦新婚要給公婆做甚麼？表示甚麼？

二、活動 (Activities)

去圖書館查資料，或者到外邊跟人了解一下老北京的地方風俗。

三、討論題 (Topics for discussion)

1、從東北大姑娘叼煙袋，你能看出東北女性的社會地位嗎？
2、你能談談你所了解的中國女性嗎？她們的社會地位、她們的權利，她們的工作機會和生活經歷。
3、和美國女性比，中國女性有甚麼不同？

四、報告 (Presentations)

《一個北京的老風俗》

语言实践 : Practice

一、根据课文回答问题 (Answering questions based on the dialogue)

1、东北的三大怪是什么？
2、为什么记者说男人们叼个烟袋没什么奇怪的？
3、抽烟袋和抽烟有什么不同？抽烟有什么好处？
4、为什么东北的大姑娘跟男人一样抽烟？
5、在东北大山里抽烟有什么好处？
　　(1)
　　(2)
　　(3)
6、在东北姑娘出嫁要用什么做陪嫁？
7、新媳妇新婚要给公婆做什么？表示什么？

二、活动 (Activities)

　　去图书馆查资料，或者到外边跟人了解一下老北京的地方风俗。

三、讨论题 (Topics for discussion)

1、从东北大姑娘叼烟袋，你能看出东北女性的社会地位吗？
2、你能谈谈你所了解的中国女性吗？她们的社会地位、她们的权利，她们的工作机会和生活经历。
3、和美国女性比，中国女性有什么不同？

四、报告 (Presentations)

　　《一个北京的老风俗》

五、看圖討論 (Picto-discussions)

五、看图讨论 (Picto-discussions)

1

2

3

4

5

6

An Advanced Chinese Multimedia Course

China **Scene**

補充課文

第十六課

學做中國菜

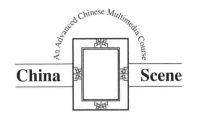

China Scene
An Advanced Chinese Multimedia Course

补充课文

第十六课

学做中国菜

課文

一、簡介 (Introduction)

　　中國的菜譜跟世界上的其它菜譜一樣，也有自己的獨特詞彙與文體。中國菜譜的特點是用詞簡潔、文法省略很多，文言詞、書面語也很多。中國菜譜的文體大同小異，所以學會一個菜譜，就能看得懂大多數的中國菜譜。

生詞

菜譜	(cài pǔ)	N.	recipe
獨特	(dú tè)	Adj.	unique, individual
詞彙	(cí huì)	N.	vocabulary
文體	(wén tǐ)	N.	writing style
用詞	(yòng cí)	VO.	to select one's words
簡潔	(jiǎn jié)	Adj.	succinct, terse
文法	(wén fǎ)	N.	grammar
省略	(shěng lūè)	V.	to omit, omission
文言詞	(wén yán cí)	NP.	archaic expression, classical expression
書面語	(shū miàn yǔ)	NP.	written language
大同小異	(dà tóng xiǎo yì)	VP.	similar in major principles but differing on minor points, almost the same

二、對話 Dialogs

毛璐：你會做中國菜嗎？

徐千：不會。我喜歡吃中國菜。我很想學做幾個菜，以後回美國去，可以給我媽媽炒炒。

课文

一、简介 (Introduction)

中国的菜谱跟世界上的其它菜谱一样，也有自己的独特词汇与文体。中国菜谱的特点是用词简洁、文法省略很多，文言词、书面语也很多。中国菜谱的文体大同小异，所以学会一个菜谱，就能看得懂大多数的中国菜谱。

生词

菜谱	(cài pǔ)	*N.*	recipe
独特	(dú tè)	*Adj.*	unique, individual
词汇	(cí huì)	*N.*	vocabulary
文体	(wén tǐ)	*N.*	writing style
用词	(yòng cí)	*VO.*	to select one's words
简洁	(jiǎn jié)	*Adj.*	succinct, terse
文法	(wén fǎ)	*N.*	grammar
省略	(shěng lūè)	*V.*	to omit, omission
文言词	(wén yán cí)	*NP.*	archaic expression, classical expression
书面语	(shū miàn yǔ)	*NP.*	written language
大同小异	(dà tóng xiǎo yì)	*VP.*	similar in major principles but differing on minor points, almost the same

二、对话 Dialogs

毛璐: 你会做中国菜吗？

徐千: 不会。我喜欢吃中国菜。我很想学做几个菜，以后回美国去，可以给我妈妈炒炒。

毛璐：那我來教你一個容易的，炒雞丁，行嗎？

徐千：好啊，太好了。我們需要甚麼？我先去買。

毛璐：要做炒雞丁，首先要有雞脯，有蔥、薑、蒜、油、鹽等。

徐千：唉呀，要這麼多東西才行啊？

毛璐：還有呢，你有鍋嗎？有火嗎？

徐千：甚麼都沒有。

毛璐：算了，算了，下次再説吧。

生詞

毛璐	(máo lù)	N.	Mao Lu, name of a person 人名
徐千	(xú qiān)	N.	Xu Qian, name of a person 人名
雞丁	(jī dīng)	N.	diced chicken
雞脯	(jī pú)	N.	chicken breast
蔥	(cōng)	N.	green onion
薑	(jiāng)	N.	ginger
蒜	(suàn)	N.	garlic
油	(yóu)	N.	cooking oil
鹽	(yán)	N.	salt
鍋	(guō)	N.	wok

三、電視原文 📺 TV original

一雞三菜

第一個菜是炒雞片。先將雞脯剔下，片成薄片放入盤內，黃瓜切片，筍切片，薑和蔥要切成末。用蛋清、鹽、澱粉將雞片調勻，放入溫油中劃開，出鍋控淨油，蔥和薑爆鍋，加上配料、雞片，加入鹽、味精、料酒、少許湯，翻炒出鍋即可。

第二個菜是辣子雞丁。將雞腿剔下，去骨頭，打上花刀，切成方丁。黃瓜、紅辣毛璐: 那我来教你一个容易的，炒鸡丁，行吗？

徐千: 好啊，太好了。我们需要什么？我先去买。

毛璐: 要做炒鸡丁，首先要有鸡脯，有葱、姜、蒜、油、盐等。

徐千: 唉呀，要这么多东西才行啊？

毛璐: 还有呢，你有锅吗？有火吗？

徐千: 什么都没有。

毛璐: 算了，算了，下次再说吧。

生词

毛璐	(máo lù)	N.	Mao Lu, name of a person 人名
徐千	(xú qiān)	N.	Xu Qian, name of a person 人名
鸡丁	(jī dīng)	N.	diced chicken
鸡脯	(jī pú)	N.	chicken breast
葱	(cōng)	N.	green onion
姜	(jiāng)	N.	ginger
蒜	(suàn)	N.	garlic
油	(yóu)	N.	cooking oil
盐	(yán)	N.	salt
锅	(guō)	N.	wok

三、电视原文 💻 TV original

一鸡三菜

第一个菜是炒鸡片。先将鸡脯剔下，片成薄片放入盘内，黄瓜切片，笋切片，姜和葱要切成末。用蛋清、盐、淀粉将鸡片调匀，放入温油中划开，出锅控净油，葱和姜爆锅，加上配料、鸡片，加入盐、味精、料酒、少许汤，翻炒出锅即可。

第二个菜是辣子鸡丁。将鸡腿剔下，去骨头，打上花刀，切成方丁。黄瓜、红辣椒要切成丁。蔥、薑、蒜切末。將雞丁加上鹽、蛋清、澱粉調勻。放入溫油劃開，撈出控淨油。蔥、薑、蒜爆鍋，放入配料、雞丁，再加醬油、味精、料酒，輕拌翻炒，勾上芡，淋上花椒油便可盛盤了。

土豆做法

涼拌土豆絲

將土豆洗淨、去皮，切成細絲。香菇、辣椒、蔥、薑均切成絲。土豆絲用開水焯一下備用，勺內放香油燒熱，加入辣椒絲、蔥、薑絲翻炒。加鹽、味精、料酒、高湯，然後倒入盛有土豆絲的盤中調勻，燜兩分鐘左右，即可食用。

幹燒土豆條

將土豆洗淨去皮，切成長條。紅辣椒切丁，豬肉切丁，蔥薑切末，勺內放油燒至八成熟時，將土豆條入油，炸至淺黃色撈出。另起勺，加少許油燒熱，放入白糖炒汁，至血紅色時迅速倒入蔥、薑末、辣椒、肉、烹高湯。一次加入酒、鹽、白糖、味精，倒入土豆條，澱粉勾芡，淋上辣椒油，翻炒幾下，即可出勺。這個菜鮮香、辣嫩、甜鹹、軟爛。

生詞

炒雞片	(chǎo jī piàn)	N.	stir fried chicken slices
剔	(tī)	V.	to peel off, to take off
片	(piàn)	V.	to slice
薄片	(báo piàn)	N.	thin slice
盤內	(pán nèi)	Prep.	on the plate
黃瓜	(huáng guā)	N.	cucumber
切片	(qiē piàn)	VP.	to cut into slices

椒要切成丁。葱、姜、蒜切末。将鸡丁加上盐、蛋清、淀粉调匀。放入温油划开，捞出控净油。葱、姜、蒜爆锅，放入配料、鸡丁，再加酱油、味精、料酒，轻拌翻炒，勾上芡，淋上花椒油便可盛盘了。

土豆做法

凉拌土豆丝

将土豆洗净、去皮，切成细丝。香菇、辣椒、葱、姜均切成丝。土豆丝用开水焯一下备用，勺内放香油烧热，加入辣椒丝、葱、姜丝翻炒。加盐、味精、料酒、高汤，然后倒入盛有土豆丝的盘中调匀，焖两分钟左右，即可食用。

干烧土豆条

将土豆洗净去皮，切成长条。红辣椒切丁，猪肉切丁，葱姜切末，勺内放油烧至八成熟时，将土豆条入油，炸至浅黄色捞出。另起勺，加少许油烧热，放入白糖炒汁，至血红色时迅速倒入葱、姜末、辣椒、肉、烹高汤。一次加入酒、盐、白糖、味精，倒入土豆条，淀粉勾芡，淋上辣椒油，翻炒几下，即可出勺。这个菜鲜香、辣嫩、甜咸、软烂。

生词

炒鸡片	(chǎo jī piàn)	*N.*	stir fried chicken slices
剔	(tī)	*V.*	to peel off, to take off
片	(piàn)	*V.*	to slice
薄片	(báo piàn)	*N.*	thin slice
盘内	(pán nèi)	*Prep.*	on the plate
黄瓜	(huáng guā)	*N.*	cucumber
切片	(qiē piàn)	*VP.*	to cut into slices

筍	(sǔn)	N.	bamboo shoots
末	(mò)	V.	to chop up in fine pieces
蛋清	(dàn qīng)	N.	egg white
澱粉	(diàn fěn)	N.	corn starch
調勻	(tiáo yún)	V.	to stir well
溫油	(wēn yóu)	NP.	warm oil
劃開	(huá kāi)	V.	to separate
出鍋	(chū guō)	VP.	to pour out of the wok
空淨	(kòng jìng)	V.	to drain completely
爆鍋	(bào guō)	VP.	to cook in hot oil
配料	(pèi liào)	N.	ingredients
味精	(wèi jīng)	N.	MSG
料酒	(liào jiǔ)	N.	cooking wine
少許	(shǎo xǔ)	Adj.	a little
翻炒	(fān chǎo)	VP.	to stir and fry
即可	(jí kě)	VP.	that is all, that will do
辣子	(là zi)	N.	hot pepper
骨頭	(gǔ tóu)	N.	bone
花刀	(huā dāo)	N.	chopping on top of the meat
方丁	(fāng dīng)	N.	subgum
紅辣椒	(hóng là jiāo)	N.	red chili pepper
醬油	(jiàng yóu)	N.	soy sauce
拌	(bàn)	V.	to mix
勾芡	(gōu qiàn)	VO.	to make starchy gravy
淋	(lín)	V.	to pour
花椒油	(huā jiāo yóu)	N.	pepper flavored oil
盛盤	(chéng pán)	VP.	to put on a plate
土豆	(tǔ dòu)	N.	potato
絲	(sī)	N.	shred
洗淨	(xǐ jìng)	V.	to wash clean
去皮	(qù pí)	VO.	to peel the skin off
細絲	(xì sī)	N.	shredded pieces
香菇	(xiāng gū)	N.	mushroom
開水	(kāi shuǐ)	N.	boiled water
焯	(chāo)	V.	to boil briefly in hot water

笋	(sǔn)	N.	bamboo shoots
末	(mò)	V.	to chop up in fine pieces
蛋清	(dàn qīng)	N.	egg white
淀粉	(diàn fěn)	N.	corn starch
调匀	(tiáo yún)	V.	to stir well
温油	(wēn yóu)	NP.	warm oil
划开	(huá kāi)	V.	to separate
出锅	(chū guō)	VP.	to pour out of the wok
空净	(kòng jìng)	V.	to drain completely
爆锅	(bào guō)	VP.	to cook in hot oil
配料	(pèi liào)	N.	ingredients
味精	(wèi jīng)	N.	MSG
料酒	(liào jiǔ)	N.	cooking wine
少许	(shǎo xǔ)	Adj.	a little
翻炒	(fān chǎo)	VP.	to stir and fry
即可	(jí kě)	VP.	that is all, that will do
辣子	(là zi)	N.	hot pepper
骨头	(gǔ tóu)	N.	bone
花刀	(huā dāo)	N.	chopping on top of the meat
方丁	(fāng dīng)	N.	subgum
红辣椒	(hóng là jiāo)	N.	red chili pepper
酱油	(jiàng yóu)	N.	soy sauce
拌	(bàn)	V.	to mix
勾芡	(gōu qiàn)	VO.	to make starchy gravy
淋	(lín)	V.	to pour
花椒油	(huā jiāo yóu)	N.	pepper flavored oil
盛盘	(chéng pán)	VP.	to put on a plate
土豆	(tǔ dòu)	N.	potato
丝	(sī)	N.	shred
洗净	(xǐ jìng)	V.	to wash clean
去皮	(qù pí)	VO.	to peel the skin off
细丝	(xì sī)	N.	shredded pieces
香菇	(xiāng gū)	N.	mushroom
开水	(kāi shuǐ)	N.	boiled water
焯	(chāo)	V.	to boil briefly in hot water

備用	(bèi yòng)	V.	to be ready to use
勺	(sháo)	N.	spoon, spoon-like wok with a handle
香油	(xiāng yóu)	N.	sesame oil
高湯	(gāo tāng)	N.	thin soup
燜	(mēn)	V.	to keep the lid on
幹燒	(gān shāo)	V.	to stew after frying
長條	(cháng tiáo)	NP.	a long narrow piece
八成	(bā chéng)	NP.	80%
炸	(zhá)	V.	to deep fry
淺黃色	(qiǎn huáng sè)	Adj.	light yellow
起勺	(qǐ sháo)	VO.	to start (with a different wok)
白糖	(bái táng)	N.	white sugar
炒汁	(chǎo zhī)	VO.	to make gravy
血紅色	(xiě hóng sè)	N.	color of blood
迅速	(xùn sù)	Adj/Adv.	rapid, swift, prompt; rapidly, quickly
烹	(pēng)	V.	to boil, to cook
甜	(tián)	Adj.	sweet
鹹	(xián)	Adj.	salty
爛	(làn)	Adj.	soft, tender

备用	(bèi yòng)	V.	to be ready to use
勺	(sháo)	N.	spoon, spoon-like wok with a handle
香油	(xiāng yóu)	N.	sesame oil
高汤	(gāo tāng)	N.	thin soup
焖	(mēn)	V.	to keep the lid on
干烧	(gān shāo)	V.	to stew after frying
长条	(cháng tiáo)	NP.	a long narrow piece
八成	(bā chéng)	NP.	80%
炸	(zhá)	V.	to deep fry
浅黄色	(qiǎn huáng sè)	Adj.	light yellow
起勺	(qǐ sháo)	VO.	to start (with a different wok)
白糖	(bái táng)	N.	white sugar
炒汁	(chǎo zhī)	VO.	to make gravy
血红色	(xiě hóng sè)	N.	color of blood
迅速	(xùn sù)	Adj/Adv.	rapid, swift, prompt; rapidly, quickly
烹	(pēng)	V.	to boil, to cook
甜	(tián)	Adj.	sweet
咸	(xián)	Adj.	salty
烂	(làn)	Adj.	soft, tender

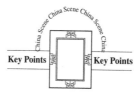

課文要點

一、詞語解釋 Words and Phrases

> 1、少許＝一點兒
>
> ☞ 加入鹽、味精、料酒、少許湯。
>
> 2、即可＝就可以了
>
> ☞ 淋上花椒油便可盛盤了。
>
> 3、至＝到
>
> ☞ 勺內放油燒至八成熟。

二、文化背景知識 Cultural Notes

As is well known, Chinese food is organized into various regional styles and flavors. Among the most popular of these are: Cantonese (Yuècài 粵菜), Sichuan (川菜), Hunan (Xiāngcài 湘菜), Shanghai (Shànghǎi cài 上海菜), Northeastern (Dōngběi cài 東北菜), and Northern (Běifāng cài 北方菜; this term is used loosely, but more often than not it refers to the food styles popular in and around Beijing and Tianjin). In general, the most staple foods from the north are wheat-based (dumplings, noodles, and so on), while those from the south are rice-based. Sichuan and Hunan dishes are more hot and spicy (là 辣) than those in other parts of China.

课文要点

一、词语解释 Words and Phrases

> 1、少许 = 一点儿
>   ☞ 加入盐、味精、料酒、少许汤。
> 2、即可 = 就可以了
>   ☞ 淋上花椒油便可盛盘了。
> 3、至 = 到
>   ☞ 勺内放油烧至八成熟。

二、文化背景知识 Cultural Notes

> As is well known, Chinese food is organized into various regional styles and flavors. Among the most popular of these are: Cantonese (Yuècài 粤菜), Sichuan (川菜), Hunan (Xiāngcài 湘菜), Shanghai (Shànghǎi cài 上海菜), Northeastern (Dōngběi cài 东北菜), and Northern (Běifāng cài 北方菜; this term is used loosely, but more often than not it refers to the food styles popular in and around Beijing and Tianjin). In general, the most staple foods from the north are wheat-based (dumplings, noodles, and so on), while those from the south are rice-based. Sichuan and Hunan dishes are more hot and spicy (là 辣) than those in other parts of China.

練習

語言結構 Structures

一、短語翻譯 (Phrase translation)

1. chicken breast and legs
2. thin slices of bamboo shoots
3. stir fried chicken slices
4. onions, ginger, and garlic
5. salt and sugar
6. MSG and cooking wine
7. cucumber and red pepper
8. soy sauce and sesame oil
9. chestnut and chicken
10. corn starch
11. shredded potatoes
12. to mix thoroughly
13. to peel off the skin
14. crispy and delicious

二、閱讀 (Reading comprehension)

酸辣黃瓜

材料：小黃瓜、大蒜、紅辣椒、油、醋、糖、鹽
做法：

1、選新鮮小黃瓜，切段，大蒜切片，紅辣椒切小段
2、鍋中燒熱油，放下大蒜、紅辣椒段，炒至有香味，放下黃瓜片，隨即放下醋、糖
　　及鹽拌炒半分鐘
3、將黃瓜裝入一隻大碗中燜至涼透

练习

语言结构 Structures

一、短语翻译 (Phrase translation)

1. chicken breast and legs
2. thin slices of bamboo shoots
3. stir fried chicken slices
4. onions, ginger, and garlic
5. salt and sugar
6. MSG and cooking wine
7. cucumber and red pepper
8. soy sauce and sesame oil
9. chestnut and chicken
10. corn starch
11. shredded potatoes
12. to mix thoroughly
13. to peel off the skin
14. crispy and delicious

二、阅读 (Reading comprehension)

酸辣黄瓜

材料：小黄瓜、大蒜、红辣椒、油、醋、糖、盐
做法：

1、选新鲜小黄瓜，切段，大蒜切片，红辣椒切小段
2、锅中烧热油，放下大蒜、红辣椒段，炒至有香味，放下黄瓜片，随即放下醋、糖及盐拌炒半分钟
3、将黄瓜装入一只大碗中焖至凉透

語言實踐: Practice

一、根據課文回答問題 (Answering questions based on the dialogue)

1、用你的話説説怎麼做炒雞片。
2、用你的話説説怎麼做辣子雞丁。
3、用你的話説説怎麼做幹燒土豆條。
4、用英文寫出怎麼做涼拌土豆絲。

二、問題 (Questions)

1、用你的話説説怎麼做涼拌土豆絲。
2、用英文寫出幹燒土豆條和蜜汁土豆泥的菜譜。

三、活動與報告 (Activities and presentation)

按照所學菜譜做兩個菜然後報告。

四、看圖討論 (Picto-discussion)

1

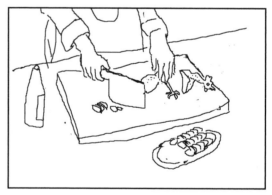

2

语言实践 ⋮ Practice

一、根据课文回答问题 (Answering questions based on the dialogue)

1、用你的话说说怎么做炒鸡片。
2、用你的话说说怎么做辣子鸡丁。
3、用你的话说说怎么做干烧土豆条。
4、用英文写出怎么做凉拌土豆丝。

二、问题 (Questions)

1、用你的话说说怎么做凉拌土豆丝。
2、用英文写出干烧土豆条和蜜汁土豆泥的菜谱。

三、活动与报告 (Activities and presentation)

按照所学菜谱做两个菜然后报告。

四、看图讨论 (Picto-discussion)

1

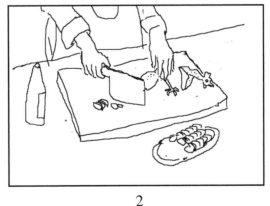

2

3

4

5

6

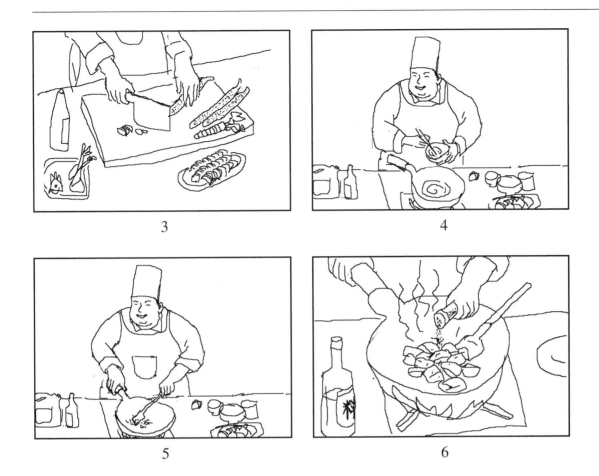

3

4

5

6

附录
Appendixes

句型索引

A

A 使（／讓）B 活躍起來 (A makes B active) L3 （五）

A 迎合 B 的＋N（口味／心理／興趣／需求） (to please, to satisfy) L13 （九）

A 誇 B (A praises B) L14 （九）

A 把 B 命名為 C; B 被 A 命名為 C (A names B after C) L14 （五）

A 被 B 拋棄（／領養）or B 拋棄 A or B 領養 A (to be deserted by) L2 （二）

A 對 B 有（很大的）影響／A 對 B 影響很大 (A has an influence on B) L1 （六）

B

把……浸注在……上 (to devote something to, to dedicate something to) L5 （十三）

把注意力放在…… (to focus one's attention on) L13 （十二）

擺脫……的束縛（／困難／限制） (to break away from the restrictions of) L4 （一）

伴隨（著） (accompanying, along with) L9 （五）

包括 (to include) L4 （五）

被稱為 (to be referred to as, to be called) L11 （五）

……被視為……／A 被 B 視為…… (to be considered) L8 （四）

被譽為 (to be honored as) L13 （八）

比得上／比不上……（條件／情況） (can/cannot be compared with) L4 （二）

步入（／進入）……的行列 (to step into the ranks of, to be among) L7 （一）

C

操（／帶）……口音 (to speak with an accent) L11 （四）

成為／是……的組成部分 (to become/to be an integral part of) L3 （六）

初期，中期，後期 (the beginning, middle, and end periods) L5 （九）

出現……（的）現象 (there occurs a phenomenon of) L1 （五）

出於……（的）目的 (stemming from the motive of, for the purpose of) L8 （十）

處於……的情況 (to be in the situation of) L13 （十一）

從……（中）選拔（出）…… (to select from, to choose from) L5 （七）

從……角度＋V（反映／描寫／考慮／表現） (from the perspective of) L13 （七）

（從）……引進…… (to introduce, to import from) L7 （七）

從來沒（有）像今天這樣…… (something has never been like this before, never like today) L13 （四）

從事……（工作／事業／研究／活動） (to engage in a particular kind of work or cause) L12 （六）

從心底裡 (from the bottom of one's heart) L9 （十）

促進……（的發展／進步／交流） (to promote) L5 （八）

句型索引

A

A 使（／让）B 活跃起来 (A makes B active) L3（五）

A 迎合 B 的＋N（口味／心理／兴趣／需求）(to please, to satisfy) L13（九）

A 夸 B (A praises B) L14（九）

A 把 B 命名为 C；B 被 A 命名为 C (A names B after C) L14（五）

A 被 B 抛弃（／领养）or B 抛弃 A or B 领养 A (to be deserted by) L2（二）

A 对 B 有（很大的）影响／A 对 B 影响很大 (A has an influence on B) L1（六）

B

把……浸注在……上 (to devote something to, to dedicate something to) L5（十三）

把注意力放在…… (to focus one's attention on) L13（十二）

摆脱……的束缚（／困难／限制）(to break away from the restrictions of) L4（一）

伴随（着）(accompanying, along with) L9（五）

包括 (to include) L4（五）

被称为 (to be referred to as, to be called) L11（五）

……被视为……／A 被 B 视为…… (to be considered) L8（四）

被誉为 (to be honored as) L13（八）

比得上／比不上……（条件／情况）(can/cannot be compared with) L4（二）

步入（／进入）……的行列 (to step into the ranks of, to be among) L7（一）

C

操（／带）……口音 (to speak with an accent) L11（四）

成为／是……的组成部分 (to become/to be an integral part of) L3（六）

初期，中期，后期 (the beginning, middle, and end periods) L5（九）

出现……（的）现象 (there occurs a phenomenon of) L1（五）

出于……（的）目的 (stemming from the motive of, for the purpose of) L8（十）

处于……的情况 (to be in the situation of) L13（十一）

从……（中）选拔（出）…… (to select from, to choose from) L5（七）

从……角度＋V（反映／描写／考虑／表现）(from the perspective of) L13（七）

（从）……引进…… (to introduce, to import from) L7（七）

从来没（有）象今天这样…… (something has never been like this before, never like today) L13（四）

从事……（工作／事业／研究／活动）(to engage in a particular kind of work or cause) L12（六）

从心底里 (from the bottom of one's heart) L9（十）

促进……（的发展／进步／交流）(to promote) L5（八）

D

打那以後 (since then) L13　（一）

打這以後…… (from now on) L9　（九）

（大）約……的時候…… (it is about) L10　（十）

但願 (to wish, to hope, if only) L12　（十二）

得益於 (to benefit from) L12　（四）

……的含義 (the meaning of) L1　（八）

……的特點是…… (the characteristics of something are) L5　（二）

……的餘地 (room for, margin of, leeway to) L7　（五）

對……（負）有（……的）責任 (to have a certain responsibility for someone) L2　（八）

對……抱……的態度 (to take an attitude toward something) L3　（九）

對……採取……（的）態度 (to adopt an attitude toward something) L5　（三）

對……的奠念 (to honor someone, to commemorate someone) L9　（十一）

對……給予……的評價 (to offer an evaluation of someone or something) L9　（八）

對……來說，…… (to, for) L2　（六）

對……滿意／不滿意 (to be satisfied/dissatisfied with) L1　（三）

對……深惡痛絕 (to detest, to abhor, to hate) L10　（六）

對……有獎勵；A 獎勵 B (to reward someone, to award something to someone) L3　（十五）

（對）……起……（的）作用 (to play a role in, to function as, to have an effect on) L8　（二）

多虧（了）(thanks to, owing to, luckily) L12　（三）

F

發生（了）……的變化 (to undergo change, changes take place) L1　（一）

分為……種（／類／樣）(to be divided into, to be apportioned into) L8　（八）

G

給……帶來（了）…… (to bring something for someone) L3　（三）

給……起（／取）……名字 (to give someone the name of) L2　（四）

給（／為）……奠定……基礎 (to establish a foundation for, to lay a foundation for) L6　（十一）

估計 (to estimate, to guess, to reckon) L2　（三）

刮起（一股）……風 (to start a new fad in) L13　（五）

歸功於 (to give credit to, to attribute one's success to) L13　（六）

H

毫無技術（／能力／自信心）(to lack the slightest amount of) L10　（三）

D

打那以后 (since then) L13 （一）

打这以后…… (from now on) L9 （九）

（大）约……的时候…… (it is about) L10 （十）

但愿 (to wish, to hope, if only) L12 （十二）

得益于 (to benefit from) L12 （四）

……的含义 (the meaning of) L1 （八）

……的特点是…… (the characteristics of something are) L5 （二）

……的余地 (room for, margin of, leeway to) L7 （五）

对……（负）有（……的）责任 (to have a certain responsibility for someone) L2 （八）

对……抱……的态度 (to take an attitude toward something) L3 （九）

对……采取……（的）态度 (to adopt an attitude toward something) L5 （三）

对……的奠念 (to honor someone, to commemorate someone) L9 （十一）

对……给予……的评价 (to offer an evaluation of someone or something) L9 （八）

对……来说，…… (to, for) L2 （六）

对……满意／不满意 (to be satisfied/dissatisfied with) L1 （三）

对……深恶痛绝 (to detest, to abhor, to hate) L10 （六）

对……有奖励; A 奖励 B (to reward someone, to award something to someone) L3 （十五）

（对）……起……（的）作用 (to play a role in, to function as, to have an effect on) L8 （二）

多亏（了）(thanks to, owing to, luckily) L12 （三）

F

发生（了）……的变化 (to undergo change, changes take place) L1 （一）

分为……种（／类／样）(to be divided into, to be apportioned into) L8 （八）

G

给……带来（了）…… (to bring something for someone) L3 （三）

给……起（／取）……名字 (to give someone the name of) L2 （四）

给（／为）……奠定……基础 (to establish a foundation for, to lay a foundation for) L6 （十一）

估计 (to estimate, to guess, to reckon) L2 （三）

刮起（一股）……风 (to start a new fad in) L13 （五）

归功于 (to give credit to, to attribute one's success to) L13 （六）

H

毫无技术（／能力／自信心）(to lack the slightest amount of) L10 （三）

免費＋V (to do something free of charge) L2　（十二）

……面對……＋N（困難／壓力／問題）(to face) L14　（八）

面臨 (to be faced with) L13　（十）

莫過於＝沒有一個比得上 (nothing surpasses, nothing is better than) L9　（三）

P

跑（起）……＋N（運輸／買賣／批發）來 (to run around doing business, to do business, to run a business) L10　（四）

憑……VO. (to rely on something to do something, to use something as proof) L7　（六）

R

讓……吃驚 (to surprise someone) L10　（五）

讓……感到……（的）氣氛 (to give someone a sense of something) L5　（十一）

讓……驚喜（／吃驚）的是…… (what amazes someone is, what is surprising is) L12　（九）

S

捨得＋VO/N (to be willing to part with, to not grudge) L5　（五）

涉及到…… (to involve, to touch upon, to be tied to) L6　（八）

使……得到……（／平衡／健康／快速）發展 (to cause something to develop) L5　（六）

使（／讓）……得到……好轉 (to improve something, to make something take a turn for the better) L6　（四）

……是 A 對 B 的稱謂 (to be the term of address used by A for B, is what A calls B) L12　（五）

……是……的獲得者（／主力隊員）(to be the winner or key player in) L14　（四）

（是／）由……創辦的 (to be established by; to be created by) L3　（八）

……是不可想像的…… (to be unimaginable) L3　（四）

……是一個（很好的）例子 (to be a [good] example of) L2　（一）

……是指…… (to refer to) L5　（一）

適應 (to fit, to adjust to, to be adaptable to) L7　（十）

受……的委托 (to be entrusted by) L8　（十二）

受（到）……（的）熏陶 (to be cultivated by, to be nurtured by) L12　（十）

受（到）……的矚目（／關注／批評／重視／歡迎）(to receive attention from) L13　（二）

受到……的限制 (to be limited by, to be restricted by) L1　（二）

說到底 (ultimately, the bottom line is) L3　（十）

說來也巧 (it just so happened that) L12　（一）

說來有點兒（／些）慚愧（／不好意思／讓我臉紅）…… (I'm a little...to say) L12　（二）

說老實話 (to tell you the truth) L12　（八）

隨著……的（變化／發展／改善／進步）(accompanying, along with, related to) L6　（九）

免费＋V (to do something free of charge) L2 （十二）

……面对……＋N（困难／压力／问题）(to face) L14 （八）

面临 (to be faced with) L13 （十）

莫过于＝没有一个比得上 (nothing surpasses, nothing is better than) L9 （三）

P

跑（起）……＋N（运输／买卖／批发）来 (to run around doing business, to do business, to run a business) L10 （四）

凭……VO. (to rely on something to do something, to use something as proof) L7 （六）

R

让……吃惊 (to surprise someone) L10 （五）

让……感到……（的）气氛 (to give someone a sense of something) L5 （十一）

让……惊喜（／吃惊）的是…… (what amazes someone is, what is surprising is) L12 （九）

S

舍得＋VO/N (to be willing to part with, to not grudge) L5 （五）

涉及到…… (to involve, to touch upon, to be tied to) L6 （八）

使……得到……（／平衡／健康／快速）发展 (to cause something to develop) L5 （六）

使（／让）……得到……好转 (to improve something, to make something take a turn for the better) L6 （四）

……是 A 对 B 的称谓 (to be the term of address used by A for B, is what A calls B) L12 （五）

……是……的获得者（／主力队员）(to be the winner or key player in) L14 （四）

（是／）由……创办的 (to be established by; to be created by) L3 （八）

……是不可想象的…… (to be unimaginable) L3 （四）

……是一个（很好的）例子 (to be a [good] example of) L2 （一）

……是指…… (to refer to) L5 （一）

适应 (to fit, to adjust to, to be adaptable to) L7 （十）

受……的委托 (to be entrusted by) L8 （十二）

受（到）……（的）熏陶 (to be cultivated by, to be nurtured by) L12 （十）

受（到）……的瞩目（／关注／批评／重视／欢迎）(to receive attention from) L13 （二）

受到……的限制 (to be limited by, to be restricted by) L1 （二）

说到底 (ultimately, the bottom line is) L3 （十）

说来也巧 (it just so happened that) L12 （一）

说来有点儿（／些）惭愧（／不好意思／让我脸红）…… (I'm a little...to say) L12 （二）

说老实话 (to tell you the truth) L12 （八）

随着……的（变化／发展／改善／进步）(accompanying, along with, related to) L6 （九）

T

騰出空兒十V (to spare the time or space to do something) L10 （十一）

同意……的意見（／意思／作法／説法／看法）(to agree with someone's opinion) L4 （六）

頭一回……(the first time, the first instance) = 第一次 L5 （四）

W

圖的是／圖……(what one pursues is, the purpose of doing something is; to pursue, to seek) L8 （十一）

為……而……(to do something because of something, to be in a particular state because of something) L7 （九）

為……服務 (to serve) L9 （一）

為……傷腦筋 (to be troubled, bothered, or annoyed by something; to have a headache over) L8 （一）

為……作（出）貢獻 (to contribute to, to dedicate to, to make a contribution to) L14 （三）

位於……(to be located at or in) L7 （四）

我想問一下……(may I ask, I would like to ask) L4 （四）

無論……都……(regardless of, no matter what) L9 （二）

無疑 (undoubtedly, without a doubt) L6 （十）

X

享受……的禮遇（／生活／待遇／條件）(to enjoy) L10 （九）

向……邁進 (to march toward, to forge ahead) L7 （三）

向……提出 (to bring up something, to suggest something to someone) L3 （十四）

行駛在……／在……上行駛……(to travel on, to drive on) L9 （四）

Y

一個偶然的機會，……(by chance, accidentally) L2 （五）

以……的名義 (in the name of) L2 （七）

以……起家 (to start out as) L11 （一）

以……為主 (to focus primarily on something) L11 （二）

以（／用）……的毅力（／態度／服務）＋V (to use one's willpower) L14 （七）

由……（決）定 (to be decided by someone) L11 （七）

由……組成 (to be composed of) L5 （十二）

由（／從）……發展到……(to develop from A to B) L6 （七）

由／為……譜寫的 (to be composed by/for someone or something) L9 （七）

由於……的（增多／影響／變化／問題）(because of, due to) L1 （四）

有消息説 (it is said that, the news says that, word has it that) L9 （十三）

與……形成反差（／對比）(to form a contrast between) L6 （六）

T

腾出空儿 + V (to spare the time or space to do something) L10 （十一）

同意……的意见（／意思／作法／说法／看法）(to agree with someone's opinion) L4 （六）

头一回…… (the first time, the first instance) = 第一次 L5 （四）

W

图的是／图…… (what one pursues is, the purpose of doing something is; to pursue, to seek) L8 （十一）

为……而…… (to do something because of something, to be in a particular state because of something) L7 （九）

为……服务 (to serve) L9 （一）

为……伤脑筋 (to be troubled, bothered, or annoyed by something; to have a headache over) L8 （一）

为……作（出）贡献 (to contribute to, to dedicate to, to make a contribution to) L14 （三）

位于…… (to be located at or in) L7 （四）

我想问一下…… (may I ask, I would like to ask) L4 （四）

无论……都…… (regardless of, no matter what) L9 （二）

无疑 (undoubtedly, without a doubt) L6 （十）

X

享受……的礼遇（／生活／待遇／条件）(to enjoy) L10 （九）

向……迈进 (to march toward, to forge ahead) L7 （三）

向……提出 (to bring up something, to suggest something to someone) L3 （十四）

行驶在……／在……上行驶…… (to travel on, to drive on) L9 （四）

Y

一个偶然的机会，…… (by chance, accidentally) L2 （五）

以……的名义 (in the name of) L2 （七）

以……起家 (to start out as) L11 （一）

以……为主 (to focus primarily on something) L11 （二）

以（／用）……的毅力（／态度／服务）+ V (to use one's willpower) L14 （七）

由……（决）定 (to be decided by someone) L11 （七）

由……组成 (to be composed of) L5 （十二）

由（／从）……发展到…… (to develop from A to B) L6 （七）

由／为……谱写的 (to be composed by/for someone or something) L9 （七）

由于……的（增多／影响／变化／问题）(because of, due to) L1 （四）

有消息说 (it is said that, the news says that, word has it that) L9 （十三）

与……形成反差（／对比）(to form a contrast between) L6 （六）

與（／跟／和）⋯⋯相比 (as compared with) L11 （八）

與（／和／跟）⋯⋯告別 (to say good-bye to someone, to bid someone farewell) L9 （六）

Z

在⋯⋯（的）情況下 (under the circumstances of) L14 （六）

在⋯⋯的關懷下 (under the care of) L1 （九）

在⋯⋯的眼裡 (in the eyes of) L9 （十二）

在⋯⋯度過＋N （假期／時期／時間） (to spend a period of time somewhere) L14 （一）

（在⋯⋯方面）超過 (to surpass someone or something in the area or field of) L12 （十一）

（在⋯⋯方面）存在⋯⋯問題 (problems exist in an area or aspect) L3 （十二）

在⋯⋯方面有⋯⋯（的）優勢 (to have the advantage in an area) L3 （十一）

在⋯⋯中 (in the middle of, in the process of) L7 （八）

（在）⋯⋯之餘 (in one's spare time, when not doing something) L12 （七）

（在）⋯⋯左右 (approximately, about) L11 （三）

在乎／不在乎 (to care/not care about) L1 （十）

早就聽說⋯⋯ (I heard it said long ago, it was said long ago) L5 （十四）

造成／導致（⋯⋯的問題／情況／困難） (to lead to the consequences of, to result in) L6 （一）

直至（／到）⋯⋯（為止） (up until) L2 （九）

⋯⋯值得⋯⋯ (to be worthwhile) L5 （十五）

重視 (to emphasize, to place emphasis on) L6 （二）

走上⋯⋯的道路 (to take the road of, to get on the path of) L3 （七）

作為⋯⋯ (as, being, to serve as) L3 （十三）

与（／跟／和）……相比 (as compared with) L11 （八）

与（／和／跟）……告别 (to say good-bye to someone, to bid someone farewell) L9 （六）

Z

在……（的）情况下 (under the circumstances of) L14 （六）

在……的关怀下 (under the care of) L1 （九）

在……的眼里 (in the eyes of) L9 （十二）

在……度过＋N （假期／时期／时间） (to spend a period of time somewhere) L14 （一）

（在……方面）超过 (to surpass someone or something in the area or field of) L12 （十一）

（在……方面）存在……问题 (problems exist in an area or aspect) L3 （十二）

在……方面有……（的）优势 (to have the advantage in an area) L3 （十一）

在……中 (in the middle of, in the process of) L7 （八）

（在）……之余 (in one's spare time, when not doing something) L12 （七）

（在）……左右 (approximately, about) L11 （三）

在乎／不在乎 (to care/not care about) L1 （十）

早就听说…… (I heard it said long ago, it was said long ago) L5 （十四）

造成／导致（……的问题／情况／困难） (to lead to the consequences of, to result in) L6 （一）

直至（／到）……（为止） (up until) L2 （九）

……值得…… (to be worthwhile) L5 （十五）

重视 (to emphasize, to place emphasis on) L6 （二）

走上……的道路 (to take the road of, to get on the path of) L3 （七）

作为…… (as, being, to serve as) L3 （十三）

生詞索引 [1]

A

阿姨們	(ā yí mén)	*N.*	nurse, aunt, nursemaid, L2
哀思	(āi sī)	*N.*	grief, sad memories, L9
艾利	(ài lì)	*N.*	Ai Li, name of a person 人名, L9
愛人	(ài rén)	*N.*	wife or husband (used on the mainland), L4
鞍馬	(ān mǎ)	*N.*	sidehorse, L14
安魂曲	(ān hún qǔ)	*NP.*	music played in a burial ceremony, L9
安麗沙	(ān lì shā)	*N.*	An Lisha, name of a person 人名, L10
安靈	(ān líng)	*VO.*	to rest in peace, L9
安喜	(ān xǐ)	*N.*	An Xi, name of a person 人名, L7
奧運會	(ào yùn huì)	*N.*	Olympic Games, L14

B

八成	(bā chéng)	*NP.*	80%, L16
巴塞羅那	(bā sài luó nà)	*N.*	Barcelona 地名, L14
巴松	(bā sōng)	*N.*	bassoon, L12
白溝	(bái gōu)	*PlaceP.*	White Gully 地名, L11
白蘭	(bái lán)	*N.*	Bai Lan, name of a person 人名, L12
白領人	(bái lǐng rén)	*NP.*	white collar worker, L7
白毛女	(bái máo nǚ)	*N.*	*The White Haired Girl* (a popular play in China), L12
白石	(bái shí)	*N.*	Bai Shi, name of a person 人名, L13
白糖	(bái táng)	*N.*	white sugar, L16
白頭偕老	(bái tóu xié lǎo)	*Idiom.*	to live together until death, L8
百姓	(bǎi xìng)	*N.*	people, L5
擺滿	(bǎi mǎn)	*V.*	to place all over, L8
擺攤	(bǎi tān)	*VO.*	to set up a stand, L4
擺脫	(bǎi tuō)	*V.*	to get rid of, to shake off, to cast off, L4
拌	(bàn)	*V.*	to mix, L16
伴隨	(bàn suí)	*V.*	to accompany, L9
辦	(bàn)	*V.*	to run, to handle, L3
包括	(bāo kuò)	*V.*	to include, to contain, L4
包子	(bāo zi)	*N.*	steamed buns with meat, vegetable, or sweet filling, L7
薄片	(báo piàn)	*N.*	thin slice, L16
保定道	(bǎo dìng dào)	*Place N.*	name of a street, L6

✏️ **Notes** [1]The index contains 1,192 entries (including the ones in supplementary texts) and is arranged alphabetically according to the pinyin system. On each line, first listed is the Chinese character, then its pinyin (in parenthesis) and its grammatical category, and then its English translation, and finally the lesson where the vocabulary entry first appears.

生词索引⁽¹⁾

A

阿姨们	(ā yí mén)	*N.*	nurse, aunt, nursemaid, L2
哀思	(āi sī)	*N.*	grief, sad memories, L9
艾利	(ài lì)	*N.*	Ai Li, name of a person 人名, L9
爱人	(ài rén)	*N.*	wife or husband (used on the mainland), L4
鞍马	(ān mǎ)	*N.*	sidehorse, L14
安魂曲	(ān hún qǔ)	*NP.*	music played in a burial ceremony, L9
安丽沙	(ān lì shā)	*N.*	An Lisha, name of a person 人名, L10
安灵	(ān líng)	*VO.*	to rest in peace, L9
安喜	(ān xǐ)	*N.*	An Xi, name of a person 人名, L7
奥运会	(ào yùn huì)	*N.*	Olympic Games, L14

B

八成	(bā chéng)	*NP.*	80%, L16
巴塞罗那	(bā sài luó nà)	*N.*	Barcelona 地名, L14
巴松	(bā sōng)	*N.*	bassoon, L12
白沟	(bái gōu)	*PlaceP.*	White Gully 地名, L11
白兰	(bái lán)	*N.*	Bai Lan, name of a person 人名, L12
白领人	(bái lǐng rén)	*NP.*	white collar worker, L7
白毛女	(bái máo nǚ)	*N.*	*The White Haired Girl* (a popular play in China), L12
白石	(bái shí)	*N.*	Bai Shi, name of a person 人名, L13
白糖	(bái táng)	*N.*	white sugar, L16
白头偕老	(bái tóu xié lǎo)	*Idiom.*	to live together until death, L8
百姓	(bǎi xìng)	*N.*	people, L5
摆满	(bǎi mǎn)	*V.*	to place all over, L8
摆摊	(bǎi tān)	*VO.*	to set up a stand, L4
摆脱	(bǎi tuō)	*V.*	to get rid of, to shake off, to cast off, L4
拌	(bàn)	*V.*	to mix, L16
伴随	(bàn suí)	*V.*	to accompany, L9
办	(bàn)	*V.*	to run, to handle, L3
包括	(bāo kuò)	*V.*	to include, to contain, L4
包子	(bāo zi)	*N.*	steamed buns with meat, vegetable, or sweet filling, L7
薄片	(báo piàn)	*N.*	thin slice, L16
保定道	(bǎo dìng dào)	*Place N.*	name of a street, L6

✏️ **Notes** ⁽¹⁾The index contains 1,192 entries (including the ones in supplementary texts) and is arranged alphabetically according to the pinyin system. On each line, first listed is the Chinese character, then its pinyin (in parenthesis) and its grammatical category, and then its English translation, and finally is the lesson where the vocabulary entry first appears.

保險	(bǎo xiǎn)	N.	insurance, L8
寶貴	(bǎo guì)	Adj.	precious, valuable, L14
報名	(bào míng)	V.	to register, L5
爆鍋	(bào guō)	VP.	to cook in hot oil, L16
悲劇	(bēi jù)	N.	tragedy, tragic, L13
悲傷	(bēi shāng)	N.	sorrow, sadness, L1
背景	(bèi jǐng)	N.	background, L13
備用	(bèi yòng)	V.	to be ready to use, L16
被稱為	(bèi chēng wéi)	VP.	to be called, L11
被視為	(bèi shì wéi)	VP.	to be considered as, L8
被譽為	(bèi yù wéi)	VP.	to be honored as , L13
被子	(bèi zi)	N.	quilt, L6
奔忙	(bēn máng)	VP.	to hurry around, to be busy doing something, L10
本	(běn)	Pron.	this (including the speaker), L4
本次	(běn cì)	Pron.	this time, L6
本科	(běn kē)	N.	undergraduate, L3
本錢	(běn qián)	N.	capital, L4
本事	(běn shì)	N.	ability, capability, L3
比率	(bǐ lù)	N.	rate, L11
比如	(bǐ rú)	Adv.	for example, L5
比試高低	(bǐ shì gāo dī)	Idiom.	to compete, L15
閉	(bì)	V.	to close (eyes), L12
便	(biàn)	Adv.	then, L7
變遷	(biàn qiān)	N.	historical changes, vicissitudes, L4
表情	(biǎo qíng)	N.	facial expression, L8
表示	(biǎo shì)	V.	to express, L9
表演	(biǎo yǎn)	V.	to perform, to act, L12
別提了	(bié tí le)	VP.	don't ask me, L9
賓館	(bīn guǎn)	N.	guest house, hotel, L7
播音	(bō yīn)	V.	to broadcast, L9
波浪	(bō làng)	N.	wave, L12
伯父	(bó fù)	N.	uncle, father's elder brother, L4
渤海	(bó hǎi)	N.	name of the sea near East China, L9
補充	(bǔ chōng)	N.	supplement, addition, complement, L7
補習	(bǔ xí)	V.	to take lessons after school, L1
不斷	(bù duàn)	Adv.	continuous, constant, ceaseless, L11
不盡	(bù jìn)	VP.	unrest, always flowing, L12
不可想像	(bù kě xiǎng xiàng)	Adj.	unthinkable, unimaginable, L3
不滿足	(bù mǎn zú)	Adj.	not satisfied with, L10
不起眼	(bù qǐ yǎn)	Adj.	unnoticeable, L4
不幸	(bù xìng)	Adj.	unfortunate, L2
不願	(bù yuàn)	V.	to be unwilling, L1
不在乎	(bù zài hu)	VP.	not care, L1
不知不覺	(bù zhī bù jué)	Adv.	unconsciously, without noticing, L7

保险	(bǎo xiǎn)	N.	insurance, L8
宝贵	(bǎo guì)	Adj.	precious, valuable, L14
报名	(bào míng)	V.	to register, L5
爆锅	(bào guō)	VP.	to cook in hot oil, L16
悲剧	(bēi jù)	N.	tragedy, tragic, L13
悲伤	(bēi shāng)	N.	sorrow, sadness, L1
背景	(bèi jǐng)	N.	background, L13
备用	(bèi yòng)	V.	to be ready to use, L16
被称为	(bèi chēng wéi)	VP.	to be called, L11
被视为	(bèi shì wéi)	VP.	to be considered as, L8
被誉为	(bèi yù wéi)	VP.	to be honored as , L13
被子	(bèi zi)	N.	quilt, L6
奔忙	(bēn máng)	VP.	to hurry around, to be busy doing something, L10
本	(běn)	Pron.	this (including the speaker), L4
本次	(běn cì)	Pron.	this time, L6
本科	(běn kē)	N.	undergraduate, L3
本钱	(běn qián)	N.	capital, L4
本事	(běn shì)	N.	ability, capability, L3
比率	(bǐ lǜ)	N.	rate, L11
比如	(bǐ rú)	Adv.	for example, L5
比试高低	(bǐ shì gāo dī)	Idiom.	to compete, L15
闭	(bì)	V.	to close (eyes), L12
便	(biàn)	Adv.	then, L7
变迁	(biàn qiān)	N.	historical changes, vicissitudes, L4
表情	(biǎo qíng)	N.	facial expression, L8
表示	(biǎo shì)	V.	to express, L9
表演	(biǎo yǎn)	V.	to perform, to act, L12
别提了	(bié tí le)	VP.	don't ask me, L9
宾馆	(bīn guǎn)	N.	guest house, hotel, L7
播音	(bō yīn)	V.	to broadcast, L9
波浪	(bō làng)	N.	wave, L12
伯父	(bó fù)	N.	uncle, father's elder brother, L4
渤海	(bó hǎi)	N.	name of the sea near East China, L9
补充	(bǔ chōng)	N.	supplement, addition, complement, L7
补习	(bǔ xí)	V.	to take lessons after school, L1
不断	(bù duàn)	Adv.	continuous, constant, ceaseless, L11
不尽	(bù jìn)	VP.	unrest, always flowing, L12
不可想象	(bù kě xiǎng xiàng)	Adj.	unthinkable, unimaginable, L3
不满足	(bù mǎn zú)	Adj.	not satisfied with, L10
不起眼	(bù qǐ yǎn)	Adj.	unnoticeable, L4
不幸	(bù xìng)	Adj.	unfortunate, L2
不愿	(bù yuàn)	V.	to be unwilling, L1
不在乎	(bù zài hu)	VP.	not care, L1
不知不觉	(bù zhī bù jué)	Adv.	unconsciously, without noticing, L7

不足	(bù zú)	Adv.	less than, L7
步入	(bù rù)	V.	to step into, L7
部	(bù)	Classifier.	classifier for movies, TV plays, etc., L12
部分	(bù fèn)	N.	part, L5
部門	(bù mén)	N.	department, L9

C

裁判	(cái pàn)	N.	referee, L14
才能	(cái néng)	N.	capability, ability, talent, L3
財富	(cái fù)	N.	property, L9
採訪	(cǎi fǎng)	V/N.	to interview, to gather material; interview, L3
採納	(cǎi nà)	V.	to adopt, to take in, L3
採取	(cǎi qǔ)	V.	to adopt, to take, L5
菜譜	(cài pǔ)	N.	recipe, L16
蔡長安	(cài cháng ān)	N.	Cai Changan, name of a person 人名, L15
參加者	(cān jiā zhě)	N.	participant, L9
殘疾	(cán jí)	Adj/N.	handicapped, L2
殘酷	(cán kù)	Adj.	cruel, L1
慚愧	(cán kuì)	Adj.	to feel ashamed (of), L12
操……口音	(cāo...kǒu yīn)	VO.	with an accent of, L11
操持	(cāo chí)	V.	to take care of, to manage, L1
曾經	(céng jīng)	Adv.	once, in the past, formerly, L1
差	(chà)	Adj.	lacking, poor, L6
產生	(chǎn shēng)	V.	to occur, to appear, L6
場	(chǎng)	Classifier.	measure word for a period of time, L1
嘗試	(cháng shì)	N.	attempt, try, L13
長處	(cháng chù)	NP.	strong point, advantage, L3
長江	(cháng jiāng)	N.	Yangzi River, L12
長條	(cháng tiáo)	NP.	a long narrow piece, L16
暢快	(chàng kuài)	Adj.	joyful, carefree, L10
焯	(chāo)	V.	to boil briefly in hot water, L16
超過	(chāo guò)	V.	to pass, to surpass, L9
超前	(chāo qián)	V.	ahead of time, L11
超人	(chāo rén)	N.	beyond the ability of an ordinary person, L14
炒	(chǎo)	V.	to stir fry, L7
炒雞片	(chǎo jī piàn)	N.	stir fried chicken slices, L16
炒汁	(chǎo zhī)	VO.	to make gravy, L16
車身	(chē shēn)	N.	car body, L10
車水馬龍	(chē shuǐ mǎ lóng)	Idiom.	incessant stream of horses and carriages, heavy traffic, L11
徹底	(chè dǐ)	Adv.	thoroughly, completely, L9
沉默	(chén mò)	N/Adj.	silence, silent, L1

不足	(bù zú)	*Adv.*	less than, L7
步入	(bù rù)	*V.*	to step into, L7
部	(bù)	*Classifier.*	classifier for movies, TV plays, etc., L12
部分	(bù fèn)	*N.*	part, L5
部门	(bù mén)	*N.*	department, L9

C

裁判	(cái pàn)	*N.*	referee, L14
才能	(cái néng)	*N.*	capability, ability, talent, L3
财富	(cái fù)	*N.*	property, L9
采访	(cǎi fǎng)	*V/N.*	to interview, to gather material; interview, L3
采纳	(cǎi nà)	*V.*	to adopt, to take in, L3
采取	(cǎi qǔ)	*V.*	to adopt, to take, L5
菜谱	(cài pǔ)	*N.*	recipe, L16
蔡长安	(cài cháng ān)	*N.*	Cai Changan, name of a person 人名, L15
参加者	(cān jiā zhě)	*N.*	participant, L9
残疾	(cán jí)	*Adj/N.*	handicapped, L2
残酷	(cán kù)	*Adj.*	cruel, L1
惭愧	(cán kuì)	*Adj.*	to feel ashamed (of), L12
操……口音	(cāo...kǒu yīn)	*VO.*	with an accent of, L11
操持	(cāo chí)	*V.*	to take care of, to manage, L1
曾经	(céng jīng)	*Adv.*	once, in the past, formerly, L1
差	(chà)	*Adj.*	lacking, poor, L6
产生	(chǎn shēng)	*V.*	to occur, to appear, L6
场	(chǎng)	*Classifier.*	measure word for a period of time, L1
尝试	(cháng shì)	*N.*	attempt, try, L13
长处	(cháng chù)	*NP.*	strong point, advantage, L3
长江	(cháng jiāng)	*N.*	Yangzi River, L12
长条	(cháng tiáo)	*NP.*	a long narrow piece, L16
畅快	(chàng kuài)	*Adj.*	joyful, carefree, L10
焯	(chāo)	*V.*	to boil briefly in hot water, L16
超过	(chāo guò)	*V.*	to pass, to surpass, L9
超前	(chāo qián)	*V.*	ahead of time, L11
超人	(chāo rén)	*N.*	beyond the ability of an ordinary person, L14
炒	(chǎo)	*V.*	to stir fry, L7
炒鸡片	(chǎo jī piàn)	*N.*	stir fried chicken slices, L16
炒汁	(chǎo zhī)	*VO.*	to make gravy, L16
车身	(chē shēn)	*N.*	car body, L10
车水马龙	(chē shuǐ mǎ lóng)	*Idiom.*	incessant stream of horses and carriages, heavy traffic, L11
彻底	(chè dǐ)	*Adv.*	thoroughly, completely, L9
沉默	(chén mò)	*N/Adj.*	silence, silent, L1

沉重	(chén zhòng)	Adj.	heavy, serious, L13
陳舊	(chén jiù)	Adj.	outdated, obsolete, L4
陳凱歌	(chén kǎi gē)	N.	Chen Kaige, name of a person, a famous film director in China 人名, L13
稱謂	(chēng wèi)	N.	term of address, L12
城鎮	(chéng zhèn)	NP.	cities and towns, L6
成長	(chéng zhǎng)	N/V.	growth, development; to grow, L1
成就	(chéng jiù)	N.	accomplishment, success, L14
成人	(chéng rén)	N.	adult, L2
成熟	(chéng shú)	Adj.	mature, maturity, L3
程度	(chéng dù)	N.	degree, L6
承包	(chéng bāo)	V.	to contract, L3
承包地	(chéng bāo dì)	NP.	contracted land, L3
盛盤	(chéng pán)	VP.	to put on a plate, L16
吃驚	(chī jīng)	V.	to be surprised, to be startled, L10
蟲	(chóng)	N.	insects, L15
崇拜	(chóng bài)	V.	to adore, L1
重返	(chóng fǎn)	V.	to go back, to return, L9
重新	(chóng xīn)	Adv/V.	again, to start anew, L9
抽	(chōu)	V.	to smoke, L15
出差	(chū chāi)	VO.	to be on a business trip, on business, L1
出鍋	(chū guō)	VP.	to pour out of the wok, L16
出嫁	(chū jià)	V.	to marry (for women only), L15
出沒於	(chū mò yú)	VP.	to be in and out of, L7
出門	(chū mén)	VO.	to go out, to get out of one's house, L4
出色	(chū sè)	Adj.	outstanding, remarkable, L14
出於…的目的	(chū yú...de mù dì)	Prep.	out of, L8
出租汽車	(chū zū qì chē)	N.	taxi, L10
處理	(chǔ lǐ)	V.	to handle, to deal with, L13
傳統	(chuán tǒng)	Adj.	traditional, L13
闖世界	(chuǎng shì jiè)	VO.	to explore the world, L4
創辦	(chuàng bàn)	V.	to start, to found, to open, L3
創傷	(chuāng shāng)	N.	wound, L1
創業	(chuàng yè)	VO.	to do pioneering work, to start an undertaking, to start a business, L3
創作	(chuàng zuò)	V.	to create, creation, L13
春節	(chūn jié)	N.	Spring Festival (New Year's), L8
春種秋收	(chūn zhòng qiū shōu)	Idiom.	to plant in spring and harvest in fall, L15
辭去	(cí qù)	V.	to resign, L3
辭職	(cí zhí)	V.	to resign, L10
詞彙	(cí huì)	N.	vocabulary, L16
此	(cǐ)	Pron.	this, L7
此刻	(cǐ kè)	Adv.	at this time, now, L10
此致	(cǐ zhì)	VP.	a salutation used at the end of a letter to indicate closure, L1

沉重	(chén zhòng)	Adj.	heavy, serious, L13
陈旧	(chén jiù)	Adj.	outdated, obsolete, L4
陈凯歌	(chén kǎi gē)	N.	Chen Kaige, name of a person, a famous film director in China 人名, L13
称谓	(chēng wèi)	N.	term of address, L12
城镇	(chéng zhèn)	NP.	cities and towns, L6
成长	(chéng zhǎng)	N/V.	growth, development; to grow, L1
成就	(chéng jiù)	N.	accomplishment, success, L14
成人	(chéng rén)	N.	adult, L2
成熟	(chéng shú)	Adj.	mature, maturity, L3
程度	(chéng dù)	N.	degree, L6
承包	(chéng bāo)	V.	to contract, L3
承包地	(chéng bāo dì)	NP.	contracted land, L3
盛盘	(chéng pán)	VP.	to put on a plate, L16
吃惊	(chī jīng)	V.	to be surprised, to be startled, L10
虫	(chóng)	N.	insects, L15
崇拜	(chóng bài)	V.	to adore, L1
重返	(chóng fǎn)	V.	to go back, to return, L9
重新	(chóng xīn)	Adv/V.	again, to start anew, L9
抽	(chōu)	V.	to smoke, L15
出差	(chū chāi)	VO.	to be on a business trip, on business, L1
出锅	(chū guō)	VP.	to pour out of the wok, L16
出嫁	(chū jià)	V.	to marry (for women only), L15
出没于	(chū mò yú)	VP.	to be in and out of, L7
出门	(chū mén)	VO.	to go out, to get out of one's house, L4
出色	(chū sè)	Adj.	outstanding, remarkable, L14
出于…的目的	(chū yú...de mù dì)	Prep.	out of, L8
出租汽车	(chū zū qì chē)	N.	taxi, L10
处理	(chǔ lǐ)	V.	to handle, to deal with, L13
传统	(chuán tǒng)	Adj.	traditional, L13
闯世界	(chuǎng shì jiè)	VO.	to explore the world, L4
创办	(chuàng bàn)	V.	to start, to found, to open, L3
创伤	(chuāng shāng)	N.	wound, L1
创业	(chuàng yè)	VO.	to do pioneering work, to start an undertaking, to start a business, L3
创作	(chuàng zuò)	V.	to create, creation, L13
春节	(chūn jié)	N.	Spring Festival (New Year's), L8
春种秋收	(chūn zhòng qiū shōu)	Idiom.	to plant in spring and harvest in fall, L15
辞去	(cí qù)	V.	to resign, L3
辞职	(cí zhí)	V.	to resign, L10
词汇	(cí huì)	N.	vocabulary, L16
此	(cǐ)	Pron.	this, L7
此刻	(cǐ kè)	Adv.	at this time, now, L10
此致	(cǐ zhì)	VP.	a salutation used at the end of a letter to indicate closure, L1

刺激	(cì jī)	V./Adj.	to excite, to stimulate; stimulating, L13
蔥	(cōng)	N.	green onion, L16
從而	(cóng ér)	Adv.	thus, therefore, L9
從事	(cóng shì)	V.	to be engaged in, L3
從無到有	(cóng wú dào yǒu)	Idom.	to spring from nothing, from nonexistence to existence, L3
湊錢	(còu qián)	V.	to collect money, to raise funds, L10
促進	(cù jìn)	V.	to promote, L5
存在	(cún zài)	V./N.	to exist, existence, L3

D

搭配	(dā pèi)	V.	to match, to balance, L7
達	(dá)	V.	to reach, to attain, L4
打柴	(dǎ chái)	VO.	to collect wood (in the mountain), L15
打動	(dǎ dòng)	V.	to move, to touch (emotionally), L2
打獵	(dǎ liè)	V.	to hunt, L15
打擾	(dǎ rǎo)	V.	to trouble, to disturb, L4
大部分	(dà bù fèn)	Adj.	for the most part, mostly, L4
大都市	(dà dū shì)	N./Adj.	big city; metropolitan, L4
大多	(dà duō)	Adv.	mostly, L11
大力	(dà lì)	Adv.	strongly, vigorously, L8
大陸	(dà lù)	N.	Mainland China, L3
大廳	(dà tīng)	N.	hall, L5
大同小異	(dà tóng xiǎo yì)	VP.	similar in major principles but differing on minor points, almost the same, L16
大霧	(dà wù)	NP.	foggy, L5
大約	(dà yuē)	Adv.	approximately, L11
大雜院	(dà zá yuàn)	N.	an enclosed compound occupied by several households, L12
代	(dài)	N.	generation, L13
袋	(dài)	Classifier.	a bag of, L15
單	(dān)	Adv.	solely, L4
單調	(dān diào)	Adj.	monotonous, L10
單槓	(dān gàng)	N.	single bar, L14
單親家庭	(dān qīn jiā tíng)	NP.	single-parent family, L1
單身	(dān shēn)	Adj/N.	unmarried, single; an unmarried person, L1
單位	(dān wèi)	N.	work unit, L3
單項	(dān xiàng)	N.	single item, L14
但願	(dàn yuàn)	V.	to wish, L12
淡	(dàn)	Adj.	light, thin, L13
蛋清	(dàn qīng)	N.	egg white, L16
當場	(dāng chǎng)	Adv.	on the spot, right there, L2
當初	(dāng chū)	Adv.	at that time, originally, L3
當地的情況	(dāng dì de qíng kuàng)	NP.	the local situation, L4

刺激	(cì jī)	*V./Adj.*	to excite, to stimulate; stimulating, L13
葱	(cōng)	*N.*	green onion, L16
从而	(cóng ér)	*Adv.*	thus, therefore, L9
从事	(cóng shì)	*V.*	to be engaged in, L3
从无到有	(cóng wú dào yǒu)	*Idom.*	to spring from nothing, from nonexistence to existence, L3
凑钱	(còu qián)	*V.*	to collect money, to raise funds, L10
促进	(cù jìn)	*V.*	to promote, L5
存在	(cún zài)	*V./N.*	to exist, existence, L3

D

搭配	(dā pèi)	*V.*	to match, to balance, L7
达	(dá)	*V.*	to reach, to attain, L4
打柴	(dǎ chái)	*VO.*	to collect wood (in the mountain), L15
打动	(dǎ dòng)	*V.*	to move, to touch (emotionally), L2
打猎	(dǎ liè)	*V.*	to hunt, L15
打扰	(dǎ rǎo)	*V.*	to trouble, to disturb, L4
大部分	(dà bù fèn)	*Adj.*	for the most part, mostly, L4
大都市	(dà dū shì)	*N./Adj.*	big city; metropolitan, L4
大多	(dà duō)	*Adv.*	mostly, L11
大力	(dà lì)	*Adv.*	strongly, vigorously, L8
大陆	(dà lù)	*N.*	Mainland China, L3
大厅	(dà tīng)	*N.*	hall, L5
大同小异	(dà tóng xiǎo yì)	*VP.*	similar in major principles but differing on minor points, almost the same, L16
大雾	(dà wù)	*NP.*	foggy, L5
大约	(dà yuē)	*Adv.*	approximately, L11
大杂院	(dà zá yuàn)	*N.*	an enclosed compound occupied by several households, L12
代	(dài)	*N.*	generation, L13
袋	(dài)	*Classifier.*	a bag of, L15
单	(dān)	*Adv.*	solely, L4
单调	(dān diào)	*Adj.*	monotonous, L10
单杠	(dān gàng)	*N.*	single bar, L14
单亲家庭	(dān qīn jiā tíng)	*NP.*	single-parent family, L1
单身	(dān shēn)	*Adj/N.*	unmarried, single; an unmarried person, L1
单位	(dān wèi)	*N.*	work unit, L3
单项	(dān xiàng)	*N.*	single item, L14
但愿	(dàn yuàn)	*V.*	to wish, L12
淡	(dàn)	*Adj.*	light, thin, L13
蛋清	(dàn qīng)	*N.*	egg white, L16
当场	(dāng chǎng)	*Adv.*	on the spot, right there, L2
当初	(dāng chū)	*Adv.*	at that time, originally, L3
当地的情况	(dāng dì de qíng kuàng)	*NP.*	the local situation, L4

檔次	(dàng cì)	N.	quality, high quality level, L7
搗蛋	(dǎo dàn)	Idiom.	to make trouble, trouble making, L12
搗亂	(dǎo luàn)	V.	to make trouble, L4
導演	(dǎo yǎn)	V./N.	to direct; director, L12
導致	(dǎo zhì)	V.	to cause, to result in, to lead to, L6
道路	(dào lù)	N.	road, route, path, L3
得益於	(dé yì yú)	VP.	to benefit from, L12
登記處	(dēng jì chù)	NP.	registration office, L8
登台亮相	(dēng tái liàng xiàng)	VP.	to appear on the stage, L5
低頭	(dī tóu)	VO.	to lower one's head, L10
地安門	(dì ān mén)	Place N.	Di'anmen, name of a street in Beijing 地名, L7
地地道道	(dì dì dào dào)	Adj.	typical, L3
地久天長	(dì jiǔ tiān cháng)	Idiom.	to last as long as heaven and earth, L8
地少人多	(dì shǎo rén duō)	Idiom.	densely populated, overpopulation with a limited amount of arable land, L4
地質	(dì zhì)	N.	geology, L3
點心	(diǎn xīn)	N.	pastry, snack, L4
典型	(diǎn xíng)	Adj.	typical, L6
電視劇	(diàn shì jù)	N.	TV play, TV series, L12
電視台	(diàn shì tái)	NP.	TV station, L4
電影節	(diàn yǐng jié)	N.	film festival, L13
奠定	(diàn dìng)	V.	to lay, to pave, to establish, L6
奠念	(diàn niàn)	V./N.	to commemorate, commemoration, L9
澱粉	(diàn fěn)	N.	corn starch, L16
叼	(diāo)	V.	to hold in the mouth, dangling from one's lips, L15
掉眼淚	(diào yǎn lèi)	VO.	to shed tears, L1
調查	(diào chá)	N./V.	investigation; to investigate, L6
疊	(dié)	V.	to fold, to make, L6
盯著	(dīng zhe)	VP.	to keep the focus on, L7
叮	(dīng)	V.	to bite, L15
訂餐	(dìng cān)	VO.	to order food, L7
東城區	(dōng chéng qū)	Place N.	east district, L8
東營	(dōng yíng)	Place N.	Dongying, name of a place 地名, L3
動作	(dòng zuò)	N.	movement, action, L14
獨創	(dú chuàng)	VP.	to be created solely by, L14
獨生子女	(dú shēng zǐ nǚ)	NP.	single child, L5
獨特	(dú tè)	Adj.	unique, individual, L16
度過	(dù guò)	V.	to spend, to pass, L8
鍛鍊	(duàn liàn)	V.	to train, to forge, to temper, L5
隊長	(duì zhǎng)	N.	team leader, L14
對勁（兒）	(duì jìng (er))	V.	to suit, to be fitting, L7
頓時	(dùn shí)	Adv.	at once, L5
多虧	(duō kuī)	V./Adv.	thanks to, luckily, L12

档次	(dàng cì)	N.	quality, high quality level, L7
捣蛋	(dǎo dàn)	Idiom.	to make trouble, trouble making, L12
捣乱	(dǎo luàn)	V.	to make trouble, L4
导演	(dǎo yǎn)	V/N.	to direct; director, L12
导致	(dǎo zhì)	V.	to cause, to result in, to lead to, L6
道路	(dào lù)	N.	road, route, path, L3
得益于	(dé yì yú)	VP.	to benefit from, L12
登记处	(dēng jì chù)	NP.	registration office, L8
登台亮相	(dēng tái liàng xiàng)	VP.	to appear on the stage, L5
低头	(dī tóu)	VO.	to lower one's head, L10
地安门	(dì ān mén)	Place N.	Di'anmen, name of a street in Beijing 地名, L7
地地道道	(dì dì dào dào)	Adj.	typical, L3
地久天长	(dì jiǔ tiān cháng)	Idiom.	to last as long as heaven and earth, L8
地少人多	(dì shǎo rén duō)	Idiom.	densely populated, overpopulation with a limited amount of arable land, L4
地质	(dì zhì)	N.	geology, L3
点心	(diǎn xīn)	N.	pastry, snack, L4
典型	(diǎn xíng)	Adj.	typical, L6
电视剧	(diàn shì jù)	N.	TV play, TV series, L12
电视台	(diàn shì tái)	NP.	TV station, L4
电影节	(diàn yǐng jié)	N.	film festival, L13
奠定	(diàn dìng)	V.	to lay, to pave, to establish, L6
奠念	(diàn niàn)	V/N.	to commemorate, commemoration, L9
淀粉	(diàn fěn)	N.	corn starch, L16
叼	(diāo)	V.	to hold in the mouth, dangling from one's lips, L15
掉眼泪	(diào yǎn lèi)	VO.	to shed tears, L1
调查	(diào chá)	N/V.	investigation; to investigate, L6
叠	(dié)	V.	to fold, to make, L6
盯着	(dīng zhe)	VP.	to keep the focus on, L7
叮	(dīng)	V.	to bite, L15
订餐	(dìng cān)	VO.	to order food, L7
东城区	(dōng chéng qū)	Place N.	east district, L8
东营	(dōng yíng)	Place N.	Dongying, name of a place 地名, L3
动作	(dòng zuò)	N.	movement, action, L14
独创	(dú chuàng)	VP.	to be created solely by, L14
独生子女	(dú shēng zǐ nǚ)	NP.	single child, L5
独特	(dú tè)	Adj.	unique, individual, L16
度过	(dù guò)	V.	to spend, to pass, L8
锻炼	(duàn liàn)	V.	to train, to forge, to temper, L5
队长	(duì zhǎng)	N.	team leader, L14
对劲（儿）	(duì jìng (er))	V.	to suit, to be fitting, L7
顿时	(dùn shí)	Adv.	at once, L5
多亏	(duō kuī)	V/Adv.	thanks to, luckily, L12

| 多樣化 | (duō yàng huà) | N. | to have variety, L7 |

E

| 兒童醫院 | (ér tóng yī yuàn) | NP. | children's hospital, L2 |

F

發表	(fā biǎo)	V.	to publish, L2
發愁	(fā chóu)	V.	to worry, to be concerned about, L7
發達	(fā dá)	N.	advancement, development, L9
發揮	(fā huī)	V.	to bring into play, to give play to, L3
發票	(fā piào)	N.	receipt, L10
法律	(fǎ lǜ)	N.	law, L8
翻炒	(fān chǎo)	VP.	to stir and fry, L16
繁華	(fán huá)	Adj.	flourishing, bustling, L4
繁忙	(fán máng)	Adj.	busy, bustling, L4
煩悶	(fán mèn)	Adj.	restless and lonely, L15
反差	(fǎn chā)	N.	contrast, L6
反映	(fǎn yìng)	V.	to reflect, L13
反正	(fǎn zhèng)	Adv.	anyway, anyhow, in any case, L4
返還金	(fǎn huán jīn)	NP.	refund, returning fee, L8
飯莊	(fàn zhuāng)	N.	restaurant, L12
方丁	(fāng dīng)	N.	subgum, L16
方針	(fāng zhēn)	N.	guiding principle, policy, L6
放棄	(fàng qì)	V.	to give up, to renounce, L7
非	(fēi)	Adv.	non, not, L5
氛圍	(fēn wéi)	N.	atmosphere, L8
分	(fēn)	V.	to assign, L3
分別	(fēn bié)	Adj.	separately, respectively, L8
分析	(fēn xī)	V.	to analyze, L11
紛紛	(fēn fēn)	Adv.	one after another, L7
份	(fèn)	Classifier.	classifier for reports, applications, etc., L9
豐富	(fēng fù)	Adj.	rich, abundant, L2
豐富多彩	(fēng fù duō cǎi)	Adj.	rich and colorful, L7
封	(fēng)	Classifier.	measure word for letters, L1
風俗	(fēng sú)	N.	custom, L15
風險	(fēng xiǎn)	N.	risk, L3
奉獻	(fèng xiàn)	V.	to devote to, L1
福建	(fú jiàn)	Place N.	Fujian (Province), L4
福利待遇	(fú lì dài yù)	NP.	fringe benefits, L3
福利院	(fú lì yuàn)	NP.	welfare institute, L2
撫養	(fǔ yǎng)	V.	to raise, to foster, L2
輔導	(fǔ dǎo)	V.	to instruct, to tutor, L6
副	(fù)	Classifier.	classifier for voice, L14

多样化	(duō yàng huà)	*N.*	to have variety, L7

E

儿童医院	(ér tóng yī yuàn)	*NP.*	children's hospital, L2

F

发表	(fā biǎo)	*V.*	to publish, L2
发愁	(fā chóu)	*V.*	to worry, to be concerned about, L7
发达	(fā dá)	*N.*	advancement, development, L9
发挥	(fā huī)	*V.*	to bring into play, to give play to, L3
发票	(fā piào)	*N.*	receipt, L10
法律	(fǎ lù)	*N.*	law, L8
翻炒	(fān chǎo)	*VP.*	to stir and fry, L16
繁华	(fán huá)	*Adj.*	flourishing, bustling, L4
繁忙	(fán máng)	*Adj.*	busy, bustling, L4
烦闷	(fán mèn)	*Adj.*	restless and lonely, L15
反差	(fǎn chā)	*N.*	contrast, L6
反映	(fǎn yìng)	*V.*	to reflect, L13
反正	(fǎn zhèng)	*Adv.*	anyway, anyhow, in any case, L4
返还金	(fǎn huán jīn)	*NP.*	refund, returning fee, L8
饭庄	(fàn zhuāng)	*N.*	restaurant, L12
方丁	(fāng dīng)	*N.*	subgum, L16
方针	(fāng zhēn)	*N.*	guiding principle, policy, L6
放弃	(fàng qì)	*V.*	to give up, to renounce, L7
非	(fēi)	*Adv.*	non, not, L5
氛围	(fèn wéi)	*N.*	atmosphere, L8
分	(fēn)	*V.*	to assign, L3
分别	(fēn bié)	*Adj.*	separately, respectively, L8
分析	(fēn xī)	*V.*	to analyze, L11
纷纷	(fēn fēn)	*Adv.*	one after another, L7
份	(fèn)	*Classifier.*	classifier for reports, applications, etc., L9
丰富	(fēng fù)	*Adj.*	rich, abundant, L2
丰富多采	(fēng fù duō cǎi)	*Adj.*	rich and colorful, L7
封	(fēng)	*Classifier.*	measure word for letters, L1
风俗	(fēng sú)	*N.*	custom, L15
风险	(fēng xiǎn)	*N.*	risk, L3
奉献	(fèng xiàn)	*V.*	to devote to, L1
福建	(fú jiàn)	*Place N.*	Fujian (Province), L4
福利待遇	(fú lì dài yù)	*NP.*	fringe benefits, L3
福利院	(fú lì yuàn)	*NP.*	welfare institute, L2
抚养	(fǔ yǎng)	*V.*	to raise, to foster, L2
辅导	(fǔ dǎo)	*V.*	to instruct, to tutor, L6
副	(fù)	*Classifier.*	classifier for voice, L14

副食品	(fù shí pǐn)	NP.	non-staple food, L4
副院長	(fù yuàn zhǎng)	N.	deputy director, L2
負擔	(fù dān)	N.	burden, load, L8
負有	(fù yǒu)	V.	to shoulder, to bear, L2
負責	(fù zé)	Adj.	to be responsible, L3
富裕	(fù yù)	Adj.	well-to-do, prosperous, well-off, L6

G

改編	(gǎi biān)	V.	to adapt, to revise, L1
改變	(gǎi biàn)	N/V.	change; to change, to alter, to correct, L1
改革	(gǎi gé)	V/N.	to reform; reform, L3
改善	(gǎi shàn)	N/V.	improvement; to improve, L5
幹燒	(gān shāo)	V.	to stew after frying, L16
感冒	(gǎn mào)	VO.	to catch a cold, L10
感情	(gǎn qíng)	N.	emotion, feeling, L2
敢	(gǎn)	V/Adj.	to dare; daring, bold, courageous, L4
敢闖敢幹	(gǎn chuǎng gǎn gàn)	Idiom.	to bravely explore and bravely engage in, L12
鋼琴	(gāng qín)	N.	piano, L5
綱要	(gāng yào)	N.	outline, L6
崗位	(gǎng wèi)	N.	post , L3
高邁	(gāo mài)	N.	Gao Mai, name of a person 人名, L8
高山	(gāo shān)	N.	mountain, L9
高湯	(gāo tāng)	N.	thin soup, L16
高效	(gāo xiào)	NP.	high efficiency, L7
告別	(gào bié)	V.	to say good-bye, to pay one's last respects, L9
歌劇院	(gē jù yuàn)	NP.	opera house, L9
個體戶	(gè tǐ hù)	N.	private entrepreneur, L3
各方面	(gè fāng miàn)	NP.	various aspects, L5
各種各樣	(gè zhǒng gè yàng)	AdjP.	a variety of, various kinds of, L8
給予	(gěi yǔ)	V.	to give, L9
耕地	(gēng dì)	N.	arable land, L4
工藝	(gōng yì)	N.	handicraft, technology, L6
工裝服	(gōng zhuāng fú)	NP.	work uniform, L3
工作量	(gōng zuò liàng)	NP.	work load, amount of work, L7
工作人員	(gōng zuò rén yuán)	NP.	working staff, L2
工作者	(gōng zuò zhě)	NP.	worker, L14
供應	(gòng yìng)	V.	to supply, L7
公德	(gōng dé)	N.	social morals, L5
公公	(gōng gōng)	N.	father-in-law, L15
公關部	(gōng guān bù)	N.	public relations department, L12
公頃	(gōng qǐng)	N.	hectare (approx. 16.5 acres), L4
公休日	(gōng xiū rì)	N.	week-end, public holidays, L2

副食品	(fù shí pǐn)	*NP.*	non-staple food, L4
副院长	(fù yuàn zhǎng)	*N.*	deputy director, L2
负担	(fù dān)	*N.*	burden, load, L8
负有	(fù yǒu)	*V.*	to shoulder, to bear, L2
负责	(fù zé)	*Adj.*	to be responsible, L3
富裕	(fù yù)	*Adj.*	well-to-do, prosperous, well-off, L6

G

改编	(gǎi biān)	*V.*	to adapt, to revise, L1
改变	(gǎi biàn)	*N/V.*	change; to change, to alter, to correct, L1
改革	(gǎi gé)	*V/N.*	to reform; reform, L3
改善	(gǎi shàn)	*N/V.*	improvement; to improve, L5
干烧	(gān shāo)	*V.*	to stew after frying, L16
感冒	(gǎn mào)	*VO.*	to catch a cold, L10
感情	(gǎn qíng)	*N.*	emotion, feeling, L2
敢	(gǎn)	*V/Adj.*	to dare; daring, bold, courageous, L4
敢闯敢干	(gǎn chuǎng gǎn gàn)	*Idiom.*	to bravely explore and bravely engage in, L12
钢琴	(gāng qín)	*N.*	piano, L5
纲要	(gāng yào)	*N.*	outline, L6
岗位	(gǎng wèi)	*N.*	post , L3
高迈	(gāo mài)	*N.*	Gao Mai, name of a person 人名, L8
高山	(gāo shān)	*N.*	mountain, L9
高汤	(gāo tāng)	*N.*	thin soup, L16
高效	(gāo xiào)	*NP.*	high efficiency, L7
告别	(gào bié)	*V.*	to say good-bye, to pay one's last respects, L9
歌剧院	(gē jù yuàn)	*NP.*	opera house, L9
个体户	(gè tǐ hù)	*N.*	private entrepreneur, L3
各方面	(gè fāng miàn)	*NP.*	various aspects, L5
各种各样	(gè zhǒng gè yàng)	*AdjP.*	a variety of, various kinds of, L8
给予	(gěi yǔ)	*V.*	to give, L9
耕地	(gēng dì)	*N.*	arable land, L4
工艺	(gōng yì)	*N.*	handicraft, technology, L6
工装服	(gōng zhuāng fú)	*NP.*	work uniform, L3
工作量	(gōng zuò liàng)	*NP.*	work load, amount of work, L7
工作人员	(gōng zuò rén yuán)	*NP.*	working staff, L2
工作者	(gōng zuò zhě)	*NP.*	worker, L14
供应	(gòng yìng)	*V.*	to supply, L7
公德	(gōng dé)	*N.*	social morals, L5
公公	(gōng gōng)	*N.*	father-in-law, L15
公关部	(gōng guān bù)	*N.*	public relations department, L12
公顷	(gōng qǐng)	*N.*	hectare (approx. 16.5 acres), L4
公休日	(gōng xiū rì)	*N.*	week-end, public holidays, L2

公益	(gōng yì)	NP.	public welfare, L6
公職	(gōng zhí)	N.	public post, job in a state-owned enterprise, L3
貢獻	(gòng xiàn)	N.	contribution, L14
共同	(gòng tóng)	Adj.	common, shared, L2
勾芡	(gōu qiàn)	VO.	to make starchy gravy, L16
購買	(gòu mǎi)	V.	to purchase, L8
購銷兩旺	(gòu xiāo liǎng wàng)	Idiom.	active buying and selling, L11
孤兒	(gū ér)	N.	orphan, L2
姑娘	(gū niáng)	N.	unmarried young girl, L15
古生物	(gǔ shēng wù)	NP.	paleontology, L3
骨灰	(gǔ huī)	N.	ashes of a person, L9
骨頭	(gǔ tóu)	N.	bone, L16
骨折	(gǔ zhé)	N.	fracture, L14
股	(gǔ)	Classifier.	a stream of, a classifier for wind, water, etc., L13
故土	(gù tǔ)	N.	home land, native land, L9
固定	(gù dìng)	Adj.	fixed, L7
刮	(guā)	V.	to blow, L13
瓜市村	(guā shì cūn)	Place N.	Guashicun, name of a village 地名, L4
拐角	(guǎi jiǎo)	N.	corner, L10
怪	(guài)	N.	strangeness, L15
怪僻	(guài pì)	Adj.	eccentric, weird, odd (of a person or his/her behaviors), L1
關東煙	(guān dōng yān)	N.	Northeast Chinese tobacco, L15
關懷	(guān huái)	VP.	show concern for, care, L1
關雲峰	(guān yún fēng)	N.	Guan Yunfeng, name of a person 人名, L12
關注	(guān zhù)	N.	concern, attention, L13
冠軍	(guàn jūn)	N.	championship, L14
觀眾	(guān zhòng)	N.	audience, viewers, L4
管理	(guǎn lǐ)	N/V.	management; to manage, L3
光	(guāng)	Adv.	only, L7
光顧	(guāng gù)	V.	to pay attention to, to focus solely on, L12
光陰	(guāng yīn)	N.	lifetime, time, L1
廣東	(guǎng dōng)	PlaceN.	Guangdong (Province), L14
廣泛	(guǎng fàn)	Adj.	wide ranging, extensive, L12
規範化	(guī fàn huà)	NP.	standardization, L5
規劃	(guī huà)	N.	program, plan, L6
規模	(guī mó)	N.	scale, scope, L4
歸功於	(guī gōng yú)	VP.	to give the credit to, attribute to, L13
歸宿	(guī sù)	N.	final resting place, L9
櫃台	(guì tái)	N.	sales counter, L8
貴賓級	(guì bīn jí)	NP.	the rank of VIP, L10
滾滾來	(gǔn gǔn lái)	VP.	roaring over, gurgling over, L12
鍋	(guō)	N.	wok, L16

公益	(gōng yì)	NP.	public welfare, L6
公职	(gōng zhí)	N.	public post, job in a state-owned enterprise, L3
贡献	(gòng xiàn)	N.	contribution, L14
共同	(gòng tóng)	Adj.	common, shared, L2
勾芡	(gōu qiàn)	VO.	to make starchy gravy, L16
购买	(gòu mǎi)	V.	to purchase, L8
购销两旺	(gòu xiāo liǎng wàng)	Idiom.	active buying and selling, L11
孤儿	(gū ér)	N.	orphan, L2
姑娘	(gū niáng)	N.	unmarried young girl, L15
古生物	(gǔ shēng wù)	NP.	paleontology, L3
骨灰	(gǔ huī)	N.	ashes of a person, L9
骨头	(gǔ tóu)	N.	bone, L16
骨折	(gǔ zhé)	N.	fracture, L14
股	(gǔ)	Classifier.	a stream of, a classifier for wind, water, etc., L13
故土	(gù tǔ)	N.	home land, native land, L9
固定	(gù dìng)	Adj.	fixed, L7
刮	(guā)	V.	to blow, L13
瓜市村	(guā shì cūn)	Place N.	Guashicun, name of a village 地名, L4
拐角	(guǎi jiǎo)	N.	corner, L10
怪	(guài)	N.	strangeness, L15
怪僻	(guài pì)	Adj.	eccentric, weird, odd (of a person or his/her behaviors), L1
关东烟	(guān dōng yān)	N.	Northeast Chinese tobacco, L15
关怀	(guān huái)	VP.	show concern for, care, L1
关云峰	(guān yún fēng)	N.	Guan Yunfeng, name of a person 人名, L12
关注	(guān zhù)	N.	concern, attention, L13
冠军	(guàn jūn)	N.	championship, L14
观众	(guān zhòng)	N.	audience, viewers, L4
管理	(guǎn lǐ)	N/V.	management; to manage, L3
光	(guāng)	Adv.	only, L7
光顾	(guāng gù)	V.	to pay attention to, to focus solely on, L12
光阴	(guāng yīn)	N.	lifetime, time, L1
广东	(guǎng dōng)	PlaceN.	Guangdong (Province), L14
广泛	(guǎng fàn)	Adj.	wide ranging, extensive, L12
规范化	(guī fàn huà)	NP.	standardization, L5
规划	(guī huà)	N.	program, plan, L6
规模	(guī mó)	N.	scale, scope, L4
归功于	(guī gōng yú)	VP.	to give the credit to, attribute to, L13
归宿	(guī sù)	N.	final resting place, L9
柜台	(guì tái)	N.	sales counter, L8
贵宾级	(guì bīn jí)	NP.	the rank of VIP, L10
滚滚来	(gǔn gǔn lái)	VP.	roaring over, gurgling over, L12
锅	(guō)	N.	wok, L16

國際級	(guó jì jí)	Adj/N.	internationally ranked, L14
國家	(guó jiā)	N.	country, nation, L3
國林耀	(guó lín yuè/yào)	N.	Guo Linyue/yao, name of a person 人名, L14
國慶節	(guó qìng jié)	NP.	National Day, L10
國營	(guó yíng)	Adj.	state owned, L3
過分	(guò fèn)	Adj.	excessive, over, too much, L6
過世	(guò shì)	VO.	to pass away, L9

H

海	(hǎi)	N.	sea, L9
海撒	(hǎi sǎ)	VP.	to scatter (ashes) in the sea, L9
海外	(hǎi wài)	N.	overseas, L13
海域	(hǎi yù)	N.	sea area, maritime space, L9
海葬	(hǎi zàng)	NP.	burial at sea, L9
嗨	(hài)	Interj.	hey!, L10
韓凱	(hán kǎi)	N.	Han Kai, name of a person, 人名, L2
含義	(hán yì)	N.	meaning, implication, L1
行列	(háng liè)	N.	ranks, L7
行情	(háng qíng)	N.	general price situation, L11
豪放	(háo fàng)	Adj.	unconstrained, bold, L15
毫無	(háo wú)	Adv.	not at all, L10
好轉	(hǎo zhuǎn)	NP.	positive changes, better, improvement, L6
呵呵	(hē hē)	N.	sound of laughter, L10
何茹	(hé rú)	N.	He Ru, name of a person 人名, L1
合理	(hé lǐ)	Adj.	reasonable, rational, L3
合作	(hé zuò)	N/V.	cooperation; to cooperate, to collaborate, L10
盒飯	(hé fàn)	NP.	boxed meal, L7
盒飯大王	(hé fàn dà wáng)	NP.	King of Boxed Lunches, name of a restaurant, L7
河	(hé)	N.	river, L9
嘿	(hèi)	Interj.	hey!, L12
狠心	(hěn xīn)	Adj.	cruel, heartless, L2
紅寶石婚	(hóng bǎo shí hūn)	NP.	red diamond wedding anniversary, L8
紅高粱	(hóng gāo liáng)	NP.	*Red Sorgham*, the name of a film directed by Zhang Yimou, L13
紅火	(hóng huǒ)	Adj.	busy and bustling, L11
紅辣椒	(hóng là jiāo)	N.	red chili pepper, L16
後生可畏	(hòu shēng kě wèi)	Idiom.	a youth is to be regarded with respect–the younger generation will surpass the older, L12
湖	(hú)	N.	lake, L9
花刀	(huā dāo)	N.	chopping on top of the meat, L16

国际级	(guó jì jí)	*Adj/N.*	internationally ranked, L14
国家	(guó jiā)	*N.*	country, nation, L3
国林耀	(guó lín yào)	*N.*	Guo Linyue/yao, name of a person 人名, L14
国庆节	(guó qìng jié)	*NP.*	National Day, L10
国营	(guó yíng)	*Adj.*	state owned, L3
过分	(guò fèn)	*Adj.*	excessive, over, too much, L6
过世	(guò shì)	*VO.*	to pass away, L9

H

海	(hǎi)	*N.*	sea, L9
海撒	(hǎi sǎ)	*VP.*	to scatter (ashes) in the sea, L9
海外	(hǎi wài)	*N.*	overseas, L13
海域	(hǎi yù)	*N.*	sea area, maritime space, L9
海葬	(hǎi zàng)	*NP.*	burial at sea, L9
嗨	(hài)	*Interj.*	hey!, L10
韩凯	(hán kǎi)	*N.*	Han Kai, name of a person, 人名, L2
含义	(hán yì)	*N.*	meaning, implication, L1
行列	(háng liè)	*N.*	ranks, L7
行情	(háng qíng)	*N.*	general price situation, L11
豪放	(háo fàng)	*Adj.*	unconstrained, bold, L15
毫无	(háo wú)	*Adv.*	not at all, L10
好转	(hǎo zhuǎn)	*NP.*	positive changes, better, improvement, L6
呵呵	(hē hē)	*N.*	sound of laughter, L10
何茹	(hé rú)	*N.*	He Ru, name of a person 人名, L1
合理	(hé lǐ)	*Adj.*	reasonable, rational, L3
合作	(hé zuò)	*N/V.*	cooperation; to cooperate, to collaborate, L10
盒饭	(hé fàn)	*NP.*	boxed meal, L7
盒饭大王	(hé fàn dà wáng)	*NP.*	King of Boxed Lunches, name of a restaurant, L7
河	(hé)	*N.*	river, L9
嘿	(hèi)	*Interj.*	hey!, L12
狠心	(hěn xīn)	*Adj.*	cruel, heartless, L2
红宝石婚	(hóng bǎo shí hūn)	*NP.*	red diamond wedding anniversary, L8
红高粱	(hóng gāo liáng)	*NP.*	*Red Sorgham*, the name of a film directed by Zhang Yimou, L13
红火	(hóng huǒ)	*Adj.*	busy and bustling, L11
红辣椒	(hóng là jiāo)	*N.*	red chili pepper, L16
后生可畏	(hòu shēng kě wèi)	*Idiom.*	a youth is to be regarded with respect–the younger generation will surpass the older, L12
湖	(hú)	*N.*	lake, L9
花刀	(huā dāo)	*N.*	chopping on top of the meat, L16

花卉	(huā huì)	N.	flowers and plants, floral, L3
花椒油	(huā jiāo yóu)	N.	pepper flavored oil, L16
花樣	(huā yàng)	N.	variety, L7
劃開	(huá kāi)	V.	to separate, L16
話劇	(huà jù)	N.	play, L12
話匣子	(huà xiá zi)	N.	chatter box, L10
懷裡	(huái lǐ)	N.	in someone's arms or embrace, L1
黃瓜	(huáng guā)	N.	cucumber, L16
皇帝	(huáng dì)	N.	emperor, L6
回歸	(huí guī)	V.	to return, L9
回族	(huí zú)	N.	Islamic nationality in China, L12
婚禮	(hūn lǐ)	N.	wedding, wedding ceremony, L8
活	(huó)	Adj.	flexible, L4
活兒	(huór)	N.	work, job, chore, L15
活人	(huó rén)	N.	the living, people with life, L9
活躍	(huó yuè)	Adj.	active, dynamic, L3
活著	(huó zhe)	N.	*To Live*, the name of a film by Zhang Yimou, L13
火	(huǒ)	Adj.	popular, L12
獲得者	(huò dé zhě)	NP.	winner, L14
獲獎	(huò jiǎng)	VO.	to win the award, L13
或許	(huò xǔ)	Adv.	maybe, L8

J

基本	(jī běn)	Adj.	basic, L5
基本上	(jī běn shàng)	Adv.	basically, L3
基礎	(jī chǔ)	N.	basis, foundation, L6
基地	(jī dì)	N.	base, L6
基金	(jī jīn)	N.	fund, L2
基於	(jī yú)	VP.	to be based on , L13
機關	(jī guān)	N.	office, L7
機遇	(jī yù)	N.	the opportunity of a lifetime, L11
機制	(jī zhì)	N.	system, L3
雞丁	(jī dīng)	N.	chicken subgum , L16
雞脯	(jī pú)	N.	chicken breast, L16
吉利	(jí lì)	Adj.	fortunate, lucky, auspicious, L8
集體	(jí tǐ)	Adj/Adv.	collective, collectively, L2
集團	(jí tuán)	N.	incorporation, group, L12
集訓	(jí xùn)	N/V.	to bring people together for training, L14
集訓隊	(jí xùn duì)	N.	training camp, L14
及時	(jí shí)	Adv.	on time, timely, immediately, L3
即可	(jí kě)	VP.	that is all, that will do, L16
擠進	(jǐ jìn)	VP.	to force oneself in, to squeeze oneself in, L12

花卉	(huā huì)	N.	flowers and plants, floral, L3
花椒油	(huā jiāo yóu)	N.	pepper flavored oil, L16
花样	(huā yàng)	N.	variety, L7
划开	(huá kāi)	V.	to separate, L16
话剧	(huà jù)	N.	play, L12
话匣子	(huà xiá zi)	N.	chatter box, L10
怀里	(huái lǐ)	N.	in someone's arms or embrace, L1
黄瓜	(huáng guā)	N.	cucumber, L16
皇帝	(huáng dì)	N.	emperor, L6
回归	(huí guī)	V.	to return, L9
回族	(huí zú)	N.	Islamic nationality in China, L12
婚礼	(hūn lǐ)	N.	wedding, wedding ceremony, L8
活	(huó)	Adj.	flexible, L4
活儿	(huór)	N.	work, job, chore, L15
活人	(huó rén)	N.	the living, people with life, L9
活跃	(huó yuè)	Adj.	active, dynamic, L3
活着	(huó zhe)	N.	*To Live*, the name of a film by Zhang Yimou, L13
火	(huǒ)	Adj.	popular, L12
获得者	(huò dé zhě)	NP.	winner, L14
获奖	(huò jiǎng)	VO.	to win the award, L13
或许	(huò xǔ)	Adv.	maybe, L8

J

基本	(jī běn)	Adj.	basic, L5
基本上	(jī běn shàng)	Adv.	basically, L3
基础	(jī chǔ)	N.	basis, foundation, L6
基地	(jī dì)	N.	base, L6
基金	(jī jīn)	N.	fund, L2
基于	(jī yú)	VP.	to be based on , L13
机关	(jī guān)	N.	office, L7
机遇	(jī yù)	N.	the opportunity of a lifetime, L11
机制	(jī zhì)	N.	system, L3
鸡丁	(jī dīng)	N.	chicken subgum , L16
鸡脯	(jī pú)	N.	chicken breast, L16
吉利	(jí lì)	Adj.	fortunate, lucky, auspicious, L8
集体	(jí tǐ)	Adj/Adv.	collective, collectively, L2
集团	(jí tuán)	N.	incorporation, group, L12
集训	(jí xùn)	N/V.	to bring people together for training, L14
集训队	(jí xùn duì)	N.	training camp, L14
及时	(jí shí)	Adv.	on time, timely, immediately, L3
即可	(jí kě)	VP.	that is all, that will do, L16
挤进	(jǐ jìn)	VP.	to force oneself in, to squeeze oneself in, L12

寄	(jì)	V.	to send, to mail, L1
寄宿	(jì sù)	V.	to lodge, to put up, L2
寄托	(jì tuō)	V/N.	to send to the care of someone, to leave in the care of, L9
寂寞	(jì mò)	Adj.	lonely, L10
計劃經濟	(jì huà jīng jì)	NP.	planned economy, L3
記者	(jì zhě)	V.	reporter, L2
繼……之後	(jì...zhī hòu)	V.	to follow, L9
繼續	(jì xù)	V.	to continue, to go on, L4
紀念日	(jì niàn rì)	NP.	day of commemoration, anniversary, L8
家	(jiā)	N.	specialist in a certain field, L5
家教	(jiā jiào)	N.	family teacher, special tutor, L1
家屬	(jiā shǔ)	N.	spouse, family members, L2
家務	(jiā wù)	N.	household chores, L1
加重	(jiā zhòng)	V.	to add, to increase, L8
價值	(jià zhí)	N.	value, L8
監護	(jiān hù)	N.	guardianship, L2
間接	(jiàn jiē)	Adj.	indirect, L13
簡潔	(jiǎn jié)	Adj.	succinct, terse, L16
健將	(jiàn jiàng)	N.	top player, L14
健全	(jiàn quán)	Adj.	normal and healthy, of sound mind and body, L6
建立	(jiàn lì)	V.	to establish, L5
建議	(jiàn yì)	N/V.	suggestion; to suggest, L3
姜	(jiāng)	N.	ginger, L16
江	(jiāng)	N.	river, L9
獎勵	(jiǎng lì)	N/V	award, reward; to reward, L3
醬油	(jiàng yóu)	N.	soy sauce, L16
交付	(jiāo fù)	V.	to pay for, L8
交響樂團	(jiāo xiǎng yuè tuán)	NP.	symphony orchestra, L9
交響曲	(jiāo xiǎng qǔ)	N.	symphony, L9
角度	(jiǎo dù)	N.	angle, perspective, L13
教育	(jiào yù)	N/V.	education; to teach, to educate, L1
教育局	(jiào yù jú)	NP.	education bureau, L6
街頭	(jiē tóu)	N.	on the street , L7
節假日	(jié jià rì)	N.	holidays , L2
節儉	(jié jiǎn)	Adj.	thrifty, frugal, L8
節目	(jié mù)	N.	program, L6
節奏	(jié zòu)	N.	pace, rhythm, L7
節奏	(jié zòu)	NP.	fast pace, L7
結構	(jié gòu)	N.	structure, L1
解乏	(jiě fá)	VO.	to be refreshing, to recover from fatigue, L15
解放軍	(jiě fàng jūn)	NP.	People's Liberation Army, L12
解悶	(jiě mèn)	VO.	to get rid of loneliness, L15

寄	(jì)	*V.*	to send, to mail, L1
寄宿	(jì sù)	*V.*	to lodge, to put up, L2
寄托	(jì tuō)	*V/N.*	to send to the care of someone, to leave in the care of, L9
寂寞	(jì mò)	*Adj.*	lonely, L10
计划经济	(jì huà jīng jì)	*NP.*	planned economy, L3
记者	(jì zhě)	*V.*	reporter, L2
继……之后	(jì...zhī hòu)	*V.*	to follow, L9
继续	(jì xù)	*V.*	to continue, to go on, L4
纪念日	(jì niàn rì)	*NP.*	day of commemoration, anniversary, L8
家	(jiā)	*N.*	specialist in a certain field, L5
家教	(jiā jiào)	*N.*	family teacher, special tutor, L1
家属	(jiā shǔ)	*N.*	spouse, family members, L2
家务	(jiā wù)	*N.*	household chores, L1
加重	(jiā zhòng)	*V.*	to add, to increase, L8
价值	(jià zhí)	*N.*	value, L8
监护	(jiān hù)	*N.*	guardianship, L2
间接	(jiàn jiē)	*Adj.*	indirect, L13
简洁	(jiǎn jié)	*Adj.*	succinct, terse, L16
健将	(jiàn jiàng)	*N.*	top player, L14
健全	(jiàn quán)	*Adj.*	normal and healthy, of sound mind and body, L6
建立	(jiàn lì)	*V.*	to establish, L5
建议	(jiàn yì)	*N/V.*	suggestion; to suggest, L3
姜	(jiāng)	*N.*	ginger, L16
江	(jiāng)	*N.*	river, L9
奖励	(jiǎng lì)	*N/V*	award, reward; to reward, L3
酱油	(jiàng yóu)	*N.*	soy sauce, L16
交付	(jiāo fù)	*V.*	to pay for, L8
交响乐团	(jiāo xiǎng yuè tuán)	*NP.*	symphony orchestra, L9
交响曲	(jiāo xiǎng qǔ)	*N.*	symphony, L9
角度	(jiǎo dù)	*N.*	angle, perspective, L13
教育	(jiào yù)	*N/V.*	education; to teach, to educate, L1
教育局	(jiào yù jú)	*NP.*	education bureau, L6
街头	(jiē tóu)	*N.*	on the street , L7
节假日	(jié jià rì)	*N.*	holidays , L2
节俭	(jié jiǎn)	*Adj.*	thrifty, frugal, L8
节目	(jié mù)	*N.*	program, L6
节奏	(jié zòu)	*N.*	pace, rhythm, L7
节奏	(jié zòu)	*NP.*	fast pace, L7
结构	(jié gòu)	*N.*	structure, L1
解乏	(jiě fá)	*VO.*	to be refreshing, to recover from fatigue, L15
解放军	(jiě fàng jūn)	*NP.*	People's Liberation Army, L12
解闷	(jiě mèn)	*VO.*	to get rid of loneliness, L15

屆	(jiè)	*Classifier.*	session, L6
金帆	(jīn fān)	*N.*	gold sail, L12
金婚	(jīn hūn)	*NP.*	golden wedding anniversary, L8
金熊獎	(jīn xióng jiǎng)	*N.*	Golden Bear Award, L13
錦標賽	(jǐn biāo sài)	*N.*	championship contest, L14
進	(jìn)	*V.*	to buy, L11
進程	(jìn chéng)	*N.*	process, L7
進貨	(jìn huò)	*VO.*	to buy goods wholesale, L11
浸注	(jìn zhù)	*V.*	to pour in, to devote to , L5
盡量	(jìn liàng)	*V.*	to try one's best, L4
京城	(jīng chéng)	*PlaceN.*	the capital city, L5
驚濤駭浪	(jīng tāo hài làng)	*Idiom.*	terrifying waves, hardship in one's life, L1
驚喜	(jīng xǐ)	*V.*	to be happily surprised at, L12
精力	(jīng lì)	*N.*	energy, L5
精神	(jīng shén)	*N.*	spirit, L3
經過	(jīng guò)	*V.*	to pass, to go through, to undergo, L3
經濟	(jīng jì)	*N/Adj.*	economy; economical, L8
經理	(jīng lǐ)	*N.*	manager, L12
經歷	(jīng lì)	*N./V.*	experience; to experience, L1
經商	(jīng shāng)	*VO.*	to do business, L11
經銷額	(jīng xiāo é)	*NP.*	amount sold, L11
經營	(jīng yíng)	*V/N.*	to run, to engage in (pertaining to selling); management, L3
經營方式	(jīng yíng fāng shì)	*NP.*	managerial style, L11
敬給	(jìng gěi)	*VP.*	to present with respect, L15
敬禮	(jìng lǐ)	*VO.*	a salutation used at the end of a letter, meaning "respectfully, with best wishes", L1
敬煙	(jìng yān)	*VO.*	to present the pipe with respect, L15
竟	(jìng)	*Adv.*	even, L8
竟然	(jìng rán)	*Adv.*	unexpectedly, surprisingly, even, L12
競爭	(jìng zhēng)	*N.*	competition, L5
究竟	(jiū jìng)	*Adv.*	after all, L5
90年	(jiǔ líng nián)	*TimeN.*	1990, L1
酒樓	(jiǔ lóu)	*N.*	restaurant, L7
舊情	(jiù qíng)	*NP.*	old feelings, recollections of the past, L12
就餐	(jiù cān)	*V.*	to eat, to dine, L7
居然	(jū rán)	*Adv.*	unexpectedly, surprisingly, contrary to one's expectations, L1
菊豆	(jú dòu)	*N.*	*Ju Dou*, name of a person, the name of a film directed by Zhang Yimou 人名, L13
舉辦	(jǔ bàn)	*V.*	to hold, to sponsor, L6
舉動	(jǔ dòng)	*N.*	action, L10
據統計	(jù tǒng jì)	*Adv.*	according to statistics, L10
具有	(jù yǒu)	*V.*	to have, to possess, L9

届	(jiè)	Classifier.	session, L6
金帆	(jīn fān)	N.	gold sail, L12
金婚	(jīn hūn)	NP.	golden wedding anniversary, L8
金熊奖	(jīn xióng jiǎng)	N.	Golden Bear Award, L13
锦标赛	(jǐn biāo sài)	N.	championship contest, L14
进	(jìn)	V.	to buy, L11
进程	(jìn chéng)	N.	process, L7
进货	(jìn huò)	VO.	to buy goods wholesale, L11
浸注	(jìn zhù)	V.	to pour in, to devote to , L5
尽量	(jìn liàng)	V.	to try one's best, L4
京城	(jīng chéng)	PlaceN.	the capital city, L5
惊涛骇浪	(jīng tāo hài làng)	Idiom.	terrifying waves, hardship in one's life, L1
惊喜	(jīng xǐ)	V.	to be happily surprised at, L12
精力	(jīng lì)	N.	energy, L5
精神	(jīng shén)	N.	spirit, L3
经过	(jīng guò)	V.	to pass, to go through, to undergo, L3
经济	(jīng jì)	N/Adj.	economy; economical, L8
经理	(jīng lǐ)	N.	manager, L12
经历	(jīng lì)	N./V.	experience; to experience, L1
经商	(jīng shāng)	VO.	to do business, L11
经销额	(jīng xiāo é)	NP.	amount sold, L11
经营	(jīng yíng)	V/N.	to run, to engage in (pertaining to selling); management, L3
经营方式	(jīng yíng fāng shì)	NP.	managerial style, L11
敬给	(jìng gěi)	VP.	to present with respect, L15
敬礼	(jìng lǐ)	VO.	a salutation used at the end of a letter, meaning "respectfully, with best wishes", L1
敬烟	(jìng yān)	VO.	to present the pipe with respect, L15
竟	(jìng)	Adv.	even, L8
竟然	(jìng rán)	Adv.	unexpectedly, surprisingly, even, L12
竞争	(jìng zhēng)	N.	competition, L5
究竟	(jiū jìng)	Adv.	after all, L5
90年	(jiǔ líng nián)	TimeN.	1990, L1
酒楼	(jiǔ lóu)	N.	restaurant, L7
旧情	(jiù qíng)	NP.	old feelings, recollections of the past, L12
就餐	(jiù cān)	V.	to eat, to dine, L7
居然	(jū rán)	Adv.	unexpectedly, surprisingly, contrary to one's expectations, L1
菊豆	(jú dòu)	N.	Ju Dou, name of a person, the name of a film directed by Zhang Yimou 人名, L13
举办	(jǔ bàn)	V.	to hold, to sponsor, L6
举动	(jǔ dòng)	N.	action, L10
据统计	(jù tǒng jì)	Adv.	according to statistics, L10
具有	(jù yǒu)	V.	to have, to possess, L9

劇院	(jù yuàn)	N.	opera house, L12
劇組	(jù zǔ)	N.	production team, L13
捐資	(juān zī)	VO.	to donate money, L2
決策	(jué cè)	N.	decision making, L11
絕對	(jué duì)	Adv.	absolutely, L11

K

開辟	(kāi pì)	V.	to open up, to start, L6
開放	(kāi fàng)	V.	to open up, to open, L1
開設	(kāi shè)	V.	to open, L8
開水	(kāi shuǐ)	N.	boiled water, L16
開展	(kāi zhǎn)	V.	to launch, to start, L6
開張	(kāi zhāng)	V.	grand opening, L12
考級	(kǎo jí)	VO.	to take a test to be placed at a certain level or group, L5
靠	(kào)	V.	to rely on, to depend on, L3
科學化	(kē xué huà)	NP.	"scientification", make more scientific, L5
可惜	(kě xī)	Adv/Adj.	unfortunately; of pity, to be a pity, L1
可想而知	(kě xiǎng ér zhī)	Idiom.	to know through imagination, to easily figure out, L11
可選	(kě xuǎn)	Adj.	selectable, L7
克服	(kè fú)	V.	to overcome, L14
客觀	(kè guān)	Adj.	objective, L13
客觀規律	(kè guān guī lǜ)	NP.	objective principle, L11
客流量	(kè liú liàng)	N.	number of customers, L11
客運	(kè yùn)	N.	passenger transport, L10
課本	(kè běn)	N.	textbook, L2
空淨	(kòng jìng)	V.	to drain completely, L16
控制	(kòng zhì)	N/V.	control; to control, L6
口味	(kǒu wèi)	N.	taste, L13
枯燥	(kū zào)	Adj.	dull and dry, boring, L10
苦	(kǔ)	Adj.	bitter, causing hardship or suffering, L5
誇	(kuā)	V.	to praise, L14
快速化	(kuài sù huà)	N.	to become fast-paced, L7

L

辣子	(là zi)	N.	hot pepper, L16
來之不易	(lái zhī bù yì)	Idiom.	hard to obtain, L14
爛	(làn)	Adj.	soft, tender , L16
勞動	(láo dòng)	N.	labor, work, L5
老爸	(lǎo bà)	NP.	my daddy, my dear old dad, L12
老大哥	(lǎo dà gē)	N.	old brother, L14
老將	(lǎo jiàng)	N.	old-timer, veteran, L14

剧院	(jù yuàn)	N.	opera house, L12
剧组	(jù zǔ)	N.	production team, L13
捐资	(juān zī)	VO.	to donate money, L2
决策	(jué cè)	N.	decision making, L11
绝对	(jué duì)	Adv.	absolutely, L11

K

开辟	(kāi pì)	V.	to open up, to start, L6
开放	(kāi fàng)	V.	to open up, to open, L1
开设	(kāi shè)	V.	to open, L8
开水	(kāi shuǐ)	N.	boiled water, L16
开展	(kāi zhǎn)	V.	to launch, to start, L6
开张	(kāi zhāng)	V.	grand opening, L12
考级	(kǎo jí)	VO.	to take a test to be placed at a certain level or group, L5
靠	(kào)	V.	to rely on, to depend on, L3
科学化	(kē xué huà)	NP.	"scientification", make more scientific, L5
可惜	(kě xī)	Adv/Adj.	unfortunately; of pity, to be a pity, L1
可想而知	(kě xiǎng ér zhī)	Idiom.	to know through imagination, to easily figure out, L11
可选	(kě xuǎn)	Adj.	selectable, L7
克服	(kè fú)	V.	to overcome, L14
客观	(kè guān)	Adj.	objective, L13
客观规律	(kè guān guī lǜ)	NP.	objective principle, L11
客流量	(kè liú liàng)	N.	number of customers, L11
客运	(kè yùn)	N.	passenger transport, L10
课本	(kè běn)	N.	textbook, L2
空净	(kòng jìng)	V.	to drain completely, L16
控制	(kòng zhì)	N/V.	control; to control, L6
口味	(kǒu wèi)	N.	taste, L13
枯燥	(kū zào)	Adj.	dull and dry, boring, L10
苦	(kǔ)	Adj.	bitter, causing hardship or suffering, L5
夸	(kuā)	V.	to praise, L14
快速化	(kuài sù huà)	N.	to become fast-paced, L7

L

辣子	(là zi)	N.	hot pepper, L16
来之不易	(lái zhī bù yì)	Idiom.	hard to obtain, L14
烂	(làn)	Adj.	soft, tender , L16
劳动	(láo dòng)	N.	labor, work, L5
老爸	(lǎo bà)	NP.	my daddy, my dear old dad, L12
老大哥	(lǎo dà gē)	N.	old brother, L14
老将	(lǎo jiàng)	N.	old-timer, veteran, L14

老倆口	(lǎo liáng kǒu)	N.	old couple, L15
淚水	(lèi shuǐ)	N.	tear, teardrop, L1
離異	(lí yì)	N.	separation, L1
李春陽	(lǐ chūn yáng)	N.	Li Chunyang, name of a person 人名, L14
李子慶	(lǐ zǐ qìng)	N.	Li Ziqing, name of a person 人名, L6
李奕芳	(lǐ yì fāng)	N.	Li Yifang, name of a person 人名, L14
禮品	(lǐ pǐn)	N.	gift, present, L4
禮遇	(lǐ yù)	N.	courteous treatment, L10
歷來	(lì lái)	Adv.	all along, always, L8
利潤	(lì rùn)	N.	profit, L11
利益	(lì yì)	N.	interest, L11
利用	(lì yòng)	V.	to utilize, L4
例外	(lì wài)	Adj/N.	exception; exceptional, L11
聯合會	(lián hé huì)	NP.	association, federation, union, L6
聯繫	(lián xì)	V/N.	to contact, to get in touch with, L9
連連	(lián lián)	Adv.	one after another, constantly, L13
練習曲	(liàn xí qǔ)	N.	etude, L5
梁為民	(liáng wéi mín)	N.	Liang Weimin, name of a person 人名, L8
了不起	(liǎo bù qǐ)	Adj.	extraordinary, amazing, L11
料酒	(liào jiǔ)	N.	cooking wine, L16
臨戰	(lín zhàn)	Adv.	prior to battle, before battle, L5
淋	(lín)	V.	to pour, L16
靈活	(líng huó)	Adj.	flexible, L11
聆聽	(líng tīng)	V.	to listen, L9
領	(lǐng)	V.	to receive (salary, fund), L8
領養	(lǐng yǎng)	V.	to adopt, L2
劉海明	(liú hǎi míng)	N.	Liu Haiming, name of a person 人名, L12
流動	(liú dòng)	Adj.	circulating (funds), floating, L4
流行	(liú xíng)	Adj.	popular, trendy, fashionable, in vogue, L6
輪船	(lún chuán)	N.	steamship, steamboat, L9
輪流	(lún liú)	Adv.	to take turns, L2
落後	(luò hòu)	Adj.	backward, L2
落葉歸根	(luò yè guī gēn)	Idiom.	leaves settle on their own roots, L9
駱駝祥子	(luò tuó xiáng zi)	N.	*Camel Xiangzi* (a play written by Lao She), L12
率	(lǜ)	N.	rate, L8

M

馬場	(mǎ chǎng)	Place N.	Machang, name of a place 地名, L2
馬桂茹	(mǎ guì rú)	N.	Ma Guiru, name of a person 人名, L12
麥當勞	(mài dāng láo)	N.	McDonald's, L12
邁進	(mài jìn)	V.	to stride forward, L7
滿意	(mǎn yì)	Adj/N.	to be satisfied; satisfaction, L1
滿足	(mǎn zú)	V.	to satisfy, L8

老俩口	(lǎo liǎng kǒu)	*N.*	old couple, L15
泪水	(lèi shuǐ)	*N.*	tear, teardrop, L1
离异	(lí yì)	*N.*	separation, L1
李春阳	(lǐ chūn yáng)	*N.*	Li Chunyang, name of a person 人名, L14
李子庆	(lǐ zǐ qìng)	*N.*	Li Ziqing, name of a person 人名, L6
李奕芳	(lǐ yì fāng)	*N.*	Li Yifang, name of a person 人名, L14
礼品	(lǐ pǐn)	*N.*	gift, present, L4
礼遇	(lǐ yù)	*N.*	courteous treatment, L10
历来	(lì lái)	*Adv.*	all along, always, L8
利润	(lì rùn)	*N.*	profit, L11
利益	(lì yì)	*N.*	interest, L11
利用	(lì yòng)	*V.*	to utilize, L4
例外	(lì wài)	*Adj/N.*	exception; exceptional, L11
联合会	(lián hé huì)	*NP.*	association, federation, union, L6
联系	(lián xì)	*V/N.*	to contact, to get in touch with, L9
连连	(lián lián)	*Adv.*	one after another, constantly, L13
练习曲	(liàn xí qǔ)	*N.*	etude, L5
梁为民	(liáng wéi mín)	*N.*	Liang Weimin, name of a person 人名, L8
了不起	(liǎo bù qǐ)	*Adj.*	extraordinary, amazing, L11
料酒	(liào jiǔ)	*N.*	cooking wine, L16
临战	(lín zhàn)	*Adv.*	prior to battle, before battle, L5
淋	(lín)	*V.*	to pour, L16
灵活	(líng huó)	*Adj.*	flexible, L11
聆听	(líng tīng)	*V.*	to listen, L9
领	(lǐng)	*V.*	to receive (salary, fund), L8
领养	(lǐng yǎng)	*V.*	to adopt, L2
刘海明	(liú hǎi míng)	*N.*	Liu Haiming, name of a person 人名, L12
流动	(liú dòng)	*Adj.*	circulating (funds), floating, L4
流行	(liú xíng)	*Adj.*	popular, trendy, fashionable, in vogue, L6
轮船	(lún chuán)	*N.*	steamship, steamboat, L9
轮流	(lún liú)	*Adv.*	to take turns, L2
落后	(luò hòu)	*Adj.*	backward, L2
落叶归根	(luò yè guī gēn)	*Idiom.*	leaves settle on their own roots, L9
骆驼祥子	(luò tuó xiáng zi)	*N.*	*Camel Xiangzi* (a play written by Lao She), L12
率	(lǜ)	*N.*	rate, L8

M

马场	(mǎ chǎng)	*Place N.*	Machang, name of a place 地名, L2
马桂茹	(mǎ guì rú)	*N.*	Ma Guiru, name of a person 人名, L12
麦当劳	(mài dāng láo)	*N.*	McDonald's, L12
迈进	(mài jìn)	*V.*	to stride forward, L7
满意	(mǎn yì)	*Adj/N.*	to be satisfied; satisfaction, L1
满足	(mǎn zú)	*V.*	to satisfy, L8

忙碌	(máng lù)	*Adj.*	busy, L12
毛病	(máo bìng)	*N.*	defect, L2
毛璐	(máo lù)	*N.*	Mao Lu, name of a person 人名, L16
沒有治	(méi yǒu zhì)	*Adj.*	incurable, L2
每逢	(měi féng)	*Adv.*	every (+ time expression), L2
燜	(mēn)	*V.*	to keep the lid on, L16
米飯	(mǐ fàn)	*N.*	rice, L7
免費	(miǎn fèi)	*Adv.*	free of charge, free, L2
面對	(miàn duì)	*V.*	to face, to confront, L14
面頰	(miàn jiá)	*N.*	cheek, face, L1
面臨	(miàn lín)	*V.*	to face, L13
描寫	(miáo xiě)	*V.*	to describe, description, L13
民政	(mín zhèng)	*N.*	public affairs, civil affairs, L9
民族	(mín zú)	*N.*	nation, nationality, race, L6
明顯	(míng xiǎn)	*Adj.*	obvious, obviously, clearly, L6
名單	(míng dān)	*N.*	list of names, name list, L2
名義	(míng yì)	*N.*	in the name of , L2
命名	(mìng míng)	*VO.*	to name (after), L14
模式	(mó shì)	*N.*	model, pattern, L13
末	(mò)	*N.*	end, L6
末	(mò)	*V.*	to chop up in fine pieces, L16
莫根	(mò gēn)	*N.*	Mo Gen, name of a person 人名, L5
莫過於	(mò guò yú)	*VP.*	nothing is better than, L9
默默	(mò mò)	*Adv.*	quietly, silently, L10
默契	(mò qì)	*N.*	tacit agreement, L10
某些	(mǒu xiē)	*Pron.*	some, L6
拇指	(mǔ zhǐ)	*N.*	thumb, L14
畝	(mǔ)	*Classifier.*	measurement for land, L3
目標	(mù biāo)	*N.*	goal, aim, L13

N

拿得出手	(ná dé chū shǒu)	*Adj.*	presentable, L8
難過	(nán guò)	*Adj.*	sad, sorrowful, difficult to bear, L9
腦子	(nǎo zi)	*N.*	brain, L10
腦子活	(nǎo zi huó)	*Idiom.*	smart, flexible way of thinking, L12
內容	(nèi róng)	*N.*	content, L5
能否	(néng fǒu)	*V.*	can or cannot, L9
能幹	(néng gàn)	*VP.*	capable of doing, able, L15
能手	(néng shǒu)	*N.*	a dab, a goodhand, a crackerjack, an expert, L6
泥坑	(ní kēng)	*N.*	mud pit, L10
膩	(nì)	*Adj.*	to be bored of, to be tired of, L7
溺愛	(nì ài)	*V.*	to spoil (a child), to be excessively fond of,

忙碌	(máng lù)	Adj.	busy, L12
毛病	(máo bìng)	N.	defect, L2
毛璐	(máo lù)	N.	Mao Lu, name of a person 人名, L16
没有治	(méi yǒu zhì)	Adj.	incurable, L2
每逢	(měi féng)	Adv.	every (+ time expression), L2
焖	(mēn)	V.	to keep the lid on, L16
米饭	(mǐ fàn)	N.	rice, L7
免费	(miǎn fèi)	Adv.	free of charge, free, L2
面对	(miàn duì)	V.	to face, to confront, L14
面颊	(miàn jiá)	N.	cheek, face, L1
面临	(miàn lín)	V.	to face, L13
描写	(miáo xiě)	V.	to describe, description, L13
民政	(mín zhèng)	N.	public affairs, civil affairs, L9
民族	(mín zú)	N.	nation, nationality, race, L6
明显	(míng xiǎn)	Adj.	obvious, obviously, clearly, L6
名单	(míng dān)	N.	list of names, name list, L2
名义	(míng yì)	N.	in the name of , L2
命名	(mìng míng)	VO.	to name (after), L14
模式	(mó shì)	N.	model, pattern, L13
末	(mò)	N.	end, L6
末	(mò)	V.	to chop up in fine pieces, L16
莫根	(mò gēn)	N.	Mo Gen, name of a person 人名, L5
莫过于	(mò guò yú)	VP.	nothing is better than, L9
默默	(mò mò)	Adv.	quietly, silently, L10
默契	(mò qì)	N.	tacit agreement, L10
某些	(mǒu xiē)	Pron.	some, L6
拇指	(mǔ zhǐ)	N.	thumb, L14
亩	(mǔ)	Classifier.	measurement for land, L3
目标	(mù biāo)	N.	goal, aim, L13

N

拿得出手	(ná dé chū shǒu)	Adj.	presentable, L8
难过	(nán guò)	Adj.	sad, sorrowful, difficult to bear, L9
脑子	(nǎo zi)	N.	brain, L10
脑子活	(nǎo zi huó)	Idiom.	smart, flexible way of thinking, L12
内容	(nèi róng)	N.	content, L5
能否	(néng fǒu)	V.	can or cannot, L9
能干	(néng gàn)	VP.	capable of doing, able, L15
能手	(néng shǒu)	N.	a dab, a goodhand, a crackerjack, an expert, L6
泥坑	(ní kēng)	N.	mud pit, L10
腻	(nì)	Adj.	to be bored of, to be tired of, L7
溺爱	(nì ài)	V.	to spoil (a child), to be excessively fond of,

			L6
年輕	(nián qīng)	*Adj.*	young, L14
凝聚	(níng jù)	*V.*	to embody, L14
牛肉麵	(niú ròu miàn)	*NP.*	beef noodle, L7
牛虻	(niú máng)	*N.*	gadfly, L15
農村	(nóng cūn)	*N.*	countryside, L3
農戶	(nóng hù)	*N.*	peasant, farmer, L4
農活	(nóng huó)	*N.*	farm work, L6
農民	(nóng mín)	*N.*	peasants, L3
弄	(nòng)	*V.*	to make, L12
暖和	(nuǎn huo)	*V.*	to warm up, L15
女將	(nǚ jiàng)	*N.*	female general, L14
女嬰	(nǚ yīng)	*N.*	baby girl, L2

O

偶然	(ǒu rán)	*Adv.*	accidental, by chance, L2

P

拍	(pāi)	*V.*	to produce, L12
排	(pái)	*V.*	to arrange, to put in order, L2
排場	(pái chǎng)	*N.*	ostentation and extravagance, L8
排斥	(pái chì)	*V.*	to exclude, to repel, L3
排隊	(pái duì)	*VO.*	to line up, to form a waiting line, L7
牌照	(pái zhào)	*N.*	license plate, L10
派出所	(pài chū suǒ)	*NP.*	the security office, L2
盤內	(pán nèi)	*Prep.*	on the plate, L16
拋棄	(pāo qì)	*V.*	to abandon, to dump, to desert, to forsake, L1
拋撒	(pāo sǎ)	*V.*	to throw, to scatter, L9
培養	(péi yǎng)	*V.*	to cultivate, to nurture, to foster, cultivation, L5
裴婉	(péi wǎn)	*N.*	Pei Wan, name of a person 人名, L15
賠錢	(péi qián)	*VO.*	to lose money, L11
陪嫁	(péi jià)	*N.*	dowry, L15
配餐	(pèi cān)	*V.*	to provide meals , L7
配料	(pèi liào)	*N.*	ingredients, L16
佩服	(pèi fú)	*V.*	to admire, L9
烹	(pēng)	*V.*	to boil, to cook, L16
批	(pī)	*Classifier.*	classifier for a group , L13
批發	(pī fā)	*NP.*	wholesale, L4
批量	(pī liàng)	*N.*	amount, L11
批評	(pī píng)	*N/V.*	criticism; to criticize, L13
片	(piàn)	*V.*	to slice, L16

			L6
年轻	(nián qīng)	*Adj.*	young, L14
凝聚	(níng jù)	*V.*	to embody, L14
牛肉面	(niú ròu miàn)	*NP.*	beef noodle, L7
牛虻	(niú máng)	*N.*	gadfly, L15
农村	(nóng cūn)	*N.*	countryside, L3
农户	(nóng hù)	*N.*	peasant, farmer, L4
农活	(nóng huó)	*N.*	farm work, L6
农民	(nóng mín)	*N.*	peasants, L3
弄	(nòng)	*V.*	to make, L12
暖和	(nuǎn huo)	*V.*	to warm up, L15
女将	(nǚ jiàng)	*N.*	female general, L14
女婴	(nǚ yīng)	*N.*	baby girl, L2

O

偶然	(ǒu rán)	*Adv.*	accidental, by chance, L2

P

拍	(pāi)	*V.*	to produce, L12
排	(pái)	*V.*	to arrange, to put in order, L2
排场	(pái chǎng)	*N.*	ostentation and extravagance, L8
排斥	(pái chì)	*V.*	to exclude, to repel, L3
排队	(pái duì)	*VO.*	to line up, to form a waiting line, L7
牌照	(pái zhào)	*N.*	license plate, L10
派出所	(pài chū suǒ)	*NP.*	the security office, L2
盘内	(pán nèi)	*Prep.*	on the plate, L16
抛弃	(pāo qì)	*V.*	to abandon, to dump, to desert, to forsake, L1
抛撒	(pāo sǎ)	*V.*	to throw, to scatter, L9
培养	(péi yǎng)	*V.*	to cultivate, to nurture, to foster, cultivation, L5
裴婉	(péi wǎn)	*N.*	Pei Wan, name of a person 人名, L15
赔钱	(péi qián)	*VO.*	to lose money, L11
陪嫁	(péi jià)	*N.*	dowry, L15
配餐	(pèi cān)	*V.*	to provide meals , L7
配料	(pèi liào)	*N.*	ingredients, L16
佩服	(pèi fú)	*V.*	to admire, L9
烹	(pēng)	*V.*	to boil, to cook, L16
批	(pī)	*Classifier.*	classifier for a group , L13
批发	(pī fā)	*NP.*	wholesale, L4
批量	(pī liàng)	*N.*	amount, L11
批评	(pī píng)	*N/V.*	criticism; to criticize, L13
片	(piàn)	*V.*	to slice, L16

片段	(piàn duàn)	N.	excerpt, L12
貧困	(pín kùn)	Adj/N.	poor; poverty, L11
貧困戶	(pín kùn hù)	NP.	poor household, L11
品質	(pǐn zhì)	N.	quality, character, L5
品種	(pǐn zhǒng)	N.	variety, assortment, L7
聘請	(pìn qǐng)	V.	to invite, to hire, L6
平衡	(píng héng)	N/V.	balance; to balance, L5
平衡木	(píng héng mù)	N.	balance beam, L14
平均	(píng jūn)	N/Prep.	average, L14
坪米	(píng mǐ)	N.	square meter, L7
憑卡	(píng kǎ)	V.	to use a card, L7
評價	(píng jià)	N/V.	evaluation, to evaluate, L9
評委	(píng wěi)	N.	the evaluation committee, L5
婆婆	(pó pó)	N.	mother-in-law, L15
撲	(pū)	V.	to throw oneself into, L1
普遍	(pǔ biàn)	Adj.	widespread, common, L4
普普通通	(pǔ pǔ tōng tōng)	Adj.	common, ordinary, L12
普通	(pǔ tōng)	Adj.	ordinary, common, L2
普通話	(pǔ tōng huà)	NP.	Mandarin, standard Chinese language, L10
譜寫	(pǔ xiě)	V.	to compose (music), L9

Q

期望	(qī wàng)	N/V.	expectation; to expect, L6
奇才	(qí cái)	N.	unusual talent, L13
起	(qǐ)	V.	to become, to take (the effect of), L8
起步	(qǐ bù)	VO.	starting step, initial step, L3
起家	(qǐ jiā)	VO.	to build up, to grow and thrive, L11
起名字	(qǐ míng zì)	V.	to name (someone), L2
起勺	(qǐ sháo)	VO.	to start (with a different wok), L16
企業	(qǐ yè)	N.	enterprise, business, L3
企業家	(qǐ yè jiā)	N.	entrepreneur, L3
氣氛	(qì fèn)	N.	atmosphere, L5
氣派	(qì pài)	Adj.	stylish, extravagant, L4
簽訂	(qiān dìng)	V.	to sign, L2
前景	(qián jǐng)	N.	future, prospects, L3
前台	(qián tái)	N.	front desk, L12
淺黃色	(qiǎn huáng sè)	Adj.	light yellow, L16
強烈	(qiáng liè)	Adj.	strong, intense, L5
悄悄地	(qiāo qiāo de)	Adv.	quietly, L5
巧	(qiǎo)	Adj/Adv.	coincidental, fortuitous, L12
切片	(qiē piàn)	VP.	to cut into slices, L16
親朋好友	(qīn péng hǎo yǒu)	NP.	friends and relatives, L8
親戚	(qīn qì)	N.	relative, L4
親情	(qīn qíng)	N.	blood relationship, L13

片段	(piàn duàn)	*N.*	excerpt, L12
贫困	(pín kùn)	*Adj/N.*	poor; poverty, L11
贫困户	(pín kùn hù)	*NP.*	poor household, L11
品质	(pǐn zhì)	*N.*	quality, character, L5
品种	(pǐn zhǒng)	*N.*	variety, assortment, L7
聘请	(pìn qǐng)	*V.*	to invite, to hire, L6
平衡	(píng héng)	*N/V.*	balance; to balance, L5
平衡木	(píng héng mù)	*N.*	balance beam, L14
平均	(píng jūn)	*N/Prep.*	average, L14
平米	(píng mǐ)	*N.*	square meter, L7
凭卡	(píng kǎ)	*V.*	to use a card, L7
评价	(píng jià)	*N/V.*	evaluation, to evaluate, L9
评委	(píng wěi)	*N.*	the evaluation committee, L5
婆婆	(pó pó)	*N.*	mother-in-law, L15
扑	(pū)	*V.*	to throw oneself into, L1
普遍	(pǔ biàn)	*Adj.*	widespread, common, L4
普普通通	(pǔ pǔ tōng tōng)	*Adj.*	common, ordinary, L12
普通	(pǔ tōng)	*Adj.*	ordinary, common, L2
普通话	(pǔ tōng huà)	*NP.*	Mandarin, standard Chinese language, L10
谱写	(pǔ xiě)	*V.*	to compose (music), L9

Q

期望	(qī wàng)	*N/V.*	expectation; to expect, L6
奇才	(qí cái)	*N.*	unusual talent, L13
起	(qǐ)	*V.*	to become, to take (the effect of), L8
起步	(qǐ bù)	*VO.*	starting step, initial step, L3
起家	(qǐ jiā)	*VO.*	to build up, to grow and thrive, L11
起名字	(qǐ míng zì)	*V.*	to name (someone), L2
起勺	(qǐ sháo)	*VO.*	to start (with a different wok), L16
企业	(qǐ yè)	*N.*	enterprise, business, L3
企业家	(qǐ yè jiā)	*N.*	entrepreneur, L3
气氛	(qì fèn)	*N.*	atmosphere, L5
气派	(qì pài)	*Adj.*	stylish, extravagant, L4
签订	(qiān dìng)	*V.*	to sign, L2
前景	(qián jǐng)	*N.*	future, prospects, L3
前台	(qián tái)	*N.*	front desk, L12
浅黄色	(qiǎn huáng sè)	*Adj.*	light yellow, L16
强烈	(qiáng liè)	*Adj.*	strong, intense, L5
悄悄地	(qiāo qiāo de)	*Adv.*	quietly, L5
巧	(qiǎo)	*Adj/Adv.*	coincidental, fortuitous, L12
切片	(qiē piàn)	*VP.*	to cut into slices, L16
亲朋好友	(qīn péng hǎo yǒu)	*NP.*	friends and relatives, L8
亲戚	(qīn qì)	*N.*	relative, L4
亲情	(qīn qíng)	*N.*	blood relationship, L13

琴	(qín)	N.	piano, musical instrument, L5
輕鬆	(qīng sōng)	Adj.	light and relaxed, L10
青煙	(qīng yān)	N.	light smoke, L15
情景	(qíng jǐng)	N.	scene, situation, L1
請教	(qǐng jiào)	V.	to ask advice, to consult, L7
秋雲	(qiū yún)	N.	Qiu Yun, name of a person , 人名, L2
趨勢	(qū shì)	N.	tendency, L6
區別	(qū bié)	N/V.	difference; to differentiate, to distinguish, L3
區縣	(qū xiàn)	N.	districts and counties, L6
驅趕	(qū gǎn)	V.	to chase away, to get rid of, L15
去處	(qù chù)	N.	place to go, L7
去皮	(qù pí)	VO.	to peel the skin off, L16
全能	(quán néng)	Adj.	all around, L14

R

然而	(rán ér)	Adv.	but, however, L1
熱愛	(rè ài)	V.	to love passionately, L12
熱戀	(rè liàn)	VP.	to love passionately, L9
熱鬧	(rè nào)	Adj.	busy, crowded, L4
熱熱鬧鬧	(rè rè nào nào)	Adj.	lively and thrilling, L8
人次	(rén cì)	N.	number of people, L11
人均	(rén jūn)	NP.	average per person, L4
人類	(rén lèi)	N.	human being, L9
人士	(rén shì)	N.	people, L13
人數	(rén shù)	N.	number of people, L4
認真	(rèn zhēn)	Adj.	conscientious, earnest, L12
扔	(rēng)	V.	to throw away, to cast aside, L2
扔在	(rēng zài)	V.	to throw on, L2
仍舊	(réng jiù)	Adv.	still, yet, L11
日報社	(rì bào shè)	NP.	newspaper agency, L2
日後	(rì hòu)	Adj.	in the future, L2
日記	(rì jì)	N.	diary, L5
日趨重要	(rì qū zhòng yào)	VP.	to become more important day by day, L11
日新月異	(rì xīn yuè yì)	V.	to change by days and months, to change continuously, L7
日用小商品	(rì yòng xiǎo shāng pǐn)	NP.	everyday goods, L11
榮獲	(róng huò)	V.	to win the award of, L13
如今	(rú jīn)	Adv.	now, L3
入土為安	(rù tǔ wéi ān)	Idiom.	to settle in the earth, L9

S

| 撒葬 | (sǎ zàng) | VP. | to bury by scattering ashes in the sea, L9 |

345

琴	(qín)	*N.*	piano, musical instrument, L5
轻松	(qīng sōng)	*Adj.*	light and relaxed, L10
青烟	(qīng yān)	*N.*	light smoke, L15
情景	(qíng jǐng)	*N.*	scene, situation, L1
请教	(qǐng jiào)	*V.*	to ask advice, to consult, L7
秋云	(qiū yún)	*N.*	Qiu Yun, name of a person , 人名, L2
趋势	(qū shì)	*N.*	tendency, L6
区别	(qū bié)	*N/V.*	difference; to differentiate, to distinguish, L3
区县	(qū xiàn)	*N.*	districts and counties, L6
驱赶	(qū gǎn)	*V.*	to chase away, to get rid of, L15
去处	(qù chù)	*N.*	place to go, L7
去皮	(qù pí)	*VO.*	to peel the skin off, L16
全能	(quán néng)	*Adj.*	all around, L14

R

然而	(rán ér)	*Adv.*	but, however, L1
热爱	(rè ài)	*V.*	to love passionately, L12
热恋	(rè liàn)	*VP.*	to love passionately, L9
热闹	(rè nào)	*Adj.*	busy, crowded, L4
热热闹闹	(rè rè nào nào)	*Adj.*	lively and thrilling, L8
人次	(rén cì)	*N.*	number of people, L11
人均	(rén jūn)	*NP.*	average per person, L4
人类	(rén lèi)	*N.*	human being, L9
人士	(rén shì)	*N.*	people, L13
人数	(rén shù)	*N.*	number of people, L4
认真	(rèn zhēn)	*Adj.*	conscientious, earnest, L12
扔	(rēng)	*V.*	to throw away, to cast aside, L2
扔在	(rēng zài)	*V.*	to throw on, L2
仍旧	(réng jiù)	*Adv.*	still, yet, L11
日报社	(rì bào shè)	*NP.*	newspaper agency, L2
日后	(rì hòu)	*Adj.*	in the future, L2
日记	(rì jì)	*N.*	diary, L5
日趋重要	(rì qū zhòng yào)	*VP.*	to become more important day by day, L11
日新月异	(rì xīn yuè yì)	*V.*	to change by days and months, to change continuously, L7
日用小商品	(rì yòng xiǎo shāng pǐn)	*NP.*	everyday goods, L11
荣获	(róng huò)	*V.*	to win the award of, L13
如今	(rú jīn)	*Adv.*	now, L3
入土为安	(rù tǔ wéi ān)	*Idiom.*	to settle in the earth, L9

S

撒葬	(sǎ zàng)	*VP.*	to bury by scattering ashes in the sea, L9

三代同堂	(sān dài tóng táng)	*Idiom.*	three generations under one roof, L1
三點水	(sān diǎn shuǐ)	*N.*	water radical for Chinese characters, L12
嗓子	(sǎng zi)	*N.*	voice, L14
森林	(sēn lín)	*N.*	forest, L9
山坡	(shān pō)	*N.*	hillside, L13
山西	(shān xī)	*PlaceN.*	Shanxi (Province), L15
傷腦筋	(shāng nǎo jīn)	*VO.*	to search one's brain, to use one's brain, to think hard, bothersome, L8
傷痛	(shāng tòng)	*N.*	pain, L14
傷心	(shāng xīn)	*Adj.*	sad, L1
商量	(shāng liáng)	*V.*	to discuss, to talk over, L8
商業街	(shāng yè jiē)	*NP.*	commercial drive, L4
上班	(shàng bān)	*VO.*	to go to work, L7
上升	(shàng shēng)	*N.*	increase, L5
上漲	(shàng zhǎng)	*N/V.*	inflation, increase; to increase, L8
稍微	(shāo wēi)	*Adj.*	a little bit, slightly, L10
勺	(sháo)	*N.*	spoon, spoon-like wok with a handle, L16
少許	(shǎo xǔ)	*Adj.*	a little, L166
蛇	(shé)	*N.*	snake, L15
捨得	(shě dé)	*V.*	to be willing to part with, to not grudge, L5
攝像機	(shè xiàng jī)	*N.*	video camera, L10
涉及	(shè jí)	*V.*	to involve, to relate to, L6
社會各界	(shè huì gè jiè)	*NP.*	people from all walks of life, L6
社會化	(shè huì huà)	*N.*	to be socialized; socialization, L7
社會學	(shè huì xué)	*N.*	sociology, L5
社會主義	(shè huì zhǔ yì)	*Adj/NP.*	socialist, socialism, L3
申請	(shēn qǐng)	*V/N.*	to apply for; application, L2
身子	(shēn zi)	*N.*	body, L15
深惡痛絕	(shēn wù tòng jué)	*V.*	to hate bitterly, to detest, L10
深入	(shēn rù)	*V.*	to deepen, L7
神聖感	(shén shèng gǎn)	*NP.*	sacred sense, holy sense, L8
神童	(shén tóng)	*N.*	prodigy, L5
甚至	(shèn zhì)	*Adv.*	even, to the extent that, L1
生動地	(shēng dòng de)	*Adv.*	vividly, L14
生機	(shēng jī)	*N.*	vitality, L11
生日卡	(shēng rì kǎ)	*N.*	birthday card, L1
生涯	(shēng yá)	*N.*	career, L14
生意	(shēng yì)	*N.*	business, L4
生意稀	(shēng yì xī)	*Idiom.*	slow business, L11
省	(shěng)	*N.*	province, L14
省略	(shěng luè)	*V.*	to omit, omission, L16
盛盤	(chéng pán)	*VP.*	to put on a plate, L16
師傅	(shī fù)	*N.*	term of address, master worker, L4
時代	(shí dài)	*N.*	era, L13
食堂	(shí táng)	*N.*	cafeteria, L7

三代同堂	(sān dài tóng táng)	*Idiom.*	three generations under one roof, L1
三点水	(sān diǎn shuǐ)	*N.*	water radical for Chinese characters, L12
嗓子	(sǎng zi)	*N.*	voice, L14
森林	(sēn lín)	*N.*	forest, L9
山坡	(shān pō)	*N.*	hillside, L13
山西	(shān xī)	*PlaceN.*	Shanxi (Province), L15
伤脑筋	(shāng nǎo jīn)	*VO.*	to search one's brain, to use one's brain, to think hard, bothersome, L8
伤痛	(shāng tòng)	*N.*	pain, L14
伤心	(shāng xīn)	*Adj.*	sad, L1
商量	(shāng liáng)	*V.*	to discuss, to talk over, L8
商业街	(shāng yè jiē)	*NP.*	commercial drive, L4
上班	(shàng bān)	*VO.*	to go to work, L7
上升	(shàng shēng)	*N.*	increase, L5
上涨	(shàng zhǎng)	*N/V.*	inflation, increase; to increase, L8
稍微	(shāo wēi)	*Adj.*	a little bit, slightly, L10
勺	(sháo)	*N.*	spoon, spoon-like wok with a handle, L16
少许	(shǎo xǔ)	*Adj.*	a little, L16
蛇	(shé)	*N.*	snake, L15
舍得	(shě dé)	*V.*	to be willing to part with, to not grudge, L5
摄像机	(shè xiàng jī)	*N.*	video camera, L10
涉及	(shè jí)	*V.*	to involve, to relate to, L6
社会各界	(shè huì gè jiè)	*NP.*	people from all walks of life, L6
社会化	(shè huì huà)	*N.*	to become socialized, L7
社会学	(shè huì xué)	*N.*	sociology, L5
社会主义	(shè huì zhǔ yì)	*Adj/NP.*	socialist, socialism, L3
申请	(shēn qǐng)	*V/N.*	to apply for; application, L2
身子	(shēn zi)	*N.*	body, L15
深恶痛绝	(shēn wù tòng jué)	*V.*	to hate bitterly, to detest, L10
深入	(shēn rù)	*V.*	to deepen, L7
神圣感	(shén shèng gǎn)	*NP.*	sacred sense, holy sense, L8
神童	(shén tóng)	*N.*	prodigy, L5
甚至	(shèn zhì)	*Adv.*	even, to the extent that, L1
生动地	(shēng dòng de)	*Adv.*	vividly, L14
生机	(shēng jī)	*N.*	vitality, L11
生日卡	(shēng rì kǎ)	*N.*	birthday card, L1
生涯	(shēng yá)	*N.*	career, L14
生意	(shēng yì)	*N.*	business, L4
生意稀	(shēng yì xī)	*Idiom.*	slow business, L11
省	(shěng)	*N.*	province, L14
省略	(shěng lūè)	*V.*	to omit, omission, L16
盛盘	(chéng pán)	*VP.*	to put on a plate, L16
师傅	(shī fù)	*N.*	term of address, master worker, L4
时代	(shí dài)	*N.*	era, L13
食堂	(shí táng)	*N.*	cafeteria, L7

实行	(shí xíng)	V.	to implement, to carry out, L3
始终	(shǐ zhōng)	Adv.	from the beginning to the end, always, L14
世纪	(shì jì)	N.	century, L5
世界杯	(shì jiè bēi)	N.	World Cup, L14
事故	(shì gù)	N.	accident, L6
事业	(shì yè)	N.	undertaking, cause, L5
逝者	(shì zhě)	N.	the deceased, the dead, L9
适应	(shì yìng)	V.	to fit in, to be suitable for, L7
市场经济	(shì chǎng jīng jì)	NP.	market economy, L3
收车	(shōu chē)	VO.	to stop driving around, L10
手头	(shǒu tóu)	N.	(at) hand, L11
首都经贸大学	(shǒu dū jīng mào dà xué)	NP.	Capital University of Economics and Business, L10
首经大	(shǒu jīng dà)	NP.	首都经贸大学, L10
首批	(shǒu pī)	NP.	first group of , L2
首先	(shǒu xiān)	Adv.	first, L8
叔母	(shū mǔ)	N.	aunt, L9
叔叔	(shū shū)	N.	uncle, L9
舒坦	(shū tǎn)	Adj.	comfortable, L10
书面语	(shū miàn yǔ)	NP.	written language, L16
熟练	(shóu liàn)	Adj.	skilled, proficient, L14
属于	(shǔ yú)	V.	to belong to, to be a part of, L1
束缚	(shù fù)	N/V.	control, restriction, fetter; to control, to restrict, L4
数字	(shù zì)	N.	number, amount, L1
双臂	(shuāng bì)	NP.	both arms, L6
双杠	(shuāng gàng)	N.	double bar, L14
双双	(shuāng shuāng)	Adv.	both, both of, L1
水准	(shuǐ zhǔn)	N.	standard, level, L6
税收	(shuì shōu)	N.	taxation, L11
说到底	(shuō dào dǐ)	VP.	bottom line, L3
说了算	(shuō le suàn)	VP.	to keep one's word, L3
思念	(sī niàn)	V/N.	to miss, long for (somebody), L1
私营	(sī yíng)	Adj.	privately owned, L3
司机	(sī jī)	N.	driver, L10
丝	(sī)	N.	shred, L16
似乎	(sì hū)	V.	to seem as if, L1
送葬	(sòng zàng)	VO.	to attend a funeral, L9
艘	(sōu)	Classifier.	classifier for ships, L9
酥	(sū)	V/Adj.	to be weak, soft, L15
素质	(sù zhì)	N.	quality, diathesis, L5
宿命	(sù mìng)	Adj.	fatal, fatalistic, L13
肃穆	(sù mù)	Adj.	solemn, L9
蒜	(suàn)	N.	garlic, L16
随处可见	(suí chù kě jiàn)	Idiom.	to be seen everywhere, L11

隨著	(suí zhe)	*Adv.*	along with, accompanying , L7
筍	(sǔn)	*N.*	bamboo shoots, L16

T

踏實	(tā shí)	*Adj.*	to feel settled, steady and sure, L9
台	(tái)	*Classifier.*	a classifier for piano, L5
太陽	(tài yáng)	*N.*	the sun, L6
態度	(tài dù)	*N.*	attitude, L5
攤位	(tān wèi)	*N.*	vendor's stand, L11
彈	(tán)	*V.*	to play (musical instrument), L5
譚波	(tán bō)	*N.*	Tan Bo, name of a person 人名, L12
譚濤	(tán tāo)	*N.*	Tan Tao, name of a person 人名, L12
譚宗堯	(tán zōng yáo)	*N.*	Tan Zongyao, name of a person, a famous performer of Chinese modern plays 人名, L12
湯目	(tāng mù)	*N.*	Tang Mu, name of a person 人名, L11
淌	(tǎng)	*V.*	to fall, L1
淘氣	(táo qì)	*Adj.*	mischievous, L12
特點	(tè diǎn)	*N.*	characteristics, attributes, L5
特殊	(tè shū)	*Adj.*	special, L2
特意	(tè yì)	*Adv.*	for a special purpose, specially, L6
特有的	(tè yǒu de)	*Adj.*	specially possess, L11
騰出	(téng chū)	*V.*	to spare, L10
剔	(tī)	*V.*	to peel off, to take off, L16
提	(tí)	*V.*	to put forward, to raise, to propose, L3
提倡	(tí chàng)	*V.*	to advocate, to promote, L8
提供	(tí gōng)	*V.*	to provide, L2
提名	(tí míng)	*VO/N.*	to nominate; nomination, L13
提起	(tí qǐ)	*V.*	to mention, L15
提琴	(tí qín)	*N.*	violin, L5
題材	(tí cái)	*N.*	theme, topic, L13
體操	(tǐ cāo)	*N.*	gymnastics, L14
體現	(tǐ xiàn)	*V.*	to represent, to embody, L6
替	(tì)	*V.*	to take the place of, to substitute for, L6
天津	(tiān jīn)	*PlaceN.*	Tian Jin, name of a city in China 人名, L2
天生	(tiān shēng)	*Adj.*	congenital, to be born with, L2
天真	(tiān zhēn)	*Adj.*	naive, L1
田野	(tián yě)	*N.*	field, L15
田壯壯	(tián zhuàng zhuàng)	*N.*	Tian Zhuangzhuang, name of a person, a famous film director in China 人名, L13
甜	(tián)	*Adj.*	sweet, L16
甜美	(tián měi)	*Adj.*	sweet and beautiful, L14
挑	(tiāo)	*V.*	to select, L8
挑起	(tiāo qǐ)	*V.*	to carry, to shoulder, L1

| 随着 | (suí zhe) | Adv. | along with, accompanying , L7 |
| 笋 | (sǔn) | N. | bamboo shoots, L16 |

T

踏实	(tā shí)	Adj.	to feel settled, steady and sure, L9
台	(tái)	Classifier.	a classifier for piano, L5
太阳	(tài yáng)	N.	the sun, L6
态度	(tài dù)	N.	attitude, L5
摊位	(tān wèi)	N.	vendor's stand, L11
弹	(tán)	V.	to play (musical instrument), L5
谭波	(tán bō)	N.	Tan Bo, name of a person 人名, L12
谭涛	(tán tāo)	N.	Tan Tao, name of a person 人名, L12
谭宗尧	(tán zōng yáo)	N.	Tan Zongyao, name of a person, a famous performer of Chinese modern plays 人名, L12
汤目	(tāng mù)	N.	Tang Mu, name of a person 人名, L11
淌	(tǎng)	V.	to fall, L1
淘气	(táo qì)	Adj.	mischievous, L12
特点	(tè diǎn)	N.	characteristics, attributes, L5
特殊	(tè shū)	Adj.	special , L2
特意	(tè yì)	Adv.	for a special purpose, specially, L6
特有的	(tè yǒu de)	Adj.	specially possess, L11
腾出	(téng chū)	V.	to spare, L10
剔	(tī)	V.	to peel off, to take off, L16
提	(tí)	V.	to put forward, to raise, to propose, L3
提倡	(tí chàng)	V.	to advocate, to promote, L8
提供	(tí gōng)	V.	to provide, L2
提名	(tí míng)	VO/N.	to nominate; nomination, L13
提起	(tí qǐ)	V.	to mention, L15
提琴	(tí qín)	N.	violin, L5
题材	(tí cái)	N.	theme, topic, L13
体操	(tǐ cāo)	N.	gymnastics, L14
体现	(tǐ xiàn)	V.	to represent, to embody, L6
替	(tì)	V.	to take the place of, to substitute for, L6
天津	(tiān jīn)	PlaceN.	Tian Jin, name of a city in China 地名, L2
天生	(tiān shēng)	Adj.	congenital, to be born with, L2
天真	(tiān zhēn)	Adj.	naive, L1
田野	(tián yě)	N.	field, L15
田壮壮	(tián zhuàng zhuàng)	N.	Tian Zhuangzhuang, name of a person, a famous film director in China 人名, L13
甜	(tián)	Adj.	sweet, L16
甜美	(tián měi)	Adj.	sweet and beautiful, L14
挑	(tiāo)	V.	to select, L8
挑起	(tiāo qǐ)	V.	to carry, to shoulder, L1

條件	(tiáo jiàn)	N.	condition, L1
調節	(tiáo jié)	V.	to adjust, to regulate, L11
調皮	(tiáo pí)	Adj.	naughty, mischievous, L12
調勻	(tiáo yún)	V.	to stir well, L16
挑戰	(tiǎo zhàn)	V./N.	to challenge; challenge, L11
跳步	(tiào bù)	N.	jump, L14
婷婷玉立	(tíng tíng yù lì)	Idiom.	slim and graceful, L14
通訊公司	(tōng xùn gōng sī)	NP.	communication company, L7
痛快	(tòng kuài)	Adj.	happy, delighted, L10
投資	(tóu zī)	V./N.	to invest; investment, L3
頭等大事	(tóu děng dà shì)	NP.	the most important thing, L8
頭一回	(tóu yī huí)	Adv.	for the first time, L5
突破	(tū pò)	V.	to break through, L13
突然	(tū rán)	Adv.	suddenly, unexpectedly, L4
圖	(tú)	V.	to seek for, L8
土地	(tǔ dì)	N.	land, L3
土豆	(tǔ dòu)	N.	potato, L16
土葬	(tǔ zàng)	NP.	earth burial, internment, L9
團體	(tuán tǐ)	N.	team, L14
推	(tuī)	V.	to push, L13

W

外出	(wài chū)	V.	to go out, L10
外地	(wài dì)	Adj.	part of the country other than where one is, L7
頑皮	(wán pí)	Adj.	mischievous, L1
丸子	(wán zi)	N.	meatball, L7
完畢	(wán bì)	V.	to finish, to complete, L7
完整	(wán zhěng)	Adj.	whole, complete, entire, L1
萬元戶	(wàn yuán hù)	N.	millionaire, L11
王府飯店	(wáng fǔ fàn diàn)	N.	Palace Hotel, L12
王鐵生	(wáng tiě shēng)	N.	Wang Tiesheng, name of a person 人名, L11
王羽佳	(wáng yǔ jiā)	N.	Wang Yujia, name of a person 人名, L5
王志仁	(wáng zhì rén)	N.	Wang Zhiren, name of a person 人名, L4
微笑	(wēi xiào)	N.	smile, L14
微型	(wēi xíng)	Adj.	mini, miniature, L10
圍城	(wéi chéng)	NP.	surrounded town, besieged town, L10
唯一	(wéi yī)	Adj.	only, sole, L1
為止	(wéi zhǐ)	VP.	until, L2
委托	(wěi tuō)	V.	to entrust, L8
偉大	(wěi dà)	Adj.	great, mighty, L1
偉人	(wěi rén)	NP.	a great person, L9
未來	(wèi lái)	N.	future, L5

条件	(tiáo jiàn)	*N.*	condition, L1
调节	(tiáo jié)	*V.*	to adjust, to regulate, L11
调皮	(tiáo pí)	*Adj.*	naughty, mischievous, L12
调匀	(tiáo yún)	*V.*	to stir well, L16
挑战	(tiǎo zhàn)	*V/N.*	to challenge; challenge, L11
跳步	(tiào bù)	*N.*	jump, L14
婷婷玉立	(tíng tíng yù lì)	*Idiom.*	slim and graceful, L14
通讯公司	(tōng xùn gōng sī)	*NP.*	communication company, L7
痛快	(tòng kuài)	*Adj.*	happy, delighted, L10
投资	(tóu zī)	*V/N.*	to invest; investment, L3
头等大事	(tóu děng dà shì)	*NP.*	the most important thing, L8
头一回	(tóu yī huí)	*Adv.*	for the first time, L5
突破	(tū pò)	*V.*	to break through, L13
突然	(tū rán)	*Adv.*	suddenly, unexpectedly, L4
图	(tú)	*V.*	to seek for, L8
土地	(tǔ dì)	*N.*	land, L3
土豆	(tǔ dòu)	*N.*	potato, L16
土葬	(tǔ zàng)	*NP.*	earth burial, internment, L9
团体	(tuán tǐ)	*N.*	team, L14
推	(tuī)	*V.*	to push, L13

W

外出	(wài chū)	*V.*	to go out, L10
外地	(wài dì)	*Adj.*	part of the country other than where one is, L7
顽皮	(wán pí)	*Adj.*	mischievous, L1
丸子	(wán zi)	*N.*	meatball, L7
完毕	(wán bì)	*V.*	to finish, to complete, L7
完整	(wán zhěng)	*Adj.*	whole, complete, entire, L1
万元户	(wàn yuán hù)	*N.*	millionaire, L11
王府饭店	(wáng fǔ fàn diàn)	*N.*	Palace Hotel, L12
王铁生	(wáng tiě shēng)	*N.*	Wang Tiesheng, name of a person 人名, L11
王羽佳	(wáng yǔ jiā)	*N.*	Wang Yujia, name of a person 人名, L5
王志仁	(wáng zhì rén)	*N.*	Wang Zhiren, name of a person 人名, L4
微笑	(wēi xiào)	*N.*	smile, L14
微型	(wēi xíng)	*Adj.*	mini, miniature, L10
围城	(wéi chéng)	*NP.*	surrounded town, besieged town, L10
唯一	(wéi yī)	*Adj.*	only, sole, L1
为止	(wéi zhǐ)	*VP.*	until, L2
委托	(wěi tuō)	*V.*	to entrust, L8
伟大	(wěi dà)	*Adj.*	great, mighty, L1
伟人	(wěi rén)	*NP.*	a great person, L9
未来	(wèi lái)	*N.*	future, L5

味兒	(wèir)	N.	smell, odor, L15
味精	(wèi jīng)	N.	MSG, L16
位於	(wèi yú)	V.	to be located, to be situated, L7
溫暖	(wēn nuǎn)	Adj.	warm, L1
溫油	(wēn yóu)	NP.	warm oil, L16
溫馨	(wēn xīn)	Adj.	warm and pleasant, L13
蚊	(wén)	N.	mosquito, L15
文法	(wén fǎ)	N.	grammar, L16
文化大革命	(wén huà dà gé mìng)	NP.	the Cultural Revolution, L13
文明	(wén míng)	N.	civilization, L9
文體	(wén tǐ)	N.	writing style, L16
文言詞	(wén yán cí)	NP.	archaic expression, classical expression, L16
穩定	(wěn dìng)	Adj.	stable, steady, L8
無法	(wú fǎ)	VP.	unable, no way, L1
無私	(wú sī)	Adj.	selfless, L1
無限	(wú xiàn)	Adj.	infinite, without limit, L1
無疑	(wú yí)	Adv.	undoubtedly, doubtless, L6
舞劇	(wǔ jù)	N.	musical dance, L9
舞台	(wǔ tái)	N.	stage, arena, L12
物價	(wù jià)	N.	price, L8
物質	(wù zhì)	N.	material, materialistic, L8

X

西柏林	(xī bó lín)	N.	Xi Bolin, West Berlin 地名, L13
吸引	(xī yǐn)	V.	to attract, L12
習俗	(xí sú)	N.	custom, convention, L9
媳婦	(xí fù)	N.	wife, L12
喜悅	(xǐ yuè)	N.	happiness, L8
洗淨	(xǐ jìng)	V.	to wash clean, L16
戲劇	(xì jù)	N.	drama and opera, theater, L12
細絲	(xì sī)	N.	shredded pieces, L16
細細地	(xì xì de)	Adv.	carefully, L10
掀起	(xiān qǐ)	V.	to stir up, to start, L12
先決	(xiān jué)	Adj.	predetermined, L11
鮮花	(xiān huā)	N.	fresh flower, L9
鹹	(xián)	Adj.	salty, L16
閒聊	(xián liáo)	V.	to chat casually, L10
閒人	(xián rén)	N.	idle person, loafer, L12
顯露	(xiǎn lù)	V.	to reveal, to demonstrate, L6
顯然	(xiǎn rán)	Adv/Adj.	obviously, obvious, L4
顯示	(xiǎn shì)	V.	to indicate, to show, L6
現場	(xiàn chǎng)	Adv.	on the site, on the spot, live, L9
現實	(xiàn shí)	N.	reality, L1
現象	(xiàn xiàng)	N.	phenomenon, L4

味儿	(wèir)	N.	smell, odor, L15
味精	(wèi jīng)	N.	MSG, L16
位于	(wèi yú)	V.	to be located, to be situated, L7
温暖	(wēn nuǎn)	Adj.	warm, L1
温油	(wēn yóu)	NP.	warm oil, L16
温馨	(wēn xīn)	Adj.	warm and pleasant, L13
蚊	(wén)	N.	mosquito, L15
文法	(wén fǎ)	N.	grammar, L16
文化大革命	(wén huà dà gé mìng)	NP.	the Cultural Revolution, L13
文明	(wén míng)	N.	civilization, L9
文体	(wén tǐ)	N.	writing style, L16
文言词	(wén yán cí)	NP.	archaic expression, classical expression, L16
稳定	(wěn dìng)	Adj.	stable, steady, L8
无法	(wú fǎ)	VP.	unable, no way, L1
无私	(wú sī)	Adj.	selfless, L1
无限	(wú xiàn)	Adj.	infinite, without limit, L1
无疑	(wú yí)	Adv.	undoubtedly, doubtless, L6
舞剧	(wǔ jù)	N.	musical dance, L9
舞台	(wǔ tái)	N.	stage, arena, L12
物价	(wù jià)	N.	price, L8
物质	(wù zhì)	N.	material, materialistic, L8

X

西柏林	(xī bó lín)	N.	Xi Bolin, West Berlin 地名, L13
吸引	(xī yǐn)	V.	to attract, L12
习俗	(xí sú)	N.	custom, convention, L9
媳妇	(xí fù)	N.	wife, L12
喜悦	(xǐ yuè)	N.	happiness, L8
洗净	(xǐ jìng)	V.	to wash clean, L16
戏剧	(xì jù)	N.	drama and opera, theater, L12
细丝	(xì sī)	N.	shredded pieces, L16
细细地	(xì xì de)	Adv.	carefully, L10
掀起	(xiān qǐ)	V.	to stir up, to start, L12
先决	(xiān jué)	Adj.	predetermined, L11
鲜花	(xiān huā)	N.	fresh flower, L9
咸	(xián)	Adj.	salty, L16
闲聊	(xián liáo)	V.	to chat casually, L10
闲人	(xián rén)	N.	idle person, loafer, L12
显露	(xiǎn lù)	V.	to reveal, to demonstrate, L6
显然	(xiǎn rán)	Adv/Adj.	obviously, obvious, L4
显示	(xiǎn shì)	V.	to indicate, to show, L6
现场	(xiàn chǎng)	Adv.	on the site, on the spot, live, L9
现实	(xiàn shí)	N.	reality, L1
现象	(xiàn xiàng)	N.	phenomenon, L4

縣	(xiàn)	N.	county, L11
限制	(xiàn zhì)	V/N.	to limit; limit, limitation, restriction, L1
相連	(xiāng lián)	V.	to be connected, L9
香菇	(xiāng gū)	N.	mushroom, L16
香油	(xiāng yóu)	N.	sesame oil, L16
箱包	(xiāng bāo)	NP.	bags and suitcases, L11
箱子	(xiāng zi)	N.	suitcase, L11
想不通	(xiǎng bù tōng)	VP.	cannot think through, cannot make sense out of, L1
享受	(xiǎng shòu)	V.	to enjoy, L2
項	(xiàng)	Classifier.	one item of, L14
項目	(xiàng mù)	N.	item, a list of items , L8
銷路	(xiāo lù)	N.	market, sale, L12
小麗	(xiǎo lì)	N.	Xiao Li, name of a person, 人名, L1
小商品	(xiǎo shāng pǐn)	NP.	small commodities, L4
校長	(xiào zhǎng)	N.	president of a school, school principal, headmaster, L2
孝心	(xiào xīn)	N.	filial piety, L15
協議	(xié yì)	N.	agreement, L2
諧音	(xié yīn)	V.	to be homophonic, L12
卸給	(xiè gěi)	VP.	to shift to, to push to, L12
新婚夫婦	(xīn hūn fū fù)	NP.	newly-married couple, newlyweds, L8
新近	(xīn jìn)	Adj/Adv.	recent; recently, L8
新人	(xīn rén)	N.	newlyweds, L8
新鮮事	(xīn xiān shì)	NP.	new things, fresh things, L7
新穎	(xīn yǐng)	Adj.	new, novel, L8
心甘情願	(xīn gān qíng yuàn)	Idiom.	be most willing to, willingness, L1
心理	(xīn lǐ)	N/Adj.	psychology; psychological, L6
心靈	(xīn líng)	N.	heart and soul, L1
心血	(xīn xuè)	N.	heart and blood, L14
星期日學校	(xīng qī rì xué xiào)	NP.	weekend school, L5
興起	(xīng qǐ)	V.	to become popular, to spring up, L15
形成	(xíng chéng)	V.	to form, L5
形式	(xíng shì)	N.	form, L9
形體	(xíng tǐ)	N.	shape, physique, L12
行駛	(xíng shǐ)	V.	to travel, L9
行為	(xíng wéi)	N.	action, behavior, L6
需求	(xū qiú)	N.	need, L5
徐千	(xú qiān)	N.	Xu Qian, name of a person 人名, L16
選拔	(xuǎn bá)	V.	to select, to choose (usually of person), L5
選手	(xuǎn shǒu)	N.	athlete, L14
渲染	(xuàn rǎn)	V.	to play up, to heighten, L8
雪	(xuě)	N.	snow, L15
血紅色	(xiě hóng sè)	N.	color of blood, L16
薰陶	(xūn táo)	N/V.	cultivation, to cultivate, to influence, L12

县	(xiàn)	N.	county, L11
限制	(xiàn zhì)	V/N.	to limit; limit, limitation, restriction, L1
相连	(xiāng lián)	V.	to be connected, L9
香菇	(xiāng gū)	N.	mushroom, L16
香油	(xiāng yóu)	N.	sesame oil, L16
箱包	(xiāng bāo)	NP.	bags and suitcases, L11
箱子	(xiāng zi)	N.	suitcase, L11
想不通	(xiǎng bù tōng)	VP.	cannot think through, cannot make sense out of, L1
享受	(xiǎng shòu)	V.	to enjoy, L2
项	(xiàng)	Classifier.	one item of, L14
项目	(xiàng mù)	N.	item, a list of items , L8
销路	(xiāo lù)	N.	market, sale, L12
小丽	(xiǎo lì)	N.	Xiao Li, name of a person, 人名, L1
小商品	(xiǎo shāng pǐn)	NP.	small commodities, L4
校长	(xiào zhǎng)	N.	president of a school, school principal, headmaster, L2
孝心	(xiào xīn)	N.	filial piety, L15
协议	(xié yì)	N.	agreement, L2
谐音	(xié yīn)	V.	to be homophonic, L12
卸给	(xiè gěi)	VP.	to shift to, to push to, L12
新婚夫妇	(xīn hūn fū fù)	NP.	newly-married couple, newlyweds, L8
新近	(xīn jìn)	Adj/Adv.	recent; recently, L8
新人	(xīn rén)	N.	newlyweds, L8
新鲜事	(xīn xiān shì)	NP.	new things, fresh things, L7
新颖	(xīn yǐng)	Adj.	new, novel, L8
心甘情愿	(xīn gān qíng yuàn)	Idiom.	be most willing to, willingness, L1
心理	(xīn lǐ)	N/Adj.	psychology; psychological, L6
心灵	(xīn líng)	N.	heart and soul, L1
心血	(xīn xuè)	N.	heart and blood, L14
星期日学校	(xīng qī rì xué xiào)	NP.	weekend school, L5
兴起	(xīng qǐ)	V.	to become popular, to spring up, L15
形成	(xíng chéng)	V.	to form, L5
形式	(xíng shì)	N.	form, L9
形体	(xíng tǐ)	N.	shape, physique, L12
行驶	(xíng shǐ)	V.	to travel, L9
行为	(xíng wéi)	N.	action, behavior, L6
需求	(xū qiú)	N.	need, L5
徐千	(xú qiān)	N.	Xu Qian, name of a person 人名, L16
选拔	(xuǎn bá)	V.	to select, to choose (usually of person), L5
选手	(xuǎn shǒu)	N.	athlete, L14
渲染	(xuàn rǎn)	V.	to play up, to heighten, L8
雪	(xuě)	N.	snow, L15
血红色	(xiě hóng sè)	N.	color of blood, L16
熏陶	(xūn táo)	N/V.	cultivation, to cultivate, to influence, L12

尋常	(xún cháng)	*Adj.*	ordinary, common, L5
訓練	(xùn liàn)	*V./N.*	to train, to drill, L12
迅速	(xùn sù)	*Adj/Adv.*	rapid, swift, prompt; rapidly, quickly, L16

Y

壓	(yā)	*V.*	to weigh on (someone), to place, to press on, L3
壓力	(yā lì)	*N.*	pressure, L6
亞軍	(yà jūn)	*N.*	runner-up, L14
煙	(yān)	*N.*	tobacco or cigarette, L15
煙袋	(yān dài)	*N.*	Chinese tobacco pipe, L15
鹽	(yán)	*N.*	salt, L16
嚴格	(yán gé)	*Adj.*	strict, rigorous, stringent, L5
嚴繼英	(yán jì yīng)	*N.*	Yan Jiying, name of a person 人名, L2
研究院	(yán jiū yuàn)	*NP.*	research institute, L3
演出	(yǎn chū)	*V.*	to perform, L5
演員	(yǎn yuán)	*N.*	actor or actress, performer, L5
演奏	(yǎn zòu)	*N/V.*	performance; to perform with a musical instrument, L5
演奏員	(yǎn zòu yuán)	*N.*	player of a musical instrument, L12
燕莎友誼商城	(yàn shā yǒu yì shāng chéng)	*NP.*	Lufthansa Friendship Shipping Center, name of a shopping center, L7
楊波	(yáng bō)	*N.*	Yang Bo, name of a person 人名, L14
洋	(yáng)	*Adj.*	western, foreign, L7
樣兒	(yàngr)	*N.*	appearance, style, L15
邀請	(yāo qǐng)	*V.*	to invite, L8
要求	(yāo qiú)	*N/V.*	demand, requirement, L1
野氣	(yě qì)	*N.*	wildness, L15
業績	(yè jī)	*N.*	achievement, L14
業務	(yè wù)	*N.*	business, L4
業餘	(yè yú)	*Adj.*	amateur, L5
一塵不染	(yī chén bù rǎn)	*Idiom.*	dustless, L10
一等獎	(yī děng jiǎng)	*N.*	first prize, L12
一流	(yī liú)	*N.*	first rate, L5
一路	(yī lù)	*Adv.*	the whole way, L9
一攤子	(yī tān zi)	*NP.*	a pile of, L12
醫療保健	(yī liáo bǎo jiàn)	*NP.*	medical treatment, L2
依據	(yī jù)	*N.*	basis, deciding factor, L11
依賴	(yī lài)	*V.*	to rely on, to depend on, L6
遺願	(yí yuàn)	*N.*	will, L9
儀表	(yí biǎo)	*N.*	appearance, bearing, L12
儀式	(yí shì)	*N.*	ceremony, L2
已婚	(yǐ hūn)	*Adj.*	married, L2
以及	(yǐ jí)	*Conj.*	and, as well as, L2

寻常	(xún cháng)	*Adj.*	ordinary, common, L5
训练	(xùn liàn)	*V./N.*	to train, to drill, L12
迅速	(xùn sù)	*Adj/Adv.*	rapid, swift, prompt; rapidly, quickly, L16

Y

压	(yā)	*V.*	to weigh on (someone), to place, to press on, L3
压力	(yā lì)	*N.*	pressure, L6
亚军	(yà jūn)	*N.*	runner-up, L14
烟	(yān)	*N.*	tobacco or cigarette, L15
烟袋	(yān dài)	*N.*	Chinese tobacco pipe, L15
盐	(yán)	*N.*	salt, L16
严格	(yán gé)	*Adj.*	strict, rigorous, stringent, L5
严继英	(yán jì yīng)	*N.*	Yan Jiying, name of a person 人名, L2
研究院	(yán jiū yuàn)	*NP.*	research institute, L3
演出	(yǎn chū)	*V.*	to perform, L5
演员	(yǎn yuán)	*N.*	actor or actress, performer, L5
演奏	(yǎn zòu)	*N/V.*	performance; to perform with a musical instrument, L5
演奏员	(yǎn zòu yuán)	*N.*	player of a musical instrument, L12
燕莎友谊商城	(yàn shā yǒu yì shāng chéng)	*NP.*	Lufthansa Friendship Shipping Center, name of a shopping center, L7
杨波	(yáng bō)	*N.*	Yang Bo, name of a person 人名, L14
洋	(yáng)	*Adj.*	western, foreign, L7
样儿	(yàngr)	*N.*	appearance, style, L15
邀请	(yāo qǐng)	*V.*	to invite, L8
要求	(yāo qiú)	*N/V.*	demand, requirement, L1
野气	(yě qì)	*N.*	wildness, L15
业绩	(yè jī)	*N.*	achievement, L14
业务	(yè wù)	*N.*	business, L4
业余	(yè yú)	*Adj.*	amateur, L5
一尘不染	(yī chén bù rǎn)	*Idiom.*	dustless, L10
一等奖	(yī děng jiǎng)	*N.*	first prize, L12
一流	(yī liú)	*N.*	first rate, L5
一路	(yī lù)	*Adv.*	the whole way, L9
一摊子	(yī tān zi)	*NP.*	a pile of, L12
医疗保健	(yī liáo bǎo jiàn)	*NP.*	medical treatment, L2
依据	(yī jù)	*N.*	basis, deciding factor, L11
依赖	(yī lài)	*V.*	to rely on, to depend on, L6
遗愿	(yí yuàn)	*N.*	will, L9
仪表	(yí biǎo)	*N.*	appearance, bearing, L12
仪式	(yí shì)	*N.*	ceremony, L2
已婚	(yǐ hūn)	*Adj.*	married, L2
以及	(yǐ jí)	*Conj.*	and, as well as, L2

藝術	(yì shù)	*N.*	art, L12
意見	(yì jiàn)	*N.*	opinion, L3
意識	(yì shì)	*N.*	sense, realization, L5
意義	(yì yì)	*N.*	meaning, significance, L2
意志	(yì zhì)	*N.*	will power, will , L5
毅力	(yì lì)	*N.*	will power, L14
憶苦思甜	(yì kǔ sī tián)	*Idiom.*	to recall one's bitterness in order to appreciate the present sweet reality, L12
義務	(yì wù)	*Adj/Adv.*	voluntary, voluntarily, L2
因素	(yīn sù)	*N.*	factor, L8
音樂會	(yīn yuè huì)	*N.*	concert, L5
銀婚	(yín hūn)	*NP.*	silver wedding anniversary, L8
引進	(yǐn jìn)	*V.*	to introduce from, to import, L7
引起	(yǐn qǐ)	*V.*	to lead to, to arouse, L6
隱患	(yǐn huàn)	*N.*	hidden disease, undetected disease, L6
印	(yìn)	*V.*	to print, L12
營養	(yíng yǎng)	*N.*	nutrition, L7
營業額	(yíng yè é)	*NP.*	sales quota, L4
迎合	(yíng hé)	*V.*	to please, to satisfy, L13
迎接	(yíng jiē)	*V.*	to welcome, L11
迎來	(yíng lái)	*V.*	to welcome (a time, festival, event, etc.), L8
影壇	(yǐng tán)	*N.*	film circle, L13
影子	(yǐng zi)	*N.*	shadow, L11
擁有	(yōng yǒu)	*V.*	to possess, to have, L2
永遠	(yǒng yuǎn)	*Adv.*	forever, always, L1
用詞	(yòng cí)	*VO.*	to select one's words, L16
用品	(yòng pǐn)	*N.*	articles for use, L6
幽默	(yōu mò)	*N/Adj*	humor; humorous, L13
優勢	(yōu shì)	*N.*	advantage, strong point, L3
優秀生	(yōu xiù shēng)	*NP.*	outstanding student, L5
由此	(yóu cǐ)	*PrepP.*	from this, because of, L6
由於	(yóu yú)	*Prep.*	as a result of, due to, owing to, L1
油	(yóu)	*N.*	cooking oil, L16
油菜	(yóu cài)	*N.*	rape (a kind of vegetable), L7
有關	(yǒu guān)	*V.*	to relate to, to concern, L4
有葷有素	(yǒu hūn yǒu sù)	*VP.*	to have both meat and vegetable, L7
有模有樣	(yǒu mó yǒu yàng)	*Adj/N.*	stylish, stylishness, L8
有幸	(yǒu xìng)	*Adj/Adv.*	fortunate, lucky; fortunately, L8
有意義	(yǒu yì yì)	*Adj.*	meaningful, significant, L9
幼兒園	(yòu ér yuán)	*N.*	nursery school, kindergarten, L2
於是	(yú shì)	*Conj.*	therefore, consequently, as a result, L2
於是乎	(yú shì hū)	*Adv.*	then, L7
輿論界	(yú lùn jiè)	*NP.*	opinion poll, public opinion, L13
餘	(yú)	*N.*	surplus, L4
餘地	(yú dì)	*N.*	leeway, room, latitude, L7

艺术	(yì shù)	*N.*	art, L12
意见	(yì jiàn)	*N.*	opinion, L3
意识	(yì shì)	*N.*	sense, realization, L5
意义	(yì yì)	*N.*	meaning, significance, L2
意志	(yì zhì)	*N.*	will power, will , L5
毅力	(yì lì)	*N.*	will power, L14
忆苦思甜	(yì kǔ sī tián)	*Idiom.*	to recall one's bitterness in order to appreciate the present sweet reality, L12
义务	(yì wù)	*Adj/Adv.*	voluntary, voluntarily, L2
因素	(yīn sù)	*N.*	factor, L8
音乐会	(yīn yuè huì)	*N.*	concert, L5
银婚	(yín hūn)	*NP.*	silver wedding anniversary, L8
引进	(yǐn jìn)	*V.*	to introduce from, to import, L7
引起	(yǐn qǐ)	*V.*	to lead to, to arouse, L6
隐患	(yǐn huàn)	*N.*	hidden disease, undetected disease, L6
印	(yìn)	*V.*	to print, L12
营养	(yíng yǎng)	*N.*	nutrition, L7
营业额	(yíng yè é)	*NP.*	sales quota, L4
迎合	(yíng hé)	*V.*	to please, to satisfy, L13
迎接	(yíng jiē)	*V.*	to welcome, L11
迎来	(yíng lái)	*V.*	to welcome (a time, festival, event, etc.), L8
影坛	(yǐng tán)	*N.*	film circle, L13
影子	(yǐng zi)	*N.*	shadow, L11
拥有	(yōng yǒu)	*V.*	to possess, to have, L2
永远	(yǒng yuǎn)	*Adv.*	forever, always, L1
用词	(yòng cí)	*VO.*	to select one's words, L16
用品	(yòng pǐn)	*N.*	articles for use, L6
幽默	(yōu mò)	*N/Adj*	humor; humorous, L13
优势	(yōu shì)	*N.*	advantage, strong point, L3
优秀生	(yōu xiù shēng)	*NP.*	outstanding student, L5
由此	(yóu cǐ)	*PrepP.*	from this, because of, L6
由于	(yóu yú)	*Prep.*	as a result of, due to, owing to, L1
油	(yóu)	*N.*	cooking oil, L16
油菜	(yóu cài)	*N.*	a kind of Chinese vegetable, L7
有关	(yǒu guān)	*V.*	to relate to, to concern, L4
有荤有素	(yǒu hūn yǒu sù)	*VP.*	to have both meat and vegetable, L7
有模有样	(yǒu mó yǒu yàng)	*Adj/N.*	stylish, stylishness, L8
有幸	(yǒu xìng)	*Adj/Adv.*	fortunate, lucky; fortunately, L8
有意义	(yǒu yì yì)	*Adj.*	meaningful, significant, L9
幼儿园	(yòu ér yuán)	*N.*	nursery school, kindergarten, L2
于是	(yú shì)	*Conj.*	therefore, consequently, as a result, L2
于是乎	(yú shì hū)	*Adv.*	then, L7
舆论界	(yú lùn jiè)	*NP.*	opinion poll, public opinion, L13
余	(yú)	*N.*	surplus, L4
余地	(yú dì)	*N.*	leeway, room, latitude, L7

癒合	(yù hé)	V.	to heal, to recover, L1
譽為	(yù wéi)	VP.	to be honored as, L14
原本	(yuán běn)	Adv.	originally, L12
原諒	(yuán liàng)	V.	to forgive, to excuse, L1
原文	(yuán wén)	NP.	original text, the original, L1
原先	(yuán xiān)	Adv.	originally, formerly, L4
原因	(yuán yīn)	N.	reason, cause, L13
員工	(yuán gōng)	N.	staff member, L7
遠隔千里	(yuǎn gé qiān lǐ)	Idiom.	thousands of miles away, L1
遠近聞名	(yuǎn jìn wén míng)	Idiom.	famous far and wide, to be known far and wide, L4
約束	(yuē shù)	N/V.	control, restriction; to restrain, L8
樂曲	(yuè qǔ)	N.	musical composition, L5
允許	(yǔn xǔ)	V.	to allow, to permit, L3
運動員	(yùn dòng yuán)	N.	athlete, L14
運輸	(yùn shū)	N.	transportation, L10
蘊含	(yùn hán)	V.	to contain, L8
醞釀	(yùn niàng)	V.	under discussion, to discuss, to deliberate on, L2

Z

在……之餘	(zài... zhī yú)	PrepP.	in the spare time of, L12
攢錢	(zǎn qián)	VO.	to save money, L10
遭遇	(zāo yù)	N.	(bitter) experience, L2
早先	(zǎo xiān)	Adj.	earlier, L12
早些	(zǎo xiē)	Adj.	(in) early (years, days), L15
造成	(zào chéng)	V.	to cause, to result in, L6
責任感	(zé rèn gǎn)	N.	sense of responsibility, L5
責任田	(zé rèn tián)	NP.	land for which one is responsible, L3
責任制	(zé rèn zhì)	NP.	responsibility system, L3
增多	(zēng duō)	V/N.	to increase; increase, growth in number or quantity, L1
炸	(zhá)	V.	to deep fry, L16
占	(zhàn)	V.	to occupy, to take up, L5
戰功赫赫	(zhàn gōng hè hè)	Idiom.	with excessive awards, winning numerous titles, L14
張東和	(zhāng dōng hé)	N.	Zhang Donghe, name of a person 人名, L2
張田青	(zhāng tián qīng)	N.	Zhang Tianqing, name of a person 人名, L4
張藝謀	(zhāng yì móu)	N.	Zhang Yimou, name of a person, a famous film director in China 人名, L13
招手	(zhāo shǒu)	V.	to wave at, L10
趙華	(zhào huá)	N.	Zhao Hua, name of a person 人名, L6
趙秀梅	(zhào xiù méi)	N.	name of a person 人名, L8
照常	(zhào cháng)	Adv.	as usual, L11

愈合	(yù hé)	V.	to heal, to recover, L1
誉为	(yù wéi)	VP.	to be honored as, L14
原本	(yuán běn)	Adv.	originally, L12
原谅	(yuán liàng)	V.	to forgive, to excuse, L1
原文	(yuán wén)	NP.	original text, the original, L1
原先	(yuán xiān)	Adv.	originally, formerly, L4
原因	(yuán yīn)	N.	reason, cause, L13
员工	(yuán gōng)	N.	staff member, L7
远隔千里	(yuǎn gé qiān lǐ)	Idiom.	thousands of miles away, L1
远近闻名	(yuǎn jìn wén míng)	Idiom.	famous far and wide, to be known far and wide, L4
约束	(yuē shù)	N/V.	control, restriction; to restrain, L8
乐曲	(yuè qǔ)	N.	musical composition, L5
允许	(yǔn xǔ)	V.	to allow, to permit, L3
运动员	(yùn dòng yuán)	N.	athlete, L14
运输	(yùn shū)	N.	transportation, L10
蕴含	(yùn hán)	V.	to contain, L8
酝酿	(yùn niàng)	V.	under discussion, to discuss, to deliberate on, L2

Z

在……之余	(zài... zhī yú)	PrepP.	in the spare time of, L12
攒钱	(zǎn qián)	VO.	to save money, L10
遭遇	(zāo yù)	N.	(bitter) experience, L2
早先	(zǎo xiān)	Adj.	earlier, L12
早些	(zǎo xiē)	Adj.	(in) early (years, days), L15
造成	(zào chéng)	V.	to cause, to result in, L6
责任感	(zé rèn gǎn)	N.	sense of responsibility, L5
责任田	(zé rèn tián)	NP.	land for which one is responsible, L3
责任制	(zé rèn zhì)	NP.	responsibility system, L3
增多	(zēng duō)	V/N.	to increase; increase, growth in number or quantity, L1
炸	(zhá)	V.	to deep fry, L16
占	(zhàn)	V.	to occupy, to take up, L5
战功赫赫	(zhàn gōng hè hè)	Idiom.	with excessive awards, winning numerous titles, L14
张东和	(zhāng dōng hé)	N.	Zhang Donghe, name of a person 人名, L2
张田青	(zhāng tián qīng)	N.	Zhang Tianqing, name of a person 人名, L4
张艺谋	(zhāng yì móu)	N.	Zhang Yimou, name of a person, a famous film director in China 人名, L13
招手	(zhāo shǒu)	V.	to wave at, L10
赵华	(zhào huá)	N.	Zhao Hua, name of a person 人名, L6
赵秀梅	(zhào xiù méi)	N.	name of a person 人名, L8
照常	(zhào cháng)	Adv.	as usual, L11

照顧	(zhào gù)	*V.*	to take care of, L4
折騰	(zhē téng)	*V.*	to do, L12
浙江	(zhè jiāng)	*PlaceN.*	Zhejiang (Province), name of a province in South China 地名, L4
針對	(zhēn duì)	*V.*	to be aimed at, to be directed against, L6
睜	(zhēng)	*V.*	to open (eyes), L12
爭	(zhēng)	*V.*	to fight for, to compete for, L9
整個	(zhěng gè)	*Adj.*	entire, whole, L12
整整	(zhěng zhěng)	*Adj.*	entire, the whole, L9
正面	(zhèng miàn)	*N.*	front side, L13
正式	(zhèng shì)	*Adj/Adv.*	formal; formally, officially, L14
政策	(zhèng cè)	*N.*	policy, L2
政府	(zhèng fǔ)	*N.*	government, L3
政治	(zhèng zhì)	*N.*	politics, L1
職工	(zhí gōng)	*N.*	staff, workers, L2
直接	(zhí jiē)	*Adj.*	direct, immediate, L13
值得	(zhí dé)	*Adj.*	worth, worthwhile, L5
指	(zhǐ)	*V.*	to refer to, L5
指揮	(zhǐ huī)	*V.*	to conduct, L5
指令性	(zhǐ lìng xìng)	*N.*	quota system, L11
至今	(zhì jīn)	*Adv.*	up to today, up to now, L6
致富	(zhì fù)	*V.*	to become rich, L4
制度	(zhì dù)	*N.*	system, L5
制作	(zhì zuò)	*N.*	make, manufacture, L6
智力	(zhì lì)	*N.*	intelligence, intellect, L5
智商	(zhì shāng)	*N.*	IQ, L2
秩序	(zhì xù)	*N.*	order, L4
終於	(zhōng yú)	*Adv.*	eventually, finally, L10
種地	(zhòng dì)	*VO.*	to till, to cultivate land, L3
種類	(zhǒng lèi)	*N.*	type, variety, L7
重擔	(zhòng dàn)	*N.*	burden, L1
重視	(zhòng shì)	*V.*	to emphasize, to attach importance to, L6
周班	(zhōu bān)	*N.*	Zhou Ban, name of a person 人名, L3
周圍	(zhōu wéi)	*Adv.*	nearby, in the vicinity of, L5
朱明	(zhū míng)	*N.*	Zhu Ming, name of a person, L1 人名, L1
逐步	(zhú bù)	*Adv.*	gradually, L3
逐漸	(zhú jiàn)	*Adv.*	gradually, L3
矚目	(zhǔ mù)	*VO.*	to receive attention, to be focused closely on, L13
主觀	(zhǔ guān)	*Adj.*	subjective, L13
主力隊員	(zhǔ lì duì yuán)	*NP.*	major player, L14
主意	(zhǔ yì)	*N.*	idea, L12
注入	(zhù rù)	*V.*	to pour into, L11
祝福	(zhù fú)	*N/V.*	blessing, to bless, L1
專供	(zhuān gòng)	*V.*	to specialize in supplying, L7

照顾	(zhào gù)	*V.*	to take care of, L4
折腾	(zhē téng)	*V.*	to do, L12
浙江	(zhè jiāng)	*PlaceN.*	Zhejiang (Province), name of a province in South China 地名, L4
针对	(zhēn duì)	*V.*	to be aimed at, to be directed against, L6
睁	(zhēng)	*V.*	to open (eyes), L12
争	(zhēng)	*V.*	to fight for, to compete for, L9
整个	(zhěng gè)	*Adj.*	entire, whole, L12
整整	(zhěng zhěng)	*Adj.*	entire, the whole, L9
正面	(zhèng miàn)	*N.*	front side, L13
正式	(zhèng shì)	*Adj/Adv.*	formal; formally, officially, L14
政策	(zhèng cè)	*N.*	policy, L2
政府	(zhèng fǔ)	*N.*	government, L3
政治	(zhèng zhì)	*N.*	politics, L1
职工	(zhí gōng)	*N.*	staff, workers, L2
直接	(zhí jiē)	*Adj.*	direct, immediate, L13
值得	(zhí dé)	*Adj.*	worth, worthwhile, L5
指	(zhǐ)	*V.*	to refer to, L5
指挥	(zhǐ hūi)	*V.*	to conduct, L5
指令性	(zhǐ lìng xìng)	*N.*	quota system, L11
至今	(zhì jīn)	*Adv.*	up to today, up to now, L6
致富	(zhì fù)	*V.*	to become rich, L4
制度	(zhì dù)	*N.*	system, L5
制作	(zhì zuò)	*N.*	make, manufacture, L6
智力	(zhì lì)	*N.*	intelligence, intellect, L5
智商	(zhì shāng)	*N.*	IQ, L2
秩序	(zhì xù)	*N.*	order, L4
终于	(zhōng yú)	*Adv.*	eventually, finally, L10
种地	(zhòng dì)	*VO.*	to till, to cultivate land, L3
种类	(zhǒng lèi)	*N.*	type, variety, L7
重担	(zhòng dàn)	*N.*	burden, L1
重视	(zhòng shì)	*V.*	to emphasize, to attach importance to, L6
周班	(zhōu bān)	*N.*	Zhou Ban, name of a person 人名, L3
周围	(zhōu wéi)	*Adv.*	nearby, in the vicinity of, L5
朱明	(zhū míng)	*N.*	Zhu Ming, name of a person, L1 人名, L1
逐步	(zhú bù)	*Adv.*	gradually, L3
逐渐	(zhú jiàn)	*Adv.*	gradually, L3
瞩目	(zhǔ mù)	*VO.*	to receive attention, to be focused closely on, L13
主观	(zhǔ guān)	*Adj.*	subjective, L13
主力队员	(zhǔ lì duì yuán)	*NP.*	major player, L14
主意	(zhǔ yì)	*N.*	idea, L12
注入	(zhù rù)	*V.*	to pour into, L11
祝福	(zhù fú)	*N/V.*	blessing, to bless, L1
专供	(zhuān gòng)	*V.*	to specialize in supplying, L7

專業	(zhuān yè)	N.	specialty, major, field of study, L3
專營	(zhuān yíng)	VP.	to specialize in selling (something), L4
賺	(zhuàn)	V.	to make (money), L8
壯大	(zhuàng dà)	V.	to strengthen, L11
追求	(zhuī qiú)	V.	to seek for, L12
資格	(zī gé)	N.	qualifications, credentials, L9
資格證	(zī gé zhèng)	N.	certificate, L10
資金	(zī jīn)	N.	funds, capital, L4
資料	(zī liào)	N.	statistics, data, information, L6
自產	(zì chǎn)	N.	self-production, L11
自發成長	(zì fā chéng zhǎng)	VP.	to grow spontaneously, L11
自家	(zì jiā)	NP.	one's own family, L3
自然	(zì rán)	N.	nature, L9
自食其力	(zì shí qí lì)	Idiom.	self-supporting, self-reliant, L6
自私	(zì sī)	Adj.	selfish, L1
自由體操	(zì yóu tǐ cāo)	NP.	floor exercise, L14
自主能力	(zì zhǔ néng lì)	N.	independence, L6
字幕	(zì mù)	N.	caption, L2
總共	(zǒng gòng)	Adv.	in all, altogether, L4
走向	(zǒu xiàng)	VP.	to march toward, L11
祖祖輩輩	(zǔ zǔ bèi bèi)	Idiom.	for all generations, L4
組成部分	(zǔ chéng bù fèn)	NP.	component, L3
組織	(zǔ zhī)	V/N.	to organize; organization, L5
最初	(zuì chū)	Adv.	at the beginning, initially, L3
最終	(zuì zhōng)	Adv.	eventually, finally, L9
左右	(zuǒ yòu)	Adv.	around, approximately, L11
作曲家	(zuò qǔ jiā)	N.	composer, L9
作用	(zuò yòng)	N.	function, role, L8
座	(zuò)	Classifier.	measure word for buildings, L6

356

专业	(zhuān yè)	*N.*	specialty, major, field of study, L3
专营	(zhuān yíng)	*VP.*	to specialize in selling (something), L4
赚	(zhuàn)	*V.*	to make (money), L8
壮大	(zhuàng dà)	*V.*	to strengthen, L11
追求	(zhuī qiú)	*V.*	to seek for, L12
资格	(zī gé)	*N.*	qualifications, credentials, L9
资格证	(zī gé zhèng)	*N.*	certificate, L10
资金	(zī jīn)	*N.*	funds, capital, L4
资料	(zī liào)	*N.*	statistics, data, information, L6
自产	(zì chǎn)	*N.*	self-production, L11
自发成长	(zì fā chéng zhǎng)	*VP.*	to grow spontaneously, L11
自家	(zì jiā)	*NP.*	one's own family, L3
自然	(zì rán)	*N.*	nature, L9
自食其力	(zì shí qí lì)	*Idiom.*	self-supporting, self-reliant, L6
自私	(zì sī)	*Adj.*	selfish, L1
自由体操	(zì yóu tǐ cāo)	*NP.*	floor exercise, L14
自主能力	(zì zhǔ néng lì)	*N.*	independence, L6
字幕	(zì mù)	*N.*	caption, L2
总共	(zǒng gòng)	*Adv.*	in all, altogether, L4
走向	(zǒu xiàng)	*VP.*	to march toward, L11
祖祖辈辈	(zǔ zǔ bèi bèi)	*Idiom.*	for all generations, L4
组成部分	(zǔ chéng bù fèn)	*NP.*	component, L3
组织	(zǔ zhī)	*V/N.*	to organize; organization, L5
最初	(zuì chū)	*Adv.*	at the beginning, initially, L3
最终	(zuì zhōng)	*Adv.*	eventually, finally, L9
左右	(zuǒ yòu)	*Adv.*	around, approximately, L11
作曲家	(zuò qǔ jiā)	*N.*	composer, L9
作用	(zuò yòng)	*N.*	function, role, L8
座	(zuò)	*Classifier.*	measure word for buildings, L6

略語表

Adj P.	adjectival phrase
Adj.	adjective
Adv.	adverb
Classifier	classifier
Con.	conjunction
Idiom	idiomatic expression
Interj.	interjection
N.	noun
NP.	noun phrase
Place N.	place name
Prep P.	prepositional phrase
Prep.	preposition
Pron.	pronoun
Time N.	expression for time
V.	verb
VO.	verb object
VP.	verb phrase

略语表

Adj P.	adjectival phrase
Adj.	adjective
Adv.	adverb
Classifier	classifier
Con.	conjunction
Idiom	idiomatic expression
Interj.	interjection
N.	noun
NP.	noun phrase
Personal N.	personal name
Place N.	place name
Prep P.	prepositional phrase
Prep.	preposition
Pron.	pronoun
Time N.	expression for time
V.	verb
VO.	verb object
VP.	verb phrase